THE
RED FOX

THE
RED FOX

THE BIOGRAPHY OF
NORM SMITH
LEGENDARY MELBOURNE COACH

BEN COLLINS

visit *slatterymedia.com*

The Slattery Media Group
Level 39/385 Bourke Street Melbourne, 3000
visit slatterymedia.com

Copyright © The Slattery Media Group Publishing, 2008
First published by The Slattery Media Group, 2008
Reprint 2017
All rights reserved. No part of this publication may be reproduced, stored in
a retrieval system or transmitted in any form by any means without the prior permission
of the copyright owner. Inquiries should be made to the publisher.

National Library of Australia
Cataloguing-in-Publication data

Collins, Ben.

The red fox : the biography of Norm Smith : legendary Melbourne coach (paperback)

ISBN 9781921778742

Bibliography.

1. Smith, Norman, 1915-1973. 2. Melbourne Football Club–Biography. 3. Australian football coaches–Biography. 4. Australian football.

796.336092

A catalogue record for this book is available from the National Library of Australia

Group Publisher: Geoff Slattery
Editor: Geoff Slattery
Sub Editor: Bernard Slattery
Cover Designer: Sam Russell
Designer: Karl Chandler
Cover Photo Illustration: Tom Kearney
Photo Production: Tom Kearney, Serena Gallante, Natalie Boccassini

Printed in China by Everbest Printing Co. Ltd

Cover Photograph: AFL Archives

Photographs used with permission

CONTENTS

Acknowledgements..7
The Cast..9
Foreword – by Peter Smith...13
Smithy – by Ray Groom..15

1. The School of Hard Knocks (1915-32)..17
2. Demons (1933-38)..40
3. The First Hat-Trick (1939-41)..67
4. 'A worthy lieutenant' (1942-43)...103
5. The Best in the VFL (1944)..113
6. Captain (1945)..119
7. The Smith-Mueller Legend (1948)..149
8. Coach of Fitzroy (1949-51)...174
9. Home Again (1952-53)..224
10. The Demon Uprising (1954)..255
11. Setting Standards (1954)...281
12. The Dawning of a Dynasty (1955)..308
13. Champions of Australia (1955)..324
14. The Finest Melbourne Side of All (1956)..374
15. The Second Hat-Trick (1957)...404
16. The Most Bitter Disappointment (1958)...428
17. Order Restored (1959)...464
18. 'Put Those Shotguns Away!' (1960)...484

19.	The Party Animal	504
20.	The End of an Era (1961)	516
21.	Just Off the Pace (1962)	529
22.	'We Should Have Won The Flag' (1963)	542
23.	The Greatest Premiership (1964)	553
24.	Calm Before the Storm (1965)	597
25.	Sacked (1965)	606
26.	Severed Ties (1966-68)	662
27.	The Saviour of South Melbourne (1969-72)	689
28.	A Premature End (1973)	732
	Postscript	743
	Select Bibliography	748
	Career statistics	751

ACKNOWLEDGEMENTS

I gratefully acknowledge the 100 or so people who subjected themselves to interviews and shared their scrapbooks as well as their memories.

Special thanks go to Peter Smith, Norm's son, who was a constant source of information and direction, and Ian Thorogood, who ensured Melbourne's past players contributed to this project.

In addition to those mentioned in The Cast, I extend my gratitude to the following: veteran broadcaster Stephen Phillips, Melbourne Football Club historian Lynda Carroll, Ian Baggott, Trevor Ruddell from the MCC Library, Troy Davis, Noel Wilson, Bill Atherton, Arthur Wilson, Judy Murphy, Mary Collins and Robert D'Rozario from Dennis Cricket Club. I sincerely apologise for any oversights.

Most significantly, I express my heartfelt appreciation to my beautiful wife Bec for her support and understanding throughout a year when early-morning starts and late-night finishes were the norm. And to my precious daughter Ruby, whose spirited nature and comedic qualities provided more than just a welcome diversion when deadline pressure was bearing down.

And, finally, to Norm Smith: although I was born two years after you died, you will always be an inspiration. It has been a pleasure to have you in my head for 12 months. You have visited me twice in my dreams – once encouraging me before my 'debut' for Melbourne, and another time blasting hell out of me in front of the team. Yes, you became an obsession. More importantly, you have reinforced what my parents taught me: to be honest and tell the truth, no matter what, even if it hurts.

Ben Collins
2008

ABOUT THE AUTHOR

Ben Collins started as a cadet journalist with *The Courier* in Ballarat in 1997 before stints with Fairfax Community Newspapers and the Herald & Weekly Times. For 11 years he was a full-time writer and author for Slattery Media Group, which produced all AFL publications including the *AFL Record*. Ben has written and co-written eight books, the first being *Jason McCartney: After Bali* – the highest-selling non-fiction book by an Australian author in 2003 – which tells of McCartney's recovery from horrific burns suffered in the Bali terrorist bombings and his remarkable effort to play one last game of AFL football. Ben's other offerings include *Champions: Conversations with Great Players & Coaches of Australian Football*, Collingwood legend Nathan Buckley's life story *All I Can Be* and former Victorian homicide detective Charlie Bezzina's autobiography *The Job*. *The Red Fox* was Ben's first biography. Since 2012 he has worked as a reporter for AFL Media. Ben and his wife Rebecca have three children and live in Melbourne's west.

THE CAST

The following people were among those interviewed for this book:

Frank 'Bluey' Adams – Melbourne 1953-64.
Sam Allica (and wife Roma) – Melbourne trainer and runner in 1960s-70s.
Ron Baggott (and his late wife Phyllis) – Melbourne 1935-42 and 1945.
Ron Barassi – Melbourne 1953-64; captain 1960-64; Legend of Australian Football.
John Beckwith – Melbourne 1951-60; captain 1957-59.
Peter Bedford – South Melbourne 1968-76; 1970 Brownlow Medallist.
Harry Beitzel – Field umpire 1948-60.
George Bickford – Melbourne 1946-52.
Don Blew – Field umpire 1963-67.
Barry Bourke – Melbourne 1963-73.
Brian Bourke – South Melbourne president 1967-71.
Noel Brady – South Melbourne secretary 1967-72.
Russell Brown (and wife Thelma) – Cousin and workmate of Smith's.
Mavis Cardwell – Widow of Jim Cardwell, Melbourne's secretary 1951-75.
Keith Carroll (and wife Edna) – Melbourne 1952-58.
Geoff Case – Melbourne 1953-62.
Tony Charlton – Broadcaster; host of *The Tony Charlton Football Show* (Nine).
Bob Chisolm – South Melbourne committeeman.
Noel Clarke – Melbourne 1951-55.
Margaret Clay – Widow of Bert Clay, Fitzroy player 1940-51.
George Coates – Fitzroy 1947-54.
Mary Collins – Widow of Geoff Collins, Melbourne player 1948-54.
Don Cordner – Melbourne 1941-50.
Bob Davis – Geelong player 1948-58, and coach 1960-65.
Frank Davis – Melbourne 1964-73.

Brian Dixon – Melbourne 1954-68.
Len Dockett – Melbourne 1946-51; died January 1, 2008.
Ken Emselle – Melbourne 1962-69.
Dick Fenton-Smith – Melbourne 1957-59.
Jack Gaffney – Fitzroy 1949-53.
Terry Gleeson – Melbourne 1953-62.
Ray Groom – Melbourne 1963-68; Premier of Tasmania 1992-96.
Tom Hafey – Richmond coach 1966-76; four premierships.
Norma Harmes – Daughter of Len Smith; niece of Norm Smith.
Wayne Harmes – A grandson of Len Smith and a grand-nephew of Norm Smith; Carlton player who won the first Norm Smith Medal in 1979.
Ken Hands – Carlton player 1945-57 and coach 1959-64.
Bob Henderson – Fitzroy 1953-62.
Greg Hobbs – Football writer for *The Age* and *The Herald*.
Frank Hughes junior – Melbourne 1945; the son of 'Checker' Hughes, the famous Richmond and Melbourne coach.
Allan Jeans – St Kilda coach 1961-76.
Graeme John – South Melbourne 1964-69; coach 1973-75.
Robert 'Tassie' Johnson – Melbourne 1959-69.
Norm Johnstone – Fitzroy 1944-57.
Bryan Kenneally – Melbourne 1959-69.
John Kennedy – Hawthorn coach 1960-1963.
Neil Kerley – South Australian football legend.
Ralph Lane – Melbourne 1951-56.
Clyde Laidlaw (and wife Judy) – Melbourne 1954-62.
George Lenne (and wife Marj) – Melbourne in 1941-42 and 1945; team manager of the Demons' reserves side 1955-69.
John Lord – Melbourne 1957-64.
Geoff McGivern – Melbourne 1950-56.
Noel McMahen – Melbourne 1946-56; captain 1955-56.
Hugh McPherson (and wife Gwen) – Melbourne 1941-44; team runner 1954-63.
Hassa Mann – Melbourne 1959-68; captain 1965-68.
Len Mann – Melbourne 1960-64.
Bernie Massey – Melbourne 1960-67.
Ken Melville – Melbourne 1953-56; the priest who conducted Smith's funeral.
Kevin Murray – Fitzroy 1955-64 and 1967-74.
Garry Pearce – Assistant bootstudder at Melbourne during Smith's reign.

THE CAST

Ricky Quade – South Melbourne 1970-80.
John Rantall – South Melbourne 1963-72; North Melbourne 1973-75.
Ian Ridley (and wife Judith) – Melbourne 1954-61.
Stan Rule – Melbourne 1946-50; died in August 2007.
Bob Skilton – South Melbourne 1956-71; Legend of Australian Football.
Peter Smith – The only child of Norm and Marj Smith.
Samantha Smith – Grand-daughter of Norm Smith; daughter of Peter Smith.
Stuart Spencer (and wife Fay) – Melbourne 1950-56.
Max Spittle – Melbourne 1947-50.
Bill Stephen (and wife Betty) – Fitzroy 1947-57; coach 1955-57 and 1965-70.
Charlie Sutton – Footscray 1942-56; coach 1951-57 and 1967-68.
Ian Thorogood – Melbourne 1957-62.
Jack Toohey – Fitzroy 1947-49 and 1951-52.
John Townsend – Melbourne 1962-72.
Geoff Tunbridge – Melbourne 1957-62.
Barrie Vagg – Melbourne 1962-69.
Doug Wade – Geelong 1961-72; North Melbourne 1973-75.
Robert Walls – Carlton 1967-78.
Wayne Walsh – South Melbourne 1969-72.
Athol Webb – Melbourne 1955-59.
Murray Weideman – Collingwood 1953-63.
Mike Williamson – Renowned television and radio broadcaster.

Other notables to appear in this book include:

'Checker' Hughes – Richmond and Melbourne coach who won five premierships.
Jack Mueller – Melbourne 1934-50.
Bert Chadwick – Melbourne president 1950-62.
Jim Cardwell – Melbourne secretary 1951-75.
Ivor Warne-Smith – Melbourne's chairman of selectors 1949-60.
Jack Dyer – Richmond 1931-49; Legend of Australian Football.
Percy Beames – Melbourne 1931-44; captain-coach 1942-44; later a respected sports journalist with *The Age*.
Allan 'The Baron' Ruthven – Fitzroy 1940-41 and 1943-54.
Max Walker – Melbourne 1967-72; Australian Test cricketer.
Stan Alves – Melbourne 1965-76.

FOREWORD

by Peter Smith

It has been a difficult task and, at times, an emotional experience to read this biography on the life of my late father Norm.

Norm came from a working-class background and never forgot the principles he was taught by his parents: high moral standards, honesty, courage and loyalty. He also never forgot that the performance of the team came before individual achievement.

The contrast between his public and private lives was stark. He was a football tyrant who ruled his teams with an iron fist, but at the same time his family knew him to be a caring and loving husband, father and grandfather.

I cringed at certain stories of 'sprays' he delivered to his players throughout his coaching career, and was also heartened by the positive expressions of love for Norm, not only for the effect he had on their football careers, but for the way the standards he imposed also affected their lives away from the game.

Norm would have been well aware of the personal hurt he had caused, but it was always intended for the betterment of the team, not to humiliate the player on the receiving end. It was probably an early form of the use of psychology in football.

I was always amazed by the different personalities of Norm and his older brother, Len. Norm was hot-headed with a short fuse, and was a very forceful orator, while Len was much calmer and quietly got his message across. Norm drank and didn't smoke; Len smoked and didn't drink. Norm had enormous love and respect for Len and I saw him cry openly for the first time the day his brother died.

And so the complexities of my father are exposed in this book. No-one wanted a sanitised version of Norm's story, only honesty and truth from those who knew him.

Despite what many people might think, Norm's saddest moment in football was not his sacking as Melbourne coach in 1965, but when he stood for election for the club's committee after retiring as coach at the end of the 1967 season and was rejected by the members. This was effectively the end of his involvement with Melbourne after thirty years as a player and coach. Although Norm was mortally hurt by this rejection, it was probably a sign of the apathy that had descended on the club and continues to this day.

Norm's premature death at the age of 57 was a loss to football, but the loss was far greater to the family that loved him. I am sure the players he attacked so vociferously would have been amazed at the tenderness he showed as he nursed and cuddled his two grand-daughters in his latter years.

Although it is sad most of Norm's awards have come since his death – ie. the Norm Smith Medal, selection as coach in the AFL Team of the Century, and official Legend status – I am sure he would be embarrassed by these personal accolades. Far more important to him were the 10 premierships he achieved with teammates and players during his career.

My thanks go to the Melbourne premiership players who committed to the production of this book and revealed the true Norm Smith: the good, the bad and the very ugly. I am sure you all know how much Norm cared for you all as footballers and people.

Finally to the author, Ben Collins: your hundreds and hundreds of hours research have culminated a biography of genuine substance. Some of your accounts sent a chill down my spine, while others had tears running down my face, and ultimately prompted me to smile about the man I was proud to call my father. Ben, I believe you have produced a very fair and accurate portrayal of Norm and for that I sincerely thank you.

Peter Smith
May, 2008.

SMITHY

[1963]

"OK, in ya' go!"
The door slams fast
and we all know
We're in for a blast
Smithy's in a ripe old mood
Red hair and that stare
he stalks his brood

"OK. Quiet!"

We wait for his word
not a sound to be heard

"You've got one opportunity
only one!
If we don't take this one we're done!
Talk boys talk
never shirk or baulk
Forget drop-kicks
use the punt
And remember fellas
stay in front
Hassa, keep movin' round
Bluey, drop in short
And scout
Barass. Don't just talk,

*Shout!
Fellas,
be proud to wear the red and blue
and don't blame others
it's up to you!
Fortune favours the brave ya' know
so get out there
and put on a show"*

*We're all psyched up
ready to go
jump'n and chatt'n
urging and patting*

*The crowd gives a roar
as we crash through the door
then dash down the race
at one heck of a pace
On the hallowed turf
of the MCG
we twist and turn excitedly
Norm's words ring out loud
Despite the wild crowd*

*"Fellas it's do or die
so try, try, try!"*

– Ray Groom, Melbourne player 1963-68,
Premier of Tasmania 1992-96.

1

THE SCHOOL OF HARD KNOCKS

[1915-32]

The toughest times breed the toughest people; and so it naturally follows that Norm Smith, perhaps the greatest coach in the history of Australian Football, and certainly one of the most uncompromising of his craft, was born in one of the toughest eras endured by Australians.

Smith's formative years were dominated by two periods of extreme crisis. He was born on November 21, 1915, almost seven months after a baptism of blood for Australian soldiers, among them some of the nation's finest footballers, at Gallipoli; the first three years of his life were spent around adults enduring varying degrees of grief and alarm as horrifying news of the death toll of Aussie 'Diggers' filtered back from the killing fields; while his teenage years, which should have been a carefree time of exploration and boyish adventure, were restricted to a large extent by the economic and social strangulation of The Great Depression.

For much of Smith's youth, Australians were gripped by an unmistakable sense of vulnerability and desperation, which, for some, deteriorated even further into depths of despair and virtual hopelessness. But this overwhelming hardship not only produced a generation of folk with seemingly endless reserves of determination and bold ambition to rise above their station in life, but also many who naturally adapted to their urgent environment and hand-to-mouth existence by adopting a blunt, no-nonsense approach to both speech and action. One individual who epitomised these traits was Norm Smith.

A complex character of stark, light-and-shade contrasts – hardness verging on brutality, and compassion and generosity verging on self-sacrifice – he was of a generation that was perhaps simultaneously more hardened and yet sensitised to the fickle nature of fate, and the preciousness of life, than any generation of Australians since. Although no-one could ever describe Norm Smith as just one of the crowd, he was a classic product of the wider environment in which he was raised. There certainly was more than a little truth in Smith's joking 'boast' that he was a graduate from the school of hard knocks.

Before his 30th birthday he had already lived through *two* world wars – although, regrettably for a red-blooded man of his virility and pride, he was prevented from fighting for his country in World War II because he worked in a protected industry that assisted the war effort, and the lives of those at home. Some of Smith's friends, taking into account his gung-ho nature and compulsion to lead from the front, believe he probably owed his life to this quirk of fate.

Smith's parents, Victor and Ethel Smith, were both products of working-class families, and both, coincidentally, were the third-born in their respective families of 13 (eight boys and five girls) and 12 (six of each sex) offspring.[1]

Victor – known mainly as "Vic" or "Dick"[2] – was born in the inner-Melbourne suburb of Hotham (North Melbourne) in late 1883. Vic's father William – Norm Smith's paternal grandfather – himself had been the third-born of 12 children in Longford, Tasmania, where this particular Smith family has its deepest Australian roots.

William Smith became a farrier (a blacksmith who shoes horses), while his son Vic became an ironworker/metal stamper – trades that have an intimate relationship with the origins of the Smith name. Smith derives from the Anglo-Saxon 'smitan', meaning to smite, or strike, and was bestowed upon craftsmen who struck metal into shape. In medieval times, the skill of a kingdom's smiths to construct high quality body armour and weaponry, including swords and other killing implements, had the potential to decide the outcome of battles with foreign enemies. As such, they too were virtually in a protected industry. Smiths ply one of the oldest trades in the history of civilisation, which perhaps goes some of the way towards explaining how Smith is the most common surname in the western world.

The maiden name of Norm Smith's mother was also a very common one – Brown. Ethel May Brown was born in Collingwood on July 2, 1886. Like her mother, she worked as a machinist. Perhaps like her mother too, she became a great home cook known for her sumptuous speciality of roast lamb, vegetables and dumplings.[3]

---

[1] All information relating to the early history of the Smith family was generously supplied to the author by Norma Harmes, a daughter of Len Smith, and a niece of Norm Smith.
[2] Russell Brown, a cousin and long-time work mate of Norm Smith's. Interview with the author.
[3] Norma Harmes. Interview with the author.

Although it is not known how Vic Smith and Ethel May Brown met, they were married on April 15, 1911. The ceremony was held at the home of Ethel's parents, Thomas and Annie Brown, at 364 Rae Street, North Fitzroy, and was conducted by Baptist Church minister William Hiddlestone. Both of Vic's parents were deceased – his father William had died 14 years earlier when Vic was just 13, while his mother Lucy had passed away not long before the wedding – but Ethel's parents were in attendance. Vic, who was living at 210 Pelham Street, Carlton, was 27 and Ethel was 24. In their wedding photo, they appear straight-faced and serious – completely at odds with how relatives remember them.

Mr and Mrs Victor Smith set up house at 318 Clarke Street, Northcote, a north/north-eastern suburb of Melbourne, where Vic would live for the rest of his life, and Ethel most of hers. The Smith house was located in a small area in south Northcote called Westgarth, the main street of which, Westgarth Street, was originally proposed for the township of Northcote in the early to mid-1850s before High Street became the town's central artery. Northcote became a working-class suburb largely because a lack of public transport to and from Melbourne severely hampered its progress, slashing land values and resulting in an influx of battling families. It wasn't until 1903 that a direct rail link with the city (via neighbouring Clifton Hill) was established, but by that time the demographics of the area had been firmly entrenched, with slaughteryards, piggeries and clay pits – the latter being the source for the mass production of bricks – providing jobs for many of Northcote's citizens. Vic Smith went to work in the iron trade.

To mark their first wedding anniversary in 1912, Vic purchased a wooden, green bench seat, which took its place on their front porch and would provide family members with a comfortable rest area for decades to come. The seat, while dilapidated and rotting, is still in a family garden as a reminder of those times.[4]

On February 9, 1912, Vic and Ethel celebrated the birth of their first child, a son they named Leonard Victor. Three years, nine months and 12 days later – on Sunday November 21, 1915 – they welcomed the arrival of another boy, Norman Walter Smith. While most people would refer to him as "Norm" from that day forth, he would remain "Norman" to his mother. Len was born in North Fitzroy, Norm in Clifton Hill. Perhaps by coincidence, their maternal grandparents, Thomas and Annie Brown, had been residing in these suburbs – both adjoining Northcote – when their grandsons were born.

The Smiths' next effort provided their boys with a sister – Marjorie Florence, "Marj" – who was born on March 14, 1918.

---

[4] Norma Harmes. Interview with the author.

The two brothers were distinguished from their sister, their parents and their huge extended family by their red hair. Some people who came to know the brothers well in later life have remarked that this was perhaps the only thing they had in common. They were believed to have been the only redheads for at least several generations – no mean feat in their well-branched family tree, which included a combined 20 aunts and uncles, not to mention numerous cousins. Although Smith is an English name, and this clan of Smiths is no different, oral history passed down through the family has it that the carroty locks of Norm and Len Smith were a throwback to distant Irish heritage. So too, apparently, were the fiery temperaments of the two younger siblings, Norm and Marj, whose Vesuvius-like volatility was in stark and curious contrast to the calm and collected natures of their parents and elder brother Len. In relation to the different personalities of Norm and Len in particular, even now, people who knew them intimately marvel at the fact that they grew up in the same house and were raised the same way.

Considering the feistiness of Norm and Marj, it was perhaps inevitable that they would suffer the odd personality clash, which Vic would usually be required to quell. The fact he would do so without raising his voice was evidence of his gentle, peacemaking qualities. But eventually even their ever-loving father would fail to stop these sibling disputes, and Norm and his sister would not talk for about a quarter of a century from their twenties until middle-age – which sadly turned out to be old age for Norm Smith. The circumstances of this breakdown remain a mystery.

Also unknown at that stage was that Smith would one day coach a Victorian Football League (VFL) side that would surpass the then unprecedented effort of the all-conquering Carlton side, which, just two months before his birth, won its fifth VFL flag in 10 seasons. In the next 75 years, only two other clubs would eclipse this purple patch and Norm Smith would be closely aligned with both when they were at the zeniths in their respective club histories: as a boy he barracked for Collingwood, 'The Machine' juggernaut which won six flags in 10 seasons between 1927 and 1936; and he later coached the other, Melbourne, to the same feat as his boyhood Magpies, but went a step further by enjoying a record stretch of five premierships in six years.

But in the collective imagination of the Australian public, football had taken a back seat to World War I. Norm Smith's birth year, 1915, also marked the birth of the legend of the Anzacs[5]: the Diggers, and all their attendant virtuous

---

[5] Anzac stands for the Australian and New Zealand Army Corps, which soldiers of these countries represented in World War I.

traits of mateship, loyalty, selflessness, courage, honesty, humour, teamwork, resourcefulness, adaptability, and a never-give-in attitude that gained them a glowing reputation among allies and foes alike for their ability to fight as fiercely and honourably as any of the world's soldiers and hastened their fledgling nation's coming of age. But it was no time for celebration. The massive loss of lives of young soldiers was devastating. Everybody knew someone who had joined the fighting. Sadly, it seemed everybody also knew someone who did not return.

The Smiths had their own concerns for a loved one. One of Ethel's younger brothers, Walter Victor Brown – the man honoured by Vic and Ethel in their choice of middle name for his nephew Norm – was a 22-year-old milk carter when he enlisted on August 18, 1914.[6] Pint-sized and fresh-faced, "Wally" Brown landed at Gallipoli on April 25 (Anzac Day). When a telegram bearing the symbol of the Australian defence department arrived at his parents' house in Clifton Hill, the Browns feared the worst. The two-line telegram stated simply, with obvious haste: 'REGRET REPORTED SON PRIVATE W.V BROWN WOUNDED WILL ADVISE UPON RECEIPT FURTHER PARTICULARS.' The wait must have been agonising. As it eventuated, Wally had received a finger wound deemed serious enough for authorities to order his return to Australia for discharge.

Maybe it was partly due to their uncle's involvement in the chaos but somehow some of the character traits of the Anzacs must have seeped into the consciousness of young Norm and Len, because these phenomenal footballing brothers displayed, and came to exemplify, many of these qualities themselves throughout their lives, and have since been eulogised on numerous occasions with similar words to those used to encompass the aura of the Digger. And, of course, the Smith boys had great teachers of life's lessons at home. Their parents, Vic and Ethel, were great role models, and symbols of strong values, who encouraged their children through words and actions to show genuine care, generosity and community spirit. Smith always reflected on his childhood with great fondness. 'I was a very fortunate boy,' he said. '(I had) a father who loved his family, and a mother the same.'[7]

Vic, in particular, encouraged participation in sport. The man who would nurture the sporting talents of two boys who would become two of the most influential men in football history, and certainly the most influential brothers the game has seen, was a sports fanatic himself. Vic loved the idea of a pure-spirited contest. As was a custom even back then for many young Australians, particularly those

---

[6] Walter Victor Brown's service record, sourced on the website of the National Archives of Australia – *www.naa.gov.au*
[7] *Midweek Magazine*, August 1964.

living in the southern states, as a boy Vic Smith had played cricket – Smith later recalled that his father developed an elegant late cut[8] – and football. Now, with the sporting careers of his sons at the forefront of his mind, Vic came into his own element. Norm Smith, in reference to the origins of his own fascination with sport, always maintained that 'there is no doubt that my father... started it',[9] adding that Vic 'must have started talking sport to me when I was still in the cradle. He never forced me to take up any sport, but his enthusiasm was certainly catching.'[10] Vic encouraged his boys to play any sport on offer. Dinner-table discussions encompassed all of this, including boxing, which was another of Vic's favourites. When Norm Smith was the Victorian Football League's supercoach in 1964, he recalled his father with reverence. 'My father loved his sport and his family life,' he said, 'and I'm trying to develop my life along the same lines.'[11]

Not that the boys needed any encouragement in their sporting pursuits. Ethel Smith later told of a family holiday to Sydney when two-year-old Len went berserk. 'I think he kicked everything within reach around the room,' Ethel Smith recalled. 'He was given a soccer ball and it became the treasure of his young life.'[12] Len also tagged along to his father's cricket matches with a local side. A rare photograph, circa 1916, exists in a family collection showing Vic and 11 teammates posing in their rag-tag assortment of creams, including a couple of turtle-neck shirts – Vic, of course, is suitably attired – with the team mascot, a three or four-year-old Len, with longish locks, clinging to his father's legs as he shyly peers at the camera. Lying on the floor in the foreground is Len's pint-sized cricket bat.

However, there was nothing shy about his kid brother Norm, who was already showing signs of the fearless, confrontational – or in modern terms, 'in-your-face' – personality for which he would become widely renowned, even notorious. 'Norman was always wrestling some bigger boy,' Ethel Smith revealed, 'and he was such a full-blooded kid that he always seemed different.'[13] The Smith brothers were so different in temperament that it was both a source of amusement and bemusement, particularly where the hot-headed Norm was concerned. Not even his own mother could ignore the fluctuations in his moods. She described Norm's emotions as being 'very near the surface – (his temper) flares up like a flash; but it is soon forgotten and nobody suffers from the outburst... I never remember Len

---

[8] Russell Brown. Interview with the author.
[9] A four-part series by Norm Smith, as told to Brian Hansen, in the Melbourne *Truth* newspaper, March-April 1962.
[10] *Melbourne Truth* series, 1962.
[11] *Midweek Magazine*, August 1964.
[12] *The Sporting Globe*, June 22, 1940.
[13] *The Sporting Globe*, June 22, 1940.

saying a cross word. Never once has he answered me back. Norm, on the other hand, goes up like a rocket.'[14]

The activity that seemed to give Smith the greatest outlet for his pent-up energy was the vigorous, full-bodied sport of football. Perhaps sensing this, Vic always bought Norm, and Len for that matter, a new football at the start of each season. Vic also supplied his boys with new cricket bats when summer came around. It was a rare extravagance for a working-class family at the time, but one that Vic felt was crucial to the development of what he soon discovered were two exceptional sporting talents. Although the shiny new footballs and smooth-bladed cricket bats became annual treats, the boys had a *never-ask-for-nothin'* mentality, so typical of the time. They took nothing for granted.

Like many enthusiastic young boys with ambitions of one day playing league football, Smith would take his footy to bed with him each night[15] and – as almost every other Clifton Hill-born boy and many Northcote lads of the era did – dream of playing in the black and white of his beloved Collingwood.[16] Such a revelation might come as a shock, especially considering the Magpies later became Smith's most bitter rivals, but he often admitted with some pride that he was a 'mad Magpie supporter'[17] in his youth.

Smith did not share football allegiances with his father or brother. Vic was a long-time Essendon supporter and Len followed his father's lead, regularly accompanying him to watch the 'Dons play – Len being a proud figure in the Essendon jumper his father bought him. Essendon's 'mosquito fleet' – they had eight players who stood no taller than 165cm, or 5'5" in the old scale – won the VFL flag in 1924 and then, in a match that decided the unofficial football champions of Victoria, were suspiciously beaten by VFA premier Footscray amid allegations of Essendon players accepting bribes to 'play dead'. Such underhandedness would never have sat well with Vic Smith because if there was one thing he instilled into his sons it was to be utterly honest. At all times. Even if the truth hurt.

Honesty was a feature of Vic Smith's working life. He harboured ambitions beyond a life working for others, to be his own boss, master of his own destiny. In 1923, at the milestone age of 40, he finally gathered the courage to break away from the clock-on, clock-off monotony of factory work to realise a dream he had held for some time – to start his own business. Trading simply as 'V. Smith', with

---

[14] *The Sporting Globe*, June 22, 1940.
[15] *The Sporting Globe*, June 22, 1940.
[16] Pollard, Jack (editor), *High Mark: The Complete Book on Australian Football*, Murray, 1964. The book contains a chapter co-written by Norm and Len Smith.
[17] *Melbourne Truth* series, 1962.

no 'Pty Ltd' or such attached, Vic ran a one-man operation making parts for prams – mainly the hood joints – in a shed he had built in a rear corner of his backyard. Apart from being his own boss, Vic enjoyed the lifestyle advantages that working from home afforded him – he wasted no time or money on travelling to and from a workplace; he could have lunch lovingly prepared by Ethel, an excellent cook; and he could spend more quality time with his family.

The Smith children attended the Gold Street State School (now Clifton Hill Primary School), some two kilometres south in Clifton Hill, where Len captained the school football team. There must have been enormous excitement and relief when it became official that a new school would be built almost directly opposite the Smith house in Clarke Street. In March 1925 – just after the VFL admitted three new clubs: Footscray, Hawthorn and North Melbourne – 13-year-old Len, nine-year-old Norm and soon-to-be seven-year-old Marj walked across the road to continue their education at the red-brick building of Westgarth Central School (now Westgarth *Primary* School). Number 4771 in the Victorian education system, the school would educate at least two generations of Smith children.[18] Norm Smith was to maintain lifelong pride in his origins: that he had grown up in a working-class family in a working-class town and had received a state school education. He believed his initial desperation to simply survive and eke out an existence in the deprived times of his youth soon generated a hunger for success. First, though, Smith had to survive – and succeed in, as best he could – school lessons.

Discipline at the Westgarth school was 'extremely strict'.[19] It had to be with just one teacher responsible for up to 60 children in a classroom. Children were taught to respect God, Australia and the British Empire – and of course, authority figures such as teachers. Naughty pupils received lashes on their hands with the feared strap, and one male teacher would 'roll up his strap and throw it at the culprit, the boy had to return it, then he got the strap on his hand'.[20] In the schoolyard and after school, Norm would tag along with Len as much as he could.[21] Although he would eventually achieve more in the sporting sphere than Len, Norm always looked up to his older brother, initially idolising him for his efforts on the football and cricket fields, but always holding an enormously high regard for Len's knowledge and opinions. But back in their Westgarth school days, as soon as the bell rang to signal the end of

---

[18] The original school building was demolished in the 1980s and was replaced by several smaller buildings.
[19] Sylvia Ratcliffe (formerly Sylvia Ray), a student at Westgarth Primary School from 1927-35, in *Westgarth Memories*, produced by Westgarth Primary School in 1992.
[20] Mrs P.O'Donnell, *Westgarth Memories*, 1992.
[21] *Melbourne Truth* series, 1962.

lessons for the day, the Smith boys would drop their bags off at home before making their way back across Clarke Street to join a large group of boys from around the neighbourhood on a vacant piece of land behind the Westgarth school known as 'Smith's Paddock'.[22] As fitting as it might have been, the paddock was not named after this particular Smith family; that honour went to a man who shared the same name as Norm and Len's paternal grandfather, William Smith, a Glaswegian who ran nearby Smith's Bacon Factory – which was also known locally simply as 'the piggery'.[23]

Those afternoons in the ruggedly-surfaced Smith's Paddock provided young Norm Smith with a tough initiation to football. Most of the boys owned just one pair of boots, which they wore for all occasions, and when it came to football they simply hammered some stops into their soles so they could grip the uneven turf better. For some time at least, their 'football' was made of rolled-up newspaper tied into shape with string.[24] Although they were not organised matches against a hostile opposition from a neighbouring suburb and were played largely among friends, and friends of friends – one of whom was Alphonsus "Phonse" Kyne, little more than two months older than Smith, and destined to become a Collingwood champion – they were anything but kick-and-giggle affairs. Many of the boys were three or four years older than Smith, and much bigger, and the lack of proper umpiring and the virtually no-holds-barred nature of these 'scratch matches' ensured young Smith's adrenalin and fear levels were pumping overtime. Adding to his difficulty in getting a kick, as he later admitted, 'they nicknamed me "Fatty" because I was short and fat'.[25] So overweight, in fact, that once when he tried to climb over the side gate at home, he got stuck up there because he couldn't haul his bulk over to the other side.[26] Although he must have struggled with the physical requirements and pace of the game on account of his body shape, it was in this dog-eat-dog atmosphere that Smith developed the quick wits and hard-edged competitiveness that were to serve him so well later on in his distinguished playing and coaching careers. Also, as he was the most junior player in the team, it would have been crucial to gain all-round acceptance by passing the ball to the older

---

[22] Smith's Paddock no longer exists. Part of its expanse has since been absorbed into the grounds of Westgarth Primary School, while the remainder has been replaced by residential development.
[23] According to the Darebin Historical Encyclopedia website – *dhe.darebin-libraries.vic.gov.au* – William Smith, who served as the mayor of Northcote in 1893, built a superb home he named 'Grand View', at 25 Prospect Grove, Northcote, about a kilometre from the Smith house. The house still stands, with many original features, on Northcote Hill, which enabled Smith a 'grand view' of his bacon factory.
[24] Norma Harmes. Interview with the author.
[25] Melbourne *Truth* series, 1962.
[26] Len Smith mentioned this detail to his daughter Norma, who related it in an interview with the author.

boys and being ultra-team-conscious – another trait that is synonymous with the legendary team-first legacy of Norm Smith. Smith later recalled this brutal football baptism as follows:

> That ground grew boulders better than grass. To get a kick you had to get in and take it. It was rough and tumble and you learned to take the knocks. The bigger boys used to give me a few welts across the ears. I was a pretty cheeky little brat when it came to football. I was the youngest and that ground was nice and hard.[27]

Once Norm and Len's enthusiasm for football was established, their father assumed more of a guiding, coaching role with them – coaching that would have even more impact than those character-building matches at Smith's Paddock. Smith later attributed his and Len's success entirely to those early one-on-two coaching sessions, writing: 'Whatever Len and I have developed we owe to Dad'.[28]

Vic Smith had one central notion of team sport: that teamwork was greater than the individual; and no success could be achieved without every individual component of the team working together, in near-perfect harmony, to the same plan, towards the same goal. Such was Vic's non-negotiable stance on this aspect of football that Smith wrote in 1962, at the height of his coaching career, 'he drummed teamwork into us all the time. His motto... is reflected in both (of) our coaching techniques'.[29]

Smith's performances on the football field were also improved by his sudden and dramatic physical development. In 1929, his last year at Westgarth Central School, his fleshy body underwent a dramatic growth spurt that helped transform him from a rotund try-hard into an athlete better suited to the demands of the game. That year, "Fatty" Smith 'shot up a foot (30.5 cms) but didn't put on any weight',[30] in the process shedding both his unwanted, ridiculed 'puppy fat' and his equally unwanted, unflattering nickname. (Of course, in the notorious way of brothers, Len kept the moniker alive, privately at least, calling Norm "Fatty" for the next four decades until his own death.[31]) It was a stunning make-over with two major benefits. Suddenly Smith was tall enough to play in a key position, and he boasted enough pace and stamina to keep up with the flankers. As a direct result of this, and with his father's coaching and the concept of team ringing in his ears, Smith so impressed the football coach at his school that he was elevated

---

[27] Melbourne *Truth* series, 1962.
[28] Melbourne *Truth* series, 1962.
[29] Melbourne *Truth* series, 1962.
[30] Melbourne *Truth* series, 1962.
[31] Norma Harmes. Interview with the author.

to the captaincy of a 'pretty good' Westgarth school side.[32] Smith became one of the dominant state school footballers in the Northcote district and beyond, and was officially recognised as such when he was selected in the initial Victorian state school squad of about 40. He played a trial match for a North of the Yarra side against South of the Yarra, but was not considered good enough to play for the Victorian state schoolboys' side in the national carnival.[33] The youngster was obviously disappointed, but there was no doubt that he had made stunning inroads in little over a season. It would not be the end of his aspirations to play for his state. Continued improvement at a steadier rate over the next decade or so would result in Smith earning the first of two state guernseys for the country's strongest football state.

Norm Smith's rise to local prominence as a footballer coincided with the onset of The Great Depression, which sucked the wealth, life and spirit out of many Australians from 1929, with its effects felt deep into the '30s. The vicious cycle started with the scarcity of work, which in turn resulted in a scarcity of money, food, clothing and shelter. These were just the tangible problems. The *in*tangibles – such as the distinct lack of dignity and self-esteem caused by their pathetic circumstances and the constant, seemingly hopeless fight of husbands and fathers to do the most basic of manly things – to provide for their families – were similarly significant and degrading. But while some men left their families to find work in the country or interstate, or attempted to escape reality by hitting the bottle, Vic Smith was a tower of strength for his family as the main breadwinner. By now Len, aged 17, had journeyed into the workforce. After further schooling at Collingwood Technical School, he had started an apprenticeship as a fitter-and-turner with Alex Mackie in Victoria St, Melbourne, and was contributing to the family funds. Norm was to follow him into the workforce soon after. Meanwhile, Ethel continued to cast her matronly eye over the family unit to ensure everyone was catered for in at least the most basic manner. Many children wore 'hand-me-downs' – clothes passed down from older siblings – and seeing Len and Norm were now similar in physique, this would have been a natural, practical course to take.

At school, teachers asked students if they could spare any food to feed the unfortunate children who had not eaten that day. The vast majority of children left school by the time they had turned 14 so they could work and help their families financially, and Norm Smith was no exception, leaving Westgarth Central School at the end of 1929.

---

[32] Melbourne *Truth* series, 1962.
[33] Melbourne *Truth* series, 1962.

Smith's first job out of school was as an apprentice engineer. His first foreman, a stern taskmaster, left a lasting impression on him in that climate of despair, as he recalled nearly 40 years later:

> I thought he was tough at the time. But I know that the discipline he taught me was the discipline I have passed on to the players in my teams...You have to slave and slog. Don't be ashamed of falling, as long as you can get up and go on trying.[34]

Nothing, it seemed, escaped the wrath of the Depression, and local football was no different. Smith discovered this at the age of 13 when he made his debut at junior level for Dennis in the Northcote & Junior Rechabite Football League, a Victorian Football Association sub-district competition.

Finances were so tight that to cover umpires' fees and equipment each week every player had to pay a shilling[35] (10 cents) – which was worth much more than it sounds today; in fact, many would-be players wouldn't have afforded it. Such a predicament meant that the only players who took the field during this particularly trying period were those who played for the love of the game, and perhaps the jumper, and little else. Not only that, clubs had to be resourceful and look within their own ranks to ease the financial burden. To this end, Dennis Football Club used the same football for every home game, after which one of Smith's teammates, a bootmaker, would take the ball home, clean it and 'polish it up on a boot polishing machine'[36].

Although it was the quintessential period of playing football for love alone, Smith remembered that 'those junior games were played harder and were more vicious than League matches'.[37] One match in particular from Smith's youth demonstrated the ferocity and true depth of passion which existed in the suburbs. The Dennis junior side, which would win the 1931-32 flags with Smith as one of its stars, was playing neighbouring arch-enemy Thornbury at Thornbury in what was a typically spiteful clash. As was always the case, the match attracted a huge crowd, comprising mainly Thornbury supporters, who became increasingly incensed with the decision-making of the sole field umpire. When Dennis hit the front in the third quarter and appeared to have gained the ascendancy, an unruly mob of Thornbury supporters stormed onto the field to remonstrate with the man in white. Understandably feeling threatened, the umpire declared the game over

---

[34] Norm Smith's speech at his testimonial dinner, held by Melbourne Football Club at Melbourne Town Hall on December 20, 1967.
[35] Melbourne *Truth* series, 1962.
[36] Melbourne *Truth* series, 1962.
[37] Melbourne *Truth* series, 1962.

and awarded the points to Dennis before wisely bolting for an exit. The umpire later reported the entire Thornbury team but when the accused players fronted the tribunal the Thornbury spokesman explained in defence that: 'We were only chasing the umpire so we could pay him'.[38]

🏆🏆🏆🏆🏆🏆🏆🏆🏆

Norm Smith would kick a football at every opportunity – before school, during breaks in lessons, after school at Smith's Paddock, and virtually all weekend. The only time he wasn't kicking a footy on a weekend was when he was watching it. On Saturday afternoons, he often travelled by train to watch Collingwood play.

In adopting Collingwood as his VFL team, Smith had gone with the strength – both in terms of supporter numbers and supporter toughness. The Magpies were, and probably still are, the most fanatically-followed and yet most passionately-despised football club in the land. Smith once said: 'In other clubs you would call it enthusiasm; at Collingwood it is fanaticism'.[39]

Although Collingwood was named in honour of Admiral Cuthbert Collingwood, who fought alongside Admiral Horatio Nelson against the French in the famed Battle of Trafalgar, there was little of what one could describe as nobility about the suburb. Collingwood was a rough industrial suburb – in some ways just a more populated version of Northcote. Aside from Melbourne itself, Collingwood was also the brewing capital of Victoria. It was blue-collar to its roots. Perhaps that was part of the allure for Smith, who only knew working-class living and would always 'have a soft spot for the fella who was doing it a bit harder than he was'.[40]

Initially, being a Collingwood supporter must have been a heart-wrenching experience for Smith. Around the time that he reached football consciousness, the Magpies lost four Grand Finals between 1920 and 1926. By this stage the dictatorial genius, and patience, of coach Jock McHale was severely tested as he had won just two premierships from eight Grand Final appearances.[41] But thankfully for Smith and the rest of the mad Magpie army, Collingwood was simply enduring the pain of defeat before it could experience the ecstasy of sustained glory. Like McHale, Smith would also experience – both as a player and then a coach – painful finals defeats before achieving success.

---

[38] Melbourne *Truth* series, 1962.
[39] Melbourne *Truth* series, 1962.
[40] Stan Rule, a teammate of Norm's at Melbourne. Interview with the author.
[41] Jock McHale took over as Collingwood coach in 1912 and won premierships in 1917 and 1919, and lost Grand Finals in 1915, 1918, 1920, 1922, 1925 and 1926.

Smith became a teenager in November 1928, in the middle of Collingwood's greatest era; indeed, the greatest era of any VFL/AFL side. The Magpies won a record four successive premierships between 1927 and 1930, and 70 of a possible 81 matches, to boost their premiership tally to nine. Nearly 40 years later, Smith's Demons would become the first of only two clubs since to threaten the Magpies' record of successive flags, the other being the Brisbane Lions of 2001-02-03.

'The Machine', driven by the stern Jock McHale, left an indelible imprint on the football psyche of Norm Smith. Although he admitted to being a young, impressionable lad at the time,[42] Smith rated those mighty Magpie sides as among the best he had the privilege of witnessing in action.[43] And his assessment was not confined to Saturday afternoons. On the odd Tuesday or Thursday afternoon after school, Smith would catch a train to Victoria Park to watch his heroes go through their paces under the eagle eye of McHale.[44] Smith recalled the Magpie coach as a figure to be feared; a tough taskmaster who made his players frightened to lose, at the sheer prospect of facing the coach's wrath: 'When Collingwood lost, McHale would stand at the front of the players' race and glare at his men coming off the ground. They would be running in slowly, then quicken their pace as they got near McHale. They were frightened of him. No doubt about that. On the Tuesday night, McHale would sulk and not speak to players, but he would let loose with all his fury on the Thursday night'.[45]

Witnessing such hard-line antics first-hand – probably for the first time – and marrying it with the success McHale's approach reaped, might well have been a pivotal moment in Norm Smith's mental approach to the game. If nothing else, it was an early lesson that coaches are perhaps better served erring on the side of cruelty rather than kindness.

After McHale had sent his players off the ground after training, Smith would wait around outside the dressing-room door[46] with other young fans in the hope he would get an up-close glimpse of his heroes, including the brothers Coventry (captain Syd and goalkicking machine Gordon) and Collier (Harry and Albert),

---

[42] Pollard, Jack (editor), *High Mark: The Complete Book on Australian Football*, Murray, 1964.

[43] Norm made this declaration in various publications and series, including previously mentioned sources like the *Truth* series in 1962 and *High Mark: The Complete Book on Australian Football*, published in 1964.

[44] A six-part series on Norm Smith in *The Sun*, written by Barrie Bretland, from Saturday September 30 to Friday October 6, 1967. Bretland's interviews with Smith were recorded at Smith's home.

[45] *Allsport Weekly*, August 2, 1973. The story referred to a talk Norm gave to a class of physical education teachers at Melbourne University in 1966.

[46] *The Sun* series, 1967.

and maybe even score an autograph or a golden word of advice that he might be able to apply to his own game. Not satisfied with that, he would then follow several of the players across Lulie Street and over the walk-bridge above the railway tracks to Victoria Park Station, virtually opposite the ground, and catch the exact same train home as his idols. However, Smith's hero worship knew some bounds because he would never travel in the same carriage as the players.[47]

Above all else, those Collingwood sides reinforced in Smith's mind what his father had taught him about the benefits of teamwork – the Magpie version of which, Smith later wrote, 'made an everlasting impression on me.'[48] Perhaps unbeknown to Smith at the time, the Magpies were so tight-knit as a playing group that their team ethic extended to their off-field attitudes. For instance, after each home game they took it upon themselves to tidy up the rooms for their social dances.

Smith was heavily influenced by the attitude and values of the Collingwood hierarchy, with the largely McHale-inspired decision to follow the adage that all men are created equal, and as such should be treated and paid the same – an all-encompassing philosophy that Smith adopted as one of his guiding principles when he became a VFL coach some 20 years later.[49] In the twilight of his coaching career, Smith declared: 'I have always been a tremendous admirer of Collingwood's team discipline, their spirit and the fact that each player was treated in exactly the same way as his teammate. I carried this idea into my coaching... I never played favourites or gave any single player preferential treatment. I believed what was good for one player was good for the other'.[50]

The Magpie modus operandi heavily influenced both Norm and Len Smith's ideas on how the game should be played: individually, positionally and collectively. They both admired Collingwood for daring to break the prevalent 'stop and prop' mould of play and regarded the Magpies as 'the pioneer of the play-on, fast-flowing style' that they themselves became renowned for in their own coaching careers. Norm Smith was particularly impressed with 'their discipline and their total unselfishness' and would never cease to marvel at seeing Collingwood players 'sacrifice their own game... for the good of the side', which he also tried to incorporate into his playing and coaching.[51]

---

[47] *The Sun* series, 1967.
[48] *Melbourne Truth* series, 1962.
[49] *The Sun* series, 1967.
[50] *The Sun* series, 1967.
[51] Pollard, Jack (editor), *High Mark: The Complete Book on Australian Football*, Murray, 1964.

Even in later years, when he proudly stated he was 'Melbourne through and through',[52] he was able to reel off the names of his Collingwood idols from his youth as easily as if he was reading them from an old team sheet. 'What material Jock (McHale) had to work with,' he wrote. 'Gordon Coventry was the champion full-forward of that era... (he) was so big and bulky he looked like the side of a house, and he was just as hard to get around. In 1929, he became the first full-forward ever to kick 100 goals in a season...[53] (Also) Syd Coventry, Harry and (Albert) "Leeter" Collier, Billy Libbis, Jack Beveridge, Harold Rumney, (John) "Jiggy" Harris and Charlie Dibbs, combined with a dozen others of almost equal ability... Players who, on paper, appeared mediocre blended into the team perfectly.'[54] He also fondly recalled the efforts of the likes of Len and Frank Murphy, Percy Bowyer, Bruce Andrew, Fred Froude and George Clayden.[55]

'They proved to me,' Smith recalled, 'that 18 players playing as a team were better than 18 champions playing for themselves.'[56] This observation was to remain firmly entrenched in Norm Smith's blueprint for success.

Another key to Collingwood's success, according to Smith, was its versatility, and occasional unpredictability, which added a refreshing element of surprise to the ruthless efficiency. Smith boasted such an acute sense of observation, even as an immature teenager, that he noticed, for example, that captain Syd Coventry would at times contest the ruck duel at a centre bounce and then cover the opposition centreman to allow the Magpies' actual pivot man, Jack Beveridge, to 'go on a walkabout'.[57] Even at this early stage, Smith was becoming aware that football was not simply a game of man-on-man; it was a battle of strategic manoeuvring. Players and positions were pawns to be manipulated on a grassy chessboard.

One of the Magpies' most versatile players was champion centre half-back Albert 'Leeter' Collier – Smith's favourite player of all time, and the best team player he ever saw.[58] Furthermore, Smith often said that if he had to select a greatest-ever team, the younger, bigger Collier sibling would have been his No. 1 pick, 'not so much for his brilliance ... as for his intelligent, protective ruck play'.[59] Superbly-muscled and proportioned, and boasting a lethal mix of strength and speed for

---

[52] Norm Smith on *The Tony Charlton Football Show* on Channel Nine on Sunday July 25, 1965.
[53] Gordon Coventry kicked 124 goals in 1929 to surpass his own previous record of 97, which he had set two years earlier.
[54] Melbourne *Truth* series, 1962.
[55] Pollard, Jack (editor), *High Mark: The Complete Book on Australian Football*, Murray, 1964.
[56] *Midweek Magazine*, August 1964.
[57] *Midweek Magazine*, August 1964.
[58] *Midweek Magazine*, August 1964.
[59] Pollard, Jack (editor), *High Mark: The Complete Book on Australian Football*, Murray, 1964.

a big man, Collier was more than just a mobile wrecking ball. He could play in any key-position on the field with equal distinction. In 1962, Smith remembered Collier as follows: 'He would make his team work around him... How fascinated I was watching him play... A pointer to his greatness was his Brownlow Medal win in 1929 (as) it is considered almost impossible for a player in a premiership team to win the medal (because) he has too many teammates cutting his throat. I first saw him play at centre half-back. I can still remember his great pace, soaring high marks and wonderful kicking... His teamwork made him one of the greats of football. He could do more with a handpass than most players. In a match, he might have had less than 10 kicks...but he would wreck his opponents with uncanny handpassing. He protected his team and did the bulk of the heavy work. The way he could make his team play around him was something to see'.[60]

Imitation is said to be the greatest form of flattery and Smith began imitating Albert Collier in his own way by injecting more thoughtful, constructive handball into his game to release quicker teammates into the clear. For Smith, Collier's playing style was another clear example of the virtues of self-sacrificing, almost self-effacing teamwork. An undeniable pattern was emerging, and Norm Smith was perceptive enough to heed the signs. It was becoming blatantly obvious to him that this was *the* way to succeed in football.

▼▼▼▼▼▼▼▼▼

Although he always kept a copy of the Bible in a drawer beside his bed,[61] and was later known to quote the Holy Book in the odd pre-match address,[62] religion never played much of a role in the life of Norm Smith. Like many Australians, he rarely set foot in a church.[63] However, as a 14-year-old Smith was a weekly attendee at the Northcote Church of Christ, albeit as a member of that church's affiliated boys' club. The boys' club was not religiously based anyway; it was simply a meeting place for local youth – they gathered at 7pm every Friday – to give them something to do and keep them off the streets.

Two of the other notable members of the boys' club were Richard Emselle and Ronald Idris Baggott – the latter being perhaps the only person alive who can recall Norm Smith as a 14-year-old. In years to come, Richie Emselle and Ron Baggott –

---

[60] Melbourne *Truth* series, 1962.
[61] Peter Smith, Norm's son. Interview with the author.
[62] Brian Bourke, South Melbourne Football Club president from 1967 to 1971. Interview with the author.
[63] Peter Smith. Interview with the author.

younger than Smith by two years and 14 months respectively – would become closely entwined with Norm Smith, both in friendship and football; the former developing first. The pair hit it off immediately with Smith, sharing a mutual interest in sport and mischief. Baggott also had the occasional kick among the neighbourhood toughs at Smith's Paddock – only occasional because he lived more than a kilometre away.

Standing at the top of Rucker's Hill in High Street, Northcote Church of Christ was a small church shielded by a large bush, which could easily conceal both boys from passers-by. 'When someone was walking past,' Baggott recalled, 'we'd drop a penny on a brick and just wait for their reaction to the tinkling sound. Almost without fail, regardless of how well-off they looked, they'd stop dead and say: 'Ooh!' and start looking for the coin they thought they'd dropped. It was a prank that worked on a lot of people, and you couldn't blame them because they were tough times in the Depression and every penny counted.'[64]

Another thing that counted in such times was mateship, and Baggott could always rely on that from Smith, whom he described as 'a terrific mate, very loyal and honest. He treated people well, and he would help anyone out of a bind.'

But Baggott was also well aware of Smith's hot temper. 'He was quite volatile,' he said. 'There were plenty of occasions where even he and I fell out with each other for a day or two for whatever reason. He'd look you straight in the face and tell you what he thought. And if anybody did something nasty to Smith, they'd live to regret it because he wouldn't just accept it and forget about it; he'd get back at them one way or another.'[65]

In 1931, the boys' club entered a team in the Northcote and Preston Churches' Cricket Association in the Sunday School Grade – the lowest grade possible – and adopted as their home ground a vacant area in nearby Fairfield. Their first act as a team was to dig a centre-wicket area with shovels, after which they arranged for the purchase of some matting to cover the pitch. But on the day of the first game, for some inexplicable reason, the matting was no longer available. The boys, led by Smith, did their best to salvage some sort of surface that would be playable, but the harder they tried to level it out the worse it became. Baggott recalled: 'We talked the opposition into playing. Unfortunately, we lost the toss and were sent in to bat on this absolute minefield. We were all out for 3! Norm Smith made two, there was one sundry and 10 ducks! We then dismissed the opposition for about 20 and called it a day. Twenty wickets for 23 runs – in less than an hour!'[66]

---

[64] Ron Baggott. Interview with the author.
[65] Ron Baggott. Interview with the author.
[66] Ron Baggott. Interview with the author.

During this period, Ron Baggott and Norm Smith were also among a large contingent of youngsters who flocked to Northcote Park to barrack for the town's VFA side. The hero of many local lads was the Brickfielders' star centre half-forward, Len Smith. Len had attracted Northcote's interest after starring for the Fairfield Band of Hope side, which also contained Herbie Matthews, who would eventually win the 1940 Brownlow Medal with South Melbourne. In 1931, while Matthews was impressing the Bloods, Len Smith started turning heads at Northcote while continuing to play for Fairfield Band of Hope. After playing some brilliant football, Len Smith was selected to make his senior debut for Northcote. However, he was soon dropped to the reserves. (At one point, perhaps a year or two later, both Smith brothers played in Northcote's reserves side under the coaching of former Port Melbourne star Bob Skilton – the father of Bob junior, who would later win three Brownlow Medals and play under Smith in Victorian sides in 1958 and 1964, and at South Melbourne from 1969-71.) Len Smith was then in serious consideration for another senior call-up for the VFA Grand Final against Oakleigh at Port Melbourne, but was named as one of three emergencies. Although, understandably, 'very disappointed' at not being selected for what would have been his senior debut in the distinctive green and gold, he took it in 'the right spirit'.[67]

A consolation for Len Smith was the news he had won the VJFA's 'fairest and best' award. Northcote secretary R.L. Walsh sent him the following note:

> Dear Len
> On behalf of the Committee, Players and Members... I desire to convey to you our heartiest congratulations on your success in winning the trophy for the 'Fairest and Best' player in the V.J.F.A.
> We are all highly pleased with your success and feel sure that the honor was richly deserved. We all look forward to next season when you should be assured of a permanent place in our team.
>
> Yours faithfully
> R.L. Walsh (Hon. Secretary)

As expected, Len Smith became a regular senior player with Northcote in 1932 and it didn't take long for him, despite standing just 5'11" (180cms), to make the

---

[67] Hec de Lacy, *The Sporting Globe*, 1940.

centre half-forward post his own. 'A brilliant exponent of key position play',[68] Len Smith boasted a 'superb leap', which enabled him to take 'sky-scraping marks'.[69] Renowned football writer Hec de Lacy. *in The Sporting Globe*, added that 'at times he was sensational'.[70] Len Smith – who some believed had more natural football ability and 'greater possibilities'[71] than his brother – became, according to Ron Baggott, 'the outstanding player for Northcote'[72] – no mean feat considering the Brickfielders were the powerhouse of the VFA. He was such an important player to the line-up that he alternated between centre half-forward and centre half-back depending on the direction of the wind.[73] Captain-coached by former Collingwood premiership player Percy Rowe (whose son Des later captained Richmond for six seasons and coached it for a further three), they played in seven Grand Finals between 1929 and 1936 for five flags, of which Len Smith would play in three (1932, 1933 and 1936). He also finished runner-up to Williamstown's Charlie Standbridge in the 1933 Recorder Cup (the precursor to the Liston Trophy), which recognised the best player in the VFA.

Apart from the prestige and local celebrity of being a star in a superstar team, Len Smith would also have enjoyed the financial aspect of playing VFA football, which made it an even more worthwhile pastime. Northcote paid its players £1 a game, which amounted to about half the average weekly wage – a godsend in the Depression. Although happy to be paid for doing something he loved, and something he would have actually paid to do, as his brother was doing with Dennis, Len Smith had ambitions to play on a bigger stage, for more prestige and, as an afterthought, more money.

In 1930, the season before Len Smith started in the VFA, former Northcote player Stan Judkins, then with Richmond, won the Brownlow Medal. In Len's mind, and perhaps even Norm's, the success of Judkins represented a clear pathway from the VFA to the VFL, which, if followed correctly, could result in a VFL career.

But not everyone was confident in Len Smith's ability to handle himself on a football field. His mother held grave concerns for him. Although Norm was apparently playing in a more spiteful football league – the Northcote and Junior Rechabite League, where off-the-ball sniping was commonplace – Ethel Smith was

---

[68] Hec de Lacy, *The Sporting Globe*, 1940.
[69] Ron Baggott. Interview with the author. Two other stars for Northcote in this golden era were full-forward Frank Seymour, who kicked 880 goals in 201 games, and Aboriginal speedster Doug Nicholls, who went on to a VFL career with Fitzroy and a crusading role for his people.
[70] Hec de Lacy, The Sporting Globe, 1940.
[71] Hec de Lacy, *The Sporting Globe*, 1940.
[72] Ron Baggott. Interview with the author.
[73] *Footy Fan*, June 27, 1964.

always more worried about the on-field welfare of her eldest son. Ethel, who once confessed she 'never liked football' because it 'involved far too many risks',[74] first became concerned when the prospect of Len playing senior football for Northcote was raised. She tried valiantly to persuade her husband and Len that it was a bad idea, but Ethel was fighting a losing battle because Len had his heart set on a football career and the ever-encouraging Vic was not about to stand in the way. Although Ethel resigned herself to that fact and started to go along to Northcote matches, she never overcame her anxiety about the possibility of Len getting hurt. Every time she watched him play she would nervously ride the bumps in a constant state of panic, and return home completely exhausted, a 'nervous wreck'.[75]

Watching Norm play, however, was a completely different, more relaxing proposition. Ethel was blasé about Norm getting in the thick of the action, and was far more confident about his on-field survival instincts because he was 'more robust... (and) more able to stand up against the hard knocks of a game'.[76] In fact, Ethel actually took a strange, perverse delight in seeing Norm – the little firebrand who regularly tested her patience – cop the odd bone-jarring crunch. With a smile, Ethel revealed: 'When Norman gets a knock – not a bad knock, of course – I always say to myself with a laugh: "That's one I should have given you when you were younger". Norman is such a pickle that he probably deserved it'.[77]

In what would be a continuing pattern throughout her sons' playing careers, Ethel Smith would usually choose to watch Norm play to save herself the grief of worrying what might happen to Len. There would later be perhaps only two or three occasions in Norm Smith's entire 16-year VFL playing career that his mother would have concern for his safety, the most serious of those being in the 1940 second semi-final when he came off second-best after receiving a murderous bump from Richmond ironman Jack 'Captain Blood' Dyer.

ŸŸŸŸŸŸŸŸŸ

Vic Smith always encouraged his boys to get involved in their community, particularly the sporting scene. Vic and his mates – who regularly gathered at a corner store in South Crescent, next to Dennis Station, just a short walk from the Smith home – were already heavily involved in the Dennis Football Club. Vic was the president of the football club, with Ron Baggott's father Ted

---

[74] *The Sporting Globe*, June 22, 1940.
[75] *The Sporting Globe*, June 22, 1940.
[76] *The Sporting Globe*, June 22, 1940.
[77] *The Sporting Globe*, June 22, 1940.

(a local barber and SP bookmaker) being his vice-president. With winter sport catered for, the men discussed the lack of a cricket team in the Dennis/Westgarth area. Vic Smith decided it was time to get on the front foot. These discussions soon resulted in the formation of Dennis Cricket Club in 1932.[78] The Smith patriarch was duly elected vice-president of the fledgling club (and became president the following season).

The club joined the Jika Cricket Association and started the 1932/33 season in B-Grade, establishing their home base at Smith's Paddock, where they trained each Wednesday night and played their home games on Saturday afternoons. At this stage, Len Smith might have been the star footballer of the family, mainly on account of his more mature age and consequent level of development, but his younger brother hogged the spotlight when it came to the summer game (although he was certainly no cricketing slouch). At just 17, Norm Smith opened both the batting and the bowling. Naturally, the main dilemmas for opposition sides centred around combatting the young prodigy, who 'hit the ball like a rocket',[79] and sent down occasionally hostile, fast-medium cutters, which provided Len, who was 'like a cat' in the field,[80] with so many catches at short-leg.[81]

Norm's scintillating finish to that first season was a case in point. In the last home-and-away round, Smith smashed 102 not out, followed by – in the semi final against Highview – an unbeaten 161 out of a total of 334, before finishing it all off with a sensational all-round performance which almost single-handedly won Dennis the B-Grade premiership[82]. In a low-scoring B-Grade Grand Final against Penders Grove Footballers, Smith snared 4/22 to rout the opposition for just 105, then compiled 87 in Dennis's reply of 139. He then claimed 6/46 to bundle out Penders Grove Footballers for 166, before applying the finishing touches with 68 not out in a second-innings total of 2/134 to lead Dennis to an eight-wicket victory. In the Grand Final, he had made a total of 155 runs while being dismissed just once (to boost his four-innings' run splurge to 418 runs for just once out), and had bagged match bowling figures of 10/68. Such performances became an almost weekly event, even after Dennis earned promotion to A-Grade in the Jika competition, with either or both of the Smith brothers dominating with bat and/or ball to pilot Dennis to five A-Grade premierships by the end of the 1945/46 season.

---

[78] Dennis Cricket Club website – dennis.cricketvictoria.com.au
[79] Russell Brown, a cousin and long-time work mate of Norm Smith's. Interview with the author.
[80] Russell Brown. Interview with the author.
[81] Peter Smith. Interview with the author.
[82] All statistical and historical information relating to Dennis Cricket Club was sourced from the club's website – dennis.cricketvictoria.com.au– and a booklet celebrating the club's 50th anniversary, published in 1982.

Norm played 17 seasons for Dennis, only giving cricket away when he became a VFL coach at Fitzroy in 1949. Len donned the creams for at least a decade longer.

Both brothers were renowned for their fast scoring – Norm once hammered 117 not out in just 50 minutes, with eight sixes and 10 boundaries, while on a separate occasion Len clobbered 135 not out in 55 minutes. In all, Norm amassed 14 centuries (six of them unbeaten) for Dennis, including five of 150-plus. His highest score was a then competition record of 205 (which stood for 59 years), which he plundered in a semi-final in the premiership season of 1943/44. That year, in 20 one-day games, Norm Smith set a still-standing competition record for the most runs in a season – 1235 – which he made at the exceptional average of 64. He also won four competition batting awards. Len Smith made five centuries.

Intriguingly, their mode of bowling reflected their characters perfectly: Norm was a fiery, aggressive type who tried to intimidate batsmen, while Len was a leg-spinner who relied on his wits and subtle variations in flight, spin and pace.[83] Norm's best bowling efforts in an innings were 9/19, 8/19 and 8/20, while Len's best was 9/16. Norm snared two hat-tricks and Len one.

The sheer weight of their runs and wickets – it is estimated that Norm played 170 games, made 6000 runs and took 300 wickets, and that Len played 350 games for 7000 runs and 600 wickets – albeit in a local competition, makes one wonder how far the Smith brothers might have gone in cricket if they were not so serious about their football. At one point in the prime of his VFL career, Norm actually pursued a district cricket career.

Naturally, the Smith name at Dennis Cricket Club is legendary. Norm Smith is regarded as the greatest player in the club's history, followed by his brother. Fittingly, they have awards named in their honour – the Norm Smith Memorial Trophy is presented annually to the club champion player, while the Len Smith Memorial Trophy is awarded to the best clubman.

---

[83] Peter Smith. Interview with the author.

2

DEMONS

[1933-38]

One evening in 1933, there was a knock at the front door of the Smith house. Standing on the doorstep were two successful football identities from the oldest club in the land – Melbourne Football Club coach Francis Vane 'Checker' Hughes and club secretary Percy Page.

Hughes, then 39, was small in stature – he stood just 5'8" (173 cms) – but he had great presence. The dux of his state school in rough-'n-tumble Collingwood,[1] he boasted a combination of cunning and toughness that made him considerably streetsmart. In 1919, he had earned a Meritorious Service Medal for his efforts with armies in France and Flanders (Belgium).[2] Hughes had perhaps been indirectly influenced by Collingwood coach Jock McHale. He was Richmond's centreman in the 1920-21 premiership sides under captain-coach Dan Minogue, who himself had played under McHale at Collingwood for five seasons (1912-16), the last three as captain. Hughes had taken over the Richmond coaching job in 1927 and, like Norm Smith's beloved Collingwood, first acquainted himself with the emptiness of defeat before achieving the ultimate success. While Smith rejoiced in the Magpies' success, Hughes bemoaned them as his bogey side. Richmond lost three successive Grand Finals to Collingwood from 1927 to 1929. Another Grand Final loss to Geelong in 1931 – their fourth in Hughes' five seasons – was immediately, finally, followed by a premiership in 1932.

The power of Hughes' personality and coaching ability can be felt in the words of Tiger legend Jack Dyer, who played the 1931 and 1932 seasons under Hughes and in 1996 still rated him 'the greatest psychologist the game has produced'. Dyer added:

---

[1] Frank Hughes junior, the son of Francis Vane 'Checker' Hughes. Interview with the author. Hughes junior played three games for Richmond in 1944 and eight with Melbourne in 1945.
[2] Francis Vane Hughes' service record, sourced on the website of the National Archives of Australia – *www.naa.gov.au*

'If he told me to jump off a cliff I would have. He could make my skin prickle and I'd jump at the sound of his voice... He could make champions out of no-hopers'.[3]

Checker Hughes' success at Richmond was due in no small part to the work of Page, who was perhaps the most effective secretary in the competition. Page was a master recruiter who walked fast, worked fast, and employed his considerable powers of persuasion on players and their parents to gain their trust, while maintaining a genuine caring attitude.[4] Indeed, one of his oft-heard philosophies was: 'Football is an entrée to society'[5] – a philosophy each of the Smith boys would subscribe to during their coaching careers. He had been instrumental in assembling, at Hughes' request, physically powerful Richmond sides. Percy Pembroke Page, then 37, had also – in his role as the Tigers' delegate to the VFL in 1931 – been instrumental in introducing the commonsense Page-McIntyre finals system, which was adopted the following year by the VFL – and every league affiliated with the Australian National Football Council – and was to remain in the VFL until a top five was introduced in 1972.[6]

Page was singularly responsible for Hughes' defection to Melbourne for the start of the 1933 season. The gun administrator had joined Melbourne in the summer of 1932-33 – on the proviso that he could handpick the club's new coach (to replace the retired Ivor Warne-Smith). Melbourne was so desperate to have Page on board that it agreed to his condition.[7] Page approached his old mate Checker with little expectation of luring him from Richmond. That was until he learned the Tigers had been unable to find work for him. Hughes agreed to coach Melbourne on the condition the club landed him a job. Page promptly offered him a position in his printing business in Queen Street, and the old firm was reunited.[8] But the

---

[3] Dyer, Jack with Brian Hansen, *Captain Blood*, Stanley Paul, 1965. Reprinted in 1996.
[4] Frank Hughes junior. Interview with the author.
[5] Bartlett. Rhett, *Richmond F.C. – A Century of League Football*, GSP, 2007.
[6] Under the Page-McIntyre finals system, detailed in *The Football Record* in 1932, the top two sides gained a 'double-chance'. The third-placed side played the fourth side in the first semi-final, while first played second in the second semi-final. The winner of the first semi-final then met the loser of the second semi-final in the preliminary final to decide who would play the winner of the second semi-final in the Grand Final.
[7] Hobbs, Greg, *125 Years of the Demons 1858-1983*, Progress Press Group, 1984.
[8] Frank Hughes junior. Interview with the author. He added: 'That was the only reason Dad left Richmond. And it was a very good reason – if you didn't work, you didn't put food on the table. If Richmond had found him a job, he would have happily stayed. But they couldn't.' In 1933, Checker Hughes' first season at Melbourne, Richmond, under new coach Billy Schmidt, finished two games clear on top of the VFL ladder only to lose the Grand Final by 42 points to South Melbourne. But the Tigers won the 1934 premiership under another yet another coach, Percy Bentley.

Hughes-Page union didn't have immediate results in its new surrounds. In fact, the Fuschias (as Melbourne was then known) went backwards in 1933, winning just three games and finishing 10th (third-bottom), under the new regime.

Hughes and Page would have been acutely aware that they were assuming leading roles at a largely amateur football club known, and in some ways despised, as the bluebloods, the silvertails, of the VFL.[9] The playing list comprised a number of former public schoolboys who played for love alone; as opposed to financially-strapped, blue-collar players who desperately needed their match payments to put food on the table. Hughes knew exactly what was needed to lift Melbourne: an injection of hard-edged vigour, some good old-fashioned 'mongrel', to rid the club of its over-genteel, almost indifferent approach, which had produced very little success. In other words, Hughes wanted to instil some of the Richmond toughness into the Fuschias. And he started by changing their flowery nickname to something more masculine and inspirational. 'Fuchsias… hmm,' Hughes pondered, while standing in the centre of the ground at training wearing his old Richmond jumper. 'They'll be bloody Demons!'[10]

It wasn't long before Melbourne stalwart J. O. Smith penned the following verse in recognition of Hughes' influence:

> For years they turned the other cheek,
> In their "gentle Annie" days;
> 'Til Checker taught them vigour,
> And as it's fair - it pays.

A working-class boy like Len Smith certainly fitted the bill and it was no surprise that he made it on to the Hughes-Page shopping list after his performances with Northcote. The superstar coach and savvy secretary had journeyed to the Smith house with one aim in mind: to sign 21-year-old Len as a Melbourne player. But when they came knocking at the Smith house, they got more than they could ever have bargained for. They initially asked Vic Smith (who was now the president of the Dennis Football Club) for permission to talk to Len Smith. It was a request Vic Smith happily granted. The proud father added that he had a younger son who also had the potential to make the grade. Perhaps feeling obligated, and to assist their single-minded quest to get Len, they humoured Vic by agreeing to speak with

---

[9] Despite the public image of Melbourne Football Club, Checker Hughes and Norm Smith, who, between them, coached the Demons for all but six seasons from 1933 to 1967, and guided the club to 10 of its 12 premierships – were both from working-class backgrounds.

[10] Frank Hughes junior. Interview with the author.

Norm, who that year had made his senior debut with Dennis as a 17-year-old at centre half-forward, and had, as previously mentioned, made the odd appearance in Northcote's seconds. Page found Norm Smith 'kicking end-to-end on the gravel in a schoolground',[11] and was impressed by what he saw.

'The upshot,' Smith said later, 'was we were both asked to train.'[12] The real upshot, though, was that Hughes and Page had, by mere chance, stumbled upon a boy who would blossom into an infinitely better player than his older brother – a player an entire forward line could revolve around – not to mention the coaching greatness he would achieve.

Checker Hughes was to have a profound and lasting impact on Norm Smith, and the pair would form an intimate, if at times turbulent, relationship born out of mutual respect. Understandably, the respect was all one-way at that initial meeting – after all, Hughes was a supercoach, while Smith was lucky to even get a minute of his time, and that being only on the recommendation of his father.

It was not long before Len Smith left the family home. Len, 21, married Florence Wiseman, 18, on July 22, 1933. "Flo" and her family had migrated to Australia from Limerick, Ireland, in 1918. Len Smith and his bride went to live in a house at 10 Ellesmere Street, Northcote, not far from Vic and Ethel's house in Clarke Street. It was an exciting time for the Smith boys. As they embarked on their first pre-season with Melbourne in early 1934, Len and Flo became parents – and Norm Smith an uncle – with Barbara being born on February 10.

Despite their optimism about pursuing VFL careers, Norm Smith's first impression of Melbourne Football Club was not a favourable one. Generally speaking, he thought the Demons were 'snobs'.[13] By then, Norm was an apprentice engineer at the ropeworks of James Miller & Co. Pty. Ltd. (known simply as Miller's ropeworks) in Dawson Street, Brunswick. Since 1868 Miller's had become a 500-employee operation, and one of the most prominent manufacturers of rope and cordage in Victoria. It was also a Melbourne Football Club stronghold. But this did not protect Norm Smith from class-based ridicule. He would ride his push-bike to training at the Albert Ground in Albert Park, in his work clothes: black overalls and a black shirt. At the time, Smith was the only player at Melbourne who worked in such garb,[14] which bemused certain academics and white-collar professionals – teammates and club officials –

---

[11] Melbourne Cricket Club newsletter, December 1967.
[12] *Melbourne Truth* series, 1962.
[13] Stan Rule in an interview with the author.
[14] Bill Stephen in an interview with the author. Stephen played under Norm at Fitzroy, was a specialist coach under him at South Melbourne and was one of his closest friends.

around him. Smith noticed their cold stares, and there was no mistaking their disdain when someone remarked with incredulity: 'A black shirt at Melbourne? At *Melbourne*?'[15] In those early days, Smith felt he was 'more or less ostracised by the old-school-tie brigade at the club.[16] Despite his disillusionment, Smith remained 'fairly quiet' at the club.[17]

Len Smith missed the first intra-club practice matches on the Albert Ground, but his brother made a good start. Although 'heavy rain made the ball greasy and the ground slippery',[18] in one match Norm Smith was one of only two forwards mentioned on either side among the most prominent players.

Three other notable recruits to Melbourne in 1934 were Norm Smith's mate Ron Baggott and two who would become all-time greats at Melbourne: key-position player Jack Mueller, 18, (just two months older than Smith), whom Percy Page signed in Echuca at 2am one Monday (morning), just seven hours before Hawthorn scouts arrived;[19] and Allan La Fontaine, a 23-year-old who was initially known as "Little Lollies" after kicking goals by the 'hundreds and thousands' in amateur ranks[20] – he actually kicked 247 majors in 24 games in a season for University Blacks. While this pair produced solid debut seasons – Mueller headed the club's goalkicking with 52.51 in 14 matches and La Fontaine kicked 32.37 and won the best first-year player award – La Fontaine's first impressions weren't good either. He later branded the 1934 Demons 'a shocking side. In my first game at Richmond, I was all set to gather a sitter and one of my own men crashed into me. Instead of getting a good goal to open out in league company, all I got was a hard knock that had my head reeling for the rest of the day'.[21]

Len Smith's official debut for Melbourne was delayed after a clearance wrangle with Northcote. Like his brother, Len Smith played in most of the practice matches – also across half-forward – but just two days before the start of the season, Northcote, for the fourth time, rejected his application for a clearance. *The Herald* reported that the VFA heavyweight felt that 'the loss of their high-flying centre half-forward would be too much of a blow'.[22] Len Smith had to be content, at least in the short-term, with playing at Northcote until he gained a release.

---

[15] Bill Stephen. Interview with the author.
[16] Stan Rule. Interview with the author.
[17] Percy Beames, *The Age*.
[18] *The Herald*, April 1934.
[19] Taylor, E.C.H., *100 Years of Football: The Story of the Melbourne FC 1858-1958*, Melbourne Football Club, 1957.
[20] Dyer, Jack and Brian Hansen, *Captain Blood*, Stanley Paul, 1965.
[21] *The Sporting Globe*, April 17, 1943.
[22] *The Herald*, 1944.

A month later, Northcote finally relented and granted Len Smith a clearance to the Demons, who immediately showed their faith in their newest recruit by thrusting him into the senior team that very week.[23] Standing 5'11" (180cms), Len Smith was one of four inclusions with Bert Taylor, Don Hooper and Rowley Fischer each returning from injury, replacing Jack Sambell, Sid Meehl, Bill Vanthoff and the injured George Margitich. Len Smith debuted on a half-forward flank, alongside the impressive Mueller, in a remarkable round five match in which Melbourne defeated North Melbourne by two points despite kicking two fewer goals. North kicked 10.2 to 2.3 in the first quarter at Arden Street but in the last three quarters managed just 7.2 to Melbourne's 13.25 – to produce a shambolic scoreline: 15.28 (118) to 17.14 (116). Len Smith played four consecutive games – two on a half-forward flank, followed by two on a half-*back* flank – before being dropped after a 49-point loss to Carlton in round eight. Len Smith returned to the senior side in round 10 and kept his place in the senior side until the end of the season, meaning he had played 13 of the last 14 games in an improving Melbourne side that finished sixth with nine wins and nine losses, four-and-a-half games outside the final four.

Norm Smith, meanwhile, played the entire season in the reserves as a tallish half-forward flanker – he was exactly six feet tall (183cms) – under the guidance of 33-year-old captain-coach Bill "Bull" Adams. A West Australian who had played with both Northcote and Preston in the VFA, Adams also captained Fitzroy and rounded out his senior playing days at Melbourne. Smith regarded the colourful Adams as 'a wonderful coach' who, like senior coach Checker Hughes, strongly emphasised team play and club spirit.[24] In addition to the earlier influence of his father and the sensational Collingwood sides of his youth, it had a snowball effect. 'By now teamwork was a fetish with me,'[25] he revealed.

Midway through the season, Smith and Demon teammate Pat McNamara impressed enough to earn selection in a VFL seconds' team which played a VFA seconds' side in a curtain-raiser to the senior VFL versus VFA match on the MCG. Smith kicked a goal in a 102-point win.

That year, the Smith brothers and Ron Baggott experienced their first taste of premiership glory when the Demons defeated Geelong by 32 points in the MCG curtain-raiser. Amazingly, it was the club's fourth reserves flag in a row – an achievement commemorated by Melbourne's committee with a special dinner.

---

[23] Len Smith was one of 13 debutants for Melbourne in 1934.
[24] *Melbourne Truth* series, 1962.
[25] *Melbourne Truth* series, 1962.

However, the Demons hadn't been impressed with Norm Smith's efforts in 1934. Bull Adams later said: 'Not many people know this, but at the beginning of 1935, Norm, along with some other players who played with the seconds in 1934... was nearly struck off the list. But he remained there, battled on and won out'.[26]

The 1935 season also commenced after the arrival of another child to Len and Flo. On March 12, they welcomed another girl, whom they named Norma Florence. 'I was named after Uncle Norm,' Norma said. 'I think they wanted to have a boy named Norman, but they got me instead!'[27] Almost 25 years later, Norma would give birth to Carlton premiership star and inaugural 1979 Norm Smith Medallist Wayne Harmes.

Again both Smiths started the season in the seconds before Len Smith received a senior call-up in round five. Dropped back to the reserves for round seven, Len Smith returned to the seniors in round eight to kick the only three goals of his stint at Melbourne, and that being in a lowly Demon total of 7.12 (54), in a two-goal loss to eventual finalists Carlton at the MCG. Len Smith played the next three games in the seniors – to make it six of the previous seven – but had played his last senior game for Melbourne after a comprehensive loss to South Melbourne's star-studded 'Foreign Legion' side in round 11. Sadly, the Smith brothers never played senior VFL football together. Len Smith returned to Northcote in 1936. Five years later, in an interview with Hec de Lacy from *The Sporting Globe*, both brothers were 'outspoken' in declaring that the manner in which Len was 'chopped about' from one position to another with the Demons 'almost ruined his football'.

But just as Len Smith's career with the Demons was fading, his brother's began to gather momentum. He and Baggott began to develop what would become a fruitful on-field relationship. Baggott was the reserves' full-forward and in the first 11 rounds of 1935 kicked 70-odd goals – he finished with 81 in 14 games – including 13 of the side's 16 goals in a one-goal win over St Kilda. Baggott recalled: 'The main reason I was able to kick so many goals was because my mate Norm Smith was playing (on a) half-forward flank and would put the ball right down my throat every time I made a lead. He just kept feeding the ball to me. It was fantastic service for a full-forward. He was a lovely drop-kick – he never seemed to miss'.[28]

With friendly rivalry developing between Smith and Baggott for key forward positions and a senior promotion, 18-year-old Baggott (14 months Smith's junior)

---

[26] *Trident Monthly*, Vol. 1, No. 1, April 1968. The publication commemorated Norm Smith's testimonial dinner, which was held at Melbourne Town Hall on December 20, 1967.
[27] Norma Harmes. Interview with the author.
[28] Ron Baggott. Interview with the author.

was first to get the nod of the selectors, and repaid their faith with 26.25 in the last seven rounds. Importantly, Baggott's development as a full-forward prompted Checker Hughes to move Maurie Gibb to a half-forward flank where he became one of the best in the business.

Norm Smith, then 19, was finally selected to make his senior debut in round 15 – just four rounds after Len Smith's final axing. Wearing the No. 4 guernsey, he became the 543rd player to represent Melbourne. The opponent that day was none other than the fearsome Richmond side, still indoctrinated with Checker Hughes' blood-and-guts style and widely regarded as the toughest in the competition. Smith was named 19th man[29], and started on the bench beside Hughes, whom Smith always regarded as 'probably the greatest strategist the game has known'.[30] While he could easily have spent his afternoon watching on, Smith didn't have to wait long for his first run. Teammate Gordon Jones broke an ankle early in the opening minutes of the match and was carried off the ground, allowing Smith to take up his position on a half-forward flank, opposed to a fearless Tiger half back flanker, Basil McCormack. Smith, who later admitted to being 'a bundle of nerves',[31] recalled: 'The first chance I had for a kick in League football was in front of the MCC members' stand. I tried to run around my mark and Basil McCormack grabbed me and I lost the ball. It's hard to say how silly I felt. But that's what nerves do, and I can understand it when newcomers make the same mistake'.[32]

Although he was one of only four multiple goalscorers on either side – he kicked two of Melbourne's 10 goals in a seven-point loss – Smith was 'moved from opponent to opponent, and it wasn't because I was beating them'.[33] In order, he was opposed to McCormack, dashing defender Martin Bolger and Jack Baggott (who was 10 years older than his brother Ron). In 1962, Smith described the Tigers defence as the strongest he had seen. 'Each was an expert in his position,' Smith marvelled, 'so much so that Richmond adopted the unusual tactics of not resting its ruckmen in defence. The rucks and rovers changed with the forwards.'[34]

Smith's next game was just as 'awe-inspiring'.[35] He made the familiar journey to Collingwood's Victoria Park, but this time his old idols were the sworn enemy.

---

[29] The VFL introduced the 19th man in 1930. When a player was replaced by the 19th man, he could not return to the field.
[30] *Melbourne Truth* series, 1962.
[31] *Melbourne Truth* series, 1962.
[32] *Melbourne Truth* series, 1962.
[33] *Melbourne Truth* series, 1962.
[34] *Melbourne Truth* series, 1962.
[35] *Melbourne Truth* series, 1962.

And he came to know the meaning of parochialism, which even manifested itself in the visitors' changerooms, where the showers were cold, and a low-wattage light-globe provided only dim light so that when the opposition side ran onto the ground the sun would, theoretically, burn their eyes and affect their sight.

That day Smith played against six of his boyhood heroes – survivors from those great Magpie sides – in Harry and Albert Collier, Gordon Coventry, Percy Bowyer, Charlie Dibbs and Len Murphy. Remarkably, this first clash with Collingwood resulted in a draw, 79 points apiece – Melbourne's inaccurate 10.19, boosted by a goal after the final siren by Ron Baggott, equalling Collingwood's 11.13. Smith was goalless against the eventual premiers and conceded, 'I soon realised it was no kindergarten to play League football. It's very hard to diagnose your own form, but I don't think I went very well that day.'[36]

Over many battles at Victoria Park, Smith formed the view that a visiting team's best tactic was to take the ball along the outer wing and avoid the grandstand side of the ground, no matter which way the wind was blowing. He believed that the masses of indignant Magpie fans in the stands unfairly influenced umpiring decisions, and also lifted their side.

Smith's third and final senior game in 1935 was against a very competitive St Kilda at the Junction Oval in round 17 – the penultimate home-and-away match. Although he kicked two goals, the Demons lost by that margin and Smith was dropped to the seconds – the first of only two such demotions in his career. Smith at least felt 'some consolation' that he and Ron Baggott – who that year won the club award for most improved junior player – were eligible for another reserves' finals campaign[37] under inspirational playing coach Bull Adams. The campaign ended in a phenomenal record of five successive reserves' premierships. Again the victim was Geelong, this time by 23 points.

After serving an apprenticeship in the reserves, Smith was ready to stake his claim for a regular senior berth in 1936. Checker Hughes, in an editorial on forward play a decade later, provided an insight into the set-up Smith was entering and what would have been expected of forwards like him:

> A forward division without method is hopeless... A forward line that crowds itself kills itself. The half-forward who crowds down to the goal base plans the funeral. The wing/half-forward should be on the fence and must stay always wide out... to create a space or area either for them to run into to receive a pass, or for other attacking players

---

[36] *Melbourne Truth* series, 1962.
[37] *Melbourne Truth* series, 1962.

of the side to stream through without interruption... The centre half-forward (should position himself) within, say, 15 yards of the circle... The (full) forward line should be well back and well spread. There must also be considerable space between the half-forward and the full-forward line(s). This enables the forwards to make a break into the clear... Forwards should never be standing still, but should be always on the move... A forward should never allow the defender to engage him in conversation. If a forward is close enough to his opponent to engage in conversation, the opponent certainly knows where he is. It is part of a forward's role to create uncertainty in the defender's mind... Play on the forward line is a game of quick movement. Anything static makes the defence easier, while a mobile attack tends to disorganise defence.[38]

Unbeknown to Smith, a behind-closed-doors conversation between Checker Hughes and new Essendon captain-coach Jack Baggott was about to alter the course of his footballing destiny. Baggott was concerned about his new club's lack of playing depth – the Bombers' had won just 14 games in their previous three seasons – so he asked Hughes, his old Tiger coach, if there were any players at Melbourne he was likely to axe, but who might be of value at Essendon.

Hughes said: 'You could possibly have Len Smith.'

But Baggott wasn't interested in Len. In fact, he was of the same opinion as Hughes: that while Len had been a terrific footballer in the VFA, he had not been able to translate that form into the VFL.

Hughes then floated an idea: 'I think you could probably have Len's brother Norm. But he's a bit slow for the half-forward flank.'

Baggott was quite keen about recruiting the younger Smith – perhaps *too keen*. Hughes asked him: 'So, where would you play Norm?'

Baggott replied promptly, and with certainty: 'Oh, he'd be my full-forward.'

Hughes said he would think about it and get back to Baggott.

The exchange must have influenced Hughes' thinking because in the next intra-club practice match he placed the established spearhead Ron Baggott at full-forward in the 'Probables' side and Norm Smith at full-forward in the 'Possibles' side.[39] As fate would have it, Smith, despite never having previously played at full-forward,[40] performed brilliantly in that trial match and impressed Hughes,[41] who decided, in time, to incorporate both players into his forward plans.

---

[38] Checker Hughes, editorial titled 'Fast Attack Beats Defence', published in *The Sporting Globe Football Book* in 1946.
[39] Ron Baggott related this story as his brother Jack told him. Interview with the author.
[40] Craven, John (editor), *Football The Australian Way*, Lansdowne Press, 1969.
[41] Ron Baggott. Interview with the author.

Hughes gave Jack Baggott a courtesy call, but delivered the Bombers coach news he didn't want to hear. 'You were right, Jack,' Hughes said. 'Norm Smith has potential as a full-forward. But bad luck, he's not going to Essendon. In fact, he's not going anywhere. He's staying put.'[42]

Smith wasn't interested in joining Essendon anyway. The sticking point was Smith's insistence to play with his brother. He had made it clear to Baggott that he would only transfer to the Bombers if they also agreed to take on Len Smith.

Baggott was similarly adamant. 'Well,' he said, 'we don't want Len.'

'Well,' Norm said, 'you don't want me then.'[43]

Although Hughes viewed Norm Smith as a long-term option at full-forward, in the meantime, however, he continued to play Ron Baggott there in the seniors. This allowed Smith to grow into his new role in the reserves, where he could learn some of the pre-requisites of the full-forward position: decisive leading, smart positioning, strong body work, pack marking and, of course, goalkicking. But Hughes' hand was forced to an extent when Baggott was suspended for four matches after an indiscretion in round six.[44] An option was to pinch-hit in the short term with a more experienced player like the versatile Jack Mueller or even new captain Allan La Fontaine – who, incidentally, had kicked four and five goals respectively in his previous two outings. But Hughes resisted that temptation and went for the logical replacement, Norm Smith, who had impressed all with his work ethic at training. The move was most successful. Smith was a multiple goalscorer in each of the next eight matches, which netted him 26 goals (2, 4, 4, 3, 3, 4, 2, 4).

It was not simply the number of goals he managed to slot himself that was so praiseworthy; it was the number he created for teammates around him, like Eric "Tarzan" Glass, who kicked 31 goals in the same period, and a club-high 56 for the season. When Baggott returned in round 12, Hughes had a decision to make about the structure of the Demons' attack. With Baggott enjoying only moderate success before his suspension – he had kicked 13 goals in the first six games – Hughes left Smith in the goalsquare and moved Baggott out to centre half-forward. Far from being disappointed, Baggott recalled the excitement they shared:

---

[42] Ron Baggott. Interview with the author.
[43] Garry Pearce related this to the author after hearing Jack Baggott tell the story at a function at the MCG in the late 1970s, early 80s.
[44] Baggott was suspended after being reported by three umpires on the curious charge of 'retaliating' against Footscray's George Bennett and was suspended for four matches. Bennett was found not guilty of striking but guilty of using 'threatening behaviour' and received a six-week ban.

Norm and I were always great mates, so there was no real rivalry between us for the full-forward spot. We were just happy to play together in the forward line. And because Norm had fed me so much before that, naturally I wanted to return the favour when it was my turn to play across half-forward. I didn't have as good disposal as Norm, but I did my best to get the ball to him. But it must be said that while he became the full-forward, he still gave away a lot of goals, and I still managed to get on the end of a lot of his good work.[45]

The effectiveness of the Smith-Baggott combination – which was to become one of the most renowned forward pairings in VFL history – was evident right from their very first senior match together. The emerging Demons, who had risen to fourth on the VFL ladder after winning eight of their 11 matches, faced the daunting prospect of taking on red-hot top side South Melbourne, which had an imposing 10-1 record. It was only Smith's ninth VFL match, and Baggott's 14th, but they directly contributed six goals between them – four to Smith, two to Baggott – as Melbourne transformed a two-goal deficit at three-quarter-time into a 52-point win, courtesy of a 10-goal to nil last-quarter avalanche. While South Melbourne's 'Foreign Legion' side is generally regarded as one of the most brilliant in history, Smith didn't rate it a great team in the true sense. 'On paper,' Smith later wrote, 'the team read like a page out of Who's Who in football... (But) they failed to put the results on the board so they cannot rank as a great... It always appeared to me that South's players played too much as individuals and not enough as a team.'[46]

As is often the case with young players, Smith's form dipped late in the season and he kicked just two goals in the last three rounds – 1, 1 and 0. With competition fierce for senior berths as the Demons entered their first finals campaign in eight years, Smith was dropped back to the reserves. The demotion no doubt hurt Smith, particularly so when the Demons' senior side eliminated Carlton in the first semi-final, before succumbing to South Melbourne in the preliminary final.

Despite the setback, Smith had made huge strides in his development. 'I finally made it,' he later wrote.[47] In 11 senior matches that season, Smith kicked 28.36 – a wayward tally on paper, but not as bad as it sounds when one considers that Ron Baggott kicked 26.38 and, the same year, South Melbourne superstar Bob Pratt, fresh from kicking centuries of goals in the preceding three seasons, could manage only 64.79, (at) a similar conversation rate. Smith's routine approach to goal was

---

[45] Ron Baggott. Interview with the author.
[46] *Melbourne Truth* series, 1962.
[47] *Melbourne Truth* series, 1962.

not to 'merely line up and sight the goals', but to 'look for an object behind the goals and aim for it'.[48]

Rather than wallow in self-pity over his axing, Smith helped the reserves qualify for another Grand Final. The Demons, however, failed in their attempt to win their sixth flag in a row, suffering a 51-point loss to Footscray.

At the club's presentation night, Norm Smith and Pat McNamara were recognised for their dedication when they received 'special training awards'. The same evening, Smith's father Vic, an ardent follower of the Demons since his sons joined the club, presented awards to reserves players Ken Feltschier and Archie Roberts for their performances in the finals. The next year, Vic presented a semi-final award to Smith's long-time mate Richie Emselle.[49]

※※※※※※※※※

In 1936, Norm Smith formed a strong friendship with a teammate; a friendship that was to have an enormous, and continuing, influence on the game that has not been equalled, or broken, in the 70-odd years since. That year Smith struck up a close relationship with a 22-year-old – two years Smith's senior – from the small community of Guildford, 130 kilometres north-west of Melbourne, between Castlemaine and Daylesford. Despite playing just four senior games as a mature-age recruit that season, he won the 'best club man' award' and was a gutsy small man who would become a valuable rover/goalsneak. He was Ron Barassi (senior).

Barassi was a second-generation Australian-born Italian. His paternal grandfather, Mario Giuseppe Barassi, migrated from his native northern Italy to Australia via Switzerland in 1855. Like so many thousands of other foreigners, Mario Barassi had made the arduous journey hoping to strike it lucky on the Victorian goldfields, but eventually had to be content with carving out a living as a farmer.[50] Many migrants received ribbing, and worse, in their adopted country. And Ron Barassi was no different, as his son, Ron junior explained. 'Everyone with ethnic names copped it back then – even a third-generation Australian-born Italian like me,' Ron Barassi junior said. 'They called my father "Mussolini" (pronounced "Muscle-ini"), in reference to the Italian dictator of the time. But as much as you mightn't have liked it, you almost accepted it and used it as a spur to do better.'[51]

---

[48] Peter Smith, *The Sporting Globe*, Saturday September 7, 1974.
[49] Melbourne Football Club Annual Report, 1936.
[50] Ron Barassi junior. Interview with the author.
[51] Ron Barassi junior. Interview with the author.

Barassi junior also elaborated upon what he described as one of the main reasons for Melbourne's rise to superpower status in the late 1930s. 'They were the first club to formed a businessman's support group, called the coterie,' he said. 'They were influential people who could find jobs for players. This was towards the end of the Depression and after it, when jobs were like gold. My father was one of the many beneficiaries of this scheme – they got him a job in the parks and gardens department on the Melbourne City Council.'[52]

Smith and Barassi, along with two other members of the Demons' 'Northcote connection', Ron Baggott and Richie Emselle, became inseparable mates. They were all clean-living teetotallers. Emselle and Barassi even played cricket with Smith at Dennis. Emselle and his wife Belle also opposed the Smiths in regular mixed-doubles tennis matches. Baggott recalled those days with great fondness: 'We were probably the four closest players in the club. Thick as thieves, and we always stuck together. Our wives were very close too. They were all bonzer blokes, very loyal mates you could trust with your life, and I've got no doubt it helped us on the field. You'd always back each other up, that's for sure'.[53]

Smith was the only Melbourne player at the time who owned a car – a grey Ford.[54] He happily drove the other three, along with teammates like Jack Mueller, to their various destinations. After dances held by Melbourne Football Club at the MCG, Smith would drive his mates to Northcote for supper, then drop them off home in suburbs like Middle Park and Windsor, before driving back home to Northcote – without ever asking for petrol money.[55] Smith even drove several reserves teammates to an end-of-season jaunt in Castlemaine.

Norm Smith 'wasn't a material person'. He saw money as one of life's necessities, but it was 'nowhere near as important as mateship', and his strong value system demanded – among other things – honesty, and compelled him to help others.[56]

This trait was later borne out in Smith's relationship with Ron Barassi's son. Barassi senior's wife Elza gave birth to their first child on February 27, 1936. They named him Ronald Dale Barassi. He became known as Ron junior or 'Young Ronny'. Norm Smith took a genuine interest in him and discovered that he possessed remarkable determination even as a toddler. For decades, Smith dined out on his favourite story about young Ronny, who later became an Australian icon. Smith's retelling of the yarn went something like this:

---

[52] Ron Barassi junior. Interview with the author.
[53] Ron Baggott. Interview with the author.
[54] Ron Baggott. Interview with the author.
[55] Jack Mueller on *The Tony Charlton Football Show* on Channel Nine, on Sunday July 25, 1965.
[56] Ron Baggott. Interview with the author.

When Ronny was three, he hacked down the family's favourite rose tree with a tomahawk. His father gave him his first hiding, but throughout his punishment, while his father's hand came into heavy contact with his rump, young Ronny raised his bottom lip, stuck his chin out and refused to cry. Even at that tender age he had spirit. He was born strong-willed and the characteristic has grown with him.[57]

▼▼▼▼▼▼▼▼▼

Season 1937 loomed as a significant one for the Smith brothers. While Norm Smith was determined to command a regular senior game after a poor finish to a promising 'breakthrough' season, Len had reached the crossroads in his football career and had to decide whether he wanted to star in the VFA or have another crack at the elite level.

After Len's career had stalled at Melbourne in 1935, he returned to Northcote, where he played under one of his brother's Collingwood heroes, five-time premiership champion Harold Rumney, and won his third VFA premiership. Len played much of the 1937 season with Northcote but found he still harboured dreams of becoming a regular VFL player. Late in the season, after notching a total of 72 senior games at Northcote, Len agreed to join his former Northcote teammate Doug Nicholls at nearby Fitzroy.[58] Hec de Lacy, the chief football writer at *The Sporting Globe*, enthused that Len was 'likely to be a champion' with the Maroons, and had 'the hallmark of a footballer all over him'. He also wrote:

> 'Norman confessed to me that Len was the better footballer of the two. That may or may not be proved, but certainly the jinx that prevented these brothers from playing side by side in the Melbourne attack was not kind to the... Demons. Both are natural forwards. Both have similar cleverness in luring a full-back out of position. Both are excellent marks and long, accurate kicks. If you've seen one, you've seen the other. Fancy the Melbourne attack with two Norman Smiths'.[59]

Len Smith played his first game for Fitzroy in round 15, 1937, against fourth-placed Richmond at his new footballing home, the Brunswick Street Oval.

---

[57] *The Sun* series, 1967.
[58] Doug Nicholls was a most notable individual. A brilliant Aboriginal footballer who stood just 157cms tall and weighed 65kgs, he played 54 games with Fitzroy from 1932-37 and was selected for Victoria in 1935. He was also a professional runner who became a pastor and was later appointed Governor of South Australia. He was knighted in 1972.
[59] *The Sporting Globe*, 1937.

With the middle-of-the-road Maroons bereft of genuine key forwards, Len Smith was selected at full-forward and contributed two goals to a total of 11.13 (79) in a four-goal loss to the finals-bound Tigers. The following week Len Smith played one of his finest games, bagging six of Fitzroy's 15 goals in a 22-point win over fellow battler South Melbourne at the Lake Oval. Len Smith was easily the Maroons' best player and if it were not for a nine-goal haul from South's Roy Moore at the other end, he would have been best-afield. That same day, Norm Smith also kicked five goals in a superb win over Collingwood.

Len Smith continued to play reasonably well in the final two games, despite receiving limited opportunities. In a shock 49-point loss to the 10th-placed Essendon at Windy Hill in round 17, Len Smith was one of the few Maroons to shine, kicking three of his side's 10 goals. In the last round against a star-studded Geelong, he kicked two of Fitzroy's 12 majors in a 28-point loss at home. In the last four rounds of the season, Len Smith kicked 13 goals (2,6,3,2), a club-high in that period, with the next best being Jock McKenzie with 11, followed by his skipper, the brilliant Haydn Bunton, with seven. Bunton, the League's first triple Brownlow Medallist, having won medals in 1931, 1932 and 1935, won the club goalkicking for the second successive season with 37 goals in 16 games, following his previous effort of 33. Not surprisingly, Len Smith later rated Bunton the most talented player of his time 'by far', adding that the Fitzroy superstar would 'get the ball, bounce it and weave gracefully through the opposition'.[60] However, Len Smith was disappointed that Bunton – who had been replaced by Gordon Rattray after just one season as captain-coach – 'wasn't a team man, and would rather shoot for goal than pass to a teammate'.[61]

While Len Smith's time with his new club would be punctuated by injuries and the odd stint in the reserves, Norm Smith, who had played 44 reserves games[62], would never return to the lower grade. However, he would remain eternally proud of the fact he had served a footballing apprenticeship and earned his spot in the senior side after something of a slog. While Smith's development had been, at worst, slow, and at best steady, following his breakthrough effort in 1936, he now became almost overnight, hot property. Smith's star potential was even realised by Collingwood – the winner of the past two premierships – which made a serious approach to him.[63] It was an approach Smith would have gleefully accepted just a year or two earlier. While flattered by the Magpies' interest, Smith rejected their

---

[60] Pollard, Jack (editor), *High Mark: The Complete Book on Australian Football*, Murray, 1964.
[61] Pollard, Jack (editor), *High Mark: The Complete Book on Australian Football*, Murray, 1964.
[62] *Melbourne Truth* series, 1962.
[63] Newspaper report, September 13, 1941.

offer to play in a star-studded attack alongside Gordon Coventry (who was about to enter his final season) and the precociously talented Ron Todd. He had just started to feel comfortable at Melbourne, a club on the rise with a swag of young stars, and while it must have been tempting to move closer to both his home and his footballing roots, he could not bring himself to make the move to Collingwood, which was seemingly in the twilight of its dominant era with ageing stars like Gordon Coventry and the Colliers getting towards the end of their careers.

Smith vindicated both Collingwood's overture and his decision to remain with the Demons by producing his first full season of senior football in 1937. He played 20 games, including two finals, in a side that finished second in the minor rounds, but equal top in terms of wins (15), just four percent behind top side Geelong. Smith's tally of 45.55 (with three 'posters' and 22 kicks that sailed out of bounds[64]) was second among the Demons, behind only Baggott who had moved out to centre-half-forward and kicked 51.40 (including one poster and 16 out of bounds). The Smith-Baggott duo, which produced a combined 191 scoring shots for the season, had become recognised as a double-act that would – considering their respective ages of 21 and 20 years – pose headaches for defenders for many seasons to come. Indeed, Smith and Baggott would, more than 60 years later, be selected in Melbourne's 'Team of the Century' in their respective positions.

Smith later joked: 'I'd lead out and Baggs would kick it over my head. I'd lead out again and he'd ignore me. I'd call out: Baggs, you so-and-so, you never bloody pass it to me! The full-back would be grinning, thinking: These two blokes can't stand each other. But the next time I went to make a lead I'd take two steps and Baggs would put the ball on my chest. We'd fool the full-back'.[65]

The pair also had their opponents arguing among themselves. Baggott said:

> 'We moved around so much that we confused them at times. Smithy was the key to it; he was the general – a real genius at it. The backmen from the other side would be blaming each other and saying: "That was your fault", and one of his teammates would go back at him and say: "No it wasn't, it was *your* fault". Smithy would just look at me with a wry grin. We knew we had them then'.[66]

---

[64] It is unknown how many of these kicks were actual shots at goal. This tally was second at Melbourne to Percy Beames, who sent 23 kicks over the boundary line. Importantly, from 1925 to 1939, free kicks were awarded against players who simply kicked the ball out of bounds, provided it had not been touched in transit.

[65] Keith Carroll, a Melbourne premiership player under Norm Smith in the 1950s, recalled Norm telling him this. Carroll related this to this author.

[66] Ron Baggott. Interview with the author.

Baggott explained that their mateship – obvious in team photos, with the pair often standing next to each other – was the main factor in their success, adding:

> 'We knew how each other played the game and we adapted to it. It probably stemmed from being great mates. Whenever we got the opportunity we'd try to hit each other on the chest. We didn't really talk about it too much; it just seemed to happen naturally. When we were at our best, things seemed to run like clockwork. You could almost call some of it uncanny, because it wasn't rehearsed; it just happened. Norm wasn't quick but he was very mobile, and I wasn't slow, so that certainly helped; it made it harder to find opponents for us, and harder to shut us down. They needed two blokes who were not only mobile enough to run with us, but also strong enough to knock the ball away in the air. At times, the play would be such that Norm would lead up the ground and I'd notice it so I'd drop back deeper towards the goalsquare, which proved a successful move because I got a lot of goals like that. Norm couldn't care less who kicked the goals, as long as we were the side kicking them!'[67]

Although Smith was hot-headed off the field, he was one of the coolest and most calculating players on it, which was exemplified in the way he approached his role in Melbourne's forward line. He was the chief avenue to goal – whether it be directly as a leading target, or indirectly with the numerous 'assists' he provided teammates – but he was, by and large, a decoy full-forward.

As was customary at the time, and for decades after, the full-back was duty-bound to follow the full-forward, and Hughes and Smith fully exploited this. In an almost unheard-of scheme devised by Hughes, Smith would take his often bigger and slower opponent on hard leads well up the field, as far as the centre, to lure the full-back out of his comfort zone. Perhaps from Hughes as well, he gleaned and subscribed to the philosophy that: 'Play is made by the player *without* the ball, not the player with the ball'.[68] Smith often provided dummy leads in the knowledge that while he himself would not get the ball, he would create valuable space behind him for teammates like Baggott, Glass, Maurie Gibb, and opportunist rovers like Barassi, Lou "Pop" Reiffel and Percy Beames. In the process, he would sometimes 'lose' or out-position the full-back in upfield traffic and would suddenly be unattended or have the 'drop' on his opponent, and become a damaging option himself. Not only was Smith the fulcrum of this

---

[67] Ron Baggott. Interview with the author.
[68] Related by John Lord in an interview with the author.

multi-pronged system of attack, but, not surprisingly, he also became a staunch believer in its merits when he later joined the coaching ranks. 'In this manner,' he later wrote, 'no one man can be bottled up. Or if anyone has a bad day, somebody else can come good.'[69]

Smith's unorthodox role became evident in the second round of 1937, when the Demons slaughtered Jack Baggott's Essendon – 25.20 (170) to 13.7 (85). Smith kicked four goals and was rated second-best on ground in *The Sporting Globe* by Jim Abernethy. 'Smith was scouting as far as the centre line,' Abernethy observed. '(He) was proving an elusive forward, and was a problem for the 'Dons' defence, continually leading well out, he never neglected his scoring opportunities, while his tactics provided the other forwards with chances with which Essendon were unable to cope… Melbourne's full-forward not only possesses football brains but must rank as the most unselfish forward in the game.'[70] A few days of reflection later, Abernethy emboldened his opinion of Smith, declaring to readers: 'Never before have I seen a full-forward quite as unselfish as Norman Smith'. (Fittingly, Smith claimed club awards as both the 'most unselfish player' and the 'best forward' that season.) Hec de Lacy, Abernethy's senior colleague at *The Sporting Globe*, was also captivated by Smith's refreshing team-first attitude:

> When Melbourne decided to experiment with their attack, they had to place unqualified confidence in the unselfishness of the man they placed (at) full-forward. They chose Smith. Every forward likes to kick goals… A large tally assures him of a place in the side… The temptation, therefore, is for a centre forward to be selfish. (But) Melbourne wanted a man who would forget about his tally of goals – a man who would decoy the defenders into false positions while his teammates nipped in behind and got the score. Smith plays the role to a nicety. Melbourne scored 25 goals on Saturday and Smith… got only four. But, as Jim Abernethy says, he could well be credited with creating the opportunity for Glass getting four, Gibb three, Beames four, Barassi two and Reiffel one.
>
> Smith leads the defenders far from their ground, and the other forwards work behind him. Yet, as if to prove his own ability to get goals (himself), he occasionally stops and adds a goal here and there. He thus proves himself far too dangerous to be allowed a free leg… (His) ability to lead his backman out and then pop up unattended that makes him so formidable, (and) so unsettling to a defence…

---

[69] Norm Smith's coaching notes, supplied by Clyde Laidlaw, who played under Norm at Melbourne and later coached South Melbourne reserves during Norm's reign as senior coach.

[70] Jim Abernethy, Melbourne 1926 premiership player and correspondent with *The Sporting Globe*, May 3, 1937.

> He is an average player in the air, safe rather than brilliant. The same describes his ground work. There is nothing, in fact, that makes him a champion footballer except the greatest attribute of all – a cool head and football brains.[71]

If there had been some semblance of mystery over Smith's tactics, there were no secrets three weeks later when Melbourne encountered the perennially strong Collingwood side in front of 44,623 people at the MCG. The Magpie with the job on Smith was none other than Collingwood's 'Prince of Full-Backs', the high-flying, long-kicking Jack Regan. But Checker Hughes decided to reverse the roles and assign Smith the job of nullifying Regan, a fellow Northcote boy. There could be few tougher tasks in the game than to shut down Regan, the established full-back in the Victorian side who, the previous season, had won his first club best-and-fairest and for the second time had earned 17 votes in the Brownlow Medal to finish equal sixth to Fitzroy's 'Dinny' Ryan. The plan was for Smith to take off on searching leads and lure Regan away from his comfort zone and thus rob the Magpies of much of their marking strength and rebound ability deep in defence. Hughes told Smith: 'Take Regan walkabout. Finish up in front of the grandstand and talk about the girls or the pictures.'[72] Smith must have known that such a role would severely limit his own effectiveness as an individual, but as Percy Beames later wrote, 'it was just part of his unselfish nature to do what suited the needs of the team best', and 'he never stopped doing the right thing' by the team.[73] Not surprisingly in his tussle with Regan, Smith went goalless, but the typically theatrical text that accompanied a newspaper cartoon summed up how well he had performed his role:

> A factor in Melbourne's success was the perplexing of 'Long' John Regan. John went to the MCG and met a forward named Smith. Smith is fond of taking long walks up the ground. He was out to lead John away from home!! If necessary he was prepared to walk right off the ground. Up the stairs of the Members' Stand. And sit among the Members!! However while John was out walking with Smith a young man named Baggott kicked six goals![74]

---

[71] Hec de Lacy, *The Sporting Globe*, 1937.
[72] Percy Beames, in a souvenir brochure for the Norm Smith Commemorative Dinner, which was held on July 12, 1979, to inaugurate the Norm Smith Medal.
[73] Percy Beames, in a souvenir brochure for the Norm Smith Commemorative Dinner, which was held on July 12, 1979, to inaugurate the Norm Smith Medal.
[74] Contemporary newspaper cartoon contained in the private files of Peter Smith.

Checker Hughes was chuffed with the efforts of his developing forward, who had perfectly executed the coach's well-conceived plans. 'Regan liked to get the last "drop" at the ball,' Hughes explained. 'He had beaten the best of them without redress, but that day he met trouble in plenty. Smithy led him out to centre half-back and created a big open space behind him. Regan was neither at home nor visiting, and soon the famous Magpies were chattering to themselves, each blaming the other. Out of that day grew a forward system that has never been beaten'.[75]

Smith's performance drew acclaim from the harshest critics. Hec de Lacy, the often provocative chief football writer at *The Sporting Globe*, wrote: '(Smith) was opposed to Jack Regan… (who was) recognised as one of the greatest fullbacks Australian football has produced. Here was a test for a young player. But… Smith handled Regan like a veteran. Before quarter-time, Regan was wondering just where he was'.[76]

In the return duel with top side Collingwood – which was without Regan, who was sidelined with injury – Smith was more conspicuously triumphant. The round 16 clash at Victoria Park was remarkable on two other fronts: Melbourne's last-quarter revival, the unprecedented goal-feast, and the negative tone of certain media reports. With about 10 minutes left, the Magpies, who had been in front all day, held a seemingly insurmountable 31-point lead. But the third-placed Demons then piled on 6.6 to nothing to win by 11 points – their first victory at Collingwood since 1921. The scoreline – 22.21 (153) to 21.16 (142) – also produced a then-record aggregate score of 295 points,[77] which would have been even more imposing had it not been for 10 'posters'. Although the game was played at a frenzied speed, football writers roundly bemoaned the distinct lack of defensive pressure, with former Carlton champion Rod McGregor informing readers of *The Sporting Globe*: 'There was no pretence at organised defence by either side… in this orgy of scoring'. Despite the negativity, Smith, free from Regan's clutches, kicked five goals and was praised by the same scribe: 'Lock-Smith-Reiffel sounds something like a mechanical contrivance, and the machine-like movements of these three working together won the game for Melbourne against Collingwood… Smith on Saturday's game reminded me of Laurie Nash in marking and elusiveness, and could take the centre half-forward position and make a success of it… Lock and Smith made most of the bullets for Reiffel to fire'.[78]

---

[75] *The Sporting Globe*, 1949.
[76] *The Sporting Globe*, 1949.
[77] According to *The AFL Record Guide to Season 2007*, there are now 46 aggregate scores above 300 points.
[78] *The Sporting Globe*, August 16, 1937.

Smith's strong, reliable, marking was made more remarkable by the fact he had 'fractionally smaller hands than he should have had for a man of his size'.[79] The following matter-of-fact description of Smith appeared in *The Argus* in 1937. Smith was unsure if he was fond of the correspondent's observations.[80]

> Norman Smith, the Melbourne full-forward, is of middle-class size, and is an unobtrusive personality. He's red-headed but a placid footballer. He neither bumps nor executes fancy turns, but strolls about the field in a quiet sort of way, and one does not notice him particularly. The ball comes near him, and he picks it up, handballs it to somebody nearby, or stab-kicks it neatly. He has the strange complex for a full-forward of not wanting to kick goals himself, and is quite happy as long as someone else is putting the ball through. Smith moves beautifully when required, can kick long distances, and is the most dangerous and effective forward in the game today. That nonchalant manner covers a great deal of cleverness, a quick-thinking football brain and a very cool head.

But Smith didn't have it all his own way. His accuracy when shooting for goal, while usually more than acceptable for the time, was occasionally a problem. In round seven, North Melbourne's Bill Findlay kicked 0.7, which Smith might have watched with some amusement from the other end, especially as he bagged six majors himself in a landslide 122-point win at the MCG. Ironically, just three weeks later, Smith also kicked 0.7 – against Fitzroy at the Brunswick Street Oval. Admittedly, he had been out of practice after kicking one goal in each of his previous two matches. Smith and Findlay still share the third worst conversion rate in an AFL/VFL match for players who have gone goalless. In that round 10 match, Smith was the main culprit in a horribly inaccurate scoreline of 11.23 (89), but Percy Beames (five goals) and Ron Baggott (four) kicked straighter and the Demons won by 29 points.

The Demons entered their second successive finals series full of running with a 15-3 record after winning their last four games by an average of 30 points. But with several players missing with injuries in each match – namely Ray Wartman, Maurie Gibb, Les Reiffel, Frank Roberts and Bert Chandler – the Demons were rapidly disposed of. They went down to eventual premier Geelong by just 12 points in the second semi-final – the then highest scoring finals match in history with an aggregate of 238 points – before suffering a 55-point hammering from Collingwood

---

[79] Bill Stephen. Interview with the author.
[80] *Melbourne Truth* series, 1962.

in the preliminary final. Melbourne was within a point of the Magpies at half-time but was outscored 10.7 to 1.7 after that, with Smith snapping the Demons' only goal in the second half. Once again opposed to Jack Regan, and once again employing the roaming tactics that had been so successful earlier in the season, Smith 'played a leading part in restoring Melbourne's morale'[81] in the third quarter but this time lowered his colours to the champion full-back, who hauled in several 'grand' marks, including one in particular in the centre, and, according to *The Sporting Globe*, was one of the best players afield. Smith later ranked Regan as the best full-back he confronted,[82] and doubted if the game had seen a better backman.[83] He wrote: 'Regan could run close to even time in his prime, he was tall, with a mighty spring and magnificent judgment, and he was essentially a ball player. And he capped off all this equipment with a glorious kick.'[84] At a bar one night during his coaching career, Smith introduced Regan to one of his awestruck Melbourne players, who gushed that Regan had been the great Bob Pratt's 'master'. Smith expanded the compliment, emphasising: 'Jack was *everyone's* master'.[85]

Collingwood progressed to the Grand Final and, in what has long been regarded as one of the most stunning battles for the premiership in history, was defeated by a fast-finishing Geelong. An interested onlooker at the MCG that day was Norm Smith. The match made such an impression on Smith that 25 years later, as a coach with seven Grand Finals' experience, he marvelled: 'If it was not the greatest (Grand Final), it was certainly one of them. Collingwood matches are usually bone-crushing affairs, but not this one. It was a game completely free of spite... The pace was a cracker, the marking and kicking scintillating.'[86]

A notable retiree after the 1937 Grand Final was Magpie goalkicking machine Gordon Coventry, who, with 1299 goals, was the greatest goalkicker in the history of the game until Tony Lockett broke the 1300-goal barrier in 1999.

♆♆♆♆♆♆♆♆♆

Although Norm Smith would eventually look back on the 1938 VFL season as 'a muddling sort of year', studded with stirring wins against three of the four eventual finalists, yet pock-marked with 'unaccountable losses' to several battling

---

[81] Ivan McAlpine, Hawthorn captain, in a column in *The Sporting Globe*, September 20, 1937.
[82] Pollard, Jack (editor), *High Mark: The Complete Book on Australian Football*, Murray, 1964.
[83] *Melbourne Truth* series, 1962.
[84] Pollard, Jack (editor), *High Mark: The Complete Book on Australian Football*, Murray, 1964.
[85] Keith Carroll, Melbourne player of the 1950s. Interview with the author.
[86] *Melbourne Truth* series, 1962.

sides, he would also recognise it as a watershed in his football career, his best season to date.[87] In truth, he had made a quantum leap.

Smith and the Demons 1938 in the best way possible, upsetting reigning premier Geelong by 17 points at Corio Oval, with the Demon full-forward bagging six goals against virtually the same miserly defence that, just seven months earlier, had restricted Collingwood to just four goals in the second half of the Grand Final.

After four rounds, the inconspicuous-but-effective Norm Smith had raced to 20 goals (6, 4, 4, 6). His second haul of six majors, in a 52-point win over South Melbourne at the MCG, inspired Hec de Lacy to write in *The Sporting Globe*:

Norman Smith - The Ideal Forward
Norman Smith, Melbourne's full-forward, was easily the outstanding player in the Melbourne-South Melbourne game... His kicking with either the drop (kick), which he used for long distances, the stab-pass or punt, is usually accurate. His marking is always safe. To evade his opponent, he frequently uses the double turn to advantage, and is rarely caught in possession. With his perfect balance and coolness, Smith is the ideal forward. His six goals against South on Saturday were well deserved, not so much for their numerical value, but for the manner in which they were gained and the openings he made for the other forwards by his long, dashing leads... Interstate honours should soon come his way.[88]

At the halfway mark of the season, Smith had kicked 43 goals and the Demons were 7-2 after recording narrow wins over the eventual Grand Finalists, Carlton and Collingwood. Against the latter, Smith booted seven of Melbourne's 17 goals to outgun Gordon Coventry's brilliant successor Ron Todd, who kicked six. The respective merits of both star forwards would be debated throughout the season. But on this particular day, a newspaper report described Smith's effort as follows:

'His ability to kick goals from almost any angle makes Norman Smith a very live wire in the Melbourne attack, but his unselfishness is even more valuable to his side. Smith showed the team spirit on Saturday when he always looked for a teammate in a better position immediately he got possession. Melbourne scored two certain goals in this fashion, although there would have been only a slight doubt had Smith taken a shot himself on each occasion'.[89]

---

[87] *Melbourne Truth* series, 1962.
[88] *The Sporting Globe*, May 18, 1938.
[89] Contemporary newspaper report.

The very next week, Smith kicked his first bag of eight goals – out of a Melbourne total of 18 – in a 30-point win over North Melbourne. Although Smith's form remained solid throughout, the Demons lost three games in a row to slip back to the pack. But just when his side was being discounted as a finals contender, Smith exploded into his best form. Over a three-week period from round 13 to 15, he contributed 18 (5, 5, 8) of the Demons' 37 goals – the next best were Barassi and Beames with three apiece – to pilot Melbourne to crucial wins by one, three and 29 points respectively and resurrect the club's finals aspirations. The last part of that trilogy was an eight-goal virtuoso performance against the lowly South Melbourne at the Lake Oval in round 15. The Swans were within eight points at half-time, but in a match that produced just one other multiple goalkicker – that being South's Owen Evans, who kicked five goals – Smith rose to another level to take the game away from the home side in the second half. A newspaper report raved: 'Smith was in brilliant form… Each of the eight goals he scored was the result of his own ability, whether by making position, marking in the pack or by snatching the ball from a scrimmage. Smith is not spectacular but he is a deadly kick'.[90] Football writer Kevin Hogan from *The Sun* also marvelled at his display:

A Cool Redhead
Full-forward play of distinctive type and method lifted Norm Smith to top place for effectiveness in Melbourne's win from South. Methodical in technique and brilliant in his tactics, Smith was a will-o'-the-wisp South's defenders could never counter. Long leads alternated with stay-at-home methods, backed by faultless marking and sure kicking, gave him eight goals. He had a hand in at least four others. Smith's coolness is rare in a player of his years (22).[91]

In round 17, the Demons defeated eventual premier Carlton for the second time, by 17 points. Smith kicked four goals in each of these victories. His performance against the Blues drew praise in the press: 'Smith… gave a magnificent exhibition of high marking… Opposed to Frank Gill, one of the high flyers of the League, Smith waged some thrilling aerial duels with the Carlton man. Wandering far down the field, Smith presented a problem that Carlton was unable to solve, and when he was not kicking goals himself, he was passing the ball on to another high mark in Ron Baggott. Between them they accounted for nine of Melbourne's 14 goals'.[92]

---

[90] Contemporary newspaper report.
[91] *The Sun*, 1938.
[92] Contemporary newspaper report, 1938.

Melbourne's season came down to the last-round clash at Collingwood. This time, Todd slotted four goals while Smith managed just two, and this was also the difference between the two sides, with the Demons squandering several scoring opportunities in the dying minutes and suffering a shattering nine-point loss.

At season's end, there was intriguing discussion about who of Todd and Smith was the more valuable forward. Todd had kicked a league-high 102 goals for the season, and would finish with 120.78 (36 percent of Collingwood's total goals) after playing three finals – he kicked a record-equalling 11 goals in the preliminary final against Geelong – while the more team-orientated Smith had been Todd's nearest rival with a club record of 80.53 (15 out of bounds), which eclipsed the old mark of 73 set by George Margitich in 1930. Smith's exploits accounted for 31 percent of the Demons' productivity. (Percy Beames was second in the club goalkicking with 37.34; Baggott was next with 32.14.) Smith had been one of only two Melbourne players – Ray Wartman was the other – to play all 18 games, and he had kicked at least four goals on 14 occasions. But the argument could not be won by quoting statistics alone. Making a comparison was difficult because observers were not comparing like with like. In fact, probably the only thing Todd and Smith had in common was their position. In many ways they were the antithesis of each other: Todd the spectacular individualist, the entertainer, who ran like a hare, kicked miraculous goals from all angles and distances and jumped like a kangaroo to take sky-scraping marks, completely at odds with the no-nonsense figure of Smith, who was simply the ultimate team man. *The Sporting Globe's* Jim Abernethy wrote of Smith: 'This man isn't a tradesman, he's a designer. I have never seen a more unselfish player'.

Abernethy and his colleagues at *The Sporting Globe* boldly selected Smith over Todd in their team of the year, explaining: 'It's a moot point which of the two is better. However, we gave the vote to Smith because he has the true sense of creating a forward system about him. He helps teammates to almost as many goals as he gets himself. Todd, on the other hand, is essentially a spearhead. The whole fabric of the team works about Todd. He is brilliant and undoubtedly a match winner. Smith is little behind Todd in the air and a much safer ground player'.[93]

Another esteemed observer who publicly bought into the argument was North Melbourne captain-coach and Essendon great Keith Forbes, who said: 'Smith is the best forward in the game today. Put him in front of the Collingwood attack and he'd get no end of goals – 160 in a season… I don't believe Baggott could hold his place in the team if it were not for Smith. Smith gives him everything. Smith

---

[93] *The Sporting Globe*, August 24, 1938.

absolutely kills his own play to make Baggott and (other) men nearer the goal.... I have seen a lot of full-forwards in my time, but this fellow Smith is outstanding, a regular tiger, and the hardest man to overcome that could be pitted against a defence. Put Smith where Ron Todd stands in front of the Collingwood line-up and then see who gets most goals. I'd put pounds to gooseberries on Smith'.[94]

Smith capped off a superb individual season with his first club best-and-fairest award, which was a clear indication of the esteem with which Checker Hughes and his coaching staff regarded their selfless full-forward.

---

[94] *The Sporting Globe*, 1938.

3

THE FIRST HAT-TRICK

[1939-41]

As has always been the case when a player undergoes a meteoric rise to prominence and becomes a one of his side's most important cogs – and there is little doubt that Norm Smith was by now the pivotal Demon forward – opposition teams spent more time devising ways to nullify his influence. Consequently, in terms of individual performance, the 1939 season was a trying one for Smith. Collectively, however, as the leader of a superbly functioning forward line, his value was further underlined.

The Demons, boasting seven players who contributed more than 20 goals that season, became the heaviest scoring team in the competition. They piled on more than 100 points in a record 15 games, all of which was due in no small part to the creativity and direction of Norm Smith. In response to the ultra-negative tactics of even closer-checking opponents, Smith's answer was to provide more long leads and attempt to 'lose' his man when he doubled back. This, of course, meant that when he won the ball on a lead he was often too far out from goal to have a shot, even allowing for his prodigious drop-kicking. (Smith was one of the few full-forwards who favoured the drop-kick when shooting at goal, even from point-blank range. Most others used either the flat-punt or the torpedo-punt.) But Smith wasn't perturbed by this subtle evolution in his role, later explaining: 'I would then find it necessary to pass to a teammate, such as Jack Mueller, who would drop back into the pocket. It is not impossible to play this way, and it still enables you to contribute towards the goals kicked for your side, even if you are not the one to kick them'.[1]

---

[1] Norm Smith in *The Sun*, 1973.

It was precisely this attitude that made Smith such a popular footballer – among both his teammates and fans. *The Argus* detected this sentiment as it introduced a new award to the football public before the start of the 1939 season: 'Every successful full-forward in League and Association football has a high place in the hearts of the followers of his club. This is particularly true of Norman Smith... Smith's ability and fairness were demonstrated last season... Melbourne has other exceptionally popular players. However, Smith is regarded by his friends as being the strongest contender for The Argus Popular Player Quest'.

Despite spending much of his time outside scoring range, Smith still had 126 shots at goal for the season – just seven shy of his stellar 1938 – to again win the Demons' goalkicking award. However, he kicked 54.72, a conversion rate of just 43 percent. He still enjoyed several standout performances: six goals in a 94-point win over second-placed Collingwood at the MCG in round 10;[2] five goals in a 24-point win over first-time finalist St Kilda at the Junction Oval in round 14; and a bag of seven in a comprehensive round 16 win over Geelong at the MCG. But he endured two uncharacteristically barren periods – in seven matches between rounds three and nine, he kicked just 14 goals (1, 2, 2, 2, 3, 2, 2), and in five matches between rounds 11 and 15, he managed just 11 goals (0, 4, 0, 5, 2). The seven-goal haul against the Cats therefore came as a relief, as was reported in the media: 'After a rather lean period, Norman Smith, Melbourne's talented forward, returned to his best form against Geelong on Saturday. Never the type of player to be judged solely on the number of goals he kicks in a game, Smith, in addition to getting seven himself, probably was directly responsible for five others. One incident appreciated by the crowd as typical of his unselfish play was when he was within easy range of the sticks himself, but made doubly sure by passing to Beames running ahead of him into the open goal'.[3]

Beames, who represented Victoria in both football and cricket and later became a renowned sports writer for *The Age*, was often a beneficiary of Smith's creativity. The superstar rover was effusive in his praise of his full-forward, describing Smith as the most unselfish player he had seen.[4] 'He'd make opportunities for everyone in the team, to the detriment of himself,' Beames said.[5] Decades later, Beames provided the following enlightening insight into what it was like to play alongside Smith, capturing his uncompromising attitude towards team play:

---

[2] The Demons inflicted Collingwood's heaviest defeat in its history to that point.
[3] Contemporary newspaper report, 1939.
[4] *The Age*, Monday July 30, 1973.
[5] *Red and Blue: The History of the Melbourne Football Club*, written and narrated by Stephen Phillips and produced by Australian Football Video in 2005.

Give any footballer one wish and it is a safe bet about the answer – to be the best player in League football. (But) Norm Smith was one player you would have lost your money on. Individual achievement played a secondary role in... (his) football make-up... In every way, Smith typified that very true football philosophy – a champion team will always beat a team of champions. It was what the team did and how it achieved success that meant everything to Smith...

(He) was no champion, nor did he claim to be. His movements never rivalled the grace and dexterity of Robert Flower, there was nothing of the spectacular, breathtaking Peter Knights' marking feats, nor could it be said his ball-handling ability matched the brilliance of Alex Jesaulenko. But you don't have to be over-endowed with special and particular skills to be a champion team player and that is exactly what Smith was – a champion team player. Without question, Smith was the best team player I played with or have seen at Melbourne.

It was a pocket forward's dream to play alongside (him).... Smith was a fierce and desperate competitor, not just for part of the game, but from the first bounce to the final siren. His relentless fierceness in going after the ball, regardless of physical risk or weight of opposition, told not so much in the possessions he won as in the wealth of opportunities (he) opened up for Jack Mueller, myself and others alongside him. Time and again, goals kicked by Mueller and myself were set up by Smith. Shrewdly, Smith, with perfect timing, would drift across and block the spoiling attempts of opponents and leave the way clear for the telling marking ability of Mueller... There was... no "soft side" in his football make-up. Some players, like Bruce Doull...produce almost a maximum effort, week in, week out... (and) Smith belonged to that special breed of footballers...

While you received all the help needed, don't believe it was all proper and respectable playing alongside Smith. It was if you did the right thing by the team, if you were a genuine trier and, regardless of the odds, put in. But if anyone loafed or put in those few short steps... then Smith became brutally frank in saying his piece. Teammates didn't need to be thin-skinned. He didn't just stop with team players. Umpires and opponents were also quick to get abuse and criticism. His praise and encouragement came just as spontaneously and if and when trouble started, as it often did with me, then it was Smith who was the first teammate to the spot. Smith in every possible way did more than his duty as a Melbourne player.[6]

---

[6] Souvenir booklet for the Norm Smith Commemorative Dinner, held on July 12, 1979, to inaugurate the Norm Smith Medal.

The Demons finished the home-and-away rounds as minor premiers, with 15 wins and three losses, but while they were just 6.4 percent clear of Collingwood, it didn't curb their confidence. As many as five weeks before the finals, skipper Allan La Fontaine told *The Sporting Globe*:

> 'We should have a repetition of the 1926 season – a premiership year'.[7] One of the major reasons for La Fontaine's optimism was the form of Smith and Baggott – the latter being selected to represent Victoria for the first time during the season, albeit as a reserve player: 'The forwards are just beginning to display the understanding that I have been desiring for some time. Most improvement has been shown by the key men, Norm Smith and Ron Baggott, and I am certain we will see that co-operation between these two comrades'.[8]

Melbourne faced Collingwood in the second semi-final and it was clear from the outset that the Magpies wouldn't be the easybeats they were in round 10. In fact, the Magpies led by 13 points at half-time before the Demons overwhelmed them with a 27-point turnaround in the second half. Norm Smith booted three goals and was among the Demons' best players as they advanced to their first Grand Final in 13 years. Collingwood then disposed of St Kilda in the preliminary final thanks largely to Ron Todd's 11.4 from 16 shots.[9] Todd totalled 121.74 in 1939 to again head the VFL goalkicking table.

On September 30, 1939 – almost four weeks after the eruption of World War II – Melbourne and Collingwood waged a ferocious battle of their own at the MCG. Both combatants were desperate to win, but for vastly different reasons. The Demons' hunger was purely based on their starvation of success, having been bundled out in preliminary finals in 1936 and 1937, and missing the finals altogether in 1938. The Magpies, meanwhile, were entering their 11th Grand Final in a 15-year period which had netted them six premierships.

The two teams played contrasting styles of football: Melbourne's long and direct kicking to key positions being at odds with Collingwood's short game and relative prominence of handball. As he had several times before, Checker Hughes

---

[7] *The Sporting Globe*, August 9, 1939.
[8] *The Sporting Globe*, August 9, 1939.
[9] It was the second successive year that Todd had kicked 11 goals in the preliminary final. The previous year, 1938, he kicked 11.3 against Geelong. He is one of only four players to have kicked 10 or more goals in a final, the others being Carlton's Harry 'Soapy' Vallence, who kicked 11.3 against Collingwood in the 1931 first semi-final, and 11.9 against the Magpies in the 1932 preliminary final; Geelong's George Goninon, who kicked 11.3, also against Collingwood in the 1951 second semi-final; and Melbourne's Garry Lyon, who kicked 10.4 against Footscray in the 1994 first semi-final.

urged the Demons: 'Use strength, take advantage of high marking ability, develop the long game and don't be fooled and taken in by Collingwood's handball. Once Collingwood starts handball, meet the player with shirt-front football'.[10]

Early in the match, Collingwood appeared set to cap the careers of veterans like the Collier brothers – the only survivors from the 1927-30 premiership sides – with a seventh flag. The Demons' main threat was Ron Todd, who continued his rich vein of form by kicking 3.2 (including a poster) of Collingwood's 6.5 in the opening term to give the Magpies an 18-point lead by the first break. But as was the case in the semi-final, the Demons again came back hard, slamming on 18 goals to eight in the last three quarters to win by 53 points with a record score for a VFL Grand Final – 21.22 (148).[11] It was just their third flag, and only their second since 1900.

Smith played a terrific game that would have been far better if only he had kicked straighter. His return of 1.6 and one out of bounds – including a 'sitter' and at least one other very gettable chance in the third term alone – was horrific, but as usual was not indicative of Smith's overall performance. Hec de Lacy wrote in *The Sporting Globe*: 'I don't know whether you could find anywhere in the game a more unselfish player than Norman Smith. He had missed several goals himself, but his clever handball had given Melbourne fully eight others'.[12]

A series of passes from Smith, mainly handballs, directly resulted in goals to the likes of Alby Rodda (who kicked 4.5), Percy Beames, Harold Ball and Jack Mueller, and far outweighed his frustrating inaccuracy, and ensured he was feted as one of the Demons' best in a drought-breaking premiership.[13]

Smith must have gained great satisfaction in triumphing over an adversary as traditionally strong as Collingwood; an adversary he was obsessed with as a boy, and one from which he had gleaned so much knowledge on how to succeed. In an almost ritualistic gesture after the match, Smith and some of his teammates swapped guernseys with their Collingwood opponents. It must have been a moment of irony. As a boy, Smith had dreamt about playing in a premiership for the Magpies, in their black-and-white guernsey. Now he won one against them, and was celebrating in their jumper, and the feeling was just as good as he had expected it would be. 'We had a wonderful team,' he reflected. 'One of the best of all time... We romped in the Grand Final. What a thrill it was.

---

[10] Percy Beames, *The Age*, Monday September 18, 1955.
[11] The Demons' effort eclipsed Richmond's 1934 total of 19.14 (128). Carlton's 1972 premiership side still holds the record with 28.9 (177). The Demons' 1939 score remains the ninth highest in Grand Final history.
[12] *The Sporting Globe*, Saturday September 30, 1939.
[13] Norm Smith again won the Demons' 'most unselfish player' award in 1939.

Even the thrill of your first League match has no comparison. That first bounce is electrifying, the roar of the crowd deafening, and, when you know it's won and there are only seconds to go, you shiver... The clanging of a bell and the deafening roar of a crowd gave me the greatest thrill of my life... I will never forget the shiver of excitement'.[14]

Melbourne's reserves side also won the premiership – the Demons' sixth seconds' pennant in nine years – resulting in just the third instance in VFL history of a club claiming both flags. The other clubs to achieve this rare feat were Collingwood in 1919 and Geelong in 1937.[15]

♉♉♉♉♉♉♉♉♉

Norm and Len Smith were always strong in their belief that football was at its best, and produced the most heroes, in the 1930s. The main reason they cited related to the old boxing adage that became particularly telling during the Depression – a hungry fighter is the best fighter.[16] Players simply *had* to be good because they desperately needed their match payments. They saw the game as a lifeline, and a way to rise above the pack, or at least exist in reasonable living conditions, so they clung to it with all they had.

To indicate how much it meant financially, Norm Smith later used the example of Checker Hughes' Richmond premiership side of 1932. After the Grand Final, almost half the team applied to receive "The Susso".[17] When Smith made his senior debut in 1935, senior players received £3 ($6) a game. While it sounds like a pittance compared to modern standards, it almost doubled Smith's weekly wage of £3/5/- ($7), elevating him into a 'high earning bracket'[18] – 'almost... into the bank manager class', said Smith.[19] However, there was no payment for playing in the 'stiffs' (the reserves). The stakes had risen. It was not just about the prestige and the love of the game any more. Missing senior selection might also mean missing your next meal. The result was that while the general standard of living

---

[14] *Melbourne Truth* series, 1962.
[15] Between 1940 and 1999, after which the reserves competition was terminated, there were seven further instances of clubs winning both the senior and reserves premierships – Fitzroy in 1944, Essendon in 1950, Melbourne in 1956, Geelong in 1963, Richmond in 1973, Carlton in 1987, and North Melbourne in 1996. Melbourne was the only club to achieve the feat twice, and Norm Smith was involved in one as a player and the other as coach.
[16] Pollard, Jack (editor), *High Mark: The Complete Book on Australian Football*, Murray, 1964.
[17] Colloquial abbreviation for 'The Sustenance' welfare payment. The modern-day equivalent is 'The Dole'.
[18] *Melbourne Truth* series, 1962.
[19] Pollard, Jack (editor), *High Mark: The Complete Book on Australian Football*, Murray, 1964.

fell, football exploded like never before. The standard of play also sky-rocketed, satisfying a hunger of sorts for fans.

The Smith brothers also felt that two major rule changes introduced in 1939 made it harder for players, particularly full-forwards, to excel to the extent of stars like Gordon Coventry and Bob Pratt. The changes, which the Smiths believed detracted from the game as a spectacle, revolved around rules relating to holding-the-man/holding-the-ball and out-of-bounds.[20]

Previously, where players had been allowed to simply drop the ball when tackled, suddenly they were forced to dispose of it with either a kick or handball. Although they realised that the game had been slower and more deliberate under the old rule, the Smiths pointed out that players had much more time to dispose of the ball properly. Thus, the abolition of the 'dropping the ball' rule sped up the game and made stab-kicks generally more haphazard, and the player who felt it most was the poor old full-forward.

And until then, a free kick was awarded against players who kicked the ball out of bounds, provided the ball was not touched. But the new rule stipulated that the ball would be thrown in by the boundary umpire. This meant play was taken wide more often from defence, rather than through the middle of the ground, creating fewer opportunities for forwards.

The Smiths felt that these changes made it difficult to compare players of different eras, particularly full-forwards like Bob Pratt with Essendon's John Coleman. Interestingly, they agreed that Coleman's effort to kick 120 goals in 1950 compared 'at least on equal terms' to Pratt's record feat of 150 goals in 1934.[21] '(It) proves what a great forward John Coleman was to have kicked so many goals in this era, when it is harder to score,' Norm Smith wrote. 'Backmen can now defend to the boundary with no worry of a penalty kick. Years ago... backmen were loathe to go near the boundary line with the ball. This means the ball was kept in play more on the forward lines.'[22]

ᵞᵞᵞᵞᵞᵞᵞᵞᵞ

While Norm Smith matured into one of the game's most valuable forwards, Len Smith, by comparison, had faded quietly into the background. Through no lack of effort, Len had played just 48 games in his first five seasons of VFL football

---

[20] Pollard, Jack (editor), *High Mark: The Complete Book on Australian Football*, Murray, 1964.
[21] Pollard, Jack (editor), *High Mark: The Complete Book on Australian Football*, Murray, 1964.
[22] *Melbourne Truth*, Saturday April 8, 1961.

to the end of 1939 – 19 at Melbourne, and 29 in his three seasons at Fitzroy. After being tried as a key forward with initial success, he found his niche in defence. But, as was so often the case during his career, he seemed to suffer an injury just when he was striking his best form.

In 1940, though, at the age of 28, Len Smith finally clicked at VFL level. And it was no coincidence that he did so after a virtually injury-free season, which enabled him to play 17 of the 18 games and sustain such a high standard of performance that he polled nine votes in the Brownlow Medal (just one fewer than Norm Smith's career-best in 1938). Len Smith had arrived as a footballer. And it was plain for all to see in the round eight clash that year between Melbourne and Fitzroy at the MCG, when he was able to melt Norm's ice-cool temperament and provoke an unusually violent reaction, the kind which brothers indulge in at a much younger age.

The Demons, the reigning premiers, were 5-2 going into the match; the middle-of-the-road Maroons 3-4. An upset looked possible when Fitzroy stormed to a four-goal advantage by quarter-time, and although the Demons powered back into the lead, they simply could not shake their persistent opponent. Norm Smith had entered the match in typically consistent form, with 30 goals in the opening seven rounds, including six hauls of four to six majors (2, 4, 6, 4, 5, 5, 4). However, the previous match probably provided the seed to his frustration. Smith had kicked an atrocious 4.11 against North Melbourne at Arden Street and was the main culprit in Melbourne posting the most inaccurate total in its history, and the third worst in VFL history – 12.34 (106). The Demons had 46 scoring shots to North's nine – 8.1 (49) – yet won by only 57 points. *The Sun* ran a cartoon depicting Smith and Baggott wearing spectacles, with the inference that they should have their eyes tested because they clearly couldn't see the goalposts!

Like many teammates in the match against Fitzroy, Norm Smith was not going well. At some point in play, with frustration building in a match that Melbourne was expected to win comfortably but was lucky to win by two points, tensions erupted between the Smith brothers. And considering the contrasting natures of the brothers, it is no surprise to learn who was largely responsible for the dust-up. Len later recalled: 'I had to speak to Norm about something and, before I realised it, he wanted to fight me. Naturally, it never came to that; but I often wonder what I would have had to tell the tribunal if he had cracked me'.[23]

The contrasting personalities of the brothers continued to fascinate those around them, including their mother. In an interview with Hec de Lacy in *The Sporting Globe* in 1940, Ethel Smith said: 'I am more proud than I can tell you of my boys.

---

[23] *The Sporting Globe* in 1940.

They are both good boys, but I have often wondered how they could be so different in temperament. Both are very considerate to me. Len never forgets to drop in on his way home from work. Norman has other ways of showing it. He doesn't do things the same way as Len.' It was no surprise that this was evident on the football field. Len was not prone to sibling jealousy. So although Norm had gone past him as a player, and would continue to do so, he was never resentful of Norm's rise to prominence. On the contrary, in fact; there was no-one prouder of Norm's achievements than Len, who revealed: 'There's no player I admire more than Norman. He is as game as they come, and he is always fighting it out. Quit? He wouldn't know how. Football is a battle to him, and he plays it as if his life depends on it… No better type could be included in an attack, for he… protects his other forwards and he is always working like a Trojan. He is never beaten. He is strong and very robust in a fair way. I like to see him succeed, for he is the type of player who deserves success'.[24]

Success was almost a constant companion for both Norm Smith and the Demons in 1940. The team dropped just five of its 21 games, while Smith kicked 86 goals, including bags of eight, seven and six (three times). He had originally been accredited with 85 goals until it was discovered that a goal early in the season, the result of a quick kick-off-the-ground in a pack of players, had actually come from Smith's boot and not Maurie Gibb as was initially recorded. Smith was so consistent that he kicked at least three goals in 18 of the 21 matches. Even on the rare afternoon where Smith struggled to have an influence, he still managed to perform the odd special feat, as he produced in a 19-point win over Footscray at the Western Oval in round 14. The wind was so strong towards one end of the ground that the Bulldogs kicked a total of just 2.3 in its two quarters into the gale-force breeze. But in the third quarter – Melbourne's second against the wind – Smith found a way where others had failed. Bulldog defender Hugh McPherson vividly remembered one of Smith's three goals: 'Norm got the ball about 50 yards out. He was too far out to have a shot – you could barely kick 30 yards into that howling wind – so he ran all the way in, bouncing the ball as he went, and kicked a goal from the goal square. A lot of players would have been a bit lazier or slower thinking and had a shot a lot sooner. But not Norm. He was so smart, and always seemed to know the right thing to do in every situation. And that's one of the things that made him a great coach later on – he set rules for players to follow for what they should do in the various situations they faced out on the ground'.[25]

---

[24] *The Sporting Globe* in 1940.
[25] Hugh McPherson, Footscray and Melbourne player, later Melbourne's and the VFL's first official team runner, and a close mate of Norm Smith. Interview with the author.

Melbourne faced a huge challenge from Richmond in 1940. Although the Demons won their round two clash by 23 points at the MCG, the Tigers were an entirely different team in the return match at Punt Road in round 13 and appeared to have the Demons' measure when they charged to a 38-point lead in the third quarter. But Melbourne rallied, keeping Richmond to just two points in the final term to win by seven points, with Smith kicking four goals. It was not the last time the Smith-inspired Demons would be forced to rally against the Tigers, and the odds.

Richmond forward Jack 'Skinny' Titus won the VFL goalkicking award with 92 goals (100 including finals), with Smith runner-up on 75 goals (86 including finals). Hec de Lacy was forced to choose between the pair when naming his much-anticipated team of the year in *The Sporting Globe*:

> 'Here I buy into many arguments, for the man I have chosen as full-forward is not the leading goalkicker for the season. However, those who have been fortunate enough to see the Melbourne forwards in action will agree that the greatest forward in the League today is Norman Smith... Smith is robust – a great fighter but unselfish to a fault. He does not rely on the other fellows to feed him. He reverses the forward order and feeds them. Sometimes he overdoes it. But Smith makes the Melbourne attack revolve around him. He is a difficult mark to counter, with a remarkable sense of where the ball will drop. Seldom do his feet leave the ground as he settles himself under a mark. Yet so awkwardly does he spread himself that defenders can't get at the ball either to outmark (him)... or to punch it away from him'.[26]

Hec de Lacy found a compromise in his selection dilemma, which was resolved by the fact that Titus was a small forward and easily be slotted into a forward pocket alongside Smith. Former Collingwood stars Bruce Andrew and Percy Bowyer – colleagues of de Lacy – also plumped for Smith ahead of his Tiger counterpart. Either way, there would not have been any argument from Titus. Ten years later, the Richmond legend declared Smith 'one of the greatest exponents of handball the game has ever seen, and perhaps the greatest master of the decoying type of forward play'. Titus believed Smith could easily have beaten him in the goalkicking award had it not been for his 'remarkable unselfishness in sacrificing all personal glory in making sure goals were gained for his side.'[27]

---

[26] *The Sporting Globe*, August 1940.
[27] *Sports Novels* magazine, September 1950.

THE FIRST HAT-TRICK [1939-41]

Despite Titus' admirable deflection of praise to his Melbourne counterpart, there were no concessions from the Tigers to the Demons come finals time. For the second successive season, Melbourne finished on top of the VFL ladder at the end of the minor rounds, two games clear of second-placed Richmond, and was heavily favoured to win back-to-back flags.

The two teams met in the second semi-final at the MCG, with both camps supremely confident. The Tigers' tactics became obvious soon after the first bounce. Statistically, it had been the most brutal season since the 1920s – 47 players had been reported – and Richmond planned to take the brutality to a new level against Melbourne. The ringleader would be fearsome Tiger ruckman Jack Dyer.

In the lead-up to the match, Alan Killigrew – St Kilda's skipper and a cheeky rover – expressed surprise that the previous week Dyer had spared him and several of his Saints teammates when he could easily have split them open. Killigrew proclaimed Dyer 'the greatest and fairest big man playing the game', adding that he had 'never seen Dyer do anything deliberately unfair'.[28] It was a timely statement, and one that was to be vigorously debated in the football world just three days later, when Dyer spared no-one.

Dyer was hell-bent on claiming casualties – even more so than normal; a dangerous mindset aggravated by a claim that a Melbourne player had kicked him in the opening minutes. Dyer, 'whose massive arms… (were) displayed to best advantage in a sleeveless guernsey',[29] ploughed through any Demon unfortunate enough to cross his path, and with his teammates employing similar rough-house tactics at every opportunity, Melbourne stars like Norm Smith were prime targets. Smith described it as 'the roughest game I've played in'.[30] He came to know that more than any other player on the field that day.

Nearing half-time, Smith had kicked 1.4 and been well held by George Smeaton, a miserly full-back and a superb spoiler. It just didn't seem to be Smith's day. At one point early in the second quarter, just after Richmond had regained the lead, a La Fontaine pass dropped short of him and in his attempt to gather the awkwardly bouncing ball he accidentally kicked the ball back (from) whence it came, causing a turnover, and the Tigers took the ball forward and scored their sixth goal.

Smith's afternoon was about to become even quieter. Just before the main break, with the Demons trailing by three straight kicks, Smith suffered a bone-crunching

---

[28] *The Sporting Globe*, Wednesday August 28, 1940.
[29] *The Sporting Globe*, September 30, 1940.
[30] *Melbourne Truth* series, 1962.

bump that had Melbourne fans calling for vengeance. Smith later admitted he had been playing the ball in a 'careless' fashion when he suddenly felt 'a chilling sensation of fear, the hair prickled on the back of my neck. I couldn't see the danger, but I sensed it.'[31] The 'danger', as always, was Dyer. The Richmond enforcer, known as 'Captain Blood', was in his prime, and on his way to his fifth Tigers best and fairest award – and fourth in a row. Smith later rated Dyer alongside Albert Collier and Jack Mueller as one of the three greatest footballers he saw, 'probably *the* greatest',[32] and a player 'totally without mercy' who had some of Smith's teammates 'in total awe and fear of him.'[33] Dyer mused that he had never known a season where so many players had 'strayed' into his path.[34] 'My timing was immaculate,' he recalled, 'and I did litter the fields with quite a few careless, flat-footed opponents.' It was in this atmosphere of imminent violence that Smith strayed into Dyer's destructive path, as the Tiger assailant later recalled:

> There is always a special tingle when you get one of the smart guys – the guys who are so slick and skilled they think they'll never be caught. Like Norm Smith. Norm was a fiery, dangerous player with a savage will to win. I wasn't fiery but I had a will to win and played the game like Norm did – hard, hard, harder...
>
> Norm had the ball. I had the hip and shoulder... I saw a blazing red-head weave through a pack... I had a clear shot at Norm Smith, the elusive Demon full-forward who could cost Richmond the 1940 premiership. Norm made that one mistake he would regret for the rest of his life. He balanced himself for a kick at goal without taking a quick look around. He was positioned perfectly for a legitimate shirtfront. I gathered speed and got fully into stride as he lined up his shot. I hunched my shoulder as Norm bent a little low in his turn.[35]

Dyer described the hit with the term, 'Whhaam!'[36]; Smith preferred 'Crash!'[37] It was a unique experience for each, although with entirely opposite emotions and consequences. It was the hardest shirtfront Dyer ever delivered. It was also the hardest bump Smith had received – and he took the main brunt of it flush on his jaw. Dyer's

---

[31] Dyer, Jack and Brian Hansen, *Captain Blood*, Stanley Paul, 1965. Norm Smith wrote the foreword.
[32] Dyer, Jack and Brian Hansen, *Captain Blood*, Stanley Paul, 1965.
[33] Dyer, Jack and Brian Hansen, *Jack Dyer's The Greatest: The Most Sensational Players of the Century*, Brian Hansen Nominees, 1996.
[34] Hansen, Brian, *The Jack Dyer Story*, Brian Hansen Nominees, 1996.
[35] Hansen, Brian, *The Jack Dyer Story*, Brian Hansen Nominees, 1996.
[36] Hansen, Brian, *The Jack Dyer Story*, Brian Hansen Nominees, 1996.
[37] Dyer, Jack and Brian Hansen, *Captain Blood*, Stanley Paul, 1965.

adrenalin was pumping furiously as he absorbed the euphoria of inflicting the heaviest and most perfectly-timed hit in a career defined by such acts. He had delighted in feeling 'Fillets of Norm' mould around his body, and hearing that massive expulsion of air, and agony, from bursting lungs – Whoof! 'That's when you know it's perfect,' Dyer explained. 'It's like a giant gas leak.'[38] The Richmond ruffian later enthused that he had bumped Smith 'so sweetly hard' that 'his vertebrae and ribcage would have been found hanging over the boundary fence.'[39] Dyer's immediate thought when he saw Smith motionless on the ground, was: 'He won't get up from that one in a hurry.'[40] Smith was in a world of pain; the shock of the impact – which lifted him off the ground – unlike anything he had experienced.[41] He later grimaced about the day Dyer – who he said 'would do anything to help Richmond win, and I mean anything' – 'damn near killed me'.[42] 'There was a floating sensation of unreality as I crashed face-first into the turf,' Smith recalled. 'A yellow light flashed across my eyes. No human could hit that hard, but then I have often wondered if Jack was human'.[43]

While incensed Melbourne fans 'hooted wildly',[44] Smith's teammates rushed in to remonstrate with Dyer. Umpire Alan Coward reprimanded the Tiger ruckman and awarded a free kick against him for using his elbow, but, strangely, did not deem it a reportable offence. Dyer was adamant that he had delivered a legitimate bump, later claiming he pointed to his bleeding shoulder and told the umpire: 'Look at his teeth marks.'[45]

Hec de Lacy provided an impartial view of the hit in *The Sporting Globe*. '(It) caused considerable comment,' de Lacy wrote, 'but from what I saw of it, and I had a good view, he was hit by a forearm bump, the forearm neither being "swung nor delivered", as we know the term in boxing. Incidents like these are to be regretted... I thought that the knock Smith received was unfortunate but due to the fortunes of war.'

After what seemed like hours to Smith, 'gradually life stirred in his body and he struggled gamely to his feet'.[46] Staggering and swaying on wobbly knees, Smith was so scatterbrained that even he conceded, 'I had no idea what was going on... I sagged

---

[38] Hansen, Brian, *The Jack Dyer Story*, Brian Hansen Nominees, 1996.
[39] Hansen, Brian, *The Jack Dyer Story*, Brian Hansen Nominees, 1996.
[40] Hansen, Brian, *The Jack Dyer Story*, Brian Hansen Nominees, 1996.
[41] Dyer, Jack and Brian Hansen, *Captain Blood*, Stanley Paul, 1965.
[42] Dyer, Jack and Brian Hansen, *Jack Dyer's The Greatest: The Most Sensational Players of the Century*, Brian Hansen Nominees, 1996.
[43] Dyer, Jack and Brian Hansen, *Jack Dyer's The Greatest: The Most Sensational Players of the Century*, Brian Hansen Nominees, 1996.
[44] Gerald Brosnan, former Fitzroy champion, in *The Sun*, September 16, 1940.
[45] Hansen, Brian, *The Jack Dyer Story*, Brian Hansen Nominees, 1996.
[46] Hansen, Brian, *The Jack Dyer Story*, Brian Hansen Nominees, 1996.

as I was handed the ball... I didn't know where I was'.[47] Despite being presented with what would normally be a regulation shot at goal, Smith turned to his nearest teammate, Ron Baggott, and asked, 'Which way do I kick, Baggs?' But Baggott, who was also recovering from a heavy knock, merely replied, 'Oh, just anywhere.'[48]

Dazed and confused, Smith kicked 'weakly'[49] and just missed. He had another shot soon after and was again astray.

In his groggy state, Smith was 'useless' in the few remaining minutes of the quarter.[50] But Hughes was reluctant to take him off the ground – and Smith was reluctant to leave – because he would have been unable to return. Hughes hoped a pep-up at half-time would do the trick and Smith would be back to his former self in the second half. At half-time, Smith collapsed in the changerooms with a severe bout of concussion. He couldn't remember anything of the match after Dyer had collected him.[51] He was taken to the nearby Prince Henry Hospital, where he spent several hours under observation before being allowed to go home at 8pm.

Smith and Dyer always disagreed – on one occasion almost violently – about the legitimacy of the bump. Smith believed, as umpire Coward did, that he had been hit 'unfairly' with an elbow[52], while Dyer maintained he had acted within the laws of the game. His comment to *The Sporting Globe* immediately after the match was: 'It is the first time that I knew that you could not use the shoulder in meeting a player.' And he stuck to his version of events. For decades after, he cited scars of teeth imprints on his shoulder as proof of his innocence. Smith's response was: 'I'll bet my teeth marks wouldn't have matched'.[53] During one such debate between the high-profile pair in a bar in Surfers Paradise about 20 years later – when they were still two of the biggest names in the game – their words became so heated that Dyer claimed Smith was 'all for having a fight with me over the incident'.[54] On *World of Sport* in 1972 – 32 years later! – Smith told Dyer: 'You could have been an even better player if you'd played the ball more'. But on other occasions Smith described them as great mates who had shared 'a million beers and ten thousand laughs together'.[55]

---

[47] Dyer, Jack and Brian Hansen, *Captain Blood*, Stanley Paul, 1965.
[48] Hansen, Brian, *The Jack Dyer Story*, Brian Hansen Nominees, 1996.
[49] Percy Taylor, *The Argus*, September 16, 1940.
[50] *The Age*, September 16, 1940.
[51] Percy Taylor, *The Argus*, September 16, 1940.
[52] Dyer, Jack and Brian Hansen, *Jack Dyer's The Greatest: The Most Sensational Players of the Century*, Brian Hansen Nominees, 1996.
[53] Dyer, Jack and Brian Hansen, *Jack Dyer's The Greatest: The Most Sensational Players of the Century*, Brian Hansen Nominees, 1996.
[54] Hansen, Brian, *The Jack Dyer Story*, Brian Hansen Nominees, 1996.
[55] Dyer, Jack and Brian Hansen, *Jack Dyer's The Greatest: The Most Sensational Players of the Century*, Brian Hansen Nominees, 1996.

But Smith and the Demons did not see anything humorous about Richmond's methods at the time. Smith's replacement, fellow redhead Keith 'Bluey' Truscott, injured a leg within just a few minutes of taking the field, while Baggott and Dowsing were also suffering from the effects of heavy knocks; but with no 19th man available, the trio was forced to stay on the ground. Either that, or play with fewer than 18 men. Truscott and Baggott responded to their difficult predicament magnificently. But although Truscott kicked four second-half goals in a magnificent cameo, and Baggott – Smith's positional replacement at full-forward – also finished with four goals, the loss of Smith for the entire second half of the 1940 second semi-final was probably the single most influential factor in Richmond upsetting Melbourne by a goal to advance to the Grand Final. Skipper La Fontaine described it as a handicap that proved insurmountable.[56]

Then, of course, there was the Dyer factor. 'Richmond were just a team,' Smith said. 'That was the effect of Dyer. His strength and courage was a spur to his side. He lifted and inspired them to unbelievable heights.'[57] Despite being bitterly criticised for years after his hit on Norm Smith, the end justified the means for Dyer, who said simply: 'We achieved our purpose – we won the game.'[58]

That day, according to Smith, a 'vastly inferior' Richmond had toppled the greatest side he ever saw.[59] And they had accomplished it by employing the most primitive methods imaginable, forcing the Demons to operate with just 15 fit men for practically the entire second half. Although the match had been close, Smith's brutally honest assessment was that 'Richmond steamrolled us. Their plan was to put us off our game and how well it succeeded.'[60]

Nursing battered and bruised bodies – and heads – the Demons had to regroup quickly for the preliminary final against Essendon. And although Smith needed to convince Checker Hughes that he was fit to play, it is doubtful that Hughes would have put much, if any, thought to playing such an important game without his star forward. *The Sun* reported that Smith had been 'well' on the Sunday, and he quashed any doubts surrounding his condition by training as normal during the week. These, of course, were the days long before players were given a mandatory week off after receiving a severe concussion.

Smith resumed at his usual position at full-forward and was a prominent player against the Bombers, kicking three goals and being among the best handful of

---

[56] *The Age*, September 16, 1940.
[57] Dyer, Jack and Brian Hansen, *Captain Blood*, Stanley Paul, 1965.
[58] Hansen, Brian, *The Jack Dyer Story*, Brian Hansen Nominees, 1996.
[59] Dyer, Jack and Brian Hansen, *Captain Blood*, Stanley Paul, 1965.
[60] Dyer, Jack and Brian Hansen, *Captain Blood*, Stanley Paul, 1965.

players for the Demons. He would have been far more prominent if he had kicked straighter. Percy Taylor told readers of *The Argus* that 'the cooperation between Smith and Baggott was masterly, and had Smith kicked reasonably accurately Melbourne would have had such a great lead in the early stages that Essendon would have been toiling all day'. Smith kicked 1.5 in the first quarter – the one goal being a purist's delight: a perfectly-struck drop-kick – and 3.7 for the match. He could have kicked at least another certain goal, according to Percy Beames: 'Smith had broken clear of the pack inside the goalsquare. He simply had to run another five metres or so to tap the ball over the line for a certain goal. Instead, he handballed to me no more than a metre or two away, because he believed it was the right thing to do'.[61]

In the final analysis, teamwork such as this was critical, with Melbourne getting down to just 16 fit men in the final term. Heavy rain turned the MCG into a quagmire and helped the Demons bottle up play to an extent, but the Bombers twice stole the lead, before goals to Beames and Baggott gave Melbourne a gritty five-point win and another crack at the Tigers.

Richmond was confident about producing a repeat of its semi-final performance while the Demons – the glamour side of the competition until that defeat – had slipped dramatically in the public's estimation. The Demons had injury woes, with Rowley Fischer, Wally Lock and Jack Furniss being forced to withdraw from the Grand Final after each had played in the preliminary final – when Fischer had been best-afield – while Hughie Murnane had been missing since round 14. Even Smith felt the odds were heavily stacked against his side. 'We were outsiders,' he said. 'But that's when a good side shows its worth.'[62]

After two physically and mentally draining finals, Checker Hughes took what must have been a revolutionary attitude towards training in Grand Final week. The master coach gave his side the night off on the Tuesday – a decision that was met with round criticism from the players, who had been conditioned to training hard. Then, on the Thursday night, Hughes called a halt to training after a mere 10 minutes – the sum of their work for the week. But Hughes was widely regarded as a genius when it came to assessing how much – or in this case, how *little* – work his players needed. On this occasion he felt they had been so sharp with their skills – by this stage of the season, fitness was not a factor – that they were primed for action. He simply wanted to keep them fresh for what was certain to be a bone-

---

[61] Souvenir booklet for the Norm Smith Commemorative Dinner, held on July 12, 1979, to inaugurate the Norm Smith Medal.
[62] *Melbourne Truth* series, 1962.

jarring rematch with his old club. 'The fellows were very disappointed,' Hughes later said of the player reaction. 'They wanted to go on, but that was the way I wanted to hold them.'[63] Even in today's anything-goes environment where new training methods and philosophies are regularly adopted and modified, and often dispensed with just as quickly, Hughes' thinking would be regarded as, at the very least, unconventional.

Much of the attention leading up to the 1940 Grand Final – among both the Demons' inner sanctum and the football public – focused on how Melbourne might try to tame Jack Dyer. After the brief training session on the Thursday night, Checker Hughes called together eight of his most senior players to discuss this very problem. 'We were very worried (about) whether Dyer would go berserk again,' Beames said.[64] Several players, including Smith's good mate Dick Hingston, grimly volunteered to do the job on Dyer, and other names were suggested. Hughes caused a surprise when he assigned the task to tough follower Jack O'Keefe. A policeman mate of Dyer's, and a former Thornbury and Northcote player, O'Keefe had played just one of the previous five games in the seniors. Hughes' explanation was: 'Some years ago I saw a Collingwood man upset Jack by playing shoulder-to-shoulder with him in a semi-final. I remembered that.'[65] The Demons were also told to kick the ball wide of Dyer to keep him stretching in the hope of tiring him.

The O'Keefe move was a masterstroke. As per Hughes' instructions, O'Keefe ran shoulder-to-shoulder with Dyer, who became increasingly frustrated with the constant 'jostling, niggling and interfering'[66] and had no influence on the match. Of course, it helped O'Keefe's cause that the match was played in soggy conditions, which made it difficult for his quarry to cope on his battle-scarred knees. Dyer, who thought O'Keefe 'couldn't play football to save himself', and even claimed much later that umpire Coward had failed him, lamented it as the most humiliating game of his career[67]. Adding insult to the humiliation, O'Keefe also kicked two goals in the second quarter.

Dyer – who had received hate mail after the second semi-final (even his wife and mother were subjected to poison-pen letters) had been flabbergasted that Smith had been passed fit to play in the preliminary final. 'How they put him back together again in time… is a tribute to modern science and Smithy's guts,' he marvelled. Dyer actually tried to repeat his devastating hit on Smith in the opening minutes

---

[63] *The Sporting Globe*, October 4, 1940.
[64] *Red and Blue* documentary, 2005.
[65] *The Sporting Globe*, October 4, 1940.
[66] Hansen, Brian, *The Jack Dyer Story*, Brian Hansen Nominees, 1996.
[67] Hansen, Brian, *The Jack Dyer Story*, Brian Hansen Nominees, 1996.

of the Grand Final. The result was another vicious bump, but this time the contact was not fierce enough to put Smith out of the match. '(Smith) was spitting mad,' Dyer said, 'but he was to have the last laugh.'[68] Indeed Smith did.

A pre-match concern for Hughes was Smith's opponent, George Smeaton who, Hughes felt, 'had the measure of Norm' in the second semi-final 'with his punching-the-ball-away tactics'. In an attempt to curb Smeaton's effectiveness and maximise Smith's body work, Hughes instructed Smith to 'play up to Smeaton', shoulder-to-shoulder and told him 'there was always to be a small man waiting for the punch'.[69]

While Dyer got away the first clear kick of the match – one of his few decisive touches – Ron Baggott soon received a free kick and drove the ball long and high to Smith, who marked in front of Smeaton and goaled from 30 metres. It was a sign of things to come.

Smith's brilliant effort to kick the Demons' second goal – an effort which proved once and for all just how skilful and persistent he was – has fortunately been preserved on black-and-white newsreel film. The footage shows Smith – after competing in a marking contest about 20 metres out from goal – outmanoeuvring two Richmond players on the ground, and paddling the ball in front of him before quickly taking possession and throwing it onto his left boot with a swift snap shot, while being sandwiched between a tackle from behind and a bump from the front. It all happens so quickly that it must be viewed in frame-by-frame slow-motion to fully appreciate the effort. The ball bounces through for a goal in the fashion that later became the trademark of Collingwood genius Peter Daicos. It was the perfect way to break his own club goalkicking record.[70]

Soon after, Smith cleverly shepherded Beames for another goal before Richmond steadied somewhat. By quarter-time, the Demons led by just 14 points, but they had reigned supreme in general play, firing 12 scoring shots to three for the term. The margin would have been bigger if Smith had not muffed a chance to kick what would have been an easy goal. In that instance, a rare lapse in his acute awareness, he unsuccessfully tried to get his boot to a waist-high ball in mid-air in the goalsquare, when he actually had more time than he realised. But in the third term, when he out-bodied Smeaton and drilled two consecutive goals – a snap and a tight-angle set shot, among three goals and a poster for the quarter to take his tally to six – the game was as good as over.

In the final term, the prolific Baggott – who won the Demons' best-and-fairest

---

[68] Hansen, Brian, *The Jack Dyer Story*, Brian Hansen Nominees, 1996.
[69] *The Sporting Globe*, October 4, 1940.
[70] Norm had kicked 81 goals, passing the 80 he had kicked in 1938.

award that season and was described by *The Sporting Globe's* Hec de Lacy as 'streets ahead' of all other centre half-forwards in the competition – delivered a superb pass across his body to Smith for his seventh goal.

Richmond added a few late consolation goals – including Titus's third, which brought up his century – but the Demons won by 39 points. Smith's seven goals was equal second to the nine-goal effort of Collingwood's Gordon Coventry in the 1928 Grand Final.[71] He is believed to have actually kicked eight goals, with one incorrectly awarded to Baggott. While Smith was typically 'reluctant to comment',[72] Baggott later could not recall the truth of the matter. 'Although I would never want to deny Smithy his due,' Baggott said, 'I wouldn't want to rob myself of a goal in a Grand Final either!'[73]

Smith's full scoreline for the afternoon was 7.3 – the reverse of his preliminary final return. In three finals against high quality opposition, Smith had fired 25 scoring shots – and, as usual, created many more – for a total of 11.14. Although his conversion rate could have been far better, he had confirmed his status as one of the most prized forwards in the game.

During the Demons' premiership celebrations at the MCG that night, various victory speeches were made by the likes of chairman Joe Blair, coach Hughes and captain La Fontaine. Although Ron Baggott and Percy Beames were generally regarded as the best players afield that day, Sir Stephen Morell – a former Lord Mayor of Melbourne and a vice-president of the Melbourne Cricket Club who once entertained the Duke (later King George VI) and Duchess of York on their 1927 trip to Australia – presented Norm Smith with a gold medal in recognition of his performance.

Presentations were also made to Harold Ball and Ron Barassi, both of whom had enlisted and would join the fighting soon after.

The Demons had achieved great things, but they were not done yet, as their annual report stated: 'Perhaps we may be forgiven for visualising in our more determined moments three parallel pennants flying in a row after the end of the coming season'.

YYYYYYYYY

---

[71] Ten other players have kicked seven goals in a VFL/AFL Grand Final: 1930 – Gordon Coventry (Collingwood); 1943 – Dick Harris (Richmond) and Tom Reynolds (Essendon); 1946 – Gordon 'Whopper' Lane (Essendon); 1954 – Jack Collins (Footscray); 1965 – Ted Fordham (Essendon); 1972 – Alex Jesaulenko (Carlton); 1980 – Kevin Bartlett (Richmond); 1988 – Jason Dunstall (Hawthorn) and 1993 – Stephen Kernahan (Carlton). Dermott Brereton (Hawthorn) kicked eight goals in 1985, while Gary Ablett (Geelong) equalled Coventry's 1928 record in 1989.
[72] *Melbourne Truth* series, 1962.
[73] Ron Baggott. Interview with the author.

Just a few weeks shy of his 25th birthday, Norm Smith married his sweetheart, Marjorie Victoria Ellis, the couple exchanging vows in a Methodist ceremony at Wesley Church in Lonsdale Street, Melbourne, on October 19, 1940. Marj, 21 (three years and eight months younger than Norm), was a softly-spoken, blue-eyed brunette who worked as a typist. She also boasted impressive sporting ability, having been a junior badminton champion.

Marj had originally dated another Melbourne footballer, Jack Maher, a wingman who played 28 games for the Demons from 1938-40 and again in 1944. Ron Baggott recalled: 'Jack Maher didn't play many games for us but he cut quite a figure. He was a real handsome bloke, always well-dressed, and we looked at him as a cut above us. He and Marj were going together as boyfriend and girlfriend, then there was a split-up and the next thing we knew Norm and Marj were together. But there was no funny business, and no problem between Jack and Norm either. That's just the way it worked out. Everyone moved along, and got along'.[74]

Another who can remember Norm and Marj during their courting days was Mike Williamson, who later achieved fame as a football commentator. Williamson grew up in the same street as Marj – Molesworth Street, Coburg – and was just a boy when Smith would visit the Ellis house. 'Marj and her family lived quite a few doors up from us,' recalled Williamson. 'I'd see Norm turn up in his car. He would take Marj out at night. I was fascinated by him – he was Melbourne's full-forward and a big star. I mustn't have disguised my fascination too well either because, later on, Norm reminded me that I'd called him "Mr Smith".'[75]

On their wedding day, the inner circle of family members met at Victor and Ethel Smith's house before making their way to the church together. Arthur Ireland not only supplied the wedding cake, but also doubled as Smith's best man. A photograph taken of the happy couple as they left the church shows them arm-in-arm and heavily-confettied: Smith, with his hair slicked-back, toothily smiling, in a dark suit and tie, his gloved left hand holding the other glove; a head taller than the shyly smirking Marj, who wore a long-sleeved, white lace dress and clutched a white floral bouquet.

According to Melbourne's annual report, 'Cupid was particularly active' in 1940. Smith was one of 12 Demons to wed that year. The others were Ron Baggott, skipper Allan La Fontaine, George Archibald, Jack Atkins, Bill Baxter, Gerry Daly, Roy Dowsing, Jack Furniss, Hughie Murnane, Frank Roberts and Ray Wartman. The club's committee extended its 'very best wishes for long life and happiness to each of them and their good ladies, who are asked to use their influence to

---

[74] Ron Baggott. Interview with the author.
[75] Mike Williamson. Interview with the author.

ensure that their husbands attend as promptly and punctually to their training and playing obligations as they formerly did'.[76]

Norm and Marj moved into a house in Raglan Street, Preston, about three kilometres north of the Smith house in Clarke Street, Northcote.

From the time they became an item, Marj rarely missed a football match Smith was involved in – either as a player or a coach – over the next 30-odd years. She knew how important football was to Smith and she became actively involved in social activities at Melbourne. It also helped that three of her best friends – Belle Emselle, Phyllis Baggott and Elza Barassi – were married to three of Smith's closest mates and were also very much part of the club's social scene.[77]

After each home game at the MCG, the players and their partners would scrub the liniment off the floor so they could hold the club dance,[78] which took care of half of the Saturday nights in football season. Afterwards, the Smiths and any or all of the other three couples might go to a restaurant for supper, which would be washed down with soft drink or a warm beverage. Ron Baggott explained: 'There was no real yahooing or playing up – just some clean fun. Everyone in our circle of friends led pretty simple lives – there was family, work and football. We didn't have the money to gallivant around either – player payments were cut in half during the war. And we wanted to get the best out of ourselves as footballers too. You can't very well do that if you're out drinking 'til all hours'.[79]

♈♈♈♈♈♈♈♈

Shortly after starring in the 1940 VFL Grand Final, rather than relaxing in the fame and afterglow of becoming a two-time premiership player, Norm Smith was pushing himself to explore new boundaries in his cricket career.

When asked by a reporter about his love of cricket, Smith modestly said: 'Don't say anything about that. I'm a very ordinary batsman, believe me. In fact, I think it's my football reputation that keeps me in the side'.[80] But he didn't fool anyone. As 'the gun bat of the Jika competition',[81] Smith had little else to achieve from an individual perspective with the Dennis side. And while football would always be his first priority, and love, and he would never allow cricket to impact

---

[76] Melbourne Football Club *Annual Report*, 1940.
[77] The Smiths, Baggotts and Emselles were married within months of each other.
[78] Phyllis Baggott, wife of Ron. Interview with the author.
[79] Ron Baggott. Interview with the author.
[80] Newspaper report, September 13, 1941.
[81] Ron Baggott. Interview with the author.

upon it – even though those were the days when you could combine the two at a high level without too much difficulty – the last thing Smith wanted was to be perceived as 'a big fish in a small pond'.[82]

Smith and Richie Emselle, who also played cricket together at Dennis, would often drive around to Ron Baggott's place in Regent (a small locality in the Preston/Reservoir area, north of Northcote) where the three childhood friends and Demon teammates would practise on a pitch Baggott had made in his backyard. These Sunday sessions would start late in the football season, to give them enough time to get in 'reasonable nick' for the start of the cricket season in October.[83]

Baggott and his brother Jack played in the first XI for Northcote in Melbourne's district cricket competition, the premier cricket competition in Victoria. Jack, who had made his debut in the 1924/25 season as an 18-year-old and eventually played 127 games, was an accomplished opening batsman who had captained the side. Ron had played his first game only the previous season. The Baggott brothers, and others at Northcote Cricket Club, had been trying to lure Smith to Northcote for several years. At the start of 1941 – after playing the first half of the season with Dennis – Smith finally relented and decided to find out if he could actually match it against the best players in the state.

Interestingly, two of Smith's more prominent teammates at Northcote were also two of his greatest enemies on the football field – Collingwood superstars Des Fothergill and Ron Todd. Fothergill, then a 20-year-old, three-time best-and-fairest winner, had just tied with South Melbourne's Herbie Matthews in the 1940 Brownlow Medal. Todd, meanwhile, was one of the most controversial and talked-about figures in football. After kicking a combined total of 241 goals in the 1938 and 1939 seasons, Todd sensationally transferred – without a clearance – from the Magpies to VFA club Williamstown for a virtual king's ransom, thus ending his VFL career at the age of 23.

Fothergill and Todd were no cricketing slouches either. In Smith's season at Northcote, Fothergill, who was captain of the side, won both the club batting award with 494 runs at an average of 44.91 and the bowling award with 20 wickets at 13.3 per scalp. In 14 summers from 1938/39 (when Fothergill was just 18) to 1951/52, Fothergill – who represented Victoria 27 times in Sheffield Shield cricket – made 15 centuries for Northcote and won the club's batting average 10 times (with a best run tally of 762 and a best average of 67.13). Todd won the batting award three times (with a best of 599 runs at 66.55).

---

[82] Ron Baggott. Interview with the author.
[83] Ron Baggott. Interview with the author.

Northcote immediately selected Norm Smith in its first eleven side for its match at Fitzroy. As though the pressure of making his long-awaited district debut was not enough for Smith, the cricketing gods conspired to send him to the crease at No.6 after his side had lost four cheap wickets, and with former Australian Test opening bowler Morrie Sievers baying for his blood. As expected, Smith received a torrid welcome from Sievers, who had played three Tests in the 1936/37 Ashes series against England on home soil. In that series, Sievers headed the Australian bowling averages with nine wickets at an average of 17.88. His claim to fame was bagging 5/21 in the first innings of a famous Test victory at the MCG – a match in which he twice claimed the prized scalp of English superstar Wally Hammond. Still only 28 years old, Sievers was in what was to be his last season in the Victorian side.

An incident in that debut innings planted the seed for Smith's discontent at his new cricket club. Smith was at the crease with a more senior batsman – not Fothergill or Todd – who was struggling to survive against Sievers, who was moving the ball considerably and regularly beating the bat. At one point, Smith despatched a rare loose ball down to deep third man and set off for a run, but was stunned when his partner sent him back. Peter Smith repeated what his father had told him: 'The other batsman didn't want to take the strike. He was happy just to stand at the bowler's end and watch Dad scratch around and try to survive. Dad didn't like that. It left a pretty bitter impression in his mind. He thought it was a selfish way to play. It went against everything he'd been taught about playing team sport. If there was one thing Dad despised, it was blokes who played for themselves; blokes who would rather protect their position than do what was right for the team. That's why, when he coached, he loved footballers who sacrificed their own games, and individual glory, for the benefit of the team'.[84]

Smith's brief innings ended when he was caught-and-bowled by Sievers for just six. But in a meagre total of 129, in which the highest score among the top eight batsmen was only 22, he wasn't disgraced. Sievers tore through the Northcote batting line-up to snare 8/61. In reply, Fitzroy passed their target just one wicket down. In the meaningless second innings, Smith batted at No.4 and was out caught-and-bowled, again to Sievers, this time for 12.

Neither Smith nor his teammates fared much better in their next match, against Hawthorn-East Melbourne at Northcote Park. After being sent in to bat, they were bundled out for 81, with Smith, dropping to No.7, contributing eight. The visitors won easily.

---

[84] Peter Smith. Interview with the author.

After three successive failures, Smith finally produced an innings of substance at Preston, compiling 57 in a total of 7/354, in which Fothergill smashed 149. Smith opened the bowling in the first innings and finished with 0/19, but didn't bowl again in the match as Northcote won outright.

In the last match of the season, Smith returned to the MCG for a match against Melbourne. From a team perspective it was be a triumphant return – Northcote totalled 258, with Fothergill making 46 and No.9 batsman Donohue hitting a match-winning 105 – but it was a personal disappointment. Going to the wicket at No.5 after Northcote had lost three cheap wickets, Smith was quickly sent back to the pavilion for a duck. Just five months earlier, Smith had walked off the MCG and been hailed a hero; now he trudged off the same hallowed turf with zero.

It was to be Smith's last game of district cricket. After just four first XI matches – in which he made 83 runs (6, 12, 8, 57 and 0) at an average of 16.6 – Smith turned his back on a promising district cricket career and left Northcote. He strongly objected to what he perceived as a 'cliquey' environment,[85] and teammates who placed an unhealthy focus on their individual performance above that of the team, as was highlighted in his debut. According to Ron Baggott, Smith's attitude was: 'Bugger this, I'm going back to my mates at Dennis'. This turn of events, and the fact he had not succeeded, was 'a great disappointment' to Smith.

'If he had've stayed on,' Baggott speculated, 'I'm sure he would have made it. He certainly had the ability. Northcote didn't want Smith to go; they thought he'd eventually be a very good district player. But it wasn't all to Norm's liking.'[86]

🏉🏉🏉🏉🏉🏉🏉🏉

Melbourne's quest to become just the third side to win a hat-trick of VFL premierships appeared to be in grave danger after just seven rounds of the 1941 season. The Demons were 4-3 and at the crossroads. Their only win of merit was a 40-point win over finals aspirant Collingwood at Victoria Park in round five, but even that victory had its downside. The Demons had led by 76 points at half-time – with a league record first half total of 19.7 (121) to 7.3 (45) – to which Smith had contributed six goals. However, a second-half fadeout was indicative of what was to come in the next fortnight. In rounds six and seven, Melbourne built quarter-time leads of 30 points and 21 points respectively against Footscray and Carlton, only to go down by 28 and 27 points.

---

[85] Russell Brown. Interview with the author.
[86] Ron Baggott. Interview with the author.

Admittedly, much of the Demons' plight could be attributed to being without as many as 12 senior players at various stages because of war service and injury. But Melbourne's dicey predicament was in contrast with the efforts of Norm Smith, whose output had remained first class. In the first seven rounds, Smith had kicked 30 goals, including two hauls of five and six each. In their three losses, he had netted 12 goals– two against brother Len's Fitzroy side, four against Footscray and six of Melbourne's 14 majors against the Blues in his 100th senior match.

With his team under pressure, Smith increased his productivity, kicking six of the Demons' 12 goals in a 40-point win over Hawthorn in round eight; eight of Melbourne's 20 majors in a 13-point victory over North Melbourne; and five of a total of 16 in an eight-goal win over eventual Grand Finalist Essendon. In four matches, Smith's contribution was 25 of his side's 62 goals – 40.3 percent of the Demons' productivity. The next best during this period was Ron Baggott with nine goals (3, 0, 3, 3), followed by Jack Mueller with eight (2, 2, 2, 2).

With the Smith-Baggott show commanding attention, the Demons were beginning to look ominous again. A newspaper report summed up the threat posed by this revered duo: 'If any single factor will win Melbourne the 1941 League premiership, it is the forward combination between Ron Baggott and Norm Smith. Firm pals from their schooldays, these two are the greatest menace opposing teams have to face'.[87]

Smith's form was so impressive that he was selected to make his debut for Victoria. There was only one other Demon chosen for the side – defender Frank Roberts. In the opening minutes, Smith showed he belonged at the elite level when he kicked the Vics' third goal – described by *The Sporting Globe* as 'a mighty kick from the half-forward line'.[88] He was not the standout forward for his state. Victoria won a high-scoring contest by 10 points, with Richmond's Dick Harris bagging eight goals and North Melbourne spearhead Sel Murray slotting six.

The dual absence of Smith and Roberts appeared a case of poor timing for the Demons, who faced a Grand Final rematch against Richmond, which entered the clash with a 9-1 record for the season. But representative duties had hit the Tigers even harder, with captain-coach Jack Dyer and goalsneak Dick "Hungry" Harris earning state jumpers. The Demons belted the Tigers by 47 points. It was their fourth successive win and they were suddenly 8-3. The Demons were back, and so was Norm Smith the following week. Smith's form on resumption was solid without being startling; kicking 19 goals in his next five games (2, 3, 5, 5, 4) as Melbourne continued on its merry way against average opposition; the only

---

[87] Contemporary newspaper report.
[88] *The Sporting Globe*, Saturday July 12, 1941.

opponent of any note being Collingwood, which the Demons disposed of by 23 points despite having seven fewer scoring shots. There was little to indicate that this was a precursor to his greatest goalkicking performance in a VFL match.

In the lead-up to Melbourne's round 17 encounter with Footscray, Melbourne great Albert Chadwick told *The Sporting Globe*: 'Smith is undoubtedly one of the best forwards we have seen. He is a forward machine in himself with his clever handball, shepherding and heady tactics. He is entirely unselfish, and has the happy knack of making everyone around him play well. The manner in which he develops an attack is brilliance itself. He is so neat and effective in everything he does'.[89] Chadwick's comments could not have been more timely.

When the Demons took on the Bulldogs at the MCG, they were aiming at their 10th straight win to remain atop the VFL ladder and secure the double chance. The Bulldogs had already been eliminated from finals contention, but were still a dangerous opponent – they had, after all, beaten Melbourne earlier in the season – and now had the added incentive of achieving a rare distinction: beating the reigning back-to-back premier twice in a season. From the outset, two things became clear: Footscray would be no easybeat, and Norm Smith was set for a big day.

In the first term, 'swift and deadly exchanges between Gibb, Baggott and Smith set the Footscray backs a problem which they could not solve... The Footscray backs pinned down every Melbourne forward except Smith with close smothering play.'[90] With the Demons trailing by seven points early, Smith had the next five shots at goal, slotting three of them to wrest back the ascendancy. Melbourne drove the ball straight down the centre to Smith at every opportunity. 'Marking with superb judgment' he drilled four 'great' goals[91] in the second quarter to give the Demons a three-point lead at half-time, by which time he had kicked seven of Melbourne's nine goals. In the second half, Smith was similarly dominant, and almost monopolised the scoreboard, kicking four of the Demons' six goals in the third quarter, and one of their two in the last.

Although his teammates could have been accused of becoming too Smith-conscious, as they 'neglected scoring chances in attempts to feed' him 'with handpasses to impossible positions',[92] there was logic in their thinking. Smith, 'incredible in his cool judgment of the ball's flight... marked everything that came his way'.[93] He did, however, miss almost as many shots as he nailed, at one

---

[89] *The Sporting Globe*, Saturday August 23, 1941.
[90] Contemporary newspaper report.
[91] Contemporary newspaper report.
[92] Contemporary newspaper report.
[93] Contemporary newspaper report.

point goaling just once from four attempts, while his last two shots were also behinds. But by that stage Smith had thrashed three opponents and amassed a personal scoreline of 12.10 (82). His teammates mustered a further 5.10, there was only one other multiple goalscorer, Jack Mueller, who kicked two majors, and the Demons triumphed by 17 points. The Bulldogs, with a total of 16.9 (105), could conjure just three more scoring shots than Smith. Indeed, it was a virtuoso performance worthy of a much bigger crowd than the 11,232 in attendance.

Smith's tally was a record at the MCG – surpassing Ted Freyer's 12.4 for Essendon against Melbourne in round one, 1935 – and was just the 18th instance of a player kicking 12 or more goals in a VFL match.

MOST GOALS IN A VFL MATCH (to the end of 1941)

Goals	Player	Club/Opponent	Venue	Season
17.4	Gordon Coventry	Coll v Fitz	Victoria Park	1930 (rd 12)
16.5	Gordon Coventry	Coll v Haw	Victoria Park	1929 (rd 13)
15.8	Gordon Coventry	Coll v Ess	Victoria Park	1933 (rd 11)
15.3	Bob Pratt	S Melb v Ess	Lake Oval	1934 (rd 3)
14.5	Gordon Coventry	Coll v Haw	Victoria Park	1934 (rd 14)
14.2	Doug Strang	Rich v N Melb	Punt Rd Oval	1931 (rd 2)
14.1	Harold Robertson	S Melb v St K	Lake Oval	1919 (rd 12)
13.5	Harry Davie	Melb v Carlton	Princes Park	1925 (rd 14)
13.3	Horrie Clover	Carlton v St K	Junction Oval	1921 (rd 12)
12.10	**Norm Smith**	**Melb v Foots**	**MCG**	**1941 (rd 17)**
12.6	Jack Baggott	Rich v S Melb	Punt Rd Oval	1928 (rd 9)
12.4	Ted Freyer	Ess v Melb	MCG	1935 (rd 1)
12.3	Jack Moriarty	Fitz v N Melb	Arden St Oval	1928 (rd 11)
12.2	Bob Pratt	S Melb v Foots	Lake Oval	1934 (rd 15)
12.2	George Margitich	Melb v N Melb	MCG	1931 (rd 17)
12.2	Bob C. Johnson	Melb v Haw	MCG	1933 (rd 11)
12*	Bob Merrick	Fitzroy v Melb	Brunswick St Oval	1919 (rd 16)
12*	George Moloney	Geel v St K	Corio Oval	1931 (rd 2)

(* denotes behinds not recorded.)

Far more notable, though, was Smith's remarkable tally of 22 scoring shots, which was only one behind record-holder Gordon Coventry, who had 23 shots eight years earlier in a return of 15.8. Smith is equal third on the all-time list.

MOST SCORING SHOTS IN A VFL MATCH

Shots	Player	Club/Opponent	Venue	Season
24 (15.9)	Kelvin Templeton	Foots v St K	Western Oval	1978 (rd 13)
23 (15.8)	Gordon Coventry	Coll v Haw	MCG	1933 (rd 11)
22 (17.5)	Jason Dunstall	Haw v Rich	Waverley Park	1992 (rd 7)
22 (12.10)	**Norm Smith**	**Melb v Foots**	**MCG**	**1941 (rd 17)**
22 (11.11)	Fred Fanning	Melb v Haw	Glenferrie Oval	1944 (rd 11)

NB: To 1953, behinds were not recorded on 30 of the 102 occasions in which players had kicked 10 or more goals in a match – which may, or may not, have impacted upon this list.

The performance encouraged *The Sporting Globe*'s Hec de Lacy to reconsider Smith's status in the game in the following editorial:

NORMAN SMITH – THE DADDY OF THEM ALL

I am wondering if football has produced a better forward than Norman Smith. Smith has introduced something new into the work of a centre forward – something that it is best described as a decoy and convoy system.

Talk of full-forwards usually ranges around the number of goals they obtain... Smith has scorned all such stuff. 'I don't get the goals, WE get the goals' is his policy, and a good policy it is, too. Consequently, Smith never 'rates' in goals scored more than round about the leaders, but add up the goals Melbourne scores through Baggott, Maurie Gibb, Beames, Wartman, Dowsing or any other second rover, (and) credit two-thirds of them to Smith, and see how the tallies work out. There is no exaggeration that Smith is directly or indirectly responsible for two-thirds of the goals obtained by other Melbourne forwards.

He leads away from goal, gathers the ball in his stride, (and) despatches it with a flashing handpass... In his next stride, he doubles back to cleverly block the opposition. Then when the incident is closed, he is as pleased about it, and shows it, as if he had got the goal himself.

He is robust, game as a couple of pebbles... hard to unbalance, and difficult to attack because of his protective body contortions.

Alternatively, he leads to a blind. While the defence troops after him, the ball is kicked high to Mueller, whose patrol is not more than five yards from the posts. Often he (Smith) runs out to centre half-forward, while Baggott... doubles back to full-forward. They move – these Melbourne forwards – like a hair-trigger machine operated from a central control. Smith is the central control. He moulds... (and) operates the mechanism of the finest attack we have seen for many years.

> To master the Melbourne attack, every forward has to be checked. Nothing else is good enough. Goal getting is the key to success. That is why this master technician might well be the greatest genius in attack we have seen.[94]

Smith was in the kind of form that prompted even the most merciless of opponents to praise him, albeit privately. Carlton sledgehammer Bob Chitty gave the following pre-match advice to first-year defender Vin Brown before their last round clash with the Demons: 'Norm Smith is the only player I've played against who, when he marked the ball and I punched it, I could not dislodge the ball from his grip. It's like a vice. So when you're playing on him you've got to beat him to the ball, otherwise he'll kill you because you just won't be able to punch the ball out of his hands'.[95] Chitty's guidance had only moderate success – Smith kicked five of Melbourne's 11 goals. But the Smith dilemma was a secondary issue for the Blues who, capitalising on the Demons' pitiful half-time score of 3.17 (35), recorded a stirring 25-point win at Princes Park to steal top spot from the Demons, who clung to second place and the double chance by a mere 0.5 percent. Smith had taken his season tally to 85 (at an average of five a game), only three behind the league leader, North Melbourne's Sel Murray, and one clear of Richmond's Jack Titus. Smith and Murray had played 17 games, Titus 18.

On the eve of the 1941 finals series, Jack Regan, now the captain of Collingwood, declared his admiration for Smith, rating him 'the greatest worry to teams opposing Melbourne'.[96] Indeed, as one newspaper reported of Smith: 'There is no "headier" player in Australian Rules football today'.[97]

Hec de Lacy went even further in his appraisal of the relative merits of the top three goalkickers of 1941: 'Whatever can be said for the claims of other full-forwards – Sel Murray (N.M.) and Jack Titus (Rich.) in particular – I think, in the final summing up, Smith stands alone'.[98]

In an interview with reporters before Melbourne's clash with Carlton in the second semi–final, Smith conveyed an upbeat attitude when asked of the Demons' chances for a third successive flag. 'Carlton look like being the danger,' Smith said, 'but with our team at full strength I think we'll be a pretty good bet.'[99]

---

[94] *The Sporting Globe*, August 1941.
[95] Vin Brown related this to his cousin, Bill Stephen, who in turn passed it onto the author.
[96] *The Sporting Globe*, August 1941.
[97] Contemporary newspaper report.
[98] *The Sporting Globe*, 1941.
[99] Contemporary newspaper report.

The result was a complete role reversal – for both Norm Smith and his team – from their round 18 clash just a fortnight earlier. Smith, who in the two minor-round matches against the Blues had netted 11 of Melbourne's 25 goals, was restricted to just one goal – his worst return for the season. Ironically, Smith's direct opponent for three quarters was Bob Chitty, who was swung into the ruck in the last quarter in a best-afield display. It was a tough day for Smith. At one point, he flew for a mark and was the victim of such a fierce 'stranglehold' that 'it was a wonder Smith's head didn't come off in the Carlton man's hand'.[100] Yet Smith received no free kick.

However, Melbourne boasted enough winners to cover Smith's lack of output. The Demons led by 33 points at quarter-time and were never seriously threatened on their way to a 26-point win. Filling the void were Baggott and Mueller, who bagged six and five goals respectively.

When the Blues went down to Essendon in the preliminary final, they became the first minor premier in 40 years to miss the Grand Final, and the first under the double-chance system. In 1901, Geelong finished two games clear atop the ladder but, without a double-chance, was eliminated after losing its semi-final.

In the days leading up to the Melbourne-Essendon Grand Final, no less a judge than Norm Ware – Footscray's captain-coach and that season's Brownlow Medallist – used the example of Norm Smith as a key plank of his reasoning for tipping the Demons for the premiership. 'The rucks and key men very nearly match up... until you start to ask (Cec) Ruddell, full-back, to hold Norman Smith... Then you begin to wonder'.[101]

The 1941 Grand Final showcased one of the gutsiest triumphs in the long and decorated history of Melbourne Football Club. The Demons were severely depleted – they were missing about 12 players due to war service and injury – and faced a full-strength Essendon, and were on the wrong end of an astonishingly lopsided free kick count, which favoured the Bombers 52-20. But the Bombers posed no threat to the Demons, who put the premiership beyond doubt with an 11-goal to two first half. While the Bombers piled on 7.8 in the last quarter to finish with one more scoring shot than the Demons, the 29-point margin flattered them. As Smith simply stated: 'We won the premiership easily.'[102]

Melbourne's attack had functioned superbly. Percy Beames booted six goals in what was perhaps his third successive best-on-ground performance in

---

[100] *The Sporting Globe*, Wednesday, September 13, 1941.
[101] *The Sporting Globe*, Wednesday September 24.
[102] *Melbourne Truth* series, 1962.

a Grand Final, while Norm Smith and Jack Mueller kicked three apiece. Smith had missed his first shots – regulation chances – but kicked a goal in each of the second, third and fourth quarters. Smith's last goal came after a pack-mark and a calmly slotted drop-kick from near the behind post. For the first and only time in his career, he had ended a season at the head of the VFL's goalkicking list. Smith had also created other goals. He cleared a path for Mueller to goal in the first term, and in the third quarter handballed off for another major to Gerry Daly, who kicked one of only two goals he managed in his brief VFL career.

Smith's three goals boosted his season tally to 89 goals. In achieving this, he became (and remains) the only Melbourne player to have kicked at least 80 goals in a season three times. It would be the closest, and the last time, Smith would come within striking distance of a century of goals. Such is the aura attached to century goalkickers that one cannot help but wonder how much greater Norm Smith would have been regarded as a player had he notched the elusive three figures: had he somehow managed to slot 14 more goals in 1940; or a further 11 in 1941. Many judges felt he would have achieved such distinction if he had not been so utterly selfless. But ultimately, to those like Checker Hughes who knew his true value, such statistics were irrelevant. Hughes proudly elaborated on the mechanics of his devastating forward set-up, marshalled by the cunning Norm Smith.

> When Smithy led out, Ron Baggott, one of those loosely put together players who was always hard to beat, ran in. Smithy sometimes took the pass, but a quick handpass to the running Baggott created more trouble for the defenders. Then we played a trump by keeping 'Big Jack' (Mueller) hanging around the goalsquare. One of the best marks in the game, he was a problem child in himself. No defence could leave him for a second.
>
> Les Jones and Percy Beames, two brilliant rovers, were always on the move, and if that wasn't sufficient we had that amazing fellow Maurie Gibb doing the cleverest things (at) half-forward right (flank). At half-forward left (flank) was that red-headed bullet, 'Bluey' Truscott. Smith, who was football brains from his thatch to his toes, was in clover.
>
> La Fontaine, our centre, diverted play to Gibb's flank or to Truscott, or maybe he drove direct to the fast-moving Smith, or again he might ignore the Smith lead and pass to Baggott, who would have doubled round just behind centre half-forward.

Smith became a genius at handball. He flipped the ball like a flash to the man running in, and then never forgot to block. The things that fellow did still amaze me. Smith was different from the others; he made a team work *around* him. Others made the team work *for* them.'[103]

Hec de Lacy later placed his hard-earned credibility on the line in *The Sporting Globe* by making a massive statement about Norm Smith's standing among the elite forwards in the history of the game:

Norman Smith was the greatest forward I saw in the football period between the two wars... He created a deadly forward system, while others like Collingwood's Gordon Coventry and South's Bob Pratt were mostly spearheads of a machine... For years, Collingwood won premierships, or nearly won premierships, by practising the slogan: 'Kick it up to Gordon'... Members of their famous teams were not all necessarily good kicks. They would have killed a smart little fellow like Fitzroy's Jimmy Freake. He wanted the daisy-cutter type of pass. But Gordon liked them comfortably high, punt or drop (kick). Consequently, big fellows drove a lofty punt in his direction and once Gordon got those vice-like fingers on to the ball it was all over. He, too, cleverly cooperated with smart rovers - Harry Collier, Billy Libbis, Alby Pannam and, in his later days, Des Fothergill. They got goals from the crumbs that Gordon, often deliberately, spilled. He used his big back and shoulders to block and shepherd for his scouts and there were few finer players than the same Gordon.

Bob Pratt was sensational - a landmark in a game. When they have forgotten Norman Smith, fans will still look at photos of Pratt's amazing leaps and wonder. Thousands went to games just to see the phenomenon in action. Such a man could not help but be famous. He broke highest individual goal tallies - 150 in 1934... But here again was the star turn of a troupe. When he took the trapeze, the band stopped and the people gaped.

Smith never attempted records. He never thought of his own football. He was (both) the clever architect, and the faithful builder... No spotlights for Smith, no hushed crowd, but afterwards always the warm feeling of another good show tucked away, another match won.

Smith searched for the opportunities. Pratt and Coventry had to have them given (to) them.[104]

---

[103] *The Sporting Globe*, 1949.
[104] *The Sporting Globe*, 1949.

THE FIRST HAT-TRICK [1939-41]

Seeking to support his claims, de Lacy asked Checker Hughes if Smith was in fact the greatest full-forward between the wars, to which Hughes replied: 'Well, that depends. In straightforward work – spearhead stuff – give me Gordon Coventry before even Pratt. But "Bluey" Smith was a real master at creating play. He was a wily bird, old "Ginger".'[105] The respect between Smith and coach Hughes was immense and mutual. Smith later paid tribute to Hughes, who was 'right at his peak then, and there was nothing he would ask the boys to do that he could not do himself on the training track'.[106] Hec de Lacy also credited the Demons' success to Hughes, who he described as 'unruffled in adversity, never overlooking detail, never blinded by success'.[107]

Smith rated the 1939-41 Demon sides as 'the equal of any team ever to play League football'. In those three golden seasons, the Demons won 49 of their 61 matches, posting totals of 100-plus points on 46 occasions while their opposition could muster only 15 centuries.

In doing so, the Demons achieved the phenomenal distinction of winning their fifth premiership in as many attempts. After winning their first flag by just four points over Fitzroy in 1900, the Demons had cruised to victory in their next four Grand Finals by an average of 44 points.

And they had done it with a quintessential team effort, which did not escape Smith's attention. Although Melbourne boasted recognised champions like Allan La Fontaine, Jack Mueller and Percy Beames – each of whom, in the public mind at least, overshadowed the subtle, understated brilliance of Norm Smith – no Demon came any closer than 12 votes to the Brownlow Medal winner in the 1939-40-41 premiership seasons. In 1939, Demon best-and-fairest Mueller, although ineligible after being suspended, was equal 10th highest vote-getter with 11 – 12 shy of Collingwood's Marcus Whelan. In 1940, another best-and-fairest recipient, Ron Baggott was Melbourne's best, also at equal 10th with 11 votes, a tally dwarfed by the 32 amassed by joint winners Des Fothergill (Collingwood) and Herbie Matthews (South Melbourne). And in 1941, there were no Demons in the top 13 vote-winners when Footscray ruckman Norm Ware took the honours.

---

[105] *The Sporting Globe*, 1949.
[106] *Melbourne Truth* series, 1962.
[107] *The Sporting Globe*, Wednesday, September 31, 1941.

The Demons laboured through the latter part of the 1941 season with heavy hearts following the death of Ron Barassi (senior), who was killed in action at Tobruk, in north-eastern Libya.

Barassi had played 58 games and kicked 84 goals in the No. 31 jumper for the Demons, winning the club's 'most unselfish player' award in 1938, and was the 19th man in the 1940 premiership side, replacing the injured Ray Wartman at quarter-time and playing the last three quarters. He had enlisted on July 15, 1940, but was dead little more than 12 months later.

On the morning of July 31, 1941, Corporal Barassi volunteered to relieve a sick driver of an Army truck, but shortly after getting behind the wheel he drove over a landmine which exploded and inflicted mortal wounds. Barassi, 27, lingered on for a few hours before dying of his injuries. He was the first VFL player to be killed in action in World War II.

Elza Barassi and five-year-old Ron junior had been staying with Elza's brother and sister-in-law, along with their three children in a weatherboard cottage at 20 Coral Avenue, Footscray. One early August day, Norm and Marj Smith visited the Barassis. They had kept in close contact with Elza and 'young Ronny', particularly since Ron senior's departure on war service. Elza had been forced to attend the Smiths' wedding on her own because the previous day her husband had boarded the *Queen Mary*, which set sail for the battlefields of Africa. On this particular day, they were sitting and talking in the loungeroom when a telegram arrived bearing the insignia of the Department of Defence. Its grim contents, regretfully informing them of Ron senior's tragic death, devastated everyone in the room. 'It was a scene of desolation and human grief that I will never forget,' Ron Barassi junior recalled.[108] In an effort to comfort the grieving widow – the wife of one of his best mates, and a woman he and his wife were extremely fond of – Smith took Elza on his knee and embraced her. Ron junior knew his mother was in pain, and he instinctively 'snuggled' up to her.[109]

While his mother cried uncontrollably, young Ron didn't shed a tear – not then anyway. He was too young to realise what had happened, and the ramifications it would have on his life, and he had already had a year to become accustomed to living without his father. He did, however, feel 'an indescribable emptiness'.[110] Little did they know at the time that in another decade Smith would pay the ultimate tribute to his fallen mate by becoming Ron junior's virtual foster father.

---

[108] Collins, Ben, *The Champions: Conversations with Great Players and Coaches of Australian Football*, GSP, 2006.
[109] Ron Barassi. Interview with the author.
[110] Barassi, Ron and Peter McFarline, *Barassi: The Life Behind The Legend*, Simon & Schuster, 1995. Ron junior first visited his father's grave in the Tobruk War Cemetery in 1984.

Smith later reflected on that 'sad day' when he learned of the passing of 'one of my close friends... a fine man and a good footballer'.[111]

Ron Baggott lowered his eyes and shook his head when he recalled the heartache: 'To lose a close mate like that, who was such a bonzer bloke, and a family man, was just terrible. It made you feel sick in the guts. All of the players felt that sadness, but especially Norm, Richie Emselle and myself because we'd been a real foursome, and all of our wives were great friends too'.[112]

Before the round 16 clash between Melbourne and Collingwood, 16 days after Barassi's death, players from both sides wore black armbands and formed a guard of honour in the middle of the MCG. A lone bugler played a moving rendition of *The Last Post*, after which everybody present observed a minute's silence. Smith and Baggott stood side by side, their heads bowed in honour of their fallen mate. 'There were a few tears shed,' Baggott revealed. 'Tough footballers who tried to knock your block off, were crying. It had that effect on everyone.'[113] The emotion of that afternoon was captured in *The Sporting Globe*. '(Barassi) departs a man honoured by his peers and those who cheer. In dying at Tobruk, he perpetuated his memory in a way that years of brilliant service with Melbourne could not have done.'[114]

Before the end of the war, at least six more Melbourne players would give their lives for their country. They included premiership heroes in Keith 'Bluey' Truscott (50 games and 31 goals from 1937-40 and 1942), wingman Sid Anderson (52 games from 1939-41) and ruckman Harold Ball (33 games and 33 goals in 1939-40), former Geelong star Clyde Helmer (two games in 1942) and fringe players John Atkins (four games in 1940), Noel Ellis (three games in 1940-41) and John Fraser. Melbourne was easily the hardest hit club in World War II.[115]

🏆🏆🏆🏆🏆🏆🏆🏆🏆

To his lasting regret, Norm Smith did not go to the war. He was granted an exemption from service because he worked in a protected industry – Miller's

---

[111] *Melbourne Truth* series, 1962.
[112] Ron Baggott. Interview with the author.
[113] Ron Baggott. Interview with the author.
[114] *The Sporting Globe*, 1941.
[115] Truscott, a redhead, earned a DFC (Distinguished Flying Cross) and had flown into battle with the figure of a red demon emblazoned on his fighter plane. Melbourne Football Club honoured Truscott's memory by naming its best-and-fairest award after him. Checker Hughes donated the 'Bluey' Truscott Memorial Cup to the club in 1943. Don Cordner was the first recipient of the award. The Sid Anderson Memorial Trophy is presented to the runner-up in the best-and-fairest, the Ron Barassi Snr Memorial Trophy to the third place-getter, and the Harold Ball Memorial Trophy recognises the Demons' best first-year player.

ropeworks was supplying rope for the war effort; rope that was put to good use by the Royal Australian Navy, for instance. And Smith was viewed as a valuable member of the company's engineering department. So valuable, in fact, that at some point in the early 1940s he initiated a major change in operation. Melbourne teammate Hugh McPherson, who first gained employment at Miller's in 1940, marvelled at Smith's achievement: 'Norm was a brilliant engineer – very clever mechanically – and he managed to do something which they said could not be done: he changed all the belt-driven machines to gear-driven. He turned the whole system around at Miller's. In no time at all – within about 12 months – he had the whole factory working on gears. He was very cluey and methodical. He had the best brain and skills in the world'.[116]

Len Smith was also a talented engineer. But he went to war; or rather, it found him. Len joined the Royal Australian Air Force and was stationed at the Laverton base in Melbourne's western suburbs before being transferred to Darwin. Len's wife Flo gave birth to their third and final child, Kevin, on January 25, 1942, and just a few weeks later Len and hundreds of fellow Australian serviceman in Darwin were under attack from the Japanese. On the morning of February 19, 1942 – just 10 weeks after their massive strike at Pearl Harbor – the Japanese launched two separate air attacks which claimed the lives of at least 243 people and injured up to 400, destroyed military planes, battleships and many of Darwin's buildings. Len's daughter Norma Harmes repeated what her father recalled of the attacks:

> The Japanese planes were flying directly overhead and most people, if they were in the same situation, would probably have run the other way, but Dad climbed up a tree to watch it all! But I think what happened that day had quite an effect on him because he even years later he would never watch the Anzac Day parades. I think it was just too sad for him because he lost a few mates in Darwin."[117]

---

[116] Hugh McPherson. Interview with the author.
[117] Norma Harmes. Interview with the author.

4

'A WORTHY LIEUTENANT'

[1942-43]

Melbourne had just enjoyed three of its greatest seasons, but now it would endure three of its most challenging.

When the euphoria associated with their trio of premierships subsided, the Demons faced a harsh new reality that would not only end any hope they harboured of equalling Collingwood's record of four successive premierships, but bring an abrupt end to their golden era and keep them a long way out of finals contention until 1946. But the fact they suffered such a dramatic fall from grace was not entirely surprising; indeed, it was probably half expected, given the desperate circumstances they confronted.

Firstly, Checker Hughes was no longer coach. The master mentor had promptly resigned after the 1941 Grand Final to concentrate solely on his expanding business interests in the hotel industry. Hughes' replacement was swiftly appointed. Club chairman Joe Blair summoned 30-year-old Percy Beames to his office and virtually forced the captain-coaching role upon him. Beames, a dyed-in-the-wool Demon who would do anything to help his beloved club, accepted the role as his duty.

Beames recognised Norm Smith's leadership qualities and football knowledge and gave him more responsibility around the club. The new coach instated Smith as a member of his five-man selection committee. The other three members of the brains trust were chairman of selectors Fred Ince, former champion centreman Dick Taylor and Jack Mueller, who was in his fifth season as vice-captain.

In addition to the departure of Checker Hughes and powerhouse secretary Percy Page – who later excelled in the position of honorary secretary of the Australian National Football Council – there was the overwhelming effect of the war, the state of which became graver by the telegram. There was some doubt, and serious debate, about whether the 1942 VFL season should in fact go ahead. But eventually the League and 11 of its 12 clubs – Geelong did not compete in 1942-43 due to wartime travel restrictions – agreed that football played an important role in maintaining morale and a sense of normality, and decided they owed it to the public to forge on, albeit in a season reduced from 18 to 16 rounds, with a bye for each side.

The war robbed the Demons – and many other clubs for that matter – of many of their star players. Norm Smith later lamented: 'The war intervened and wrecked our chances of equalling and bettering Collingwood's record'[1] of four successive premierships. The majority of available players was made up of soldiers on leave, of whom there was a particularly high turnover rate, and men working in essential services or munitions like Norm Smith. Half of the Demons who played senior football in 1941 – 18 of their 36 players – were unavailable in 1942. The club blooded 19 first-year players in the senior side.

Winning was more a matter of good fortune than good management, as it simply came down to who was available on any given Saturday. For this very reason, many supporters of the day – predominantly those who supported unsuccessful clubs – refused to fully acknowledge team and individual performances from 1942 to 1945. Even the VFL, in its decision to abandon the Brownlow Medal during these four seasons, conceded, albeit tacitly, that the competition had been weakened.

Public interest in the game plummeted, as it did during World War I. The average attendance at home-and-away games in 1942 dipped to just 8238 people – well short of the 1941 average of 10,715; well adrift of the pre-war (1939) mark of 15,236; and less than half the high watermark average of 20,494 back in 1924.

The Demons' on-field performances deteriorated to such an extent that they endured their poorest season since 1933. Under Beames, the Demons won just two of their first 10 matches in 1942; their eight losses being by an average of 44 points. In the opening two rounds against the eventual Grand Finalists, Essendon and Richmond, they conceded a total of 55.30 (360) to their own 34.23 (227).

It didn't help that the US army had commandeered the MCG, leaving the Demons to find an alternative ground to train and play at. As was reported in Melbourne's annual report, 'our good neighbours, Richmond, readily came to the rescue with the kind offer for us to share the Richmond ground (Punt Road Oval), and this proposition was gratefully accepted'. While the Demons found a training base at the Albert Ground, training attendances were down. 'It was a problem getting

---

[1] *Melbourne Truth* series, 1962.

players to the ground in time to train,' Beames recalled. 'A good crowd would be say about eight or 10 (players) – that's all we'd have on a training night.'[2]

After being a disastrous 2-8, Melbourne won three of its next four matches, claiming the scalp of that season's premier Essendon by 20 points in round 12. But it was not enough to lift the Demons higher than eighth (of 11 sides) – five games and 40.8 percent out of the top four. It was their worst season since 1933.

Frustratingly for Norm Smith, he could do little to stop the downward spiral. After proving himself one of the most resilient players in the competition by playing five full seasons without missing a game – and kicking 361 goals in 101 consecutive games in that period[3] – Smith finally succumbed to injuries. He was restricted to just 10 of the 16 games in 1942. However, when he was available he was a solid contributor, kicking 30 goals, including 15 in three games (5,4, 6) late in the year, and only once failed to be a multiple goalscorer, that being when the Demons kicked just 10 majors in a round 10 loss to Carlton. Teammate Hugh McPherson said that despite limited opportunities, Smith was as brilliant as ever:

> Whenever Norm got the ball – and he got it quite often – all you could hear was (Jack) Mueller, (Ron) Baggott and the other forwards, who would suddenly get excited and start chirping like birds who wanted to be fed. They'd be screaming: 'Norm! Norm! Norm!' And he'd put it right down their throats. No wonder they got excited when Norm got the ball. He was a magnificent footballer. Honest to God, he was the best footballer I've ever seen. The whole forward line lived off his uncanny ability to get the ball and give it out to someone in a better position.[4]

During the war, Smith also played an exhibition match for a League side against a Combined Services side. Among Smith's teammates in the League side, selected by the Lord Mayor of Melbourne, Sir Frank Beaurepaire, were two of his meanest opponents, Jack Dyer and Bob Chitty, while the opposition featured Demon mates Allan La Fontaine and Jack Mueller. The League team won by five points.

He played another couple of 'kick-and-giggle' matches, this time more novelties than exhibitions, against US servicemen at Punt Road. They contested a hybrid game called 'AUSTUS' – a cross between Australian Rules and American gridiron, in which the Australians kicked the ball and the Americans threw it. Smith's young Demon teammate Don Cordner recalled the Americans proving tougher opponents

---

[2] *Red and Blue* documentary, 2005.
[3] These figures include one appearance for Victoria in which Norm kicked two goals.
[4] Hugh McPherson. Interview with the author.

than expected. 'With their throwing, they were deadly accurate in front of goal – they didn't miss – so we were allowed to throw as well,' Cordner said.[5]

After the first round of the 1943 season, Jack Mueller was posted up north with the AIF (Australian Imperial Force). Between 1943 and 1945 Mueller would play just 11 games for the Demons. Mueller's replacement as vice-captain was none other than his good friend, Norm Smith. Smith was suddenly the right-hand man of captain-coach Percy Beames. Although the promotion was gained by default, it was viewed as a natural progression for a natural leader. He 'proved a worthy lieutenant, and set an inspiring example to the younger players'.[6]

Although Smith was, according to Cordner, 'initially a quiet, well-spoken, respectful fellow who was very pleasant to talk to; an agreeable personality',[7] he treated football as a deadly serious business. Even Hugh McPherson, a work colleague and a mate of Smith, incurred his wrath. McPherson, one of only four Demons to play all 15 games in 1943, was a hard-hitting follower and defender whose fierce attack on opponents came under scrutiny from umpires:

> Before a game one time, the umpires approached me and warned: 'Watch yourself today, McPherson, because we're after you.'
>
> I thought: 'That's a bit rough; the game hasn't even started and I'm already in the gun with the umps. We have to do something about this; it just isn't right'.
>
> Percy Beames wasn't playing that day, and Norm was our acting captain, so I approached Norm and told him what the umpires had said. I appealed to him to sort it out. But I should've known that I'd get no sympathy from him. You didn't go whinging to Norm; he wouldn't have it. He looked me straight in the eye and said: 'Forget the damn umpires! Forget the opposition and everybody else! They won't matter a damn if you *just play the bloody ball!*'
>
> He could talk like that with a clear conscience because that's what Norm did: he *just played the bloody ball*.[8]

Smith played *on* the ball for the first time in 1943. It didn't start out that way though, with Smith assuming his customary position in a Melbourne attack minus Ron Baggott, who had gone to war. In round one, the Demons played Fitzroy at Punt Road and for the first of only two such instances in head-to-head clashes

---

[5] Don Cordner. Interview with the author. Cordner could not recall if Norm took up the throwing option.
[6] Melbourne Football Club Annual Report, 1943.
[7] Don Cordner. Interview with the author.
[8] Hugh McPherson. Interview with the author.

in their careers, Len Smith, who was on leave from armed service, outscored his brother – five goals to three – as Fitzroy won by three points. On the other occasion, in round nine, 1945, the count was two to one. This particular match in 1943 was to be Len Smith's only VFL game for the season before returning to Darwin.

Norm Smith made amends the next week when he kicked six of the Demons' 15 majors in a 23-point win over South Melbourne. But soon after he was forced to reinvent himself as a VFL player as a 27-year-old. For coach Beames, there were two major motivating factors behind the move.

Firstly, Fred Fanning – who worked with Smith in the engineering department at Miller's – had emerged as a prolific full-forward. Fanning, 21, possessed a body that horrified full-backs. He was a man-mountain, who stood at 6'4" (193cms) and grew to about 16.5 stone (105kgs). As a 17 and 18-year-old in the reserves, Fanning had kicked a total of 220 goals in two seasons (109 in 1938, and 111 in 1939), including 12 goals in the 1939 reserves Grand Final. He had since missed much of the 1940 and 1941 seasons with injury. A senior return of 37 goals in 15 games in 1942 was followed by 62 goals in 15 games (including bags of 11, 8, 7 and 6) in 1943. He actually led the VFL goalkicking that season.[9]

Fanning's mother, a charismatic Englishwoman, was also pleased with her son's development. In a match against Fitzroy at Punt Road, Mrs Fanning, in her broad English accent, was quite vocal in her encouragement of the Melbourne players. Fed up with her urging, a Fitzroy-supporting woman of a similar vintage said: 'I've got six sons away fighting for the likes of you'. Mrs Fanning said: 'Well I've got two – one's away fighting for you, the other is out there entertaining you'.[10]

Fanning's impressive development offered a solution to an important problem. The retirement of Allan La Fontaine had, for the first time in eight years, left Melbourne without a top-class centreman. Beames' answer was to experiment with Norm Smith – his chief playmaker in attack – by thrusting him into the key 'pivot' role. The experiment was regarded as a success. Smith performed well enough to convince Beames it would be worth playing him permanently in the middle where his awareness, nous, quick hands, deadly drop-kicking, marking ability and mobility for his size were enormous assets.

The Demons finished seventh (of 11 sides) with a record of 7-8, two games and 36.3 percent out of finals contention. It was a meritorious effort considering

---

[9] Fanning's tally of 62 goals in 1943 was the lowest for a VFL leading goalkicker since 1922 when Carlton's Horrie Clover kicked 54 goals in 16 games.

[10] Marj Lenne, the wife of George Lenne (a Melbourne player in the 1940s), and later a member of Melbourne's ladies' social committee. Interview with the author.

a further 18 players made their senior debuts for Melbourne in 1943, and that after six rounds they had been on the bottom of the ladder with just one win. Amazingly, just seven players from Melbourne's 1941 premiership side were still at the club. They were Percy Beames, Norm Smith, Don and Ted Cordner, Maurie Gibb, Richie Emselle and Adrian Dullard.

ϒϒϒϒϒϒϒϒ

Vic Smith was sitting at his dining table and had just taken a bite from a pear when he suffered a massive heart attack and dropped dead.[11] It was a Monday, August 9, 1943. Vic was just 59. It was a horrible shock for the entire family, especially as Vic had always been a healthy, active man who had strong sporting interests. A devastated Len returned from air force duties in Darwin to join the rest of the family in its grieving.

Vic's obituary, which appeared in a local newspaper, gave an insight into just how significant a loss he would be to not only his family and friends but the Northcote community which he had embraced and enhanced:

> A well-known Northcote resident... the late Mr Smith is survived by his widow, daughter and two sons (who are) well-known in football circles. Len, who commenced his football career with Northcote, then later with Melbourne and Fitzroy, is now a sergeant in the R.A.A.F. at a distant operational station, and Norman, who for many years has played with Melbourne. As President of the Dennis Cricket Club, which he fostered for many years... (Mr Smith's) experience as a cricketer in his younger days was eagerly sought. A popular follower of all sporting activities in or around Northcote, he never hesitated to assist a club in distress. His presence as a spectator or player was always warmly welcomed... The death of so popular a sportsman will be a severe loss to many in Northcote.[12]

Vic's funeral was conducted three days after his death. His obituary also recorded that 'representatives of the Melbourne and Fitzroy football clubs, and Northcote and Dennis cricket clubs acted as pallbearers and a large attendance was at the graveside'.[13] The Smiths paid £10 for their patriarch to be buried in the Church of England section of the Melbourne General Cemetery.

---

[11] Norma Harmes. Interview with the author.
[12] An obituary of Victor Smith. Source unknown.
[13] An obituary of Victor Smith. Source unknown.

'A WORTHY LIEUTENANT' [1942-43]

Known simply as "Pop" to his grandchildren, Vic was so fondly regarded, and remembered, that Norm Smith would name his own son Peter *Victor* Smith, while Len Smith's daughter, Norma would name one of her sons Wayne *Victor* Harmes.

The sudden, unexpected death of Vic Smith raised questions about the future of his backyard engineering business, which had supplied parts to pram manufacturers for 20 years. Virtually on the spot, Norm Smith decided to leave Miller's ropeworks to take over the family business, which was classified as belonging to a protected industry that provided an essential service for Australian mothers.

It wasn't exactly a step into the unknown for Smith, as he had grown up with the business, and had helped his father at various stages, particularly in his young life; therefore he knew what to expect. But with his football commitments, he felt he needed some help, even if it was only on a part-time basis. When his 13-year-old cousin Russell Brown visited the Smith house with his family to console his Aunty Ethel, Norm Smith came up with an idea. Smith asked young Brown – whose father Les was a younger brother of Ethel – if he'd like to lend him a hand after he'd finished his school day at Collingwood Tech. Although they did not know each other very well, the youngster was a Melbourne fan and his number one idol was none other than Smith.[14] Not surprisingly, Brown jumped at the double bonus of spending time with his hero and making some pocket-money at the same time.

Perhaps as a tribute to his dearly departed father, Smith continued to trade under the business name, 'V. Smith'. Shortly after his father's death, Smith and his young cousin took over where the old man had left off, operating two heavy hand-presses to make pram parts – metal, folding hinges for the hoods, and the folding component at the bottom.[15] The hand-presses were such hard, physical work that Smith even enlisted the help of Demon colossus Fred Fanning, along with another teammate, Col Bradley, for a few hours a week. Their workshop was Vic's old, unpainted, weatherboard shed, which was so roughly finished it would 'scrape and splinter' anyone who accidentally brushed against it. 'The whole set-up was so antiquated at the start,' Brown recalled, 'you'd grab a hammer and it'd be so old and worn that the head of the hammer would be only half-an-inch deep, and it'd be worn away at the thumb too, from being banged so much for 20-odd years.'[16]

---

[14] Russell Brown told the author that Vic Smith, whom he knew as "Uncle Dick", had influenced him as a child to barrack for the Demons. 'I didn't really barrack for a VFL club at the time but Uncle Dick told me: "Barrack for Melbourne." With Norm being my idol, I said: "Yeah, OK, Uncle Dick, I'll barrack for Melbourne." He wasn't a forceful character, but he certainly made sure I supported the right club.'

[15] Norma Harmes fondly recalls having lunch at "Nanna's place" every Tuesday. 'Uncle Norm would sit in Pop's old chair at the dining table,' she told the author.

[16] Russell Brown. Interview with the author.

Russ Brown proved such a competent assistant that when he turned 14 just two months later Smith asked him: 'Russ, why don't you come and work for me permanently?' Brown gratefully accepted. The only obstacle was the Manpower Directorate, established in January 1942, which empowered the government to determine, and enforce, where workers would be best used in assisting the war effort. People couldn't simply take any job they liked. With children routinely leaving school at 14, they were subjected to the same scrutiny as adults. For all that, Brown was allowed to take Smith up on the offer. Brown's recollections of their long working relationship provide fascinating insights into Smith's character:

> When I started, I had stars in my eyes because Norm was my hero. But that barrier was broken down through working side by side, just the two of us, and talking to him all day every day for 48 hours a week, over many years. Despite the 14-year age gap, we became mates. Of course, we still had our disagreements along the way. Norm couldn't work with anyone for any period without having a tiff at some stage. And with us coming from the same family and the same mould – fire in the guts – we were bound to clash occasionally.
>
> Norm hated lateness. He caught me a couple of times and if it wasn't for Aunty Ethel I might've been sacked. Norm would be having a go at me – 'You're bloody late!' – but Aunty Ethel would cover for me; she'd say: 'No, he wasn't, Norm'.
>
> Norm was a hard boss but what you learnt, you learnt properly. He'd show you how to do something and make sure you did it right and then leave you to do it. If you constantly made mistakes, he'd naturally go crook. When I was 14, I made a mistake and he said: 'You silly bastard!' I stood up to him: 'I'm not a bastard! My parents were married when I was born!' He just laughed. It was my way of showing him he couldn't stand over me. He respected me for that.
>
> I'd sulk, whereas he'd blow up quick and cool down quick. Five minutes after we'd had a blue, I'd still be sulking and he'd say: 'What's wrong with you?' But he'd soon talk me around and have me laughing. He'd put his point across strongly but once he'd made it he'd be onto the next thing. He didn't dwell on anything.
>
> Norm was a man of integrity, so he'd get most upset if you questioned that integrity. He was so honest and upfront that he'd tell you straight out what he thought of you. You always knew where you stood with him. Sometimes that was good, other times it was bad! One time, we both got fired up and I called him a liar. He went all blue in the face and glared at me like he was burning holes through me with his eyes. He said: 'Don't you ever call me a liar!' He grabbed me by the collar

and started choking me. I thought: 'He's going to strangle me!' But it was over just as quick, and nothing was mentioned about it again.[17]

Although Smith ran a business, he didn't have a passion for business. But he could certainly play hard ball with business associates, as Brown remembered:

> He hated it when people were slow to pay their bills. Small businesses need money coming in constantly to pay the bills, so when someone didn't cough up what they owed in time, Norm would go crook. One day, this late-paying bloke turned up in a flashy Jaguar. When he came in to pay, Norm was disgusted with him; he said: 'Sell your bloody Jag and you might be able to pay your bills on time!' Another time he gave a bloke such a serve that he virtually made him shrink before our eyes. He said: 'You shouldn't be in business until you learn to pay your bloody bills!'
>
> He was so direct, but it wouldn't have affected the business relationship after that. As soon as the bloke paid up, Norm would move on. He wasn't a person to hold grudges. He was confident enough in himself to confront a problem, handle it with the person or people concerned and then put it behind him. I respected him so much for that when I became an adult because it's such a difficult thing to do.

Smith and Brown would also work on Saturday mornings and then Smith would leave to play football. He often took Brown with him to Melbourne matches and always ensured he got finals tickets. 'But regardless the result, Smith never seemed to bring his moods to work,' Brown revealed. 'He didn't allow a loss in the footy on the weekend to affect his work or the way he treated people. He was a good loser. He'd do his best to win, but if he lost he accepted it and moved on.'[18]

▼▼▼▼▼▼▼▼▼

Norm Smith's coaching career had the humblest of beginnings – in a back alley in Northcote. But it had nothing to do with football and was of the one-on-one variety rather than a group situation. As expected though, in light of Smith's later coaching feats, his early mentoring was to have a profound effect.

In August 1943, his young cousin Russ Brown expressed an interest in cricket, despite having never played the game. When Smith took him for a hit with a tennis ball in an alley adjoining the Smith property in Clarke Street, Brown's complete

---

[17] Russell Brown. Interview with the author.
[18] Russell Brown. Interview with the author.

lack of experience was obvious. 'I was utterly hopeless,' Brown admitted. 'I didn't even know which end of the bat to hold! I can only imagine what Smith must have thought, seeing he was probably the best player in the local Jika competition.' But Smith took it upon himself – as a personal project – to coach the youngster.

Each day, the pair would devote most of their lunch break to improving Brown's cricket skills, particularly his batting. They practised across the alleyway, using a banana box or a tin as the stumps, batting becoming very difficult when the ball steepled or grubbed after hitting the join between concrete blocks. Smith's first task was to equip his enthusiastic charge with the basics of batting: stand up straight, keep your front elbow up, get your foot to the pitch of ball, play straight, keep the ball on the ground, etc. 'He drilled those basics into me the whole time,' Brown said. 'He thought if you couldn't do the basics well, what hope did you have?'

Smith introduced a system of scoring that ensured his fundamentals were adhered to. The only way Brown could score was to hit the ball straight, past Smith, through a narrow gap between the shed and the garage. 'But Norm was such a good fielder,' Brown admired, 'you'd hit it like a rocket, only an inch off the ground, and he'd catch it in one hand.' It became even tougher when Smith batted. 'If I wanted to have another bat myself, I'd have to get Norm out, which was extremely difficult. A lot better, more experienced bowlers had a hard enough time doing that themselves, so how was I going to do it? He knew it was hard for me, but that's what forced me to improve. He was testing my character too.'

Within six months – by February 1944 – Smith had transformed the rawest of novices into an A-Grade player for Dennis. Brown made double figures in his first two innings and, little over a month later, was a member of a premiership side with Smith and his Melbourne teammate Richie Emselle.

Brown played at A-Grade level for more than 30 years and didn't retire until he was 60. In that time he made four hundreds, including 140 in a semi-final win in 1953/54 and a whirlwind 100 in 71 minutes in 1960/61. He also coached Dennis for eight seasons and led the club to a premiership.

As Brown pondered the impact of those private coaching sessions, tears moistened in his eyes, and he needlessly apologised. 'Forgive me… Norm was a great man. He had an enormous effect on my life. My cricket career – not that I reached any great heights – was all due to Norm. And when I coached – from kids up to senior players – I taught the Norm Smith way. It's amazing how successful it was at local level over a long period of time.'[19]

---

[19] Russell Brown. Interview with the author.

5

THE BEST IN THE VFL

[1944]

Norm Smith kicked a career-low of three goals in the 1944 season – including just one goal in the last 13 rounds – yet it was probably his best season. That year, as a permanent centreman, Smith won his second Melbourne best-and-fairest award and was widely recognised as the best player in the VFL that season. Indeed, it was generally acknowledged that the Demon vice-captain would have won the Brownlow Medal if it had not been suspended since 1942.

Smith did, however, win a consolation prize. He was voted *The Herald*'s 'League Star Footballer' – an award regarded by many as the substitute of the Brownlow. Teammate Don Cordner believed Smith 'thoroughly deserved' the award.[1]

Smith was one of the few positives to emerge from another disappointing season for the Demons in which they never recovered after slipping to 2-7, eventually finishing eighth – five-and-a-half games out of the top four. With 22 of the previous season's players unavailable, the Demons had been forced to blood 16 debutants and use 46 players – the most in the club's history.[2] In all, 55 new players had been tried since the 1941 flag.

Another positive was Fred Fanning's second successive league goalkicking award. The monstrous full-forward kicked 87 goals in 14 games (including 50 of the Demons' 101 goals in the first seven rounds) – a tally that showcased two hauls of 11 majors, in landslide wins over the bottom teams, Hawthorn and Geelong – to take him within two goals of Smith's club record. Fanning, who was a prodigious and extraordinarily accurate torpedo-punt kick, was the beneficiary of Smith's

---

[1] Don Cordner. Interview with the author.
[2] There have since been four other instances of Melbourne using 46 players – in 1966, when the Demons finished 11th under Norm Smith; in 1979, when they also came 11th in Carl Ditterich's first season at the helm; in 1981, when they finished on the bottom (12th) under new coach Ron Barassi; and in 1986, when they again ended up 11th in the first year of John Northey's reign.

skills and tutelage. After the Demons' unexpected loss to St Kilda in round five at Punt Road – a match in which Fanning kicked four of Melbourne's 10 goals but the Demons' 'forward work broke down'[3] – *The Herald* reported on the Tuesday that Smith would give Fanning 'special tuition in full-forward play at training this evening and on Thursday. At his top, Fanning is almost invincible in the air, but he needs more finesse'.[4] Fanning kicked nine and eight goals in the two matches immediately after receiving Smith's 'tuition'.

Smith was also the chief supplier of scoring opportunities for Fanning, and the rest of the side for that matter. This was one of the aspects of Smith's game that rarely altered, regardless of the position he played. Smith's high-quality disposal skills came in for special praise from *The Herald's* renowned football writer, Alf Brown, who felt his main asset as a centreman was 'his superb kicking', which 'made him a star',[5] just as it had when he played as a roaming forward. His captain-coach, Percy Beames, later wrote that 'it was a delight to see him drop-kicking the ball as a centreman in 1944. From any distance up to 50 metres, Smith, in that season, threaded the ball through the proverbial needle' to teammates.[6] Hugh McPherson, who was recognised with Beames as Melbourne's 'most determined players' that season, recalled how Smith would 'shark the ball from the centre bounce and put it down someone's throat in a flash.'[7]

Percy J. Millard, writing for *The Herald*, raved that as a centreman Smith was 'an artist', and took particular notice of his 'adroitness, crisp marking and deft disposal'.[8] Even bitter opponents like Collingwood rover Lou Richards became grudging admirers:

> (Norm Smith) had a razor-sharp football brain. He was an extremely cagey player... He was a wily and tough customer who always had you guessing what he was going to do next; even more important, he was a quick-thinking team man.[9]

That Smith was able to produce such a superb season in a previously foreign position underlined his versatility and the depth of his football brain. At the age of 28, he had transformed himself from being the Demons' fulcrum in attack to being

---

[3] Percy J. Millard, *The Herald*, June 6, 1944.
[4] Percy J. Millard, *The Herald*, June 6, 1944.
[5] *The Herald*, May 4, 1979.
[6] Souvenir booklet for the Norm Smith Commemorative Dinner, held on July 12, 1979, to inaugurate the Norm Smith Medal.
[7] Hugh McPherson. Interview with the author.
[8] *The Herald*, May 19, 1944.
[9] Richards, Lou with Ian McDonald, *Boots And All!*, Stanley Paul, 1963.

their fulcrum in the centre – a role he had first experienced and familiarised himself with in the latter part of the previous season. Smith was one of only six Demons to play all 18 games – his first full season since 1941. Don Cordner was impressed, but not surprised, with how easily Smith made the transition from goalkicker to ball-getter:

> Norm was a very good centreman. Well, he was a very good footballer wherever he played. He was a natural. He always seemed to know where to go and what to do in any given circumstance. He wasn't a dominating player but he was always in the play and always doing the right thing, and he brought other players into the game like very few others.[10]

Smith didn't immediately dominate the voting in *The Herald* award. After seven rounds, Fanning led with 10 votes, with Smith on six. But Smith accumulated 16 votes in the next eight rounds, missing votes in just two games during this period. After scoring his sixth best-on-ground performance against Geelong in round 15, Smith had sprinted to 22 votes to lead by six votes from his nearest challenger, Essendon ruckman/defender Percy Bushby. Interestingly, Smith collected four best-afield honours among the 14 votes he won in losing teams.

In announcing Smith as the winner of the prestigious trophy – which was presented to Smith at a club social and dance at Rainbow Hall, Prahran, on September 14 – *The Herald*'s Percy J. Millard observed:

> By his consistent excellence in a team that finished eighth, Norm Smith, who played in all 18 games, clearly proved his right to the title (of *The Herald's* Star League Footballer). With his intelligent anticipation for "football sense", quick and sound judgement, safe marking and sure disposal by hand and foot, he gave polished, masterly displays. His unerring stab-kicks to comrades stamped him as a sort of "Football Lindrum". He was undoubtedly a big factor in giant Fred Fanning heading the League goal list, another honour to the Demons with 87 for the season...
>
> In the Melbourne dressingroom on Saturday, it was announced that he had won the "Bluey" Truscott Memorial Cup... A club supporter, Mr (J.) Beeching, also gave Smith a trophy "as the leading Melbourne player in *The Herald* vote".[11]

---

[10] Don Cordner. Interview with the author.
[11] *The Herald*, Monday September 4, 1944.

THE RED FOX – NORM SMITH

THE HERALD STAR LEAGUE FOOTBALLER AWARD – 1944
Top 10 vote-getters

23	**Norm Smith (Melbourne)**
20	Percy Bushby (Essendon)
17	Lou Richards (Collingwood), Don Cordner (Melbourne)
16	Arthur Olliver (Footscray), Allan Ruthven (Fitzroy)
15	Reg Garvin (St Kilda), Sid Dyer (North Melbourne)
14	Alan Crawford (North Melbourne), Jim Munday (Geelong)

NORM SMITH'S 1944 SEASON
(As assessed by the football staff at The Herald)

Rd	Opponent	Result	In Melb's best	Votes
1	Richmond	L 40	NO	-
2	Essendon	L 20	1st	3
3	Carlton	L 15	2nd	-
4	Geelong	W 73	2nd	-
5	St Kilda	L 13	1st	3 (6)
6	Coll'wood	W 30	4th	-
7	Nth Melb	L 28	NO	-
8	Fitzroy	L 25	1st	2 (8)
9	Footscray	L 2	1st	3 (11)
10	Sth Melb	W 3	NO	-
11	Hawthorn	W 105	1st	3 (14)
12	Richmond	L 41	1st	3 (17)
13	Essendon	L 20	3rd	-
14	Carlton	W 16	2nd	2 (19)
15	Geelong	W 13	1st	3 (22)
16	St Kilda	L 39	NO	-
17	Coll'wood	L 19	NO	-
18	Hawthorn	W 62	2nd	1 (23)
TOTAL				23

In Melbourne's annual report, the committee lauded Smith for his brilliant season.

Norm Smith, vice-captain for the second year... is deserving of the highest praise for his services as deputy leader and a player. For many years regarded as a champion goalkicker, he is now generally accepted as (the) outstanding centreman in the League... (He) set the rest of the team an inspiring example with his brilliant but unselfish play, ever ready to assist and encourage the younger lads.'[12]

From Smith's perspective, it was perhaps also pleasing that while the competition was still a considerable way from being back to its former glory, at least there were more fans on hand than in any of the previous four seasons to witness his stunning rebirth. On average, almost 3000 more people attended each home-and-away match in 1944 than in the previous season; while average crowds had swelled by almost 5000 since 1942.

Another prestigious honour came Smith's way at the Melbourne Football Club's Annual General Meeting, which was held at Kelvin Hall in Collins Place. Smith was awarded life membership of the club after becoming just the 10th player to complete 10 years' service.[13] The club's annual report enthusiastically recorded his achievement – 'Hearty congratulations to you, Smith, and thanks also for the wonderful service you have given the club... A brilliant player and a splendid clubman!'[14]

Despite leading a busy lifestyle – which accommodated the running of the family business, a VFL career and home life with Marj – Smith still found time to help friends in need.

Smith's old mate Richie Emselle had retired at the end of 1943 after succumbing to knee problems. On June 17, 1944 – the same day that Smith played in a round seven loss at North Melbourne – Emselle's wife Belle gave birth to their first child, a son they named Ken. The Emselles and Smiths were present at most of the significant events in each other's lives and this was no different – Smith and Marj were among the close circle of family and friends to visit the mother and baby at the hospital in High Street, Preston. 'Norm had a car, my parents didn't,' Ken Emselle said, 'so when it was time for me to go home with my parents for the first time, Norm was there to pick us up from the hospital.'[15] The newest arrival in the Emselle family would come to know his chauffeur that night as Uncle Norm, and later, his premiership coach in 1964.

---

[12] Melbourne Football Club *Annual Report*, 1944.
[13] The nine other Melbourne players to have been awarded life membership after 10 or more years' service was Herb Fry (1889-1900), Harry Brereton (1907-15 & 1918), Charlie Lilley (1913-15 & 1919-25), Robert Corbett (1920-29), Dick Taylor (1922-31 & 1935), Gordon Ogden (1928-37), Percy Beames (1931-44), Jack Mueller (1934-44*) and Maurie Gibb (1934-43). *Denotes still playing at the time.
[14] Melbourne Football Club Annual Report, 1944.
[15] Ken Emselle. Interview with the author.

Norm Smith wasn't the only Smith brother to earn individual accolades in 1944. While stationed in Darwin that year, Len Smith played football for the RAAF in the Northern Territory Combined Services' Sports Carnival and won the Coates Medal after being adjudged the best-and-fairest player in the competition. Among his teammates were Collingwood's tough, goalkicking rover Alby Pannam, who captained the side, star Carlton ruckman Jack 'Chooka' Howell, Collingwood and Williamstown full-forward Ron Todd, Essendon defender Cec Ruddell, Footscray wingman Jim Thoms, and Geoff Spring who later played for Richmond. In a congratulatory letter from the RAAF's sports office, Len Smith was praised for his 'outstanding displays' which 'reached the highest standard', and were 'at all times consistent with the sportsmanship expected when the Services meet on the field of play'.

Len Smith's award was also a minor consolation for a much bigger prize. Due to RAAF service, he played just 30 VFL games between 1941 and 1945, and agonisingly missed out on a chance to play in Fitzroy's 1944 premiership side – the club's last flag. One day, though, Len would take the Maroons to within striking distance of a flag as a coach.

6

CAPTAIN

[1945-47]

The retirement of Percy Beames as Melbourne's captain-coach at the end of the 1944 season not only brought an end to an illustrious career – comprising 213 games, 323 goals, and 10 Victorian guernseys over 14 seasons[1] – but also cleared the path for the pairing of one of the most formidable leadership combinations in AFL/VFL history.

In 1945, Demons fans welcomed back several favourite sons from their now distant, golden past – former skipper Allan La Fontaine, Ron Baggott, Adrian Dullard, and last but not least, their messiah, Checker Hughes, for his second stint as coach of the club. One of Hughes' first decisions was to appoint a new captain, and he wisely chose his greatest team player, Norm Smith – a move which proved similarly popular. It was a well-deserved promotion for Smith, who described it as the realisation of 'one of my greatest football ambitions'.[2] It was also a seemingly inevitable one, Hughes later revealing: 'He was my greatest pupil'.[3]

Smith was 29, had played 152 games, kicked 430 goals, represented Victoria, and won two best and fairests. He was in his prime as a player, but more importantly, he had earned the unwavering respect and support of teammates, like Hugh McPherson, who said: 'If ever a man was ready to captain a football side, it was Norm Smith. Every player looked up to him as a player, for his great skills as a forward and a centreman, and for the selfless way he played the game. And when

---

[1] In 1996, Percy Beames became one of the 136 original inductees into the Australian Football Hall of Fame. He was also selected in a forward pocket, alongside Norm Smith, in Melbourne's 'Team of the Century'. A talented all-round sportsman, he also captained the Victorian cricket team, playing 18 first-class matches and making 1186 runs, including three centuries, at the exceptional average of 51.56 and taking seven wickets at just 22.42.
[2] *Melbourne Truth* series, 1962.
[3] *Trident Monthly*, Vol. 1, No. 1, April 1968. The publication commemorated Norm Smith's testimonial dinner, which was held at Melbourne Town Hall on December 20, 1967.

he spoke we all listened intently. But, of course, he had been a great on-field leader well before they made him captain'.[4]

Unfortunately, Smith's debut season as captain was a disappointing one. The Demons won their first two games, defeating eventual premier Carlton by 21 points in round one, but lost 12 of the last 18 games to finish ninth – five games out of the top four. Perhaps it was to be expected with the playing list undergoing continual reconstruction. Indeed, a third of the players on the Demons' 1945 list were 'straight from the paddocks',[5] and 10 of the club's 14 debutants were no older than 20 years of age. In the four seasons since the 1941 flag, the Demons had, on average, used 42 players a season, including 17 newcomers; compared with the previous six-year period (1936-41) of relative stability where they averaged just 34 players and seven debutants.

It had not taken long for Hughes, in his first season back with the Demons, to revert to old habits by swinging his new skipper Smith back into more familiar territory – the forward line – where he had been such a dominant force for the last four years of Hughes' original reign. Smith's response was reasonable in the circumstances. He kicked 33 goals in 17 matches – being a multiple goalkicker on 10 occasions – in a support role to Fanning, who won the League goalkicking award for the third successive season with a total of 67 goals. Although Smith was never driven by individual awards, he must have seen irony in the fact that Fanning had won league goalkicking awards with tallies of 62 and 67 goals while he himself had had kicked 80-plus on three occasions yet never led the league after the minor rounds.

Although Smith had not been as dominant on the field as he had been in the past, largely due to a lack of opportunities in the forward line, teenage teammate George Bickford, in his first year with the Demons, was in awe of his skipper's drop-kicking at goal:

> Norm was a very good drop-kick. He'd go straight back from the man on the mark, run in straight and kick straight through the ball, and in most cases the ball would start on line and not waver – it would literally go straight through the goals. There was none of this business of kicking around corners like they do in rugby. He was a beautiful, pure kick; almost perfect technically.[6]

---

[4] Hugh McPherson. Interview with the author.
[5] Melbourne Football Club *Annual Report*, 1945.
[6] George Bickford. Interview with the author.

The general consensus was that Smith simply continued to be a great role model and was the type of player who was ideally suited to captaincy. Melbourne's annual report praised Smith's selection as skipper and stated the he 'cooperated fully with the coach, and his determination and teamwork on the field were an inspiration to his teammates. He was ably assisted by Dr Don Cordner, vice-captain, who proved a worthy deputy'. Cordner recalled:

> The greatest influence a captain has is with his example, and Norm Smith certainly set a great example for us to follow. He wasn't interested in trying to be flashy or doing spectacular things, just whatever was best for the team at any given time. You'd really struggle to find fault with what he did on the field; his intentions were always honourable.[7]

Smith, who won yet another club award as the 'most unselfish player', expected his teammates to be just as 'honourable' in their efforts. While Smith's example was generally louder in actions than words, there were times when the opposite was true. George Bickford remembered Smith was 'always talking, encouraging and directing' and made his presence felt as 'a disciplinarian' in the heat of battle. Bickford recounted an incident at Fitzroy which left no doubt in his mind that Norm Smith could eventually make a successful transition to coaching:

> My opponent in the centre got the ball and started racing away, with me in pursuit about five yards behind him. I wasn't making any ground so I gave up the chase. I'd taken the practical point of view that I was never going to catch him. Norm ran right down the field from the forward line to abuse me for not chasing. In my defence, I told him: 'I was never going to catch him,' but that didn't satisfy Norm. He was quite right because I was in the wrong – my opponent could have slipped or dropped the ball. Norm was never afraid to let a player know if he thought they weren't doing the right thing, which was fair enough; he'd earned that right because he always seemed to do the right thing. He practised what he preached.[8]

One of Smith's worst pet hates was teammates who lacked the physical and mental strength to keep their feet in a contest; players who needlessly went to ground and let the side down. Teammate Stan Rule discovered this the hard way.

---

[7] Don Cordner. Interview with the author.
[8] George Bickford. Interview with the author.

If you ever got knocked down and didn't bounce back up straight away, Norm would scream at you: 'Get up or get off!' It was a command. If it came from a bloke who was a bit slow getting to his feet himself, you wouldn't take as much notice, but you did with Smithy. He called me 'Autumn Leaves' because if I flew for a mark or someone bumped me, I'd fall down. He'd say: 'Get up, Autumn Leaves – you're always on the bloody ground!'[9]

Smith also instructed opponents on how they should play. Collingwood prodigy Len Fitzgerald debuted for the Magpies in 1945 at the tender age of 15 and received some light-hearted advice from Smith early in his career. On another occasion, a young Hawthorn opponent made a mistake and Smith told him what he should do in the same situation next time. Some observers interpreted it as Smith arrogantly 'standing over' opposition players. But this description was proven wrong when the young Hawk let it be known that Smith had genuinely tried to help him. 'Norm got a real kick out of helping a player improve, especially a young player,' teammate Hugh McPherson said.[10]

Sometimes Smith's frustration with a teammate's performance compelled him to take the player aside for a chat. One such occasion had humorous consequences. Star ruckman Don Cordner was playing one of his worst games. At half-time, Smith – who later described Cordner as 'just about impossible to beat… he couldn't contemplate the possibility of being downed'[11] – approached his ruckman and said: 'Don, what's the matter with you? You haven't had a kick. You're a better player than that bloke, but you look as though you're frightened of him. What the hell's going on?'

Cordner – a recently graduated 23-year-old doctor who only ever regarded football as 'a pleasant Saturday afternoon's entertainment'[12] – *was* frightened:

> For the previous fortnight, I had been treating a footballer for his third bout of gonorrhoea, the venereal disease. Just before the opening bounce, I realised he was standing opposite me, ready to contest me in the ruck. I got out of his way – and I stayed out of his way. So when Norm demanded an explanation, I had a moral dilemma. In accordance with medical ethics, a doctor is bound to keep details of his patients confidential. But there is also a thing called personal pride, and that's what won out on this occasion. I took Norm into a corner and said: 'Look, Norm, this is the story…'

---

[9] Stan Rule. Interview with the author.
[10] Hugh McPherson. Interview with the author.
[11] **Pollard**, Jack (editor), *High Mark: The Complete Book on Australian Football*, Murray, 1964.
[12] Don Cordner. Interview with the author.

He was completely taken aback. He said: 'Jesus!' And from that point on he didn't get a kick either![13]

More angst followed. In the round 18 clash with North Melbourne, Smith was opposed to North tough man Ted Jarrard, who gave him a particularly hard time. Smith kicked two of Melbourne's eight goals in a 25-point loss, and also allowed frustration to overwhelm him on one of the rare occasions in his career. He later said: 'The only time I ever lost my cool on a football field was one day against North Melbourne. Jarrard was frustrating hell out of me, goading me, harassing me, belting me'. Smith had reached his limit of tolerance. In a wild-eyed departure from his normal air of calculation, he turned to Jarrard and, with fists clenched, roared: 'I'll fight you now.'[14] The result of the confrontation is not recorded.

Melbourne officials vented their frustration over the treatment of Smith by state selectors. Along with Fred Fanning, Smith was chosen to represent Victoria for the second time against South Australia at the Adelaide Oval. While Fanning was one of only two Vics to kick three goals – Richmond's Alby Pannam was the other – Smith spent most of the afternoon on the bench. Mercifully, he was given a belated, albeit brief, run in the last quarter, but by then the match had been decided – Victoria was thumped by 52 points. In Melbourne's annual report that year, club officials could not contain their disgust about the demeaning role assigned to their captain, tersely stating: 'The selection of Norm Smith as 19th man... was disappointing. That a player of the calibre and vast experience of Smith should have been taken interstate to "look over the fence" appears to be illogical and unfair to the player and our club'. For Smith, it was a sad final appearance – a virtual *non*-appearance – for the state.

Compounding the Demons' frustration was that, despite the fact they lacked the firepower of Fanning and Smith in attack, they came within a whisker of toppling eventual premier Carlton for the second time that season. The Demons went down to the Blues by a point at Punt Road, leaving most experts to logically conclude that while the Blues had been without ruck star Ron Savage, who was also on state duties, the Demons would have won if Fanning and Smith had been available.

In round 17, with the war all but over – and the Demons facing the more fancied Footscray at Punt Road – Checker Hughes delivered one of his most inspiring and emotional addresses of his illustrious coaching career. Fortunately *The Sporting Globe* was there to record it for posterity. Hughes told his players:

---

[13] Don Cordner. Interview with the author.
[14] Bill Stephen. Interview with the author.

> This will possibly be the last game of football you will play during the war period. During the war, many of you young players have been wearing the numbers of players who have made this club famous. Some of them made the supreme sacrifice. Those players were champions because they would never admit defeat. You are playing a team above you on the premiership list. You have the ability to win. Now get out there and win![15]

Melbourne turned a 19-point half-time deficit into a nine-point victory, with Fanning slotting four goals and the old firm of Norm Smith (two goals) and Ron Baggott applying the finishing touches in the final term. It was one of the last times Smith and Baggott would play together, with Baggott leaving at the end of the season to captain-coach VFA club Brunswick. In the meantime, however, World War II ended – on Tuesday August 14, 1945 – before they played their next match.

When the 1945 season ended, Smith continued to be a driving force for his teammates. He became a member of the organising committee for Melbourne's Footballers' Summer Social Club, which arranged regular functions and outings to keep the players together as a group and help them get to know each other better in the off-season. These events were crucial in bonding a club that for several years had been ravaged by high influxes, and exoduses, of players.

🏉🏉🏉🏉🏉🏉🏉🏉🏉

Len Smith's VFL career ended in 1945. As a 33-year-old that season, he made nine senior appearances for Fitzroy and kicked 20 goals. Although he did not break into the side until round three, Len immediately proved that even in the twilight of his career he was still worthy of a spot in the Maroons' senior side.

In his first three games of the season, all in losing sides against quality opposition, Len slotted 13 goals – four against Footscray (the eventual fifth side) in round three, three against Carlton (premier) in round four, and six against North Melbourne (fourth) in round five. His goal tally in this three-match period was five more than his next best teammate – Jack Symons, who kicked eight goals (3, 4 and 1) – to again provide a glimpse of what he might have produced at the top level if he had enjoyed just an ounce of luck with injury.

Len played his last VFL game in round 12 against Geelong on July 7 in round 12. A competitive contributor to the very end, he kicked three of Fitzroy's 17 goals in a 96-point win over Geelong at home. He had succumbed one last time to injury.

---

[15] *The Sporting Globe*, 1945.

It would not be the last Fitzroy would see of Len Smith. He would return to the club a little over two years' later to start what would be a superb coaching career.

In 1946, the VFL competition started its steady return to former glories as ex-servicemen returned to football. Among them was a large contingent of mature-age recruits aged in their early to mid-20s; competitive men hardened mentally and physically on the battlefields, where they had to put their bodies on the line for their mates, and watched on helplessly as some of them were cut down in their prime. The ranks of Melbourne's returning servicemen included five premiership players – Ted Cordner, Gerry Daly, Dick Hingston, Wally Lock, Shane McGrath and Alby Rodda.

The Demons also recruited 22-year-old former soldier Stan Rule, who was snapped up on the recommendation of tough defender Lock, who had served with him in New Guinea, where Rule kicked seven hard-earned goals on Lock in a Services match. Rule recounted a fascinating conversation he and his father had with Demon captain Norm Smith before the start of the 1946 season:

> My father asked Norm: 'Did you go to *la guerre*?'
>
> Norm turned to me and said: 'What's your old man talking about?'
>
> I said: 'Well, he's a First World War "digger" and he's talking in French. "*La guerre*" is French for "the war", and he's asking you: "Did you go?"'
>
> Norm said: 'No, I didn't.'
>
> Dad was a bit annoyed that Norm hadn't served his country. He said: 'What?! You didn't go to *la* bloody *guerre*?!'
>
> Norm was hurt by that, so he turned to me and said: 'Is your old man drunk or something?'
>
> I said: 'No, he's just curious; he just wants to know.'
>
> Then Norm spilled his guts. He said: 'The reason I didn't go was because I was in a protected industry. And it's a very sorry part of my life that I didn't go; like something's missing. I only wish that I did go with all the other fellas. I lost some mates there.'
>
> Dad then told Norm about how I'd gone to the war as a teenager. From that point on, we got on very well.[16]

---

[16] Stan Rule. Interview with the author.

Perhaps out of a sense of duty towards a young man who had put his life on the line for his country, and maybe even out of a sense of guilt, Smith took a shine to Rule, who was eight years his junior. It didn't take long for Smith to also learn that Rule – who slotted into Melbourne's senior side in round three and was to become a regular senior player – had endured a rough upbringing devoid of education and was living in hardship. Since returning from the war, Rule had been unable to find a job and was living in a dirt-floored hovel in Brighton (an south-eastern suburb of Melbourne) with no gas or electricity and just one water-tap out the back. 'My background and circumstances,' Rule conceded, 'caused me a quite a bit of embarrassment at Melbourne. There were a lot of educated fellas down there from much better backgrounds. But Norm Smith didn't give a damn where you came from: whether you were a rich man with everything, or a pauper with only the shirt on your back; if you were decent to him, he was decent to you.'

Something within Smith – and Rule believes it was a combination of the way he himself was initially treated at Melbourne, allied with his compulsion to help those who were less fortunate – prompted him to offer assistance to his new mate. After training every Tuesday and Thursday night at the Albert Ground, Smith insisted that he drive Rule home to Brighton before doubling back to his own house in the northern suburb of Preston. Their houses were in virtually opposite directions from the city but Smith kept up this ritual for four months. Eventually, Rule insisted: 'You're not doing this for me any more, Norm. It's too far out of your way.'

On those car rides, the pair would talk more about life than football. Conversation topics included Rule's ill mother. 'Norm was very sensitive about Mum's condition,' Rule said. 'He was also very interested in where I'd been and what I'd done in the war.' Rule soon formed the opinion that:

> It was probably for the best that Norm didn't go to the war. I told him once: "With your attitude, if you went to the war, you wouldn't have made it back – you'd be dead." He was a real man. He would've wanted to be the one leading the charge, the one to score first blood, which a lot of blokes tried to do and didn't live to tell the tale. He was too courageous and confrontational for his own good.[17]

It was a view shared by Ron Baggott, who said: 'There's no way known there'd be any tight situation that Smithy would have tried to avoid. If he went to the war, he'd have been right amongst it, in the thick of the action.'[18]

---

[17] Stan Rule. Interview with the author.
[18] Ron Baggott. Interview with the author.

Rule recalled that Smith once asked him: 'You went to the war; what's courage?'
Rule replied: 'When fear runs out, that's when courage starts.'
Smith thought hard about the remark and concluded: 'I reckon you're pretty right'.
Smith also tried to solve Rule's employment problems – to his own detriment. Rule has vivid recollections of Smith's generosity:

> I didn't have a trade but I was offered a job carting bricks on the condition that I get a truck. The coterie committee at Melbourne said they'd give me £300 as a deposit for a truck. When I went to collect the truck, the coterie committee reneged on the deal. They said: 'Checker Hughes said you'd be too tired to train if you're carrying bricks, so we're not going to give you the truck.' When Norm found out, he offered me £400 to get the truck. I was quite moved by that, but I said: 'Thank-you for the offer, Norm, but on principle I can't let you do that. It's not your obligation.' Some time later, his wife Marj told me: 'Stan, you remember the £400 Norm was going to give you?' I said: 'Yes I do; how could I forget?' She said: 'We didn't have it.' But that's the kind of man Norm was – he was prepared to give it to me anyway. He was no wealthy man, but he was the best man I've ever known. A man of honour who lived by his word.[19]

Smith's charitable nature also manifested itself in his relationship with his young apprentice, Russ Brown. Brown said Smith helped him buy his first motorbike, and build his first car:

> Jack Semoff, an old fella at Miller's ropeworks, had a little two-stroke motorbike and when I was 17 (in 1946), Norm took me to old Jack's place in Essendon (at 6 Woodvale Grove) – which Len later bought (in the 1950s). Norm checked out the motorbike to make sure it was in working order and then paid for it. He let me give him a little bit out of my pay each week to cover it. He didn't have to do that, so I really appreciated it.
>
> Later on, in 1950, Norm bought two Morris sedan chassis – one for him and one for me – which had come out here on a shipment. There was the chassis and the windscreen with no glass in it, and no car body. We built the bodies. My wife Thelma and I drove it around on our honeymoon, but without Norm we wouldn't have been able to do that. He was a hard man but generous and thoughtful.

---

[19] Stan Rule. Interview with the author.

Incidentally, when Thelma and I originally got engaged, Norm told me: 'If you want to buy her a better ring and you're a bit short, there's money here for you to borrow if you need it.' I asked Thelma if she wanted a better ring but she didn't, so I didn't take Norm up on that.[20]

Smith later helped the Browns in a manner that, Thelma Brown recalled, 'went way beyond anything anyone could possibly imagine from another person':

When we were building our house, we took out a second mortgage, which we really couldn't afford and we were getting deeper and deeper into trouble with it. Norm found out about our situation, had a look over things and put us onto his solicitor, (Melbourne Football Club committeeman) Charlie Loughrey, who got us out of that commitment. Norm also told him: 'I want you to watch these people all the way with this builder.' More than 50 years later, there's not even a crack in a wall – all thanks to Norm.[21]

YYYYYYYYY

Melbourne's annual report of 1945 wasn't far wrong in its optimistic forecast for the Demons for season 1946:

What club, irrespective of its performances during a season, does not aspire to the premiership of the following year? Melbourne? Well, it's a long step in a season from 9th position to 1st on the list, and although much work has been done and much good material introduced into the club wherewith to gain the honours, yet much remains still to do. Old Demons returning from the forces will add valuable experience to our side, but should not be expected to step straight into their brilliant stride of former years, and must be given time to settle down. Our young blood, several having given indications of reaching stardom in League football, will have to be taken along steadily. Confidently, however, we believe that 1946 will find Melbourne greatly improved.

In reality, 'greatly improved' was perhaps a little conservative. But if, after eight rounds of the 1946 season, someone predicted that Melbourne would make the finals, let alone the *Grand* Final, they would have been dismissed with contempt.

---

[20] Russell Brown. Interview with the author.
[21] Thelma Brown. Interview with the author.

The Demons began the season well, winning three of their first four matches, with the highlight being a six-point victory over reigning premier Carlton in round two. Their single loss came against rising power Essendon at Windy Hill in round three, when the Bombers kicked 10.5 to 2.1 in an opening-quarter blast to set up a 56-point win. Norm Smith, who had again become the Demons' centreman, said he was 'not worrying a great deal' about the crushing defeat; in fact, he viewed it as an aberration. 'When a side begins like the Dons did that day by kicking 10 goals in the first quarter – well, no team could do much about that.'[22]

Melbourne's slump really started, though, in round five against Footscray at Punt Road. The Demons bombarded the goalmouth in the first quarter to lead 6.8 (44) to 2.0 (12), but in the last three quarters were outscored 20.14 to just 6.5 and went down by 61 points. Footscray found an unlikely hero in Ron Grove, who, despite kicking just 57 goals in an 82-game career, became just the third Bulldog to bag 10 goals. Smith said: 'I'll never forget that game... I don't know if we were stunned by Grove's performance or what it was.'[23]

After further losses to bottom side Hawthorn – which kicked three late goals to come from behind and record their first win of the season – and similar battlers Fitzroy and North Melbourne, the Demons slumped to 3-5 and ninth position on the VFL ladder, their losses being by an average of 43 points. In rounds seven and eight – when Smith was sidelined with injury, and Fred Fanning also missed a match – Melbourne kicked a combined total of just 8.20 (68), including their worst total in 14 years, and the lowest by any side that season – 3.9 (27) – in a 29-point loss to North Melbourne at Arden Street.

Smith was nonplussed at his side's dramatic loss of form. 'I can't say why we lost those games,' he said. 'Certainly we had some good players out, but we should have done much better than we did. Some of our best players couldn't strike it, and nothing seemed to go right. It was certainly a bad trot. Of course there were the usual stories that we weren't a happy family at Melbourne, but nothing could have been further from the truth. Actually I have not seen such good feeling in the club for years.'[24] Smith felt that this high level of camaraderie among the Demons was hard-earned:

> Melbourne are at a disadvantage training at the Albert Ground. We have to undress in three small rooms, (so) new men don't get to know their teammates

---

[22] *The Herald*, July 1946.
[23] *The Herald*, July 1946.
[24] *The Herald*, July 1946.

as they would in one big clubroom, and it is harder to foster that necessary club spirit. And Melbourne need and have to work harder for this club spirit than other sides. We have no big local districts to draw on like Collingwood, Essendon and Footscray, and we recruit a large proportion of our chaps from the country and the outer suburbs beyond other clubs' residential areas. This means that many of the lads arriving at Melbourne are complete strangers. They have not played with or against each other in junior competitions, and naturally it takes them a while to settle down and get to know their teammates. But... the club spirit at Melbourne is the best for many years.[25]

Smith's return from injury, and to his old role at full-forward, coincided with the Melbourne's improvement, the skipper slotting five and six goals in respective wins over lowly St Kilda (39 points) and competitive Richmond (16 points). The Demons were on their way. While there was some talk about the merits of Smith displacing Fred Fanning – who had kicked 27 goals in the first seven rounds – Smith assured fans that he and the three-time league leading goalkicker were comfortable with the arrangement. 'Fred Fanning is very happy at centre half-forward,' Smith told Alf Brown, the chief football writer at *The Herald*. 'He is giving me plenty of opportunities at full-forward, and so far I have been fortunate enough to be fairly well on the target.'

Although Melbourne's chances of earning a finals berth appeared slim, Smith presented a positive outlook in the in-depth interview with Brown:

> Melbourne are seventh, but I think we still have a chance of making the final four. Footscray and Essendon look safe, so to get in we have to displace either Collingwood or Carlton, who are both eight points ahead of us. It's a big task but Melbourne are just about at their top and I think we will manage it.
>
> Anyway we'll soon know if we are going to make it or not. Our next six games are really tough – we meet Collingwood, Geelong at Geelong, Carlton, Essendon, South Melbourne and Footscray. To have a chance, we must win every one of those six games, and that's a big order for any side...
>
> The four leading sides are in a happy position – believe me, it's a great feeling to be eight points or more ahead of the opposition with half the home-and-home games gone. It means that you can afford to drop a game or two, but the teams chasing you can't lose any if they are going to remain in the race.

---

[25] *The Herald*, July 1946.

Look at it this way. In the next six weeks Melbourne must meet the four teams at present in the four. Even if we win the six games, and Collingwood and Carlton lose two each, we will still only be level with them on premiership points. But, just the same, I am confident we will do it. One good thing, we won't be in doubt for long – the next couple of games should decide our 1946 prospects.

Smith's forecast was to prove prophetic. The Demons won their next four matches, again accounting for Carlton – which Smith had earlier described as a side that 'did not impress me at all'[26] – this time by 17 points; before upsetting top side Essendon by five points at Punt Road after kicking just 1.13 in the second half, and 9.24 for the match, *and* surviving a late shot at goal by Bomber Jack Jones, who had the chance to tie the match.

A new Demon making an impact was follower/defender Stan Rule. During what he termed a 'promising start to an unpromising career', Rule 'played a blinder'. He admitted: 'I probably let it be known too loudly, and too often, that I thought I'd played pretty well. Smithy got that attitude out of me quick-smart.' Smith took Rule aside and said:

Now you listen to me, Stan, and you listen good. OK, you played well, very well in fact – you know it, I know it, and everyone knows it. But we all knew it before you started big-noting about it. Sure, gain confidence from it, and let it be a point of reference in your mind, but don't live on it. You can't achieve great things in the future if you live on past glories.

Aside from that, by telling blokes how good you think you are you're setting yourself up for a big fall, because everyone will expect you to do the same this week and the next and the next, and when you fail – and you will fail at some stage; everyone does – by Christ they'll give it to you.

A way to guard against big-headedness – and I strongly suggest it to you – is to take the attitude that: 'You're only as good as your next game'. If you live by that, and truly believe it, it will always keep you striving to be better. And your poor games will be better. Understand?

Rule reflected: 'I was disappointed to hear that at the time, but he was right on the money. I'd heard the saying: "You're only as good as your *last* game", but never "your *next* game". Great philosophy. Smithy spoke to me with all the wisdom of a bloke who'd been coaching for 20 years. It might as well have been Checker

---

[26] *The Herald*, July 1946.

telling me. You could imagine (Kevin) Sheedy saying that. That was probably the first time I seriously thought to myself: 'Smithy will be a great coach one day'. Not just a good one, a *great* one'.[27]

The Demons' mindset was they could not wait for the next game. They were in the midst of a famous winning spree, their only other loss in the minor rounds being against South Melbourne in at the Junction Oval in round 15 after they had led by four points at the last change. Despite that blemish, the Demons found ways to win when it appeared matches, and their finals hopes, were all but lost. Their victory over top-four side Footscray was the performance of a team with special fighting qualities. And with the side needing to win virtually every match to make the four, the Demons' sense of urgency was evident before the match, with the players pressuring their skipper, Norm Smith, to go against the orders of coach Checker Hughes, as Don Cordner revealed:

> It was blowing a gale this particular day. In the rooms before the game, Checker addressed us and then he said to Norm: 'Now, Norm, if you win the toss, kick with the wind.' I hated kicking with the wind first because you often waste the advantage because you're still settling down, and I especially hated the idea of doing it at Footscray because the wind usually picked up and blew a gale in the last quarter. But the risk with my theory was that if the wind changed you lost a quarter with the advantage of the breeze. But I was adamant that we shouldn't kick with the breeze first. I said to a couple of teammates: 'We've got to do something about this,' so when we got out onto the ground we surrounded Norm and said: 'We don't care what Checker said; if you win the toss, kick *against* the wind.' Norm said: 'You're right; I think that's a good idea.' As it turned out, he actually did win the toss and we kicked against the wind. I'm not sure how Checker handled the news, but all the players agreed with it.[28]

At three-quarter-time, the Demons trailed 8.8 (56) to 12.12 (84), but as Cordner anticipated, the wind became even stronger and Melbourne exactly doubled its score in the last quarter – kicking five goals in five minutes after the 15-minute mark – to win 16.16 (112) to 13.13 (91). The next week – in the first football match at the MCG since the 1941 Grand Final – Melbourne was nine points behind a determined Hawthorn at the last change but, inspired by Norm Smith's seven goals – he kicked three of his side's four first-quarter goals – the Demons celebrated

---

[27] Stan Rule. Interview with the author.
[28] Don Cordner. Interview with the author.

their return to the hallowed turf by piling on 7.7 to three behinds in the final term to win easily. In round 18, the Demons endured their third scare in as many weeks when they beat Fitzroy by four points after scoring just 3.7 after quarter-time, as another late shot from an opposition boot went astray.

Smith missed the last home-and-away round after experiencing stomach pain. A medical examination revealed that he needed an operation to remove his appendix. Suddenly, Smith's hopes of leading the Demons into their first finals series in five years were in serious jeopardy. Such a prospect was inconceivable for Smith. After discussing it with his doctor and weighing up the risks, he chose to delay the operation until the end of the finals campaign… unless, of course, the pain became too severe to bear.

In the Melbourne rooms at half-time of an earlier match, Smith was 'keeled over' and obviously in pain. Stan Rule asked him: 'Are you all right, Smithy? Did you cop it in the guts or the nuts?'

Smith was in no mood for jokes.

'No, no, I've just got a crook stomach,' Smith sighed through clenched teeth. 'If you want to clown around, I'll rip your nuts off!'

'Well, maybe you should sit out the second half,' Rule suggested.

Smith looked at him as though he was from another planet.

'Are you mad?' said Smith. 'I have to get back out there – I'm the bloody captain. And you'd do well to worry about yourself – you've hardly had a bloody kick!'

Rule took no offence. His only thought was: 'Well, Smithy with a crook guts would still play a lot better than most fully-fit blokes'.[29]

ŸŸŸŸŸŸŸŸŸ

Before the 1946 finals series began, Don Cordner became the first post-war Brownlow Medallist, and the first Melbourne winner since Ivor Warne-Smith won his second medal in 1928.[30] Cordner, a young veteran at just 24 years of age and with 86 games' experience, claimed he was fortunate to win the medal, as he believed that umpires must have mistakenly awarded him votes that were meant for his similarly talented eldest brother Ted. In a sign of the times – pre-glitz and glam Brownlow Medal Count times – Cordner found out about his victory in a phone call from the authorised informant, his old coach Percy Beames.

---

[29] Stan Rule. Interview with the author.
[30] No other Melbourne player won the Brownlow Medal until 1982 when Brian Wilson triumphed.

With an ounce of luck, Norm Smith could have been both a League leading goalkicker and a Brownlow Medallist. Now, though, he had two teammates – Fanning (goalkicking) and Cordner (Brownlow) – who each had one of these titles.

By virtue of other results falling their way, the Demons scraped into fourth position to set up a first semi-final clash with Footscray at the MCG. Smith passed himself fit for the clash and boldly told *The Sporting Globe*'s Hec de Lacy of the Demons' desire to not only win the first final but claim another flag. 'Melbourne were never fitter,' Smith said. 'I am confident, without being foolishly so, that we will win it. The players are anxious to take up football where we left it off on the Melbourne ground – with a premiership in 1941.'[31] Not long into the match, Smith might have wanted to retract this statement.

After the players and umpires formed a 'hollow square' in the centre of the ground and led the crowd of 61,277 in a mass rendition of *God Save The Queen*, Footscray kicked the first two goals with the breeze, while Melbourne kicked atrociously. Smith's first three shots at goal resulted in a snapped behind from the boundary, a rushed behind and a kick that slammed into the man on his mark. Even one of his normally precise passes failed to find its target. Finally, though, he slotted Melbourne's second goal with a drop-kick.

Melbourne produced a withering eight-goal to three burst in the second-quarter to lead by 24 points at half-time. Percy Beames observed in *The Age* that: 'Employing direct methods through Smith... Melbourne's many excursions forward were eventually fruitfully rewarded.' Hec de Lacy wrote that Smith was 'in everything', and was 'the inspiration' behind the Demon domination.

But just when most thought Melbourne would streak away, the Bulldogs dominated the third quarter to take a one-point lead by the last change. Just before the three-quarter-time siren, Smith marked and his long shot for goal sailed out of play where a policeman 'leapt to take a high mark, amidst a great round of applause.'[32] But Smith would not have been in any mood to laugh at this strange sight.

Footscray maintained its ascendancy for the first 20 minutes of the last quarter, by which time they had added 8.5 to Melbourne's 3.4 after half-time, to lead by seven points. Early in the last quarter, Smith made, according to Percy Beames, 'his only mistake' for the match when, 'forced to come well afield because of the non-cooperation of the wingmen and a weak half-forward division', he marked within scoring distance but played on and handballed to Fanning, who was unable to gather the ball, which was quickly whisked away.

---

[31] *The Sporting Globe*, Saturday September 7, 1946.
[32] *The Age*, Monday September 9, 1946.

CAPTAIN [1945-47]

Two minutes into the time-on period, and with just four minutes left, Melbourne trailed by seven points, and when Bulldogs captain-coach Arthur Olliver was paid a dubious mark deep in attack, the Demon dream appeared over. Olliver – who later admitted: 'I thought we had it in the bag'[33] – lined up for a set shot at goal from, depending on the source, somewhere between 10 and 25 yards out. In any case, everybody agreed that it was an easy shot, especially for a star who had been his side's best player that day and had already kicked three goals. But instead of covering himself in glory by kicking his fourth goal to put his side 13 points clear – and leading his club to its first finals win since it had joined the VFL in 1925 – Olliver let either exhaustion or the big occasion get to him, and he missed everything. 'He was so tired that he couldn't kick the ball,' Don Cordner, one of Olliver's ruck opponents, recalled. 'As he swung his leg back to kick, his other leg collapsed under him and the ball trickled out of bounds',[34] drawing 'audible groans of despair' from Bulldogs fans.[35]

From the throw-in, the Demons rushed the ball forward, towards the Punt Road end, and centreman Len Dockett sent one of his trademark left-foot passes to Norm Smith, who marked on the boundary line, on the 'wrong' side of the ground for a right-footer. Teammate Stan Rule, who was standing nearby, marvelled:

> Norm was 30 or 40 yards out and on the tightest possible angle. As he went back to take his kick, we were saying: 'God, we hope you bloody kick this.' It was a pressure situation, everything was riding on that kick, but Norm looked like a bloke who didn't have a care in the world. He said: 'Don't let it worry ya'.' It was like he was just having a kick in the park. I thought: *'Don't let it worry ya'*?! We're flat out trying to win this bloody final, and we're almost gone – we've got every right to bloody worry!' But Norm just relaxed, took a few seconds to steady himself and then calmly kicked it straight through. He had nerves of steel.[36]

Smith's goal, his third, revived the Demons. 'As if someone had given the signal,' Percy Beames told readers of *The Age*, 'the whole side sprang into action, and, playing with uncanny precision, added three further goals – to Jim Mitchell (also his third), Ernie O'Rourke (third) and Dockett – 'in almost unbelievable fashion, to leave supporters of Footscray dumbfounded, and those of Melbourne beside themselves with excitement.' In those frantic last four minutes, the Demons had

---

[33] *The Sun*, Monday September 9, 1946.
[34] Don Cordner. Interview with the author.
[35] Percy Beames, *The Age*, Monday September 9, 1946.
[36] Stan Rule. Interview with the author.

kicked 4.1 – more than they had managed in the previous 50 minutes of play – while keeping the Bulldogs scoreless, to win by 18 points. It was the second time in four weeks that Melbourne had run over the Bulldogs with a barnstorming finish, and the fourth time Footscray had failed to progress beyond the first semi-final.

Melbourne's final burst was described as 'paralysing',[37] and 'breath-taking',[38] while Percy Beames hailed it one of the most dramatic finishes seen in final series'.[39] Both Norm Smith and Jack Mueller (four goals) received special praise from Hec de Lacy in *The Sporting Globe*: 'The best Melbourne man was either Mueller or Norman Smith – both in attack were resourceful, and never suppressed. It was this pair that won the game.'

Arthur Olliver graciously, and manfully, accepted the criticism for the defeat, lamenting: 'If anyone has to take blame for our defeat, it is me.'[40] Smith, meanwhile, admitted the Demons had been lucky. 'It was a typical semi-final game, played in the best spirit. I would like to congratulate Footscray on its fine showing. Considering injuries to star players and replacements it had to make for the game, I think Footscray did a good job and was unlucky. (But) any side with men like Don Cordner, Fanning, Mitchell, Dullard, Mueller and Rule to change in ruck must take beating. Throwing Fanning into the ruck in the last five minutes gave us wonderful drive. Our finishing efforts recently have been wonderful and show Melbourne does not lack grit or determination.'[41]

In the other semi-final the next week, Essendon and Collingwood played out a thrilling draw, which meant they had to replay the match the following week. Melbourne suddenly had another weekend off. The situation must have frustrated Smith, as it meant the operation to remove his appendix would have to be delayed by another week, barring – and at the risk of – further complications.

In the second semi-final rematch, Essendon defeated Collingwood by 19 points to go straight through to the Grand Final, while the Magpies faced a clash with Melbourne in the preliminary final. After training on the Thursday night before the match, a confident Norm Smith said: 'No team, more than Melbourne, has a healthier respect for the ability and resourcefulness of Collingwood in final(s) games. Setbacks... fail to disturb its poise or confidence. Nevertheless, I have no hesitation in saying Melbourne will play off for the premiership. We possess a greater array of ability, have all the physical advantages, are fit and well, and

---

[37] Gerald Brosnan. *The Sun*, Monday September 9, 1946.
[38] Kevin Hogan. *The Sun*, Monday September 9, 1946.
[39] *The Age*, Monday September 9, 1946.
[40] *The Sun*, Monday September 9, 1946.
[41] *The Sun*, Monday September 9, 1946.

will be meeting a team which obviously is feeling the effects of a gruelling season'. Meanwhile, Collingwood captain Phonse Kyne was similarly keen on the Magpies' chances: 'I have not lost confidence in our ability to make history by playing four (finals) games... to win this year's premiership'.

Smith's old sparring partner, Richmond captain-coach Jack Dyer, wrote in his preliminary final preview in *The Sun* that Smith was 'not quite so elusive as he used to be', but that 'no player in the game knows better than Smith how to lure away the full back – and sometimes other defenders too – and give Mueller space to manoeuvre for marks.' However, Percy Beames reminded readers of *The Age* that Smith, 'with his clever, unrivalled manoeuvring and use of the body in taking standing marks, accurate drop-kicking and dexterous handpassing, although opposed to a capable, experienced defender in (Jack) Green, is likely to prove more than a nuisance value.' Both eminent men proved correct.

Norm Smith led the Demons onto the MCG having donned black armbands as a mark of respect for their late chairman, Joe Blair, who had died on the Monday before the game after a short illness. Blair, whose initials, JCB, formed his nickname, was a vice-president of the VFL, and in his 18th season as Melbourne's chairman. He would be remembered as 'a forceful and skilful administrator'[42] who 'spared neither time nor energy in furthering the advancement of an organization to which he was so devoted'.[43]

Smith won the toss and elected to kick to the Punt Road end and in the opening minutes smartly gathered the ball and kicked the first goal of the match. But the Magpies quickly took control, steaming to a 29-point lead early in second quarter, and still holding sway by 23 points at three-quarter-time. But as they had done several times during the season, the Demons produced a stunning last quarter assault, piling on 7.4 to 1.4 to win by 13 points. The match-winner was Jack Mueller, who, despite a thigh injury, was 'unbeatable in the air'[44] and kicked eight goals. Mueller – who shared best-afield honours with Collingwood rover Lou Richards – had been, as was often the case, well fed by Norm Smith, whose precise passing had created several other scoring opportunities for teammates but only behinds resulted.

After the match, Smith paid tribute to the Magpies. 'I admire Collingwood as I admire no other team,' he said. 'They have amazing spirit and take adversity in their stride. Undaunted by the loss of star players in (Bill) Twomey, (Des) Fothergill

---

[42] Melbourne Football Club Annual Report, 1946.
[43] Taylor, E.C.H., *100 Years of Football: The Story of the Melbourne FC 1858-1958*, Melbourne Football Club, 1957.
[44] Former Collingwood star Bruce Andrew, in *The Sporting Globe*.

and (Norm) Campbell, they gave their all against the superior strength of their opponents and took their defeat like true sportsmen. The Magpies have given the football public some grand, exciting football and must have won many supporters and sympathisers by their courageous football in the final series.'[45]

Collingwood skipper Phonse Kyne praised Norm Smith for playing his decoy role to perfection:

> Without detracting from Mueller's sterling display... I must pay tribute to the captain's part played by Norm Smith, who repeatedly and deliberately went upfield, taking opponents with him so that Mueller had only one opponent to beat and not fight for his marks with the packs. It was a grand show by both players.[46]

When Checker Hughes was asked before the start of the 1946 season how his Demons would fare, he remarked cryptically that his players were: 'A nice rosy pink at the moment – not quite red – bright pink.' There was no denying now that the Demons were red-hot. They needed to be, as they would encounter a devastating Essendon side led by the triple Brownlow Medallist captain-coach Dick Reynolds.

The Demons' leaders, Smith and Hughes, both expressed their optimism about the prospect of securing another premiership. Three days before he would skipper the Demons in a Grand Final for the first time, Smith told *The Sporting Globe*: 'We should beat Essendon because we play a similar type of game and I believe we are individually stronger in most departments. I would rather meet the Dons than Collingwood, whose pace and play-on game always worries us. Saturday's game has brought us right to our top and with so many men playing well we feel very confident. Our attack is the most effective of the four final(s) teams and I think it will make greater use of its opportunities than the Essendon forwards.' Smith followed it up in the Friday edition of *The Sun* with: 'I feel confident we can pull it off... As all our big men are showing wonderful form at training, I feel sure they will strike it on Saturday. All the same, we expect a hard fight.' Hughes echoed Smith's sentiments in the same publication, saying: 'The side is fit, well and confident. We hope to take up where we left off in 1941 – as premiers'. Melbourne had every right to feel confident – they had defeated every side in the competition at least once.

While Collingwood captain Phonse Kyne tipped the Demons to topple the Bombers – 'not because I think they are a better team, but because they have

---

[45] *The Sporting Globe*, September 28, 1946.
[46] *The Sporting Globe*, September 28, 1946.

a greater variety of talent among their big men'[47] – he and Jack Dyer, in their columns in *The Sporting Globe* and *The Sun* respectively, warned of the threat posed by Essendon big man Gordon 'Whoppa' Lane. Kyne believed Lane 'may be too much of a problem for Ted Cordner',[48] whom Dyer described as 'slightly out of touch'[49]. Dyer ominously added that Lane – a big-occasion player who kicked six goals in Essendon's 1942 premiership – had matured and was playing 'robustly as well as brilliantly', and 'could easily take hold of the game at centre half-forward'.[50]

In perfect conditions, the Demons got away to a flying start, thanks largely to the influence of Fred Fanning in the ruck. At the first bounce, Fanning palmed the ball down to Len Dockett, who kicked long into the forward zone where Adrian Dullard swooped to register the first goal – all of which took just six seconds. In the opening minutes, Melbourne slammed on the first four goals to nothing to lead by 26 points.

In a first term shootout – primarily between Melbourne and Essendon, and secondarily between forward counterparts Mueller and Lane – Melbourne kicked 8.3 (51) to Essendon's 7.2 (44). Mueller had four goals, Lane three. Both sides had eclipsed the previous highest quarter-time score in a Grand Final of 6.6 (42), set by Melbourne against Essendon in the 1941 Grand Final – a match contested by the same two coaches and 15 of the same players.[51] Logically, the Demons and Bombers also achieved the highest first-term aggregate in a Grand Final – 15.5 (95) – and it remains a record. The next best is 13.8 (86) in the 1972 Grand Final between Carlton (8.4) and Richmond (5.4). Indeed, it is a better aggregate than most *half*-time scores in Grand Finals. The Demons' 8.3 was also a record, and even now stands just a point behind the efforts of Carlton in 1972, and Hawthorn in 1989, both of which had kicked 8.4 by the first break.

A more scrappy second quarter meant the Demons held a three-point lead at half-time – 10.4 (64) to Essendon's 9.7 (61), with Mueller's contribution now five goals and Lane's four. Few could have predicted what happened next. As Don Cordner recalled: 'We were in front and playing well but then the wheels well and truly fell off.'[52]

---

[47] *The Sporting Globe*, September 28, 1946.
[48] *The Sporting Globe*, September 28, 1946.
[49] *The Sun*, Saturday September 5, 1946.
[50] *The Sun*, Saturday September 5, 1946.
[51] Those who played in both the 1941 and 1946 Grand Finals were: Essendon – Dick Reynolds, Gordon Abbott, Wally Buttsworth, Jack Cassin, Harold Lambert, Gordon Lane and Cec Ruddell; Melbourne – Norm Smith, Don Cordner, Ted Cordner, Adrian Dullard, Wally Lock, Shane McGrath, Colin McLean and Jack Mueller.
[52] Don Cordner. Interview with the author.

A central figure in Melbourne's downfall was "Whoppa" Lane, who had kicked his fourth goal early in the second quarter, prompting Checker Hughes to move Ted Cordner off the Bomber star and give Dullard the unenviable task of shutting him down. While Lane had destroyed Ted Cordner early in proceedings, teammates like Len Dockett and Stan Rule simply could not believe Hughes' logic in replacing him with Dullard, a handy utility who, Dockett recalled, 'could take a big mark but had a bad habit of trying to out-mark his opponent from behind instead of going the punch, even when he was on a big fella like Lane'.[53] The result was that Lane kicked another two goals as the Bombers produced the most devastating quarter in Grand Final history. After starting the third term with five straight behinds to take a two-point lead, Essendon finished the quarter with 19 scoring shots to two for a return of 11.8 to 1.1, to storm to an unassailable 64-point lead by the final change. The 11 goals had come in a 20-minute frenzy.

Norm Smith did not lead the Demons as well as he would have liked in what would be both his biggest yet most disappointing afternoon as captain of the Demons. After resuming after half-time with his right knee bandaged, he forlornly hobbled off the ground at three-quarter-time – goalless and, unusually in a final, after having little impact on proceedings. By then, many Melbourne fans had left the stadium in despair after – as Alf Brown observed in *The Herald* – watching Essendon 'kicking goals with ease against a side that had stopped to a walk and were playing with little heart'. It was perhaps a harsh judgement. Without detracting from the Bomber blitzkrieg, the Demons' previous two finals had been last-man-standing affairs and must have taken a toll.

Although the Demons managed to reduce the margin by a point by the final bell, to make it 63 points, they had suffered the worst defeat in Grand Final history, overwhelming their own 57-point win over Collingwood in the 1926 Grand Final. It was also Melbourne's first Grand Final loss after winning at their first five attempts. Essendon's final score of 22.18 (150) also toppled the Demons' 21.22 (148) against Collingwood in 1939.

While Lane kicked seven goals and was the undisputed best player on the ground – Smith described it as 'one of the greatest football performances I have ever seen'[54] – at the other end of the ground, Mueller kicked six goals to complete a sensational finals series in which he kicked 18 goals in three matches and was the Demons' best player in each match.

---

[53] Len Dockett. Interview with the author.
[54] *Melbourne Truth* series, 1962.

Smith, who kicked 33.33 in 13 games after resuming at full-forward, won another 'best clubman' award. When the agony of the Grand Final thrashing, and his own poor showing, had subsided, he adopted a fatalistic attitude, explaining that while the Demons had boasted a strong line-up, they had encountered a Bomber side that was in its 'golden era'.[55] Like most other fair-minded judges, Smith realised the Demons still had much to be proud of. Just when their season appeared over, they embarked on a winning spree that was impeded just twice in four months. They had thrilled their fans with two remarkable, come-from-behind wins in the finals, and had led a first-rate opponent for the entire first half in a Grand Final. They had much to anticipate.

YYYYYYYYY

Two months after the 1946 Grand Final, when Melbourne Football Club was still adjusting to life without their dearly departed chairman Joe Blair, the Demons were rocked by another tragedy.

On December 8, the club's most experienced committeeman, Fred Ince, died from injuries sustained in a car accident. Ince had served on Melbourne's committee for 21 years, and the selection committee for 18 years, the majority of which was spent as the chairman of selectors.

Norm Smith had participated in numerous selection committee meetings chaired by Ince over the previous five seasons. He was another untimely loss for the Demons, who suddenly had to find new men to fill the roles of club chairman and chairman of selectors. These positions were eventually taken by Bill Flintoft (42 games for Melbourne from 1909-12, and one game with St Kilda in 1913) and former star centreman Dick Taylor (164 games from 1922-31 and 1935) respectively.

YYYYYYYY

After a couple of minor, early-season hiccups, Melbourne attacked the 1947 season like a side determined to take the next step.

The Demons lost two of their first three games to the vastly improved Carlton (by 13 points) and Fitzroy (nine points) – their first win being against Geelong in round two after starting the match with 13 straight behinds – but they had been without Jack Mueller against the Blues, and minus Fred Fanning against the Maroons. In their absence, Norm Smith performed admirably, kicking 12 goals –

---

[55] *Melbourne Truth* series, 1962.

5, 3 and 4 – before suffering a hamstring injury, which kept him sidelined for the next five weeks.

In Smith's absence, Fanning lifted himself like rarely before, kicking 47 of Melbourne's 70 goals (a remarkable 67 percent of the total output) in the next six matches – 9, 9, 6, 7, 10 and 6 – to pilot the Demons to six consecutive wins and equal top position with Carlton. But then, as Smith later described, 'the skids were under us... despite the brilliance of Fred Fanning'[56]. The selection committee, boosted by the expertise of La Fontaine and Ivor Warne-Smith, had its share of headaches, with injuries to the likes of George Bickford, Len Dockett, Stan Rule, Jim Mitchell and Norm Smith – who sat out another three games – taking their toll. The Demons immediately followed their six straight wins with six straight losses, and after 15 rounds had plummeted to ninth.

The Demons finished the season with four consecutive victories, but it was a case of too-little-too-late. They finished sixth, missing the finals by just one game. After suffering six losses by 13 points or less, and with a healthy percentage of 117.1 – eight percent clear of fourth-placed Richmond – it was a bitter pill to swallow.

Fred Fanning provided the highlight of the season – and one of the biggest highlights in the history of the game. After kicking 10.4 of Melbourne's 24.11 in a 75-point win at Footscray in round 18, Fanning produced what Smith described as 'the greatest piece of full-forward play I have seen'.[57] What Smith failed to mention was that he himself played a vital role in Fanning's legendary, almost mythical performance.

Going into the last-round match against bottom side St Kilda at the Junction Oval, Fanning had kicked 79 goals (in 15 games) – 10 behind Smith's club record. Smith was desperate to play, after experiencing the most injury-interrupted season of his career, having played just eight of 18 matches, and missing the previous two games with more hamstring trouble. While he was accepting of his injury problems – 'I suppose I was due for injury,' he explained, '(because) it had pretty well by-passed me until then'[58] – Smith was not about to allow them to sideline him for Fanning's tilt at his record. Although only half-fit, he convinced the selection committee selection to pick him on a half-forward flank.

As the Demons ran onto the field, Fanning boldly announced to Don Cordner: 'I'm gonna kick 18 goals today'.[59]

---

[56] *Melbourne Truth* series, 1962.
[57] *Melbourne Truth* series, 1962.
[58] *Melbourne Truth* series, 1962.
[59] Dr Don Cordner. Interview with the author.

CAPTAIN [1945-47]

Understandably, the Melbourne vice-captain dismissed the prediction as more than a little fanciful. But it was apparent very early in the match that Fanning was set for a busy afternoon. After the big spearhead had slotted four goals in the first term, getting the extra seven goals he required to break Smith's record seemed a strong possibility, especially as he had kicked 10 of Melbourne's 15 goals against the Saints in round eight.

With the result of the match never in doubt, Smith, like every other Demon, made a concerted effort to get the ball to Fanning at every opportunity. 'Our men passed to Fred on occasions when they could quite easily have kicked goals themselves,' Don Cordner said. 'If you were running into an open goal, you'd almost turn around to look for Fred'.[60]

Young teammate Noel McMahen, who regards Norm Smith as the best team player he has ever seen, said his skipper's cameo performance that day perfectly reflected his selflessness:

> Smithy sent Fanning three or four magnificent passes where he didn't even have to break stride. The moment Fanning passed Smithy's record, Smithy hobbled off the ground. He was unfit; he really shouldn't have played, but he worked his gut out to help Fanning to the record and his job was done. Smithy's unselfishness that day was typical of him.[61]

According to Smith, Fanning 'popped them through from all angles',[62] kicking seven goals in the second quarter, three in the third, and four in the last, to amass 18.1 – the first 13 straight, then a poster, followed by another five without a miss – from 20 kicks. Eerily, Fanning's pre-match remark to Don Cordner had proved remarkably prophetic. His effort not only surpassed the Demons' previous club record of 13 by Harry Davie in 1925, but also eclipsed Gordon Coventry's League record of 17.4 for Collingwood in 1930. And the honours did not end there – Fanning won his third league goalkicking award, ending the season with 97.38 (39 percent of Melbourne's goals), which remains the best season tally for a Melbourne player. It was a pity that only 6000 people were at the Junction Oval to witness what remains the greatest goalkicking effort in a VFL/AFL match.[63]

---

[60] Dr Don Cordner. Interview with the author.
[61] Noel McMahen. Interview with the author.
[62] *Melbourne Truth* series, 1962.
[63] The WAFL record belongs to South Fremantle superstar Bernie Naylor, who kicked 23 goals against Subiaco at Fremantle Oval in 1953, while the SANFL record is 23, jointly held by Anthony 'Bos' Daly (for Norwood against Adelaide in 1893) and Ken Farmer (for North Adelaide against West Torrens in 1940).

In the 93-point win over the Saints – who were captain-coached by Allan Hird, the grandfather of Essendon superstar James Hird – Melbourne kicked 27.9 (171). Besides Fanning, only four other Demons kicked goals: Frank O'Connor 4, Frank Scanlan 3, and Jack Mueller and Adrian Dullard one apiece. Norm Smith was goalless. But amid the euphoria of the history-making performance, not everyone was happy with Fanning, as Len Dockett revealed:

> "Spud" Dullard had a go at Fanning after the game. He said: 'You're a bloody greedy bugger. We passed (the ball) to you every chance we got, but after you'd already kicked 15 I'm all alone in the goalsquare and you didn't even think of passing the bloody thing to me!'
> Fanning wasn't a good team man. Not like Norm was, for example. But very few were.[64]

There was some resentment towards Fanning. While his teammates recognised his matchwinning abilities, they felt he was a fair-weather superstar, exceptional on an easy day but liable to go missing when the pressure was on: like when the Demons played fellow finals aspirant Richmond in a must-win round 15 clash at the MCG. Fanning's teammates would have loved him to have contributed even five goals that day; instead, he kicked three – to give him just five goals in his previous three outings – and Melbourne lost by nine points, and their finals' hopes virtually vanished.

Even Smith – who had worked with Fanning at Miller's ropeworks, employed him part-time in his pram-parts business, and from all reports got along well with him socially – was frustrated with several issues relating to Fanning. They were, namely, the one-out forward set-up required for Fanning to thrive, his lack of consistency, and, worst of all, his individualistic and occasionally petulant attitude.

Smith felt that while Fanning was 'a great forward',[65] Checker Hughes had foolishly 'put all his eggs in one basket' by allowing him to become a 'one-man show' in attack, thus placing an unhealthy reliance on the performance of one player.[66] Under this system, if the opposition stopped Fanning they were almost assured of winning. Smith had always been in favour of a more flexible, multi-pronged forward structure with several viable avenues to goal, as the Demons had

---

[64] Len Dockett. Interview with the author.
[65] *Melbourne Truth* series, 1962.
[66] Clyde Laidlaw – a Melbourne player from 1954-62 – repeating what Norm Smith had told him. Interview with the author.

proudly boasted during their hat-trick of premierships. That way, if one or two forwards were blanketed, another one or two could generally be relied upon to fill the void.

And, according to Smith, Fanning had his share of 'bad days', citing a humorous incident one afternoon at Fitzroy's Brunswick Street Oval as an example. 'Once he was scratching for a kick and a dog ran on to the ground,' Smith said. 'Fred picked it up and was dumping it over the fence when a Fitzroy supporter yelled, "Leave the dog on and take yourself off!"'[67]

The criticism of Fanning didn't end there. If there was one thing Norm Smith despised above all else it was selfishness in a team environment – a failing he was disappointed to discover in Fanning. Smith said privately: 'If we lost the game but Fred kicked seven or eight goals, he would be laughing and all cheery; but if we won and he only kicked one or two, he'd be down in the dumps.'[68] Smith also felt that when things didn't go Fanning's way he would carry on like a 'big baby', a 'sook'.[69]

At the end of 1947, Fanning shocked the football world when he applied for a clearance to coach Hamilton in the Western Border League. Hamilton had offered Fanning £20 a game – a huge increase on the £3 he earned each week in the VFL under the Coulter Law. Fanning had accepted the Hamilton job after going into business with his father-in-law in the town.

Surprisingly, not everyone thought Fanning would be a great loss. Len Dockett felt that while Fanning could be sensational on his day, the Demons would never win a premiership while he almost monopolised the forward zone:

> Most of us thought the club should let Fanning have his wish and give him the clearance. We had Smithy and Jack Mueller anyway, and Smithy was a team player; Fanning wasn't. But one night at training (early in 1948), Checker Hughes told us: 'Leave that bloody decision to us! Stay right out of it! We'll decide what's best for this club, and if that means we refuse to clear Fred Fanning, then you'll all just have to bloody well accept it!'[70]

Despite the anti-Fanning sentiments of at least some of his players, Hughes was desperate to retain the gargantuan forward. According to Kevin Hogan in *The Sun*,

---

[67] *Melbourne Truth series*, 1962.
[68] Keith Carroll – a Melbourne player from 1952-58 – repeated what Norm Smith had told him. Interview with the author.
[69] John Beckwith, who played for Melbourne from 1951-60 and captained the club from 1957-59. Interview with the author.
[70] Len Dockett. Interview with the author.

Hughes believed the Demons had the potential to 'steal' the 1948 premiership; a belief which prompted him to 'expend great, but unsuccessful, efforts' to persuade Fanning to play at least one more season with the Demons.[71] But, Dockett said, 'it was a great relief to the players when common sense prevailed and eventually the club agreed to clear Fanning'.[72]

In his footballing prime at the age of just 25 – and after amassing 28.5 in his previous two matches – Fred Fanning turned his back on the VFL, never to return. But his exploits in his last game for the Demons ensured he would never be forgotten.

☘☘☘☘☘☘☘☘☘

On Monday, September 22, 1947 – just five days before Carlton pipped Essendon by a point in the 1947 Grand Final – Norm and Marj Smith became parents. Marj, then 28, gave birth to their first child, a son they named Peter Victor Smith.

Despite arriving five weeks early, Peter was a big baby, particularly for the times. He hit the scales at 8lb. 7oz. (3.83kg). It had been a particularly difficult pregnancy for Marj, who, at some stage of her term contracted blood poisoning and endured severe kidney problems. She became considerably ill and also had to cope with such swelling that her rings had to be cut from her fingers. Although Peter was the clichéd happy, healthy, bouncing baby, doctors advised Norm and Marj against trying to have another baby. They reluctantly, sadly, but probably wisely, accepted medical opinion and resigned themselves to the fact that Peter would grow up an only child. Whenever the subject was raised in a social atmosphere, the couple would mask their disappointment by joking: 'We tried it once and didn't like it!'[73]

The same year Peter arrived, the Smiths relocated. After six years in Raglan Street, Preston, they moved into a maisonettte in Shedden Street, Pascoe Vale – a suburb they would call home for the rest of their lives.

---

[71] Kevin Hogan, *The Sun*, Monday October 11, 1948.
[72] Len Dockett. Interview with the author. Incidentally, the previous coach of Hamilton, former Melbourne teammate, Jack O'Keefe (the man who blanketed Jack Dyer in the 1940 Grand Final) had taken the club to the 1947 flag and had apparently been told he could coach again if he desired. The controversy caused a split in the club – literally. At a special club meeting, Fanning won a vote of members and O'Keefe and his supporters stormed out and soon formed the Hamilton Imperial club. (Source: Fred Fanning, *The Sun*, 1956.)
[73] Margaret Clay, the widow of Fitzroy player Bert Clay, and the best friend of Mary Smith. Interview with the author.

CAPTAIN [1945-47]

ŸŸŸŸŸŸŸŸŸ

One Autumn afternoon before the start of the 1948 season, Melbourne Football Club held a picnic for players, officials and their families at Park Orchards. The Demons' annual report later described it as 'a happy affair', adding that 'the sporting events' had been 'a pleasure to watch'.[74]

The event that took Norm Smith's eye was the goalkicking contest. One of the competitors was Ron Barassi junior – the 12-year-old son of his late mate.

In the seven years since his father had passed away, young Barassi and his mother Elza had remained in contact with the Demons, and the Smiths. In fact, young Ronny – as the son of a premiership player, and a popular one at that – had been given the rare privilege of being able to wander around the changerooms on match-days. Barassi admitted he probably took the situation for granted, but that he didn't know any different either. 'It was obviously a thrill for me but it wasn't such a big thing; not as big as it would have been for a kid who'd just come into the club for the first time,' Barassi said. 'I was very lucky, but it just felt natural, and that probably meant I wasn't overawed when I started league football myself later on.'[75]

From the age of about six, Barassi had lived with his paternal grandfather, Carlo Guiseppe Barassi, and his Aunt May on the family farm at Guildford. His mother, who ran the canteen at Miller's ropeworks, had sent him there with his best interests at heart after he had become too difficult to handle for another aunt – the wife of Elza's brother Arthur Ray. 'It became a bit much for my aunty in her small house in Footscray, and I suspect I was also causing trouble with my cousins,' Barassi admitted.[76] Elza Barassi would visit her son every six or eight weeks.

Barassi was now attending Castlemaine Technical School and was, he conceded, 'a rough-'n-tumble type of kid; a bit accident-prone'.[77] But he had also started to develop his football skills to a point where he could kick with real purpose – a fact to which all who witnessed the goalkicking competition at Park Orchards would testify.

It was a light-hearted event – even Smith said: 'I don't know if we were all

---

[74] Melbourne Football Club Annual Report, 1948.
[75] Ron Barassi. Interview with the author.
[76] Ron Barassi. Interview with the author.
[77] Collins, Ben, *The Champions: Conversations with Great Players and Coaches of Australian Football*, GSP, 2006.

flat out or not'.[78] But like any contest – serious or not – between red-blooded, competitive males, pride was on the line.

While the Demons senior players lined up from a considerable distance, Barassi was allowed to shoot from about 25 or 30 metres – the limit of his own kicking power. As his big-name opponents dropped out of the competition after muffing their attempts, young Barassi continued to hold his nerve. Eventually it came down to two – Barassi and Albie Rodda. That year Rodda, 27, was to play the best football of his career, representing Victoria, winning the Demons' best-and-fairest and playing a starring role in the finals. A raw 12-year-old didn't appear much of a match. 'Alby was one of my favourites,' Barassi said, 'even though he had kept my father out of the side on a few occasions during their careers because he was a rover/goalsneak too.'[79] But the youngster was not overawed.

While Smith recalled that Barassi 'dead-heated' with Rodda,[80] Barassi believed he finished second. Regardless, it was an attention-grabbing effort. Smith was pleasantly surprised. 'Ronny impressed me with his determination to win the prize,' Smith later said. 'There was something in the boy's make-up that made me want to do something more for him.'[81]

Smith did do something more for him. When Barassi came down to Melbourne during his school holidays or on weekends away from the farm, Norm and Marj would often keep him company and offer to assist his mother in any way they could. It was during these times that Barassi discovered that Smith was 'rather quiet and retiring away from football'.[82]

---

[78] *Melbourne Truth* series, 1962.
[79] Ron Barassi. Interview with the author.
[80] *Melbourne Truth* series, 1962.
[81] *The Sun* series, 1967.
[82] Ron Barassi's speech at the Australian Football Hall of Fame dinner, July 19, 2007.

7

THE SMITH-MUELLER LEGEND

[1948]

As the 1948 season neared, Norm Smith looked forward to captaining Melbourne for a fourth season – an achievement that would have equalled the captaincy records of turn-of-the-century skipper Bill McClelland[1] and club legends Bert Chadwick and Ivor Warne-Smith, and been bettered by only Allan La Fontaine, who led the Demons for six seasons (1936-41). Not that individual achievements meant much to Smith. But with his body beginning to fail him in a football sense, he was limbering up for what would most likely be his final season as a player in the VFL. As such, it would be a season to savour – even more so than he normally, and naturally, did anyway – before pursuing another football dream: a senior coaching career.

It was not until about a fortnight before the start of the season that Smith gained the first inkling that his captaincy was under threat. The Demons were training at the MCG when club chairman Bill Flintoft walked onto the field and approached Smith's deputy, Don Cordner, who was shocked by what followed:

> Flintoft, an objectionable fellow, asked me: 'Would you accept the captaincy?' Now, I was very loyal to Norm Smith, so I said: 'I will not stand against Norm Smith for the captaincy. If Norm Smith is not captain, then yes I'm available. But I will not compete with him.' I'd been put in a delicate situation, so I decided that the

---

[1] McClelland was Melbourne's captain from 1901 to 1904, club chairman for 14 years and the VFL president from 1926 to 1955. The W.C. McClelland Trophy, introduced in 1951, was awarded to the club which earned the most premiership points in the thirds (later the under-19s), reserves and senior grades combined. With the disbanding of the reserves and under-19s in 1991, the trophy has since been awarded to the AFL's minor premier.

best policy was to be upfront and entirely honest about it. Immediately after that conversation with Flintoft, I went straight over to Norm and said: 'Norm, this is what's happened. I have been asked by the chairman to accept the captaincy. I have told him I am your loyal supporter, but that if for any reason you are not captain, then I'm available.' Norm was very gentle about it. He said: 'Fair enough.'[2]

The decision came down to a simple question of Smith's fitness – his ability to lead the Demons in the vast majority of matches. Despite pledging his full support of Smith, Cordner felt that his skipper was starting to become 'a little bit wobbly, and at times was almost getting (around) on one leg'[3] – an observation he kept to himself, but a view that was shared by Demon officials.

Smith was also acutely aware of the injury woes that had restricted his availability and output the previous year, when he broke down three times in 1947 and missed a total of 10 matches. But he was adamant he should remain captain, and that he could still provide the leadership and inspiration that the role required. Smith later said he was told: 'We want you to resign from the captaincy'.

'Resign from the captaincy?' Smith said. 'I want it. Sack me by all means, but don't ask me to give up something I want.'[4]

Despite Smith being vehemently opposed to losing the captaincy, the club saw fit to install Don Cordner as his successor. The club gained almost immediate vindication for its decision, and Smith also admitted the move had been made in the best interests of the Demons. 'The club proved right,' Smith conceded. 'Injuries were catching up with me.'[5] Smith played just three of the first 11 matches, and only 13 of 23 for the season. Cordner, meanwhile, hadn't been sidelined since round 12, 1942, and by the end of his first season as captain had played 117 consecutive matches. Cordner was so impressive in the leadership role that he also skippered Victoria against South Australia at the MCG. And there would be an even greater captaincy honour later in the year.

Smith maintained his dignity throughout the committee's deliberations on his tenure as captain. Once the decision was made, he showed no outward signs of bitterness or resentment, not even when he was overlooked for the vice-captaincy – that honour went to another of Smith's close mates, tough full-back Shane McGrath. Smith's reaction to his demotion attracted even more respect from Cordner, who recalled: 'Norm gave me his full and utter support, just as I had given him. The fact

---

[2] Don Cordner. Interview with the author.
[3] Don Cordner. Interview with the author.
[4] *The Tony Charlton Football Show*, Channel Nine, Sunday July 25, 1965.
[5] *Melbourne Truth* series, 1962.

that I'd taken over the captaincy from him didn't affect our relationship – he certainly didn't take it out on me – and we remained firm friends. That was a sign of the man that he could put his personal hurt aside for the sake of the team and the club.'[6]

‌‌‌‌‌‌‌‌‌ ŸŸŸŸŸŸŸŸŸ

Melbourne's forward line took on a vastly different and, it must be said, less potent look in 1948. At the start of the season, they were without three of their trump cards from the previous season. Fred Fanning had left, Jack Mueller was now coaching the seconds, and Norm Smith was injured. More was suddenly asked of centre half-forward Lance Arnold and utility Adrian Dullard, while the inclusion of young Bob McKenzie injected some much-needed zip and an element of surprise to the attack. McKenzie, who had spent the previous season in the Demons' under-19s side, had an immediate impact. In round one against the star-studded Essendon side, the precocious 19-year-old produced one of the best debut quarters in VFL/AFL history, kicking four of Melbourne's five goals in the first term. But while he finished with five for the game from a half-forward flank, the Demons were overpowered by 19 points.

Despite their gallant loss to the Bombers, the Demons struggled without key targets in attack. They notched their first win against hapless bottom side St Kilda but then suffered a 38-point belting at the hands of Fitzroy after scraping together just six goals. Melbourne rebounded with a five-goal to two last-quarter burst to pip Richmond by five points at Punt Road, a venue many of the Demons regarded as a second home after playing there for the majority of the war years.

Norm Smith's long-awaited return was short-lived. He came back in round five, at the start of a three-week block of comfortable wins over North Melbourne (by 45 points), South Melbourne (46 points) and Carlton (51 points). Smith's contributions were one, three and two goals respectively. The round seven clash with the Blues at the MCG marked his 200th game. He became just the third Demon to reach the milestone – after Percy Beames and Jack Mueller (who had reached it in 1947). While his big day was capped with a win, which lifted the Demons to third, Smith would remember it for all the wrong reasons.

In the first half, with the Demons trailing, Smith chased the ball along the boundary line and just as he gained possession the field umpire, Jeffrey Jones, deemed it out of bounds. Smith turned to umpire Jones and snarled: 'You didn't

---

[6] Don Cordner. Interview with the author.

bloody well see that!'[7] Jones took exception to Smith's reaction and reported him on a charge of using obscene language to him. At the tribunal hearing on the Tuesday night, Smith protested the charge and pleaded his innocence, but was stunned when what he described as 'untrue evidence' was sworn against him.[8] He was even more stunned by the verdict – he was suspended for four matches!

'Norm was furious,' said George Bickford. 'We couldn't believe it either.'[9] Neither could most people. Melbourne secretary Alex Gray protested that four matches was 'a colossal sentence for a man who has played 200 games and has such a fine record'.[10] A dumbfounded Alf Brown commented in *The Herald*:

> Why Norman Smith was not given the benefit of the doubt by the League Tribunal last night and what caused its two members to impose such a severe term of disqualification on him are questions that are puzzling football followers today... It was Smith's word against Jones's. Smith, a League veteran playing his 200th game, had never been disqualified. While everyone agrees that the authority of an umpire must be strongly upheld, this would surely have been met by a reprimand from the tribunal. The sentence was much stiffer than provided for in a court of law. Section 24 of the Police Offences Act imposes a fine of not more than £10 on a person found guilty of using obscene language. Smith last night was 'fined' £22. This sum is made up of £12 for playing (£3 a match) and club (£4) and League (£6) provident fund payments.[11]

It was to be Smith's first and only suspension. He never forgot nor forgave umpire Jones. Some, including Alf Brown, believe the injustice forever distorted Smith's opinion of umpires; that it poisoned him for life and he became an 'umpire-hater'.[12] At the least, he eyed the men in white as a necessary evil of the game.

During Smith's month of enforced absence, the Demons fell to top four sides Collingwood (at Victoria Park) and Footscray (at the Western Oval) – both by just seven points. The Demons had lost their place in the four, but regained their standing with wins over lowly Hawthorn and Geelong.

On his return from suspension, Smith kicked four of Melbourne's nine goals in a 26-point loss to league powerhouse Essendon, which had just completed the

---

[7] Related by George Bickford in an interview with the author.
[8] Alf Brown, *The Herald*, 1958.
[9] George Bickford. Interview with the author.
[10] *The Herald*, Wednesday June 2, 1948.
[11] *The Herald*, Wednesday June 2, 1948.
[12] *The Herald*, 1958.

fourth win of a 12-game streak that would stretch into the finals. The Demons rebounded hard, belting St Kilda by 105 points – a win that came at a cost. After Smith had kicked three goals, another hamstring strain sidelined him for the next two matches. The Demons struggled without him, suffering a 62-point loss to Richmond after totalling just 6.8 (44).

In a welcome return to the Melbourne line-up, Smith kicked seven goals (4 and 3) in wins over the battling North Melbourne (by 32 points) and South Melbourne (49 points). The Demons then faced a huge round 18 clash with Carlton. They had to win to keep alive their hopes of securing second spot and the double-chance. Melbourne trailed all day and went into the last quarter eight points down. But then Smith ignited a season-defining Demon onslaught when he kicked his fourth goal, as Dockett recalled:

> We really needed to lift and Norm seemed to take it upon himself to do it. He took this beautiful high mark near the centre of the ground, and went back and kicked a drop-kick that went a mile – straight through for a magnificent goal. That stirred up Bobby McKenzie.[13]

For three quarters, McKenzie had been well held by dashing Blues defender Jim Clark, but he exploded in the last quarter, slamming on the Demons' next five goals, including three in time-on – some of which came courtesy of Norm Smith – to pilot them to a truly inspirational nine-point win.

In the final round, with McKenzie bagging another six goals, and Smith two, the Demons claimed their biggest scalp – Collingwood, by 30 points at the MCG – and the coveted double-chance was theirs. Twice that afternoon, McKenzie passed to a leading Norm Smith and received a handball back and goaled. The McKenzie-Smith combination received its due praise. In a three-match purple patch, McKenzie had kicked 17 goals (4,7,6) and Smith nine (3,4,2). A brilliant opportunist, McKenzie had often been the beneficiary of Smith's clever play, as George Bickford recalled:

> Norm combined well with Bob McKenzie across the half-forward line. Norm would lead out and quick as a flash handball to Bobby, who would run on and have a shot at goal. In the main, Bobby would feed off Norm, but the feeding went both ways. Bobby would put these beautiful, low torpedo passes out in front of Norm and he would mark them in his hands without any trouble – which was quite a difficult thing to do. When Norm took the mark, he would often give off the handball to his

---

[13] Len Dockett. Interview with the author.

left, to Bobby, who'd followed up his kick, and he would kick these torpedoes for goal. It was quite a sight, and it showed off the great skills of both players.[14]

Even in later years, Smith would marvel at McKenzie's quirky penchant for running towards the boundary and taking a final step in-board to steady and straighten up before he had a shot at goal.[15] Smith had a fatherly affection for McKenzie that extended into the Demons' social scene. Teammate Stan Rule observed an incident that exemplified this:

> Young Bobby turned up to the ground for the after-match dance and he had a few of his mates with him. The man on the gate told him: 'You can come in, but they can't.'
> Bobby said: 'If they can't come in, I'm not coming in'.
> Norm saw the commotion and went over and said: 'What's the trouble?'
> Bobby said: 'This bloke won't let my mates in.'
> Norm wouldn't have any of that. He said to the man on the gate: 'Open that bloody gate up; they're coming in!'
> Done! Norm was a man of action and he looked out for people, especially young blokes or players who'd just started at the club.[16]

Melbourne finished second, three-and-a-half games behind Essendon, and was logically at long odds to beat the Bombers in the second semi-final. Checker Hughes was concerned about his players suffering an inferiority complex about Essendon, and so devoted a training night to improving the mental approach of his players, aiming to boost their confidence by humanising their seemingly invincible opponent. Hughes took the team to the Public Schools' Club for a talk, which made a marked impression on Noel McMahen. 'Checker hadn't been speaking long when I realised what he was doing,' McMahen said. 'He was pairing us off with the Essendon players and giving us the confidence to beat them individually, so that we might beat them collectively. Most importantly, he was gearing us up to give Essendon a tough time. For instance, he might describe a particular Essendon player as being "six feet two", runs like a greyhound, strong as an ox, drop-kicks it a country mile, but I think he has a heart the size of a pea. You'll look after him won't you Walter (Wally Lock)?" It was very clever from a psychological perspective

---

[14] George Bickford. Interview with the author.
[15] John Beckwith. Interview with the author.
[16] Stan Rule. Interview with the author.

because by showing their individual weaknesses, we suddenly started to believe that we might actually be capable of beating them. It didn't have an immediate impact on the way we played, but I'm certain it did a few weeks later.'[17]

Hughes also recognised the need to bolster the forward line, to give greater support to Smith and McKenzie. Norm Smith was still widely regarded as a very good player but being the sole linchpin in attack had never really been his forte. And now he had a torn thigh muscle to contend with. And while McKenzie had been on a spree of late, he was a flanker, an opportunist, not a powerful key target who would cause sleepless nights for the Bomber defence. And after the heroics of his stunning debut against the Bombers in round one, McKenzie had kicked just one goal against them in round 12. The Demons needed a new dimension – something, *anything* – to rattle Essendon.

Hughes later gave an insight into his thought processes on the matter, revealing: 'When I saw McKenzie playing so well, I knew we could win (the premiership), but not through McKenzie. He was a marked man. He had shown his wares.'[18]

After much thought, Hughes hatched a plan to bring back veteran Jack Mueller and get the old firm back together. It was a huge gamble, but one that Hughes felt he had to make. The problem was that Mueller, 33, had been the playing coach of the seconds for the vast majority of the season, was not anywhere near as mobile as he had been even 12 months before, and was physically almost finished as a League footballer. Hughes had actually brought Mueller back for two senior games in rounds 13 and 14, and the old superstar had responded well, kicking six goals and two goals respectively. But, like Smith, the old champ was battling a torn thigh muscle. Amazingly, and it was as much a sign of the Demons' desperation as a testimony to the mental strength to play with injury of both Smith and Mueller, the Demons were considering playing two key forwards – both veterans and seeming liabilities – who were literally on their last (footballing) legs.

Captain Don Cordner elaborated on a fateful selection meeting prior to the clash with the Bombers:

> Checker told us that he wanted Jack Mueller in the side. It was a very good plan, to have Mueller and Smith, the two major focal points, working together up forward. But I didn't think it was a wise idea to bring Jack back for the second semi-final. We had a very long meeting that night discussing the pros and cons of such a move. I said: 'But Mueller's only got one game left in him, perhaps two

---

[17] Noel McMahen. Interview with the author.
[18] *The Sporting Globe*, Wednesday October 13, 1948.

if we're really lucky. If he plays in the second semi-final and we lose, to win the premiership Jack has to play three.' We argued. Checker said: 'Well, we'll make him 19th man.' I said: 'No, we should wait until the preliminary final. We'll throw everything we've got at Essendon this week, Checker, but we'll most likely get beaten and that's probably the wrong attitude to take, but if we beat them this week they'll do us in the Grand Final.' Essendon had beaten us twice already that season and I knew that we could only beat them once; we couldn't beat them twice. So it would have been foolish to win the second semi-final, but you just couldn't go into a match to lose it. Checker eventually saw my point of view and agreed to keep Jack in cotton wool for the preliminary final. It was the only time I ever prevailed on Checker.[19]

Melbourne did lose. Badly. Essendon was five goals clear at half-time and, although the Demons fought hard in the second half, they never threatened the Bombers. But as a minor consolation to Checker Hughes, particularly after the thrust of his mid-week address, the Demons dished up a bruising and physically taxing game. The Bombers looked forward to the luxury of a week off as they waited for Melbourne and first-semi final winner Collingwood to fight for the right to play off against them in the Grand Final, and there is little doubt they hoped the less physical Magpies would be their opponent.

While Dullard and Eddie Craddock kicked three goals apiece in the loss to Essendon, chief forwards Norm Smith and Bob McKenzie were restricted to just one each, and Smith found the going tough as the sole focus in attack, heightening the urgency for Mueller's return. Even Smith admitted: 'We were struggling up forward... We were desperate for a full-forward.'[20]

As was discussed behind closed doors the previous week, the entire six-man selection committee – chaired by 1926 premiership captain-coach Bert Chadwick – was unanimous that Mueller be recalled to the senior side for the preliminary final. The old Smith-Mueller duo, which had been so successful as recently as 1946, was reunited. The news 'was actually welcomed in the Collingwood camp' by 'Magpie strategists (who) reckoned that the veterans had lost so much of their former speed and skill that they were more likely to be Melbourne liabilities than matchwinners'.[21] But the move proved a masterstroke, and the Magpies had 'failed to profit' from the 'lesson' Mueller had given them in the preliminary final two years earlier.

---

[19] Don Cordner. Interview with the author.
[20] *Melbourne Truth series*, 1962.
[21] Kevin Hogan, *The Sun*, Monday, September 27, 1948.

Although Collingwood started the preliminary final with three quick goals and led by eight points at the first change – by which stage Mueller had kicked 0.3 – the game took on a completely different complexion after quarter-time. With Mueller bagging seven goals in the second and third quarters combined, followed by an eighth in the last, and Norm Smith contributing 6.3, Melbourne piled on 21.10 to 9.9 in the last three quarters to win by 65 points. The aggregate of 267 points – 25.16 (166) to 15.11 (101) – remains a preliminary final record. The Demons' total was also a record for a preliminary final, surpassing Carlton's 23.19 (157) in 1932.[22] Smith was pleasantly surprised that Mueller had not lost much of his spring and marking ability. 'He'd take off straight up, like a rocket, with both legs together, and a perfect stretch,' Smith said.[23] Collingwood's feisty and usually talkative rover Lou Richards could only say: 'Mueller and Smith mauled us.'[24]

The Demons' star centreman George Bickford, a penetrating kick, provided an insight into the 1948 version of the decoy system:

> Checker Hughes encouraged me to kick long drop-kicks to the goalsquare – 'like a hot knife through butter'. That was the style of play that suited Norm and Mueller. Norm would lead out, sometimes deliberately away from the ball, to give maximum room for Mueller to work around the goalsquare. Norm's movement usually took him 50 or so metres away from goal, which created the space for our centreline and half-forwards to give Mueller open slather on where he wanted the ball.[25]

Dockett, who played alongside Bickford on the wing, said that while Mueller was the chief target, the Demons occasionally directed the ball to Smith. 'But if there was a choice between kicking to Smith's lead or going long to Mueller,' Dockett said, 'Checker would go stone-mad if we didn't kick to Mueller.' Dockett believed the ploy was successful mainly because Smith 'never thought about himself. It was all about the team. You wished you had 10 Norm Smiths in your side.'[26]

The Demon duo seemed to share a rare telepathy. Smith later demystified the hysteria created by their 14-goal preliminary final. 'The critics had us figured as a team with a remarkable set of signals,' Smith said. 'Jack and I had no signals, but we understood each other perfectly.' Indeed, there was very little that was

---

[22] The current record belongs to Essendon, who tallied 28.6 (174) against Collingwood in the 1984 preliminary final.
[23] Pollard, Jack (editor), *High Mark: The Complete Book on Australian Football*, Murray, 1964.
[24] Richards, Lou with Ian McDonald, *Boots And All!*, Stanley Paul, 1963.
[25] George Bickford. Interview with the author.
[26] Len Dockett. Interview with the author.

mysterious or subtle about Mueller, whom umpire Harry Beitzel described as 'the most frightening and loudest talker on the field' he ever came across.

Smith later revealed the true extent of Checker Hughes' gamble:

> I do not think that many people know the risks that ... Checker Hughes had to take in playing Jack Mueller and myself in the 1948 finals. We both had torn thighs, which were likely to go on us at a second's notice. After each match we could hardly stand. For the final practices, we begged Checker to just let us trot round the ground. He did.[27]

Richmond antagonist Jack Dyer later noted that 'the Smith-Mueller combination was a strange coupling'[28] and its success had been a 'football mystery' because 'they were complete opposites. Smith was a colossal team man and Mueller an individualist with a supercilious sneer'.[29] Dyer also made the observation that 'probably the combination clicked because Smith teamed with Mueller, rather than Mueller with Smith. Smith knew every move the giant forward would make and he moulded his game to suit his more spectacular comrade'.[30]

Despite their contrasting on-field styles, the pair appeared to have much in common off the field. Much like the Smith-Baggott alliance, the Smith-Mueller combination was built on a solid friendship, and a mutual respect that went back to 1934 when they both started with the Demons. Their strong relationship survived some merciless ribbing. Shortly after his debut season, Mueller – whom Smith occasionally referred to as 'The Big Hun' – caught his right hand in a machine at work and severed two middle fingers above the knuckles and also damaged his little finger. While he returned with a protective glove and his superb marking remained seemingly unhindered, years later, when the subject of the war came up in conversation, Smith would joke that Mueller had cut his fingers off on purpose – so he didn't have to join the fighting![31]

During the war years, Mueller had also copped more than his share of insults from over the fence. At a time when the Nazis were the most reviled ogres imaginable in the minds of those living in Allied countries, hatred was directed at anything and everything German. Even the dog breed, German Shepherd, was given to a more

---

[27] *The Sporting Globe*, early 1952.
[28] Dyer, Jack and Brian Hansen, *Jack Dyer's The Greatest: The Most Sensational Players of the Century*, Brian Hansen Nominees, 1996.
[29] Dyer, Jack with Brian Hansen, *Captain Blood*, Stanley Paul, 1965.
[30] Dyer, Jack and Brian Hansen, *Jack Dyer's The Greatest: The Most Sensational Players of the Century*, Brian Hansen Nominees, 1996.
[31] Sam Allica, Melbourne runner in the 1960s. Interview with the author.

politically-sensitive name – Alsatian. So a footballer of German descent playing football in a country that had sent a whole generation of young men to fight the aforementioned Germans would naturally be targeted. But, Smith marvelled, 'the more abuse Mueller got, the harder he went into the play'.[32]

Mueller's on-field persona differed markedly to Smith's cool calculation. Mueller often fuelled the abuse. Len Dockett said: 'Mueller would take a mark on the half-forward flank and the opposition supporters would be hanging over the fence and yelling: "You'll miss this, ya' German bastard!" Mueller would turn and leer at them and then put it through from about 60 yards out. The opposition supporters loved to hate him, and he didn't seem to mind it either. He half-smiled and half-sneered at them, and that made them hate him even more. Norm wasn't like that at all – he'd just go about his business very quietly, almost embarrassed to take the limelight or any accolades.'[33]

As usual, Mueller was a target for Essendon supporters in the 1948 Grand Final. After accounting for the Demons in each of their three meetings that season – and winning by an average of 27 points – the Bombers were primed to make amends for squandering a golden premiership opportunity the previous season. At three-quarter-time in the 1947 Grand Final, Essendon had fired 11 more scoring shots than Carlton but led by just 11 points, and eventually lost by one point. The Bombers had redemption on their minds in 1948, and all had gone to plan… so far.

A crowd of 85,658 jam-packed the MCG to such an extent that the Health Department, worried about the potential for injuries in the crush of people, ordered the entry gates closed just before the start of the game. If those who missed out knew in advance the kind of match that would be played that day, they would have made sure they were there early.

When the two skippers, Don Cordner and Dick Reynolds, shook hands before the toss of the coin, Cordner – well aware his side had been beaten by the Bombers in each of their three meetings that season – told his rival: 'Well, Dick, this is our last shot at you.' Reynolds' reply was: 'Unless it's a draw, Don.'[34] This was to be the 50th VFL Grand Final and there had never been a draw.

Norm Smith sensed that 'Essendon was still cocky'.[35] But by half-time any cockiness on the Bombers' part had disappeared. The Bombers had dominated, and had fired eight more scoring shots than the Demons, yet still trailed by two

---

[32] *Pollard*, Jack (editor), *High Mark: The Complete Book on Australian Football*, Murray, 1964.
[33] Len Dockett. Interview with the author.
[34] Don Cordner. Interview with the author.
[35] *Melbourne Truth* series, 1962.

points. Their scoreline was unforgivably inaccurate – 2.15 (27) to Melbourne's 4.5 (29). Smith had slotted the Demons' second goal after receiving a free kick when Bomber backman Percy Bushby fended him off with a push to the face.

The Sun's chief football writer, Kevin Hogan, made the following observation about the respective forward lines:

> Too often when an Essendon man secured the ball in shooting range he was hemmed in by teammates who clustered inexcusably in front of goals. Melbourne's forward zone, in which traffic was shrewdly directed by Norman Smith, was a striking contrast in (its) freedom from congestion. Smith worked about 80 yards out, leaving the front-of-goal area open for Jack Mueller, who again played splendidly. McClure halved Mueller's effectiveness by outmarking him cleanly, but Bushby's negative tactics of punching from behind succeeded only when the ball was kicked high and straight to Mueller. Bushby was badly stranded several times when Smith, a genius in forward play, sent cleverly controlled kicks wide or short to give Mueller the short run he needs before rising for high marks.[36]

The Bombers, their pride stung by their embarrassing incompetence in front of goal, produced a big third quarter to take a 13-point lead – they had literally kicked 13 more points than Melbourne. Smith realised how lucky the Demons were to be still in the contest. 'If Essendon had kicked straight it would have been all over,' he said. Noel McMahen attributes Essendon's horrific inaccuracy to the speech Checker Hughes gave the Demons before the second semi-final. 'They were kicking the ball before they had it – they were waiting to get thumped,' McMahen asserted. 'Checker Hughes was responsible for that. His brain was at its brilliant best in that finals' series.'[37]

By time-on in the last quarter, the Demons had reduced the margin by just a point – the scores were Essendon 7.27 (69) to Melbourne's 8.9 (57) – before a remarkable Demon fightback took the game into previously uncharted territory. The man who sparked the revival was Norm Smith, as Don Cordner recalled:

> Norm took a mark on the left half-forward flank about 35 yards out and he drop-kicked a goal – right through the middle. *Drop*-kicked it. Mind you, he was a very accurate drop-kick, but thinking back, with the state of the game as it was, and it being a Grand Final of all things, it appeared a gutsy decision to use

---

[36] *The Sun*, Monday October 4, 1948.
[37] Noel McMahen. Interview with the author.

that type of kick. Norm kicked only one goal in that game but it was one that really mattered.[38]

Moments later, the Demons rushed the ball forward from the centre bounce and "Spud" Dullard marked at half-forward, seemingly outside scoring range. 'Spud didn't look for anyone; he just launched into this torpedo-punt – he couldn't have struck it any better in his dreams – and it sailed through for a goal,' Cordner marvelled. 'Spud wasn't all that bright, and to his dying day I don't think he realised what he actually did. He'd levelled the scores. We didn't know how much time there was left, but we knew that the next score wins.'[39]

Melbourne again won the ball and this time Norm Smith – who had been one of the best-afield, gifting Mueller at least three of his six goals – marked 50-odd metres out. Instead of wasting valuable time by going back for his kick, and risking not covering the distance, Smith played on immediately and blazed away at goal, his kick drifting across the face of goal and out of bounds just a few metres from the behind post.

Cordner has such a vivid memory of the frantic final moments that, at 85 years of age, and almost 60 years after the event, he relived the experience as though it was happening before his very eyes:

> The crowd noise is unbelievable. There can only be seconds left. I'm beside myself with excitement that: 'We could actually *pinch* this!' I'm about 50 yards away from where the throw-in is going to take place, and the boundary umpire is still making his way to the ball. You're never tired in a situation like that; you get new legs. As I'm rushing over there, I make up my mind that: 'I'll try to punch the ball through for a behind. No, I won't just try – *I can do this!*' I envision it happening: 'I'll jump on that bloke's back and go bang with my fist and we'll be premiers.'
>
> But Norm Smith is standing there thinking he has to contest the throw-in, and he's got other ideas. I can almost read Norm's mind – he wants to grab it out of the ruck and kick a goal. But it wasn't necessary – we just had to score. I'm screaming: 'Leave it Norm! Leave it Norm!' because I've got the run at it and I can hit this thing through for a point. But Norm gets in front of me. I can't blame him though; he can't hear me because the crowd is going absolutely bananas. I can hardly even hear myself. Norm gets his hands to the ball and I hit it at exactly the same moment and the ball spills to the ground and comes within a few feet of the goal line.

---

[38] Don Cordner. Interview with the author.
[39] Don Cordner. Interview with the author.

Norm makes another attempt at the ball on the ground but slips and (Essendon full-back) Cec Ruddell grabs it and kicks it, and then the bell rings.

From being a screaming match, there is suddenly dead silence. It was like (Don) Bradman making a first-ball duck there, which I saw years earlier. We had played in the first drawn Grand Final in VFL history.[40] And the inescapable fact was that after Essendon had thrown the game away, Norm and I had cost us the win.[41]

Just as inescapable was the fact that the Demons had squandered three vital scoring chances in the last minute of play, and Norm Smith had been the common denominator in each instance. Smith noted later that he had the *same* idea as Cordner when they tangled at the boundary throw-in.[42]

Smith, like most of his teammates, was simultaneously disappointed, elated and confused, and he summed up the atmosphere on the field after the final siren when he said: 'We didn't know who to congratulate.'[43] Cordner's immediate thought was: 'We've blown our chance. Essendon should have thrashed us by 10 goals. They won't let us get that close in the replay.'[44]

Although Smith had been brilliant – *The Sporting Globe*'s Hec de Lacy hailed him as 'the greatest player in the game... He was thwarted but never defeated, and he rallied his side magnificently at vital points'[45] – he couldn't wait for the replay... it was an opportunity to *redeem himself*. Checker Hughes later observed: 'It was grand to see the determination of Smithy after the drawn game. He had the bad luck in those last few minutes to miss the chance to clinch the premiership. He made up his mind that there'd be no slip-up (the next week).'[46]

The odd Demon was actually happy with the result. Smith said later: 'Some wag said: "Good show, chaps. Now we can come back for another tenner next week".'[47] The 'wag' might have been Noel McMahen, who recalled: 'Three of us were sharing a big bath after the game, and I said: "Isn't this beautiful – we're in another Grand Final!" The older pre-war blokes like Wally Lock and

---

[40] There has been just one other drawn Grand Final in the VFL/AFL, and that was in 1977, when Collingwood tied with the Ron Barassi-coached North Melbourne – 9.22 (76) to 10.16 (76). The Kangaroos won the Grand Final replay by 27 points – 21.25 (151) to 19.10 (124).
[41] Don Cordner. Interview with the author.
[42] *Melbourne Truth* series, 1962.
[43] *Melbourne Truth* series, 1962.
[44] Don Cordner. Interview with the author.
[45] *The Sporting Globe*, Saturday October 2, 1948.
[46] *The Sporting Globe*, Wednesday October 13, 1948.
[47] *Melbourne Truth* series, 1962.

Shane McGrath were so unimpressed by my enthusiasm that they screamed: "You bastard!" and acted like they were going to drown me!'[48]

Demon great Percy Beames was also upbeat, writing in *The Age*: 'In spite of Essendon's 34 scoring shots to 19, there was little difference between the two sides. Individually the Dons were superior, but Melbourne's teamwork was better. With the Smith-Mueller combination, the Demons also came nearer to revealing a winning strategy'.[49]

Tensions were also running high in the Demon camp in the hours after the dramatic draw. After a meat-pie-and-sauce dinner, Norm Smith and "Spud" Dullard had a violent disagreement. It is thought that perhaps they clashed over what transpired in those frantic final moments. In any case, it escalated, or deteriorated, into a fist fight. The strapping, similarly-sized pair – Smith was 6' (183cms) and 14 stone (89kgs), while Dullard was 6'2" (188cms) and 13st. 7lbs. (86kgs) exchanged blows while standing on a bar-table. 'After the fight, there was an uneasy silence,' Don Cordner said. 'Smith and Dullard had both played a large part in our revival in the last few minutes of the match – in fact, they had kicked our last two goals – yet here they were, at each other's throats. And we still had another Grand Final to play the following week. That's how tense everybody was.'[50]

Everybody – players and officials from both clubs, and their supporters – remained on edge in the lead-up to the first ever Grand Final replay. The strain continued to show on Norm Smith. '(It) was a week of tension,' he later recalled. 'Essendon were pronounced favourites. Most people declared they should have won the previous week. (And) Mueller and I were getting long in the tooth and many thought the hard game would have taken it out of us.'[51] With both Smith and Mueller carrying niggling leg injuries, they were strapped up accordingly. A Melbourne trainer concerned about their supposed frailty warned: 'Don't undo the bandages, they might fall apart.'[52] In reality, a warning should have been delivered to the Bombers: expect more fireworks from the old Demon duo.

Despite all the hype, the Grand Final rematch was attended by a crowd of just 52,226 – 33,000 down on previous week. Bad weather would have deterred some fans, with rain falling for an hour before the match, and the odd shower expected to intervene throughout the afternoon. Perhaps the football public was simply sick

---

[48] Noel McMahen. Interview with the author.
[49] *The Age*, Monday October 4, 1948.
[49] Don Cordner. Interview with the author.
[50] *Melbourne Truth* series, 1962.
[51] Dyer, Jack and Brian Hansen, *Jack Dyer's The Greatest: The Most Sensational Players of the Century*, Brian Hansen Nominees, 1996.

of Essendon-Melbourne matches. In 1948, they became, and remain, the only two clubs in VFL/AFL history to play each other five times in a season. Melbourne also became the first club to play 23 games in a season. Although 'massed bands tried to whip up the enthusiasm of the people with community singing... it fell flat'.[53] It was a sign of things to come. The match was an anti-climax. But Demon fans were ecstatic, as their heroes pulled off one of the great Grand Final heists.

With Melbourne continuing its relentless assault on ball and body, 'no Essendon man was allowed to take the ball unchallenged'.[54] The Bombers played 'panic football' and the 'timidity of some of their players to go near the pack'[55] allowed the Demons to play the match on their terms. Checker Hughes ensured 'especially good care was taken to dog the steps'[56] of Essendon's chief playmakers – particularly Dick Reynolds and Bill Hutchison and, 'without a counter for (centreman) Bickford, who showed his usual appreciation of wet turf... and clearly outwitted by Smith's baffling passing in the forward zone, Essendon had lost the match before many of its players got properly warmed up'.[57] Late in the first term, Smith delivered a pass to Mueller, who brought up his second goal and Melbourne's sixth, to extend the Demons' lead to 35 points – 6.2 (38) to 0.3 (3).

Essendon fought back with five goals to two in the second term before Bob McKenzie bombed long to the goalsquare where Smith briefly 'departed from his job of "feeder" to Mueller'[58] to outmark Ruddell. Smith's 'clever use of the hips' had 'completely unsettled' the Essendon full-back.[59] His simple goal – its level of difficulty seemingly increased by his use of the drop-kick – put Melbourne 22 points up. Although the Demons were clearly on top, there was still plenty of fire in the contest. Ruddell, Smith's opponent, was reported by umpire Jack McMurray junior and a boundary umpire for elbowing Mueller, in retaliation after Mueller, after arriving late to a marking contest had crashed into a vulnerable Norm McDonald. Norm Smith also reacted angrily to a poor umpiring decision, as Hec de Lacy observed in *The Sporting Globe*:

> McKenzie again got the ball to Smith. Umpire McMurray made a very bad mistake when he awarded a free kick against Smith, who had been held by (Bob) Syme when he tried to kick. Even if Smith had been guilty of playing on, he could not

---

[52] Hec de Lacy, *The Sporting Globe*.
[53] Kevin Hogan, *The Sun*.
[54] Hec de Lacy, *The Sporting Globe*.
[55] Kevin Hogan, *The Sun*, Monday October 11, 1948.
[56] Kevin Hogan, *The Sun*, Monday October 11, 1948.
[57] Kevin Hogan, *The Sun*, Monday October 11, 1948.
[58] Hec de Lacy, *The Sporting Globe*, Saturday October 9, 1948.

be attacked by players from behind. The half-time siren then sounded, but Smith, evidently incensed, attempted to argue with umpire McMurray as he came off the ground. Ruddell and (teammate) McMahen pushed him away.

Dick Reynolds again reduced the margin to 16 points early in the third term. But after 10 minutes of 'wild play' punctuated by 'fumbles and slips in every part of the field... it was Smith who settled Melbourne down'.[60] Smith marked and quickly played on and found Bickford, who assisted Alby Rodda for a steadying goal. Soon after, Smith took a freakish one-handed mark. With his left arm retarded by Ruddell, Smith worked his right arm free and clutched the ball to his chest. Alas, his long shot at goal resulted in a behind. However, Smith's subtle brilliance was having an enormous influence in the premiership quarter, in which he 'led the defence a merry dance and kept the goal under clever pressure'.[61] He was the main reason the Demons restored their advantage to 30 points by three-quarter-time.

The Bombers were hell-bent on upsetting the Demons' momentum, and their two veteran forwards, so they reverted to their last resort – all-out aggression, with particular focus on Smith and Mueller. The belated tactic backfired. Reynolds was penalised for charging Smith, and then Ruddell gave away a free kick when he illegally crashed into Mueller. Reynolds conceded another free kick when he cuffed Demon forward Craddock; the kick being awarded downfield to Norm Smith, who promptly delivered to Mueller, who in turn slotted his sixth goal to give the Demons a 39-point lead and their first premiership in seven years. It was the conclusion to a season Smith hailed as "the most remarkable I... played in.'[62] As was the case in the only other drawn Grand Final scenario in 1977, the side that reprehensibly squandered its opportunities in the drawn match lost the replay by a considerable margin.

Triumphant skipper Don Cordner was chaired off the ground by Mueller, with some assistance from Cordner's younger brother Denis. Cordner had become just the third of seven players in VFL/AFL history to both win a Brownlow Medal and captain a premiership team.[63]

According to some, Norm Smith had remained a kind of spiritual leader of the Demons, as George Bickford revealed:

---

[59] Hec de Lacy, *The Sporting Globe*, Saturday October 9, 1948.
[60] Hec de Lacy, *The Sporting Globe*, Saturday October 9, 1948.
[61] *Melbourne Truth* series, 1962.
[63] The others are Syd Coventry (Brownlow 1927, premierships 1927-30) Harry Collier (Brownlow 1930; premierships 1935-36), Dick Reynolds (Brownlows 1934, 1937-38; premierships 1942, 1946, 1949, 1950), James Hird (Brownlow 1996; premiership 2000), Michael Voss (Brownlow 1996; premierships 2001-03) and Chris Judd (Brownlow 2004; premiership 2006).

Norm's maturity and leadership was instrumental to our success in 1948. Just because he'd lost the title of captain, he didn't stop setting the example for the rest of us on how the game should be played. Norm's experience was invaluable. Our captain, Don Cordner, was playing in the ruck and changing out of a back-pocket, while Norm controlled the forward line and was virtually a pseudo-captain in the forward half the ground. His sharing style of play, where he brought others around him into the game, was quite inspiring.[64]

Indeed, Norm Smith had been inspirational throughout the Demons' four-final campaign, but never more so than in the premiership decider. He 'drew the defence upfield and (then) shattered it with his clever passes... (and) made rabbits of the defenders'.[65] When asked later about his stunning contribution to the success, all he revealed was: 'Teamwork was our answer'.[66] Fortunately, others weren't so brief and modest on his behalf. Opposing captain-coach Dick Reynolds wrote: 'Norm Smith was the best player on the ground. He was the brains of the Melbourne attack, and rarely wasted an opportunity of unselfishly sending the ball forward to Mueller.' It was a view endorsed by *The Sporting Globe*'s expert, Hec de Lacy, who wrote: 'My best player is again Norman Smith. There wasn't an Essendon defender who could put a shadow on him... Ruddell battled against Smith, but he was outwitted.' Alf Brown of *The Herald* lauded Smith for playing 'one of the greatest games of his brilliant career'.

It was a recurring theme throughout Smith's career, but it deserves to be emphasised: the quality of his performance could never be judged simply on the number of goals he kicked; it was always about how many he *created*. Playing in his regular position at full-forward – albeit as a decoy who generally worked much further out from goals – he had kicked a grand total of just two goals in the two Grand Finals of 1948. However, he had been arguably in the top three on the ground in the drawn match, indisputably best afield in the replay.

Smith's work in tandem with Mueller became the stuff of legend. The two battle-weary warriors had pooled all their rat-cunning, experience and superb skills to conquer an old enemy on one last tour of duty. After winning his fifth premiership as a coach, Checker Hughes told Kevin Hogan from *The Sun* that he had been confident that the old Smith-Mueller pairing would again be a significant factor in the Demons' quest for the premiership. But, as was his penchant, Hughes had

---

[64] George Bickford. Interview with the author.
[65] *The Sporting Globe*, Wednesday October 13, 1948.
[66] *Melbourne Truth* series, 1962.

kept his cards close to his chest because, he felt, 'it would do no harm to allow our opponents to bask in the sun of assumed superiority'.[67]

Don Cordner commemorated the pair's heroics in song, adding the following verse to the Demons' theme song, *A Grand Old Flag*:

> Oh the Demons they were great,
> In the year '48,
> Because we didn't just know how to lose.
> And it was thanks to Norm and Jack,
> That we won the flag back,
> And gave it to 'Checker' Hughes.

Demons fans who thought Mueller could not play any better than he did in the 1946 finals' series were gleefully surprised. The inner sanctum at Melbourne had placed a two-game limit on Mueller's comeback, but he had risen to extraordinary heights for the third successive cut-throat final. And he had done it under considerable physical pressure. 'Despite constant attention, much of it unfair',[68] Mueller had kicked 20 goals in three finals – two more than he managed in 1946. Most of his goals had been, directly or indirectly, the result of Smith's team play.[69] Sixteen years later, Smith still rated Mueller the greatest big occasion player he ever saw, adding that he never saw him fail in a Grand Final.[70]

No-one was more appreciative of the old firm's output than Checker Hughes, who told *The Sporting Globe*:

> When I think of old 'Ginger' Smith and Jack Mueller giving me football like that after many hard years in the game, I realise that the lifetime I have given to football will... be my golden years in friendships. They're old bones, you know; old bones, when I think back to 1936 and know they were with me then. It cost those coves something to come up week after week for the physical hiding they took. They never conceded a yard. They never flinched a clash. They never batted an eyelid under irritation. They out-thought and out-played everything the opposition threw at them... I doubt whether there has been a finer display of forward combination and self-control than that given by Jack and Normy.[71]

---

[67] *The Sun*, Monday October 11, 1948.
[68] Hec de Lacy, *The Sporting Globe*.
[69] In 1948, Norm Smith kicked 35.31 in 13 games, while Mueller netted 28.15 in five games.
[70] Pollard, Jack (editor), *High Mark: The Complete Book on Australian Football*, Murray, 1964.
[71] *The Sporting Globe*, Wednesday October 13 1948.

Hec de Lacy, perhaps Smith's greatest admirer among the scribes, ultimately rated him as the best forward he had seen – ahead of Essendon's John Coleman, Gordon Coventry and Bob Pratt, each of whom are official Legends of Australian Football. In 1955, de Lacy sparked debate among readers of *The Sporting Globe* when he wrote an article titled: 'Who was the best League full-forward? You can have them all, I'll take Smithy'. He then compared Smith with the two gun spearheads of the day – Coleman and Footscray's Jack Collins – explaining:

> Footscray can have their Jack Collins and Essendon can have their John Coleman, but if I were planning the perfect football team Norman Smith would be the spearhead of my attack... Both (Collins and Coleman) are superlative forwards... but view... (them) in the rosiest lights and they both lack something that Norman Smith brought to football... Smith organised – and I mean organised – a band of marauders that had every defence snatching at shadows.

Smith's efforts also reinforced Don Cordner's opinion of his playing prowess:

> Norm Smith was the best player that I played with. That assessment is probably helped by the fact I played more with Norm than anyone else. I played about 100 games with him, and I don't think I ever saw him play a bad game. He was consistently the best player I played with. I never saw him play a completely dominating game either, but he was always reliable and always there, always thinking and moving; he was very active, almost in constant motion.
>
> It's also important to realise that, up until (David) Neitz broke the record (in 2006), Norm Smith was the greatest goalkicker in the history of Melbourne Football Club. And he did it playing no more than two-thirds of his career at full-forward. He started on a half-forward flank, and then (Fred) Fanning played at full-forward for five or so years and in that time Norm played a lot in the centre. Fanning could be both a match-winner and a match-loser who couldn't be relied upon, whereas you could utterly rely on Norm. I think Norm could have kicked 300 more goals if he had been at full-forward the whole time. With him, it was never a case of: 'Kick it to me so I can kick a goal'. Mueller's attitude was: 'Kick it to me and leave me alone on the forward line. Stay out of my way'. Smithy fed so many goals to others like Fanning and Mueller, and didn't think anything of it.[72]

---

[72] Don Cordner. Interview with the author.

THE SMITH-MUELLER LEGEND [1948]

Although Smith and Mueller had been the headline acts, Melbourne's success over a seemingly superior opponent was the result of Checker Hughes's intuition, and his rare ability to identify just what his team needed at just the right time, whether it be in training, team balance, or a timely speech. Kevin Hogan from *The Sun* summed it up aptly when he wrote: 'Melbourne's 1948 League title will probably always be known as Checker Hughes's premiership. Melbourne, an inferior side to Essendon throughout the season, won... because (of) better discipline and planning'. Noel McMahen said: 'It was a wonderful coaching effort from Checker. He'd already coached four premiership sides, but I reckon this one was his finest moment because he won when he shouldn't have. He pinched it – through his strategies. He manipulated that Grand Final. He manipulated the psychology of players on both sides: he lifted us and had us believing in ourselves, while he had the Essendon players looking over their shoulders.'[73]

At the age of 54 and after demonstrating that he was still at the peak of his powers, Hughes stepped down from the coaching position. This time, though, despite coaching Victoria from 1949-51 and again in 1953, Hughes would not return to coach a VFL club on a permanent basis. Remarkably, it was the third time he had resigned as the reigning premiership coach. He had done it at Richmond in 1932 and Melbourne in 1941. Very few others have done this even once. But certainly no-one has done it twice, let alone three times. Hughes had left to spend more time running hotels. With the professionalism of the modern game and the salaries of the best coaches climbing towards $1 million, it is not conceivable that Hughes' effort will be repeated.

One of the Demons' premiership celebrations was held at the famous Tivoli Theatre in Bourke Street. At the end of the evening, a triumphant quartet – Checker Hughes, Don Cordner, Norm Smith and Shane McGrath – was coaxed into stepping onto the stage. To the cheers of those in attendance, the three players wrapped their coach in the 1948 VFL premiership flag.

Norm Smith had long been an integral part of – and one of the keenest participants in – the social scene at Melbourne Football Club. Even Marj had joined Smith on the Demons' social committee in 1947.

Smith wasn't a drinker... initially. It is believed that he did not touch alcohol until his early 30s. At least one teammate remembers him getting merrily tipsy on an end-of-season footy trip in the late forties. Smith's social drink of choice was beer. According to Peter Smith, just once did his father drink a shot of whisky –

---

[73] Noel McMahen. Interview with the author.

and that was only after someone told him it would help cure the effects of a cold.[74] Later, he also sampled copious amounts of the beverages on offer on a tour of the Barossa Valley wine region while on a football trip in Adelaide.

Smith was a central figure at the Demons' after-match functions – or simply 'after-matches', as they were known – after home games at the MCG. After the players had bathed – generally sharing one of the three large tubs with a team-mate – they met the opposition side in the social rooms for a drink and a chat. After an hour or so, they headed off to a players' dinner at Phair's Hotel, at 329 Collins Street. It was there that a player was assigned the task of MC, among whose tasks it was to introduce the musical entertainment and arrange the tallying of the bill. Also, if a player was caught reading that evening's edition of 'the pink paper', *The Sporting Globe*, and perhaps reading about themselves without asking permission, they would be fined 'two bob' (20 cents), which would go towards the players' fund for the end-of-season trip.[75] The players then picked up their wives or girlfriends and went back to the MCG for the club dance, where Smith was totally in his element, as Len Dockett recalled: 'Norm would be holding court with the young players and old players around him. He was very popular. We would always congregate around him and he'd take over for the night. He was a good talker, very entertaining, very friendly, very social, but very humble too.'[76]

One of the customs of the evening – which was feared by some – was that every player had to stand up and sing a song. Any song. Smith loved singing on these occasions. When asked about Smith's vocal abilities, Don Cordner said: 'He made a noise.' But Smith did not care that he did not have the greatest voice. It was about participating and being involved, and even being prepared to be the subject of laughter for the benefit, and amusement, of the group.

ŸŸŸŸŸŸŸŸŸ

Although he had just produced perhaps the best football of his career, and received wide acclaim for his role in one of the greatest premierships in VFL history, Norm Smith knew his playing career was over. He had spent a lot of time nursing injuries on the sidelines in the previous two seasons – he played just 22 of 42 games in 1947-48 – and carried other niggles into the few games he did play. Such acts required enormous courage, the mental strength to play with pain,

---

[74] Peter Smith. Interview with the author.
[75] Len Dockett. Interview with the author.
[76] Len Dockett. Interview with the author.

and a willingness to limp through the working week. On the cusp of turning 33, Smith felt it appropriate to end his career at its zenith. The 1948 Grand Final replay, in which he had been adjudged best afield by most judges, would be his last appearance in a VFL match. At the age of almost 33, he had played 210 games, just three behind Percy Beames' club record. He had also kicked 546 goals, which *was* a club record, one that stood for almost 58 years until David Neitz surpassed it in his 271st AFL game in 2006.

Smith's ambition was to replace Checker Hughes as Melbourne's senior coach – in a *non*-playing capacity. It would be a tough act to follow – the Demons could only go down the ladder from here – but Smith believed he was ready for the challenge. Many of his teammates agreed. The other candidate for the job was his former captain Allan La Fontaine. Both possessed brilliant football brains and probably could not be separated in this area. Noel McMahen regards La Fontaine as the best football brain he came across. La Fontaine had an edge in experience, and as the chairman of selectors for the previous two seasons he had dealt with selection issues in a manner that had brought success. But the respect factor also appeared telling. La Fontaine was regarded by a number of the players as aloof, arrogant and a loner who was not a good communicator, whereas Smith was respected by all of the players for the way he approached his football and for his capacity to gather them together. Stan Rule summed up the feelings of his teammates:

> Norm was respected and accepted by the players, while La Fontaine was respected for his fantastic playing record and nothing else. They were completely opposite characters. I had all the confidence in the world that Norm could have done the job straight away without any problems. It wasn't as though he was wet behind the ears and they would have been taking a chance – he was 33 and he'd been a great leader out on the field, and off it. In most of our minds he was a certainty; a shoe-in, and we were happy for him to coach us.[77]

What followed was the tightest possible tussle to decide Hughes' successor. After a ballot of committee members, Smith and La Fontaine had polled the same number of votes. The constitution gave club chairman Bill Flintoft the power to deliver the casting vote. Flintoft was in hospital with illness, so a messenger had to be was sent to his bedside to gain his deciding vote. He voted for La Fontaine.

Smith was hurt, and seething. Years later, he diplomatically conceded: 'Allan La Fontaine had the service on the board and the committee was fully

---

[77] Stan Rule. Interview with the author.

justified in appointing him. He had been a great player and had captained the side well.' However, he still described the result as 'the greatest disappointment of my football career... (It) was an even greater disappointment than the previous year (1947) when I lost the captaincy'.[78] The common denominator in both decisions was Flintoft. While even Smith admitted that stripping him of the captaincy had proved an astute move, very few, apart from those who actually voted for La Fontaine, believed that installing the triple-premiership captain was the correct decision. Smith never forgave Flintoft.

A sad quirk of fate for Smith was that a notable absentee from the vote was Frank 'Pop' Vine, the owner of Miller's ropeworks, a 1926 premiership player, Melbourne captain in 1932-33, and a staunch Norm Smith supporter. Vine had been overseas. Max Spittle, one of Smith's teammates who worked under Vine at Miller's ropeworks, revealed: 'Pop wasn't very happy. He was a Norm Smith man – 100 percent. He was disappointed in his fellow committeemen for appointing La Fontaine – it was the worst thing that ever happened to Melbourne. But Pop was even more disappointed that he hadn't been able to cast the vote that would have given Norm Smith the coaching job.'[79]

Like many of his teammates, skipper Don Cordner was bewildered by the appointment of La Fontaine: 'I was captain of the team but I don't recall the committee ever consulting me for my opinion. In those days, all the captain did outside playing and training was to be a member of the selection committee on a Thursday night. I certainly didn't get any say in the coaching appointment. I don't know how the conclusion was reached that La Fontaine was the favourable alternative to Norm. It's still a mystery, even after all these years.'[80]

Stan Rule revealed that religion could have been a factor in the Smith snub: 'There was a rumour that, before the announcement of the senior coaching position, Norm made a comment that got back to the committee. They were mainly Protestants at Melbourne, but there were a few Catholics on committee. Apparently Norm had remarked: "A Catholic flag will never fly over Melbourne." If it was true, it might have killed his hopes of getting the job. That comment might have turned a few committeemen against him.'[81] If Smith made this remark, it may well have been misinterpreted. Smith could never have been described as religious. In fact, religion never played a significant role in his life. According to Terry Gleeson – who, by his own admission, was one of the few Catholics to later play under him

---

[78] *Melbourne Truth* series, 1962.
[79] Max Spittle. Interview with the author.
[80] Don Cordner. Interview with the author.
[81] Stan Rule. Interview with the author.

at Melbourne – Smith 'always sang with the Catholics'.[82] However, Smith was not religiously biased one way or the other. 'Norm and Checker Hughes took me to the Freemasons' Club for dinner one night,' Gleeson said. 'They said: "You've got to leave your rosary beads out the front!" In the engineering industry, freemasonry was a big part of it back then.'[83]

Regardless of the reason – whether it was based on religion, personality or simply that La Fontaine would make a better coach – the fact was that Norm Smith faced a dilemma. He didn't want to leave Melbourne. He had been there for 15 seasons – almost half his life – and many of his mates were still at the club. But what were his options if he stayed? He could hang around the club in a background role, and perhaps secure a position on the selection committee, and basically bide his time until La Fontaine's reign ended. This was not really an option. Or he could attempt to play another season and hope his failing body held out. But at the end of the season, unless the Demons endured a disastrous year and La Fontaine proved completely incompetent in which case Melbourne might rethink the coaching position – not a situation Smith would wish for, much less want to be part of – he would find himself in the same position as he was in now. And Smith wanted to coach now. He arrived at the logical conclusion that the only way he could do that was if he coached elsewhere. Understandably, Smith found it a 'difficult decision', but he felt he had no other option. 'I was forced to leave Melbourne,' he later lamented. 'I was getting too long in the tooth to play and to fulfil my coaching ambitions I had to go walkabout.'[84]

The Demons committee welcomed La Fontaine with the following words in its annual report: 'With his wealth of football experience and his active connection with the club as a member of the selection committee, it is felt that he will prove a worthy successor to Checker Hughes.' But, generally speaking, the playing group he was about to inherit was not so enthusiastic, as Len Dockett revealed:

> It was a bad situation all round for the club. First of all, Norm missed out on the coaching job, and then it was a terrible shame that we lost him from the club completely. He wanted to coach, and you couldn't blame him for that. And then we were stuck with La Fontaine, who I knew didn't have the personality to be a good coach, just as I knew Norm did.[85]

---

[82] Terry Gleeson. Interview with the author.
[83] Terry Gleeson. Interview with the author.
[84] *Melbourne Truth* series, 1962.
[85] Len Dockett. Interview with the author.

8

COACH OF FITZROY

[1949-51]

At the end of the 1948 season, Fitzroy Football Club was a place of discontent. The Maroons had just endured the most dramatic form slump in VFL history. It was a stark contrast with the jovial, upbeat atmosphere that had permeated the club just two months earlier.

Midway through the 1948 season, first-year coach Charlie Cameron[1] was being lauded as a revelation. Admittedly, Cameron had taken command of a strong team, which – under the guidance of 1944 premiership captain-coach Fred Hughson[2] – had led the mighty Essendon by a point at three-quarter-time of the 1947 preliminary final, only to succumb by 13 points. Cameron, then 39, had exceeded most expectations when, after each side had played each other once, his Maroons had climbed to the top of the VFL ladder with a 9-2 record – the nine wins being by an average of 38 points, and the two losses being to eventual finalists Footscray (by seven points) and Collingwood (17 points).

But just when the critics began to rate the Maroons serious premiership contenders, they imploded. They lost the last eight games to finish seventh – three games out of the final four. The knockout blow had been a soul-destroying round 15 defeat at the hands of hapless cellar-dweller St Kilda, an inexperienced and incompetent side which had just a draw to show for its previous 30 matches. Fitzroy had led by four goals at the final change, by which time it had fired 17 scoring shots to eight, but was completely blindsided by St Kilda, which more than doubled its own score with a devastating burst of 6.3 to 1.1.

---

[1] Charlie Cameron represented Victoria 11 times as a wingman from 1929-32 and played 122 games as a wingman for North Melbourne from 1926-34 and 23 games (for 52 goals) as a goalsneak for Fitzroy from 1934-36. Before becoming the Fitzroy coach, he had coached the club's reserves and served on the committee.

[2] Hughson, a 164-games champion full-back, left Fitzroy at the end of 1947 to coach South Warrnambool in the Hampden league.

There appeared no logical explanation for Fitzroy's late-season fade-out, described by one newspaper as 'one of the most unexpected and amazing happenings in senior football for many years'.[3] It is believed in some quarters that in-fighting at committee level had had an unsettling effect on the players. Another theory revealed an alleged rift between the leaders of the club's football department – coach Cameron and first-year captain Allan Ruthven. The pair is believed to have clashed heavily – albeit behind closed doors and away from other players and club officials – which no doubt affected morale. However, any disharmony certainly did not affect on Ruthven's form – the champion rover collected his fourth club best-and-fairest award.

Charlie Cameron resigned as coach, claiming he found it too difficult to combine business and football.[4] Ruthven might have been relieved, perhaps even happy… but not for long.

Fitzroy moved decisively in its search for a new coach for season 1949. The club quickly identified Collingwood captain Phonse Kyne as its preferred option. It was astute thinking. Kyne – one of the lads who played scratch matches with Norm and Len Smith at Smith's Paddock – was a 33-year-old centre half-forward/ruckman who had starred in the Magpies' 1935-36 premiership sides, and had represented Victoria eight times. More importantly, Kyne was a natural leader of men who thrived on the responsibility of leadership. Indeed, he had won best-and-fairests in each of the previous three seasons he had captained Collingwood. Kyne was a coach in waiting, and Fitzroy was sick of waiting for success. However, it was an ambitious bid, as the Magpies would have had Kyne in mind as a potential successor to coaching legend Jock McHale, who was in the twilight of his incomparable career. Nevertheless, the Maroons gave it their best shot to lure Kyne the one and a half kilometres to their headquarters at the Brunswick Street Oval. Kyne was believed to have been keen to make the switch as captain-coach. But, after much negotiation, Fitzroy's bid failed when Collingwood doggedly refused to grant their skipper a clearance. It was a disheartening development for the Maroons, who had been confident about sealing what would have been a coaching coup.

Fitzroy soon found a solution to its coaching problem. Upon hearing of Melbourne's appointment of Allan La Fontaine, and the consequent rejection of Norm Smith, the Maroons smartly approached the retired Demon. Fitzroy was a club Smith felt he knew reasonably well, albeit on a second-hand basis, after hearing

---

[3] A contemporary newspaper report.
[4] Charlie Cameron must have had business interests in the vicinity of Ballarat as he coached East Ballarat to the Ballarat league premiership in 1949.

much about it through Len. When Smith indicated he was interested in coaching the club, the Maroons could not believe their luck. A sticking point, though, had been Smith's playing future. Fitzroy wanted him to join the club as a playing-coach, as his glowing example would no doubt inspire the players. But Smith felt his playing days were over and he was keen to concentrate on mentoring from the sidelines. He later gave the following critical self-assessment of his diminishing playing abilities: 'I was past my best as a player. I was too heavy and was slowing up. I could no longer do the things needed to inspire a side.'[5]

But Fitzroy did not want to waste whatever Smith had left in the tank. Perhaps influenced by the performances of their previous two coaches – Hughson's success as a playing-coach, and Cameron's turbulent lone season in an off-field capacity – the Maroons refused to compromise on this point, and eventually convinced Smith to play on. With heavy hearts, the Demons agreed to sign his clearance papers; doing so in the hope that 'the big redhead' would one day return.

Smith was appointed captain-coach for two seasons – an appointment that was generally met with excitement among Fitzroy players, officials and fans. A contemporary newspaper report summed up the consensus, stating that Fitzroy 'has been fortunate in securing the services as playing-coach of Norman Smith, brilliant and astute Melbourne champion... His experience, leadership and capabilities will help the Maroons in their bid for success. Smith has carefully analysed Fitzroy's prospects and players available since his recent appointment, and is quite confident that with last year's promising players, and the wealth of promising local and country talent unearthed, he will be able to mould together a strong combination'.

Third-year Fitzroy player Jack Toohey, then 23, recalled being 'over the moon' about Smith's appointment:

> Norm Smith was a legend who'd helped Melbourne win all these premierships, and when a legend like that comes to a little old club of battlers like Fitzroy, people become part-mesmerised, and I was one of them. We all looked up to Norm. His quality was higher than what we'd had. Charlie Cameron was a great orator – boy, could he make a speech – but Norm had won premierships and knew what was required and I was looking forward to him teaching us how to be successful.[6]

But not everyone was happy with the decision... initially anyway. Emerging star Bill Stephen, 20, felt that Smith was the lesser of the two coaching candidates.

---

[5] *Melbourne Truth* series, 1962.
[6] Jack Toohey. Interview with the author.

'I personally wanted Phonse Kyne to coach us,' Stephen recalled. 'I was disappointed when he didn't get the job. I didn't know either him or Norm Smith, but I just felt that I knew less about Norm Smith than I did about Phonse Kyne. We didn't know a lot about Norm apart from the fact he had been a very good player with Melbourne. But later on, I was so grateful that Phonse Kyne didn't get the job because of the strong friendship I formed with Norm over the next 20-odd years until his death.'[7]

Perhaps the most disillusioned individual was Allan Ruthven. After nine superb seasons, which produced four best-and-fairests (the first of which came during the premiership year of 1944) and nine state matches (for 29 goals since 1946), the 26-year-old was Fitzroy's best player, in his prime, and had richly deserved the captaincy. He understandably felt, as did certain others, that he didn't deserve to lose the honour he so dearly coveted. But he had little choice in the matter when Norm Smith was appointed *captain*-coach. For Ruthven, the best he could hope for was the vice-captaincy. Ruthven was so upset by this development that he entertained lucrative offers to coach in the country. Soon, he resolved to leave Fitzroy.

Such a decision, by today's standards, sounds like a melodramatic over-reaction. But captaincy was perhaps a bigger deal in those days. Although it was still essentially a title, it officially recognised the best leader in a side and more prestige was attached to the position. This is in contrast with the recent trend of AFL clubs implementing 'leadership groups' of as many as eight players, and even multiple and rotating captains – all of which honourably aim to spread the leadership load and dilute the importance of a single captain. In 1949, other experienced players might have set an example for others to follow, but the official leadership group comprised merely the captain and vice-captain.

A lifelong Fitzroy supporter, as a youngster Ruthven would attend the Brunswick Street Oval on training nights and fetch balls that were kicked through the goals. He loved Fitzroy deeply. In fact, in the minds of many, he *was* Fitzroy. He was even given the famous No.7 that Haydn Bunton had worn with such distinction from 1931-42. The aura surrounding him also held the fascination of fans – a most necessary ingredient for a club seemingly on the skids. A flamboyant character, Ruthven wowed his teammates by arriving at training in tailored suits and an array of eye-catching shirts and ties. As a 17-year-old in his debut season, 1940, he was given the nickname 'The Baron' – not for his fine taste in clothes, but after Australia's Governor-General from 1936-45, Sir Alexander Gore Arkwright Hore-Ruthven, the 1st Baron of Gowrie. Despite his aristocratic moniker, Ruthven

---

[7] Bill Stephen. Interview with the author.

was still a courageous rover – he missed virtually two seasons from 1942 after experiencing blood in his urine and defied medical advice to return to the game. The condition recurred throughout his career.

Norm Smith knew that he, and Fitzroy, could ill-afford to lose Ruthven, who was a key to any success the club might enjoy in the near future. He could have been the difference between Smith's coaching debut being a success or failure. But with the big money that country clubs were offering, it was always going to be tough to convince him to stay. Imperial Football Club in Hamilton offered Ruthven £18-a-week to be its playing coach – a position he accepted in January 1949. But Fitzroy steadfastly refused to release him on the grounds that Imperial had ignored its strict instruction not to approach their star. Broken Hill then doubled Imperial's offer to £36-a-week, but Fitzroy stood firm and Ruthven remained at Brunswick Street – to the infinite relief of the entire club, including its new coach.

Smith had, as player George Coates explained, 'come to Fitzroy at a difficult time, and taken on a bad situation'.[8] Perhaps to have even more of a say in the operations of the club, particularly off-field matters relating to the team, Smith became one of only two player representatives on Fitzroy's committee. The other was his star defender, state representative Reg Nicholls. Smith had an almost immediate influence in this role.

When Smith lost the vote for the coveted Melbourne coaching job and joined Fitzroy, he had also lost out in the standard of club facilities at the Brunswick Street Oval. While Allan La Fontaine enjoyed the relative luxury of a coach's room and second-to-none training, playing and social facilities at the MCG, Smith began his coaching career in far less opulent surrounds. So poor were Fitzroy's facilities that after training and matches sweaty, muddy players had to share one bathtub! The committee, coerced by Smith, undertook 'extensive and badly needed improvements to the club training rooms'.[9] Bill Stephen recalled: 'By leaving Melbourne to join Fitzroy, Norm had to adapt to a completely different environment at the Brunswick Street Oval to what he'd been used to at the MCG for 15 years. In the changerooms – training sheds would be a better term – there were just these little boxes which you put your clothes in. They were like lockers but they weren't locked. The coaches had lockers next to the players – they didn't have any special coaches' rooms. But with Norm being the kind of man he was, a little thing like that was never going to bother him. But, just the same, it must have taken some getting used to'.[10]

---

[8] George Coates. Interview with the author.
[9] A contemporary newspaper report.
[10] A contemporary newspaper report.

But not everything was unfamiliar. Like Melbourne, Fitzroy was one of the most successful clubs in the VFL. The Maroons had won eight premierships – two more than the Demons, the same number as Essendon and Carlton, and behind only Collingwood, which had collected 11 flags.

Smith had also inherited a Fitzroy culture that was very much in tune with the working man; the honest battler – the kind of salt-of-the-earth stock that Smith had been raised among, worked with, and best related to. He felt immediately comfortable in his new environment, and pleasantly discovered that all Len had told him about the virtues of the club tallied entirely with his own impressions.

Smith soon had Len in mind for another reason. There was a vacancy on Fitzroy's coaching panel. The reserves were catered for – they would be guided by Norm Hillard, the former centre half-back who was best-on-ground in the 1944 premiership. The under-19s – or 'thirds', as they were known since their inception in 1946 – were a different story. As late as early March – just six weeks before the start of the season on April 16 – Fitzroy still had not found a suitable man to coach the thirds. It was an important role, and similar to Hillard's, where performance was judged more on player development than mere wins and losses. The Maroons initially advertised for the job, but eventually gave it to one of their own. Len Smith accepted his brother's offer to coach Fitzroy's thirds. Distance was no issue for Len Smith, who continued to work as a foreman in charge of about 45 people in maintenance engineering at Miller's ropeworks in Brunswick, and lived with his wife and three children – daughters Barbara, 15, and Norma, 14, and seven-year-old son Kevin – in Roseneath Street, Clifton Hill.

Smith held his first pre-season training session as the Fitzroy coach at the Brunswick Street Oval on Tuesday, March 8. Although it was just a month and eight days before the start of the VFL season – in complete contrast with the five or so months of pre-season training undertaken by today's professional footballers – this was common for clubs of the era who generally played four intra-club practice matches before the season proper.

Any Maroons who thought their new coach would ease himself into the coaching caper to win them over, and perhaps take it easy on them on the training track, were in for a rude awakening. Those who had played under Charlie Cameron, and Fred Hughson before him, were shocked by the intensity that Smith demanded at training. For most, it was unlike anything they experienced before or since. But if any new coach had the right to place sizeable demands on his players, it was Norm Smith, who epitomised the old saying: 'Don't ask anyone to do anything you can't do yourself'. Smith had done it, and could still do it, albeit in a more limited manner. He was one of the most selfless players the game had seen, and as such, he was qualified to ask his players for a lot in return.

Like most training sessions of the day and for some time after, Smith's sessions were very basic affairs. He ordered his players to jog a few warm-up laps, and perhaps stride out into a few sprints, followed by end-to-end kicking and an hour or so of circle-work around the oval. 'It was all circle-work in those days,' player George Coates recalled. 'We did so much of it that you'd almost get dizzy running around and around the ground.'[11] To add some spice to circle-work, Smith often paired similarly-matched players and demanded they make it difficult for each other to get a touch.

But while the structure of the sessions was easy to comprehend, completing them often required vast reserves of physical and mental toughness. In fact, it soon became well known in football circles that training under Norm Smith could be termed a form of torture. Tuesday and Thursday nights at the Fitzroy ground were anything but kick-and-giggle sessions. There was plenty of kicking, and running, but very little to giggle about. To Smith, football was serious business and training was a crucial component for success, so it had to be treated with the respect and effort it deserved. It all revolved around Smith's unwavering belief that: 'You must train as you play'. Bill Stephen elaborated:

> Norm felt: 'If you train with intensity, you'll carry it into games. But if you train with a relaxed attitude, it is impossible to maintain your intensity on a Saturday.' He would rather train absolutely intensive for half-an-hour rather than have two-and-a-half hours of casual, flat training. He emphasised 'quickness'. He *loved* quickness. Blokes who didn't go flat-out on the track were either shown the door or just weren't accepted.

Smith immediately impressed the likes of Stephen with his ability to impart his wealth of knowledge:

> Norm was a great teacher of football. He taught you how to train, why you trained, how you could get the best out of yourself at training, how to improve your pace or your kicking or marking. He didn't only tell you what to do, he told you how to do it. And it all came back to one thing – hard work.
>
> One night after training, he told me about how I could improve myself at training and how I could make myself better by just striving that little bit harder,

---

[11] George Coates. Interview with the author.

and pushing myself to the point of exhaustion. He felt that: 'If you don't exhaust yourself at training, how are you going to be able to do it in a match?' He said: 'If you can just run that little bit harder to get to an extra ball a quarter, and then make it stick, that's four extra kicks a game you wouldn't have got.' It helped me. If you apply a philosophy like that, it can only improve you.'[12]

It could also take a player to the brink of collapse. Despite being in just his first season of VFL football, Jack Gaffney[13] won the club award for 'most attentive to training' that year and, as such, was well qualified to comment. Gaffney, then 19, explained: 'Under Norm, there were no half-measures with training – you trained to improve and to get fit. And he felt that when you were fit, you could always be fitter, so you had to work even harder. It was a never-ending cycle of hard work. He'd try to make you push through exhaustion, through the pain barrier.' Gaffney was one of a number of players who, 'on quite a few occasions after being pushed by Norm', actually vomited during training.[14]

Emerging ruckman Alan "Butch" Gale, then 18, recalled a particularly harrowing session. Gale had arrived late to training and so, as punishment, Smith ordered him to run laps of the oval until he was told to stop. 'Norm ran me around the ground so much,' Gale said, 'that I became so sick that I was going blind and didn't know where I was. I was almost delirious. I couldn't even find the (players') race.'[15]

Smith also pushed his players to strive for perfection in skill execution. 'He believed in quality training,' Bill Stephen said. 'He wanted us to eliminate all casual things and keep mistakes to a minimum. That required complete concentration, and that's exactly what he demanded.'[16] Smith often told his players: 'Anything you do is worth doing well – anything less than that and you're wasting your time'. Two other catch-phrases of Smith's along these lines were: 'The skill to do comes from doing', and he also demanded that his players 'do the common things uncommonly well'. He believed in constant repetition of skills until the action became second nature, so that when players were confronted with a certain situation in a match they would react instinctively through habit.

Smith had no time for players who bludged at training, or worse still, those who were shamefully referred to as 'psychos', who invented and exaggerated injuries to

---

[12] Bill Stephen. Interview with the author.
[13] Jack Gaffney served as the chairman of the VFL tribunal from 1985 to 1987.
[14] Jack Gaffney. Interview with the author.
[15] Gale told this story to Keith Carroll, a Melbourne player of the 1950s. Carroll related it to the author.
[16] Bill Stephen. Interview with the author.

get out of training. 'Baron' Ruthven frustrated Smith no end in this department. A known 'loper' who was 'most un-Smith-like in that he hated training',[17] Ruthven performed accordingly in this environment – when he did in fact subject himself to it. In Ruthven's defence, he worked as a country traveller which prevented him from attending training at times. Bill Stephen recalled Smith's struggles with his champion vice-captain:

> Norm and Baron and got along OK, but Norm had to push Baron to train because while he was a wonderful player he wasn't a great trainer. Norm had difficulty getting his point across to Baron. Baron didn't become one of Norm's great subjects like perhaps I did because I knew a lot of his philosophies and I knew what he was trying to do. Baron never got to that point. His brilliance got him through and he'd never had to battle much, so he didn't see much point in changing.[18]

It is a wonder anyone could see at all at training in 1949. A constant bane of football coaches at the time was that they had limited light to work with at training. In those days, few, if any, teams trained under lights, and all the players and coaches had full-time jobs. With the onset of winter, most training was conducted in fading light at best. In these circumstances, the eagle eye of Norm Smith came to the fore and, importantly, reminded his players that they had nowhere to hide, to bludge, not even in virtual darkness. George Coates marvelled: 'I was sure Norm couldn't see anything out there – because I certainly couldn't – but he would always be barking orders like: "Go harder!"; "You didn't run hard enough!" or: "You should have called louder!"'

Another of Norm Smith's pet hates was players who took chest marks at training. He regarded it as lazy, mentally weak and even dumb. Jack Toohey recalled:

> Norm said: 'You must learn to mark the ball in your hands out in front of you. Never take a chest mark. Your opponent then has to try to punch the ball from over your shoulder – he'll struggle to reach the ball and you might also get a free kick for over-the-shoulder or in-the-back. Trying to mark on your chest is the easy option, and it's the silly option because you're making it much easier for your opponent to punch it away. Besides, it might bounce off your bloody chest'.[19]

---

[17] Jack Gaffney. Interview with the author.
[18] Bill Stephen. Interview with the author.
[19] Jack Toohey. Interview with the author.

The practice match series unveiled a reinvigorated Fitzroy line-up which adapted well to Smith's demand to 'kick it a bit longer'. Compared to the MCG, many VFL grounds, including Fitzroy headquarters at the Brunswick Street Oval, were reasonably short and often players fell into the trap of simply chipping the ball to the next line, the next pack of players. Smith wanted to get some of his players out of this habit by going for extra distance. His theory was based around the fact that the finals were played on the wide open expanses of the MCG. If the Maroons were to succeed, they would need to master a long-kicking game and develop sturdy, key-position players who, while they didn't necessarily have to haul in swags of marks, could compete fiercely in the air and at least bring the ball to ground to provide crumbs for classy opportunists like Ruthven and Coates.

Smith later described his preferred style of play as 'safety-first in defence and straight for home in attack'.[20] His preferred movement pattern of the ball was in a virtual diamond shape, as follows: take it out wide in defence – never through centre half-back, and *never* across goal – and move it along the boundary line with long kicking until the ball is forward of the wing and only then start moving it in a direct line toward goal. Don't centre the ball too soon because a turnover will open up the whole field for the opposition to attack on the rebound. If there is a choice between going short or long, always take the long option. He also encouraged his players to 'snowball' up the field; in other words, he wanted his players to outnumber the opposition. He would say: 'I don't want to see just one of our men and one of theirs; I want to see our man, their man, and another one of ours'. Smith stuck to this basic formula for his entire coaching career.

Of course, there was the odd exception, like when there was a strong cross-breeze. In that case, he would instruct his defenders to kick to the 'dead', or defensive, side of the ground, and when the ball had been steadily centred, subtly move it into an advantageous position on the other side, the attacking side, where goalscoring was easier. But if the breeze eased or started to blow in the opposite direction, no player was empowered to change tack themselves – Smith would call the changes. The last thing he wanted was a divided approach where some players were doing one thing and the rest were doing the opposite.

The Maroons' forward line was an area of concern for Smith. In 1948 – the year before Smith arrived at Fitzroy – the Maroons' lightly-built, fast-leading full-forward Eddie Hart had finished third on the VFL goalkicking list with 61 goals – behind Geelong's Lindsay White (86) and Richmond's Jack Dyer (64). The next best Maroons were Ruthven (42), Coates (21) and Norm Johnstone (19). Smith knew only too well that he had to find more viable avenues to goal. The blueprint

---

[20] *The Sun* series, 1967.

to success was Melbourne's 1948 premiership side, which boasted eight players who had kicked 15 or more goals.

The pre-season form of Fitzroy, and its new coach, impressed many onlookers. Smith had successfully alternated between full-forward and centre half-forward with Hart, and provided his side with another much-needed source of goals. Crucially, he was a taller, stronger target in an attack mainly comprising small opportunists. The round one edition of *The Football Record* enthused: 'Maroons coach Norm Smith is in such good form that he is expected to revitalise the forward line, giving it the balance and drive it has lacked in recent years. With Eddie Hart alongside, they will be a problem for defenders. Their co-operation in practice games has been an outstanding feature.' Hec de Lacy told readers of *The Sporting Globe* that Smith was 'trying to create the same forward force around him at Fitzroy' as the one he had marshalled at Melbourne. 'It doesn't seem the same at the moment,' de Lacy wrote. 'But every now and again we see that beautiful cooperation that won for Melbourne the premierships of 1939-40-41 and 1948.'

Fitzroy began the 1949 season in far more impressive fashion than even the Demons had in 1948. Smith's coaching career got off to the perfect start, when he guided the Maroons to wins on each of the first three rounds, including consecutive one-point victories over quality opponents in Carlton and Collingwood (at Victoria Park). The forward set-up was flourishing, with Hart kicking 12 goals (3,6,3) and Smith kicking five (2,2,1) but creating other opportunities with slick handball, deft tap-ons and cunning use of space. Smith was not starring but he was certainly contributing. His opponent against Carlton had been 22-year-old, two-time premiership player Ken Hands, who shared the following recollection of the duel:

> Norm was playing at centre half-forward and I was centre half-back. It was blowing a gale at the Fitzroy ground – the wind was howling across to one side of the ground. Norm turned to me and said: 'I'll stand here and keep the wind off you.' Rubbish! While it sounded like he was doing a good deed, he was actually trying to get the advantage! I was awake to that one. Norm was very cunning.
>
> He was also a very methodical player. When he ran somewhere, and even when he *walked* somewhere, it was always done for a reason, with some plan in mind. Mentally, he never rested out on the field. He might have only been walking or even standing still, but he was very alert. As an opponent, he would keep you thinking and worrying about him the whole time. And he was always a physically hard player. His opponent needed to be smart, strong and fairly mobile.[21]

---

[21] Ken Hands. Interview with the author.

Despite a disappointing 12-point loss to an average Geelong side at home in round four, Smith got his players back on track with wins over the lowly Hawthorn and Footscray. Suddenly, the Maroons were 5-1 and outright second on the ladder – just a game behind Carlton, whose only loss had been inflicted by the Maroons. At this point, Smith's defection to Fitzroy was a roaring success – made all the more bittersweet by the fact his old club Melbourne was 2-4 and struggling.

A concern of Smith's, though, was the Maroons' poor last quarters. They had been outscored in the final term five times out of six. Smith's answer was to train his players even harder. It backfired. The following week against Richmond, the Maroons were competitive for a quarter before the Tigers piled on 8.7 to nothing in the second term on their way to an 81-point win at Punt Road. On a personal front, the match highlighted both the benefits and shortcomings of Norm Smith the veteran player. He played a lone hand up forward, kicking four of his side's nine goals, but he was now almost unable to compete with any confidence against capable, athletic opponents. Jack Toohey said Smith had particular problems handling Tiger wild man Don 'Mopsy' Fraser, a fellow redhead who was arguably the most feared player in the game:

> Norm was playing at centre half-forward on 'Mopsy' Fraser, and Mopsy was beating Norm. Norm was getting old and he couldn't keep up with him. At half-time (with Fitzroy 64 points down), Norm told me: 'Jack, you pick up Mopsy. I can't handle him; he's too young, too quick and too good for me. He's jumping all over the bloody place. You're younger; you can look after him'. Norm did that to me a couple of times. At Essendon one day he said: 'I want you to pick up (Essendon's champion full-forward John) Coleman.' I said: 'You must be crook on me, Norm'. He just laughed and said: 'Get on with it'.[22]

Smith's individual performance in attack was a rare highlight for Fitzroy fans in such a disappointing loss, but it meant nothing to the man himself. Alarm bells were ringing for the Maroons' coach, and they became even louder at quarter-time the next week when they trailed battling South Melbourne by 11 points at the Lake Oval. But the Maroons, inspired by eight goals from Eddie Hart, managed to save face with a scrappy 19-point win.

The scene was set for Smith to play against his old mates from Melbourne for the first time. It was a tough time for Smith, who was not looking forward

---

[22] Jack Toohey. Interview with the author.

to opposing men with whom he had forged such cherished bonds; men with whom he had won a remarkable premiership little more than eight months earlier; men who believed, as he did, that he should have been coaching them. But as well as he had managed to publicly mask his personal anguish, Smith failed miserably to contain his true feelings on the private front. On the morning of the match, Elza Barassi and 13-year-old Ron arrived at the Smith house to offer moral support and attend the clash with Norm and Marj. Barassi recalled:

> Norm said: 'Ronny, do you want to come for a drive with me; I'm going to see Mum'. I said: 'OK, Norm', so off we went in his little duck-mobile to his Mum's place, which wasn't far away. We stopped there for a cup of tea and a chat, then we got in the car and drove off. About a minute later we were back in the same spot. We just pulled in to Norm's Mum's driveway again and sat there. I looked across and Norm was just staring blankly ahead. Not a word was spoken. After a brief pause, we took off again. A minute later we were back there again. He was driving around in circles. This time I looked across at Norm for some kind of explanation and he was crying. This so-called tough, fearsome man was actually *crying*. I was only a kid – I didn't know what to do – but it was pretty obvious that he was hurting like hell that he had to play against his mates in a few hours' time. He was an emotional wreck. We nearly had a few accidents because Norm's mind was elsewhere, and he probably couldn't see past his tears.[23]

Smith's day lurched from bad to worse. Unbeknown to him, in the visitors' changeroom Melbourne coach Allan La Fontaine had hatched a plan to humiliate him in front of his home crowd. Demon midfielder George Bickford recalled: 'La Fontaine had given us strict instructions not to shake his hand or even acknowledge him. He wanted us to embarrass him. I thought that was unnecessarily cruel. I really felt sorry for Norm that day'.[24]

Although he accepted that almost anything goes on a football field, Smith was completely blindsided, shocked even, by crowd activity off it. Many Melbourne fans who had travelled to the Fitzroy ground expended great energy booing and heckling him. Smith's shock fermented into disgust, then hardened into anger. The fans who had fawned over him for so many years – and as recently as the previous October – bared what could only be described as misguided contempt. Smith later

---

[23] Ron Barassi. Interview with the author.
[24] George Bickford. Interview with the author.

confided: 'I pride myself on my loyalty to Melbourne, so that was pretty rough treatment.'[25] It was a harsh lesson in the fickle nature of fans.

Fitzroy's season also continued to take a fickle turn that afternoon. The Maroons entered the match with a 6-2 record – two games clear of the improving Demons, who had won their previous three games. Fitzroy was within eight points at the last change but went down by 22 points.

Despite recording an upset three-point victory over Essendon the next week and improving their record to 8-4, the Maroons were on the slide. They lost six of their last nine games to finish seventh with 10 wins – three games outside the final four. Smith simply said: 'I did not perform any miracles in my first year as coach'.[26] That may have been true, but the Maroons had not simply endured a form slump, as they had in 1948. They had encountered a bad run with injury, which started in round one when promising half-forward Eric Moore suffered a season-ending broken wrist, and was exacerbated by the loss of the likes of veteran ruckman Bert Clay, Eddie Hart (who had kicked 52 goals in the opening 12 rounds),[27] young star Bill Stephen (who still won Fitzroy's most determined player award) and utility Harold Shillinglaw crippling Smith's campaign for a first-up finals appearance.

To fill the vacancies, Smith had been forced to delve deep into the Maroons' stocks of youngsters – he blooded 10 new players – which prevented continuity and robbed the side of experience. But from a positive standpoint, the blooding process – which unearthed talented players like tough half-back flanker Jack Gaffney, on-baller Don Furness and another defender, Eddie Goodger – was an investment for the future.

Smith missed six matches with continuing hamstring troubles – in his absence, Ruthven proudly resumed the mantle of captain – but kicked 22 goals in his 13 appearances, including four in a 49-point win over South Melbourne in the final round. Despite playing just two-thirds of the season, Smith 'earned his keep on the field',[28] and even 'played a couple of *very* good games'.[29] He might not have played as much as he would have liked but the players still regarded him as a genuine, natural leader of men. Restricted by the increasing limitations and immobility of his body, Smith was forced to rely more on his considerable cunning than physical ability. He still used, to great effect, his old tactic of leading out, taking possession

---

[25] Related by Keith Carroll in an interview with the author.
[26] *Melbourne Truth* series, 1962.
[27] Eddie Hart still finished equal third with Geelong's Lindsay White on the league goalkicking table, behind Essendon's debutant century goalkicker John Coleman and North Melbourne's Jock Spencer (65).
[28] George Coates. Interview with the author.
[29] Bill Stephen. Interview with the author.

and handballing to teammates running past. He also opened paths for the likes of Hart, Ruthven (33 goals), Dick Kennedy (23) and Coates (20).[30] Jack Gaffney gave the following picture of a battle-weary Norm Smith:

> Norm was a very powerful man with big thighs and a big body, and he liked to play in front and he was hard to shift out of the way when he went for a mark. He was a good target to kick to - you always felt he would, at the very least, hold his own against his opponent. He was a great competitor - he never gave up - and he led by example. Norm tried to do everything that he asked us to do, which made it easy for us to follow him.[31]

Easy is a word rarely associated with Norm Smith's coaching methods. Those who played under him used words like 'hard', 'tough', 'uncompromising', 'stern', 'blunt', even 'cruel', but, more often than not, he was 'fair'. He was also 'honest' – brutally so. In fact, he believed that the two most important traits in coaching were frankness and honesty – and he felt a great sense of duty, of responsibility, and indeed a compulsion, to remain true to this belief. A favourite saying of Smith's was: 'I walk a straight line and I never deviate'.[32] It is doubtful if anyone could challenge him on this point.

Bill Stephen said a conversation with Smith – which was usually a one-way affair – could be a confronting experience, especially for younger players:

> When Norm spoke to you, he looked you very strongly in the eye - straight down the barrel - and he didn't take his eyes off you. And that was the case when you were just having a normal conversation with him, without copping a spray. You always had his full attention when he spoke to you. That was part of his honesty. He was quite nice to me, polite - hello-how-you-going type of thing. Deep down he was probably a little bit wary too because it was his first coaching stint.[33]

The 'sprays' became commonplace and were at times quite cutting. If Smith thought a player was not working hard enough at training or in a match, or had not run hard enough at the ball, or, worst of all, had pulled out of a contest, he let him know his feelings in no uncertain terms. The Maroons quickly discovered

---

[30] It was the first time in Fitzroy's 53 seasons in the VFL that they had boasted five players who had kicked 20 or more goals in a season.
[31] Jack Gaffney. Interview with the author.
[32] Bill Stephen. Interview with the author.
[33] Bill Stephen. Interview with the author.

Norm Smith's first rule of football, which went something along the lines of: 'Attack the ball with ferocity at *all* times. Don't, under *any* circumstances, shirk a physical clash. Don't even flinch. Otherwise, suffer the consequences'. This has always been – and always will be – the key tenet for success in the game, but Smith was perhaps more aggressive in his demand for it.

Smith had very definite ideas on the value of courage. For starters, every League player must have it. He estimated that 'League football is 70 percent guts. Split up the other 30 percent any way you like.'[34] Although he felt that 'every man's a squib at heart',[35] guts – or courage – 'isn't the absence of fear, but the mastery of it'. He had little time for players who allowed fear to dictate their actions. A favourite rebuke was: 'You look like Tarzan, but you're playing like Jane'. But that was reasonably tame. In a verbal sense, Smith tore them to shreds. But he did it in a loyal and protective way. 'I do not lie in my pep talks and I don't like outsiders listening in,' Smith declared. 'If a player is shirking, I'll tell him so and I won't spare him. (But) it is between myself, the team and the player. I do not like spectators tuning in because it can be very embarrassing for the player under fire.'[36]

Smith took the loyalty theme a step further by prohibiting players from criticising each other, or repeating any criticisms he had levelled behind closed doors. There were even occasions where he had blasted a player, and later overheard a teammate talking in a similarly disparaging way about the same player, and Smith defended him quite aggressively. 'His attitude was: "I can level criticism at a player, but not you",' Jack Gaffney said. 'And he would do you the courtesy of always telling you to your face. You never heard it second-hand from anyone. Even though he often gave a player a burst in a team setting, Norm always went straight to the source of his frustration.'[37] Jack Toohey vividly recounted one such Smith blast in 1949:

> At half-time one day, he kicked everyone out of the committee room so that it was just him and us players in there. He had a go at one of the players – I can't recall who it was. He said: 'There are 17 other blokes out there slaving their guts out for the team, yet here you are – you jibbed it! You've let the whole side down! *You let 'em down!*' We all froze. After half-time, we had 18 blokes running through brick walls and winning VCs, because we didn't want to be named as a squib!
>
> Most blokes who ever played the game have pulled out at some stage, but you just hoped it wasn't noticed by anyone. But nothing ever escaped Norm.

---

[34] Recalled by Alf Brown in *The Herald*, May 4, 1979.
[35] Newspaper report, 1965.
[36] *Melbourne Truth* series, 1962.
[37] Jack Gaffney. Interview with the author.

> He noticed *everything*. There was nowhere to hide. Norm set a high standard and it made us try to lift ourselves higher too. If you squibbed it, you wouldn't get a game. There weren't many who did anyway, because a lot of us had been to the war, where we had to show real courage.[38]

Smith defended his merciless style by explaining that he realised very early in his career that you can't get results from 'being kind or kidding' players, and that a coach can actually 'ruin' a player by adopting the easy approach and mollycoddling him,[39] rather than taking the less popular route and bluntly telling him exactly where he had erred. Smith also felt that self-deception was a particularly insidious trait, and he preached to his players sayings like: 'The best judge of your performance is you'; and: 'The biggest lie is the one you tell yourself'. The translation of which goes something like: 'If you don't go full-steam ahead, and only go 99 percent instead of 100 percent, there are no excuses, and there is nowhere to hide, so don't kid yourself, just cop the consequences and don't dare let it happen again'. Typically, Smith made no apologies for his methods:

> Are you being kind to a player when you go up to him, scratch his back and say, 'Come on, son, you can do better', when you know in your own heart the boy may be hanging out? He may be making an exhibition of himself and he may be getting himself into a position where he's not admired by his fellow men. Are you being honest when you let that boy continue playing that way? I don't believe so. You are more honest if you take him aside and tell him what you think is wrong. If this is ruthless or tactless, then I'm both. But this is the way I am.[40]

In later years, Smith provided another rounded insight on courage:

> The word 'jib' is a title that, if applied to a footballer, is ruinous to his career, yet I feel it is handed out far too indiscriminately, often by people without the experience of feeling the fear sometimes experienced by all league footballers. Having to stand your ground for a mark, knowing that a pack of players is descending on you, calls for the ultimate in courage. Although one may have moments of apprehension and fear, a coach demands that his players overcome these and develop the courage to stand their ground and take the mark. If you can't do this, it means you can't

---

[38] Jack Toohey. Interview with the author.
[39] *Midweek Magazine*, August 1964.
[40] *The Sun* series, 1967.

overcome your fear and show your true courage. It's important to remember the saying: 'You can't be a hero without having the feelings of fear'.[41]

But beneath the unforgiving exterior emerged a man who had more tools in his coaching kit-bag than mere fire-and-brimstone. Smith generally tried to convey the image that he was trying to implement the legendary Collingwood ethos that all players should be treated equally – with equal doses of honesty and bluntness – regardless of their background, experience and abilities. This was true… to a point. Jack Gaffney believed Smith treated players *differently*, and that he tailored the delivery of his message according to the personality of the individual:

> Norm was a great psychologist. He'd study the individual and he picked his mark. He knew he could roast certain players in front of the team and they would respond to that humiliation in the precise manner he was looking for – they would take their anger out on the opposition. But he knew that if he took that approach with others, they would just sulk and he'd get no result, so he took a gentler approach with those players and spoke quietly to them. He had the rare ability to get the best out of every player he came into contact with. Some of them hated him so much at times that they played well to spite him. But it was Norm who provoked them to perform. Without the roast, they mightn't have performed as well. One way or another, Norm inspired players. It was a real gift of his.[42]

Smith's explanation supported Gaffney's view. He once said: 'Psychology has always been a part of football. Only, in my playing days, we didn't call it psychology. We called it bullshit. Some players you have to bullshit to (to) get results'.[43] He also elaborated:

> Guidance, perhaps using the fatherly way, may have the desired effect. But if it doesn't, you've got to… come at him another way, perhaps hammering it into him… You needle them sometimes, you kid them other times; you lead them along, depending on the way they're playing… It's not an easy thing.[44]

---

[41] From an article by Ian McDonald titled 'Why we all miss Norm', published in *The Sporting Globe* on August 11, 1973, shortly after Smith's death.
[42] Jack Gaffney. Interview with the author.
[43] *Allsport Weekly*, August 2, 1973.
[44] *Midweek Magazine*, August 1964.

Smith's generally hard-edged methods were always going to put him on a collision course with certain people. For some, Smith could be *too* honest – or too scathing, depending on the viewpoint of the individual. His most vocal detractor at Fitzroy was emerging ruck star Alan 'Butch' Gale. Despite Gale's youth and inexperience – he had played just two games in his debut season of 1948 – he was 'his own man',[45] and it was almost inevitable that he would clash with Smith. George Coates elaborated on the rift:

> Norm was disappointed with Butch's attitude. Butch was the most mature young bloke I've met anywhere. He came to the club as a 17-year-old and he immediately carried himself like he'd been there forever. He was 17 going on 25. He bounced off the older fellas and treated them like they were young blokes. And he progressively went more that way. He was very brash, and that wasn't Norm's style. With Norm, you toed the line; and young blokes like Butch, no matter how good they were, had to earn respect; they weren't automatically given it. But Butch didn't like Norm's approach either. He felt that Norm went over the top with some of his ear-bashing. I never did though. What Norm gave was more often than not warranted. That was his style and the rest of us, besides perhaps only Butch, copped it and accepted it because we respected him so much. I can't recall Norm ever going crook and getting it wrong. In football clubs, there is always someone who doesn't like the coach, and in this case it happened to be Butch Gale.[46]

A decade after Smith's death, Gale revealed: 'Norm Smith and I had a running fight from the day we met… I deeply resented the way Norm embarrassed and humiliated (me).'[47] Their differences did not seem to affect Gale's form, however, with the cocky youngster playing 17 games in 1949 and winning Fitzroy's award as the 'most improved' player. His form was such that he was described in the Fitzroy annual report as follows: 'Not yet nineteen, but possessing the assurance of a veteran, his services to the club will be invaluable for many seasons'. But his running disputes with Smith brought question marks over his ability to accept authority and follow instructions. 'One day in particular,' Jack Toohey recalled, 'Butch took real offence to something Norm said to him. I didn't hear exactly what was said but they had a fair-dinkum crack at each other – a screaming match – behind closed doors.'[48]

---

[45] Bill Stephen. Interview with the author.
[46] George Coates. Interview with the author.
[47] Sutherland, Mike. Rod Nicholson and Stewart Murrihy, *The First One Hundred Seasons: Fitzroy Football Club 1883-1983*, Fitzroy Football Club, 1983.
[48] Jack Toohey. Interview with the author.

The young Norm Smith was so robust that his older brother Len called him 'Fatty', even into adulthood. He threw his weight around, too. His mother Ethel later remarked that her Norman was 'such a full-blooded kid' he was 'always wrestling some bigger boy'. *(Peter Smith)*

Victor Smith married Ethel Brown in North Fitzroy on April 15, 1911. They set up house at 318 Clarke Street in working-class Northcote, where they raised their children: Len (*back right*, 1912-67), Norm (*front right*, 1915-73) and Marj (1918-96). Vic was a sports fanatic who encouraged his sons to play any sport on offer. Norm Smith later surmised that his father 'must have started talking sport to me when I was still in the cradle'. *(Norma Harmes)*

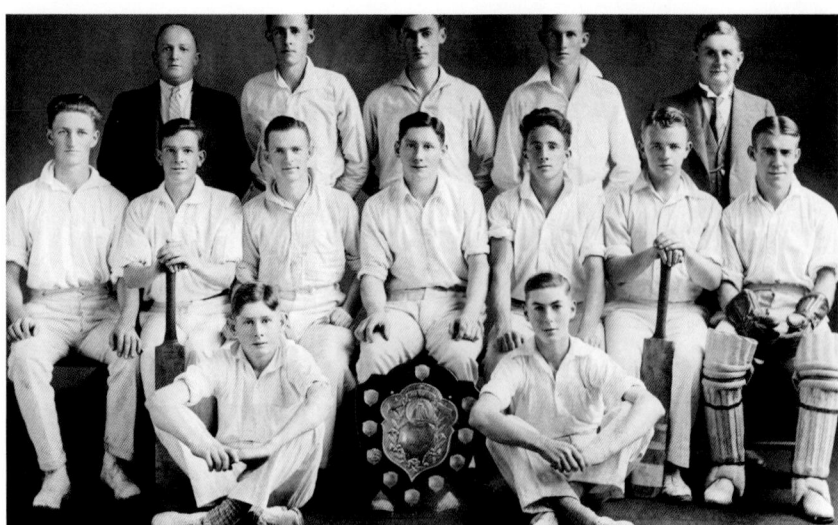

Vic Smith (*back row, far right*) was the founding vice-president of Dennis Cricket Club in Northcote in 1932. His sons were the club's two guns: Norm (*bottom left*) opening both the batting and bowling, while Len (*middle row, centre*) was a leg-spinner, short-leg specialist. Dennis played on a rough paddock near the Smith home. *(Dennis Cricket Club)*

Childhood mates become premiership heroes. Norm Smith, Ron Baggott (*left*) and Richie Emselle (*right*), seen here on a Melbourne Football Club trip in the late 1930s, were inseparable. The trio knew each other from their early teens in Northcote and reinforced their strong bond by playing together in the Demons' 1939-40-41 premierships. Smith and Baggott formed a lethal forward combination. *(Ken Emselle)*

A superb exponent of the drop-kick, Smith was capable of launching the ball prodigious distances. He was one of the few forwards of his era to favour the drop-kick for set shots, regardless of the angle or distance. He could actually 'bend' his kicks to suit the situation. *(Herald & Weekly Times)*

On October 19, 1940, just weeks before his 25th birthday, Smith married Marjorie ('Marj') Ellis at Wesley Church in Lonsdale Street, Melbourne. Marj, then 21, had originally dated another Melbourne footballer, Jack Maher. A loyal supporter of her husband, Marj rarely missed a football match Smith was involved in – either as a player or a coach – over the next 31 years. She was also a mother figure to the partners of players coached by Smith. *(Norma Harmes)*

Smith marking at training in 1937. This is the sight Melbourne fans became accustomed to – a fast, intelligent lead complemented by a reliable pair of hands. That he was such a strong mark was made more remarkable by the fact he had 'fractionally smaller hands than he should have had for a man of his size'. *(Herald & Weekly Times)*

Smith, the Melbourne captain, leads his side onto the MCG for the 1946 Grand Final against Essendon. The Demons were thrashed, but they got revenge two years later when they upset the seemingly invincible Bombers, with Smith arguably best-afield in both the drawn Grand Final and the replay. *(Melbourne Football Club Collection)*

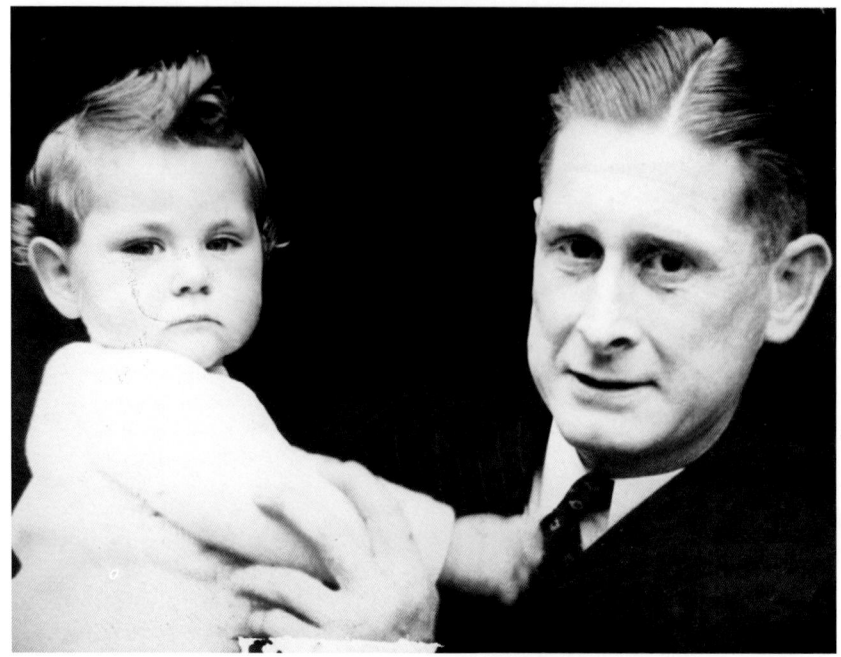

Smith with son Peter, who was born on September 22, 1947. Marj endured complications during her pregnancy and was warned against trying for more children. *(Peter Smith)*

After former skipper Allan La Fontaine pipped him for the Melbourne coaching job by one vote at the end of 1948, Smith took over an in-fighting Fitzroy. Under Smith, the Maroons failed to make the finals, finishing seventh, fifth and fifth respectively.

When Smith was in the midst of a heated debate, he was known to exclaim: 'I mightn't be right in what I say but I've got a bloody right to say it! And if I'm wrong, I'm not far wrong!' He was certainly 'right' where George Coates was concerned. Smith once said: 'I know what players can do and less than their best upsets me'[49] – a statement that Coates admitted was applicable to him in mid-1949:

> I played footy like an amateur – I loved just running around and getting a kick, and wasn't overly tough or courageous. But I made the Victorian side in 1949.[50] In my first couple of games back with Fitzroy, I did fairly well – or at least I thought so. But Norm took me into the boardroom at Fitzroy – that was probably the only private room we had at the club – and he said: 'What's wrong with your game?' I said: 'I thought I was going pretty well'. He said: 'No, you're not playing anywhere near as well as you were before you went away with the state side'. I said: 'Well I'm surprised to hear that. I've been named in the best players in the papers'.
>
> Norm said: 'Well I'm telling you you're not. You were selected in the state side for playing up to a certain standard each week – you can't let yourself slip below that standard. You won't if you want to play in my team anyway. Something you need to learn is to set your own standard. It doesn't matter what the papers say, and what the supporters say; if you set your own standard and you're honest with yourself, you'll know how well you're going. If not, I'll tell you. You know what your best is, I know what it is because you've displayed it, but I want it every week'.
>
> It was a fair ask. It was also a great lesson because after that I set my sights a bit higher and worked harder. Norm toughened my approach and made me more determined, and my game lifted accordingly.[51]

Although it was widely acknowledged that Norm Smith favoured no-one, he made the odd concession. Fitzroy hard man Norm Johnstone was notorious for being late to games and team meetings – he said: 'I wasn't late; I just wouldn't get there too early!' – but he was a rare exception to Smith's cast-iron guidelines. 'I knew what Norm was going to say,' Johnstone said, 'because his message was always the same to me – "Run straight through" – so I'd duck out to the toilet. Norm would sing out: "Come on, 'Johnno', get out here!" I'd call back: "Don't

---

[49] *Melbourne Truth* series, 1962.
[50] Besides George Coates, Fitzroy had three other Victorian representatives in 1949 – Reg Nicholls, Eddie Hart and Bert Clay.
[51] George Coates. Interview with the author.

worry about me; I know what I've got to do!" He had no problems with that. I think he put up with it because he realised what suited me best.'[52]

Likewise, Johnstone suited Smith as a player. While Smith demanded that his players overcome fear on the field, in Johnstone he boasted a human wrecking-ball who could instil great fear in opposition players. Smith wanted his players to be hard and tough at the ball, and he had a fascinating philosophy on retaliation – 'If you take it once, you will always take it, so come back as hard as you can immediately, but keep playing football at the same time'[53] – but the menacing presence of Johnstone enabled Smith to use aggression as an offensive weapon.

Johnstone, who won the Maroons' most consistent player award in 1949, revealed: 'In most games, and particularly if we were struggling and our blokes weren't getting the ball, Norm would tell me: "Get in there, Johnno, and knock a few blokes over. Rough 'em up a bit, and the other blokes will follow you". He wanted you to do it fairly of course. He never asked you to do anything dirty. You had to focus on the ball. If someone got in the way while you were going for the ball, that was their bad luck. I didn't get rubbed out anyway. I had a bit of speed and weight, and that was my natural game anyway. He'd usually have me at either centre half-forward or centre half-back, depending on how we were going, but either way I was coming straight through'.[54]

ŸŸŸŸŸŸŸŸŸ

On the six occasions Norm Smith was forced to coach from the sidelines in his first season, he found it to be an enlightening experience on several fronts. He learnt that a coach must put himself in the players' shoes and become completely absorbed, and emotionally involved, in the contest. He believed:

> Before the match you've got to become worked up. During the match you've got to feel that everything that's happening to them out there is happening to you, and, all in all, you become part and parcel of the team. I believe that this is the only way that anybody can coach a side. You can't be removed from it. If you try to be removed and you just take it casually, then I don't think that has the desired effect. But if the boys see that you're enthusiastic, your enthusiasm can become infectious and they take it from there.[55]

---

[52] Norm Johnstone. Interview with the author.
[53] *The Herald*, 1958.
[54] Norm Johnstone. Interview with the author.
[55] *Midweek Magazine*, August 1964.

The transition from captain-coach to non-playing coach also severely tested Smith's patience, and his ability to restrain himself. Despite his best attempts to act in a controlled manner, Smith admitted that he failed miserably. His emotions consumed him, and often boiled over, as he felt an overwhelming urge, a compulsion, to express himself. With his slicked-back red hair and almost permanently furrowed brow, Smith became easily recognisable to crowds as he sat on the bench, brooding, gesticulating, growling. He provided the following insight into his character transformation into what he termed 'that worrisome creature',[56] which he became as he called the shots from outside the boundary line:

> I have been described as a quiet redhead. (But) I'm far from quiet on that coach's bench. Somehow I'm a different person. In a match (as a player), I was always able to control myself. If you lose control of yourself, particularly up forward, you are playing right into your opponent's hands. (But) when I am sitting on that bench, I find it hard to restrain myself. You feel so helpless when you see mistakes being made and there is nothing you can do. So I just wait and get more and more excited... I do not see football as a spectacle. I cannot sit on the boundary and be casual. I have to watch tactics and most games are 100 minutes of agony. All the same, it is agony I enjoy.[57]

Smith increasingly took the 'agony' home with him, much to the frustration of his wife. Although Marj loved her football, she certainly did not enjoy her husband's company as much as usual now that he had become a VFL coach. Marj confided to several friends: 'Norm is terrible to live with in the football season.' Smith had always been intense about the game, but now that he was coaching, and as such was the individual most accountable for the team's performance, he accordingly took the intensity to another level. Smith spent considerable time on weeknights (although he often went to bed as early as 8pm), and Saturday mornings, studying and scheming for the next match, formulating possible teams and talking to players on the telephone. Although Marj later told a reporter that her husband 'didn't eat and sleep football', she knew this to be a white lie. Smith was obsessed with football, and it was an obsession that only intensified over the years.

It came back to honesty, and his unrelenting desire to be better. He felt it no use being honest with players if you were unable to give an honest self-assessment. 'You go home at night and analyse the things you have done (and), more often

---

[56] Craven, John (editor), *Football The Australian Way*, Lansdowne Press, 1969.
[57] *Melbourne Truth* series, 1962.

than not, if you are honest with yourself, you fail to measure up to the standard you set yourself.'[58]

When it came to coaching, Smith was never satisfied and always restless:

> I couldn't stop thinking about the coming game. I would start thinking about next week's game on the night the last one ended. All through the week the build-up would go on in my mind. Then on Friday night the thoughts and ideas would come into my brain while I slept. Into my subconscious, I suppose you could say. They would build up and build up and my mind would be full of the game when I woke up... I would be tense on the morning of the game. And just before it started I would be very edgy, very toey.[59]

Despite his pre-match anxiety, and his strong sense of morality, Smith still found time for a light-hearted giggle – and a rare risqué remark – before a match. Jack Toohey recalled: 'You'd walk into the ground with your wife and Norm might playfully say to her: "You didn't let him take liberties with you last night, did you? I need him to be full of beans today." But nobody ever took offence to him because that wasn't how it was intended'.[60]

This kind of banter, however, was uncommon for Smith. Marj told friends that he would become so tense and highly-strung that there was no point mentioning football to him from the time the team had been announced on a Thursday night. She felt she could talk to him about other things, though, except on Saturday mornings, when his mind was so consumed with football that she decided it was best to leave him to his own devices. Conversation, even basic small-talk, just made him irritable, if in fact he listened at all. Smith was so edgy on the morning of a match that he could rarely even stomach breakfast.

While Marj no doubt would have preferred Smith to have been more pleasant and easy-going during the winter months, she accepted it because she loved him and naturally wanted him to be happy. She also knew him – and what made him tick – perhaps better than anyone, and, begrudgingly or otherwise, she understood how important football was to him. She also realised early on that Norm was particularly good at this coaching caper and that it was likely he would continue to coach on a part-time basis for at least a few years to come. She unselfishly decided to take the path of least resistance; to support her husband in his pursuit of success; to go along for the roller-coaster ride and embrace it as best she could.

---

[58] *Melbourne Truth* series, 1962.
[59] *The Sun* series, 1967.
[60] Jack Gaffney. Interview with the author.

While Smith's moods were prone to fluctuate with the team's performances, Marj remained balanced in her outlook. She was a symbol of emotional stability and even-mindedness in Smith's cut-throat world of VFL coaching. She became even more than that, according to Bill Stephen:

> Marj was Norm's receptionist at home. If you rang to speak with Norm, you had to get past Marj first. Norm would never answer the phone first. And on a Saturday morning there was about a two-hour block when he could not be disturbed. From about 9am to 11am, he'd sit down and go into a deep-thinking mode about that afternoon's match. By then, he'd have the teams, and he'd have a fair idea of how the opposition would line up through the newspapers – back then, teams lined up pretty much the way the appeared in the paper; tricks hadn't really come into it then – and he'd finalise what he wanted from the players that day. Marj was under strict instructions to ensure nothing interrupted that time Norm had to think to himself. No-one was allowed in the house, and he required virtually dead silence. If you rang during that two-hour period, even if it was an emergency, you'd have to wait until later. Marj manned the phones and manned the door, and made sure nothing got through. She was so loyal to Norm, and such a great support to him.[61]

For Marj, things would return to normal on a Saturday night. 'Normal' was actually the exception to the rule in football season, because Saturday nights – and to a lesser extent, Sundays – were the only times of the football week that Smith allowed himself to relax. Although he could be a 'cantankerous, aggressive and intolerant character' for some time after a match,[62] he generally composed himself by the time he had showered and entered the clubrooms. Over a few beers, Smith would congratulate, or commiserate with, opposition coaches and players. He would pick their brains, and have his picked, and quickly earned a reputation for being – as went one his guiding mottoes – 'humble in victory and gracious in defeat'. As South Melbourne great Bob Skilton would later explain: 'There was no worse loser than Norm Smith, but there was also no better loser'.[63] Although a loss might prompt him to unleash a vitriolic tirade at his players, he soon changed modes, and would say something like: 'We can't change the result, so let's go and have a drink with the opposition and show them the respect they deserve'.

---

[61] Bill Stephen. Interview with the author.
[62] Barrie Bretland, *The Sun*, Monday July 30, 1973.
[63] Bob Skilton. Interview with the author.

These 'after-matches', particularly those after home games at the Brunswick Street Oval, were great bonding sessions. Under the six o'clock closing laws, these sessions also provided a venue for players to have a few drinks on a Saturday night.[64] The Maroons boasted a tight-knit social scene, which Smith wholeheartedly embraced and seamlessly blended into. 'Norm loved winning and success, but he also loved the social side of football,' Bill Stephen said. 'He loved nothing better than celebrating a win with the players and their partners. But even when the side lost, he liked to ease the disappointment by socialising with them.'[65]

Jack Gaffney said Smith was a staunch believer that players should stick together at every opportunity: 'He felt that in that relaxed setting after matches we could gain something from one another's company, and learn about each other as people, which would draw us all closer together and help us out on the ground. And Norm wasn't only interested in encouraging interaction between the players. He loved everyone being together on a Saturday or Sunday night, and that included the women'.[66]

On these occasions – with baby Peter being looked after by his Aunt 'Dorry' (Marj's sister Dorothy) – people saw a different Norm Smith to the drill-sergeant they became accustomed to during the week. Later in the night, as the function became a dance, Smith would drop his guard, albeit ever so slightly, in the company of his players and their partners. It was at these times, when Smith 'let his hair down'[67] over a few ales, that people caught a rare glimpse of the man behind the football tyrant. His players discovered that he was great company, and far removed from his abrupt coaching persona. Jack Toohey was one of a number of players who were quite taken with him:

> He was quite the opposite to what people perceived. He wasn't the rough 'n ready fella that people thought he was, and liked to say he was. He was very likeable, loveable even. He was a paternal fella, who cared for you and was very wise. So was Len. Norm wasn't from the country, but he was very countrified. Country people are generally very warm, friendly, modest and genuine – and that was Norm. He had an inner charm that drew people to him. Sure, he'd call a spade a spade, but he was gentle at heart. He called me 'Jack-a-boy', and I called him 'Knackers'.

---

[64] From 1915 to 1966, Australian hotels, by law, had to close by 6pm.
[65] Bill Stephen. Interview with the author.
[66] Jack Gaffney. Interview with the author.
[67] Bill Stephen. Interview with the author.

He wasn't a Christian but he had great Christian qualities. He was a quality human being; a fine, moralistic man. The players and the women respected him because he was a gentleman.[68]

Margaret Clay, the wife of ruckman Bert Clay, recalled: 'It was lovely having Norm at the club. He was very popular with everyone. You were never "just a wife" or "just a girlfriend" to him – he saw everyone as an important part of the place. He always had a hello and a bit of a chat with you. And he got along very well with my Bertie'.[69]

George Coates was similarly captivated by Smith's presence: 'Everything about Norm was impressive – except when he was upset about somebody. But underneath the fiery exterior, he was really a cool customer. He had such a good rapport with most people. He had that sort of air about him where he bonded people to him. He gave you the feeling you were in the hands of a good man'.[70]

Smith soon became one of the ringleaders in the social shenanigans, all the while conducting himself in a responsible manner. 'Norm led by example in all areas of his life and he expected you to follow him,' Gaffney said. 'He was a man of character and he instilled that character into his players. He would say: "You have a responsibility to lead by example and be decent people and behave properly." If you stepped out of line, he'd tell you.'[71]

Smith also enforced the odd social-night custom, such as making each player sing a song of their choice. His own choice was either *The Barrow Boy* or *Champagne Charlie*, and often he sang both, numerous times over, prompting even some of the women to say: 'What about a change of song?' Towards the end of the evening, some players would have the alcohol-induced confidence to 'act out' the lyrics. It was entertaining, and amusing, for all in attendance.

Often, the festivities didn't end with the dance at the football club. Smith usually coaxed Marj into allowing him to invite some revellers back to their house to 'kick on'. These gatherings were much smaller and more intimate, but just as hazily memorable, as Coates recalled. 'There would be a bunch of us sitting on the floor with our backs to the wall, drinking beer and talking about footy until the wee hours of the morning,' Coates said. 'Norm would be the centre of it all because he had such a big personality. He was a wonderful character; so accommodating.'[72]

---

[68] Jack Toohey. Interview with the author.
[69] Margaret Clay. Interview with the author.
[70] George Coates. Interview with the author.
[71] Jack Gaffney. Interview with the author.
[72] George Coates. Interview with the author.

After the traditional 'pleasant Sunday morning' session – during which players would receive a rub-down and 'rehydrate' with beer – the Smiths regularly invited the senior players, and partners, back to their Pascoe Vale home, where the socialising would continue from about 4pm to 11pm. Young Ron Barassi also took the opportunity to ride his push-bike over from West Preston and soak up the intimate football atmosphere. Occasionally, Barassi recalled, 'Melbourne players like Shane McGrath and Fred Fanning... (would also) drop in. There would inevitably be a goalkicking competition between the clothes-line and the corner of the garage. Is it any wonder that I grew up to be a football fanatic myself?'[73]

Bill Stephen's wife Betty marvelled at the Smiths' generosity. 'Somehow we'd all squash in there, and Marj would prepare salads and cook roast legs of lamb for dinner,' she said. 'They were really wonderful get-togethers, and went way beyond what anyone could have expected them to do. They just loved company.'[74] Bill Stephen said the Smiths were 'great at encouraging involvement' and admired their thoughtfulness to 'include shy people and make them feel part of it'.[75]

Marj had been welcomed by the Fitzroy women on her first visit to the clubrooms for a Christmas function in December 1948. Margaret Clay recalled:

> I still remember Marj arriving with Norm and Peter, who was the most beautiful baby in the pusher. Of course, Marj was naturally very shy on her first time at the club, so I went over to her and said: 'Would you like to come and sit with us (wives and girlfriends) over here?' Marj said: 'I'd love to. Thank you'. That was the start of our friendship, which lasted about 50 years until Marj passed away.[76]

The Smiths also continually overwhelmed people with their inclusive nature, as Gaffney recalled: 'Norm and Marj gave everything to the people they were associated with. (In August 1950), they threw a 21st birthday party for me at their home in Shedden Street, Pascoe Vale. That was just a wonderful gesture. You never expect those kinds of things, but in another way you came to expect it because that's the kind of people Norm and Marj were. They were wholesome people, and a very loyal couple, who gained great satisfaction from doing things with, and for, others'.[77]

Consciously or not, Marj became a mother figure to the Fitzroy women, their unofficial leader. 'If any of the girls was having trouble, Marj would do her bit to

---

[73] *The Sun*, August 1973.
[74] Betty Stephen. Interview with the author.
[75] Bill Stephen. Interview with the author.
[76] Margaret Clay. Interview with the author.
[77] Jack Gaffney. Interview with the author.

help without interfering,' Betty Stephen said. 'But she did it in such a quiet way that it probably looked like Norm did a lot of it.'

While Marj was immensely proud of her husband's growing achievements in football, it is little known that he also admired her sporting achievements. Smith told anyone who listened that his unassuming, quietly-spoken wife had been a champion badminton player in her youth. It is believed that Marj actually won a state title. 'But Marj would never tell you that,' Betty Stephen said. 'She might say: "I played a bit of badminton", but she wouldn't say she was the Victorian champion. She played into her fifties.'[78]

The Smiths had an enormous influence on life at Fitzroy Football Club. The Maroons' annual report noted 'a very marked improvement... in the harmonious relationship between officials, players and staff... We feel sure that the great team spirit... will lift the club to unprecedented heights'.[79] The annual report enthused that while the Maroons had failed to make inroads in terms of ladder position, there was 'a spirit of optimism' around the club. 'Although we missed a place in the final four,' it stated, 'our confidence to reach that goal next year is unshaken.' The Fitzroy committee told its members of its satisfaction with its first-year coach:

> The appointment of Mr Norm Smith to the position of captain and coach for seasons 1949-50 was a wise one, and should materially benefit the club, not only for the term of his appointment, but for many years to come. Enjoying the full confidence and support of all players, his leadership has been no small factor in creating that determined team spirit, so evident during the season. Undaunted by the serious loss of star players, your coach has never shown the slightest sign of despair, and faced up to the unenviable task of welding together a balanced team combination from the material available with such enthusiasm that not only inspired the players in his charge, but all actively connected with the club... and we take this opportunity to express our thanks to the (Melbourne) committee... for their unselfish attitude and sportsmanship in granting permission to Norman to accept the position of coach to our club.[80]

Len Smith also received a mention for his efforts with the thirds. Incidentally, Len had enlisted Arthur Ireland – a mate of his and Norm's from Dennis

---

[78] Betty Stephen. Interview with the author. Peter Smith can also recall, as a boy in the 1950s, his parents playing as a mixed doubles combination in a mid-week badminton competition at Miller's ropeworks.
[79] Fitzroy Football Club *Annual Report*, 1949.
[80] Fitzroy Football Club *Annual Report*, 1949.

Cricket Club – as his team manager. The annual report stated: 'Mr. Len Smith… did a remarkably good job with the material that was available.'

🏆🏆🏆🏆🏆🏆🏆🏆🏆

Norm Smith knew he was 'past it' as a footballer. He also felt he had made a natural and relatively seamless transition to coaching. The next logical progression in his mind was to retire as a player and focus entirely on coaching. He stated his case to the Fitzroy committee, explaining the futility of trying to play on with chronic hamstring problems, and the benefits a non-playing coaching role would reap. But the men on Fitzroy's committee would not hear of it. They had appointed him as *captain*-coach for two seasons, and prevailed upon him to honour the deal and at least attempt to play in 1950. On those terms, a man of such honour and integrity as Norm Smith felt a sense of duty to pull on the boots for another season.

But Smith did not want to simply make up the numbers. He decided to get as fit as his weary body, and failing hamstrings, would allow. He approached one of his most talented young players, Bill Stephen, for help. Smith had already done Stephen a favour. The 22-year-old lived in Normanby Avenue, Thornbury – which was on Smith's way home from the Fitzroy ground – and so, at some stage during the 1949 season, Smith offered to drop him off at home after training. Stephen gratefully accepted, and so started a friendship that would remain strong for the duration of Smith's life. On those twice-weekly rides in Smith's little home-made utility, the pair discussed football and a genuine master-and-apprentice relationship evolved.

In the summer of 1949-50, the master asked the apprentice if he would like to play squash with him once a week until the 1950 season started. Stephen thought it such a good proposal that it became a Monday night summer tradition for the pair for the next 'seven or eight years'.[81]

Even on the squash court, Smith continued his tough brand of coaching. And, of course, he was so hell-bent on winning that he pushed gamesmanship to the absolute limit. Another Fitzroy player, George Coates, also joined them on occasions. Smith was, according to Coates, 'a big fella with a big stretch' and 'mighty hard to beat'.[82] It was yet another example of there being no such thing as a 'social' game of anything if Norm Smith was involved. The initial idea might have been to get together – or in this case, get fit – but once there, he was serious. During these hour-long sessions in the hot-box of the squash court, literally no

---

[81] Bill Stephen. Interview with the author.
[82] George Coates. Interview with the author.

quarter was asked and none was given. 'They were tremendously competitive games of squash – battles, really,' Stephen said.[83] Such was the last-man-standing nature of these contests that it was not uncommon for them – i.e., Stephen and Coates – to walk off the court at the end of the match, drenched in not only sweat but also blood. 'Claret' ran freely from their noses, and they also wore assorted grazes and bumps – the result of 'accidental' backhanders and the like – while black-and-blue welts appeared on various parts of their bodies after their manic opponent had drilled the ball into them. Stephen recalled:

> Norm would often tell me: 'You're not callous enough. You need to become more callous.' He didn't think I had enough killer in me. He'd put his foot out to trip me, or put his elbow out to try to put me off. But I wouldn't look at him; wouldn't even acknowledge it. I'd just jump his leg, or dodge his elbow, and keep playing the game. I didn't retaliate or try to return the favour either. He obviously wanted to win but he was probably also testing my character to see if I could take it. It never affected our friendship though. We were always firm friends.[84]

Coates, too, was taken aback – although not entirely surprised – by Smith's ferocity on the squash court:

> Norm would take the centre of the court and he'd hold onto that position with everything he had, because if you do that you control the game and your opponent struggles to get back into the point. He made you realise that if you were going to hit the ball, you were going to have to pay a price for it. It was very difficult to get past him without getting whacked – either with the racquet or the ball. If you got in front of him, between him and the wall, look out. WHACK! He'd belt the ball into you to get you out of the road and make you think twice about doing it again. It was a legitimate tactic, quite within the rules – but a tough one though.
>
> If he dropped the ball in short and you tried to get past him to the ball, he would make it very difficult. He'd also have a big back-swing, so you'd have to watch out for that too. His racquet would be flailing about, but if you didn't go for it, you knew that he knew that you knew you'd shirked it. He was merciless. But you just accepted that that was just Norm. Either you played to his rules or you didn't play at all. It was his way of toughening blokes up, and winning.[85]

---

[83] Bill Stephen. Interview with the author.
[84] Bill Stephen. Interview with the author.
[85] George Coates. Interview with the author.

Stephen didn't beat Smith for three years. 'He wasn't the type to let someone win for the sake of it,' Stephen said. 'Wins had to be earned, and if you were going to beat him you knew you'd have to battle like mad to do it.'[86] But Stephen eventually had his day, recalling: 'We'd pre-arranged to play our regular game of squash one Christmas Eve, but that day he'd had a few beers at a luncheon. I took advantage of the fact he was a bit under the influence and I beat him. I didn't let him go. Maybe he'd finally made me a bit more callous!'

Smith employed his engineering expertise in squash – he advised his inexperienced opponents: 'Don't hit the side wall first; it takes the pace off the ball. Hit the front wall first and angle it to the side wall'[87] – and also used it in football. He memorised the dimensions of every ground and was aware of the unique characteristics of each. In team meetings – which he described as 'not a discussion group with the players contributing, but a lecture that… (I) alone give' – he educated his players on spatial matters like 'Hawthorn with its narrow wings, (and) Footscray with its cemetery corner (or 'dead' pocket),' and, although it had no connection to engineering, 'even Collingwood with its celebrated grandstand supporters'.[88] Stephen said:

> Norm knew how deep the pockets were and the best spots to have shots at goal; and it would vary from ground to ground. Particularly at the MCG, where the breeze tends to swirl around. He always thought the Members' Stand side (on the northern side of the ground) was the best place to kick goals from. Logic said it was best to attack on that side because it was protected by the stand, but Norm had also worked out that it was a shorter distance home because the goals weren't perfectly central – they were a bit off-centre. He was highly attuned to little things like that, which could make a big difference, and he was absolutely driven to exploit them.

Stephen added: 'While Norm was ruthless in sport, he wasn't ruthless in life. When it came to winning and getting to the top, he was the most ruthless individual imaginable, but he had a lot of compassion. I know for a fact he was financially helping people out. He did things like pay school fees for children of ex-teammates who had either died or fallen on hard times, and he helped their widows. When I think of Norm Smith, words like generous and compassionate come to mind as well.'[89]

---

[86] Bill Stephen. Interview with the author.
[87] Bill Stephen. Interview with the author.
[88] Norm Smith's personal notes for a speech he made while on a football trip to Western Australia in 1957.
[89] Bill Stephen. Interview with the author.

COACH OF FITZROY [1949-51]

🏆🏆🏆🏆🏆🏆🏆🏆🏆

The 'spirit of optimism' at Fitzroy intensified after the Maroons produced a magnificent performance against reigning premier Essendon in the 1950 season-opener. In the Bombers' most recent outing, the 1949 Grand Final, they had pummelled Carlton by a then-record 73 points. A journey to the Brunswick Street Oval was expected to produce a similarly dominant display from the VFL heavyweight, which had played off for the flag in seven of the previous nine seasons and claimed three premierships. But the Maroons – with Norm Smith showing the benefits of his off-season fitness regime – were undaunted by the reputation of their opponent. The home side led by a point at quarter-time and trailed by 14 points at half-time, but remained within striking distance until the final siren signalled a six-point win to eventual premier Essendon. In 1950, very few sides would come so close to toppling the Bombers.

Optimism quickly turned to despair. The Maroons suffered a 42-point belting from Collingwood at Victoria Park – the game was over at half-time when they trailed by 41 points – and a 10-point loss to Richmond at Punt Road. Although they recovered with big wins at home over the two bottom sides, South Melbourne (by 66 points) and Hawthorn (81 points), it was mere papering over the cracks. Fitzroy won just two of its next seven matches to slump to 4-8. The most damning indictment was that their wins had been against four of the eventual bottom five sides. Their finals chances appeared over. Even if they won their last six games, they would finish with just 10 wins. Just once before in an 18-round season had a team made the finals with such a meagre tally of victories.[90]

Once again, injury had cruelled the Maroons' finals hopes. At one point in the opening rounds, they had just 16 fit players to choose from and had to bring in others to fill gaping holes left by the likes of big men in Bert Clay and Butch Gale, star full-back Vic Chanter, Harold Shillinglaw and Norm Smith. But with players returning as the season progressed, and with the pressure off, the Maroons won the last six games of the 1950 season – by an average of 23 points – but missed finals by 13.9 percent. (Geelong made the four with 10 wins.) Most encouragingly from a future perspective, the Maroons played their best football in the last two rounds, upsetting finals-bound Melbourne by five points, and inflicting a 24-point defeat on eventual Grand Finalist North Melbourne. It was the Kangaroos' first loss at the Arden Street Oval since round two, 1949. The 'Roos had won their previous 17 matches there by an average of 28 points.

---

[90] Collingwood finished fourth at the end of the 1908 home-and-away season with just 10 wins.

Norm Smith played just four games and kicked four goals in 1950. He played the first two rounds before tearing one of his troublesome hamstrings and missing the next six matches. He returned in round nine but called it quits after round 10. 'He had to give it away,' Bill Stephen said. 'He said: "It's no good." He realised he couldn't go on because his body wouldn't go any more for him.'[91]

When Smith retired as a player, he was equal 17th on the all-time games list:

MOST VFL GAMES – as of round 10, 1950	
312	Jack Dyer (Richmond)
309*	Dick Reynolds (Essendon)
306	Gordon Coventry (Collingwood)
294	Jack Titus (Richmond)
265	Arthur Olliver (Footscray)
263	Percy Bentley (Richmond)
262	Vic Thorp (Richmond)
261	Jock McHale (Collingwood)
253	Harry Collier (Collingwood)
249	Frank Curcio (Fitzroy)
245	Reg Hickey (Geelong)
239*	Phonse Kyne (Collingwood)
236	Rod McGregor (Carlton)
234	Percy Wilson (Collingwood)
232	George Todd (Geelong)
230	Dick Lee (Collingwood)
227	**Norm Smith (Melbourne/Fitzroy)**
227	Jack Graham (South Melbourne)
227	Syd Coventry (Collingwood)

Denotes still playing at the time.

As a non-playing coach, Smith seemed constantly agitated on the sidelines. One of the more humorous sources of his agitation was utility Ken Ross. 'A bit of a wag',[92] Ross was a superb athlete but an unreliable kick. One day he marked within range of goal and shocked all at the ground – particularly his coach – when he put the ball on the ground and set up for a place-kick. Place-kicks were almost extinct by then, and Smith certainly wasn't calling for their rebirth. 'Norm was nearly having a fit at what he was seeing,' Stephen said.

---

[91] Bill Stephen. Interview with the author.
[92] Bill Stephen. Interview with the author.

'He screamed out: "Tell him to kick it, not to *place*-kick it!" Kenny picked it up and kicked it normally. I don't think he was game to go through with a place-kick.'[93]

Even Stephen himself – the loyal protégé of Smith's – became a subject of the coach's frustration. With just three rounds left, Stephen – arguably the best back-pocket in the game – was leading *The Herald's* £100 best player award. The prospect of more votes loomed when the Maroons fronted up to the winless bottom side Hawthorn for their round 16 clash at Glenferrie Oval. Hawks coach Bob McCaskill pulled a surprise move when he assigned his own regular back-pocket player, Norm Black, the task of nullifying Stephen. Current AFL sides often use 'defensive forwards', but this ploy was relatively unheard of in 1950. Black – who was given the now politically-incorrect nickname of 'Nigger' – was instructed to stand on the boundary line to not only drag Stephen away from the play but also to separate him from his great defensive ally, Vic Chanter. Stephen recalled his predicament:

> I stood with Black on the boundary line and thought to myself: 'If he doesn't move, I'm not going to get a kick. How am I supposed to win the Herald award, and the £100, if I don't get a kick?' So I started to sneak in a bit to try to get a kick, thinking: 'He (Black) isn't going to get the ball out there.' But at half-time, in front of everyone, Norm tore shreds off me. He basically said I was being selfish and undisciplined. He said: 'I don't care where he stands! You bloody well stand next to him! Got that?!' I didn't get a kick in the second half either and I never won *The Herald* award – I was runner-up three times![94]

Stephen – who could 'justly be claimed as the No. 1 back-pocket player of the League'[95] – enjoyed a landslide win in Fitzroy's best-and-fairest count, and was one of the favourites for the 1950 Brownlow Medal. But he had to be satisfied with 12 votes as Allan Ruthven – who had taken over the captaincy from Smith – became the Maroons' sixth Brownlow Medallist. Ruthven received 21 votes, to finish three clear of Geelong star Fred Flanagan, and a further vote clear of three other players – Footscray's pocket battleship Charlie Sutton and the 1948 winner, Richmond ruckman Bill Morris. Ruthven was to be one of just two players to win a Brownlow Medal under Norm Smith.[96] Apart from that, the next-best Brownlow placing by

---

[93] Bill Stephen. Interview with the author.
[94] Bill Stephen. Interview with the author.
[95] Fitzroy Football Club *Annual Report*, 1950.
[96] The other was South Melbourne midfielder Peter Bedford in 1970.

one of Smith's players was equal fourth (which was achieved by three players – Denis Cordner in 1955, and Ron Barassi and John Beckwith in 1956). It was an indication of Smith's focus: it was all about the team, never the individual.

Jack Gaffney largely attributed Ruthven's Brownlow success to his belated acceptance of Smith's demand for intensity at training. 'Norm rode the Baron that hard at training,' Gaffney said, 'that eventually the message sank in and he became fitter than he'd ever been, and the results of Norm's methods were there for all to see in the Baron's performances that year.'[97]

Smith believed much of the credit for his skipper's medal win had to go to veteran ruckman Bert Clay. Smith said: 'Clay was such a terrific ruckman that Ruthven could run anywhere and call for the ball and he'd turn himself inside out to palm it to him and make him look good.'[98]

Although Smith was delighted with Ruthven's achievement, he must have also been a little bemused. In late July, Stephen and Ruthven had been members of the all-conquering Victorian side – coached by Checker Hughes – in the 'wet' carnival in Brisbane. Ruthven had struggled to that point, compounded by the fact he was 'half-a-stone overweight',[99] but after playing four games in 14 days on grounds made heavy by constant monsoonal rain, the champion left-footer shed the excess flab and hit career-best form. 'Baron dominated the second half of the season,' Stephen said. 'I can imagine Norm would have been thinking: "If only the Baron had trained harder earlier he might have played well the whole season and we'd have been better off – we might have made the finals".'[100]

Smith's two seasons at the Brunswick Street Oval had not gone to plan. He appeared to have players of sufficient quality to play finals football, but he had been unable to lift the Maroons into the final four in either season. It was widely acknowledged that he had been forced to contend with a mounting injury list – a factor that even gained understanding from a Fitzroy committee that was becoming increasingly impatient for September action. The committee reappointed Smith for a third season. This time there would be no excuses.

YYYYYYYYY

Norm Smith always said what he meant, and, as many Fitzroy players attested, he *always* meant what he said. But, on the odd occasion, he still used reverse

---

[97] Jack Gaffney. Interview with the author.
[98] Related by Keith Carroll in an interview with the author.
[99] Bill Stephen. Interview with the author.
[100] Bill Stephen. Interview with the author.

psychology with his players. An early example of this was Smith's treatment of half-back flanker Jack Toohey in the pre-season of 1951.

Toohey and Smith became good mates soon after Smith's arrival at Fitzroy, but their association was interrupted when Toohey was forced out of VFL football with a shoulder that dislocated too easily and too often. Toohey took a coaching job up at Cobram in the Murray league in 1950 and got through the season unscathed. At the age of 25, he decided to attempt a VFL comeback at Fitzroy, and Smith agreed to give him a trial. Toohey recalled:

> Norm said: 'Jack-a-boy, I doubt very much whether you'll make it back. It's very rare that a bloke leaves League football and gets back'. He was testing whether I was fair dinkum or not; and he was throwing me a challenge. Some blokes might have pulled the pin there and then, but he must have known how I'd respond to that kind of comment. And he took that hard line with me even though I was one of his best mates at Fitzroy. He was always very good at drawing that line and deciding when to be your mate and when to be your coach. I played OK in the practice matches and when the sides were selected for the first game, he said: 'Jack-a-boy...' – and there was a pause – 'you've made it back; you're in.'[101]

Fitzroy was back too. The Maroons were the only undefeated side after four rounds – they won their games by an average of 22 points, while conceding a total of just 34 goals – to extend their winning sequence from 1951 to 10. They had claimed the prized scalps of Geelong and Footscray at home, and also recorded victories against the struggling St Kilda and Melbourne. In the four-goal win over the Demons at the MCG, Norm Smith displayed a touch of cunning that was so subtle it would have been noticed by very few who played the game that day, and even fewer who watched from the stands. But one man who did was Smith's former team-mate Noel McMahen, who had developed into a tough half-back flanker:

> Norm put Donny Furness on me, which was a very astute but sneaky move. Norm knew that Donny was my younger cousin and I wouldn't hit him because I wasn't allowed to. Donny would whack me and kick me without any fear of reprisal, and I just had to put up with it, because my mother wouldn't let me hit 'little Donny'.[102]

---

[101] Jack Toohey. Interview with the author.
[102] Noel McMahen. Interview with the author.

A positional move in round five, however, had some Fitzroy, players, officials and supporters none-too-subtly questioning Smith's sanity.

In the week leading up to that match against Carlton at Princes Park, Smith approached his star back pocket, Bill Stephen, and said: 'You've got too much skill to be playing in the back pocket. I'm going to try you at half-forward. How do you feel about that?' Stephen was a consummate team man who would always do as his coach requested. He had also been a forward in his junior days, so he agreed to go ahead with the experiment. When the switch became public knowledge, it caused a mini-furore. The VFL had several high-class full-back/back pocket duos – Geelong had Bruce Morrison and Bernie Smith, Footscray had Herb Henderson and Wally Donald, while Fitzroy had Vic Chanter and Bill Stephen.

'The committee were up in arms and the Fitzroy fans went mad,' Stephen said. 'They were saying: "What the hell is Smithy doing?!" Vic Chanter was quite upset about it as well – upset enough to have a go at Smithy before the game about breaking up our combination.'

Stephen kicked two goals on his cousin, Jack Brown, but admitted that the move 'wasn't successful'. After just one game, Smith reluctantly aborted his plan for Stephen, to the relief of all at Fitzroy, including Stephen himself, who 'returned to the back-pocket and stayed there happily ever after'.

However, Stephen believed it would have worked if he had not had a lifelong hip restriction, which did not allow him to run with any pace, or stretch out with his left leg, over more than about 20 metres. 'It wasn't that Norm's gut instincts were wrong because, all things being equal, I would have been able to play at half-forward because I knew how to play the position; it's just that I physically couldn't,' Stephen said. 'My hip wouldn't allow me to play in positions where you had to be continually running. Norm was naturally disappointed, but he quickly accepted it and moved on.'[103]

The clash with the Blues produced an even bigger disappointment – the Maroons' first loss of the season. After leading by a goal at half-time, they were outscored 14.9 to 4.6 in the second half and were crushed by 57 points. But it was written off as a minor stumble, an aberration, when the next week, in an inspiring display of controlled vigour, the Maroons toppled reigning premier Essendon by 23 points at the Brunswick Street Oval. However, this week-to-week inconsistency was to punctuate Fitzroy's season. Just seven days after upsetting the Bombers, the Maroons let themselves down badly. Hosting 1950 Grand Finalist North Melbourne, Fitzroy trailed by 25 points at quarter-time and managed just 1.9 in the second half to go down by 33 points.

---

[103] Bill Stephen. Interview with the author.

The Maroons bounced back the following week against Richmond at Punt Road, kicking 4.6 to 1.2 in the last quarter to win by 22 points and break the Tigers' six-game hot streak. In the visitors' changerooms after the match, *The Sporting Globe*'s Jim Blake approached Maroons skipper Ruthven, who was lying on a table in the hands of the trainers. 'Naturally, he was a little weary,' Blake noted, 'but he was all grins.' Ruthven confidently predicted a finals campaign for Fitzroy, which, he said, was thriving under Smith's influence: 'Often we've been at the other end of the stick in my 11 years at Fitzroy, but now that's all changed. We are certainly a new side and playing a different brand of football. Norm Smith has done all this for us. He will do me as a coach... (He) has helped us... (with) his patience and encouragement. From the day he came to the club three years ago, there has been a steady lifting (both) on and off the field.'[104]

However, the wider football public's opinion of the Fitzroy side changed dramatically in the next fortnight. The Maroons served up a pathetic first half against a mediocre South Melbourne at Brunswick Street in round nine, trailing by 32 points at the long break. That was the cue for Norm Smith to conjure one of the most memorable speeches of his time at Fitzroy. The club's annual report recorded that it was a classic example of where Smith, 'by his indomitable courage infused into his charges that will to win', after which he 'sent his team out with a grim determination to retrieve the position, and in the words of a very famous coach who was present, he lifted the team from rags to riches in five minutes. This was one of many such instances, and put the hallmark on Norman's ability, and stamped him as one of the best mentors in our national game'.[105]

Smith's 'stirring address' worked to an extent. His Maroons did not win, but did not lose. They drew with South Melbourne – 12.13 (85) apiece. Apart from the thrilling finale, the contest became known as 'Clegg's Match' – after South's champion centre half-back and 1949 Brownlow Medallist Ron Clegg had virtually monopolised the ball, taking either 27 or 32 marks (depending on the reporter). 'It was the best game I saw from an opposition player,' Bill Stephen declared. 'It didn't matter where we kicked the ball – the wings or up the centre – he marked the lot. We couldn't get the ball past him. He virtually played us on his own, which must have frustrated Smithy because he felt that you can't win a game on the strength of just one player, so neither should you lose a game that way either.'[106]

---

[104] *The Sporting Globe*, June 16, 1951.
[105] Fitzroy Football Club *Annual Report*, 1951.
[106] Bill Stephen. Interview with the author.

Above everything, Smith felt it was totally unacceptable, and almost unforgivable, to lose a game through lack of intensity. He wasn't in a forgiving mood during the round 10 clash with the lowly Hawthorn at Brunswick Street. Fitzroy was third, four games clear of the 11th-placed Hawks, whose seven losses had been by an average margin of 41 points. Smith was again angry at half-time. Although his side led by 24 points and had fired 16 scoring shots to seven, he sensed many of his players were going through the motions as if they simply expected to win. One of the culprits was Bill Stephen, who had arrived late after spending the morning looking for an engagement ring with then fiancée Betty:[107]

> Norm told us quite sternly: 'If you don't lift yourselves, this mob will hang in and hang in and they'll beat you!' As Norm said, Hawthorn hung on, hung on and beat us by a point. And I hardly got a kick after arriving late. I wasn't mentally ready to play – my mind was anywhere but on the footy. It was one of my worst ever games. I walked off the ground and Norm was standing there at the door, glowering and glaring, with steam coming out of his ears! I thought: 'I'll take my jumper off and throw it in your face!' That's how I felt. But I wasn't game enough to do it.[108]

Fitzroy's season, and their hopes to make the finals for the first time since 1947, was fast reaching crisis point. A rare 32-point win over the strong Collingwood side at Victoria Park returned the Maroons to second spot, and set up a top-of-the-table clash with Geelong at Kardinia Park in round 13. The Maroons led by five points at the first change – 1.1 (7) to 0.2 (2) – but were swamped in the remaining three quarters, with the Cats piling on 11.8 to just 3.4 to win by 47 points. Although Smith was terribly disappointed by the efforts of his players, he realised they had been beaten by a mighty opponent, which went on to win the 1951-52 flags and finish runner-up to Collingwood in 1953. Smith later declared: 'The Geelong team coached by Reg Hickey in 1951 borders on greatness. Reg set a new standard and a new style of football. That Geelong side saw the birth of sustained pace, the fast play-on football. The side was laced with stars. Bernie Smith, John Hyde, Bob Davis, Peter Pianto and "Nipper" Tresize are just a few. They were unlucky not to win three premierships on end.'[109]

Comfortable wins over bottom side Melbourne and Footscray – the Maroons' main rival for a finals berth – meant the Maroons had won four of their previous

---

[107] The Smiths hosted a kitchen tea for Bill and Betty Stephen before they were married in March 1952.
[108] Bill Stephen. Interview with the author.
[109] *Melbourne Truth* series, 1962.

five games and consolidated third position. With three rounds remaining, this is how the ladder stood:

	W	L	D	Pts	%
Geelong	12	3	-	48	137.8
Collingwood	11	4	-	44	127.7
Fitzroy	**10**	**4**	**1**	**42**	**110.8**
Essendon	10	5	-	40	113.0
Footscray	9	6	-	36	107.6
Richmond	8	7	-	32	115.0

The Maroons had a reasonable draw. They had two very winnable games to come against Carlton (at home) and North Melbourne (away), and a tough one against Essendon (away), although, of course, the Maroons had beaten the Bombers in round six.

All was going to plan when Fitzroy led the Blues by 23 points at half-time, before Carlton produced a five-goal to one third quarter. In the end, the Maroons were fortunate to walk away with their second draw of the season after a goal to Carlton ruckman Bill Milroy was disallowed because it was deemed to have been kicked a split-second after the final siren.[110] Fitzroy was still fourth – a game clear of Footscray. But not for long.

After a 26-point loss to third-placed Essendon, the Maroons surrendered their spot in the four to Footscray by just 2.3 percent. They were then left with the challenge of having to beat eighth-placed North Melbourne at Arden Street, while praying for seventh side South Melbourne to upset Footscray at the Western Oval. The first part appeared the easier to fulfil, but even that proved too difficult. The Maroons trailed North Melbourne all afternoon and lost by 20 points, while Footscray had sewn up its match against South in the third quarter. After appearing odds-on for a finals berth for most of the season, the Maroons had finished a game and 7.8 percent out of the four. In the last 10 rounds, Footscray had won eight matches and collected 32 premierships points, while Fitzroy had won four and drawn two for a total of 20 points.

In Fitzroy's annual report to its members, the now impatient committee bemoaned the side's fatal inconsistency as follows: 'The season... proved to be another mixture of brilliance and mediocrity; at times it was hard to believe the brilliant team of a week previous... could perform so poorly against moderate

---

[110] Fitzroy became just the 14th team in history to draw two matches in the same season.

opposition a week later. No explanation of such reversals of form can be given, but your committee is confident that each player gave his best at all times... At the end of the season it seems to be the custom to paint a picture of dogged bad luck and what might have been if key players were not out of the team through injuries. Your team has had its share of bad luck during the season in this respect, but this alone cannot account for such inexplicable reversals that have been experienced during the season.'[111]

However, there was no mistaking the fact that the Maroons had – for the third successive season under Norm Smith's reign – been forced to battle injuries to key players. An indication of this was that, unusually, not one Fitzroy player appeared in all 18 games, although Ruthven and best-and-fairest award winner Chanter probably would have if not for interstate duties. Ruthven was one of three Maroons to battle thigh injuries – the others were Jack Gaffney and Bill Stephen – and, despite finishing runner-up to Chanter in the club award, he did not come close to producing his Brownlow form of the previous season. Towards the end of the season, full-forward Eddie Hart suffered a severe head injury which had such far-reaching consequences for the Maroons that the committee, in the annual report, stated its firm belief that it was 'the main factor in our loss of fourth place'.[112] Before the heavy knock, Hart had kicked 57 goals in the first 13 rounds, including an equal career-best of nine goals against Hawthorn at Brunswick Street in round five – an effort that remained the greatest individual haul of any player in Norm Smith's 23-year coaching career. He finished the season with 65 goals – 34 percent of Fitzroy's goals – which, remarkably, was to be the most by a player under Norm Smith in his three-club, 23-season coaching career.

In his three seasons at Fitzroy, Smith had coached the club in 55 games for 30 wins, 23 losses and two draws – for respectable but frustrating ladder placements of seventh, fifth and fifth.

At times, the situation wasn't helped by friction between the coach and certain committee members, whom Smith accused of being unsupportive. The source of most of Smith's angst was committeeman Oliver 'Buller' Hornsby. Strangely, despite having no discernible background in football, Hornsby doubled as Smith's chairman of selectors, having been appointed to the important role by his fellow committee members when Smith arrived at the club. Although Hornsby 'always had the best interests of the club at heart', he 'wasn't easy to get along with because

---

[111] Fitzroy Football Club *Annual Report*, 1951.
[112] Fitzroy Football Club *Annual Report*, 1951.

he was a testy sort of bloke'[113] – which set him on an inevitable collision course with Smith. It was no surprise that the equally obstinate pair clashed angrily, and often.

Bill Stephen recalled: 'Buller Hornsby wasn't a football person, but he had a bit of power, and probably got a bit carried away with it. Norm told me that he found it very hard to deal with because he was trying to get his ideas across but he felt he was being restricted, hindered. Buller interfered in team selection, and would argue and try to block Norm to get his own way'.[114]

Although he came to love Fitzroy Football Club, and many of the individuals within it, Smith became increasingly frustrated by the attitude of people like Hornsby. In fact, it made his next decision about his football future far easier.

ΥΥΥΥΥΥΥΥΥ

As his younger brother steadily built a reputation as a coach at the highest level, Len Smith was steadily making people aware that his brother was not the only capable coach in the Smith family at Fitzroy. A side 'recognised as one of the best in the third eighteen competition',[115] Len's lads appeared finals-bound mid-season before a few narrow defeats ruined their hopes. Nonetheless, the club's annual report enthused: 'Len Smith is to be highly congratulated for the... progress many of these young players are making.'[116]

One such youngster under Len's guidance in 1951 was 13-year-old Kevin Murray. Len had played with Kevin's father Dan, who had been the 19th man in Fitzroy's 1944 premiership side. It was only through this friendly association that Len allowed a boy as young as Kevin to train with the older boys. 'There was never any hope of Len giving me a game at that age,' Murray recalled. 'He wouldn't have thrown me to the wolves that early – I was just there for experience. I didn't get a game until I was 15.' Murray recalled: 'Len Smith had a system of how he wanted us to play and I was lucky that I was able to learn that system as a 13-year-old. It was quite simple stuff compared to today – mainly to do with moving the ball quickly – but one of Len's real strengths was the way he imparted it at training'.[117]

At the end of the 1951 season Len received an added bonus – life membership of Fitzroy Football Club. He had become eligible after 10 years' service with

---

[113] George Coates. Interview with the author.
[114] Bill Stephen. Interview with the author.
[115] Fitzroy Football Club *Annual Report*, 1951.
[116] Fitzroy Football Club *Annual Report*, 1951.
[117] Kevin Murray. Interview with the author.

the Maroons – seven as a player and three as the under-19s coach. The Fitzroy committee commended him for being 'an extra fine clubman' who had 'given great service in tutoring many young players to senior ranks'.[118]

ϒϒϒϒϒϒϒϒϒ

When Norm Smith left Melbourne Football Club at the end of 1948, the Demons had soared to one of their highest peaks – in both on-field performance and off-field fraternising. But by the middle of 1951, this once great club had deteriorated, almost to the point of anarchy.

The source of most angst among the players was their coach, Allan La Fontaine. Although it was indisputable that La Fontaine had been a brilliant player and possessed a wealth of knowledge of the game – Noel McMahen described him as 'the best football brain I had anything to do with'[119] – it was just as indisputable that he was a poor coach. The consensus was that he was a poor mixer who lacked the ability to inspire his players and was simply unable to impart his genius.

The most glowing description – if it could be called that – of La Fontaine came from Don Cordner, who captained the Demons in La Fontaine's first season, 1949, and retired the following season. 'He was a nice bloke, but a soft bloke,' Cordner said. 'He wasn't hard enough on players, and not forceful enough in getting his message across. He was probably too nice to be a good coach. You probably have to be a bit of a bastard to be a successful coach, and there's no doubt Norm was a bastard at times. No-one could doubt his discipline or call him soft.'[120]

La Fontaine *had* been 'a bit of a bastard' when he took a hard line on after-match functions. George Bickford said: 'La Fontaine, he cut out the social get-togethers we had, and enjoyed, at Phair's Hotel. He said: "From now on, we'll just have a players' dinner at the ground." But that meant those dinners were as flat as a tack, particularly when we lost, because we'd just be sitting around reading *The Sporting Globe*. La Fontaine put a dampener on those nights. His attitude was that we had to bond a different way – a way that was more to his liking and his personality – but not necessarily to the players' liking. It just didn't work.'[121]

La Fontaine's character did not endear him to his players, who described him variously as aloof, arrogant, a shameless egotist, a loner, and a poor mixer who rarely spoke to his players outside team addresses. He also set what some regarded

---

[118] Fitzroy Football Club *Annual Report*, 1951.
[119] Noel McMahen. Interview with the author.
[120] Don Cordner. Interview with the author.
[121] George Bickford. Interview with the author.

as impossible standards. 'He measured you against his ability, which was unfair,' recalled Melbourne player Max Spittle. 'If you weren't as good as he was, you were nothing to him. Very few were as good as he was because he was one of the all-time great centremen. He was sarcastic, and he'd sooner criticise you than praise or encourage you. He wouldn't help you like a coach should. He didn't have our respect because he didn't respect us.'[122]

Most disturbing were the events that took place during a match against a lowly opponent in 1950. Stan Rule recounted what happened next. 'We were down at half-time and not playing real well, and La Fontaine brought us in close, stood up on a bench and let rip at us,' Rule said. 'He said something like: "*You* players aren't doing this, this and this. When I played, I would never have played like *you players* are today." Here we were, supposed to be a team all together as one with the players and the coach, but the coach is talking about how good he was and how poor we are. It didn't sit well with us. Lenny Dockett and Bobby McKenzie took their jumpers off and said: "If you're that bloody good, why don't you go out there and bloody well do it yourself?! We had to physically force the pair of them down the race to get them onto the ground to play the second half. McKenzie went to the forward flank, folded his arms and just stood there. His opponent thought it was Christmas. That's what it had deteriorated to.'

Rule sensationally revealed that he reached his own breaking point with La Fontaine after the 1950 first semi-final when he became embroiled in an alleged bribery scandal. The third-placed Demons had finished two games clear of their opponent, Geelong, but had their score doubled in a humiliating 44-point defeat at the MCG. Shortly after retiring to the showers, Rule was alerted to a hot rumour that had swept the changerooms. 'I was told that there was a story going round that I had accepted a bribe to "play dead",' he said. Rule pleaded his innocence; then he became 'ropeable'. He confronted La Fontaine and asked him whether he believed the rumour. La Fontaine 'went along with it', telling Rule: 'You did not play your best.' Rule – a 26-year-old Victorian representative at the time – replied: 'I'll never play under you again.'

Rule received moral support from Norm Smith. 'Even though Norm was coaching Fitzroy at the time, he heard what was going on so he rang me and begged me to stay at Melbourne. He said: "For Christ's sake, stay there. If I have my way I'll be coaching Melbourne in 12 months." If I'd known that beforehand, I'd have stayed and put up with La Fontaine for a year.'[123]

---

[122] Max Spittle. Interview with the author.
[123] Stan Rule. Interview with the author.

Melbourne fans also reached boiling point in 1951, when their side struggled like rarely before. The Demons faithful turned on their own, booing their players off the ground several times during the season.[124] Their anger reached flashpoint at the MCG in round nine when Footscray hammered them by 103 points – Melbourne's worst loss in 32 years. McMahen lamented: 'It was probably the worst day of my football career. The terrible crowd reaction had such an impact on me that I had tears streaming down my face. Melbourne supporters booed us like mad as we walked off the ground, and quite a few of them tore up their membership tickets right in our faces.' McMahen, who won the Demons' best-and-fairest that season, added: 'I played on temper. I was so annoyed with what was happening at my club. *Wild* is perhaps a better description.'[125]

La Fontaine copped a savage backlash from supporters. One wet afternoon someone slashed the back of his raincoat.[126] Checker Hughes was also upset. Midway through the season, with the Demons at the foot of the ladder, Hughes was invited, without notice, to address the team at an after-match players' dinner. McMahen recalled: 'Straight off the cuff, Checker said: "In all goodly business organisations, the 30th of June is time for a stocktake. It's about time we had a bloody stocktake in this football club!" For the next 20 minutes, he went through every player individually and told him where he stood. Apart from Checker's voice, you could have heard a pin drop. It was magnificent. Just what we needed.'[127]

By the time Hughes had delivered his memorable speech, La Fontaine had already started the rebuilding process that was to prove crucial to Melbourne's success over the next decade. At the end of 1950 – after recalling 35-year-old Jack Mueller for one last fling in the semi-final – La Fontaine concluded: 'We can't win another premiership with pre-war players'.[128] A mass exodus of retirees – including Mueller, Don Cordner, Shane McGrath, Alby Rodda, Stan Rule, Max Spittle and Billy Deans – represented a massive loss of experienced finals players. It opened up gaping holes, and numerous opportunities, for rookies to fill.

In 1951, La Fontaine blooded 18 first-year players, among them John Beckwith, Neil Clarke, Ralph Lane, Ian McLean and Ken Christie. Two other notable youngsters who had made their VFL debuts under La Fontaine were Stuart Spencer and Geoff McGivern. It was always going to be a tough transitional period. McMahen observed: 'The foundations were laid in 1951, but they had to be built

---

[124] Len Dockett. Interview with the author.
[125] Noel McMahen. Interview with the author.
[126] George Bickford. Interview with the author.
[127] Noel McMahen. Interview with the author.
[128] Noel McMahen. Interview with the author.

upon. And La Fontaine was never going to see it all come to fruition because reformations never get the due reward for their labour.'[129]

Beckwith, one of the Demons' most talented rookies, recalled: 'Most of us were young and didn't think anything other than: "Gee, wouldn't it be nice to win a game", and: "Gee, wouldn't it be nice to play in the finals one day". Even though we were losing, the mere fact that we were playing League football was very exciting. Little did we know what the football gods, and Smithy, had in store for us.'[130]

♟♟♟♟♟♟♟♟♟

The Demons' 'stocktake' also involved a re-evaluation of the coaching position. Midway through the 1951 season, the club moved decisively on this issue. With Fitzroy entrenched in the top four and Melbourne languishing on the bottom, newly-appointed Melbourne secretary Jim Cardwell approached Norm Smith with a burning question.

'Would you come back and coach Melbourne?' Cardwell asked.

Smith was flattered, but refused to discuss the idea at such a crucial time.

'Jimmy, that is not…(the) right question to ask me because while I've got 36 men giving their all for me, I've got to be loyal to them,' Smith said.

Never one to take no for an answer, Cardwell repackaged his proposition.

'Would you be interested in coming back to Melbourne at the finish of this year?' he asked.

Smith did not discount the idea, and he also did not leave any doubt in Cardwell's mind about where his allegiances lay.

'Look, at the finish of this year, you come and talk to me,' Smith said, leaving the door slightly ajar before once again slamming it shut, for the time being. 'But while I've got a job to do, I'll do it. If players support me, I support my players.'[131]

Despite Smith's stern retort, Melbourne officials remained confident of luring him back to Demonland – if a little perversely so. In the gloom of the visitors' changeroom at the Brunswick Street Oval, after the Demons had been soundly defeated by Fitzroy, a Melbourne selector made a staggering remark to a devastated player. 'Don't worry,' the selector said, attempting to console the player, 'we're one game closer to the redhead coming home.' Despite being barely able to move after

---

[129] Noel McMahen. Interview with the author.
[130] John Beckwith. Interview with the author.
[131] Norm Smith recounted this conversation on *Tony Charlton's Football Show*, which screened on Channel Nine on Sunday, July 25, 1965.

a tough slog on a gluepot, the player jumped to his feet and wrestled the selector, and chastised him for his disloyalty, smearing mud on his suit in the process.

By the end of the 1951 season, Melbourne's predicament had become even more desperate. The club had finished on the bottom of the VFL ladder – three games adrift of 11th-placed Hawthorn – after winning just one of its 18 games. The Demons' 17 losses had been by an average of 31 points, and on 13 occasions they had failed to kick more than 11 goals. It was the Demons' first wooden spoon in 28 years; their fifth in total. Statistically, it had been their third worst season ever.[132]

When Cardwell made another overture to Smith at the end of the 1951 season, he found him to be far more receptive. In fact, Smith agreed to stand against incumbent Demon coach Allan La Fontaine for the job. His motivations were multi-faceted. Above all was the emotional attachment to his beloved Melbourne, where many of his close friends and acquaintances remained. He had also weighed up the respective futures of both clubs, and analysed their playing lists and such issues as administration, finances and facilities, and arrived at the overwhelming conclusion that Melbourne was by far his preferred option. On the playing side of the equation, Smith felt the Demons had more 'promising young players', 'good team players' and 'the nucleus of a good side'.[133]

However, Smith's willingness to return to Melbourne still raised a few eyebrows. Alf Brown later wrote in *The Herald*: 'Some people, knowing Smith, were surprised. Having been overlooked once, they thought it was foreign to his nature to give Melbourne another chance. But they forgot two things: Smith's humility – a contradictory facet in his trigger-tempered, straight-talking character – and his great love for Melbourne.'[134]

La Fontaine and Smith were the only coaching candidates seriously considered by the Demons. Most Melbourne players, particularly those who were former teammates of Smith, believed his appointment was inevitable: 'a fait accompli',[135] which would signal the return of a favourite son. But it was a much closer contest than that. In fact, it could not have been any closer. On this issue, two distinct factions remained at committee level. The pro-Smith camp, championed by the likes of Checker Hughes and 'Pop' Vine, opposed a pro-La Fontaine group.

For Smith, the vote conducted by the Melbourne committee in late 1951 had a poetic twist. After missing out on the job by one vote (to La Fontaine) late in

---

[132] Melbourne's 1951 season (one win and 17 losses, and a percentage of 70.5) was only slightly better than the club had performed in 1919 (0-16 and 43 percent) and 1906 (1-16, 48 percent).
[133] *Melbourne Truth* series, 1962.
[134] *The Herald*, 1958.
[135] Noel McMahen. Interview with the author.

COACH OF FITZROY [1949-51]

1948, he won it by the same margin three years later. It was rumoured among the players that the ballot had swung on the preference of a single committeeman who had voted against Smith in 1948 but had changed allegiances and voted for him this time. Whatever the case, this tight result led to Smith – either consciously or subconsciously – trying to please too many people at Melbourne early in his time as coach of the club. But others are not so sure that this was the case – or, at least, they did not notice Smith appearing to try to 'please' anyone as such. Several players made comments to the effect that: 'Smithy only ever did it his way – he knew no other way'.

Smith was so thrilled to be the new Melbourne coach that money – his coaching fee – had not even been a consideration. It had not even been discussed. Smith always maintained – and subsequent events would prove it – that money was never a motivating force at any stage of his coaching career, or indeed his life. Smith had simply wanted the job so badly that he had not even mentioned remuneration during negotiations. The day after his appointment, he rang Jim Cardwell and asked in an innocent, almost naïve manner: 'Jimmy, I am getting paid for this, aren't I?'[136]

He was told he would receive £250 ($500) for the season plus a £25 ($50) expense allowance, and that it would be reviewed if the team made the finals.[137]

A few months later, when he accompanied Cardwell on a recruiting trip to Shepparton and Albury, Smith asked Cardwell: 'What was that amount of money I was getting?'[138]

His love for the job, without a thought for the material gain – not that there was much on offer at that time anyway in League football – was refreshing.

Before Smith could officially return to Melbourne, he had to gain a clearance from Fitzroy. But, courtesy of a rare gesture of respect from Fitzroy towards both Smith and the Demons, this process was neither painful nor protracted. Although the vast majority of Maroons wanted to retain Smith as coach, they chose not to block his clearance. Their decision – which reciprocated Melbourne's decision to release Smith to them three years earlier – was as admirable as Smith's was logical. It was official – Norm Smith was the new Melbourne coach. The man himself described it as a case of 'better late than never'.[139]

---

[136] John Lord, a Melbourne player from 1957-65, relayed to the author what Jim Cardwell had told him.
[137] Melbourne Football Club, Minutes of Committee Meetings, courtesy of the Melbourne Cricket Club Library.
[138] *Midweek Magazine*, 1964.
[139] *Melbourne Truth* series, 1962.

One of the key agitators for Smith's return was Checker Hughes, who was on a family holiday in Europe when he found out that Smith was the new Demon coach. His son, Frank Hughes junior, said: 'My father was quite happy about Norm's appointment because he was one of the people working behind the scenes to get him there.'[140] Checker Hughes later said: 'I am proud that as well as having a hand in recruiting Norm for Melbourne, I also played some part in having him appointed as coach of Melbourne in 1951.'[141]

But at Fitzroy, Smith's departure sparked bitter disappointment for players and close friends like Bill Stephen:

> When Norm left Fitzroy to go back to Melbourne, I felt very annoyed and hurt. Betrayed even. Especially after Norm had preached so much loyalty to us, and all of a sudden he turned his back on us. I told him that, too. Our team was mainly made up of young players who thought the world of Norm, and we didn't want him to go. But when he explained his side of the story to me – about the problems he'd had at committee level, how he'd always loved Melbourne, and he saw a better future there – I understood then.
>
> Norm had a great affection for Fitzroy, particularly for the people who supported him in his three years there, and he gave everything he had to Fitzroy while he was there. But Melbourne was his love, which was natural after playing there for 15 years – almost half his life.[142]

Other Maroons believed their committee should have ignored the 'gentleman's agreement' with Melbourne. George Coates described Smith's leaving as 'in hindsight, a very important moment in the club's history':

> We shouldn't have let him go so easily. I would've fought like buggery to keep him, and then signed him for another five years! We certainly lost out because of it.
>
> I enjoyed the time Norm had at Fitzroy and what we were able to learn under him. He hardened us up as a club and showed us what was required to be successful. Norm had taken over after our disastrous, roller-coaster year under Charlie Cameron, and he started from scratch to get the team rolling again, and he did it pretty well. If he had stayed on, we might have gone on and had some success, because not everybody gets the message at the same time; it takes some longer than others.[143]

---

[140] Frank Hughes junior. Interview with the author.
[141] *Trident Monthly*, April 1968.
[142] Bill Stephen. Interview with the author.
[143] George Coates. Interview with the author.

COACH OF FITZROY [1949-51]

The Fitzroy committee farewelled Smith with the following praise:

> During his three years at Fitzroy, he has made many friendships which will continue for all time. His relations with the players were always excellent and the progress of many of the younger players has been solely due to his advice and encouragement. Although his sojourn at Fitzroy has only been of short duration, he will always be remembered as a true sportsman and natural gentleman. Good luck, Norman, may much success come your way in your new appointment.[144]

The ultimate tribute, though, came from courageous defender Jack Gaffney, who later served as the chairman of the VFL tribunal (1985-87):

> I admired and respected Norm so much – it wasn't love, but it was close to it.
>
> He was a players' man. While he expected the players to give everything for him, it was a two-way thing, because he gave to his players, and he gave himself to his players. He was so loyal to you that you were automatically loyal to him – often without even thinking about it. Norm engendered such loyalty that if he called me at three o' clock in the morning and told me to drive to Sydney, I'd have jumped straight in the car and done it without any questions asked. I had total faith and trust in Norm.
>
> He was so much more than a football coach. He made a great contribution to society by shaping and influencing people's lives – not only in how to play sport, but in the way you live. And he did it through his example and the disciplines he imposed, which people then – perhaps without even thinking about it – applied to their own lives. Many players who were coached by Norm can credit him for much of the success they gained in their later lives. He certainly had a tremendous influence on me.
>
> He was very enthusiastic, a very powerful character, and a man of great sincerity and integrity. His word was his bond. He was strong, honest and straight – a fundamentally good man. You were either a Smithy man or you weren't, and I was a Smithy man. I felt that as a man, he was tops. Still is.[145]

---

[144] Fitzroy Football Club annual report, 1951.
[145] Jack Gaffney. Interview with the author.

9

HOME AGAIN

[1952-53]

Contrary to what one might think, coaches generally prefer to join clubs that are struggling, or off the pace. The idea is that it gives them the opportunity to start from scratch and put their own stamp on the club. Norm Smith's appointment as the coach of Melbourne marked the second time he had accepted such a coaching position, and it would not be long before he put his stamp on the entire Demon outfit.

Admittedly, Smith had little choice in either circumstance: Fitzroy had been his only VFL coaching option for the 1949 season, and while he had the pick of the Fitzroy and Melbourne jobs for 1952, his emotional attachment to the Demons sealed his decision to return to the MCG.

The Demons, though, were in a far deeper pit of despair than Fitzroy had been three years earlier. But when Smith got back to Demonland, he had a mighty support crew waiting for him; one that inspired great confidence in him that whatever needed to be done, he wasn't going to bear the load alone; and one that was perhaps unprecedented in its quality, football nous, business acumen, experience, no-nonsense approach and drive for success.

Bert Chadwick, then 54 and in his second season as Demon chairman, was the complete package as the club figure-head. Firstly, he had been a champion footballer: a rugged centre half-back and ruckman, he captain-coached Melbourne to the 1926 premiership, captain-coached Victoria 10 times and was runner-up in the first Brownlow Medal in 1924 (just one vote behind Geelong's Edward 'Carji' Greeves) and equal third the following year. Chadwick was also one of Australia's most powerful businessman, later becoming chairman of both the Australian division of the Overseas Telecommunications Commission (1963-68) and the Gas & Fuel Corporation in Victoria (1963-73). A strong personality who always seemed to have the perfect solution to any problem, he was on his way to a knighthood (in 1974) – although when he was then respectfully referred to as 'Sir Albert', he said: 'Just call me Bert'.

The chairman of selectors was an even bigger Demon legend – the VFL's first dual Brownlow Medallist, Ivor Warne-Smith, also 54. A much quieter, low-key character than Chadwick, he was a great calming influence around the club, and one who could take the heat out of any conflict.

Second-year secretary Jim Cardwell, 36 (little more than two months Norm's junior), was regarded as perhaps the best in the caper even at this early stage. A high-powered official with seemingly boundless energy and 'the gift of the gab' – proven by his successive victories in the Victorian Solo Debating Championships of 1934 and 1935 – he was a master diplomat who maintained friendly links with people in all areas of the club. He was a great backstop for any coach.

Checker Hughes assumed more of a background role but still exerted enormous influence at the club, and was to be a confidant and mentor to Smith.

Aside from Cardwell (who had won a best-and-fairest for North Brunswick Amateurs in 1938 before trying out with Melbourne's reserves), the other three had coached VFL sides (Chadwick and Warne-Smith had also captained Melbourne), while all four had been further toughened by going to war.

The Demons also boasted, as their recruiting officer, former player Ken Carlon (1949-50: 30 games), who had great success, with Cardwell, in luring players from all parts of the state, but particularly from country and regional areas. Generally, Carlon located the talent and then left it to Cardwell to do what he did best: negotiate with the player, and often his parents, sometimes until midnight, until he got a commitment from the player that he would join the Demons. But Cardwell did more than his share of scouting. He believed that young reserves players should be groomed for specific positions in the senior team, so that when a player retired or left the club, the transition would be as seamless as possible. One of Cardwell's philosophies was: 'Recruit for the seconds; don't recruit for the firsts. Then compare firsts and seconds players in their respective positions. For example, is the centre half-back from the seconds better than the centre half-back from the firsts? If he is, he gets a game'.[1]

Old stars Dick Taylor and Pop Vine were among other credentialled stalwarts working towards lifting the Demons.

The football planets had aligned to bring this high-powered group of men together. Noel McMahen said: 'At Melbourne, there's a photo of four heads – Sir Albert Chadwick, Ivor Warne-Smith, Jim Cardwell and Norm Smith.

---

[1] John Lord. Interview with the author.

If we ever match it, the club will again be as successful as we became. How could you not succeed with those men in charge? They had stability, strength, character – everything you wanted in your club leaders. And there was also a man of Checker Hughes' experience on hand as well.'[2]

Frank 'Bluey' Adams, who joined the Demons the following year, gave an insight into the effect such a combination had on the lives of impressionable young players. 'All of us were so lucky to play with Melbourne in those years, not so much because we ended up playing so many finals, but in terms of having your character moulded and developed in an environment that was full of first-class people who knew a thing or two about winning and life,' Adams said. 'One could learn how to conduct oneself in one's life.'[3]

With the Demons' off-field fortunes seemingly secure for quite some time, now it came down to how quickly, and sustainably, Smith could – with the help of his wise officials – rehabilitate the playing list. *The Football Record*, which described Melbourne as 'the flop of 1951', acknowledged Smith's coaching abilities but emphasised the difficulty of his task. 'Norm Smith is expected to make a world of difference,' the *Record* reported, 'but he has the job ahead of him to bring this team from the bottom of the ladder to near the top. It looks like a tough road'.[4]

The Herald's Alf Brown expected Smith to have an immediate impact:

> Norman Smith... has the sort of job coaches dream about. Melbourne were last this year... However, they have the framework of sufficiently good and experienced players to become a final four possibility next year. It means that even if Smith were a coach of only ordinary ability he could lift Melbourne up the League premiership ladder. But there is nothing ordinary about Smith's coaching. He is a fine leader, an astute coach and a dynamic personality. He will get the best out of Melbourne. He gave Melbourne wonderful service for many years, and starred in several positions...
>
> With so many good players in the side this year Melbourne's continued lack of success was disappointing. Many players were half-hearted, and some could have 'gone in' with more determination. Smith will be impatient of this attitude, and any player who does not give Smith – and Melbourne – everything he has throughout the game will soon be looking around for another club.[5]

---

[2] Noel McMahen. Interview with the author.
[3] Frank 'Bluey' Adams. Interview with the author.
[4] *The Football Record*, April 19, 1952.
[5] *The Herald*, late 1951.

Smith told *The Sporting Globe* of his joy at being back at his footballing home. 'I was very happy at Fitzroy. They treated me well,' he said. 'But I must confess I am happier back at Melbourne. When you play 15 years with a team, as I did with Melbourne, no matter where you go, you never forget your old club. Melbourne has been a big part of my life. I will certainly not feel strange when I get togged in the room(s) again.'

In the same interview, Smith expressed pleasure at Fitzroy's decision to replace him with Allan Ruthven. 'He should do well,' Smith said. 'Allan is a great sportsman and a gentleman. In addition, he knows the game. What is more important, he will have the confidence of his men for, after all, Allan is almost Fitzroy itself.'[6]

Although Smith did not expect overnight success, he was confident the young Demons would improve with experience. 'When I left Melbourne three years ago, we were at the top of the tree,' he recalled. 'Under normal circumstances, you would expect a premier team of only three years back to be still with the leaders. But on studying last year's list, it is not difficult to see the reason for the drop. For 1951, Melbourne had 19 first-year players. Only nine of them had been with them since 1948. Just look at the players Melbourne lost last year – Shane McGrath, Don Cordner, Alby Rodda, Deans and Rule. A quintette *(sic)* of really brilliant players who would still dominate a League game. Rule, McGrath and Deans formed the full-back line. And a really brilliant backline it was in every sense of the word. Don Cordner, as a follower... (was) top class. Alby Rodda could be used as second rover and still be one of the best.'[7]

Smith was undaunted about taking charge of the 1951 wooden spooner. 'Coming back from the ruck is not new to Melbourne,' he said. 'We dropped right down after our 1939-40-41 premierships when almost all the side served in the Second World War. But by 1948 we were back again, and so we can rise again.' He was excited by the prospect of an even higher standard of football – 'The lag caused by the war has almost been overcome,' he said – but warned that most teams in 1951 had appeared to be 'on the up' and a Demon revival would be hard-earned.[8]

ŶŶŶŶŶŶŶŶŶ

On a beautiful summer's day early in 1952, Norm Smith joined a host of his Melbourne players at the wedding of recently retired wingman Len Dockett.

---

[6] *The Sporting Globe*, early 1952.
[7] *The Sporting Globe*, early 1952.
[8] *The Sporting Globe*, early 1952.

Dockett, a 31-year-old former teammate of Smith's and one of the heroes of '48, was an ardent admirer of his from way back. A measure of Dockett's admiration was the fact that he would have invited Smith to the wedding even if he was still coaching Fitzroy.

The ceremony was conducted at The Holy Trinity Church in Kew and was followed by a reception at The Dauphine in Ivanhoe, where Dockett stole the night with his wedding speech. The content of the speech became a talking point, and a source of amusement, for many in attendance. The crux of the matter was that Dockett usually referred to his bride, Norma, simply as 'Norm'. When he praised 'Norm' for 'turning up', there were mild giggles, and Dockett was not sure why. He went on to pay tribute to Smith for being a supportive captain and teammate who had always been willing to lend a helping hand. By this point, there was muffled laughter as most of the gathering realised that Dockett was not referring to his blushing bride, but the guest who had just become the new Melbourne coach:

> I was speaking straight from the heart about a man who had helped me so much, but people thought I was talking from the heart about Norma. I would have done that at some point too, but I felt Norm Smith deserved to be praised – even in my wedding speech! Norm was great to me. If you were being beaten by your opponent, he'd come over and have a quiet word to put you on the right tram, like he did for me in a final against Footscray in 1946. I wasn't going too well and Norm came up to me at half-time and gave me a bit of a talk about how I could get myself into the game. After half-time, I was a completely different player – and it was all because of Norm Smith. I never forgot that because Melbourne Football Club meant the world to me and Norm Smith helped me make a name for myself and succeed there.[9]

Smith's first speech to the Melbourne players was just as memorable. He eyeballed the players as though he was staring into their souls, and he laid down the law in no uncertain terms. Anyone who dared smirk or giggle risked a severe reprimand. Smith told his new charges, among them former teammates:

---

[9] Len Dockett. Interview with the author. The happiness of the Docketts was relatively short-lived. A tragic chain of events followed. In 1956, Norma Dockett suffered severe burns in a kitchen accident at home when, unbeknown to her, she was pregnant with twins. Perhaps as a result of their mother's injuries, both twins died shortly after birth. The Docketts bore two healthy children – one either side of the twin tragedy – but worse was to come. After 12 years of marriage, Norma Dockett succumbed to cancer at the age of 35. (Source: Norma Dockett's sister, Noel Axton.)

HOME AGAIN [1952-53]

I am a disciplinarian. I expect every man to give his utmost for the club. With me, it is Melbourne first and the player second. Any player who does anything to upset the harmony of the club is out.[10]

First-year player Keith Carroll – a country boy from Romsey who didn't even know what Smith looked like until 'this big redhead with strong features' stood up and addressed the players – recalled some other stern words from the coach:

Norm spelt it out for us immediately. He said: 'My name is not Smithy, and it's not Mr Smith. My name is Norm.' Behind his back, blokes would say: 'Smithy did this', but they didn't say it to his face though. Or if you did, you only did it once because he'd let you know about it. He came across as a good, solid, upstanding man straight off, but very serious of course. I thought: 'We're in the real world now. There'll be no mucking about here.'

ŸŸŸŸŸŸŸŸŸ

The Demons' skipper was star ruckman Denis Cordner, who had captained the side for one season after taking over the job from champion fullback Shane McGrath. Melbourne's poor season could hardly be blamed on their new leader, with Cordner polling 14 votes and finishing equal fifth in the Brownlow Medal. But while Smith and Cordner were great friends, Smith was thinking of replacing him as captain. His candidate was another former teammate, Stan Rule – the man who had been tainted with the bribery allegations after the 1950 semi-final. Rule, then 27, had spent a season as captain-coach of Albury in the Ovens and Murray league, where he had been one of the competition's best recruits in years. Norm Smith was keen for Rule to return to Melbourne and even offered him the captaincy as an inducement:

Norm came up and saw me at Wodonga. He turned up with Checker Hughes, Jim Cardwell and two blokes by the names of (Dick) Taylor and (Norman) King. They gave me a big crystal lamp as a present on leaving Melbourne the year before. Norm didn't beat around the bush. He said: 'We want you to be captain of Melbourne. Will you take the job?'
  I was quite flattered, but I said: 'I'll have to have to talk it over with my wife because if I'm to come back to Melbourne we'd have to change what we're doing in our life. Leave it with me. I'll get back to you'.

---

[10] *Melbourne Truth* series, 1962.

I talked to my wife, and she said: 'Well what do you want to do?'
I said: 'I'd like to do it'.

Being captain of a VFL club is a prestigious thing. But my wife said: 'They accused you of taking a bribe and they give you only £3 a week, whereas up here you're getting £15 a week, free rent, and you've got a job at the SEC worth £17 a week.' When she mentioned those things, the decision was pretty easy. I had to knock Norm back. A part of me regrets it, but my wife would have made me regret it more if I decided to take it!"

Smith admitted to having 'no set plan' on how he would go about lifting the Demons, and it had a lot to do with being unfamiliar with many of the players. 'I had been away for three years and there were many new players,' he said. 'Most of the old names I had known had gone. There were very few left of the 1948 premiership side, so I had to concentrate on getting to know the form, style and ways of the new players.'[12]

One Demon he had formulated ideas about – and had been extremely impressed with as an opposition coach – was Noel Clarke who, he said, 'seems to be a champion'.[13] Smith had gained his first glimpse of Clarke when he coached Fitzroy to a round 14 win over the Demons at Brunswick Street. 'He was in the centre, where he showed brains and pace,' Smith enthused.[14] Clarke, a Tasmanian in his first season of VFL football, highlighted his potential with 18 goals (6,6,6) in the last three rounds of the 1951 season. That was enough for Smith to foreshadow a permanent forward role. 'He may be our focal point in attack,' he said. 'I will have to pay special attention to this department. Up forward, (a) combination will have to be built. I was so long in attack myself... that I know only too well what combination means. The full-forward alone does not get all the goals. He can, however, help the rest to get them.'[15]

But in the absence of a detailed plan, Smith decided the best approach to help the Demons become competitive again was to go back to basics – discipline, teamwork, courage, percentage play. These would be the starting points from which all else would, hopefully, flow. Smith taught second-year player John Beckwith an immediate lesson in an early intra-club practice match. Beckwith recalled:

---

[11] Stan Rule. Interview with the author.
[12] *The Herald*, late July, 1955.
[13] *The Sporting Globe*, early 1952.
[14] *The Sporting Globe*, early 1952.
[15] *The Sporting Globe*, early 1952.

I was playing on the half-back flank and I was getting a bit lazy and letting my opponent lead me to the ball. I distinctly remember Norm telling me: 'If you don't beat him to the ball, you'll never become a player'. It was a simple thing, but very important. He elaborated on it – 'You've got to start off level with the bloke, just so you can feel him, but if you don't get to the ball first, you'll never be any good.' That stuck in my mind and I used that as a starting point to build my game around.[16]

Before one such pre-season encounter, Smith also had some advice for club chairman Bert Chadwick. Smith 'quite liked' Chadwick,[17] but with both being fiercely proud, indomitable men, they were prone to suffer the odd personality clash. Second-year player Ralph Lane was nervously putting his playing gear on when he overheard Smith and Chadwick engaged in a heated conversation, which culminated in Smith saying: 'Listen, Bert; you look after the administrative side of the club and I'll look after the football side. I won't interfere with your side of it, but don't you interfere with mine either'.[18]

Smith was loathe talk to anybody except his players on match-days. Occasionally Chadwick – known by many as "Chaddy" – would approach Smith in the changerooms and mention something Smith regarded as trivial or irrelevant. Those in earshot could almost predict Smith's firm response – 'Bert, don't bother me with that at this time'.

Smith later told close friends, with great pride: 'Who would ever have thought that when I first went to Melbourne in a black shirt, and I was alienated, that one day I'd be able to talk to the president of the MCC, a very powerful businessman, and tackle him on issues, and even beat him occasionally to get what I want?'"[19]

While Smith's reputation as one of the sternest of taskmasters had preceded him – Lou Richards wrote that Smith 'had fiery red hair that matched the Fuchsia socks of his team, and penetrating eyes which made the heart of many a player thump with fear'[20] – he still raised a few eyebrows when he applied his methods at Melbourne. Former teammates like Noel McMahen found Smith's dictatorial approach quite confronting:

> Norm's approach to coaching was totally the opposite to the way Checker Hughes went about it. I started under Checker, so Norman's coaching style gave me a bit

---

[16] John Beckwith. Interview with the author.
[17] Bill Stephen. Interview with the author.
[18] Ralph Lane. Interview with the author.
[19] Bill Stephen. Interview with the author.
[20] Richards, Lou with Ian McDonald, *Boots And All!*, Stanley Paul, 1963.

of a shock to the system. Checker would give you a lolly or a kick up the backside according to your temperament, but Smithy ruled by fear. I think some players were scared to make a mistake, which inhibits a lot of people. It probably helps a lot of people too. It can go either way.[21]

But Smith was not always a scary, deadly-serious ogre. He still tried to lighten the mood at times. An example of this was when a young recruit from the country was receiving a rub-down in the changerooms. A quirk of those days was that players, particularly those at VFL level, were massaged in the nude. The youngster was not used to such an invasion of his privacy – and his private parts – after coming from country club where most players turned up at games with their football shorts under their trousers. He was shy and embarrassed; emotions that snowballed when Smith walked past, flicked the young man's genitals and said: 'Jeez, that nearly finished me. Nice size, son.' It was enough to deter the rookie from having another rub-down for weeks.

Melbourne showed dramatic improvement under their new coach in the season-opener against reigning premier Geelong at the MCG. Melbourne led by nine points at quarter-time, but was outlasted by the star-studded Cats' line-up to go down by just six points. However, the effort appeared a fluke when the Demons slumped to a three-goal deficit at three-quarter-time of their second-round match against eventual bottom side St Kilda at the Junction Oval. A 3.9 to 1.1 last quarter gave them a face-saving two-point win and got their season started. Worse was to come. The Demons were defeated by lowly Hawthorn, which had kicked a combined tally of just 10 goals in its opening two matches.

In times of need such as this, Norm Smith got into the habit of making a telephone call to Checker Hughes at his hotel on a Monday morning. For up to half-an-hour, the pair would discuss the fortunes of the side and how it could be enhanced. The Demons lifted their game with a 24-point win over 1951 finalist Footscray at the Western Oval, a narrow loss to a handy South Melbourne, and consecutive wins over North Melbourne (at Arden Street) and that season's runner-up Collingwood, by 32 points – 82 to 50 – at the MCG.

The Demons were suddenly 4-3, with a clash against Smith's mates at Fitzroy looming. The Maroons were 3-4. With the VFL promoting the code by scheduling matches at various interstate and country venues,[22] the Demons and Maroons

---

[21] Noel McMahen. Interview with the author.
[22] The round featured the first night match played for premiership points – Essendon versus Geelong at the Brisbane Exhibition Ground.

travelled to North Hobart. On the flight down to Tasmania, Smith 'put the wind up' young Keith Carroll, who was on his first plane trip:

> We were on a four-engine Skymaster plane and the turbulence was unbelievable. It was a pretty rough trip. Norm was sitting beside me and he pointed out the window and said: 'Keith, when the wings start moving that much, you have to start to worry. They could snap off.'
> I think he was having me on, but with his engineering knowledge, he sounded like he knew what he was talking about. I must have been as white as a ghost because an air hostess came up to me and said: 'Are you all right?'
> I said: 'Yeah, I feel good.'
> She said: 'You don't look too good,' and she put the air vent on me. Norm had contributed to my condition![23]

It did not take long into the match for Smith's agitation to boil over. With his side trailing by 26 points at half-time, he made it decidedly uncomfortable for the likes of Hughes, Warne-Smith and Cardwell, who were seated beside him on the bench. 'I bounced about so much I knocked some officials off the bench and they fell into the mud,' Smith later recalled. 'I was too worked up. When Noel McMahen and Fitzroy's Norm Johnstone clashed, I automatically swung my hips and sent the others flying. The dose was repeated in a later match and I suddenly found myself short of partners... I had to sit on my own.'[24]

Smith probably felt like sitting on his own anyway – to reflect upon a 20-point loss to the Maroons. But he was far from despondent. There was no disgrace in the loss as Fitzroy was to become a top-four side, and there was a major positive to come out of the afternoon – the emergence of John Beckwith as a high quality defender. Beckwith had joined the Demons as a centreman/half-forward flanker, but admitted he didn't have the stamina to play in the middle: 'Norm switched me onto a half-back flank and it suddenly clicked for me. I started to go for my marks and it just felt different; it felt right – and I was a better player for it. Norm had found my niche. At one stage, he threw me to full-back for half-a-season to fill a gap, and I played on all the gun full-forwards despite the fact I was giving away six inches every week. But it was a learning curve and Norm felt I could handle that responsibility. But then he moved me

---

[23] Keith Carroll. Interview with the author.
[24] *Melbourne Truth* series, 1962.

to the back pocket, where I played for the rest of my career, and played my best football.[25]

With no rules in place for deliberate out-of-bounds or out-of-bounds-on-the-full, Beckwith turned the rugby-like 'kick for touch' into an art form. The tactic had its origins in Smith's game plan:

> Norm always had this theory that when you defend you keep the ball wide, out to the boundary, then the rucks came in and you regrouped and started again. He actually had a rule that you didn't start straightening up until you got towards the half-forward line. A few times, blokes brought the ball back too early and miscued and goals were kicked against us and, oh gee, Norm went bananas; absolutely right off. We never kicked it into the middle of the ground from defence. To Norm's mind, that was a punishable sin. And I'd usually be *deep* in defence, so I wasn't taking any chances. Pretty much whenever I got the ball I'd kick for the boundary.[26]

Smith later joked that Beckwith executed this tactic 'so well and so consistently they used to say he was picking out the woman in the green hat in the first row of seats'.[27] But there were some influential people who opposed the 'Becky special'. Beckwith later said: 'At one point (*The Herald*'s) Alf Brown blew it up into a bigger issue than it was. Sometimes I miscued and the ball would end up in the crowd, but most of the time it landed in play and bounced out. Alf Brown wrote one day: "John Beckwith got 20 kicks and 19 of them went out-of-bounds". The public inherits opinions from sportswriters, who can build you up but just as easily cut you to pieces'.[28]

Melbourne bounced back from the loss in Hobart by claiming a big scalp, Essendon, which had contested 10 of the previous 12 Grand Finals (including the draw of 1948). The Demons were 17 points behind at the last change but stunned the Windy Hill faithful by kicking 3.4 to 0.4 in the final term to win by a point. They followed it up with a 37-point win over Richmond at the MCG, despite losing the free kick count 42-16. The Demons also won when it came to the physical clashes, as 21-year-old centre half-forward and 1952 best-and-fairest winner Geoff McGivern recalled:

---

[25] John Beckwith. Interview with the author.
[26] John Beckwith. Interview with the author.
[27] *The Sun* series, 1967.
[28] John Beckwith. Interview with the author.

HOME AGAIN [1952-53]

Norm didn't burden me with any instructions. In his first year back at Melbourne, all he said was: 'I've watched you play a couple of times – just keep on doing what you're doing'. But he gave we some advice before we played Richmond. Everyone knew 'Mopsy' Fraser was going to retire at the end of the year. In previous games, Mopsy had belted the living daylights out of me. But by this stage, I'd worked in a quarry for almost 12 months, I'd become a lot bigger and stronger and I fancied my chances of finally giving Mopsy a couple back. I thought: 'If this bastard retires without me giving him one – just one – I wouldn't forgive myself'. Norm knew this. He took me aside before the game and said: 'Now listen. I know this bloke has given you a pretty torrid time in the past, but we might just sneak into the finals, and we need you, so don't do anything stupid.'

I said: 'I wouldn't do anything like that, Norm.'

He said: 'I know what you're thinking.' He didn't want any player putting himself before the interests of the team. And just before we ran out onto the ground, Norm said: 'Don't forget!'

By the third quarter, Mopsy had ripped my strides off me twice. That was how angry the beast would get. But late in the third quarter, I got my chance. I thought: 'He's going to turn to his right when he gets out of the pack', and I decided: 'This is it'. Sure enough, he went to his right and I flattened him. It wouldn't have been 10 seconds later when the message came out: 'That's enough!'[29]

With four wins from their past five matches, the Demons had moved to 6-4. Another crucial clash with Fitzroy beckoned, this time at the MCG. The Demons led by five points at three-quarter-time before being overpowered by 10 points. Although the loss – Smith's second to Allan Ruthven for the season – hurt Smith and his side's chances of scoring a finals berth, he was still keen to catch up with his former Maroon charges. Fitzroy backman Jack Toohey recalled:

I was playing on Bob McKenzie on the half-back flank, so I had a pretty big job. But in the last couple of minutes of the match, when it was clear we were going to win, the ball was up the other end of the ground and I got a tap on the back. It was a Melbourne trainer. He said: 'Knackers (Norm) said: "Don't forget the barrel (of beer) after the game, Jacka-boy".' This was quite amazing. Norm loved winning and he took his football deadly serious, but this day he was losing, yet he sent the trainer out to invite me, an opposition player, for a drink after the game. I thought that was a terrific gesture. He didn't care about protocol.[30]

---

[29] Geoff McGivern. Interview with the author.
[30] Jack Toohey. Interview with the author.

The Demons' season almost unravelled over the next fortnight. A round 12 draw with finals hopeful Carlton at Princes Park was followed by a 56-point defeat to Geelong. They rebounded with wins over the three bottom sides – St Kilda, Hawthorn and Footscray – to be within a game and 1.6 percent of fourth-placed South Melbourne with three rounds left. When they confronted South at the Lake Oval in round 17, the Demons kicked away their finals hopes with an unforgivable 2.7 to 0.3 last quarter to lose by just eight points.

The final-round match against Collingwood at Victoria Park – a daunting prospect for the most seasoned campaigner – marked the senior debut of Keith Carroll. He recalled:

> Before the game, as was his custom for first-gamers, Norm congratulated me in front of all the players. Then he said: 'Well, Keith, you've never played a game of football until you've played against this mob out here.' That was my introduction to football. It hardly filled you with confidence, but Norm was trying to get across how lucky I was.
>
> I was the 19th man, as I was on quite a number of occasions early in my career, and Norm coached me a lot on the do's and don'ts of the game while we sat on the bench. He'd nudge me and point something out and say: 'Don't ever do that.' I just took it all in.
>
> I think Norm had a fear of being penalised for the 19th man going onto the ground before they were supposed to, because he'd have hold of you by the jumper and the split-second the other bloke came off he'd push you on. It was a strange feeling because you'd been sitting down wearing a dressing-gown and all of a sudden you've had to throw off the dressing-gown, which makes you feel naked when the cool air hits you, and the coach is pushing you out there; throwing the lamb to the slaughter.[31]

Collingwood led by 44 points at half-time and although the Demons piled on five goals to one in the last quarter against the eventual Grand Finalist, they lost by 21 points – their eighth loss by no more than this margin for the season.

Melbourne finished sixth with a 9-9-1 record – two-and-a-half games out of the final four. While obviously disappointed, Smith described it as 'a good year' after the horror of 1951.[32] The Demons' annual report stated: 'Norman instilled into the side a spirit that at all times made them fight grimly and determinedly for

---

[31] Keith Carroll. Interview with the author.
[32] *The Herald*, late July, 1955.

victory. This was borne out by the fact that in 13 of the 19 games ... Melbourne scored more points in the last quarter than their opponents, the actual scoring in that quarter being 337 points for, and 248 points against. This fact reflects great credit on the players, and also on Norman. It is to be hoped that his forceful spirit will continue to be a feature of (the) Melbourne team's future performances.'[33]

Meanwhile, Fitzroy had finished the minor rounds in third position with 13 wins and six losses, and defeated Carlton by a point in the first semi-final before losing the preliminary final to Collingwood by 19 points. The Maroons – who had been superbly served in the finals by the likes of Bill Stephen, Eddie Goodger, Vic Chanter, Jack Gaffney, Norm Johnstone and Allan Ruthven – believed that Norm Smith had been partially responsible for their success. Jack Gaffney said: 'It was the result of Smithy's three years of hard work. In all due respect to the Baron, we might have even made a Grand Final if Smithy had still been in charge'.[34]

ʯʯʯʯʯʯʯʯ

One of Norm Smith's triumphs during the 1952 season was the transformation of Stuart Spencer from a plodding, albeit solid, back pocket into a high quality rover. It was a transformation that required Spencer to reprogram his mind and body to satisfy Smith's need for him to think fast and run fast.

Spencer, a star rover for Portland in the Western Border League, had debuted for Melbourne in 1950. Allan La Fontaine shifted him to a half-forward flank, and then to a wing. John Beckwith, who had just signed with the Demons in 1950, recalled attending a Melbourne-Collingwood match at the MCG that year and watching Spencer struggle on the wing. 'Stuey didn't have the fitness to run up and down the ground,' Beckwith said. 'At one point, he gave away a free kick to his opponent, Thorold Merrett, and he was lying on the ground and he gave the ball to Thorold, who just ran off!'[35]

La Fontaine finally settled Spencer in a back pocket. 'As they say,' Spencer reflected, 'the next move is usually out of the side.'[36] Smith continued to play Spencer on the resting rovers, but it was not long before he realised the 20-year-old was being under-utilised on the last line of defence. Spencer takes up the story:

---

[33] Melbourne Football Club *Annual Report*, 1952.
[34] Jack Gaffney. Interview with the author.
[35] John Beckwith. Interview with the author.
[36] Stuart Spencer. Interview with the author.

By mid-season 1952, Norm decided that I was to become Melbourne's No. 1 rover. He said: 'Stuey, there will be time for you to return to the back pocket when you are 35.'[37] Usually such a development would be met with excitement from the player concerned, but I was actually disappointed because Norm dragged me out of the back pocket at a time when I was receiving praise for my efforts in that position. I was getting votes from Alf Brown in *The Herald*, and there was some discussion that 'this Melbourne back pocket might actually challenge the great Bill Stephen for the back pocket position in the state side'. But the coach had decided, so I had to do as he said. From that point on, I became a subject of Norm's close scrutiny. He continually pressed me on the training track, screaming: 'Stuey, why didn't you do this?! Stuey, you should have done that?!'

I'd think to myself: 'Why is he picking on me?' This happened all the time. He wanted me to get the ball and take off, which I didn't naturally do. I've seen modern footballers train and they never seem to be under the pressure that Norm applied to us. It got to the point where I felt so victimised that I was about to give up, pack my bags and go home to Portland. I continually came home from training and complained to my wife, Fay: 'Why does he keep picking on me?'[38]

After one such self-pitying lament, Fay Spencer decided she had tired of both her husband's complaining and the coach's chastisements. She recalled:

We'd go to the club dances and Norm would come over to Stuart and say: 'You didn't do this, you didn't do that', and Stuart was so keen on doing well with his football that he'd be like a pricked balloon for the rest of the night. I'd be thinking: 'Gee, Norm, why did you do that? It's spoiling our Saturday night.' So when Stuart complained to me after training that night, I was fed up with both of them.[39]

Fay told Stuart that in many ways she agreed with Smith. Stuart could not believe his ears. 'Fay, you're supposed to be on *my* side,' he complained. Fay elaborated: 'Maybe Norm is at you so much because he thinks you can be so much better than you're showing.' She went on to describe her husband as 'a bit of a jogger; a plodder' – an assessment which initially mortified Stuart, as he explained:

---

[37] Spencer was actually 37 when he returned to the back pocket, in his capacity as playing coach of Tasmanian club Clarence.
[38] Stuart Spencer. Interview with the author.
[39] Fay Spencer. Interview with the author.

The definition of a jogger in football terms is that you can run all day but you rarely catch up with the play, and you are unable to initiate team play. I didn't want to hear it but that's basically what I was at the time – a jogger, a plodder. But from that point, I made up my mind to change my whole approach to develop acceleration and, as Norm would term it, 'quickness'. That was all Norm had been trying to do with me. He could see I was working hard, but I wasn't quick. As soon as I realised what Norm had been trying to achieve to make me a better player, the ensuing results were outstanding. It was such a moment of clarity, such a brilliant realisation. It was like walking from the dark shadows into bright sunshine. From that moment on, every time I got the ball I dashed. Norm had baited me, whereas I hadn't seen it myself. I think I always had pace but I never knew how to extract it and use it to its full potential. Thankfully Norm did. He not only saved my career, but he built a foundation for something that could be respected.[40]

Smith often said: 'Respect isn't automatically given; it's *earned*.' After a shaky beginning, Spencer had certainly earned Smith's respect. Fay Spencer recalled her husband being best afield shortly after he had changed his outlook and Smith approaching her at the club dance and saying: 'The boy did well today.' It was a turning point in both Spencer's football career and his relationship with his coach. In seasons to come, Spencer's transition from plodder to tireless dasher became so complete that Smith would advise young players: 'If you want to learn how to train, watch Ron Barassi, Donny Williams and Stuey Spencer.'

Beckwith added: 'Stuey Spencer proved you could improve by simply getting more out of yourself at training, which Norm drove him to do. Once Stuey started training properly, he developed tremendous stamina and he was a different player, and we were a much better team for it because he'd win the ball as a rover and he'd kick goals. Stuey was already a good player, but he became a freak – one of the best. And a lot of it can be attributed to Norm's influence on his training, and Stuey's decision to take up Norm's challenge and train harder. If Stuey continued on the way he was going he still would have been a good player, but he would never have elevated himself to greatness like he did.'[41]

---

[40] Stuart Spencer. Interview with the author.
[41] John Beckwith. Interview with the author.

Elza Barassi had found love again. While working the canteen at Miller's ropeworks, the war widow had been courted by Tasmanian-based sales agent Colin Brewster. The couple eventually married and made arrangements to settle in Hobart in 1952. Ron junior was 16 and Elza naturally wanted him to join her and her new husband. Ron did not get along with his stepfather, but in light of his youth he had little choice but to follow his mother's wishes.

For Melbourne Football Club, and Norm Smith, this was an alarming development. The club had already fought for the right to recruit young Barassi, and other sons of former Demons, after successfully campaigning for the introduction of a father-son rule to circumvent the zoning system.[42] It is believed the Demons conceived the rule and suggested it to the VFL specifically with Barassi in mind. Without it, Barassi, who had been living with his mother in Preston and then Brunswick, would have been residentially zoned to Collingwood then Carlton.

However, a move to Tasmania would pose new problems in securing Barassi – if and when he was regarded as good enough – with players from interstate clubs often refusing to clear their stars to their VFL counterparts.

But to the infinite benefit of football fans for generations to come, fate – in the form of Norm Smith – intervened.

Smith had seen Barassi play in the Demons' third eighteen – 'the same start as his father', Smith noted[43] – and believed he 'had wonderful possibilities'[44] and 'looked like being a fine player'. He felt that while the youngster 'didn't have exceptional ability', he had 'good ability'. But Smith was most impressed with Barassi's 'exceptional enthusiasm' and his 'very strong desire to succeed'.[45] Fearful that Barassi would be lost to the Demons if he relocated to Tasmania, Smith concocted a plan to keep him in Melbourne, and give him an opportunity to play football *for* Melbourne. Norm and Marj Smith would offer to accommodate Barassi at their house and act as his foster parents. When Smith put his proposal to Elza Barassi, he explained the difficulty the Demons would face in gaining a clearance for Ron. This was an important consideration for Elza, a mother who was acutely aware of her son's dreams of playing in a premiership side for the Demons, as his father had 12 years earlier. 'After a lot of discussion,' Smith later recalled, 'she reluctantly agreed to let him stay with me.'[46]

---

[42] In 1950, Carlton's Harvey Dunn junior was the first player to be recruited under the VFL's father-son rule. Barassi was to be the second, and Fitzroy's Kevin Murray the third.
[43] *Melbourne Truth* series, 1962.
[44] *Midweek Magazine*, August 1964.
[45] *The Sun* series, 1967.
[46] *Melbourne Truth* series, 1962.

A priority for Elza was Ron's schooling. 'Mum felt I wouldn't knuckle down to study,' said Barassi, who had been studying for a diploma of engineering at Footscray Senior Tech. It was decided he would continue the course at night school. Norm and Elza also used their contacts to land Ron a full-time job in a three-year cadet executive course at Miller's ropeworks, where he would spend the first year as an office boy and then spend time in each department.

Smith would solve the question of Barassi's lodgings, and give the teenager some privacy, by paying for a bungalow to be built in his backyard. Elza would not hear of her friends funding something she was quite capable of looking after. She insisted that she would pay for the bungalow and that Ron would pay board. The finer details agreed upon, Barassi settled at the Smith house – with Norm, Marj, and four-year-old Peter – where he would spend the next four years.

Elza also knew that Smith would provide much-needed discipline for her boisterous son. Elza, according to Ron, had always been 'very conscious of me not growing up too soft without a father... She was soft and tender but she was also very tough'.[47] She was also determined that her son would become a man – in the truest sense of the word. A man who would stand up for himself and those close to him; one who would never take a backward step. Elza knew that Norm Smith was such a man – an ideal role model for Ron.

The headstrong Barassi was beginning to feel 'almost bullet-proof' and, in hindsight, admitted he needed to be 'straightened out' by a strong, paternal male.[48] Smith certainly filled that role. Barassi recalled: 'Norm walked a straighter line than most people. The only deviousness he had about him was the scheming and plotting he used in his coaching to deceive the opposition, but that was legitimate deceit in the name of winning. Aside from that, you'd struggle to find a straighter man. He was utterly trustworthy.'[49]

But while Barassi acknowledged that Smith had a profound influence on him as a young man – an influence that would encompass his entire life – he disputed the belief that Smith had been responsible for forming his values and outlook:

> The Norm Smith/father-figure thing has been a bit overdone... While he was certainly my football father, I was fairly well formed mentally and psychologically before I came under Norm's influence. Mum and Norm were very similar in their attitudes towards life – they were both strict on conduct; i.e., there was a right way

---

[47] Collins, Ben, *The Champions: Conversations with Great Players and Coaches of Australian Football*, GSP, 2006.
[48] Ron Barassi. Interview with the author.
[49] Ron Barassi. Interview with the author.

and a wrong way to do things – so Norm's values only reinforced what had already been drummed into me. I was very lucky to have such great role models.[50]

When Smith was asked years later to describe his relationship with Barassi, he said: 'It's not really father-son... He was a bit difficult to handle when he was young. He was 16, and I was hard with him, I suppose, but, there again, I was fair.'[51] Barassi agreed Smith had been fair, 'although, like any independent young bloke, I didn't always think he was so fair at the time!'[52] Marj Smith later said:

> Norm and (Ron)... had their disagreements but they were mostly about football. And they were mostly out of my hearing. I remember once, though, Ronny wanted to pay his board in threepenny pieces. He brought his bottle of threepences out to the kitchen table and emptied it. Norm objected to that and told him to take it back. There were little conflicts like that. He was a strong-headed boy. His mother was fairly strong-willed, and I think his father had been, too... Ronny was just naturally a pretty determined person. He sets his mind on something and whether it is right or wrong he goes for it.[53]

Barassi revealed that Smith's demeanour at home was not what many people would expect. 'He wasn't moody or grumpy,' Barassi said. 'He wouldn't bite our heads off just because he was in a bad mood. There was always a good reason for him being annoyed. He never whinged or moaned either. Not that he didn't complain – because he did – but it was never over a trivial matter. He didn't suffer whingers or moaners either.' One night Barassi 'whinged' and duly copped the consequences. 'I either criticised Marj's cooking, or I didn't eat it because I didn't like it, and *by golly*, did Norm go *off*,' Barassi said. 'He told me how very ungrateful I was, and that I should be thankful that I get a feed at all. Like my mother, he was very big on manners and being polite.'

For Barassi, the cooking incident was also an example of the strong relationship between Norm and Marj Smith. 'What a couple!' Barassi marvelled. 'They were extremely close. They occasionally had tiffs, like anyone, but they were rock-solid. They backed each other up to the absolute hilt, and were fiercely loyal to

---

[50] Collins, Ben, *The Champions: Conversations with Great Players and Coaches of Australian Football*, GSP, 2006.
[51] *Midweek Magazine*, August 1964.
[52] Ron Barassi. Interview with the author.
[53] Barassi, Ron and Peter McFarline, *Barassi: The Life Behind The Legend*, Simon & Schuster, 1995.

each other. Marj would always look out for Norm's interests, and if ever anyone offended Marj in the slightest, he'd come down on them like a ton of bricks.'

Barassi once quipped: 'I owe Marj a lot for the better part of my better parts, (and) to Norm for some of my bad parts!'[54] While Smith admitted to having 'some violent arguments'[55] with his young boarder, Barassi said they never went beyond verbal slanging matches. 'Our disagreements never escalated into a physical thing,' he said. 'There were never any punches thrown, and not even a grab of the collar. So while Norm could be a very hard, fearsome man who could intimidate, and he'd attack various parts of your character at times, you always knew he would never attack you physically. He was above that.'[56] Also, Smith understood that he and Barassi were similar souls. 'Ronny is like me in many ways,' Smith said. 'He's strong-willed and won't back down to anyone if he believes he's right.'[57]

The volatile pair also shared a similarly dogged competitive streak, which came to the fore during some 'ding-dong games of ping-pong'.[58] They set up a table tennis table in the Smiths' dining room and, according to Peter Smith, 'would go at it hammer and tongs. It was just another outlet for their competitive natures'.[59] Smith was an excellent table tennis player. A decade earlier, he defeated Australian champion Jim Thoms (who also played 120 games as a wingman for Footscray) in a 'social' game at Miller's ropeworks. 'Norm wiped Thoms off the table,' Hugh McPherson revealed.[60]

Smith recalled his table tennis contests with Barassi with great fondness: 'I'd use the pen-holder grip and beat him, then I'd use another grip and beat him. It would always end the same way with Ron throwing the bat down with a bang in frustration and annoyance... He hated to lose... Admittedly, I played it hard with him because of his determination to succeed. These were the same traits I had myself as a young fellow. I might add that in later years when we were both down at Melbourne he improved so much that he was able to thrash me and do it regularly. I didn't mind though. He was entitled to get his own back'.[61]

Owing to this ongoing rivalry, Barassi became such a fan of table tennis as a competitive pursuit that he later ensured a table was available for the use of his players at each of the clubs he coached. 'I used table tennis as a bit of a guide,' Barassi said. 'You could get a sense of how someone would be under pressure.

---

[54] Ron Barassi's speech at the Australian Football Hall of Fame dinner, July 19, 2007.
[55] *The Sun* series, 1967.
[56] Ron Barassi. Interview with the author.
[57] *The Sun* series, 1967.
[58] Ron Barassi. Interview with the author.
[59] Peter Smith. Interview with the author.
[60] Hugh McPherson. Interview with the author.
[61] *The Sun* series, 1967.

Do they go back into their shell and play safe and just put the ball back on the table? If they do, you might surmise that they might be a bit suspect in a tight situation on the football field. Or do they rise to the occasion and really go for it? In the space of five minutes you can do a fairly accurate character assessment.'[62]

The fierce nature of these dining room struggles also reinforced another of Smith's philosophies, as Peter Smith explained:

> It's like when I played tennis with Dad. Initially I'd try to hit winners, but I'd hit a few out and lose the match. Then I realised I had to play smarter. I thought: 'I've got to make him run.' It wasn't until I was about 16 that I beat him for the first time in tennis. He wouldn't let me win. But it wasn't as though he was being cruel. He felt that if you want to win you've got to earn it. If he just let me win from the start, I wouldn't have improved at all. He forced me to think and work and improve.[63]

This philosophy, which applied to any contest, even a 'social' game, rubbed off on both Peter Smith and Barassi. When they became fathers themselves, they did not let their own children win anything, 'not even board games', according to Barassi.[64] Peter explained: 'That's the way I was brought up and I thought it had a lot of sense. People would say to me: "You never let your kids win." I'd say: "Well, they weren't good enough". That came from Dad.'[65]

Despite being at loggerheads whenever there was a contest on offer, the pair developed a rare, almost unique, sense of loyalty toward each other. 'Norm wasn't a very demonstrative person,' Barassi said. 'He would express his affection with acts. He'd back you up. You knew that if ever help was needed, he'd be there – with bells on. And you couldn't have a better man in your corner.' An early example of this took place within months of Barassi's arrival at the Smith residence.

Barassi had a girlfriend – fellow Miller's Ropeworks employee Nancy Kellett (who later became his first wife). Rather than call her from home and risk being heard, Barassi regularly walked to a public phone-booth near the corner of Gaffney and Sussex streets for some privacy. On this particular occasion, Barassi patiently waited for a person to finish his call and exit the booth, but when he did, another man pushed past Barassi to make a call. The youngster ripped open the door to verbally protest against this treatment and was stunned when the man punched him in the face. With the door being held shut by his aggressor, Barassi moped home,

---

[62] Ron Barassi. Interview with the author.
[63] Peter Smith. Interview with the author.
[64] Ron Barassi. Interview with the author.
[65] Peter Smith. Interview with the author.

his masculine pride shattered. By the time he stormed in the front door, he was fuming. His mother just happened to be visiting that night. She and Smith realised something was amiss. Smith asked Barassi: 'What's up, mate?' When Barassi told him, Smith was seething. '*Jesus*!' Smith exclaimed. 'Let's go and see if he's still there.' When their search proved fruitless, they returned home. But Barassi could not get the injustice out of his mind.

'I was out in the bungalow and I kept stewing over it,' Barassi said. 'I thought: "This bastard must live somewhere around here", so I started scouring the streets.' He even searched a nearby foundry for the man, but with no luck.

On the way home, he spotted a woman sitting on her front fence as a man worked under the bonnet of a car. Barassi asked the woman 'I left my wallet down at the phone booth; do you know anything about it?'

The woman turned to the man and said: 'Darling? This young man has lost his wallet.' The man looked up and Barassi instantly recognised him as 'the mongrel I'd been looking for'. Barassi gave him his 'best straight right', and the man did not even fight back. When Barassi got home, he told the story. 'Mum was beaming with pride and Norm thought it was fair enough – one for one,' Barassi said. 'Neither of them condoned violence, but they believed in self-respect, standing up for yourself and not letting people walk over you. That also illustrated Norm's loyalty.'

By the end of the 1952 season, Smith had earmarked Barassi for a possible VFL debut the following year. As an initiation, and to enable him to become better acquainted with the senior players, Smith took Barassi on the players' end-of-season skiing trip to Mt Buffalo, in Victoria's North East. It was to be the first of many high points they would reach together over the next 12 years.

ŦŦŦŦŦŦŦŦŦ

In the Demons' rebuilding phase, with so many players no older than 21, they could ill-afford to lose any of the few experienced players they had. But at the end of 1952, they farewelled three experienced players of note – each of whom had been teammates of Norm Smith's in 1948. They were premiership centreman George Bickford (25-years-old, 126 games), tough half-back Geoff Collins, (26, 67 games), who had been posted to Korea as a fighter pilot with the RAAF, and brilliant Aboriginal running player Eddie Jackson (27, 84 games), who had been the 19th man in the 1948 premiership side.

Bickford, Melbourne's vice-captain, revealed that Smith's uncompromising attitude had swayed him to retire:

I gave the game away because I felt that, from my point of view, Norm was too demanding. I had an amateur outlook on the game, which was fine early in my career. After the war, under Checker Hughes, we had gotten down to training just one night a week. Don Cordner was a doctor and he was training one night a week, and I was doing the same, and going down there mainly on a Thursday night. But that wasn't enough when Norm came back to Melbourne as coach. He demanded that we train more. It was becoming more regimented and less flexible for players like myself who had an amateur outlook.[66]

As he suspected, Smith found that replacing this trio 'was not easy'. It was part of a full-scale reconstruction of the playing list. 'We decided to start at the very beginning and build up a team based on youth,' Smith said. 'The list had to be drastically cut at the end of '52. Players who had been at Melbourne a few years but who had not shown the necessary improvement were passed over.'[67]

Among the 15 youngsters who made their senior debuts for Melbourne in 1953 – many of whom were elevated after playing in the thirds under that great developer of youth, Roy McKay, the previous season – were eight superb long-term prospects: Frank 'Bluey' Adams, Ken Melville, Geoff Case, Peter Marquis, Don Williams, Terry Gleeson, Trevor Johnson, and… Ron Barassi. Curiously, despite the fact that Barassi lived under the same roof as the coach, he was actually invited to train with the Demons' senior list by secretary Jim Cardwell – by letter:

> Dear Ron,
>
> This is to extend to you a warm invitation to attend training with our club for Season 1953.
>
> Training will commence on the MCG on Thursday, March 5th at about 4.45pm and I trust we can see you in attendance under Coach Norman Smith.
>
> Wishing you all the best for the Season to come.
>
> Yours sincerely,
> J.H. Cardwell
> Secretary

---

[66] There are conflicting reports over Norm's treatment of amateurs. Some, like Bickford, say he was less tolerant of them; others say he was more lenient, with some citing skipper Denis Cordner as a prime example. It is alleged that while Norm drove every other player at training, he allowed Cordner, an industrial chemist, to 'lope around' at his own pace. Perhaps this was a one-off concession for Cordner alone.

[67] *The Herald*, late July, 1955.

HOME AGAIN [1952-53]

Barassi has often said: 'Living with the coach is a good way to get a game'. But in truth, it was probably a lot harder when the coach concerned was Norm Smith. The coach always stressed that he never gave Barassi preferential treatment. Many attest to the opposite being true. Smith explained: 'I do not believe in having favourites, and having Ron live with me made no difference to my treatment of him as a footballer. In fact, I was probably harder on him than any other player'.[68]

On reflection, and even at the time, Barassi understood Smith's tough stance. 'I quite agreed with his approach to me,' Barassi said. 'I would have done exactly the same thing myself had I been in his situation. Like all coaches, Norm had his favourites, and I'm sure I was probably one of them – that's the human element of it all –but coaches can't *play* favourites. Norm didn't want to be accused of that with me.'[69] Barassi realised: 'Norm didn't want anyone to justifiably say: "Hold on, Smithy, you're saying that and acting that way towards that particular player, but with your mate's son, Ron Barassi, the 'Roger the Lodger' at your place, you're not treating him the same way. What's going on?" A coach can't afford to let that situation develop, or even be implied, and Norm wouldn't have wanted that because it would have been seen as a weakness in man-management.'[70]

So when Smith and his selection committee decided that Barassi had earned his first senior game – after the Demons had lost the opening three games of the season – it was no surprise to the 17-year-old that Smith did not tell him personally. Barassi recalled: 'It might seem strange to people that although I was living with the man, and we sat at the same dinner table every night, he didn't tell me himself that I'd made the senior side – I had to read it in the newspaper like everybody else. I didn't see anything wrong with that, though, because Norm didn't tell other people when they'd made the side, so he didn't tell me either.'

Barassi was to play his first VFL game against a strong Footscray side at the MCG in round four, 1953. It did not take him long to learn Smith's pre-match ritual. 'It was a very quiet drive to the football,' Barassi said. 'He didn't want to talk, and didn't want to be talked to. I was of a like mind anyway, so that didn't bother me. I wasn't told not to talk, but there wasn't much conversation on the way to a game.'[71] (As the relationship evolved, however, the pair would often 'argue about different things all the way to the ground'.[72])

---

[68] *Melbourne Truth* series, 1962.
[69] Ron Barassi. Interview with the author.
[70] Collins, Ben, *The Champions: Conversations with Great Players and Coaches of Australian Football*, GSP, 2006.
[71] Ron Barassi. Interview with the author.
[72] Hugh McPherson, in an interview with the author, recalled Marj Smith telling him this.

Barassi spent all but 10 minutes of his debut seated next to Smith on the bench, watching on as the Demons managed just 1.4 to three-quarter time and conceded 20 more scoring shots (30 to 10) in a 45-point loss to the Bulldogs. When Barassi finally got a run in his father's No. 31, he was so keen to impress during his belated cameo that he admitted he 'ran around like a chook with its head cut off'.[73] But he still managed to learn a crucial lesson. Rampant Footscray captain-coach Charlie Sutton had tucked the ball under his bulging arms and was charging straight at Barassi. Sutton teased the youngster by showing him the ball, and Barassi was drawn to it like a moth to a porch-light. Sutton baulked him easily and continued on his merry way down the field. 'He'd sold me a dummy and I felt like a bloody dill,' Barassi said. 'After the match, Charlie introduced himself to me and said: "Son, a player's hands are faster than his body, so always go for the body".'[74]

Barassi was to learn a far bigger, and sterner, lesson from Norm Smith later in 1953. After getting a taste of senior football in his debut, Barassi was sent back to the reserves to refine his game under the guidance of Smith's old forward partner, Jack Mueller. Barassi was recalled to the senior side in round 11 (against St Kilda at the Junction Oval) – by which stage the Demons had just one win on the board. Three weeks later, when he was demoted for the second time, Barassi was still yet to play in a winning senior side. This next stint in the reserves revealed a disturbing change in his attitude. Barassi later described Smith as 'a very personal coach' whose focus was 'mainly character stuff',[75] and the youngster was about to experience this 'personal' style first-hand.

Smith was first alerted to the problem when he received a written report from Mueller. Smith recalled: 'It was blunt and straight to the point and said: "Barassi: This player thinks he can do as he likes." The inference was that because he lived with Norm Smith, the senior coach, he could do as he pleased. I had to dress him down over that one.'[76] Barassi conceded he probably deserved whatever blast he had coming. 'Whether it was true or not that I was acting like a selfish player, I had at least given that impression,' Barassi said. 'They felt my attitude was: "I've just come down from the firsts; they should kick the ball to me". When Norm heard about it, it was like waving a red rag at a bull.'[77]

---

[73] Ron Barassi. Interview with the author.
[74] Collins, Ben, *The Champions: Conversations with Great Players and Coaches of Australian Football*, GSP, 2006.
[75] Ron Barassi on ABC Radio National program *The Sports Factor*, on September 28, 2001.
[76] *The Sun* series, 1967.
[77] Ron Barassi. Interview with the author.

HOME AGAIN [1952-53]

The confrontation between player and coach took place in Smith's car. As per usual on training days, Smith would pick up Barassi at Miller's ropeworks on his way to the MCG. It was only a matter of minutes before Smith enlightened the young tyro about the contents of Mueller's report. 'That revelation came out when we got to Fitzroy,' Barassi said, 'and the journey from that point to the MCG ensured I never got a swelled head again.'[78] Smith's recollection of what followed was typically brief – 'I can see him now. The chin came out, but he didn't argue. He took it and said nothing.'[79]

Barassi's recall of the tense car ride was far more vivid, which was understandable considering he was an impressionable 17-year-old at the time:

> It was a one-way conversation. Norm said: 'Who the hell do you think you are?! Jack Mueller reckons you think you can do what you bloody like because of your connection with the senior coach!'
>
> He proceeded to give me a lecture on concentrating on doing your best for the team, not for yourself. That way you get looked upon as a better player anyway, and your teammates are more willing to give you the ball. Today, team play has gone to extraordinary levels because they have been taught better, but back then star players, particularly those in poor teams, could rule the roost and pretty much do what they liked. But Norm would have none of that. Everyone played under the team rules, his rules, or you were out. He said: 'Don't get ahead of yourself.'
>
> I might have gotten into the car with a swollen head but when I got out 20 minutes later Norm had deflated it to half the size. Norm was very good at one-on-ones, and gauging a player's attitude and putting them back in their place. The only thing that made that lecture a little easier to bear was the fact that Norm couldn't eyeball me like he would normally – because he was driving the car at the time! And, boy, could he eyeball you. I get shivers just thinking about it now.[80]

Barassi added that Smith and Mueller were '100 percent right' to come down hard on the first sign of any complacency on his part. 'If a player acts that way and the coaches decide: "That's OK, let him have his head; he'll come around one day", that's wrong,' Barassi said. 'I was very lucky to have a bloke like Norm around to keep everything on an even keel.'[81]

---

[78] Collins, Ben, *The Champions: Conversations with Great Players and Coaches of Australian Football*, GSP, 2006.
[79] *The Sun* series, 1967.
[80] Ron Barassi. Interview with the author.
[81] Collins, Ben, *The Champions: Conversations with Great Players and Coaches of Australian Football*, GSP, 2006.

Smith also questioned the team ethic of another of his promising youngsters – Frank 'Bluey' Adams. A redheaded whippet who debuted in round 14 and played four games before being dropped, Adams said: 'Norm told me he thought I was a very selfish footballer; perhaps one of the most selfish he'd seen. It was probably true to a certain extent. It was more about my style of game than my attitude. One of my strengths was my speed, so I liked to get the ball and run with it and bounce it and take on the opposition. But in doing so, sometimes I'd ignore a lead or an opportunity to handpass. But Norm did say that his role as coach was to take advantage of my strengths, and not so much to work hard on my perceived difference from the ideal footballer. He wanted to maximise your strengths.'[82]

Smith always spoke his mind, and nothing was ever left unsaid, like the time when a fringe player asked him why he was not in the senior team. Rather than dilute or sugar-coat the criticism, Smith was as blunt as ever: 'You're not in the team because you're not bloody good enough!'[83] While it was a brutal and probably hurtful retort, at least the player walked away from it knowing exactly where he stood, and that he had not simply been 'spun a line'. Another young player who bravely asked Smith the same question was Ralph Lane, who recalled:

> I was playing well in the seconds but wasn't getting a senior game, so I went up to Norm at training one night and said: 'I reckon I should be getting a (senior) game. Why aren't I getting one?'
>
> Norm told me I wasn't fit enough, along with a couple of other things I had to smarten up on. I went away and thought: 'Jeez, he's right'. So I went pro-running in the summer of 1952-53 and ended up running in the Stawell Gift. I came back a lot fitter and faster for 1953 and eventually Norm and the selectors rewarded me and I played the next 40-odd games in a row.
>
> Norm had helped me get to that level because his words had a real impact on me. Some players didn't take too kindly to certain things Norm told them and they didn't change their ways and were dropped – and some didn't turn up to play in the seconds, which you just don't do. But they had nothing to complain about because a lot of the time it was their own bloody fault and Norm was right![84]

---

[82] Frank 'Bluey' Adams. Interview with the author.
[83] *Allsport Weekly*, August 2, 1973.
[84] Ralph Lane. Interview with the author. Lane later performed various roles with the VFL/AFL. He was manager VFL Park at Waverley, AFL finance manager and player payments director. He was also the finance director on the Melbourne board (1985-91).

Smith was also right to stand firm on Melbourne's residential hold on reluctant young recruits like 16-year-old Ian Thorogood. A Richmond supporter, Thorogood was desperate to play for the Tigers, but was zoned to the Demons, who demanded that he 'front' for training so they could assess his potential. He recalled:

> I was training with big names like McMahen and McGivern, but to me they were nobodies because my heart was set on Richmond. I didn't feel I should have been there, and didn't want to be there, so I didn't try very hard at all at training. I just cantered around on the MCG for a couple of weeks. That's when I met this big, gruff, redheaded bloke. Norm came up to me and said: 'I think you've got something'. I don't know how he could have formed that opinion because I certainly didn't think I had shown much on the training track. Norm said: 'We're going to send you down to the under-19s'. That was that. It started a steady movement through the ranks, with Norm frightening hell out of me at times.[85]

One of the standout traits Smith most admired in his growing crop of youngsters was the courage of former University Blacks star Ken Melville. A 22-year-old wingman-cum-centreman, Melville won the Demons' best-and-fairest in his first season. Smith came to describe Melville as the most courageous player he had seen. Barassi once wrote that Smith had 'made such a thing' of courage 'that some of his players who were a bit timid were also too scared to show they were scared'. But unnatural levels of courage were seemingly a natural part of Melville's make-up. 'Norm Smith was always loud in his praise of Ken Melville,' wrote Barassi.[86] Smith later said: 'Ken Melville is my No.1 player for courage... Although he lacked physical strength... he did more courageous things on the ground than any other player I have seen... Ken inspired his teammates by taking marks while running into difficult positions. Courage was something he taught himself, and yet he was such a gentle man'.[87]

Although flattered by the compliment, Melville did not think there was anything special about the way he played. 'I didn't have the natural ability and flair of a lot of other players,' he said, 'so if I saw the ball, I determined that I'd better get there before the other bloke. If a mark had to be contested, I contested it'. Melville, in turn, was in awe of Smith:

---

[85] Ian Thorogood. Interview with the author.
[86] Ron Barassi, *The Sun*, August, 1973.
[87] Newspaper report, 1965.

I followed Melbourne as a boy and as a 10-year-old, I saw Melbourne play in the 1941 Grand Final. He was one of the players I aped in kick-to-kick. I hero-worshipped him to an extent. I once ran onto the ground and got him to scrawl 'N. Smith' onto a bit of paper. I was always full of admiration for him as a player and his whole attitude to the game, in terms of his unselfishness and team-first.

I was fascinated to meet him in person when I first went to Melbourne in 1953. I found him so approachable and likeable; a thoroughly good bloke. In the early days, I was in awe of him and the whole situation I found myself in. I never even considered that I might play football with Melbourne because I never thought it would come within my realm of possibilities. I more than respected Norm. I won't say I revered him, but I felt he was a wonderful man. And that was quite apart from his football skills. To spend time with him socially was a marvellous experience. He was genuinely interested in you.[88]

Smith moved Melville into the centre midway through the season and did not see the need to give him too much direction on how to play the position. 'Norm only spoke to me once about it,' Melville said. 'He said: "You're staying too close to the centre. Move around a bit". So I did as he asked and that must have kept him happy because I didn't receive any criticism from him after that. I developed my game myself. I was very much a defensive style of centreman. I'd often drop back and cover for teammates while they ran down the field. I think that style fitted in well with what Norm wanted. I certainly didn't hear anything from him to the contrary.'

Melville also recalled a game when Smith decided not to give any instructions to any player. Leading into the round 11 clash with St Kilda at the Junction Oval, the Demons were 1-9 and on the bottom of the ladder, while the perennially battling Saints were 2-8. Melville said:

Norm was so frustrated with some of the attitudes of players, and the way we were going about it, that before the game at St Kilda he told us: 'All right, if you think you can do it your way, go out and do it your way. I won't say a word'. He gave us no instructions whatsoever. We were dumbfounded. He just let us play. I'm sure some of the players thought: 'Great, we can do what we like here'. But at quarter-time we were worse off than ever (24 points down). It was an interesting touch he had just to prove the point that we needed a coach, and we needed to take notice of what he was saying.[89]

---

[88] Ken Melville. Interview with the author.
[89] Ken Melville. Interview with the author.

By the end of the 1953 season, it was debatable whether the players were in fact listening to the coach. All the Demons had to show for their 18-round season were three wins and a draw. After a good first-up season, the Demons had plummeted to 11th – only their third double-figure finish since the VFL became a 12-team competition in 1925. It was the club's (not Smith's) second such placing in three seasons. 'Level-headed and experienced judges knew that this was no true reflection of ability,' Percy Beames later wrote in *The Age*. 'But they thought a comeback would take at least four years.'[90]

The Demons' annual report was sympathetic to Smith's predicament, stating he had 'at all times displayed keenness and ability deserving of a higher reward than the position on the list we ultimately occupied. Always seeking to develop team spirit, Norman must be in some measure rewarded by the abundance of that spirit now evident in our rooms'.[91]

But Melbourne officials who had been conditioned to success under Checker Hughes were restless. It had been – by five-and-a-half games, or 22 premiership points – the worst performance by a team coached by Norm Smith. He provided the following insight into the lot of a losing coach: '(The coach) can be the loneliest man in the world. When the team wins, the players get most of the credit. When it loses, the coach cops the abuse.'[92]

In Smith's defence, the reason for Melbourne's fall appeared obvious: the rebuilding process, which necessitated the mass blooding of youngsters – many of whom had been exposed to senior football before their time – was never going to bring immediate results. One such youngster, Geoff Case, later blamed Melbourne's slump on the inconsistency of youth. 'Us young players could fire up one week,' Case said, 'but then, for no particular reason other than our inexperience, we'd go missing the next week. That makes it pretty tough on the poor old coach. But Norm would have expected that, and been fairly optimistic that we'd eventually come up with the goods for him.'[93]

Another mitigating factor was the number of close matches that went against the Demons. In addition to the draw, they had lost five games by no more than 10 points, and another, to eventual premier Collingwood, by 15 points. Smith's view was: 'While we did not expect to be well up the list during our team-building process, we thought we would do better than the three-and-a-half games we did win. Our position on the list, second last, was a little disappointing... We lacked the

---

[90] *The Age*, Monday, September 19, 1955.
[91] Melbourne Football Club annual report, 1953.
[92] *The Sun* series, 1967.
[93] Geoff Case. Interview with the author.

experience, so, on the surface, it was not as bad as it appeared. We were consoled by the thought that there were better things to come.'[94] If, in fact, Smith would still be there to oversee the better times.

Smith's job – and, indeed, his entire VFL coaching future – was in danger. And he knew it. He later admitted: 'There was plenty of talk then that Smith was a failure as a coach. I was rather concerned about it, and I think my position was in doubt, in real jeopardy'.[95]

The Demons considered their options for what seemed like an eternity to Smith. After much discussion at board level, and a particularly long decision-making process, they eventually put Smith out of his anxious misery and reappointed him for 1954. Publicly at least, he had the full support of the committee, which enthused: 'It will only be a matter of time before his hard work and endeavour will be rewarded'.[96]

On reflection, this was a crucial moment VFL history, and, in particular, Melbourne Football Club. If the Demons had sacked Smith, many Melbourne people would have been disappointed, but few would have been surprised, and even fewer would have been outraged enough to mount a campaign for his reinstatement. Despite the extenuating circumstances, the fact was Smith's coaching record was moderate at best. At the end of 1953 it read: 92 matches, 42 wins, 46 losses and four draws, equating to a success rate of just 45.65 percent. Even worse, he had not coached a side into the finals in his five seasons in charge of two VFL clubs. An indictment on his coaching ability – probably unfair – was that even Allan La Fontaine, the largely reviled former Demon coach, had guided a team to a finals series. Despite the various glowing tributes from individuals within both clubs, Smith's CV was hardly impressive. Would another VFL club have offered him a coaching position? Perhaps. But it is certainly possible that Norm Smith's coaching career could have been over before it really began.

---

[94] *The Herald*, late July, 1955.
[95] *The Sun* series, 1967.
[96] Melbourne Football Club *Annual Report*, 1953.

10

THE DEMON UPRISING

[1954]

The Melbourne committee's review of the coaching position at the end of the 1953 season was a bittersweet experience for Norm Smith. While it was a stressful and protracted affair, it prompted Smith to make a fundamental change in his approach; one that was essentially self-centred, but would help to steer the Demons to the most successful dynasty in VFL/AFL history.

After his coaching performance had survived heavy scrutiny in the boardroom and he was appointed Melbourne coach for a third season, Smith subjected himself to a critical self-analysis in which he closely examine his strengths and weaknesses. Of course, he paid particular attention to his weaknesses. His conclusion was:

> I realised then that I'd been making a bad mistake. I'd been trying to please too many people and in fact was pleasing no-one, not even myself. I remember going to (secretary) Jim Cardwell…and telling him about my change of outlook. 'From now on,' I told him, 'I'm going to please only one person. If I fail, I'll fail on my own merits and by using my own methods.'[1]

That meant assuming, and being given, more power both on and off the field. In later years, Smith gave an idea of the level of power he sought: 'The coach must have the courage of his convictions. He must be given sole control of the team when it's on the field, and he must have the final say in team selection and placement. You sit with your four other selectors and you must listen to what they have to say. But it is no good taking someone else's selection and trying to make it

---

[1] *The Sun* series, 1967.

work your way. This is the advice I would offer to all young coaches... There were very few occasions (when) I failed to get the team I wanted, even if I had to debate the matter pretty hard to get my way.'[2]

Smith was bemused when the experts wrote Melbourne off as a declining force after the lowly finish in 1953, and remained quietly confident about the Demons' mid to long-term future. The major reason for his optimism was what he proudly described as his 'first-class bunch' of youngsters.[3] The Demons further enhanced their stockpile of youthful talent in 1954 when they recruited of another batch of brilliant boys – ruckman/forward 'Big' Bob Johnson, centreman Laurie Mithen, on-baller Brian Dixon, rover Ian Ridley, forward Clyde Laidlaw and ruckman Colin Wilson. Smith's youth policy was in full swing.

Dixon recalled a daunting first meeting with Smith: 'I was barely 17 and weighed less than 10 stone (63.5kgs). In my eyes... (Smith) was physically enormous, matching the stands which were his background. He talked like a demon, with his red hair and his nostrils flaring. I was afraid. I said clearly: "Good afternoon, Mr Smith", but my heart was thumping'.[4]

Smith later revealed some of his philosophies on dealing with young players, and his expectations of them when they entered his regime:

> Being young was certainly no barrier - if a player had the necessary attributes. I found that young players who were good enough, and yet had potential, were keen to learn, eager to train hard and...keep fit...
>
> Not all young players can break straight into a League side from junior ranks. The majority must be prepared to fight their way up from the lower sides and model their play along the lines adopted by the senior team.
>
> I expected any young player who came to Melbourne to show me every talent he possessed, both on the track and in practice games.
>
> A newcomer is expected to be able to kick and mark reasonably well. If he is small, he must have quickness of movement. If he is big, he must be patient because his type takes longer to develop.
>
> The most important thing of all is determination to succeed, and I cannot emphasise this point more. For if there is no real and honest will to succeed then a player might as well take up table tennis on Saturday afternoons...

---

[2] *The Sun* series, 1967.
[3] *The Herald*, late July, 1955.
[4] *The Age*, early 1965.

They cannot be playboys and play football. They must be prepared to make sacrifices to get to the top. And they will find the benefits and privileges they can obtain - the payments, the glamour, premiership honours, interstate trips and, above all, personal satisfaction of succeeding - make it worthwhile.

They must have the ability to take it more than give it. I have more admiration for the player who can take it, and go on playing football, than for the player who gives it and can't take it when he gets it back.

Young players should be prepared to suffer disappointments and unlucky breaks, and always place their club before themselves. They must always be completely loyal to the club they represent...

They must be prepared to play in any position without argument... Full-forward(s) and rovers are the hardest to find...

Young players... should guard against over-confidence. They will find a big difference in standard, and the hardest thing to cope with will be the quickness of senior players.

They will find themselves tackled fiercely. This, incidentally, was an important feature of our game at Melbourne...

All players should be developed along individual lines and encouraged to develop their natural style of play while being integrated into a team. This is better than having a team composed of 18 stereotyped footballers - robots who all look alike, but fail when the coach presses the button for men to play differently - because our great game is a matter of circumstances and crucial decisions. A player must be capable of changing style and tactics when he is told to.

Any coach's aim is to get a team of 18 stars. Then he must coordinate the ability of the individuals into a team effort. The players must know what they can do and what they are not allowed to do. They must do what is expected of them by their coach and teammates at *all* times... Discipline - that's what makes great players... (However) players should be encouraged to use their own initiative... while playing to the overall plan devised by the coach...

They must always realise they are playing to win and that sometimes a word or two from the coach can make the difference between defeat and victory...

A player with a lot of natural ability is never easy to tell, especially when he first joins a club. He has never had to be told before. Always accept advice, even if it hurts. When you can do this, son, you are on your way.[5]

---

[5] *Craven*, John (editor), *Football The Australian Way*, Lansdowne Press, 1969.

That Smith's autocratic coaching style met little resistance said more about Australian society at the time than anything else. Bluey Adams, then one of Melbourne's developing players, explained:

> An 18-year-old back then was a lot different from an 18-year-old today. We didn't have the level of education or maturity. We came from a Victorian background – Victorian in terms of behaviour, not the state – where children should be seen and not heard. Using me as an example, I came from a single-parent family and I was almost painfully shy. When I got to Melbourne, I trained in a sleeveless pullover for the first four nights because I didn't have the nerve to ask for a training guernsey.
>
> And all of the parents of the players at that stage had lived through the Depression, and none of us had really privileged backgrounds, so we had it drilled into us from childhood that you had work for everything you got. We had simpler, better-balanced lives than players of today – we worked 40-hour weeks, most of us played another sport in the summer, unlike today where they just play footy, and they've got a lot of money, free time and temptations, whereas we played for the love of it and there weren't all these other distractions.[6]

All young players of the generation were also required to complete compulsory national service with the Army.[7] Clyde Laidlaw described the mindset of many footballers of the day who had been 'nashos':

> All of my age group did national service, where you were punished if you stepped out of line. And you had to look out for your mates, and as a footballer, all I wanted to be was a team man. It was important to me to be looked upon like that by teammates. We were disciplined, very fit, and quite accustomed to following orders and conforming. We were ready-made to be taught and told things, which suited a drill-sergeant type of coach like Norm. Like 99 percent of players under Norm, I never questioned his decision-making. His coaching was army-style, which many of us were very familiar with. We respected authority. There weren't many who put a foot out of line.[8]

---

[6] Frank 'Bluey' Adams. Interview with the author.
[7] With several conflicts around the world impacting upon Allied interests, including the declaration of war in Korea, the Menzies government introduced the *National Service Act 1951*, which required males turning 18 from November 1, 1950, to complete 176 days of service training. Up to 1972, 300,000 'nashos' graduated from the scheme.
[8] Clyde Laidlaw. Interview with the author.

In fact, some of Smith's players believed the discipline he enforced was a lot tougher than Army discipline. It was all motivated by Smith's unwavering belief that 'weak men can't win premierships'.[9]

Although Smith tried to create an atmosphere of togetherness at Demonland, he kept his distance from most of his players, particularly, it seems, the younger ones. First-year player Ian Ridley said: 'Maybe it was because I was a naïve country boy at the time, but Norm seemed such a gruff character that you felt you should call him "Mr Smith".'[10] Laidlaw, who was 'in awe' of Smith in his first two seasons, believed his coach's stand-offish manner was a conscious ploy. 'He kept the players at bay, and kept you guessing, particularly early in the piece,' Laidlaw said. 'He wanted to constantly keep you on edge; to keep you in doubt over your spot in the team, so that you didn't feel you'd made it.'

Most of the debutants were dropped to the seconds at semi-regular intervals, and Laidlaw didn't believe the demotions were all form-related. 'We were all in and out of the side,' Laidlaw said. 'We'd play a couple of games and then we'd get dropped – and Norm never gave you much explanation. But the selectors felt that turning over so many young players, giving us a taste, dropping us and bringing us back, and testing our character and trying us in different positions, was a good thing because we would be better for it in the long run.'[11]

Smith's youthful team received a boost in experience and toughness with the return of 27-year-old war hero Geoff Collins. The Demons regained the 1948 premiership player only after some fancy political footwork by Bert Chadwick. Collins, who had been cited for bravery after flying more than 100 missions over Korea in 10 months, was permanently posted at the military testing town of Woomera, 486 km north of Adelaide. This posed a dilemma for Smith. With Denis Cordner relinquishing the captaincy due to growing business commitments, Smith had identified Collins as his preferred replacement. His best ally in bringing his plan to fruition was Chadwick. The Melbourne president 'pulled some strings' with his contacts in the RAAF, and arranged a promotion for Collins that permanently relocated him to North Melbourne. It was a bittersweet experience for Collins: he 'wasn't happy' about being forced to give up his flying career, but he was honoured to be appointed captain, which was at least some consolation.[12] In some ways it was a surprise appointment. Collins had been out of the game for a season and had just 67 games to his name. The other strong candidate for the coveted leadership

---

[9] *Melbourne Truth*, Saturday July 31, 1965.
[10] Ian Ridley. Interview with the author.
[11] Clyde Laidlaw. Interview with the author.
[12] Mary Collins, the widow of Geoff Collins. Interview with the author.

role was Noel McMahen, who, in Collins' absence, had become a superb on-field leader under Cordner. Despite having 118 games' experience and being one of the club's best players for several seasons, McMahen was unexpectedly overlooked.

Nonetheless, Collins – a premiership teammate of Smith's in 1948 (and the son of 1926 premiership wingman Jack Collins) – was a figure who commanded great respect. He certainly had the respect of his coach, who had paid for an official RAAF photograph of Sergeant pilot Collins in air force attire after returning from a mission against 'the communists of North Korea'. Collins was standing beside his Meteor jet-fighter, which was adorned with an insignia of a pitchfork-wielding Demon, along with the slogan: 'BOWL 'EM OVER'. What impressed Smith even more was that was exactly how Collins played.

ϒϒϒϒϒϒϒϒϒ

Melbourne supporters were abuzz with excitement in the pre-season period of 1954 when Fred Fanning signalled his intention to make a VFL comeback with his old club. In the six seasons since his retirement at the end of the 1947 season, Fanning had coached Western District league club Hamilton to four Grand Finals and two premierships, and continued his goal-fest. He once kicked a record 152 goals, and bagged a league record 22 majors against Heywood in 1949, and 20 against Penshurst in 1950.

The Demons had never been far from Fanning's thoughts. In recent years, he had alerted Melbourne officials to talented young local players like Ian Ridley (Hamilton Imperials), and Stuart Spencer and Clyde Laidlaw (Portland), and he occasionally caught up with Norm Smith and other former teammates for a drink when he was in Melbourne.

From the outside, it appeared that the goal-starved Demons – in 1953, Bob McKenzie had won the club goalkicking award for the third time with a total of just 38 goals, with the next best being ruckman Denis Cordner on 15 – would be boosted by the return of a goal machine.

But Norm Smith wasn't so convinced. Although well aware of Fanning's ability, Smith also acutely conscious with his shortcomings. Fanning was 32, had not played a VFL match for six-and-a-half years (since the day he kicked the League record of 18 goals), and had constant weight problems – his already massive frame had ballooned to more than 18 stone (115 kilograms). Then there was the issue of Fanning's single-minded attitude and style of play. In the event of a Fanning return, Smith would likely install him as the spearhead, but would build a multi-pronged attack that would not allow him to be the sole focus of both his teammates' forward thrusts and the opposition's defensive efforts. Indeed, one of Smith's catchphrases was: 'You don't put all your eggs in one basket'.

But Smith acknowledged his side's desperate need for more goals – from somewhere, anywhere – and warily agreed to trial Fanning. However, that was to be the extent of the 'comeback'. It soon became obvious that Fanning had lost most of his mobility and it was decided, perhaps mutually, to abort the exercise.

Although most areas of the Melbourne line-up required close attention after a disastrous 1953 season, the Demons clearly needed a revamp of its forward line. Although Noel Clarke had played further afield in 1953, Smith would switch him back to a key forward role. It was not ideal. Clarke, who had won the Demons' goalkicking in 1952 with 49 in 19 games, was brilliant on his day, and so was regular Victorian representative McKenzie, but with a lack of tall options, Smith resolved to get more goals from the likes of Stuart Spencer and 'Bluey' Adams.

🏉🏉🏉🏉🏉🏉🏉🏉🏉

Among the many new faces in the Melbourne changerooms at the start of 1954 was an old, familiar one that Norm Smith instantly recognised as his tough former teammate Hugh McPherson.

'Hughie! How are you?' Smith said, delivering a firm handshake to his old mate. 'What the bloody hell are you doing down here?'

'I've just been to see Jim Cardwell,' McPherson replied, 'and he said that seeing I was a former player he's quite happy to have me here as a trainer.'

'Trainer, be buggered,' Smith said dismissively. 'You're my runner. And there'll be no ifs or buts about it.'

McPherson didn't protest. It was just the kind of role he instantly knew he would relish.

In 1954, VFL clubs were prohibited from using runners or messengers. But most clubs used trainers for this role, sending them onto the field under the pretence of treating players for sore spots, when they were actually relaying messages from the coach. Many believed Norm Smith pushed this harder than any other coach of the era. Smith sensed the bespectacled McPherson – a strongly-built butcher – would be ideally suited for this important covert job.

Smith and McPherson had a long discussion about what the running job entailed. Smith told him: 'I want you to deliver messages to players in exactly the same manner as I give them to you. Sometimes I'll want very fierce messages delivered and you'll need to be fierce as well. Don't water it down. And don't take any back-chat.' McPherson recalled:

> Every player understood I was the ghost of Norm Smith. I was Norm's voice out on the field, his messenger, and an extension of his thoughts, and I, too, became indoctrinated with his philosophies. What I told them, and how I told them, was how Norm intended them to be told – with venom, and a pat on the back. I'd say: 'You do this', and I'd point the finger just as Norm would. He also knew I would stand up to the umpires if necessary. And it was necessary quite often because of the rules. It could be a difficult job at times. You had to be a bit sneaky and not let the umpires know what you were up to, even though they and the whole crowd knew what you were up to. As soon as the crowd realised what was going on, they'd erupt and start screaming and moaning about it. The umpires – whether they be field or boundary umpires – would often send me off the field, or at least try to, and we'd argue, and the opposition crowd would get stuck into me. But I had a thick skin and was never afraid of being involved in a bit of a ruckus – that's why Norm gave me the job in the first place.

McPherson estimated that he delivered '30 or 40' illegal messages a game. 'It was mainly to tell a player what he was doing wrong and how to fix it,' he said. 'If a player wasn't doing his job properly, the message from Norm might be: "If you don't lift yourself, you'll be off." That usually put the fear of God into them because, in those days, if you were dragged off the ground you stayed off. It wasn't an interchange system back then.'[13]

One of McPherson's most memorable early messages related to the kicking skills of former captain Denis Cordner, whom Smith greatly respected both as a player and a person. Smith later wrote: 'Denis may have lacked a little of his older brother's finesse, but he was completely tireless and dependable – and this made him just as valuable'.[14] However, Smith still tried to place some constraints on Cordner, as McPherson recalled:

> Denis was one of the best ruckmen Melbourne ever had, but he was also one of the worst ever drop-kicks. One day, Denis out-marked his opponent on the last line of defence, went back and kicked a drop-kick, which was marked by the man standing the mark a few yards away, and he kicked an easy goal from

---

[13] Hugh McPherson. Interview with the author.
[14] *Pollard*, Jack (editor), *High Mark: The Complete Book on Australian Football*, Murray, 1964.

the goalsquare. It was an embarrassing mistake. Norm sent me out to tell Denis: 'You are *NEVER* to attempt a drop-kick again!' But in another match not long after, Denis took a mark five metres out from goal and, with nobody within cooee of him, drop-kicked a goal. As he was running back to the centre for the bounce, he gave Norm a wave on the bench. It frustrated hell out of Norm, but it became a running joke between them.[15]

Incidentally, Smith actually frustrated an opponent with a wave of his own from the bench. Ralph Lane laughed as he recounted: 'One day John Brady from North Melbourne was bouncing the ball around the boundary line and as he went past, Norm jumped off he seat and waved his hands in front of him to try to put him off. Brady kept running, took another couple of bounces and kicked a goal, and stuck his thumb up at Norm. It was a bit of fun for both of them, but I think it was one of the very few occasions where Norm was made to look foolish in any way.'[16]

︎ ︎ ︎ ︎ ︎ ︎ ︎ ︎ ︎

In sport, the wonder of youth carries with it the virtues of excitement, enthusiasm and the promise of success. But, to the frustration of impatient fans, youth also brings inconsistency, which the Melbourne faithful came to know only too well in the first half of the 1954 season.

In what Norm Smith expected to be a year of redemption – and despite the presence of a sprinkling of experienced campaigners like Geoff Collins, Denis Cordner, Noel McMahen and Bob McKenzie – the Demons' early-season form fluctuated from giant-killing peaks to inexplicable failures. But then again, anything was better than the continuous disappointment of 1953 – and Melbourne's performances early in 1954 were *far* more assured than they had been the previous year.

In their season-opener against reigning premier Collingwood at the MCG, the Demons impressed 45,858 spectators with their early ferocity, leading by a goal at quarter-time and trailing by a point at half-time. However, they conceded five goals to none in the third term and eventually went down by 38 points. There was no shame in that, though, against a Magpie side which, in its previous match at the MCG, had taken on a record-breaking Geelong side in the 1953 Grand Final and had sewn up the premiership by three-quarter-time.

---

[15] Hugh McPherson. Interview with the author.
[16] Ralph Lane. Interview with the author.

Undeterred, the Demons won five of their next seven games, taking the prized scalp of the Cats at Kardinia Park in round eight. But just one victory from the next four matches had them perilously placed in seventh with a 6-6 record – a game behind Essendon, Richmond and Geelong. They needed to win virtually all of their remaining six matches to make the finals. One of the turning points was the round 10 clash with Footscray at the Western Oval. Although the Demons did not win the match – they lost to the classy Bulldogs by 16 points – they had pulled an ace from the pack. Smith had used the previously tried and failed colt, Ron Barassi, in an unorthodox and rarely before seen role as a small ruckman – or, as the position became known, ruck-rover.

As Smith later marvelled: 'It is curious to think back on it now but… (Barassi) wasn't an instant League success'.[17] In Barassi's six senior matches in 1953, he started three off the bench and endured unsuccessful stints in attack. In the Demons' round 12 draw with Richmond at the MCG, Barassi was tried at centre half-forward. His opponent that day was 27-year-old Richmond captain and star backman Des Rowe. 'I never gave him one touch,' Rowe said later. 'Norm Smith said to me as I went up the race, "Thanks very much, Des, I will never play Barassi in a key position again".'[18] On this point, Smith was not true to his word.

Barassi started his second season, 1954, in the reserves. He played at full-forward on Syd Coventry junior at Collingwood and performed well enough in front of Smith to be promoted to the seniors for the round two clash with Carlton at Princes Park. Although he managed to kick two goals and was 'robbed of at least another couple'[19] in a 19-point win, his opponent George Ferry was best-afield. The following match against Hawthorn at Glenferrie Oval produced an almost identical result: two Barassi goals and a dominant opponent, this time state full-back Len Crane, who was second-best on ground.

Stuart Spencer recalled: 'Barassi had so much energy and enthusiasm that he was jumping over everyone – even his own players – to try to get the ball. Our centre half-forward, Clyde Laidlaw, was so sick of being rammed into and jumped on that he went up to Norm and said: "Get this bloke off the ground, otherwise he'll bloody kill someone!" It got to that.'[20] Laidlaw was more circumspect but no less critical. 'Barass was so awkward at full-forward – he was mistiming his jump, misjudging the ball and leading too early,' Laidlaw said. 'He just wasn't suited to playing that type of role.'

---

[17] *The Sun* series, 1967.
[18] Bartlett, Rhett, *Richmond Football Club: A Century of League Football*, GSP, 2007.
[19] Ron Barassi. Interview with the author.
[20] Stuart Spencer. Interview with the author.

Barassi's confidence had taken a pounding. 'It wasn't a surprise to anyone that I was banished to the seconds the next week,' he said.[21] He was giving his all – perhaps too much – and now he had failed in another position. There was confusion over which position he should be tried next. Even Barassi was unsure. 'I struggled early because I wasn't quick enough to be a half-forward flanker and I wasn't tall enough to be a key-position player,' he said. 'Norm thought I would make it as a player, but he wasn't sure which position suited me best.'[22]

Back in the reserves, Barassi was picked on a half-back flank against Richmond at Punt Road. He had 'a bit of a crook knee', but the demotion to the reserves – and more so to the backline – had hurt more. He thought: 'I really shouldn't be playing, so maybe I should dodge the half-back flank and give my knee a rest at the same time.'[23] But fearing that his withdrawal would be 'another black mark' against him,[24] Barassi played, and performed moderately.

Smith was perplexed about what to do next with 'young Ronny'. Hugh McPherson recounted a fateful conversation with Smith – a conversation that Barassi remained unaware of for decades after.

> Often Norm and I would sit down and have a chat about players, and I'd make the odd suggestion, which he would take on board and either use it, do something similar or discard it completely. He always told me: 'If any of these things that you've suggested to me actually come off, I'll get the accolades; and if they don't come off, I'll take a kick in the bum.'
>
> One night, Norm told me: 'I'm having trouble with young Barassi. He's really keen to play League football, but I've tried him in three different positions but he's been hopeless in each of them.'
>
> I said: 'He's such a willing worker, why not try him in the ruck?'
>
> Norm said: 'Oh, don't be bloody silly. He's not big enough.'
>
> I said: 'Well, do you think I was big enough to ruck with Don Cordner? *The Herald* rated us the best ruck combination in the League in 1943, and Ron is two inches (5cm) taller than me.'
>
> I was 5'9" (175cms) and Ron was 5'11" (180cms). And he was a strong enough lad to do it. I just saw that Ron had it in him to do it. It was at least worth a try.

---

[21] Collins, Ben, *The Champions: Conversations with Great Players and Coaches of Australian Football*, GSP, 2006.
[22] Collins, Ben, *The Champions: Conversations with Great Players and Coaches of Australian Football*, GSP, 2006.
[23] Collins, Ben, *The Champions: Conversations with Great Players and Coaches of Australian Football*, GSP, 2006.
[24] Ron Barassi. Interview with the author.

We played entirely different games: he was full of endeavour; everything I did revolved around protecting Don Cordner. But Norm said: 'Oh, no, no, no – you must be out of your mind.' We just agreed to disagree and left it at that.[25]

For the next reserves match, against St Kilda at the MCG, Barassi was chosen as second ruck to Terry Gleeson in the reserves. Barassi regarded it as an 'interesting' selection.[26] Until that time, teams generally – and ideally – assigned the ruck duties to three big men: two ruckmen who changed out of a back-pocket, and another big 'second ruck'. The idea was that, between them, the ruckmen and the second ruck would have the stamina to contest all bounces and throw-ins around the ground. But the roles of Barassi and Gleeson were to be different. Gleeson, 'a very fit ruckman who could go all day',[27] was to do *all* the ruckwork. According to Barassi, 20-year-old Gleeson 'expressed excitement that he didn't have to share the ruck duels'.[28] This also suited Barassi, who was free 'to follow the ball around and do my own thing'.[29]

The experiment was an overwhelming success – Barassi was best-on-ground in his first game as a 'ruck-rover'. The role was custom-made for him to showcase his strength and fierce attack on the ball. Over the next three rounds, with Gleeson continuing to work tirelessly in the ruck, Barassi strengthened his credentials as an on-baller. He was selected to represent Victoria in a reserves match against South Australia,[30] in the curtain-raiser to the senior match. Again, Barassi was outstanding in his new role, with the South Australian selectors awarding him a trophy as the Vics' best player.

Smith's opinion of Barassi the footballer, and potential long-term leader, continued to rise. With regular leaders missing from the reserves line-up, Smith awarded Barassi the captaincy for the round nine match against Essendon at Windy Hill. With the senior side to play on the Monday, Norm Smith watched Barassi in action as a ruck-rover for the first time. On the short drive home, Smith asked Barassi: 'Why didn't you shift "Dicko" (Brian Dixon) out of the centre and put yourself in there?'

Barassi shrugged his shoulders. 'Well, that's the coach's job isn't it?'

---

[25] Hugh McPherson. Interview with the author.
[26] Collins, Ben, *The Champions: Conversations with Great Players and Coaches of Australian Football*, GSP, 2006.
[27] Ron Barassi. Interview with the author.
[28] Ron Barassi. Interview with the author.
[29] Collins, Ben, *The Champions: Conversations with Great Players and Coaches of Australian Football*, GSP, 2006.
[30] This is the only time an interstate reserves match has been played.

Smith said: 'You should have done it yourself.'

Barassi was surprised by Smith's comments, later saying: 'Whether he didn't think much of Jack Mueller as a coach I don't know, but I'd hate to think what would have happened to a captain who did that when Norm was coaching! I wouldn't have even thought about doing it, but here Norm was, telling me I should have basically overruled or undermined the coach.'[31]

By virtue of his brilliant form – particularly on such a big stage on a stand-alone day of football when VFL clubs had a week's break – Barassi had forced Smith and his fellow selectors to recall him for the match against Footscray. And rather than placing him on a flank or in a pocket, Smith selected him as second ruck – a decision that was received with incredulity by most of the football public. Fourteen years later, Smith wrote: 'I remember too well the ridicule we got when Ron Barassi was named as a ruckman'.[32]

Before the match, Barassi asked his senior ruck partner, Denis Cordner: 'What do you want me to do, Denis?'

Cordner's uncharacteristic response was: 'I don't care what you do; just keep out of my bloody way!'

Barassi recalled: 'That was the extent of our discussion on tactics! But I did precisely as Denis asked and it worked very well.'[33]

Hugh McPherson took special notice of Barassi that afternoon, and proudly remembered that he 'bored in all day and crashed through packs, and passed it off or kicked it long. He played a terrific game, and a star was born. I was very happy that the move had come off – if it hadn't, Norm probably wouldn't have listened to me again! – and I was full of admiration for Norm for being flexible enough to change his thinking on Barassi and consider another point of view from left-field'.[34] What's more, Barassi still managed to make an impact on the scoreboard, kicking two of Melbourne's eight goals. Smith later hailed that afternoon at the Western Oval as 'the start of a legend'.[35]

Barassi had finally found his niche, and would never return to the reserves in the remaining 15 years of his glittering career. Smith was relieved. 'He was finally fitted in as... the third leg only of a very wonderful ruck combination with Denis Cordner and Stuart Spencer'.[36] And so began the career of a player who would

---

[31] Ron Barassi. Interview with the author.
[32] *The Age*, Wednesday June 19, 1968.
[33] Collins, Ben, *The Champions: Conversations with Great Players and Coaches of Australian Football*, GSP, 2006.
[34] Hugh McPherson. Interview with the author.
[35] Newspaper report, 1965.
[36] *The Sun* series, 1967.

not only make the position his own, but produce such heroic feats that he would, in 1996, be named ruck-rover in the AFL's 'Team of the Century'.

Some have claimed that Barassi's reinvention as a ruck-rover probably saved his career; and that if Norm Smith (and Hugh McPherson) had not created the position for him, he might not have found his niche, and might have been lost to VFL football all together. But this view is too simplistic. While it is indisputable that Barassi owed his initial meteoric rise to stardom to the positional change, it does not account for the famous Barassi resolve – that bottomless pit of determination – which would likely have found a way when there appeared none anyway.

The ruck-roving position, as Smith had instructed Barassi to play it, had seldom been employed in the history of the game. Despite what many believe, Barassi was not the first ruck-rover – a fact Barassi openly admitted. Perhaps the title of the first true ruck-rover belongs to Allan 'Bull' Reval, a Port Adelaide great of the 1930s and 1940s. Others to have played similar roles were Richmond champion Jack Dyer, and Geelong's Russell Renfrey, although this pair also contested ruck duels. But regardless of the origins of the position, there is little doubt that Barassi popularised it, and took it to a new level, and in doing so became the prototype for teams the country wide to imitate in their on-ball structure.

It was no coincidence that once Barassi became a dominant on-ball presence, the Demons' form improved. 'The advent of Barass helped us immeasurably,' said John Beckwith. 'Once he got a sniff of what to do, he was a great runner – he took off. He also loved to handball over blokes' heads – not always to his teammates; sometimes just so he could run on and get it back again. That was a bit different too, and while it didn't always come off – to Norm's great displeasure at times – it was this type of initiative that created run and meant we carried the ball over the next line.'[37] Clyde Laidlaw recalled that when Barassi's 'super high levels of energy and enthusiasm' were channelled into ruck-roving, 'he left the rest of us behind individually, but as a team he helped take us forward in leaps and bounds'.[38]

Barassi also had the nerve, and confidence, to bark orders at club veterans. In a game early in his career, he felt that Noel McMahen was giving an opposition forward too much latitude, so he screamed at McMahen: 'Get back on your man, Macca!' McMahen, being a great on-field leader in his own right, accepted it without protest because the youngster had been right. This incident simply reinforced the view of those at Demonland that they had a livewire on their hands.

---

[37] John Beckwith. Interview with the author.
[38] Clyde Laidlaw. Interview with the author.

THE DEMON UPRISING [1954]

The Demons had pushed the strong Bulldogs side and followed up with a 33-point win over North Melbourne, the Kangaroos being 'regarded in many quarters as probable Grand Finalists'.[39] *The Football Record* stated: 'Melbourne could win through to the four and give the premiership a shake. But they have proved most inconsistent this year'.[40] In round 12, they faced the sternest of tests – reigning premier Collingwood, in front of 29,000 fans at the Magpie cauldron, Victoria Park. The Magpies, who were still at the head of the VFL ladder, had entered the match with an 8-3 record after defeating an impressive Footscray by 10 points. In atrocious conditions, Melbourne surprised the fanatical black and white army by dominating general play. But to their frustration, the Demons did not finish off their work in front of goal. Although Melbourne had twice as many scoring shots as the Magpies in the first half, the scores were level – 2.8 (20) to 3.2 (20). Inaccuracy cost the Demons the match, as they went down by 10 points – 8.6 (54) to 5.16 (46). Even though they had now lost three of their previous four matches – to take their record to 6-6 – the Demons were actually improving.

Although Barassi was a major driving force, and a unique point of difference for the Demons, it was by no means a one-man show. The Demons were also boosted by the improvement of the likes of Bluey Adams, 'Big Bob' Johnson, Geoff Case, Brian Dixon, and Laurie Mithen, which added greater depth to a side piloted by the almost constant output of more experienced performers like Cordner (who won his second best-and-fairest), Spencer (who averaged 23 kicks a game), McMahen, Melville, Noel Clarke, Bob McKenzie, Ian McLean, Beckwith and Peter Marquis.

'Once the young players started to play better, the whole team changed,' Beckwith said. 'We suddenly didn't have all these holes to plug. The change was quite dramatic from '53 to '54. We also had quite a few other players who were starting. At the end of '53, Norm probably decided we had to attack more. We'd always been a very good defensive side but we didn't have many attacking players, but the influx of youth, many of them quick players, certainly fixed that.'[41]

The Football Record emphasised the speed factor. 'The Demons must be regarded as one of the fastest teams in the League... It seems to be a mistaken idea that they are a long-kicking, high-marking side. Certainly they possess a number of aerial stars, but they have won their games principally through speed and stamina'.[42]

The Demons were a mere outside chance of making the finals in 1954. It appeared that they would have to win all of their remaining six matches – depending on

---

[39] *The Football Record*, July 3, 1954.
[40] *The Football Record*, July 3, 1954.
[41] John Beckwith. Interview with the author.
[42] *The Football Record*, July 17, 1954.

other results, they could perhaps afford to drop just one game – to make the final four. It was crunch times like these when Norm Smith's coaching ability came to the fore. Smith would take it upon himself to provide the spark. He later wrote: 'I cannot stress enough the importance of the coach's role. He must encourage his players to believe it is possible to do things they thought impossible, to show in their own play imagination and initiative above the ordinary. More often than not, he will have to go it alone, but if he has the courage of his convictions and is determined to put his ideas into effect, success will surely come.'[43]

The Demons, as expected, comfortably disposed of Carlton (by 35 points) and Hawthorn (77 points), but then, inexplicably, suffered a shock 11-point defeat to Allan Ruthven's second-bottom Fitzroy at Brunswick Street in round 15. The Demons slipped back to seventh, but just a game off third. They had lost any margin for error that they previously had, and would need to win the last three games to have any chance of making the finals.

The round 16 clash with finals hopeful Richmond, which was a game clear of the Demons, would prove telling. In fact, it was what *The Football Record* described as 'one of the most remarkable games of the year'. With five minutes left, Melbourne led 14.4 (88) to 5.17 (47), 'when suddenly an atom bomb hit it'. The Tigers piled on five goals in a frenzy, and, with the crowd 'hysterical with excitement',[44] surged forward yet again, with a long shot being touched in the goalsquare for a behind to reduce the Demons' lead to 10 points. A goal would have slashed the margin to five points. Although the Demons saved face with a late goal and a 16-point win, they had lost valuable percentage in the process.

With two rounds remaining, the VFL ladder stood as follows:

	Pts	%
Geelong	44	130.3
Essendon	40	111.1
Collingwood	40	107.6
Footscray	38	122.5
Nth Melbourne	38	94.3
Richmond	36	113.6
Melbourne	**36**	**113.5**

---

[43] *The Age*, Wednesday June 19, 1968.
[44] *The Football Record*, August 21, 1954.

THE DEMON UPRISING [1954]

The Demons were scheduled to play two of the three bottom sides – St Kilda and South Melbourne. After they pounded the Saints by 57 points at the MCG, they faced a tricky assignment at the Lake Oval. The rumour mill had finals aspirant Essendon offering financial inducements to South Melbourne players to down the Demons and, thus, help the Bombers into the final four. The rumours were unfounded and Melbourne won in 'cavalier fashion' by 52 points.[45]

The Demons had finished the season with a hot streak, winning five of the last six rounds, by an imposing average of 49 points. The reward was fourth spot on the ladder. They finished just half-a-game behind second-placed Footscray, and a game and healthy percentage clear of Richmond, Essendon and Collingwood. It was official – the Demons had qualified for their first finals series in four years, and Norm Smith would mount his maiden September campaign in six attempts. Immensely proud of his young side, Smith was bemused by the reactions of experts to the achievement of the Demons, and defended his side against claims it had been lucky to make the final four. 'People said we fluked it,' Smith said. 'I didn't agree. We had recruited remarkably well and had the basis of a good side in 1953.'[46]

Norm Smith's first final as a coach was the 1954 first semi-final against North Melbourne at the MCG. It was also the first time the Demons and Kangaroos had clashed in a final, and neither side had made the four since 1950. Just five Melbourne players – Geoff Collins, Denis Cordner, Noel McMahen, Bob McKenzie and Geoff McGivern – had VFL finals experience. North was no better off in this department. Similar to the Demons, North had won four of its previous five matches – albeit against the four bottom sides: Hawthorn, South Melbourne, Fitzroy and St Kilda – but the one miss was a draw with Footscray in round 16 at Arden Street.

North Melbourne's tactics became apparent immediately after the opening bounce when Demon forward McKenzie retaliated and was reported for striking North's Percy Johnson. The home side's plan worked, and they were first to settle amid the mayhem, charging to a three-goal lead, which, 'on general play, should have been greater', as Melbourne 'fumbled badly, seemed overawed by the importance of the occasion, were outpaced and outmarked'.[47] It was not until midway through the second term that the Demons finally played with the system that earned them a finals berth, and they briefly stole the lead before going in at half-time trailing by a goal. The Demons gained the ascendancy with a five-goal to two third term as the game became 'really nasty' and descended into 'a bloodbath'.[48] McGivern

---

[45] *The Football Record*, September 4, 1954.
[46] *The Sun* series, 1967.
[47] *The Football Record*, September 11, 1954.
[48] Ralph Lane. Interview with the author.

was one Demon who was decked behind play by a mystery assailant. *The Football Record* condemned North for instigating 'stupid and unnecessary physical clashes', while commending Norm Smith's Demons for their unwavering approach. 'It says much for Melbourne's courage,' *The Record* admired, 'that they never flinched, never shirked the issue, and few teams would have withstood the fierce and fiery onslaughts that met players in the second half.'[49]

Melbourne polished its performance with 7.3 to 4.2 in the final term – to total 12.7 to 6.7 in the second half – to win by 30 points. Noel Clarke starred with six goals, to go with the five he kicked against the Kangaroos in the round 11 win, while other prominent Demons included Geoff McGivern at centre half-forward, Geoff Case (three goals) on a half-forward flank and defenders Don Williams, Peter Marquis and John Beckwith. Barassi had also posed problems for North with his seemingly boundless energy around the packs.

The victory mood was tempered when it was learned that McKenzie had received a four-match suspension. It was a massive loss. McKenzie had won three of the past five club goalkicking awards. In that period since the start of the 1949 season, he had kicked 206 goals in 99 games – 79 more than the nearest Melbourne player, Noel Clarke, who had kicked 127 majors in 55 games.

The Demons advanced to their first preliminary final since 1948, but were confronted with a daunting challenge. Their opponent was Geelong, which had entered the finals on top of the ladder for the fourth consecutive season (it had won the 1951-52 flags and finished runner-up in 1953) after winning its last eight home-and away games by an average of 39 points. The Cats had stumbled in the second semi-final, succumbing to Footscray by 23 points. Stung into action by the loss to the Bulldogs, the Cats quickly set about trying to set up a rematch with Footscray in the Grand Final.

Geelong boasted 15 premiership players; Melbourne had four – Geoff Collins, Noel McMahen, Denis Cordner and Lance Arnold. The edge in experience told early in heavy conditions on a saturated MCG, with Geelong kicking two goals before Melbourne had scored. The Demons finally posted their first goal after 17 minutes. The Cats opened up a three-goal lead early in the second term, but Melbourne responded with the next two goals – both to Noel Clarke, the second from a dubious free kick – to be within a goal at half-time. Just seven goals had been kicked in first half.

The weather cleared after half-time and with an injured McMahen being replaced, the Demons appeared to be in trouble when a 60-yard punt from Cats

---

[49] *The Football Record*, September 11, 1954.

star Leo Turner sailed through for a goal. But, inexplicably, that was to be the end of the Geelong resistance, as Melbourne kicked the next three goals to take an 11-point lead by the last change, before adding 3.2 to 2.2 in the final term to win by 17 points. The likes of Denis Cordner, Don Williams and Ken Melville and Geoff Collins starred in the inspiring win.

Remarkably, after almost being out of the finals race mid-season, the Demons had made the Grand Final. Even more remarkable was the fact they had come from second-last the previous season. Although Melbourne's annual report of 1954 raved that Smith's effort was 'without equal in the records of the VFL', this was not entirely correct. It was the first such instance since the VFL had become a 12-team competition, but two other sides had previously come from second-last or last to play in Grand Finals the next year: Essendon came from last in 1907 (eight teams) to runner-up in 1908 (10 teams); and Richmond went from second-last in 1923 (nine teams) to runner-up in 1924.[50] There has been just one such instance since, with Collingwood rising from last in 1976 (12 teams) to runner-up in 1977.

The question was: 'Can the young Melbourne side stand tall for a third successive final?' The situation was not helped by a decision to take the players down to sit in the hot sea-baths at St Kilda on the Sunday morning after the preliminary final. It was thought that it might aid the recovery of their aching limbs, but it actually had the opposite effect on some players, including wingman Ralph Lane. 'I don't know why we went there,' Lane said. 'I knew it was a bad idea as soon as I stood up to get out – I could hardly stand up. It had taken everything out of me.'[51]

That day, the Bulldogs were 'primed' and 'full of beans'.[52] After having a week's rest by virtue of their victory over Geelong in the second semi-final, they had what captain-coach Charlie Sutton described as 'the best training session I've been involved with'.[53] In front of a massive crowd of about 18,500 fans at the Western Oval – where the Sydney-to-Melbourne bike race finished after Footscray's session – the Bulldogs 'trained the house down'[54], and 'the ball hardly hit the ground'.[55] The only problem Sutton had was ensuring his players did not overdo it.

---

[50] The 1916 season, when only four teams participated – and Collingwood finished the minor rounds in second place, but ended up 'last' after the finals, only to win the flag the next year – was not counted in this exercise.
[51] Ralph Lane. Interview with the author.
[52] Charlie Sutton. Interview with the author.
[53] Charlie Sutton. Interview with the author.
[54] Charlie Sutton. Interview with the author.
[55] Charlie Sutton, in *The Champions: Conversations with Great Players and Coaches of Australian Football*, by Ben Collins, GSP, 2006.

Meanwhile, Smith was struggling to get his players to do the bare minimum of track work in Grand Final week. During the Thursday night session, less than two days before the game, most of the Melbourne players 'couldn't kick the ball more than 30 yards. They were physically gone'.[56]

The Bulldogs were understandably warm favourites to win their first premiership in their 30th season in the VFL. Essendon coach Dick Reynolds added to the Bulldog aura by declaring in *The Argus* that they had the VFL's best full-back (Herb Henderson), centre half-back (Ted Whitten) and full-forward (Jack Collins). Success-starved Footscray had won just two finals in its history. Its ice-breaker was the previous season's first semi-final, when it defeated Essendon by eight points. (Before that, the Bulldogs had lost six first semi-finals – in 1938, 1942, 1944, 1946, 1948 and 1951.) They had bowed out of the 1953 finals series with a 26-point defeat to Geelong in the preliminary final. Sutton said the win over Geelong had 'really topped up the belief among the players that we could win a premiership ... We were ready to go'.[57]

Grand Final day was perfect. The MCG bathed in warm sunlight under a cloudless, blue sky. With the Northern Stand under construction in preparation for the 1956 Olympic Games, a more-than-capacity crowd of almost 81,000 crammed into the stadium. Spectators spilled over the fence and ringed the boundary line, sitting three-deep. In addition to holding actual favouritism, Footscray was also the sentimental favourite. Most of the crowd barracked for the Bulldogs that day.

As Smith tried to rev up his players and lift them to another inspired performance, Sutton was doing the same with his Bulldogs, and getting so 'worked up' that he had 'froth and spittle flying out of his mouth'.[58] In turn, Footscray players, as young star Peter Box said, went into a trance-like state. Box said: 'I would have run through the burning fires of hell for Charlie Sutton'.[59]

Sutton was acutely aware of the contrast in physical conditioning of both sides. 'We knew Melbourne would be very tired after coming from fourth and playing two tough finals, which was a pretty big effort,' he said. 'We decided we'd hit them hard and often and make them chase us. If we placed enough pressure on them, they'd eventually crack and we should run over them.'[60] Sutton emphasised that playing 'run-on football at all costs' would bring success, and – using a line

---

[56] John Beckwith, on the *Red and Blue* documentary, 2005.
[57] Charlie Sutton. Interview with the author.
[58] Herb Henderson, Footscray full-back, in an interview with the author for *The AFL Record*, April 8-12, 2004.
[59] Peter Box, in an interview with the author for *The AFL Record*, April 8-12, 2004.
[60] Charlie Sutton. Interview with the author.

he had gleaned from Checker Hughes on an interstate trip with the Victorian side – implored his Bulldogs to 'shop early and avoid the rush'. Sutton was also wary of the physical threat posed by Demon tough nuts like Collins, McMahen and Barassi. 'I told the players: "I'll look after the heavy stuff; you just concentrate on playing football".'[61]

The contrast between the sides extended to the way they entered the field. Sutton and his Footscray side were out first. They were 'fresh and fit and raring to go, and they bounced out onto the ground'.[62] Melbourne was late. So late, in fact, that umpire McMurray went to the rooms to order them out while Smith delivered his last-minute instructions. The young Demons were 'exhausted'.[63] After two hard-hitting finals in a row, particularly in the heavy conditions of the preliminary final, amid an extended run of must-win games for the previous two months, they 'just fell out' onto the field. They were 'mentally and physically buggered'.[64] Some Demons, like McMahen, limped into the game. McMahen had torn a leg muscle while representing Victoria in Perth mid-season, and, he recalled, several teammates were similarly restricted. 'We were just hanging on and Footscray were absolutely primed and playing great football,' McMahen said. 'We were always going to struggle just to compete with them in that Grand Final.'[65] However, the Demons later conceded that such explanations did not, in any way, detract from the efforts of Footscray, which they regarded as the best side of the year.

At the start of the game, a Melbourne player riled Footscray spearhead Jack Collins with the timeless, though crass, sledge: 'I slept with your mother last night'.[66] The insult was designed to provoke the volatile full-forward into fighting rather than kicking goals. Collins, the Bulldogs' wildcard, had already done plenty of the latter, having kicked a league-high 77 goals in 16 matches. He had an added incentive to perform. 'I blame myself for us not making the Grand Final the year before,' Collins lamented. 'I shouldn't have gotten myself suspended. I was very determined to atone for my misdeeds.' The sledging backfired, but not immediately. It actually appeared to have the desired effect when Collins missed his first two shots; 'easy' chances according to the man himself. 'I think nerves and the big occasion got to me,' Collins said.[67]

---

[61] Collins, Ben, *The Champions: Conversations with Great Players and Coaches of Australian Football*, GSP, 2006.
[62] Ralph Lane. Interview with the author.
[63] Noel McMahen. Interview with the author.
[64] Ralph Lane. Interview with the author.
[65] Noel McMahen. Interview with the author.
[66] Hugh McPherson. Interview with the author.
[67] Jack Collins, in an interview with the author for *The AFL Record*, April 8-12, 2004.

At the 10-minute mark, Ken Albiston hit Noel Clarke with a sizzling pass to bring up the first goal of the match. The Demons led – 1.1 (7) to 0.2 (2) – but their advantage was short-lived.

Sutton, the Bulldogs' man of steel, began to show just why he was regarded as 'a master in the scientific use of weight'.[68] Sutton had entered the match with a question mark over his left hamstring after not having played a full match for five weeks, and missing the second semi-final. But the 30-year-old veteran – he had captain-coached Victoria to victory over South Australia at the MCG in 1952 – had hatched a cunning plan to throw Norm Smith and the Demons off-guard. Sutton said: 'I made out I was injured and the plan worked… I was 100 percent fit and fully recovered for the Grand Final. But I thought we might be able to get an advantage if I wore a huge bandage around my thigh – the Melbourne boys would think I was still injured. It worked because they started a younger inexperienced opponent on me – John Beckwith. I thought I'd try to upset them a bit, so I started a dust-up with Beckwith and had another with "Barass".'[69]

In this destructive frame of mind, where he waged a virtual one-man war on the Demons while his teammates played the ball, it was almost inevitable that Sutton would prove a handful. Beckwith admitted: 'Charlie Sutton… threw his weight around and had a go at various players and that unsettled us, (and) we couldn't get going'.[70] Smith soon relieved Beckwith of his unenviable assignment. Sutton regarded it as an early moral victory. 'I knew we had them worried,' Sutton said, 'because they started shifting their backmen around and reacting to what we were doing. They put their captain, Geoff Collins, on me. I thought: "Hello, there's the crack in the armour. We've got them a little bit rattled".'[71]

Ignited by Sutton, and with 21-year-old Ted Whitten starring at centre half-back and John Kerr controlling the centre, the Bulldogs placed the Demon defence under siege. Collins kicked the next two goals, and finished with three of Footscray's six goals of the first term, to open up a 29-point lead – 6.3 (39) to 1.4 (10). The Demons were flat-footed and devoid of system, with many of their kicks missing their intended targets. The Bulldogs were sharp and purposeful. Sutton observed: 'We got the jump and they were always going to struggle to catch us after that.'[72]

---

[68] Hugh Buggy, *The Argus*, September 25, 1954.
[69] Charlie Sutton, in *The Champions: Conversations with Great Players and Coaches of Australian Football*, by Ben Collins, GSP, 2006.
[70] *Red and Blue* documentary, 2005.
[71] Charlie Sutton, in *The Champions: Conversations with Great Players and Coaches of Australian Football*, by Ben Collins, GSP, 2006.
[72] Charlie Sutton. Interview with the author.

Straight from the centre bounce at the start of the second term, the Bulldogs moved the ball with a series of slick passes to Collins, who kicked his fourth major to extend their lead to 35 points.

The Demons got no sympathy from the largely Bulldog-barracking crowd either. With spectators lining the boundary players often pulled up before the line, which they could barely see, but that didn't stop some from falling into the crowd. Bulldog ruck Arthur Edwards said: 'It was terrific if you were playing for Footscray because if you went over the boundary and into the crowd, they threw you back. I think they wanted to throw the poor Melbourne players *over* the fence.'[73]

Just when the game appeared over, the Demons rallied. Goals to Barassi, Spencer and Mithen drew them within 17 points. A Sutton goal from a free kick just seconds before the half-time siren once again gave Footscray the upper hand. Collins said: 'We were so pumped up when we went in at half-time and playing on so much confidence that we knew Melbourne would have to produce a near-miracle to beat us.'[74]

An actual miracle was required when the Bulldogs kicked two goals in the opening four minutes of the third quarter to increase the margin to 37 points. Melbourne kicked consecutive goals, including Bob Johnson's first, ironically while he was in the ruck and not while stationed in the forward pocket. But Collins' fifth goal and Sutton's third blew out the deficit to 38 points by the final change.

South Melbourne great Laurie Nash criticised Smith for being slow to react, writing in *The Sporting Globe*: 'Norm Smith reshuffled his side at three-quarter-time. Clarke and McGivern changed places, and Mithen went (from a half-forward flank) to the centre... These changes should have been made at half-time'.[75]

Melbourne responded with the first goal of the final term but that was the end of the resistance. Collins' seventh goal, courtesy of a booming 70-yard torpedo, sealed the match, with the Dogs eventually doubling Melbourne's score – 15.12 (102) to 7.9 (51). Footscray had become the first of the three former VFA clubs introduced into the VFL in 1925 – North Melbourne and Hawthorn were the others – to win a VFL premiership. It was Footscray's first and remains its only flag.

The best players in a losing Melbourne side were Cordner, Barassi, Mithen, McLean, Williams and Albiston. Although the Demons had been comprehensively beaten, they were not disgraced. Beckwith said: 'We never caught up (with Footscray), but there were good signs there with the way we played after quarter-time'.[76]

---

[73] Arthur Edwards, in an interview with the author for *The AFL Record*, April 8-12, 2004.
[74] Jack Collins, in an interview with the author for *The AFL Record*, April 8-12, 2004.
[75] Laurie Nash, *The Sporting Globe*, September 25, 1954.
[76] *Red and Blue* documentary, 2005.

Norm Smith hated losing. This is borne out by one of his oft-used sayings: 'Rarely is there honour in defeat'. Another went: 'Winning isn't everything, but it's a bloody sight better than what comes next!' But, all things considered, Smith took the Grand Final defeat well, which reinforced another Smith credo that demanded humility in victory and graciousness in defeat. Ken Melville elaborated:

> Norm was always a delighted winner, but a very gracious one. He wasn't one for crowing over opponents when he was the victor. And he always a gracious loser, and first to congratulate the opposition. That's a trait I've always valued, and it's a value that I have tried to pass on to others. If we lost a game, Norm would certainly be disappointed, but it wasn't the end of the world. He didn't castigate us for it. If we'd lost, as we walked off the ground, he would be at the head of the players' race and perhaps give you a touch on the arm and a word of encouragement. There certainly weren't any recriminations on his part.[77]

Smith later said: 'I never like to lose matches, but I did not begrudge them the win.'[78] Smith was always 'very warm towards those who succeeded against him'.[79] According to Sutton, this was exactly the attitude Smith presented over a drink after the match. Sutton recalled:

> Norm must have been hurting but he certainly didn't show it. He warmly congratulated us and complimented us on how we played the game. He told me: 'Charlie, you blokes showed us how to play premiership football today.' There's no bigger compliment or greater endorsement of the Bulldogs '54 side than that. He then said: 'You deserved your victory, but we'll be back and we'll make up for it next year.' And didn't they make up for it! Although we obviously would have loved to have gone on with the business and won more premierships after that, we're proud in a way that we had an influence on one of the greatest teams ever. Funnily enough, we can actually take some credit for helping Melbourne become a league heavyweight.[80]

Smith consoled his players, including Geoff McGivern, who recalled:

---

[77] Ken Melville. Interview with the author.
[78] *Melbourne Truth* series, 1962.
[79] Tony Charlton, *The Age*, Friday July 20, 2007.
[80] Charlie Sutton. Interview with the author.

Like a lot of our blokes, I had a bloody shocking day. (Ted) Whitten gave me a nice old touch-up. Norm came up to me at the bar and said: 'I know you've had a bad day, and that's unfortunate. But the way you played in the first semi-final got us away to a terrific start. I'll never forget that day. It was probably the best game of football you've ever played. Don't ever forget that.'

I said: 'Norm, I can't even remember it.' I'd been king-hit and knocked unconscious.

'But the point is,' he said, 'don't dwell on it. We've done well. We put on a good show. We got a lot further this year than I thought we would. Mark my words: next year'll be a good'n.'[81]

As Smith suggested in his conversation with McGivern, he was disappointed he hadn't been able to 'steal' the premiership, but he was immensely proud of his players, whom he described as 'a team to be reckoned with'.[82] Making the finals, let alone the Grand Final, had been a triumph in itself. 'We made it a year too early,' Smith said. 'We should never have been in the finals, but our young blokes kicked on a bit quicker, and better, than I thought they would.'[83] He added that considering the bad reviews they had received the previous season, their 1954 effort was 'not bad for a spent force'.[84] McMahen agreed. 'Just getting there was a huge achievement,' he said. 'It was one hell of a turnaround and Norm deserves great credit for helping to make it happen so quickly.'[85] The Melbourne committee reinforced this view in its annual report:

Norman Smith... deserves an abundance of praise for the magnificent manner in which our team fought out to the bitter end every engagement in which they played. The spirit of our players was indeed something to marvel at, and their fitness was due to his careful handling and guidance. To Norman must go the congratulations of all at Melbourne and the football world in general...

Norman's obvious love for Melbourne, with his enthusiasm for the players, communicates itself to the team which he controls, and has been a prime factor in the success he is now enjoying.[86]

---

[81] Geoff McGivern. Interview with the author.
[82] *Melbourne Truth* series, 1962.
[83] Athol Webb told the author that Norm had made this admission to him.
[84] *Melbourne Truth* series, 1962.
[85] Noel McMahen. Interview with the author.
[86] Melbourne Football Club *Annual Report*, 1954.

With Melbourne's Grand Final side containing 10 players no older than 22 years of age, including six teenagers, it was obvious that the club had a bright future. Smith enthused that in the previous two seasons the Demons had 'got hold of 14 players who were to form the backbone of a great team for years to come'.[87] Crucially, McMahen said: 'Although we lost, it was very beneficial to get that finals experience into our young players. And losing first up like that gives everyone that little bit of extra hunger for the next year.'[88] And there was still much room for improvement. 'We still had weaknesses in '54,' Beckwith said. 'Some players were just finding their feet as senior players, and we were very inexperienced, yet we had still made the Grand Final. We felt that once a number of the youngsters got 30, 40, 50 games under their belts, that's when we would really start to see the results. It was a settling-in period, and we felt there was better to come. And as it worked out there was *much* better to come.'[89]

ͲͲͲͲͲͲͲͲͲ

The growing depth, and dramatic improvement, of Melbourne's young playing list was underlined by the club's achievement in making the finals in each of the senior, reserves, thirds and fourths (under-17s) competitions.

Consequently, the Demons performed strongly in the McClelland Trophy (which was awarded to the club that won the most premiership points combined in the seniors, seconds and thirds). The Demons finished level on points with Geelong. It was the first tie since the trophy had been introduced three years earlier. However, the winner was decided on the percentage of the respective senior teams, and Geelong, the minor premier, prevailed – 133.1 to 121.4.

The Demons would remain among the top three clubs in the McClelland Trophy for the next eight years.

---

[87] *The Sun* series, 1967.
[88] Noel McMahen. Interview with the author.
[89] John Beckwith. Interview with the author.

11

SETTING STANDARDS

[1954]

Throughout Melbourne's run of solid victories in the latter part of 1954, there was increasingly stiff competition for positions in the senior team. Fringe players like Keith Carroll became so desperate to be part of the excitement that they were willing to do almost anything to get a game:

> I was a half-back in the seconds, and our half-backline in the firsts was Geoff Collins, Noel McMahen and Lance Arnold – all interstate players – so I was finding it hard to get a senior game. It really didn't matter how well I played in the seconds because I basically had to wait until one of those players got injured before I got a run in the firsts. I kept getting injuries as well, but Norm kept encouraging me, saying: 'Just keep plugging away.' But I didn't want to wait too long – I had to try something else to impress Norm and the selectors.
>
> Before a seconds game at Hawthorn, a senior player, one of my best mates, said: 'All you've got to do is run through a few blokes and you'll get a senior game'. I used that as gospel, so I went out there charging madly at blokes, unfairly even, and I had a couple of blokes carried off. I only did it to try to get a senior game.
>
> At the dance that night, Norm asked me: 'How did you go today, Keith?'
>
> I said: 'I had a few blokes carried off – that might get me a game.'
>
> I quickly realised that was the wrong thing to say to Norm. He poked me in the chest quite firmly and said: 'Don't you talk to me like that!'
>
> I poked him back and said: 'I'll say it as much as I like!'
>
> Norm said: 'If that's your opinion, I don't want you in the club! Get out!'
>
> I said: 'Right then, I'm going. You can stick your football.'
>
> He followed me out and said: 'Hey, I've had a few drinks. Just forget about it.'
>
> I didn't want to go because I loved the club. I said: 'All right then, I'll forget it.'

> At training on the Tuesday night, I came out like nothing had happened and Norm called me over and said: 'Have you still got that chip on your shoulder?'
> I said: 'No, Norm, I've forgotten about it, like you said.'
> He said: 'Well I bloody well haven't!'
> He must have been stewing on it all weekend. He said: 'I'm going to bring it up in front of all the players.'
> He got the circle of players together and he had me standing there with him and he said: 'Keith got some stupid idea in his head that I want bash. I'm just making it clear that whoever told him that, they are wrong. I do not want bash and I will not stand for it.'
> I felt smaller and smaller. But that was all that was said about it. He was a man's man and he wouldn't stand for any dirty play. Never in the seven years I played under him did I hear him target an opposition player. He never encouraged that. I wish I'd known that about him before I decided to get blokes carried off!'[1]

Skipper Geoff Collins often crunched opposition players, and now he was being targeted by his own fans. Usually a reliable defender, he was not as assured as he had once been, and Demon supporters let him, and Smith, know all about it, screaming things like: 'Hey Smithy, get Collins off and bring Carroll on!' Incensed by such blatant disloyalty to a club great, Smith turned around and roared: 'It wasn't so long ago that you were cheering him, and now you're booing him. You're too bloody fickle!' He then turned to Keith Carroll, who was seated beside him on the bench, and said: 'That's what people are like, remember that. They'll build you up and then chop you down.'[2]

Carroll was taught another important lesson that season.

> I was the 19th man and Jimmy Cardwell was telling me: 'You should be in the firsts every week. You can kick the ball a mile, so if you get a run today, kick it as hard and as far as you can'.
> I got a run early and the ball landed in my arms and I kicked it as hard as I could. The problem was that it went off the side of my boot and hit the roof of the grandstand in the outer! At half-time, Norm came straight over to me and said: 'What the bloody hell were you trying to do?!'
> I said: 'I did what Jim Cardwell told me to do.'
> Norm said: 'And what did Jimmy tell you to do?!'

---

[1] Keith Carroll. Interview with the author.
[2] Keith Carroll. Interview with the author.

I said: 'Kick it as far as I could.'

That was like a red rag to a bull. Norm glared at me and said: 'Jim Cardwell is secretary of this club, I'm the coach around here! Don't listen to anyone but me!'

He went on about it nearly all of half-time, saying that I should look where I'm kicking the ball, play my own game and not listen to anyone else, particularly the secretary, however well-meaning he was. Norm hated interference from anyone else, which was fair enough. He was the sole owner of the team.[3]

There was another uglier example of Smith reacting angrily to what he perceived as interference. It involved 19-year-old Big Bob Johnson, who was one of the Demons' major discoveries of the season.

Johnson had captained the thirds early in the year and was promoted to the senior side in round 11, when he kicked four goals in the win over North Melbourne. In his first seven matches, he slotted a team-high 19 goals (the next best in this period were Noel Clarke with 15 and both Bob McKenzie and Stuart Spencer with 11 apiece), including four contributions of at least three majors. More importantly, he had given Smith greater flexibility in an attacking sense. Johnson was a virtual two-in-one player, who generally spent 80 to 90 percent of his time in a forward pocket, but could provide crucial respite for Cordner in the ruck. Johnson's work in tandem with Noel Clarke had shades of the Mueller-Smith combination – although clearly a poor man's version of it. Clarke was instructed to perform Smith's old decoy role, providing a fast-leading option and creating space for Johnson, who, like Mueller, would drift across to the goalsquare for the long kick and use his marking skills to advantage in one-on-one contests.

While Smith could not be happier with his young charge, he was not always so pleased with Johnson's father. Bob Johnson senior was a Demon immortal, having been best-afield in the 1926 Grand Final triumph after kicking six goals from centre half-forward. Described by Bert Chadwick as the best mark of his era, he kicked 302 goals for Melbourne in 113 games and retired the year before Smith arrived at the club. He was also very supportive of his son's career, religiously attending every match he played.

Recollections vary about what caused the blow-up between Smith and Johnson senior. One version had Smith criticising Big Bob in the changerooms after a match in front of the players and other club people, and Johnson senior saying: 'Lay off the lad, Norm. Give him a go'. Smith then focused his abuse on Johnson senior. Another account had Johnson senior confronting Smith in the players' race and demanding

---

[3] Keith Carroll. Interview with the author.

that he give his son a better run in the ruck. Yet another version had Smith overhearing Johnson senior 'coaching' his son in the rooms at half-time, and Smith telling him – politely at first – to leave the coaching to him and to stay out of the rooms in future. However, each account ends the same way: secretary Jim Cardwell, ever the diplomat, sweeping a visibly upset Johnson senior away into the committee room.

The only people Smith wanted in the changerooms were those who needed to be there – preferably just the players and trainers. At times he ordered people out, as Bob Johnson senior discovered. Smith said:

> When I am talking to my players, I prefer to talk to them alone. I do not exclude my members of the match committee or my president, naturally, but at Melbourne these speeches are, in the main, for the players' instruction and not for public entertainment... There has been a tendency develop over latter years for these talks pre-match to be regarded as public entertainment. Well I won't have a bar of it, and fortunately neither will my committee.
>
> I prefer to have the players in a small room where I can have them close to me as I speak. I... have only the team in... (my) vision... Trainers and boot-studders and such people (should) all (be) out of the way. This is very vital... The same at half-time: we fight to keep people out of the rooms. We demand that the players obtain maximum rest, try and get them relaxed and lying down wherever possible. If you have people who must come into the rooms, keep them behind ropes where they can look on, but at all costs try and keep them away from the players.[4]

But there were exceptions – his son, Peter, for instance. Smith started taking six-year-old Peter to the football with him in 1954. Peter recalled his father's tenseness before games. 'In the car on the way to the ground, there was complete silence,' Peter said. 'Dad drove, Mum was in the passenger seat and I was in the back, but not a word was spoken. Dad was concentrating on the game and didn't want to be disturbed or distracted, so talking was forbidden. I knew what was good for me! That might have been at 10.30 or quarter to 11 in the morning – three hours before the start of the senior match. But in those days, the sole responsibility rested with the coach – there wasn't the coaching entourage like they have today – so he had a fair bit to mull over in his mind.'

For several seasons, Peter accompanied his father into the changerooms before the game, at half-time, and after the game, and sat on the bench beside him during

---

[4] Norm Smith's notes titled: 'My Theories and Practices For Fitness For Melbourne League Team', believed to have been written in 1959.

play. 'I was allowed to sit there but I had to keep quiet,' Peter said.[5] He was not the only young boy granted access to the Melbourne rooms. Alf Brown, the acid-penned scribe from *The Herald* who became a friend of Smith, recounted the following personal experience:

> Before a game, Smith generally was irritable. One of Jim Cardwell's jobs was to keep back-slappers and know-alls away from him. But sometimes Smith could relax and surprise everyone. It happened to my small son one day. Melbourne then had a magnificent, spacious room... and players kicked the ball around before games. Young Brown used to cover me from errant footballs. One day he took a desperate mark and saved my head from being hammered. Briefly, he was proud. Then Smith roared: "Don't admire the bloody ball! Keep it moving!" Just then a toothless mouth roared from the other end of the room, "Over here, Bruce!" and a very proud boy found Barassi with a pass. It was a big 30 seconds. After all, how many nine-year-olds have been roared at by the great Norm Smith and given a lead by Ron Barassi in one afternoon?[6]

Cardwell's own son, Geoff, later had a memorable experience of his own with Smith before a match. Geoff Cardwell had been a regular in the rooms since he was a baby, and as he grew he began to help out the Demons' support staff with minor tasks. At half-time one day, property steward Les Green asked Geoff to fetch a glass of water, which Green would routinely hand to Smith after his speech. The youngster grabbed the first full glass he saw and gave it to Green. According to Hugh McPherson, as soon as Smith poured the contents into his mouth, he 'gargled and choked and spat it out all over the place. His face went as red as his hair'.[7] The glass had contained either hair oil or liniment! Smith rushed to get a drink of water to wash the taste out, and also rinsed his mouth with Listerine mouthwash.

'Which bugger did this?!' Smith roared.

McPherson thought: 'Heaven help the poor soul who was responsible.'

When Smith found out the culprit was young Geoff Cardwell, the secretary's son, Smith said: 'I'll throttle the little bugger!'

Smith would never have followed up, in any way, on this threat. Young Geoff was like family to him. He soon calmed down when Geoff said: 'Don't do that, Uncle Norm; I'm sorry but I didn't know.'

---

[5] Peter Smith. Interview with the author.
[6] Alf Brown, *The Herald*, May 4, 1979. Bruce Brown played six games for Melbourne under Ian Ridley in 1971 before making one appearance for Essendon in 1972.
[7] Hugh McPherson. Interview with the author.

Pre-match and half-time speeches in the players' room could be eventful occasions. Smith demanded full attention from his players, as Ian Ridley recalled:

> Often when Norm was talking to us, he'd say: 'Eyeball me! Come on, I want you to look me in the bloody eye!' His eyes would be bulging and, even though looking him in the eye could almost send a shiver down your spine, only a very silly person would dare not do as he demanded. Norm was always looking for the honesty, intensity and strength of character in you. And while he was addressing us, no-one would dare speak or smile or show the slightest hint that they weren't focusing on him one hundred percent; if they did, he would go off his brain.[8]

Smith's voice also had an intimidating quality about it, as centreman Harold "Hassa" Mann (later the club captain) described:

> When Norm spoke to you with that resonance in his voice, particularly when he was really trying to drive home a message to you, you were frightened to look at him, but even more frightened *not* to look at him. When we weren't playing well and heads were dropping, he'd say: 'Get your head up. Look at me'.[9]

But there were times when it was difficult for the players to keep a straight face. Hugh McPherson said: 'Norm was giving his speech with plenty of gusto, with spittle flying from his mouth and all eyes in the room fixed squarely upon him. Suddenly, his false tooth fell out. But nobody moved or took their eyes off him. If they did, he would have had them quartered. And Norm carried on as if nothing had happened, too.'[10]

Geoff Tunbridge also recounted: 'Norm was ferociously berating someone at half-time and his top denture fell out onto his bottom denture. Cluck! It was the funniest thing I'd seen for ages, but I didn't crack a boo, and neither did anyone else. Norm stopped talking, shoved them back in and carried on with his tirade.'[11]

But some still made the fatal mistake of allowing themselves to become distracted. John Lord, who played with the Demons from 1957 to 1965, said:

> Norm was a great motivator and I loved his speeches, but for some reason one day my mind drifted off. I was daydreaming and I started to grin. Big mistake.

---

[8] Ian Ridley. Interview with the author.
[9] Hassa Mann. Interview with the author.
[10] Hugh McPherson. Interview with the author.
[11] Geoff Tunbridge. Interview with the author.

Boy, did I cop it. Norm saw me and went off: 'What are you laughing at?! You're supposed to be concentrating!'

I apparently looked stupefied and all I managed to say was: 'Sorry, I was thinking of something else.'

He was utterly disgusted. Fair enough, too.[12]

Another player who probably provoked a somewhat similar reaction from Smith was Barrie Vagg, who played under Smith from 1962 to 1969. Smith urged him: 'Let your imagination run wild out there.'

Vagg replied: 'But I haven't got much imagination, Norm.'

'Well just have a bloody go then!' Smith snapped, before walking off.

On another occasion, Smith told Vagg: 'You've got me a bit worried today, Vaggy. I never know what you're going to do.'

Vagg responded: 'I never know what I'm going to do either.' Again, Smith simply walked away.

Vagg later reflected: 'Norm must have wondered: "Why the hell did I even bother talking to him".'[13]

♟♟♟♟♟♟♟♟♟

Norm Smith the orator has been described as 'a natural',[14] 'brilliant… compelling… magnetic'.[15] A 'magnificent speaker: fluent, forceful, colourful; sometimes hurtful',[16] he was also 'very powerful in his delivery, which made you sit up and pay full attention'.[17] Bluey Adams recalled: 'Even outside of times where he addressed players, whenever he stood up to address a gathering, there was absolute silence. No-one else spoke, and there was no rattling of cutlery. You could hear a pin drop. He was the only person I ever saw who had that effect on people. That demonstrated just how much people respected the man.'[18]

Smith was never short of material for his addresses; in fact, he 'rarely, if ever, repeated anything – he didn't have to; he could think up different things'.[19] Players 'did not grow (too) accustomed' to his speeches, and '(his) words did not sail over

---

[12] John Lord. Interview with the author.
[13] Barrie Vagg. Interview with the author.
[14] Ron Barassi. Interview with the author.
[15] Clyde Laidlaw. Interview with the author.
[16] Alf Brown, *The Herald*, Monday July 30, 1973.
[17] Clyde Laidlaw. Interview with the author.
[18] Frank 'Bluey' Adams. Interview with the author.
[19] Bob 'Tassie' Johnson. Interview with the author.

the heads of the older players'.[20] But the material didn't just simply come to him on the spot. Like all good orators, he was a talented ad-libber, but most of his talks, particularly those before matches, were prepared and planned. He actively sought material to stimulate the minds of his players. Clyde Laidlaw revealed: 'Norm read a lot from eminent men – like Churchill for example – and he would weave their sentences into his speeches. Norm prided himself on reading as much on Churchill as he could.'[21]

However, there were still times when Smith lapsed back into using all-too-familiar themes in his addresses, as 'Bluey' Adams observed: 'Sometimes he would say the same old thing and, I suppose, sound like a bit of a broken record – but that's only because we were making the same old mistakes!'[22]

Alf Brown, the chief football writer at *The Herald*, wrote that Smith had an uncanny ability to 'lift a sagging side with his oratory', or 'arouse' it 'from lethargy to brilliance'. Brown added: 'Some people smirk and mock the oratory of football coaches. But they never heard Smith. He could flay a player with his tongue and if the man had any spirit he could turn him into a match-winner.'[23] Clyde Laidlaw marvelled at how Smith could inspire players just by the way he spoke. 'To my mind,' Laidlaw said, 'that was Norm's greatest strength.'[24]

Smith was 'more inspirational than tactical' in that 'he didn't deliver blackboard lectures like Checker Hughes',[25] but the players' response to his speeches was generally overwhelming.

John Townsend (who played for Melbourne in the 1960s) said: 'You'd run through a brick wall for Smithy. He virtually took over as your old man, so you just didn't want to let him down. Gee whiz, if they had some of his pre-match addresses on tape they'd really be something to look at. He was able to work you into a frenzy. He laid it all on the line. No other coach I heard ever came near him. In that regard, he was on his own.'

Ian Ridley was at times mesmerised by Smith's calls to arms. 'Maybe I was a receptive country boy, but every one of Smith's pre-match addresses held me,' Ridley remembered. 'Throughout my career, I listened to every word Smith said… (and) not once did he lose me… He could send you out starry-eyed, determined

---

[20] Alf Brown, in a souvenir booklet for the Norm Smith Commemorative Dinner, held on July 12, 1979, to inaugurate the Norm Smith Medal.
[21] Clyde Laidlaw. Interview with the author.
[22] Frank 'Bluey' Adams. Interview with the author.
[23] Alf Brown, *The Herald*, Monday July 30, 1973.
[24] Clyde Laidlaw. Interview with the author.
[25] Noel McMahen. Interview with the author.

SETTING STANDARDS [1954]

to beat the whole opposition 18 on your own.'[26] Barassi was similarly inspired: 'Even in my final season at Melbourne in 1964, after I'd been listening to Norm's addresses for 12 years, he never failed to get my competitive juices flowing. He'd always have us all fired up and ready for battle.'[27]

The Demons literally were primed for battle one day, as Ralph Lane recounted:

> Before one game, Norm used the word 'blitzkrieg' (a German word meaning 'lightning war'). The war had finished only eight or 10 years before, so it was a very powerful word to use, and it evoked some powerful images in your mind. That's how he wanted us to approach the start of the game. He really wanted us to go out there all guns blazing from the first bounce, like the Germans had done during the war. Often after Norm addressed us – and that day was a classic example – you'd feel like running through the bloody fence on your way out onto the ground. It was what he said and the way he delivered it. It wasn't just ranting and raving; it was thoughtful, purposeful stuff, and he always seemed to get the reaction he was after.[28]

Smith later said:

> I'm no Bob Menzies,[29] but I am surprised sometimes by the emotion I am capable of achieving... Players respond differently, of course. Ron Barassi was a player who would look you directly in the eye and suddenly you would detect a wild look. You had got across. The tiger was pacing in his cage.[30]

Smith's Melbourne teams slowly developed a stranglehold over Collingwood, and part of it can be attributed to the hatred of the Magpies he engendered in his players. An example of this emerged before Collingwood games, particularly those at Victoria Park, when Smith would occasionally incite his side by saying: 'This is the team that was told by their coach (Jock McHale) that (Don) Cordner is a doctor and if he puts his hand near the ball, kick it!'[31]

The visitors' rooms at Victoria Park were also the setting of an amusing incident during one of Smith's pre-match speeches. Already well-accustomed to

---

[26] Hobbs, Greg, *125 Years of the Demons 1858-1983*, Progress Press Group, 1984.
[27] Ron Barassi. Interview with the author.
[28] Ralph Lane. Interview with the author.
[29] Sir Robert Menzies is Australia's longest-serving Prime Minster, having held office from 1949 to 1965.
[30] *The Sun*, Saturday July 31, 1965.
[31] Trevor Johnson, in a facsimile to the author.

the shambolic condition of the changerooms and the notoriously unruly behaviour of the Magpie throng towards visiting teams, the Demons now had to contend with a hole in the roof which exposed them to the elements. Smith was firing up his players and about to reach a climax when a Collingwood supporter poked his head through the hole and said: 'What would you know about it, you big, redheaded bastard?!'

Utterly disgusted, but not entirely surprised, Smith turned to his players and said: 'See, boys, that's the kind of rubbish you get when you come out here!'[32]

Smith once divulged some of his theories on delivering an address:

> A coach must build himself up to a pitch before the game. You cannot go in and speak coldly to the players and expect to get your message across. The greatest speaker in the world couldn't go into the rooms before the game, talk in a normal tone and expect the players to respond. One of the things a coach must learn is to transmit the build-up within him to the players.
>
> A lot of people say coaches talk *to* their players. You don't. You talk *with* the players. You aim to get them to join in, to feel what you feel, to feel the same enthusiasm. In the successful years at Melbourne, I felt I was able to do this. It's not just a matter of shouting and roaring. I spoke loudly, but I always tried to work up to a peak, a pitch.
>
> One of our half-backs, Ian Thorogood, tells the story about these pre-match speeches of mine. He said he'd often go to a match and hate the thought of playing. He just wouldn't feel like it. But he said (that) by the time he ran down the race he wanted to murder somebody.
>
> It was easy to get some players worked up. With men like Thorogood and Barassi, for instance, you could tell from their eyes that they were getting the message and were responding. Other players like Laurie Mithen and big Bob Johnson, who were cooler types, wouldn't show much emotion. But they've often told me they were building up inside.[33]

Accordingly, Smith varied his approach to certain players. 'Norm knew who the players were that he had to put his hand on their shoulder to tell them a home truth,' Hugh McPherson said. 'But he also knew the others who he had to tell straight out: "This is what you have to bloody do", and demand it out

---

[32] Garry Pearce, assistant boot-studder at Melbourne. Interview with the author.
[33] *The Sun* series, 1967.

SETTING STANDARDS [1954]

of them.'³⁴ This was a source of mild bemusement for Keith Carroll, who said: 'In the changerooms before a game, I'd be sitting next to Geoff Tunbridge and Norm would say to me: "Now Keith, get on your man and sit on him, and keep him out of the play, and make sure you do this, this and this". But in the next breath he'd turn to "Tunner" and just say: "Browse around, Tunner", and move on to the next player'.³⁵

Assistant boot-studder Garry Pearce said:

> Norm was very good at distinguishing between the characteristics of different players. Here are two examples from opposite ends of the spectrum. The first would be a player who Norm knew was trying his guts out but was just having a bad day. Norm wouldn't tear the backside off him; he respected the guy's sensitivity and the fact he was trying, so he'd just quietly talk to him and say: 'I know you're giving your best, but just hang in there, keep putting in and it'll turn for you'. He could be sensitive to people's feelings. But any player he felt was bludging on their mates, or just wasn't performing and Norm felt would respond to being the subject of a high element of sarcasm, or from getting strips torn off them in public, that's the treatment he would mete out. No-one can argue that it didn't get results.³⁶

YYYYYYYYY

Len Smith also enjoyed his most successful coaching season to date in 1954. Furthermore, it was Fitzroy's most successful of their nine seasons in the thirds competition.

The Maroons didn't make the finals – a loss late in the season kept them a game outside the final four just when a premiership appeared a realistic possibility.

However, as Fitzroy's annual report noted: 'The standard of play showed considerable improvement on past seasons, and full credit must be given to coach Len Smith, who has been very patient and painstaking in teaching his young players the finer points of the game, and at last is reaping the rewards that his good work merits.'

The Maroons eyed the future with great anticipation. 'With the addition of a few new players next season,' the annual report continued, 'better results can

---

³⁴ Hugh McPherson. Interview with the author.
³⁵ Keith Carroll. Interview with the author.
³⁶ Garry Pearce. Interview with the author.

be expected, and as several of this year's players are expected to make strong bids for inclusion in the senior side, the efforts of Len Smith are beginning to bear very good results.'

ŸŸŸŸŸŸŸŸŸ

Whenever one of his players' wives had a baby – and there were numerous Demon children born during Smith's reign – he would supply the happy couple with a new pram. Although Smith worked in the pram industry and received a discounted rate, he would pay for the prams out of his own pocket. It was regarded as a remarkably kind gesture and was always well received.

And while his young football team was treading new ground, Smith was doing the same with his pram parts manufacturing business.

In 1954, he relocated his backyard operation from Clarke Street, Northcote, to a factory he built at 21 Allenby Street, North Coburg. The small, single-storey, brick building occupied the rear of the block, which abutted a laneway.

The move was not made because business was booming, or that it had really outgrown his mother's back shed; it was made more for practical reasons – it was a better way of operating, and it was simply time to branch out and give Ethel some well-earned peace. Smith's business never boomed anyway. Part of the reason was the comfort factor: the business already made enough money to comfortably support Marj and Peter, and then there was the personal comfort zone of running a business he had been familiar with ever since he could remember. And being his own boss, he also had no problem pursuing his coaching career – he could leave early on Tuesday and Thursday afternoons.

The enterprise never rose above the category of a small business, and was 'never a big money-maker',[37] because it was not Smith's passion. While Peter Smith said his father 'wasn't a businessman',[38] Ron Barassi believed Smith could have been a 'big-time businessman', but that 'it never appealed to him because his life was football. That was what consumed his thoughts'.[39] Smith later explained his intention to combine business and sport:

> I had to make a decision... whether to concentrate on business activities or devote more time to football, and I chose that I could work it this way... I love football,

---

[37] Russell Brown. Interview with the author.
[38] Peter Smith. Interview with the author.
[39] Ron Barassi. Interview with the author.

I love my work and my business, and naturally I want to be successful in both. But it does require a lot of time.[40]

Smith still attempted to improve his lot in business. Over the years, he progressively increased the size of the factory, adding a chrome plating plant and building a large extension at the front, which he leased to small businesses as another source of income. Through Len, he picked up extra work lathing certain items for Miller's ropeworks. His offsider, Russ Brown, said: 'Norm was always looking for a better way to do things. An example of that was when he used his engineering expertise to convert the hand-presses to power, with pulleys and so forth, and that made things a lot easier – it wasn't as physical then.'[41]

Smith originally had a small office at the back of the building where, outside of business purposes, he had his regular Monday morning chat with Checker Hughes, and often spoke to media men like Alf Brown. But, to allow for more work space in an increasingly cramped environment, Smith eventually hired a carpenter to construct an office atop a platform which could be accessed by stairs. He also installed a changeroom and a shower, so that he did not necessarily need to go home before attending an appointment or function that required him to be fresh and well-groomed, which he generally was anyway.

On training nights during the 1954 season, Smith drove down St Georges Road to a drycleaners' in Northcote where he would pick up young defender John Beckwith. 'I felt rather privileged to be going to training with the coach,' Beckwith said. 'That was well before I'd really established myself, so I was pretty lucky.'[42] On those car trips, there was generally only one topic of conversation. 'I might ask him about work and he might mutter something about that, but then it would be straight back to football,' Beckwith said. 'Soon I didn't even bother asking him about work, or anything else, because all he really wanted to talk about was football. He'd *always* be talking football – day and night. He was obsessed with it.'

Conversely, there were times when Smith spoke about work at the football club, with like-minded people such as Keith Carroll, who was employed by an engineering firm. Smith told Carroll: 'When you make a decision at work, you might have made the wrong decision, but go along with it and you'll find a way to make it work. There's more than one way of doing something. Once you make

---

[40] *Midweek Magazine*, August 1964.
[41] Russell Brown. Interview with the author.
[42] John Beckwith. Interview with the author.

a decision, do it. It's the same with football: I don't mind you making mistakes, but be decisive.'[43]

Smith also shared his wisdom with Terry Gleeson – a rough 'n' ready big man who studied commerce at university and was described by Barassi as an 'educated larrikin'. From 1956, the coach and the ruckman had lockers next to each other. Gleeson recalled: 'When you have a locker next to someone – I'm not sure if it always happens – you share things; you share personal thoughts. I'm certain there were things Norm told me that he didn't tell many other people. He was a well-organised bloke who had his business planned and organised so that he had quite an amount of flexible time, which he devoted to coaching. He'd talk to me about managing time and people because I was developing along those lines myself.'

Whenever one of Smith's players asked about his education, his stock-standard response was: 'Son, I was educated in the school of hard knocks'. While he appeared to prefer blue-collar folk to their white-collar counterparts, that didn't mean he was opposed to university types. A classic example was Gleeson: a down-to-earth, have-a-go type who was trying to better himself. But as Gleeson recalled, he still had his difficulties with Smith where football and university overlapped.

> I had lectures to attend after training on Tuesday and Thursday nights. I had to meet a timetable, otherwise I'd turn up late to a lecture and everyone would boo me because they knew where I'd been. I told Norm about my situation and I asked him: 'Can I leave training early?' But instead of giving me overall permission to leave the track early, each night he made me ask him: 'Can I leave?' Then he'd say: 'Oh, OK, bloody go', or something. He made it clear that while my studies were important, so was my footy, and that you had to be committed to it.
>
> I'd try my best to avoid asking him if I could. I'd look at the clock and quite often I'd think: 'We're going to finish in a minute – I won't ask him', so I wouldn't leave until the end of the session. I'd rather risk being a couple of minutes late to my lecture than risk Norm going crook![44]

Smith could, with a clear conscience, demand such things from his players because he willingly made the sacrifices himself. Once when he was asked how much of his spare time was devoted to football, he replied:

---

[43] Keith Carroll. Interview with the author.
[44] Terry Gleeson. Interview with the author.

It's not spare time that's given to football. It's time that's given to football. I haven't much spare time *after* football... It's quite a deal of my private life, but fortunately my wife and boy love football and my wife comes to most of the functions with me. We have a ladies' committee here and she works on the social committee and they have their entertainment after the match, allowing us to have our separate entertainment until about 8.30. Then we have our dances and we are together. It's only on training nights that I come down here on my own, and on the end-of-season trip.[45]

🏆🏆🏆🏆🏆🏆🏆🏆🏆

Ask anyone associated with Melbourne Football Club in the mid-to-late 1950s to describe the atmosphere at the time and odds are they will warmly refer to it as 'one big family'. Indeed, Melbourne was the original family club. The blossoming of this cosy, all-inclusive environment can be attributed to several key factors, including: the plethora of quality young players, and first-class citizens, joining the club at a similar time and maturing to manhood together; the Demons' unmatched pillars of administrative and coaching strength, which harnessed the youth and provided astute leadership; and success, which strengthened the bonds between individuals, although the bonding came before the success, and was one of the key reasons it was achieved.

Much of the bonding was developed at the famous after-match functions that were held after each home match at the MCG. In fact, these functions probably were not much different from what a lot of other clubs hosted, but Melbourne perhaps took the concept a step further during Norm Smith's reign. The man himself was one of the major driving forces behind the success of these occasions, which 'became more popular by the week'.[46]

The Demons' social scene had deteriorated to bare existence under Allan La Fontaine, but Smith decided, as one of the key planks of his rebuilding program, to nurture it to the levels he had experienced as a player at Melbourne, and then as a coach at Fitzroy. Smith later wrote that struggling clubs – as Melbourne was when he returned – often 'do not develop enough club spirit and loyalty'; that 'defeat becomes common to them', and 'they take it (the whole VFL experience) for granted'.[47] He added: 'These (lowly) clubs must try to build up a winning

---

[45] *Midweek Magazine*, August 1964.
[46] Stuart Spencer. Interview with the author.
[47] *The Age*, Wednesday June 19, 1968.

tradition, and develop to the highest degree a fierce pride in their team. If a club is not a proud one, it has little chance of success'.[48]

It was Smith's strong desire to create a warm, welcoming atmosphere where players – and their partners – could relax in each other's company, share some light-hearted fun and gain a greater understanding of each other as footballers and people, in the belief that the team that socialises together, wins together. Smith later elaborated:

> Team spirit is the basis of teamwork. The players at Melbourne were comrades off the field and on. We believed in keeping them together. They were real friends and always prepared to help each other. Mateship is the greatest of all morale builders. Many teams are inclined to forget there's a warm and human side to footy.[49]

The bonding that took place was immense, and was to have a profoundly positive effect on the on-field fortunes of the Demons. Bluey Adams recalled that with six o'clock closing laws still in force, 'there wasn't the opportunity to go to pubs and nightclubs, so your social life centred around the football club and your teammates'.[50]

Another factor was money. 'The money wasn't in football then,' Ian Ridley said, 'so you couldn't really afford to go out much. Spending Saturday night at the footy club was our only real option, and it turned out to be a great thing for all of us young players of that era. We didn't go off and do our own thing in small groups. We all became so close; we were best mates – and still are.'[51]

The after-match bonding started with drinks with opposition players, coaches and officials, and the umpires. It was 'one of the best cooling-off periods you could ever have'.[52]

The first step of Smith's 'cooling-off' plan was to get his hands on some refreshments. To ensure he was not short of a drink in the crowded Committee Room bar, Smith later developed a standard arrangement with a club barman to pour four pots of beer for him as soon as he entered the room. 'A couple of them would go straight down the hatch,' Allica recalled. The amber liquid provided

---

[48] *The Age*, Wednesday June 19, 1968.
[49] *Craven*, John (editor), *Football The Australian Way*, Lansdowne Press, 1969.
[50] Frank 'Bluey' Adams. Interview with the author.
[51] Ian Ridley. Interview with the author. A core of 15 to 20 Melbourne players of the era still meet for lunch each month.
[52] Sam Allica, Norm's runner after Hugh McPherson. Interview with the author.

Smith with almost instant stress relief. 'It relaxes me,' Smith once told Allica as they stood at the bar. 'It lets out some steam.'[53]

Smith believed that Saturday night socialising was also important for the sanity of his players. He told them: 'You build yourself up all week for the game, and then you play your guts out, and afterwards you have to release things. After that, you can think about what's going to happen the next week.'[54]

After being a late starter when it came to alcohol, Smith made up for lost time. He became a 'prodigious drinker'[55] who could 'down them with the best of them'.[56] But, it must be said, he was only a Saturday night, social drinker who rarely, if ever, drank during the week; and never did so on his own; it was all about socialising with people. It was also roundly accepted that while Smith could become more easily agitated, and more abrupt – and, conversely, more mellow – when he had been drinking, he could consume copious amounts of liquor yet still appear relatively unaffected; almost sober. Although he could be a 'party animal',[57] a 'larrikin'[58] and 'the most loveable drunk of all time',[59] Smith rarely, if ever, acted like a drunk. Reserves team manager George Lenne, who became a close friend of the Smiths, said: 'Norm always controlled himself. He was always very aware of the responsible position he held in the club, and he would never do anything to tarnish that.'[60]

Hassa Mann (who debuted in 1959 and later captained the Demons) recalled:

> At no stage did he conduct himself in a way that would allow you to have anything on him. He always retained his authoritative persona. He was always the coach. There was always a distance; he would keep himself slightly removed, at arm's length, and he never lapsed from that. He might get pissed with the players on a Saturday night but at the next training session on the Tuesday that was gone and it was: 'Let's get on with business'.[61]

Smith's company – especially after he had won premierships – was in high demand after matches. Opponents enjoyed picking his brain for wisdom that they

---

[53] Sam Allica. Interview with the author.
[54] John Townsend. Interview with the author.
[55] Ron Barassi. Interview with the author.
[56] Hassa Mann. Interview with the author.
[57] John Beckwith. Interview with the author.
[58] Athol Webb. Interview with the author.
[59] John Lord. Interview with the author.
[60] George Lenne. Interview with the author.
[61] Hassa Mann. Interview with the author.

might be able to apply to themselves. Smith relished this situation, and 'loved sharing his knowledge with his counterparts'.[62] Smith even indulged in the odd mind game with a rival, as Terry Gleeson recalled.

> After a game, Norm and I were having a drink with (Carlton coach) Ken Hands and he asked Norm: 'Why did you do this today?'
> Rather than keeping a trade secret, Norm gave him the answer. I couldn't believe it.
> When Ken Hands left, I said to Norm: 'Why the bloody hell did you tell him that?' Norm's matter-of-fact response was: 'We'll do something different next time.'
> He had a creative mind and he backed himself to devise a new tactic. Strategically, he was very clever.[63]

Smith also liked to pick the brains of others, and even sought suggestions from left field. After a match in the late 1950s, Smith and Fitzroy captain 'Butch' Gale were discussing ways to overcome congestion around centre bounces. Smith called over one of his boot-studders, Garry Pearce – who, despite his role, was respected by Smith for his perspectives on the game. Smith asked Pearce: 'What would you do about it?' Pearce suggested a centre rectangle be introduced, which both Smith and Gale 'politely considered and didn't think was such a bad idea'.[64]

Another regular feature of Smith's after-match cooling-off process was smoothing over any temporarily fractured relationships with his players. Just hours earlier, Smith might have savaged a player in front of the team for his lack of work or team ethic, or even his lack of courage, and sometimes the player would take exception to the blast. But in the relaxed atmosphere of the social rooms, Smith, almost without fail, would approach the player in question, perhaps put his arm around him and talk gently with him, and for a time drop the slave-driver's whip and assume the role of a mate. To self-confessed 'big softies' like John Lord, who wore their hearts on their sleeves, Smith might say: 'I didn't mean to upset you. I might have been a bit hard on you today, but this is what I was trying to do. We've got to do this right'.[65] Within a short time, the player would generally be 'eating out of the palm of Norm's hand again',[66] and they would soon be having a beer together and Smith would be 'laughing and joking and slapping you on

---

[62] Stuart Spencer. Interview with the author.
[63] Terry Gleeson. Interview with the author.
[64] Garry Pearce. Interview with the author.
[65] John Lord told the author that this was a typical Norm Smith refrain.
[66] Ian Thorogood. Interview with the author.

the back'.⁶⁷ He often bought rounds of drinks for his players, saying: 'Here's a fiver; it's about time the coach shouted'.⁶⁸ Such gestures were not expected, but nonetheless were well received.

'Norm bore no grudges,' Stuart Spencer said, 'and after a game he would be your most trusted friend, and the greatest company.'⁶⁹ Some described Smith as a different man at these times. Bluey Adams said:

> Norm could live in compartments. His attitude was: 'We lost today's game, but now we're going to put all that behind us and have a good time together'. It wasn't like he was surly and bitter after a loss. You didn't think: 'I'd better not talk to Norm tonight'.
>
> You might have made a blue or played a poor game and when Norm came over to you, you'd be thinking: 'Jeez, he's going to want to talk to me about it', but then he would surprise you by saying: 'How's the family?' and you'd think: 'You beauty, he didn't bring it up!' But on the Tuesday, he'd look at you and say: 'Hey, come over here', and you'd think: 'Damn it! He hasn't forgotten'. But that was footy time and that's when he dealt with footy issues.⁷⁰

Smith was 'at his best in a social situation',⁷¹ and was often 'the life of the party'. He 'always held the floor' in group discussions,⁷² which often lasted hours, and his disciples would 'listen to him like he was a god',⁷³ Beckwith said. 'He loved his players and he loved being with them and having them gather around him. He loved the audience, and he loved to talk about football and various other things in that environment. He loved those sorts of occasions. He really was in his element.'⁷⁴ Hassa Mann observed that Smith 'could stand out in a crowd because he had this aura about him. You knew he had something special. People who played under Barass say the same thing'.⁷⁵

Not to be satisfied with creating a friendly atmosphere for his players, Smith also instigated trainers' functions at Melbourne. 'It was a wonderful initiative on Norm's part,' said Hugh McPherson. 'It gave the trainers from both clubs a chance

---

⁶⁷ Hassa Mann. Interview with the author.
⁶⁸ *The Herald*, 1958.
⁶⁹ Stuart Spencer. Interview with the author.
⁷⁰ Frank 'Bluey' Adams. Interview with the author.
⁷¹ Clyde Laidlaw. Interview with the author.
⁷² John Beckwith. Interview with the author.
⁷³ John Townsend. Interview with the author.
⁷⁴ John Beckwith. Interview with the author.
⁷⁵ Hassa Mann. Interview with the author.

to get to know each other better and swap notes on things like how to treat certain injuries. Trainers from other clubs commented on how good an idea it was.'[76]

Quite often, when the opposition players had started to leave, Smith would say: 'Come on, boys, we'll go to the trainers' function now', and his players would invariably follow. McPherson said: 'Norm would lead us in everything, but we were quite happy for that to be the case because he was a great leader and we knew we were in good hands.'[77]

Smith had great respect for the trainers and other club staff. In fact, he 'welcomed and enjoyed their company as much as anybody's', and 'was always quick to recognise the contributions others made to the running of the club'.[78] Part of this recognition involved successfully lobbying the committee to allow the trainers and support staff to mingle and drink in the Committee Room after training and matches. 'From then on,' McPherson said, 'even the boot-studder could go into the committee room and drink with the committee members. We were all so appreciative that Norm used the power of his position to do something like that. I'm sure a lot of people in his position wouldn't have even considered it. But it was nothing for Norm to do it. He made us all one. Everyone was the same. And that was Norm's intention all along. And the committee were happy to go along with it, which was also great.'[79]

For Smith, there was an added motivation behind wanting more of the heart-and-soul Demons in the usually off-limits Committee Room. Peter Smith said: 'Dad preferred to be with his players or the trainers, rather than rub shoulders with the fancies that congregated in the Committee Room. That doesn't necessarily mean the members of the committee, but the other people who went in there.'[80] Smith also used his influence to get some closer associates into the Demons' inner sanctum, as Alf Brown later recorded:

> (Norm) had a tremendously soft spot for old cricket mates from the Jika Jika Cricket Association. He would gather them around him in the committee room after a game and listen to their obvious comments, seemingly enraptured. It used to infuriate secretary Cardwell. Each week he (Cardwell) had a room full of big names – some could be persuaded to give good jobs to players; others would part with money. And could he get Norm to mingle? No way, as long as

---

[76] Hugh McPherson. Interview with the author.
[77] Hugh McPherson. Interview with the author.
[78] John Lord. Interview with the author.
[79] Hugh McPherson. Interview with the author.
[80] Peter Smith. Interview with the author.

the boys from the old Jika Jika Cricket Association were there. Maliciously, Smith would call Cardwell over to hear a half-baked opinion from a... (JJCA) mate. 'I reckon we could do something with that,' Norm would say. Cardwell would squirm.[81]

By this stage, the night had only just started. The players then made their way up to the elaborately furnished Sheffield Room for a players' dinner. These dinners – organised and funded by the Melbourne Football Club coterie – were regarded as 'one of the cornerstones of Melbourne's great success'.[82]

A strict dress (and grooming) code was observed, with players generally required to wear their Melbourne Football Club blazers and neatly-pressed slacks. A player would then be the nominated as the evening's master of ceremonies, who would ensure all protocols – like proposing toasts, and informing their audience of any relevant information – were fulfilled and behaviour was up to standard (which it invariably was with Norm Smith in attendance). Most senior players performed the role of MC/chairman at some stage, and it proved another refreshing element of the evening, with different players sharing another form of responsibility and ownership of the team, and displaying their leadership qualities, and perhaps even emerging from their comfort zones as more confident individuals. The designated MC was also obliged to enforce fines for breaches of team rules. John Lord recalled:

> Anyone who turned up late would have to pay a fine. Norm was *always* late. But he probably did it on purpose so that he'd have to contribute a bit into the coffers for the footy trip. And he'd always bring someone with him as a guest – which he had a right to do – and it might be the opposition coach or a player. By then he was right into the fun swing of the night.[83]

As they waited for their meals to be served, another Norm Smith initiative was enforced, whereby each player had to sing a song, or, as a last resort, 'tell a yarn'.[84] As was the case with most things, Smith led his players in this vocal merriment. Apart from the fact he loved singing, it also showed the players that he was willing to do whatever they did; and that what was good enough for the players was also good enough for the coach. 'At a function like that,' said assistant bootstudder

---

[81] Alf Brown, *The Herald*, May 4, 1979.
[82] John Lord. Interview with the author.
[83] John Lord. Interview with the author.
[84] Hugh McPherson. Interview with the author.

Garry Pearce, 'Norm didn't stand on rank or anything; he was just part of the group, and that was one of the wonderful things about him.'[85]

As usual, Smith stuck with *The Barrow Boy* and *Champagne Charlie*, which he sang while standing on the bar. The assessments of Smith's singing ability had not changed. 'As far as singing went, he was a great football coach,' said reserves team manager George Lenne. 'You certainly wouldn't put him on the concert stage, put it that way. But he was fun to watch at those times when he was letting his hair down.'[86] Hugh McPherson said: 'Norm had a voice – I won't say it was a good one – but he enjoyed singing and he got the party started, and that was the main thing.'[87] However, some said Smith's bellowing was 'bearable'. One of the better performers was Jim Cardwell, whose rendition of *Some Enchanted Evening* was quite polished, 'although he'd get into trouble with the higher notes'.[88] Another notable was skipper Geoff Collins, who – fittingly, in light of his hair-raising experiences in the Korean War – would sing *Lucky Old Sun*.

Depending on their religious beliefs, players would also band together to sing numbers like *When Irish Eyes Are Smiling* (Catholics) and *I Belong to Glasgow* (Protestants). Smith 'always sang with the Catholics',[89] who were in the minority at Melbourne and were often applauded and mocked with heckles like: 'Sit down, ya' Micks!'

While everyone had a great time watching their mates slaughter the classics, it was not an entirely carefree experience for every player. Stuart Spencer, who would sing a Nat King Cole tune, *Too Young*, was referred to as 'the whispering baritone' because his teammates had trouble hearing him. But that was nothing compared to Bluey Adams, who recalled: 'I was a shy, retiring kid, so singing in front of all of my teammates took me completely out of my comfort zone. The attitude of some of the boys would be: "Sing a song – no big deal", but the first time I had to sing I was trembling. But after you did it a couple of times, you'd build some confidence.'[90]

Youngsters like Adams did not even try to boost their confidence with the free 'Dutch courage' that was on offer. Although Smith and a small crew of senior players and officials drank alcohol, most of the younger players were teetotallers, just as Smith had been for the vast majority of his playing career. 'In the early days,

---

[85] Garry Pearce. Interview with the author.
[86] George Lenne. Interview with the author.
[87] Hugh McPherson. Interview with the author.
[88] Keith Carroll. Interview with the author.
[89] Terry Gleeson. Interview with the author.
[90] Frank 'Bluey' Adams. Interview with the author.

(at) the dinners after the game,' Adams said, 'there would be so much soft-drink on the table... because so many of the younger players didn't drink – the Barassis and Dixons, etc.'[91]

Smith had very definite views on player drinking habits. 'I do not forbid my players to have a glass or two,' he said. 'But I prefer that they do not have a beer or many late nights after the Tuesday evening. After the match, we have our dinners of a Saturday evening and I have a few (drinks) with them, (because) I rather think (that) if a fellow is a drinker it is better that he does have a few with you... rather than go elsewhere where you do not know what he is doing.'[92] Although some Demons claim that Smith 'taught' them how to drink, he often recalled his own playing days when he told young players: 'If you are a non-drinker, stay a non-drinker. No-one at Melbourne will encourage you to drink.'[93]

After the players had sung their individual songs, they would all unite for a proud and passionate rendition of the Demons' theme song, *A Grand Old Flag*. 'We all belted it out with great gusto,' Hugh McPherson said. 'It only lasted for a minute, but it was a very special part of evening.'

Although some of the lyrics of certain songs verged on risqué, Smith never lapsed into vulgarity. In fact, he prided himself on not swearing (although some people were adamant they had heard him swear). 'Norm didn't tolerate swearing,' said John Lord. 'The worst word I heard him say was "bloody". He said: "You've got permission to say bloody when you get to my age. I'm now 40-bloody-one!"' (Smith didn't even believe in swearing while addressing his players. 'Bad language... is out. I never indulge in it and I do not recommend (it)'.[94]

After dinner, at about 8.30, the players would go back downstairs and collect their wives and girlfriends (who generally went home after the match, 'dolled themselves up' and ate dinner at home or in company with each other) before entering the club dance in a room alongside the training rooms. The Melbourne Football Club dance 'was the envy of every other club'.[95] There was always musical entertainment provided by a band, or mini-orchestra, and often Mike Williamson was able to use his television and radio contacts to attract the top acts from the nearby Tivoli Theatre, and talented touring international musicians – like Winifred Atwell, the prominent West Indian pianist, who played

---

[91] Frank Adams, on the *Red and Blue* documentary, 2005.
[92] Norm Smith's notes titled: 'My Theories and Practices For Fitness For Melbourne League Team', believed to have been written in 1959.
[93] *The Herald*, Wednesday April 15, 1959.
[94] Norm Smith's notes for a speech he made on a football trip to Western Australia in 1957.
[95] John Lord. Interview with the author.

free of charge to the Demons' inner sanctum of up to 80 people when she was in Melbourne.

But when it came to dancing, Smith was a standout for all the wrong reasons, as Barassi recalled:

> Norm was not a great dancer. And that's probably flattering him! I, myself, have always been a terrible dancer, so for someone of my limited dancing ability to criticise another man for his dancing is a real insult, and it shows just how bad Norm was! But it didn't make him shy away from it - he'd still get up and have a go, particularly in the barn dances, which everyone had to get in on.[96]

Smith wanted everyone 'in on' – and wholeheartedly embracing – the caring, sharing, family atmosphere of these functions. And that included their partners. 'The girls of Melbourne were always an integral part of the team,' John Lord said. 'They were a great bridge between us and Norm's highly emotional encouragement.'[97] Hassa Mann explained:

> Norm brought the wives and girlfriends into the football club environment and really made them feel part of it. He felt it was important to have players and their partners all mixing together. It made for a very tight-knit environment where life-long friendships were formed, not only between the players, but the wives too. Norm also saw enormous value in it from a football perspective. He felt that if you're close off the field, you'll be close on it. You'll know your teammates like the back of your hand and you'll put your body on the line for them, and back them up, without any hesitation. The club was a big family, because Norm basically declared that we needed to have harmony on and off the field.[98]

Smith's dealings with the ladies of the club uncovered the chivalrous side to his nature. Mavis Cardwell, Jim's wife, said: 'Nobody could be more respectful of women than Norm. He was always very courteous and discreet.'[99] He would

---

[96] Ron Barassi. Interview with the author.
[97] John Lord. Interview with the author.
[98] Hassa Mann. Interview with the author.
[99] Mavis Cardwell. Interview with the author. Smith was so respectful of women, and was at such pains to portray himself as such, that – as Ron Carter reported in *The Age*, on July 30, 1973 – on one occasion when he and Jim Cardwell were away recruiting, trying to persuade a boy's mother to let him sign with Melbourne, the woman did not believe that Smith could actually be involved in such an aggressive pursuit as football. 'And tell me, Mr Smith,' said the mother, 'are you interested in football too?' According to Carter, it took Smith 'a long time to recover from that'.

not tolerate anyone swearing in front of women; if they, did, they would be told in no uncertain terms to stop; and if it continued there would be trouble, and perhaps a punishment meted out. Thelma Brown, the wife of Smith's cousin Russ, observed Marj's influence on Smith. 'Marj tamed the lion,' she said. 'Norm might have roared like a bull with the blokes, but he was a pussycat with women. I never knew him to raise his voice or be aggressive in any way. I always found him to be a nice, pleasant man.'[100]

Smith also took great pride in getting to know, and remembering, the names of the wives and girlfriends, and, in many cases, their children. 'The girls genuinely liked Norm,' said Clyde Laidlaw. 'They thought he was first-class; a real gentleman.'[101] Laidlaw's wife, Judy, admired how 'Norm would always take time to talk to you. He was a very nice, pleasant, family man'.[102] Smith displayed such warmth that John Lord was moved to say: 'You almost felt he shared his love of Marj and Peter with us all.'[103]

Marj naturally became an even greater mother-like figure to the young Melbourne women than she had been at Fitzroy. There was now a bigger age gap between her and many of the players' partners – to some of them, she was old enough to be their mother – and she was back at a club where she had many fond memories from the days of her late teens, through the celebrations of four premierships and her gradual maturation from girl to woman, to wife, to mother. She made a genuine effort to make the women feel welcome, get to know them, and ensure their group within the club was as harmonious as any other. She and her husband also paid close attention to the relationships between players and their partners, as Mike Williamson observed:

> Norm and Marj became matchmakers and even marriage guidance counsellors to some of the players. Norm would have a chat with the player, and Marj would mother his wife. And if a player brought a girl down to the club who Marj didn't approve of, she would say so. She might tell the player: 'I don't like that girl you're with tonight'. But she'd mean well. She had great maternal instincts.[104]

One of the fondest memories of these functions was provided by charismatic schoolteacher (later principal) Geoff Tunbridge.

---

[100] Thelma Brown. Interview with the author.
[101] Clyde Laidlaw. Interview with the author.
[102] Judy Laidlaw. Interview with the author.
[103] John Lord. Interview with the author.
[104] Mike Williamson. Interview with the author.

Melbourne chairman Bert Chadwick, well-connected as he was, had entered the hall with the Australian Prime Minister, Mr Robert Menzies. Chadwick addressed the audience: 'I would like to introduce all you to your Prime Minister, Mr Robert Menzies.' The announcement drew enthusiastic applause, along with the odd mischievous hoot. In his role as the MC, Tunbridge demanded: 'Silence!'

The 'carnival atmosphere' dissipated. A hush came over the room. With all eyes on him, Tunbridge approached Mr Menzies and said: 'The entry price, sir, is £5'.

Onlookers like Hugh McPherson thought: 'What the hell is "Tunner" up to?' Chadwick leant across to Menzies and said: 'That's Geoff Tunbridge from Ballarat.' Menzies, who had attended school in Ballarat and knew of the Tunbridge family, handed over a £10 note and responded loud enough for everyone to hear. 'Ah, yes,' he said, 'I remember Geoff's family from my Ballarat days; a very honourable, hard-working family. So I know that I will receive the right change!'

Menzies' priceless retort 'brought the house down'.[105]

Such famous guests were a treat for the Demons, and so were the culinary delights. There was no shortage of club people willing to volunteer to supply and prepare supper for the dances. Two standout 'caterers' were George De Morton (a member of the social committee member who owned a delicatessen in Essendon) and Clarrie Williams (the father of young star Don), who, voluntarily, also provided hot soup and bread rolls after training on Tuesday and Thursday nights, and organised sausage nights.[106] The women often contributed a plate of food, and the smorgasbord included a variety of casseroles, sausage rolls, sandwiches, cakes and biscuits.

One of the strongest contributors was Mavis Cardwell, who said: 'Everybody did their bit and worked hard for the club. It was an absolutely wonderful club, a very happy club and I feel very lucky to have been part of it. It's something you miss very badly when it finishes. The kids of today wouldn't understand how close we were. We were like family. Outside of the football club, there wasn't time for a social life. Everything revolved around the club, and we all loved it. We'd watch the football during the day and we wouldn't leave the club until after midnight'.[107]

Almost invariably, Norm and Marj Smith would outlast everyone. 'Norm was always last to leave social events,' said John Beckwith. '*Always* last. He'd be there 'til the end with Marj.'[108] The night would usually end with Smith and Shane

---

[105] Hugh McPherson. Interview with the author.
[106] Hugh McPherson. Interview with the author.
[107] Mavis Cardwell. Interview with the author.
[108] John Beckwith. Interview with the author.

McGrath singing *Champagne Charlie*, and Smith requesting Mike Williamson, the compere, to 'Give us *That Old Black Magic*'.[109]

Occasionally they put up someone at their house, such as Ralph Lane, who lived about 45 kilometres away in Frankston and occasionally missed the last train home. Lane fondly remembered stopping in with Smith at 'Baron' Ruthven's house in Fitzroy for a few beers before making it to the Smith home in the wee hours.

Then there were what became known as 'pleasant Sunday mornings'. The players would go on a light recovery run to loosen up some sore spots and then follow it up with a few drinks. Occasionally the mornings spilled into afternoons, as Ken Emselle, the son of Smith's mate Richie, recalled:

> Dad didn't go along to the past players' reunions too often, but Norm would keep at him: 'Come on, you've got to come along', and eventually Dad relented. It was supposed to be a 10am-noon function, and I'd go along with Dad and I'd be having a kick with Peter Smith and Ian Baggott (Ron's son) out on the MCG – what a place to have kick-to-kick! – while Dad was having a drink inside. They'd still be drinking at about 3pm. Dad didn't drink very often, so by that time he was a mess. Norm would drive us home, and of course he'd been drinking too. As soon as he'd dropped us off, Norm took off, which was a wise move because Dad was full, we were three or four hours late, and Mum was on the warpath!

Past players were shown enormous respect by Smith, and he expected his players and other club people to be just as respectful. He also saw the potential for their wisdom to rub off on his Demons. 'Norm welcomed the past players into the fold, and highlighted their attendance whenever they were in the room,' said John Lord. 'And it had a very positive effect on the players. We had a situation where, rather than past greats just being names on honour boards and faces in photographs, they were almost actively sought out as great examples for us to aspire to, if we didn't already. It was awesome to be in the same room with some of the greats of the past. I always felt Jack Mueller was watching me – we were both Echuca boys – and I was never game to put a foot wrong when I knew Jack was there. I know other players had their pet past players – maybe they wore their number – and there were these bonds that developed, which was always comforting.'[110]

---

[109] Mike Williamson. Interview with the author.
[110] John Lord. Interview with the author.

12

THE DAWNING OF A DYNASTY

[1955]

The 1955 season marked the dawning of what remains the most dominant decade-long dynasty of any club in AFL/VFL history. Although Norm Smith had every right to be optimistic about the Demons' chances of winning multiple premierships, especially after proving their worth with a barnstorming second half of the 1954 season, he could not have predicted the snowballing success that lay ahead.

'We faced up to 1955 with a great deal of confidence,' Smith later said. 'All going well, I could see a long reign at the top. We had a young side loaded with talent.'[1]

Significantly, it was the promotion of one of the more experienced players to the captaincy that was to prove the first major development of Melbourne's 1955 campaign.

Geoff Collins had retired at the end of 1954, at the age of 28, but not without a concerted effort from Smith to keep his great mate at the club. After losing the Grand Final to Footscray, Smith went back to Geoff and Mary Collins' flat in Queens Road, Albert Park (where Norm and Marj Smith often found themselves late on Saturday nights), and over several late-night beers tried to coax his skipper into 'going around again' in 1955.[2] Collins rejected Smith's pleas because he felt he was finished and wanted to apply for a soldier settlement in the country. Mary Collins recalled: 'Football was something Geoff loved doing, but he felt it was only one part of his life. Norm was disappointed, but he accepted that.'

---

[1] *Melbourne Truth* series, 1962.
[2] Email from Mike Collins, brother of Geoff.

THE DAWNING OF A DYNASTY [1955]

Smith presented Geoff and Mary Collins with a pewter mug each in appreciation of their efforts.[3]

Incidentally, that night in the Queens Road flat, Smith asked Collins's 15-year-old brother Mike[4] what he thought of the loss that day. When the youngster said he was 'very disappointed', Smith told him: 'Don't be –Melbourne is on the way up.'[5]

Geoff Collins's replacement as skipper would continue this upward trend. The Demons appointed Noel McMahen to the leadership role. It was perhaps a belated honour for the frighteningly tough defender, who was desperately unlucky not to have been chosen to lead the side the previous season.

Noel McMahen and Norm Smith – who were to become Melbourne Football Club giants and, more pointedly, entwined forever as a successful coach-and-captain combination – shared a complex relationship. McMahen revealed:

> There was mutual respect between Norm and I, but no great fondness. We weren't close, but I gave him complete loyalty, and I always played hard under him. I respected Norm for many, many things, and he certainly respected me, but it was an unspoken respect. But we were civil to one another, and we made it work. And we were both successful together – he as the coach and myself as captain.[6]

McMahen admitted that at times he 'got Norm offside' with some of his on-field decision-making. 'Norm got annoyed with me when I made a few moves of my own out on the ground,' he said. 'That was a bit foolish – it was probably asking for trouble – but I felt they were necessary. I swapped the centre half-back and full-back a couple of times if I could see that their opponent was a bit quick on the lead, or a bit too strong in the air. Occasionally I'd switch half-back flanks with Donny Williams. If a bloke was getting a few kicks on me, I'd tell him: "Cut it out or I'll swap with Donny Williams and then you *won't* get a kick". Donny was a champion. Norm was OK about it in the end. We worked it out. Most of the planning was done before the game anyway, so I had a reasonable idea of the possible moves that could be made.'

McMahen's appointment was a timely one, as he was regarded by many Melbourne players of the era as 'the godfather' of the group. Indeed, Smith himself later described McMahen as one of the key ingredients of Melbourne's success.

---

[3] Mary Collins. Interview with the author.
[4] Mike Collins played four games with Melbourne in 1961-62.
[5] Email from Mike Collins.
[6] Noel McMahen. Interview with the author.

ㆍㆍㆍㆍㆍㆍㆍㆍㆍ

In Norm Smith's own words, Melbourne started the 1955 season 'with a bang'.[7]

Although their first quarter of the year was unimpressive – they trailed the previous season's wooden spooner St Kilda by three points at quarter-time at the Junction Oval, and at one stage had scored 2.11 – the Demons piled on 15.11 to 5.9 in the remaining three quarters to win by 59 points.

They faced their first test in round two, when they encountered Geelong at the MCG. But 'what had promised to be a ding-dong struggle fizzled out early',[8] with the Demons storming to a five-goal lead after just 15 minutes to shellshock the Cats. With Noel Clarke at his best with just his second bag of seven goals, Melbourne's dominance became complete in the middle two quarters when they added 7.4 while restricting the highly-rated Cats to just six behinds to charge to a match-winning 59-point lead by the last change.

The Demons had vaulted to the top of the VFL ladder – a position they would occupy for the rest of the season.

The following week, Melbourne entered the Grand Final rematch with Footscray at the MCG with injuries to five key players – Noel Clarke, Laurie Mithen, John Beckwith, Geoff McGivern (who would miss the first 11 rounds after badly tearing a thigh muscle in the last training session before the start of the season) and Ian McLean. It mattered nought. Just 12 goals were kicked from 44 scoring shots and the Demons won by 12 points – 6.22 (58) to 6.10 (46). Inaccuracy almost cost the Demons. They led by 11 points at the last change and kicked 0.9 in the final term, while the Dogs could manage just 1.2.

The Demons fought out another tight contest in round four, this time from against an unlikely opponent – North Melbourne. After making the finals in 1954, the Kangaroos had started the season disastrously: three straight losses, two of them by 11 goals. But when they hosted the Demons at Arden Street, it became clear early in the match that the League leader would not walk away with a landslide victory. In fact, they would be lucky to get away with a victory of any kind. Late in the second quarter, the Demons had fired twice as many scoring shots as North, and 'almost as many shots went out of bounds as scored points',[9] but despite their ascendancy they held only a narrow lead. The Demons 'seemed over-anxious',

---

[7] *Melbourne Truth* series, 1962.
[8] *The Football Record*, April 30, 1955.
[9] *The Football Record*, May 14, 1955.

'fought each other for the ball and spoilt one another in the air'.[10] From his vantage point on the bench, Norm Smith was becoming increasingly agitated. Young centre half-forward Clyde Laidlaw revealed what happened next:

> Just before half-time my opponent, (John) Brady, a star centre half-back, took a mark and went for a run down to the forward line and they got a goal. When the siren went, Norm attacked me in front of everybody. He abused me. He said: 'When he got the ball, you didn't chase him hard enough! You gave up!' I felt quite embarrassed about it. When Norm cooled down, he delivered his half-time speech and then our captain, Noel McMahen, came over and said: 'Don't worry, he does it to us all', which was reassuring, in a funny kind of way. I never forgot it though. From that point on, I made sure I chased hard every time because I didn't want to attract another response like that from Norm. So, from that point of view, Norm's outburst worked.[11]

It was also a tonic for Laidlaw's performance for the rest of the match. *The Football Record* reported that he 'had the better of individual tussles with Brady and was the best of the attacking division'.[12] The Demons eventually clawed their way to a hard-fought 13-point win. It was ugly but effective, and the Demons were now the only undefeated team in the VFL, but with five sides just a game behind them.

If Smith wasn't already convinced he had charge of a special team, confirmation of this fact came after his side won the next six games. Smith's conclusion wasn't merely based on results, but particularly the manner in which they won three of these contests: coming from behind in the last quarter and running over solid opposition.

The first side they shocked was a quality Essendon side at Windy Hill in round five. The Bombers had entered the game with a 3-1 record – they eventually finished fourth – and looked likely victors when they produced a third-quarter burst of 5.5 to 3.0 to move to an eight-point lead by the last change in a low-scoring match. But the Demons kept the home side to just three behinds in the final term while kicking 3.7 themselves, doing most of their attacking in the final 10 minutes, thanks largely to the work of Spencer, Dixon and Williams, to win by 14 points. *The Football Record* noted: 'This young side has proved this year that it is never beaten'.[13]

---

[10] *The Football Record*, May 14, 1955.
[11] Clyde Laidlaw. Interview with the author.
[12] *The Football Record*, May 14, 1955.
[13] *The Football Record*, May 21, 1955.

But much better was to come just a fortnight later, when the Demons recorded one of the most astonishing victories in their history.

South Melbourne hadn't been a strong team for some years, but opposition clubs often found them difficult to shift at their home at the Lake Oval. The Swans led by five points at half-time – they regained the lead just before the interval after Demon rover Stuart Spencer took a bounce in defence and watched in horror as it sprung back over his head and South kicked a goal. The Swans went into overdrive in the second half as Melbourne put in another substandard third term. South kicked six of the next eight goals to lead by 29 points with about eight minutes left. The Swans 'looked home and hosed', and 'the honour of being the first team to down the undefeated leaders appeared their for the taking', particularly as the Demons were 'playing like a beaten side'.[14] The Demons had scraped together just six goals for the afternoon and now needed five goals in as many minutes. They had played the entire second half virtually one man short. Spencer was stretchered off to hospital after being knocked out and Noel Clarke was also carted off the ground with concussion, while Dick Atkinson nursed a broken wrist in the forward pocket to fill in the numbers. The Demons looked gone. Smith later conceded: 'South Melbourne had us beaten to a frazzle.'[15] The red and white faithful let them know all about it. But the hecklers were not smug for long. This was the cue for an amazing Demon revival.

Noel McMahen described what happened next in what he hailed as 'the greatest game I've ever played in'.

> (South Melbourne vice-captain) Micky Sibun was on a half-forward flank and Billy Gunn, who I was playing on, had absolutely killed me. Billy Gunn I could never beat – he was a wonderful player. They were kissing each other. And Denis Cordner came to me and he said: 'Macca, let's give them one more twitch. Come into the ruck with me.' He's hit the ball down to the lake end so far (that) Dick Atkinson, who was on the field with a broken wrist, kicked a goal; (then) Terry Gleeson kicked a goal, Bob Johnson kicked a goal... Unbelieeeevable!'[16]

Melbourne kicked five goals in the dying stages, including three in time-on, to win by a point. 'One of those football miracles had occurred,' hailed *The Football Record*.[17] It had been a similar barnstorming victory to the one Smith

---

[14] *The Football Record*, June 4, 1955.
[15] *Melbourne Truth* series, 1962.
[16] Noel McMahen, on the *Red and Blue* documentary, 2005.
[17] *The Football Record*, June 4, 1955.

and his Demons teammates had conjured against Collingwood at Victoria Park in 1937. Smith was thrilled with the effort. 'Our players had a fantastic will to win,' he said. 'They played strong, purposeful football and, above all, played as a team. We showed our fighting capabilities.'[18]

Melbourne's other notable comeback was against Richmond at the MCG in round nine. The Tigers had won just two matches, but, prophetically, *The Football Record* gave them a chance. 'They often play well at the MCG and could cause trouble to the Demons,' *The Record* speculated.[19] But not even "Chatterer" (the nom de plume of *The Record*'s chief writer) could have predicted that the Tigers would open up a 25-point advantage early in the last quarter. The Demons were playing 'listless, dispirited football',[20] but in what had become a trademark fast finish, they more than doubled their own score by slamming on 7.6 to 1.2 to win by 16 points.[21] Again, 'the honours were with the losers, but, as at South Melbourne, the Demons proved they are a great team.'[22]

Melbourne had recorded nine successive victories – their club's best-ever start to a season in 59 attempts, eclipsing the efforts of their 1928 and 1937 sides.

A 32-point victory over Fitzroy (now coached by Bill Stephen) at the Brunswick Street Oval gave the Demons 10 wins in a row, which equalled the club record, originally set in 1927-28 and repeated in 1941. In doing so, they had conceded just 80 goals (an average of just eight a game) while kicking 124 themselves (at 12.4 goals a game). The Demons were two games clear at the head of the VFL ladder. They had indeed started 1955 with a 'bang'.

Smith was impressed. 'The side was as fit as any I have seen,' he said.[23]

Smith could take most of the credit for the supreme fitness of his players. He supervised the toughest training regime of any club in the competition, so once he had the right kind of individual in his side – the kind who did everything he asked of him, no questions asked – it became almost inevitable that the Demons would become the fittest and best-prepared combination in the VFL. He was, in fact, 'ahead of his time' in this department.[24] McMahen declared: 'That was Norm's greatest discipline and his greatest effort towards us being a great side'.[25]

---

[18] *Melbourne Truth* series, 1962.
[19] *The Football Record*, June 4, 1955.
[20] *The Football Record*, June 18, 1955.
[21] Richmond wasn't as poor a side as it seemed. It went on to win seven of its last eight games, but still missed the finals by three games.
[22] *The Football Record*, June 18, 1955.
[23] *The Football Record*, June 18, 1955.
[24] John Beckwith. Interview with the author.
[25] Noel McMahen. Interview with the author.

Pre-season training had steadily become more consuming. In the late 1950s, Smith wrote:

> The old idea that prevailed many years ago, that a player used the practice match period... to get fit is completely out. Nowadays... on the first training night, practically every player has been training for months... Ron Barassi privately, so many of the players, Athol Webb, Dixon, Case, etc. running as pro-runners, with only one reason – to get fit for the football season. But no matter how fit they might be for foot-running, they have still to be conditioned for their football, (because) they lack ball-handling, they lack balance, (and) they lack real toughness, and this can only be obtained on the track. No matter what new experiments are made, and no matter what new techniques are introduced, I do not think they will ever leave behind the sweating hours one must spend on the track at training...
>
> I endeavour to find out just what amount of work each player has been doing through the summer. In many cases, merely by looking at a man you can tell how fit he is or otherwise, and you can gauge the amount of work that is necessary for each man... I refer often to previous records on a player – his weight last year, etc. – and decide if it is necessary for him to further reduce or to be rested because he is below weight.[26]

Smith was always bemused to hear that some coaches would have their players running in sandshoes for most of the night in pre-season. 'I can't see much value in that,' he wrote. 'After all, you are training them to be footballers, not harriers.' As a result, Smith would bring out the balls on the first training night. 'I let them have a kick the first night,' he said, 'but not too much, mainly little punt passes... (with) more emphasis on handball and backing up one another.'[27] Not a pre-season went by when Smith didn't warn his players of the perils of over-kicking – i.e., kicking too much, too hard, too soon. Perhaps in light of the problems he endured in his own playing career, he remained fearful that they would damage their hamstrings or adductor muscles in their thighs – injuries that can linger for some weeks, even months, and become chronic ailments difficult to repair. One player who fell foul of Smith in this regard was Bluey Adams, who recalled:

---

[26] Norm Smith's notes titled: 'My Theories and Practices For Fitness For Melbourne League Team', believed to have been written in 1959.
[27] Norm Smith's notes titled: 'My Theories and Practices For Fitness For Melbourne League Team', believed to have been written in 1959.

> One coolish night in pre-season, Norm called us in for a chat in the centre and he spoke and spoke and spoke. After what seemed like an eternity, he said: 'That's it, boys. Sprint in.'
>
> Hassa Mann was about five metres in front of me, so I thought: 'I'll catch Hassa; I'll reel him in.' I'd just about caught him when – *ping!* My adductor muscle went. I headed straight for the medical room and Norm followed me in. He said: 'Kicking too hard too early?'
>
> I said: 'No, I pulled it when I was sprinting.'
>
> I was being honest, but in doing so I'd semi-blamed him, because if he hadn't kept us so long in the centre, and we hadn't cooled up, and he hadn't asked us to sprint in, it would never have happened.
>
> He walked away, but about 10 minutes later, as I was leaving via the toilets, Norm bailed me up and said: 'You little liar!' He really gave it to me. But in that instance he was wrong. But what can you do? Are you going to make an issue of it? He was convinced I did it kicking, so you just have to cop it because you weren't going to change his mind. I knew when to shut up and not come back at him, and that was one of those times. But one thing with Norm was that he wouldn't harp on about it the next time he saw you. He made his feelings known once and that was it; he never mentioned it again. The next time he saw you he might ask: 'How's the family? How's (wife) Noelle?' And he'd be back in your good graces again. Very few players crossed swords with him.[28]

As had been the case at Fitzroy, training under Norm Smith could be a genuine ordeal for players. Getting through a Tuesday night session was often an achievement to be proud of; surviving it for multiple seasons, or a career, was something they almost wore as a badge of honour.

The discipline started in the changerooms. 'Norm insisted that we all went out onto the training track together, as a team, just as we did on a Saturday,' John Lord said. 'He was always critical of players who turned up late to training. There was no surer way of upsetting Norm than being late – for anything.'[29] John Townsend said: 'There was no way you were ever going to be late for training. It wasn't because you were afraid of getting kicked over the fence; it was just the respect you had for the bloke, and the Melbourne jumper, which Norm always emphasised.'[30]

Ron Barassi recounted one of the lighter moments relating to lateness:

---

[28] Frank 'Bluey' Adams. Interview with the author.
[29] John Lord. Interview with the author.
[30] John Townsend. Interview with the author.

One night on the MCG, Norm was addressing us in front of the empty Members' Stand. An lot of construction work had been done to transform the MCG into a world-class stadium for the 1956 Olympics. The whole stadium had been refurbed and there was the new Olympic Stand. As Norm was addressing us, out came this ruckman from Tasmania, who never made it and whose name escapes me. Let's call him 'Jonesy'. He was late, and he tried to slip unnoticed into the back of the group. But Norm spotted him and said: 'Jonesy, where have you been?'

Jonesy said: 'Sorry, Norm, I got caught up in the sheds.'

There was silence for a few seconds as Norm looked around this brand new, state-of-the-art stadium, a monument to cutting-edge architecture of the time.

'*Sheds?*' Norm said. He was incredulous. '*Sheds?*'

We wet ourselves. Even Norm saw the funny side of it. Jonesy came out standing 6' 4" but he suddenly felt 5' 4". It showed that while football was a serious business to Norm, even he could have a laugh on the training track.[31]

There was often a stark contrast between a Tuesday night session and a Thursday session. Tuesday was set aside for the hardest, heaviest, slogging work, almost ignoring skill errors in the pursuit of 'quickness', while Thursday was usually a short-and-sharp, morale-building tune-up.

Sessions generally started with end-to-end kicking, followed by circle-work for half-an-hour to an hour, and perhaps a combination of match-practice, where players were matched up and one team wore red jumpers while the other wore blue, drills that involved one-on-one contesting, sprints, specialised ruck or forward work. 'All players need relief from monotony,' Smith later wrote, 'and I tried to vary the work I gave them.'[32] Despite Smith's best efforts to the contrary, some players still regarded this basic training regimen as 'unimaginative'[33] and, at times, even 'boring'.[34] McMahen put it into perspective when he said: 'What we actually did wasn't any different from what any other club would have been doing – it certainly wasn't revolutionary in any way – it's just that Norm had us doing *more of it*. A *lot* more of it'.[35] However, Bernie Massey, who played under Smith in the '60s, said: 'I don't think we trained any more than anyone else, I just think that we were probably more disciplined. We didn't buggerise around on the

---

[31] Ron Barassi. Interview with the author.
[32] *Craven*, John (editor), *Football The Australian Way*, Lansdowne Press, 1969.
[33] Geoff Tunbridge. Interview with the author.
[34] Ian Ridley. Interview with the author.
[35] Noel McMahen. Interview with the author.

training track; we did exactly what we were supposed to do. We played the way we trained.'[36]

Match practice was not for the faint-hearted. Back then, the idea of 'token pressure' – where teammates simply place a hand on each other to simulate match conditions while not risking injury – had not yet been conceived. Alf Brown observed in *The Herald*: 'Some mid-week practice games are rugged affairs. They are the nearest thing I have seen to legalised mayhem. Players take more hard knocks in them than in some games. Teammates have come to blows. Smith is the umpire and anything goes. I've seen him give only three free kicks. Each time it has been against the one player. "Too flash – free kick against you," Smith will yell in defiance of every rule, but in anger at a piece of brilliant but individualistic play.'[37] Smith later explained: 'When I umpire a match at training, I prefer not to blow the whistle much so the ball is kept moving. This enables players to get themselves out of awkward situations without waiting for the whistle for a free kick.'[38]

Melbourne players were constantly thrust into awkward situations when it came to coping with the training workload. The concept of 'more' was fully explored by Smith during what became known as 'Tuesday night torture'. Smith firmly believed that 'as fitness fails, so does skill'.[39] As a result, he strove to push his players into uncharted areas of exhaustion in the training environment, on the sound basis that increased fitness delays the onset of exhaustion and related skill errors in a match situation. John Beckwith said:

> Norm always maintained that: 'You have to pass through the pain barrier. If you can do that at training and get more out of yourself, you'll be better players and we'll be successful'. It proved true. I lost count of the number of times I came off the ground at training dry-retching and spewing – absolutely gone. But as much as you despised doing it, there's no doubt it helped on a Saturday knowing that you'd prepared yourself to that level.[40]

Ralph Lane described a drill in which Smith inflicted pain on his players:

> Norm would pick out two players and then he'd kick the ball 30 metres away and say: 'Righto, go and get it!' You'd sprint and fight like mad for the ball and get it

---

[36] Bernie Massey. Interview with the author.
[37] *The Herald*, 1958.
[38] *Craven*, John (editor), *Football The Australian Way*, Lansdowne Press, 1969.
[39] Related by Hassa Mann in an interview with the author.
[40] John Beckwith. Interview with the author.

back to him. But then he'd kick it away and say: 'Go again!' After about four times, you'd be thinking: 'Hell, I *can't* go again'. But you'd battle through it, and however many more times he wanted you to do it, and when it was over you'd just about be throwing up. It made you realise that you could do it if you had to; that you had more in reserve than you thought. When you thought you'd put in 100 percent, you still had more to give. And you'd be a bloody fool if you gave up.[41]

Giving up, and bludging, were sins to be punished. He demanded his players 'keep on going all the time' because he believed that 'perseverance beats brilliance'.[42] He also subscribed to the theory that: 'The harder you work the luckier you get'. Smith would 'abuse blokes badly if they took it easy and just loped along – that was like a red rag to a bull'.[43]

One wet, windy and muddy night after training, as his players trudged back to the changerooms after a gruelling session, Smith noticed that one of his young stars looked a little too fresh. 'How do you feel?' he asked.

'Fine,' the player replied.

'Well, that's because you didn't train hard enough. You can stay out here and run laps until you're tired.'

Bluey Adams also recalled:

> A few times when we were doing circle-work and I thought we were training all right as a group, Norm became quite angry with the standard, and perhaps our level of effort, and he'd say: 'Well, if you won't train properly *with* the balls, perhaps you'll train properly *without* them!' The balls would be put away and he'd run the backsides off us up and down the ground.[44]

Other times, when he was not happy with training, Smith would order his players to sprint to the boundary and back. And if they were not puffing enough, he would demand they do it again. 'That's when you can really give 'em a burst,' Smith later said, 'because they're puffing so much that they can't mouth back.'[45] Very few dared to back-chat Smith anyway. One who did, and immediately wished he had not, was Geoff Case, who revealed: 'One training night late in my career, I must not have done something incorrectly and Norm told me what I should've

---

[41] Ralph Lane. Interview with the author.
[42] Dick Fenton-Smith. Interview with the author.
[43] John Beckwith. Interview with the author.
[44] Frank 'Bluey' Adams. Interview with the author.
[45] Related by Bill Stephen in an interview with the author.

done and I made the mistake of answering him back. Boy, didn't he pay out on me! Even my father copped it afterwards!'[46]

However, Smith was still capable of showing compassion for – and even having a wry grin with – players who avoided some of the training load. Trevor Johnson credited Smith with coining his nickname. 'My day job involved heavy physical work,' Johnson said, 'and at training, because there were no floodlights in the 1950s, I often moved out to the boundary line, where it was quite dark, for a rest. The old fox would seek me out in the approaching darkness by calling: "Where are you, Phantom?"'[47]

Barassi offered the following slant on Smith's demanding training program: 'He was very strict on discipline, not for the sake of being a disciplinarian but for the sake that it does produce the best footballer... (These days) if you don't get a person who's unselfish and disciplined on field, he's regarded as a poor player. That was not the case when Norm was coaching.'[48] Smith trained his players harder as they got older,[49] but Barassi also reasoned: 'While we might have grumbled about the training he put us through, we knew that what he was saying and making us do made sense. You did not really have the chance to buck the system. We had a powerful team, and if you didn't play the team game, you were pretty quickly in the reserves. That would have helped him, too.'[50]

Another major – and surprising – feature of Tuesday night training was Smith's casual attitude to skill errors. He explained: 'Tuesday... (is) the night for the bullocking work, when you run and force yourself all the time, not worrying about skill'.[51] He challenged his players to challenge themselves – physically, mentally and skill-wise – rather than simply go through the motions. 'Let your imagination run wild,' he urged.[52] He didn't want safe play, devoid of adventure or an element of risk. He often barked: 'If you're not making mistakes, you're not trying!'[53] Smith wanted players to attempt things they were 'not sure of to build their confidence'. He later explained: 'I tell them to go for the ball and not wait for the bounce, picking up on the half-volley if necessary, but keeping on the move. The aim is to teach players to do things at full stride... Good players do not wait for the ball. They make the play. That is probably why good teams look faster than other

---

[46] Geoff Case. Interview with the author.
[47] Trevor Johnson, in a facsimile to the author.
[48] Ron Barassi, on ABC Radio National program *The Sports Factor*, on September 28, 2001.
[49] Robert 'Tassie' Johnson. Interview with the author.
[50] Sheedy, Kevin, with Warwick Hadfield, *The 500 Club*, News Custom Publishing, 2004.
[51] *Craven*, John (editor), *Football The Australian Way*, Lansdowne Press, 1969.
[52] Related by Barrie Vagg in an interview with the author.
[53] Related by John Lord in an interview with the author.

sides.'⁵⁴ He warned them: 'If you go for the ball my way and fail, you'll be OK; I can accept that. But if you do it your way and fail, you'll be out on your arse.'

Smith did not just want a fit side; he wanted a fast side. However, he believed: 'There is a vast difference between pace and quickness. Many players have pace but not quickness. (For) instance, Peter Brenchley (was) an even-time runner but not particularly quick, (while Denis) Cordner, though not a pacy runner, was never beaten at getting his foot to a ball, or... giving a quick handpass'.⁵⁵

Smith also remained adamant that players should, wherever possible, mark the ball out in front, in their hands, rather than on their chests. He even challenged them to try it on wet training nights, and promised not to chastise them for spilling the ball. 'This gives them confidence in marking a wet ball,' Smith wrote, 'and they learn to do it with reasonable certainty when the occasion arises in a match.'⁵⁶

One of Smith's disciples on the *no-chest-marks* theory was Barassi. 'It really was a no-brainer for me; I was instantly converted to Norm's way of thinking as soon as I heard him explain it,' Barassi said. 'I thought: "That makes a lot of sense. Why would you waste your time doing something you've been perfect at since you were 10 years old? Why wouldn't you test yourself by trying to do something that's more difficult, but will make you a better player?" It was pretty obvious to me. It has a lot of advantages – the ball has to travel an extra foot or two to reach your chest, giving your opponent more time to effect a spoil, and if you mark in your hands he has to reach over or around you, increasing your chances of getting a free kick; and once you've taken the ball you've also got your hands free to handball or kick.'⁵⁷ Barassi took the theory a step further when he became a coach himself in 1965. 'While Norm discouraged chest marks at training, I was so red-hot on it that I banned them all together,' he said. But that was not all – Barassi actually punished offenders by ordering them to run laps and/or complete push-ups.⁵⁸

Although Smith was keen for his players to experiment with their marking and their attack on the ball, he was not so keen for them to take chances with their kicking. He discouraged his players from drop-kicking in the first 10 or 15 minutes of a game when the play was red-hot and more conducive to mistakes. That way, he felt his players gained balance and timing and adjusted to the tempo of the game before they attempted a 'droppy'. Smith progressively discouraged drop-kicking

---

⁵⁴ *Craven*, John (editor), *Football The Australian Way*, Lansdowne Press, 1969.
⁵⁵ Norm Smith's notes titled: 'My Theories and Practices For Fitness For Melbourne League Team', believed to have been written in 1959.
⁵⁶ *Craven*, John (editor), *Football The Australian Way*, Lansdowne Press, 1969.
⁵⁷ Ron Barassi. Interview with the author.
⁵⁸ Ian Collins, who played under Barassi at Carlton, revealed this in *An Amazing Life: George by George*, by George Harris with Jim Main, BAS Publishing, 2006.

THE DAWNING OF A DYNASTY [1955]

full-stop. 'That showed how forward-thinking he was,' Barassi said. 'Just because he had been such a great exponent of the kick, and he loved it for its aesthetic qualities, he decided it had to go because the aim was to win, not to look good. He could see it was becoming a thing of the past because the game was becoming faster and there was less time and less space to steady and deliver an accurate drop-kick. He felt it was an unreliable kick under pressure. It showed what a smart man he was. He started the death of the drop-kick, and I buried it for good later on when I coached.'[59] Smith preferred his players to use the drop-punt or, what he termed, the 'mongrel punt' because 'it was quicker, safer and less prone to error'.[60]

Thursday night training had a starkly different focus. Although there were some common themes, such as going flat-out, Smith generally shortened the session – at times to barely 20 minutes – and demanded that his players attempt to delete all errors from their training. 'Thursday is... used to polish up your play, (and) develop your skill, with lighter, sharper training,' he later wrote.[61] This 'lighter' element, when players were often still recovering from the Tuesday session, came as a welcome relief. An example of what became a typical Thursday night drill – which also highlighted Smith's ability to be innovative – was described by Barassi:

> The MCC told Norm at one point that he had to protect large sections of the ground, which were too boggy to train on. The biggest section of the MCG available to us, which was firm enough to train on, was an area of only a quarter-of-an-acre or so. With 50 players, Norm needed to devise drills suited to confined spaces. We had to do end-to-end a lot closer in – over 25 or 30 metres – and he observed that we enjoyed it more because we handled the ball more often, and our skills were better too because of that fact. He made that a regular thing. 'End-to-end' used to be big long kicks and high marks, but this was over only half the distance. It was a great way for players to have a lot of touches and it also promoted a lot more interaction and voice and spirit. When you did it well, everybody was buzzing and feeling great about themselves, so it had enormous benefits. We called it 'short ends'. It was one of the early precursors to today's training, where players touch the ball every few seconds, and touch it a lot more than we ever used to before Norm introduced, through necessity, this 'short ends' drill.[62]

---

[59] Ron Barassi. Interview with the author.
[60] John Lord. Interview with the author.
[61] *Craven*, John (editor), *Football The Australian Way*, Lansdowne Press, 1969.
[62] Ron Barassi. Interview with the author.

Smith believed he could predict how well his players would perform at the weekend after watching them train on a Thursday.[63] He was 'a smart operator' who 'knew when you were fair dinkum and when you weren't, when you'd done enough and when you hadn't, and he'd train you accordingly'.[64] He would wait until his players had 'just got into the groove' and were 'training smoothly' and would then call an abrupt halt to the session.[65] He said: 'Players should leave the ground on a Thursday night wanting to do more and not feeling they have done too much'.[66] He wanted them to be 'hungry'[67] for Saturday, which he described as 'the big and all-important day'.[68]

To an extent, Smith individualised his training. 'A coach must know his players well,' he wrote, 'for different players need different training', and it is 'the duty of the coach to study all his charges and decide the right policy to be adopted with each one'.[69] John Beckwith elaborated on this point:

> Norm had a great ability to train us to a peak at the right time, particularly in the finals. We were cherry-ripe. Norm always had this theme that: 'I treat everyone the same'. But the thing was he treated players differently. He was a bit like a racehorse trainer in that respect. A real strength of Norm's coaching was analysing the type of individual he was talking to and tailoring what he said to their personality and the type of player they were. He actually eased players out of training when he thought they had done enough – he didn't want to over-train you. Quite often with me, he would say: 'Do a lap, Becky and go in early'. But he drove other players who he felt needed the work, or who he felt were lazy. He would rather train us flat-out for an hour than three hours at a leisurely pace.[70]

The flow-on effect of Smith's training program was plain to see. Ralph Lane said: 'Our supreme fitness level would show up when the Victorian sides were picked and a few players who hadn't been able to make the state training session at the MCG trained with us instead. They were struggling to keep up.'[71] Stuart Spencer, who played five games for Victoria, said: 'When you trained with the

---

[63] John Lord. Interview with the author.
[64] Ian Ridley. Interview with the author.
[65] John Lord. Interview with the author.
[66] *Craven*, John (editor), *Football The Australian Way*, Lansdowne Press, 1969.
[67] John Lord. Interview with the author.
[68] *Craven*, John (editor), *Football The Australian Way*, Lansdowne Press, 1969.
[69] *Craven*, John (editor), *Football The Australian Way*, Lansdowne Press, 1969.
[70] John Beckwith. Interview with the author.
[71] Ralph Lane. Interview with the author.

state side, it was very easy to make a comparison between how hard other teams trained and how hard we trained. It was quite evident that we were by far the best-prepared side. The only ones who could compete with us in that regard were Jack Clarke and Billy Hutchison from Essendon. The rest were hopeless. You never loped around at a training session run by Norm Smith. You had to dash, flat out, and that's what made the difference between me being a success or failure... and I was almost a failure.'[72] Spencer added: 'I used to board out at Thornbury, and on the odd occasion I'd stop at Victoria Park to watch Collingwood train under Phonse Kyne. They didn't train; they just walked around. They weren't conditioned to the same level as we were.'[73] This was also borne out when Smith later coached the Victorian team (in 1958, 1964 and 1967). Hassa Mann recalled:

> Normally, when you got picked in the state side the coach wouldn't worry about fitness because it was virtually expected that your fitness was already at a high standard. State training runs were more like get-togethers for players to get to know each other. But it wasn't like that with Norm. He didn't see it as a social thing. We trained as hard, if not harder, with the Victorian side than we did at Melbourne. (Ted) Whitten ran up beside me and said: 'Hell, do you Melbourne guys always train like this? No wonder you bastards always run over us.'[74]

At Melbourne, it also helped that Smith had some prime athletic talent to work with. In the 1950s, the Demons boasted 'nine players who could run inside even-time (100 yards in 10 seconds) in football boots'.[75] Wingman Brian Dixon explained: 'We were very fortunate that such an incredible group of young athletes were brought together in '53-'54-'55. We had the leg speed of the likes of Frank Adams, Donny Williams, Laurie Mithen, Stuey Spencer, Ian Ridley, and even our bigger blokes like Denis Cordner, Noel McMahen, and Big Bob Johnson were very quick'.[76] Beckwith believed the Demons' fast movement of the ball 'changed the whole thing' and, with 'bullocking types' like Barassi, Mithen and Laidlaw opening paths, 'transformed a good young side into a *great* side'.[77]

---

[72] Stuart Spencer. Interview with the author.
[73] Stuart Spencer. Interview with the author.
[74] Hassa Mann. Interview with the author.
[75] Athol Webb. Interview with the author.
[76] Brian Dixon. Interview with the author.
[77] John Beckwith. Interview with the author.

13

CHAMPIONS OF AUSTRALIA

[1955]

Melbourne's record-breaking 10-game winning streak came to an end against its most hated rival – Collingwood – at Victoria Park in round 11.

It was a match the Demons should never have lost. After leading by seven points at three-quarter-time, the Demons finally 'met their Waterloo',[1] suffering an eerily similar defeat to the one they received a year earlier against the same team and at the same venue. Again, dreadfully inaccurate kicking for goal – 5.15 (45) to Collingwood's 7.6 (48) – had condemned the Demons to defeat at Magpie headquarters. It was their first loss in more than nine months, since the 1954 Grand Final. However, they were still a game clear at the head of the table, with both Collingwood and Geelong nipping at their heels.

Melbourne restored its confidence with an obligatory 97-point hammering of bottom side St Kilda at the MCG in round 12. The Demons had 33 scoring shots to just six and the Saints' meagre total of 3.3 (21) was their lowest since 1921, when they managed just 0.18 (18). While the Demon demolition was not a memorable spectacle, it marked the birth of a new forward structure that was to prove a crucial component of Melbourne's success. Regular full-forward Noel Clarke kicked two early goals (to take his tally to 21 in his ninth appearance) but, in the second quarter, copped a heavy knock to a disc in his neck, which placed undue pressure on a nerve and rendered an arm virtually useless. The injury forced a reshuffle of the forward line. At half-time, Smith had a brainwave. He had just elevated Athol Webb, a 19-year-old Tasmanian, for

---

[1] *The Football Record*, July 9, 1955.

his VFL debut. Smith recalled that Webb, a lightning-fast wingman/centreman, had once filled in at full-forward for Tasmania (under coach Roy Cazaly) against a Victorian amateur team in Hobart. He would be worth a go, Smith thought. Webb said:

> Norm came to me at half-time and said: 'You played full forward for Tassie didn't ya?'
> I said: 'Yeah.'
> And, without having ever seen me play there, he said: 'Well, you've got the job.'
> And that was it. I never played anywhere else. Norm was a wizard, no doubt about it.[2]

Webb kicked two goals in the second half against the Saints and, although he and his teammates did not face much resistance that day, it was nonetheless a promising start. With Clarke sidelined for several weeks, Webb had the opportunity to prove his worth as an under-sized key-forward.

Although Webb and Clarke shared a number of striking similarities – i.e., they were both fast, lightly-built, medium-sized Tasmanians who had been asked by Smith to perform a role that 'many other coaches would never have even considered'[3] – they also proved to have striking differences in style, intent and willingness to embrace Smith's tactics.

Clarke was a left-footer who could take spectacular marks and would have preferred to have played as a pure full-forward, the spearhead. As a result, he was a reluctant participant in Smith's decoy forward system, which, inevitably, caused friction between the pair. Clarke was 'a beautiful mover and very stylish, but Norm wasn't at all interested in style'.[4] According to teammates, Clarke 'didn't conform with Norm's plan' because he 'felt that his leads should be honoured' and he 'didn't like being overlooked'.[5] Clarke would also 'get wild' with Smith because 'he wouldn't let him play his own game'.[6] Clarke himself explained:

> I originally went to Melbourne (from North Launceston) as a centreman. But they had a lot of trouble finding someone who could play at full-forward, and I think

---

[2] Athol Webb. Interview with the author.
[3] Stuart Spencer. Interview with the author.
[4] Keith Carroll. Interview with the author.
[5] Clyde Laidlaw. Interview with the author.
[6] Keith Carroll. Interview with the author.

it was Checker Hughes' idea to try me there. They really had no-one else to put there – they'd tried everyone else – and I kicked the odd goal, so they thought: 'Let's keep him there'. I did OK, but nothing to write home about. I kicked a few goals, but I might have kicked a few more if I'd been allowed to settle at full-forward, instead of being moved around. And I definitely would've kicked more goals if Norm had let me play my natural game.

We didn't see eye to eye on the decoy forward thing. I didn't want to get brainwashed into decoying and dummy-leading – that's not the way I wanted to play football, especially in a key position. Norm wanted me to lead and keep leading and not worry if I didn't get the ball. Under Norm's system, the plan wasn't for the decoy to get the ball because in his eyes that's all you were: a decoy. I didn't go along with that at all.

I thought that a good lead should be rewarded. It's very hard to get a break on your opponent, and then you'd have the resting ruckman and the back-pocket chopping across in front of you.

And when you do get a break, you expect the ball to be delivered in a reasonable fashion, but under Norm you were lucky if anyone kicked to you at all, and if they did – and I probably shouldn't say this – but Melbourne was a shocking side for delivering the ball. Very few players could deliver well. The best I could hope for was that they'd kick the ball up to the 10-yard square, so that I could at least jump at it. I missed Bob McKenzie's beautiful stab-passes – he'd drive them straight down your throat.

I was quite open about it. I said to Smithy: 'Look, I don't want to play full-forward. But if you decide to play me there, and I think I can kick a goal, it's my prerogative to do it'. I thought that might have put him off and they might have played me somewhere else further up the ground, but they didn't.

Norm got stuck into me a few times. One day when we played Geelong at the MCG, Laurie Mithen delivered the ball to me and I kicked a torpedo through for a goal from about 60 yards out. Norm abused me. He reckoned I should have passed it. I said: 'Norm, if you kick a goal, mate, you can't do much better than that'. There was always a bit of tension attached to that.

I was a pretty good kick for goal, so it wasn't like I was a liability in that department. But on the odd occasion when you had a shot inside 30 yards and you missed, he'd never forgive you. He said: 'You just don't miss goals from that distance!'

In those days, you had to have something fairly special to play full-forward. The other full-forwards at the time were fellas like John Coleman and Jack

Collins. The only way you were going to be recognised as a full-forward was to kick goals – that's what full-forwards are judged on – and you're very conscious of that. You don't want to be selfish or jeopardise the side's chances of winning, but by the same token you want to be regarded as a good player. If you don't kick goals, you'll be out. That's what I reckon playing up forward is all about. What else are you there to do?

Norm and I only argued on that one point. Apart from that, we got on very well.[7]

Webb, by contrast, was a right-footer, lighter, not as highly skilled as Clarke, but a superb ground player. He was also faster. 'No-one was quicker than "Webby" – he was like greased lightning,' said Keith Carroll.[8] More importantly, Webb was happy to do whatever Smith asked of him, and had no qualms playing as a decoy full-forward: providing virtual dummy leads up the ground to give Big Bob Johnson one-out contests in the goalsquare, and enabling other teammates to run into the space he had created. Johnson said: 'Athol Webb would lead out and I'd fall in behind him… If they couldn't find Athol, they shot it up to me. But Athol then… would come back through the front of the pack and take the chips off the front of the pack. Webb was a great player and he had a lot of pace. He was a vigorous sort of a coot, too.'[9]

Carlton captain Ken Hands described the difficulty of countering such a plan. 'Webb and Big Bob were both smart cookies,' Hands said. 'Webb would break up the defence with his leading, and Big Bob was always lurking deep in the forward line and putting himself in the right position – he was difficult to shift – and to make things even more awkward, he was a left-footer. Norm's forward line was always very mobile, with a lot of fast, smart little blokes as well, which didn't allow defenders to sit on their men.'[10]

Webb's role was one that, outside the Demons' inner sanctum, was never going to earn him the recognition he deserved. Traditionally – in this case, short-sightedly – full-forwards were judged solely on the number of goals they kicked, and in Smith's grand scheme it was always going to be difficult for Webb, or Johnson for that matter, to finish among the VFL's top goalkickers. But Webb was not concerned about not having kudos amongst outsiders. All he cared

---

[7] Noel Clarke. Interview with the author.
[8] Keith Carroll. Interview with the author.
[9] Bob Johnson, on the *Red and Blue* documentary, 2005.
[10] Ken Hands. Interview with the author.

about was pleasing his coach, keeping his place in the team and making a meaningful contribution. He usually fulfilled each of these aims, with Smith coupling him with Barassi as players who were 'exceptional in their own field', and suggesting that 'other clubs may be struggling to imitate them'.[11] Webb himself said:

> I didn't feel I was sacrificing my game in the slightest. My job was to create goals, not kick them. Norm would tell me: 'I don't care where you go to get a kick, as long as you're moving and doing something'. About 10 times during a game the runner would come out and say: 'Run, ya' bastard! Run!' That kept me moving, even late in the last quarter when I was knackered.[12]

In Webb's eight senior appearances in his debut season of 1955, he kicked 14 goals. He produced his best performance of the year when opposed to South Melbourne's champion full-back, Fred Goldsmith, in round 18, the final minor round. Goldsmith was at the peak of his powers and within days would become the first full-back to win the Brownlow Medal, after being awarded 21 votes (including five best-afields) to pip Essendon genius Bill Hutchison by one vote. But, undeterred by the reputation of his opponent, Webb kicked a mini-bag of four majors, which could easily have been a major bag, after firing 16 shots at goal. Despite his inaccuracy, *The Football Record* enthused: 'Webb gets more kicks than any other goalsneak'.[13]

Aside from the odd exception, no forward was ever going to kick bags of goals in Norm Smith's multi-pronged forward set-up. During Smith's 16-season reign at Melbourne – all 307 games of it – there were just 18 instances of Melbourne players kicking more than five goals. The breakdown was: 6 goals (11 times), 7 goals (6 times) and eight goals (once). In fact, in the premiership seasons of 1960 and 1964, no Demon kicked more than five goals in a game.

The best effort in a season in this period was 56 goals – by Webb in 1957. Furthermore, the average tally by the club's leading goalkickers was just 40, as the following table illustrates:

---

[11] Norm Smith's notes for a speech he made on a football trip to Western Australia in 1957.
[12] Athol Webb. Interview with the author.
[13] *The Football Record*, August 27, 1955.

CHAMPIONS OF AUSTRALIA [1955]

Year	Leading goalkicker	Goals	% of team goals
1952	Noel Clarke	49	25%
1953	Bob McKenzie	38	24%
1954	Noel Clarke	51	21%
1955	**Stuart Spencer**	**34**	**15%**
1956	**Bob Johnson**	**43**	**19%**
1957	**Athol Webb**	**56**	**21%**
1958	Athol Webb	44	18%
	Ron Barassi	44	18%
1959	**Ron Barassi**	**46**	**17%**
1960	**Ian Ridley**	**38**	**17%**
1961	Bob Johnson	36	16%
1962	Laurie Mithen	37	18%
1963	Barry Bourke	48	19%
1964	**John Townsend**	**35**	**15%**
1965	Barry Vagg	30	17%
1966	Barry Vagg	20	12%
1967	Hassa Mann	38	22%

• Bold denotes premiership seasons.

But while the Demons never boasted a prolific goalkicker, they were a more dangerous proposition because they developed what Smith termed as 'a widespread attack', which he believed was 'something similar' to the one that powered the Demons to the 1939-40-41 premierships.[14] Between 1954 and 1964, Smith usually had six to eight players who contributed at least 15 goals. This made the Demons less predictable and planted greater uncertainty in the minds of opponents. Even if they shut down two or three Melbourne forwards, others, it seemed, would always bob up to produce a winning total.

In teams coached by Norm Smith, the key forward posts, centre half-forward and full-forward, were almost sacrificial positions. They certainly were not the Hollywood-like glamour roles they were at other clubs, and are today. Smith rated their worth on how many goals they helped create, rather than how many they actually kicked themselves. Barassi said: 'There is a saying in football that you can't win premierships without a good centre half-forward, but I think Melbourne in the 1950s proved that wrong. In fact, they never had a name full-forward

---

[14] Norm Smith's notes for a speech he made on a football trip to Western Australia in 1957.

either.'[15] Smith's system was not conducive to a single dominant presence anyway, particularly at full-forward. He later wrote:

> Goals are hard to get when the forward line is congested, so I strove to keep play open. But this was not easy. With our style of play at Melbourne, we found that by playing a good team man who was prepared to sacrifice his own efforts at times for the good of the side, we could improvise at full-forward rather than look for one man to kick goals. After all, why give it to one man when someone else could kick goals just as well?[16]

Smith later said: 'We had a different full-forward each year.' Although this was not exactly true, it was not a major exaggeration. In 1959, Webb eventually relinquished the decoy mantle to Alan Rowarth, and, at times, Johnson was relieved in his deep forward role by the likes of Dick Fenton-Smith (in 1957), Laurie Mithen and a 'resting' Barassi. All of which proved Smith's point that: 'It is not always necessary to retain the same team set-up'.

In Melbourne's attacking zone, the small men were as valuable, and damaging, if not more so, than the big men. Opportunists of the calibre of Stuart Spencer, Ian Ridley and Bluey Adams would, as Adams recalled, 'keep the forward line open and arrive at Big Bob's feet at the last second with great momentum, so that if the ball spilled we'd hit it flat-out as we streamed through to goal'.[17] And 'if there was a crumb to be had', one of this trio 'generally got it and, more often than not, kicked a goal'.[18] Smith particularly admired Ridley, according to Hassa Mann (who, it must be said, did not play with Spencer).

> Norm's philosophy was: 'It doesn't matter who gets the goals', and he loved guys like Ian Ridley, who would put their life on the line for teammates to kick goals. He loved Barassi for that reason too, but Ridley in particular because he was so small and he would go into a pack head-first and bum up and palm it off to someone else who'd run into an open goal. Norm wouldn't care less about the guy who kicked the goal – it was all about the guy who did the hard thing to create the opportunity.[19]

---

[15] Barassi, Ron and Peter McFarline, *Barassi: The Life Behind The Legend*, Simon & Schuster, 1995.
[16] *Craven*, John (editor), *Football The Australian Way*, Lansdowne Press, 1969.
[17] Frank 'Bluey' Adams. Interview with the author.
[18] Clyde Laidlaw. Interview with the author.
[19] Hassa Mann. Interview with the author.

A mainstay of Melbourne's relatively fluid forward line was Clyde Laidlaw (the Demons' 'most improved player' in 1955), who provided the following detailed insights into Smith's expectations of him at centre half-forward:

At the start of 1955, Norm told me: 'I'm going to teach you the centre half-forward position as I want it played.' I was quite excited by that because it's such an important position in a team, perhaps *the* most important position. Anyone who plays at centre half-forward dreams of being the main target and taking 10 marks and kicking five or six goals, but that was never part of the plan with Norm. I wasn't that kind of player anyway. I was a very average, hard-working footballer. I just had to compete.

But we played to a plan. Bob McKenzie or, later on, Hassa Mann, had to be right out on the flank and Geoff Tunbridge was on the other flank. When the centre bounce took place, I was standing near the opposition ruckman. I was up there to keep the forward line open. Sometimes Denis Cordner would say: 'If the ball is in a favourable position, I'll give it a mighty punch and clear the pack, so you'd better be on the alert.' A few times that came off.

It sounds quite strange now, but Norm told me to never to go into the forward line. Even though I was the centre half-forward! No wonder I played nine years and kicked only 50-odd goals. I was told that I could move up to the centre but I wasn't to go deep into the forward line. Certainly not to the goalsquare. As a player himself, Norm led far and wide and was totally unselfish in his game and he expected others to do the same, no questions asked. He expected you to give part of your game away, and make a few sacrifices, to help the team.

Another directive from Norm was that I had to be in front of my man. If my opponent was determined to be in front, we'd keep edging in front of one another until we got to the centre and then I'd run back to centre half-forward and we'd start it all over again.

If our centreline was playing well and the instruction was: 'Kick long', I wouldn't see much of the play, but if our half-backline was playing well, that would bring me into the game. There were many games where the play went over my head because, with the way the play unfolded, I was almost in no-man's-land at times. But Norm felt that worked for us a lot as well, especially if I was playing on (Footscray's Ted) Whitten, or (St Kilda's Neil) Roberts or (North Melbourne's John) Brady, because they would be caught under the ball as well, so they'd be neutralised somewhat.

Whitten never played well against us. Norm told me to play him close, like a backman, and drag him under the ball so he couldn't use his superb marking skills.

I had to drag him up the ground and then go back and start the position again. In his notes before he died, Ted wrote that I was one of three or four opponents he had trouble with, and I attribute that entirely to Norm's tactics.

Above all, the key thing Norm wanted from me – and from every player for that matter – was a flat-out attack on the ball and a fierce contest. There were some players he always liked having in the team. He liked Keith Carroll, and Jim Sandral, because while they had no airs or graces, they attacked the ball. That was Norm's top priority. If you could convince him of that, he would accept you. Norm would say: 'I want you to run at the ball as hard as you can, and if you make an honest attempt and it bounces awkwardly in front of you, I won't go crook at you'. But if you only went 80 or 90 percent at it, or you hesitated, or looked around, or looked as if you were apprehensive, he would hammer you for it. Playing at centre half-forward, I was in that situation quite often, so I just had to do it, and I think Norm appreciated my effort.[20]

Despite all the of merits of the Demons' attack, some critics like Alf Brown from *The Herald* still found cause to launch scathing criticism. Webb recalled:

In '56, when I wasn't kicking many goals (he kicked 28 in 20 games) Alf Brown wrote a headline saying something like: 'This must be Webb's last game'. This kind of campaign went on for about six weeks and by that stage he had headlines about four inches high. I'd eventually had enough of it, so I took it to Norm and said: 'Have a look at this.'

Norm said: 'Listen mate, when we want him to pick the side, we'll make him a selector.'

Alf Brown was barred from the Melbourne rooms for 12 months after that. Norm wasn't unhappy with me – he kept giving me a game – and we were still getting by all right and winning most games. It's just that some people, such as Alf Brown, figured that if you're the full-forward you should be kicking heaps of goals. But full-forward under Norm Smith wasn't the traditional full-forward role. Some people just didn't get that I was there to create goals, not necessarily kick them.[21]

Laidlaw added: 'Alf Brown felt we had a weak forward line. Well, we didn't have superstar forwards but we had six forwards who knew their roles, and usually performed their roles, and we functioned well together. Alf Brown would

---

[20] Clyde Laidlaw. Interview with the author.
[21] Athol Webb. Interview with the author.

hammer Webby and I because we didn't kick many goals. But the way we played wasn't set up for that.'[22] Conversely, Brown also commended Smith for his ability to 'improvise' with his forwards.[23]

Smith was always creative with his forward network, but throughout the other two-thirds of the field he generally preferred consistency, continuity and predictability. Laidlaw said Smith stuck to a basic philosophy and brand of football, which perhaps deprived his players of individual glory, but enriched their lives no end from a team perspective. 'We weren't a great stab-passing side, and that's why Norm had us playing a simple style,' Laidlaw explained. 'We weren't a pretty side; we were hard-working and consistent. Nothing was left to chance. Norm hated lairising and individualism and players drawing attention to themselves by bouncing the ball and trying to take everyone on. No-one ever got away with flamboyance or individualism under Norm, and it's no coincidence that none of our players polled well in the Brownlow Medal. In that era, Brownlows tended to go to great players in weak sides.'[24]

Smith further simplified the game plan for self-confessed poor kicks like wingman Brian Dixon (a man who actually had the talent to win a Brownlow) and half-forward Geoff Tunbridge (who was so wayward he was nicknamed 'Heinz 57 Varieties'). Both Dixon and Tunbridge were left-footers with haphazard kicking techniques – they dropped the ball from an awkward height and, as a result, did not properly guide the ball onto their boot. But they were appreciative of Smith's attitude to their shortcoming. Dixon said:

> Norm was always keen for me to try to put the ball into the goalsquare, which was fortunate for me because I wasn't the world's greatest kick, and I certainly wasn't an accurate pass, and it meant I didn't have to worry so much about delivery. I rarely kicked it to the leading full-forward; I did occasionally, although it was very unusual – I only ever did it really if it was the only option. Most of the time I'd just lob it up into the square for Big Bob or Dick Fenton-Smith or Barassi or whoever had drifted back there. Norm more or less accepted the fact that I wasn't such a great kick and he just made use of my other attributes. Our strategies were very, very simple, and they were to avoid mistakes. Kicking long was the recommended, percentage thing to do; we weren't to mess around with too much handpassing or short kicking, which perhaps suited me more than most.[25]

---

[22] Clyde Laidlaw. Interview with the author.
[23] Alf Brown, in a souvenir booklet for the Norm Smith Commemorative Dinner, held on July 12, 1979, to inaugurate the Norm Smith Medal.
[24] Clyde Laidlaw. Interview with the author.
[25] Brian Dixon. Interview with the author.

At training, Smith often told players who were poor kicks: 'It's no good expecting me to teach you how to kick; if you don't know how to kick before you get here, bad luck, it's too late'.[26] Tunbridge said: 'I was a hopeless kick. Absolutely hopeless. I wouldn't last in the modern game. But Norm never spoke to me about it, or tried to coach me in it, probably because he felt I was beyond help, and that I was too old to change my natural technique. I could kick goals on the run and over the shoulder, but I was hopeless when I had a deliberate shot, which must have been a source of some frustration from a coaching perspective. Norm would obviously have preferred me to be better in that department, but he never voiced that. He never coached me in it, but he never knocked me about it either'.[27]

Smith would even playfully rib Terry Gleeson about his kicking attempts. 'Norm knew I wasn't the most skilful player in the world,' Gleeson said. 'I had an awkward kicking style and often when I had a kick at training Norm would say: "Replace your divot". I told that story on TV and Jack Dyer said: "You must have enjoyed playing under Norm", and I said: "Shit yeah", and the TV went off. The TV screens of people at home went black. I think I was the first person to say "shit" on TV! And it was in response to a question about Norm Smith.'[28]

But there were examples of Smith's ability to improve a player's kicking. A later example was Stan Alves, who started with Melbourne in 1965. Alves later wrote: 'One of my problems early on was my disposal under pressure. I could kick okay from a standing start, but on the run it was different because I was very quick and very prone to spray my kicks… (Smith) would get me alone and give me personalised coaching. Very slowly I started to get it right. The most important thing he showed me was how to become properly balanced under pressure. This meant not running in a straight line after I got the ball, but pulling back my speed to half-pace just before the moment of delivery.'[29]

Geoff Case never received any such one-on-one coaching from Smith. He said:

> Strangely, when I first started training with the senior team as a 17-year-old in 1953, Norm more or less said: 'When you get here, I don't have to teach you anything. You should already be able to play – that's why you're here'. That was a surprise to me because you'd expect that, as a young lad, you'd need plenty of tuition. I was only 17. Of course, he did give us tuition, but he felt that: 'You don't get

---

[26] Ralph Lane. Interview with the author.
[27] Geoff Tunbridge. Interview with the author.
[28] Terry Gleeson. Interview with the author.
[29] Alves, Stan with Col Davies, *Sacked Coach*, Crown Content, 2002. This book contains an insightful 30-page chapter titled 'The Norm Smith Legacy'.

any favours from any of the other guys because of your age. It's up to you to adapt yourself'.[30]

Just as surprising was Ian Ridley's revelation: 'Norm didn't actually teach me a lot about how to play the game. But he did what a good coach should do: he kept it very easy for us to understand by simply encouraging what was good and discouraging what was bad.'[31]

Conversely, Smith once said: 'Give me a player who's a poor kick, or a poor handballer or a poor mark and I'll improve him. But if he doesn't know how to get the ball, I can't teach him.' He firmly believed that ball-getting nous was an instinctive 'skill' that could not be coached. A player either had it or he did not.[32]

Ultimately, though, all Smith was interested in was producing selfless team players. Hassa Mann, who debuted with the Demons in 1959, said:

> One of the first things Norm told me was: 'I'm not going to teach you how to play football. You've been recruited by Melbourne because you've got the ability to play League football. I *expect* you to play well. I'm going to make you a good team player – if you're good enough'.
>
> Norm felt it was his role to marry that ability into a team performance. He was very big on team and team discipline, and on playing to a team plan. He said: 'I'm like the conductor of an orchestra. There are the wind instruments, the strings, the drums and so forth – my role is to combine them all into one performance.'[33]

Although individual tuition was often sacrificed in preference for the collective, team focus, Smith still expected his players to come to him for advice if they needed it. Len Mann (a Demon ruckman from 1959 to 1964, and a cousin of Hassa) recounted an occasion when Big Bob Johnson was teaching him how to shepherd in a ruck duel. Afterwards, Smith took Mann aside and 'went crook', saying: 'If you want to know anything, you come and ask me! Don't go asking anyone else!'

Mann said he did not need to know much as a ruckman under Smith. 'All he wanted his ruckman to do was get in front and bloody stay in front, and compete as hard as you can. But that was the general principle that applied to every player on the field.'[34]

---

[30] Geoff Case. Interview with the author.
[31] Ian Ridley. Interview with the author.
[32] Related by Garry Pearce in an interview with the author.
[33] Hassa Mann. Interview with the author.
[34] Len Mann. Interview with the author.

Smith's coaching skills were complemented by his ability to still execute the skills of the game. Even into his forties, Smith was still a superb kick – in fact, he appeared to have lost little of his deftness in this area since his playing days. Hassa Mann was one player who was stunned by the kicking skills Smith maintained:

> I would marvel at Norm because, even when he was well into his forties, he was one of the best stab-passes in the team! I'd heard that he had been a prodigious kick in his playing days, and you could tell by his beautiful kicking action it would have been true. He was still a magnificent stab pass over 35-40 metres. If you were going really well, he was so skilful that at times he would purposely put the ball at your toes to really test you out and see if you could pick it up.
>
> At times we'd finish training with four or five shots at goal. He would invariably kick as many, if not more, goals as any of us from 30 or 40 metres –from any angle. He'd say: 'Do it this way, son', and then go BANG - goal.[35]

Trainer-cum-runner Sam Allica, who described Smith as 'a perfect kick', shook his head in amazement as he recalled a one-on-one kicking lesson with the Melbourne coach:

> We were having a kick together after training one night, and I got Norm offside at first. I said: 'Norman, when you drop-kick at goal, I think you toe it a bit.'
> He was taken aback.
> 'I've *never* toed a football in my life!'
> I showed him what I thought he was doing wrong, but he wouldn't have it.
> He said: 'I've never ever kicked a football like that.'
> Then he proceeded to show me a few things, including something I'd never seen before, and never knew was even possible. He showed me how to kick drop-kicks which bend - like players do with banana kicks these days. He could bend these drop-kicks either way simply by tilting the ball about and eighth of an inch at the bottom of the ball. As a young fella he'd experimented and worked at it and developed it to a level that made it a deadly kick. It was amazing.[36]

---

[35] Hassa Mann. Interview with the author.
[36] Sam Allica. Interview with the author.

Full-back loomed as a problem position for Norm Smith in 1955. The retirement of Lance Arnold after the 1954 Grand Final had left a gaping hole in the Demon defence. The situation worsened when Geoff McGivern – whom Smith planned to switch from centre half-forward to the key defensive post – was injured before the start of the season.

McGivern lamented: 'Norm was just about to send me in on the Thursday night before the first game when I buggered my damn leg. It was very disappointing because I'd kept "Clarkey" to one goal in the practice matches. Clarkey had said: "Jeez, you're a bit of a bastard, 'Macca'; I can't get away from you". I said: "Well, that's the idea!" So Norm had to change his plans for full-back'.[37]

Smith and his match committee came up trumps with their second option.

'We had to reorganise,' Smith said, 'and Peter Marquis, a ruckman, was chosen to fill the breach. What a wonderful job he has done!'[38]

In a game against St Kilda, Marquis carried out Smith's instructions to the letter, with devastating results. Smith armed Marquis with some important information about his opponent, St Kilda captain-coach Les Foote (the former North Melbourne champion). 'Foote,' Smith observed, 'will try to hold the ball out and bring it back in very quickly and baulk you. But he can't change the direction of his body very smartly. So the way to fix that is when he is coming towards you, don't watch the ball, just watch his body'.

Garry Pearce recalled: 'Poor old "Footey" threw the ball out on his left had and he must have thought *The Spirit of Progress* (an express train which ran between Melbourne and Sydney) had run over him, because Marquis, who was a very solidly-built citizen, just didn't take his eyes of Foote's chest and ran straight through him'.[39]

The move of Marquis to full-back – one of the Demons' most successful for the season – had a two-fold benefit, with the Demon defence being further solidified when McGivern returned. 'When I came back,' McGivern said, 'Norm told me: "Peter Marquis is doing really well at full-back, so we'll try you at centre half-back. That'll suit you even better because you know how to play at centre half-forward; you know what they're trying to do, and how to stop them from doing it'.[40] Within a few weeks, Smith was saying: 'Now McGivern is back and is settling in at centre half-back. He has improved with each game and looks like being a star in this position'.[41]

---

[37] Geoff McGivern. Interview with the author.
[38] *The Herald*, late July 1955.
[39] Garry Pearce. Interview with the author.
[40] Geoff McGivern. Interview with the author.
[41] *The Herald*, late July 1955.

Smith once said: 'I believe football is a two-part game, that defence is equally as important as attack'.[42] He also believed: 'A backman is judged on the way his opponent plays – not on his own number of marks and kicks'.[43] Logically, his broad, typically basic instruction to his backmen was: 'Don't let your man get a kick'. Ian Thorogood said: 'I reckon that before every game I played, Norm would quietly come up and say: "Thurra, I don't care if you don't get a kick, as long as your opponent doesn't either". Maybe that's why I didn't get many kicks!'[44] Fulfilment of this instruction wasn't likely, but attempting to fulfil it was paramount. On one occasion, Smith armed one of his backmen with this most basic of instructions when he assigned him the task of stopping an opposition goalsneak. The backman in question amassed numerous possessions and was widely regarded as the best player on the ground. The problem was his opponent had kicked five goals. He was dropped the next week. The player challenged Smith: 'Why the hell have I been dropped?'

'What was your job?' Smith asked.

'To mind so-and-so.'

'Well there's your answer,' Smith pointed out. 'He kicked five goals, you didn't do your job, so you're out.'

To key defenders like Marquis and McGivern, who contested many aerial duels, Smith was more specific. 'Touch the ball first,' he emphasised. 'If you do that, you can control it, get it, then clear it. And kick it as far as you bloody well can!'[45]

The 'punch from behind' command was elementary, but both Tassie Johnson and John Beckwith incurred Smith's wrath for breaching it. In a nail-biter at Hawthorn in the 1960s, Melbourne was only a few points in front with just seconds remaining when Johnson marked from behind on the last line of defence. The Demons scraped home, and Johnson felt like the hero of the day, but, Smith was far from pleased. 'When we got in the rooms,' Hassa Mann recalled, 'Norm ripped into Tassie. He said: "Don't you ever try to mark from behind again!" Win, lose or draw, it was a sin in Norm's eyes to break a team rule, no matter what the circumstances.'[46]

Beckwith told of a similar experience:

> Norm always told us: 'If you're behind, you punch'. One day at Collingwood, Peter Marquis was at full-back on Murray Weideman, and the ball was kicked in high

---

[42] *The Sun* series, 1967.
[43] Craven, John (editor), *Football The Australian Way*, Lansdowne Press, 1969.
[44] Ian Thorogood. Interview with the author.
[45] Robert 'Tassie' Johnson, in an interview with the author.
[46] Hassa Mann. Interview with the author.

about 20 to 30 metres out from goal. I could see that Weideman was going to mark it and I thought: 'I've got to do something here', so I took off with the intention of punching it away. But as I lifted, suddenly I'm about a hand-span above them, and I've grabbed it. It was one of the best marks I ever took. And it was a complete accident. It was just before half-time and when I get in the rooms Norm's waiting for me. He said: 'You didn't punch!'

I said: 'Well, I was going to, but I reckoned I could mark it'.

He said: 'But if you'd spilt it, your bloke would have been loose on the ground and he would have kicked a goal'.

I felt like saying: 'You can't have it both ways. I had to make a decision, and it came off'.

He was more interested in the fact I had disobeyed the rules.[47]

Although Smith remained adamant in his demand for accountability, Geelong's 1951-52 premiership sides, particularly their half-back line, left an indelible impression on him. He later said: 'The rebound defence – big, quick half-backs who cut off attacks and in a flash race the ball back into the forward zone by direct play – was a Reg Hickey specialty. I was a great admirer of the Geelong attacking half-back line of (Russell) Middlemiss, (John) Hyde and (Geoff) Williams in their great sides in the early '50s. I set out to get the same results at Melbourne.'[48]

In 1955, Smith finally had three players at his disposal to duplicate this most lethal of the Cats' weapons. On one half-back flank was his brutal, ever-reliable skipper, Noel McMahen, at centre half-back was the talented Geoff McGivern, and on the other flank was brilliant 19-year-old Don Williams, whom some regarded as the equal of Barassi.

McMahen said: 'We copied Geelong, who had that wonderful, attacking half-back line. They would beat their opponents for the ball and then run off them and create enormous run down the field, rather than simply minding their men. We developed that with Donny Williams, who would run at every opportunity. But if you were doing that, someone had to cover for you, so everyone moved up a line. We had to do that. You couldn't leave a half-forward all on his own while you chased kicks. By leaving your man, you've basically told your mates: 'I'm going to get this bloody ball!' And woe betide you if you didn't. If you burnt your bridges, you had to bloody well get it. Therefore, it came down to judgment: when to leave and when to stay. There was a lot more emphasis on the leaving than

---

[47] John Beckwith. Interview with the author.
[48] *The Sun* series, 1967.

the staying, because we didn't want a negative backline. But you had to use your initiative wisely'.[49]

Smith never gave McGivern many instructions – 'Perhaps he thought: "He won't take any bloody notice anyway!"' McGivern joked – but he offered some advice on the two teammates who flanked him. McGivern said: 'Norm told me: "Noel (McMahen) won't run with the ball much – he'll generally get it and kick it – but Donny (Williams) *will* run, so you'll have to move across and back him up". Sounded pretty simple, but it wasn't always so easy.'[50]

Although the half-back line was given a licence to be creative, they still needed to be predictable for their teammates further afield. McMahen said: 'If you kicked the ball short out of the backline, you'd quickly get a message: "Are you crook on your forwards?" Ivor Warne-Smith was quite influential in this. He'd say: "Run as far as you can and kick it as far as you can in the direction you're running in, then blokes at the other end will know where it will land. If you start mucking around with it, they won't know if you're going to go long or short and the whole system will be buggered up'. Ivor was a wise old man, who, like Checker, was a great influence on Smithy. He'd say: 'Football is like tennis. It's a simple game made complicated by coaches'.[51]

Smith kept it simple for his defenders. He discouraged them from running too far down the ground, so that, in the event of a turnover, the Demons would have reinforcements. However, as Geoff McGivern discovered, Smith wasn't completely inflexible on this point.

> One day at St Kilda, I came tearing through the centre, picked the ball up and let fly with a torpedo punt - not at anything in particular - and, with the aid of a gentle, following breeze, it just went and went and it sailed through for a goal. It was a freak occurrence. In a flash, the message came out: 'That was great, but don't get carried away'. I gave Norm a wave, and he waved back.[52]

Smith also made the odd exception for Tassie Johnson – who made his name at full-back in the sixties – but under a strict proviso. Johnson said:

> Sometimes I'd kick out from full-back and follow the ball right down the field. One time, I did that and missed the mark, but I picked it up, turned around and went

---

[49] Noel McMahen. Interview with the author.
[50] Geoff McGivern. Interview with the author.
[51] Noel McMahen. Interview with the author.
[52] Geoff McGivern. Interview with the author.

whack from about 50 yards out – a big drop-kick straight through the middle. Just then, the siren went for three-quarter time. As I was walking back to the huddle, Norm came straight up to me and said: 'Just as well you kicked that'. I did that five times in my career – ran down and kicked goals.

Quite often, when I could see Dicko one-on-one with his opponent, I'd kick it out to him and go for a run to help him out. Although Dicko couldn't kick right foot or handpass at all, I would pick up a few crumbs and get it down to the forward line. Norm would go crook about it sometimes because he worried about my man being on his own, but he said: 'You always seem to get back into your position to cover your man'. But the opposition never got a goal out of it, and I think Norm tolerated it because of that. I was lucky that I had good blokes around me and they covered for me.[53]

Covering for each other was one of the key features of Norm Smith's defensive blueprint. The Demons were under strict instructions to try to 'cut out the loose man at its source',[54] by running straight at the ball-carrier, even if it meant leaving their own opponent unattended, and even if they were deep in defence. All of which necessitated the other, equally important part of the plan: for Melbourne players behind the ball to immediately push up to guard the next opponent.

Smith learnt the *attack-the-ball-carrier* rule while playing under Checker Hughes, who had drilled it into his Melbourne sides in the 1930s as a method of countering Collingwood's pacy, small-man brigade. (The same tactics had initially been introduced to Melbourne in the mid-1920s by Bert Chadwick to stop Essendon's brilliant 'Mosquito Fleet'.) Hughes would tell his players: 'Don't be fooled and taken in by Collingwood's handball. Once Collingwood starts handball, meet the player with shirt-front football'.[55] When Hughes was assisting Smith, he continued to warn young players: 'If you let them, these little blokes from Collingwood will make you look silly: they'll handball over your head and run away from you'.[56]

Smith took the tactic even further by widening its application to every opponent, not just the Magpies. He commanded his players to bump the ball-carrier heavily when he was 'wide open' after handballing.[57] Beckwith said: 'Any time a player tried to pop it over your head and create the loose man, you took off at him flat-out and dipped the shoulder and went BANG! – fairly of course – and over

---

[53] Robert 'Tassie' Johnson. Interview with the author.
[54] Ian Thorogood. Interview with the author.
[55] Related by Percy Beames in *The Age*, Monday, September, 19, 1955.
[56] Related by John Beckwith in an interview with the author.
[57] Keith Carroll. Interview with the author.

they went'.[58] The idea was to apply enough pressure to 'put them off' and cause a turnover, and perhaps even 'slow them down and make them think twice about doing it again'.[59]

The results were quite stunning. Opponents became gun-shy and 'did it a bit quicker',[60] and more carelessly, in the name of self-preservation. 'We had Collingwood bluffed in those years,' Carroll said. 'Norm would say: "They're trying to get rid of the ball before they've got it because they know they're going to cop one".'[61] Beckwith explained: 'If a bloke gets the ball and suddenly he's confronted with an opponent running 100-miles-an-hour at him, a bit of panic sets in, and we made the opposition cough the ball up, and miss easy shots at goal, time and again using that method'.[62]

Although the Demons delivered legitimate bumps, the tactics were illegal. In 1945, the VFL had introduced the downfield free kick which penalised players who interfered with opponents after they had disposed of the ball. But this didn't deter Smith. 'He still wanted us to do it,' Carroll said, 'because it stopped their run-on and it had them really looking around rather than focusing on the ball.'[63]

The *cover-for-your-mate* manoeuvre – 'a kind of swivel movement'[64] – was 'ahead of its time';[65] 'a great innovation that Norm perfected'.[66] Ian Thorogood said:

> Norm made you meet the ball-carrier and not worry about where your own opponent behind you because that was the job of the next link in the chain to cover for you, and the job of the next link to cover for him, and so on. The half-back would push up to cover the wingman, the back-pocket would cover the half-forward flanker, the full-back would move across to the pocket, the other back-pocket would go to the full-forward... you might even have your wingman on the other side of the ground dropping back a line to cover the other half-forward flanker. This didn't happen one after the other; it was instantaneous. It was a machine situation. And it was pumped into us.[67]

---

[58] John Beckwith. Interview with the author.
[59] Keith Carroll. Interview with the author.
[60] John Beckwith. Interview with the author.
[61] Keith Carroll. Interview with the author.
[62] John Beckwith. Interview with the author.
[63] Keith Carroll. Interview with the author.
[64] Noel McMahen. Interview with the author.
[65] Keith Carroll. Interview with the author.
[66] John Beckwith. Interview with the author.
[67] Ian Thorogood. Interview with the author.

Smith 'brainwashed' this two-part tactic into his players at training, so that it became second-nature in a match situation. 'We practised it a lot,' Beckwith said. 'We'd have players standing in their positions and then one of us would make a break to tackle the loose man, while, as a group, we'd immediately move up and across. It became one of the ingredients for our success because it really put the squeeze on the opposition.'[68]

It also became the subject of a heat-of-the-moment argument between two Demons. A half-back flanker had become increasingly frustrated with a wingman on two counts: his eagerness to 'run down the field trying to take speccy marks and kick goals', and his infuriating reluctance to get back and guard his direct opponent when the ball rebounded out of the forward line. The half-back flanker explained:

> On so many occasions, the ball would rebound over his (the wingman's) head to his opponent, who would turn around and run towards me, and I would immediately run towards him – as it was Norm's instruction to cut off the loose play at its source as soon as it happened – and he'd put the ball over my head and my opponent would either have a shot at goal or pass the ball. It would happen so quickly that we didn't have enough time to cover for each other. As a half-back, my job was to stop my man from getting a kick, so when a teammate continues to let you down like that, you're in a hopeless, no-win situation.
>
> In the end, I told this player during a match: 'If you don't get on your man, I'll kick your frigging head over the grandstand!'
>
> It was just before half-time and what I didn't realise at the time was that Norm had seen me remonstrate with my teammate. Hughie McPherson, the runner, came out and said: 'What's wrong?'
>
> I said: 'Nothing.'
>
> As soon as we got in the rooms at half-time, Norm said: 'I want you and you in there', and he pointed to the property steward's room. He took us behind closed doors and really laid down the law. He didn't ask what I'd said, but he knew there was upheaval between the two of us, and I think he also knew the reason why – because I was being made to look somewhat of a jackass.
>
> He gave us a real hammering about teamwork and how individuality and warring with words, particularly during a match, is not the way to go. He dismissed me from his sight and then spoke to the other guy at length. I have no idea what was said, but after that the wingman always understood there would be a problem if he didn't get back on his opponent.

---

[68] John Beckwith. Interview with the author.

I should say that we became pretty good mates after that and played a lot of footy together. Although he still tried for the speccy mark and the miracle goal, he picked up his opponent extremely quickly, which helped us all.[69]

♟♟♟♟♟♟♟♟♟

The Demons' renowned stamina failed them in their top-of-the-table clash with Geelong at Kardinia Park in round 13. Although they 'probably had 70 per cent of the play for three quarters',[70] they continued their disturbing pattern of wasting opportunities – they kicked 6.16. Melbourne led at each change, and by 10 points at three-quarter-time, but was overrun and outscored in the last quarter – 5.2 to 0.3 – to go down by 19 points. It was their second loss in three games, and suddenly the Cats were level with them at 11-2, although the Demons still held a 28.4 percent advantage.

The field umpire that afternoon, Harry Beitzel, hailed the Melbourne-Geelong clash as a defining contest in the history of the game. Beitzel said:

> Although it was relatively low scoring, I believe it helped change the face of the game. I reckon it started the modern game of all this running and play-on football. What a game! Both sides ran the ball from one end of the ground to the other at lightning speed. They took it to another level. It was so fast and free-flowing that I only awarded about 15 free kicks for the whole day.
>
> After the game, both Reg Hickey and Norm Smith were together and as soon as I came into the rooms they called me over. I was still fairly young at that time, and those two gentlemen – two of the biggest name coaches of all time – gave me an enormous thrill when they said: 'You made the game'.
>
> But truth was the game was so damn fast that I ran out of puff and didn't have enough breath to blow the bloody whistle![71]

During the tense encounter, Smith became irate when he saw his normally tough-as-nails defender Keith Carroll walking off the ground. Carroll had been assigned the important role of nullifying 'The Geelong Flyer', Bob Davis. He said:

> I was going really well on Bob Davis, but then I was badly injured – I copped a knee, which burst blood vessels in my groin. I was really struggling; I couldn't run, and

---

[69] Interview with the author.
[70] *The Football Record*, July 23, 1955.
[71] Harry Beitzel. Interview with the author.

couldn't even move my leg, so I just walked off the ground. There was nothing else I could have done. The best thing for the team was to get someone else on. Norm caught me at the race and started screaming at me: 'You're beating Davis but as soon as he gets a couple of kicks you walk off the ground!'

I passed out in front of him. I regained consciousness in the dressingrooms, but I was unconscious all the way home from Geelong to Melbourne. I was in a pretty bad way and Norm rang me later on, which was unusual. I think he felt guilty over giving me a blast. That was a big thing for him to do. It was his way of saying sorry, but it wasn't an apology.[72]

'There were,' according to Tassie Johnson, 'absolutely no excuses under Smithy.'[73] And that covered excuses as varied as sheer inability through injury, to fumbling a ball while looking straight into the sun. In regard to the latter, Smith would say: 'Don't use the sun as an excuse. Keep looking where you think the ball is and even a second before it hits your nose you've got time to see it and take it'.[74] On the former, he believed: 'Most injuries are in the mind'.[75] He 'hated seeing someone rolling around in pain on the ground – he thought it was a sign of weakness'.[76] He would say: 'No matter how hard you get hit, never let anyone see that you're hurt'.[77] After all, he would say disdainfully: 'It's only pain'. This hard-line attitude made a particularly strong impression on Ian Ridley, who vividly recalled:

Norm would say: 'If you go down, get straight back up. The only time you stay down is if you're knocked out or dead'. That had a big influence on me because whenever I got knocked over, and even if I was in all sorts of agony, I'd hear Smithy's words ringing in my head: 'Get up! Get up, you weak bludger!' When I realised I wasn't knocked out or dead, I'd force myself to get up. It wasn't easy to do it at times, but it's amazing what you can do when you are forced to do something.[78]

Hard-at-it backman Ian Thorogood concurred:

Norm believed: 'Don't concede in any way.' One time at Collingwood, just before half-time, I crashed head-on into (Magpie ruckman) Ray Gabelich. I wasn't out to

---

[72] Keith Carroll. Interview with the author.
[73] Robert 'Tassie' Johnson. Interview with the author.
[74] Related by Robert 'Tassie' Johnson in an interview with the author.
[75] Related by Clyde Laidlaw in an interview with the author.
[76] Keith Carroll. Interview with the author.
[77] Related by Keith Carroll in an interview with the author.
[78] Ian Ridley. Interview with the author.

it, but I was dazed. Hughie McPherson got me off the ground and into the rooms. I was bleeding from the mouth and nose and (head trainer) Jack McLoughlin had me lying on my back. I really didn't know where I was. But I heard Norm's voice: 'What's the matter with that weak bastard!' At one stage I was never going to forgive him for that comment. But what it made me do was get up off the table in a real huff and get back out there and play the second half. That's the kind of effect he had on me throughout my career. He knew which buttons to get the desired result. And I wanted to play football the way he wanted it played.[79]

Hassa Mann endured a similar experience in the early 1960s:

I'd been playing fairly well this day and about two minutes before half-time I had to contest for the ball right in front of Norm. I was going down to get the ball and I got cleaned up – an opposition player drove his knees into my ribs. I was winded and hurt.

Norm jumped to the boundary line and screamed: 'Get up! Get up! You're not hurt! Get up!'

I couldn't breathe and I was all over the shop, but Norm proceeded to give me a roast at half-time for showing that I was hurt. I played on, and was X-rayed after the game and found out I had two cracked ribs. But that didn't matter one iota to Norm: you weren't allowed to show the opposition that you were hurt.[80]

Smith always had the final say when it came to assessing injuries. Although the club doctor, Dr Don Duffy, and McLoughlin had the medical expertise, Smith 'controlled them', 'had them bluffed', and 'reserved the right to overrule them if need be'.[81] Laidlaw said:

If you felt you weren't right to play, Norm would force you into it, and you'd get through it OK... most of the time. That's where Ron Barassi and Denis Cordner stood out – they could both play with injuries. They could have severe injuries that would have kept me, for one, off the ground for sure, but because of their toughness, and Norm's influence, they could play with great pain. Early in your career, you don't seem to be able to play with injuries, but as you gained more experience and felt more secure in the team, and with a coach like Norm standing

---

[79] Ian Thorogood. Interview with the author.
[80] Hassa Mann. Interview with the author.
[81] Clyde Laidlaw. Interview with the author.

over you and convincing you that can get through, you felt you could still contribute even though you were dragging a bit somewhere.[82]

However, there were times when the opposite was the case; when Smith refused to be fooled by players carrying injuries he felt would jeopardise the team's performance. 'Tassie' Johnson said:

If you had a corky or a bruised rib or something, you'd get treatment through the week and train on the Thursday hoping you'd be selected. A lot of times I'd train – and I knew other people were training with injuries – and Norm would walk up to you, and he knew exactly where to tap to make it hurt. If you flinched, you weren't in the side.[83]

In light of his chronic hamstring problems during his own playing career, Smith regarded himself as somewhat of an expert on what have become known as 'soft-tissue' injuries. His theory – which still stands today – was that stock-standard torn hamstring took three weeks to repair. One training night Don Duffy declared such a player fit after just two weeks. 'OK, then,' Smith told the player, 'go and warm up and then come and see me.' When the player returned, Smith immediately – without notice – hurled a ball at his feet. Just as he suspected, as the player bent down, he groaned in pain and clutched his leg. Regrettably vindicated, Smith muttered: 'Go and tell Dr Duffy that you're *not* fit'.[84]

While Smith 'could relate to players who had hamstring problems, he couldn't relate to those battling other injuries'. Barry Bourke (who joined Melbourne in the early 1960s) said: 'At one point I was struggling with a crook wrist and an ankle, and Norm was constantly into me about the whole thing being in my head. In the end they discovered I had a crack in my wrist and a crack in my ankle'.[85]

There was also the odd misunderstanding between Smith and an injured player. Keith Carroll said:

Another time when I injured my thigh, Norm approached me at the dance and said: 'Keith, I want you to train on Tuesday night but only at half-pace'.

I said: 'Oh, OK, but I have to be a bit careful because I want it to heal properly'.

---

[82] Clyde Laidlaw. Interview with the author.
[83] Robert 'Tassie' Johnson. Interview with the author.
[84] Noel Brady, South Melbourne secretary from 1968 to 1972. Interview with the author.
[85] Barry Bourke. Interview with the author.

I did as Norm said and trained at half-pace, but Norm must have forgotten what he'd told me. We trained terribly and he was in a shocking mood and getting more and more agitated with what he was seeing. He called us into the centre and said to me: 'What do you think you're doing?'

I said: 'You told me to train at half-pace'.

He said: 'Are you calling me a *liar*?! Get off the ground!'

I walked off the ground, went into the dressing room, had a shower and was getting changed. By then training had finished and Norm came in, sat down beside me and said: 'You must have misunderstood me the other night, Keith'.

I said: 'No way, I did *not* misunderstand you. I've got witnesses who heard you tell me to train at half-pace'.

He said: 'Oh, forget it,' and he got up and walked away. He was in the wrong then and he knew it, but that was as close to an apology as you'd get.

Smith was also cautious about leaking any information about injuries or the like to the media. Carroll inadvertently found this out the hard way.

I was injured and the club knew it, and at training one of the reporters from *The Sun* asked me: 'How are you going?'

I replied honestly: 'I can't play on Saturday'.

When the paper came out, the headline read: *Leave Me Out, Says Flanker*. It sounded like I just didn't want to play when I was actually physically unable because I was injured.

When Norm saw me, he said: 'What's this "leave me out" rubbish?! I'll damn well tell you when you're out!'

I tried to explain that the newspaper had created that, but I was wasting my breath.[86]

ϒϒϒϒϒϒϒϒϒ

The round 13 defeat at Geelong came at an even greater cost, with Ron Barassi struck own with a bout of chicken-pox, which he had contracted from seven-year-old Peter Smith.

Barassi said: 'Peter and I got along very well. In time, as he got older and our age difference was less pronounced, we became very close mates. But our friendship soured a bit when he gave me chicken-pox and I missed a game because of it.

---

[86] Keith Carroll. Interview with the author.

CHAMPIONS OF AUSTRALIA [1955]

I played shithouse at Geelong and, after the game, I was shivering under a hot shower. The lumps started coming out the next day. It was all quite accidental of course, and quite funny looking back on it, but I don't think Norm was too happy about it at the time!'[87]

Smith said that during the 1955 season 'it became obvious' that Barassi had emerged as 'a new star' of the VFL,[88] which led him to drive the 19-year-old even harder, to firstly ensure there could be no perception of favouritism, and secondly to squeeze every last ounce of effort from him. Barassi said: 'I was very pragmatic about it all – if that's the way it is, that's the way it is. If someone was in charge and I could see his aim was noble, I wouldn't have to be convinced of much more than that and he could do almost anything to me. Not that Norm and I didn't have arguments because we got fairly animated at times; our strong personalities would inevitably clash on the odd occasion'.[89]

Home life, though, presented no serious issues between the fiery pair. Smith had no real cause to discipline Barassi for his off-field conduct. 'I had no trouble getting him home early at night or any difficulty getting him to train,' Smith said. 'He is a clean-living type and his conduct has always been excellent. But he is exuberant and you have to clamp down on him or his exuberance will take control of him.'[90] In turn, Barassi described the at-home, away-from-football Norm Smith as 'a man of very simple interests and tastes. He wasn't into flashy things, or material things. He was a real homebody. He wasn't into travel. Outside of footy trips, he didn't leave the country. He led a very simple life. I never even remember him going out to theatre or the movies. He enjoyed a quiet home life and liked entertaining friends'.

Smith also impressed upon Barassi the importance of being able to 'roll with the punches', and adapt quickly to any circumstance that was thrown at him. A minor example of this was when Smith took Barassi for his first hit of golf at the Royal Park course. 'You couldn't hire clubs back then,' Barassi said, 'so I had to borrow Norm's clubs. The problem was I was a left-hander and Norm had right-handed clubs. But his attitude was: "What's wrong with you? So what if you're a left-hander? You can still have a hit. Play right-handed". I know that if the roles had been reversed he would have changed hands without any problems.'[91] (This quality

---

[87] Ron Barassi. Interview with the author.
[88] *Melbourne Truth* series, 1962.
[89] Collins, Ben, *The Champions: Conversations with Great Players and Coaches of Australian Football*, GSP, 2006.
[90] *Melbourne Truth* series, 1962.
[91] Ron Barassi. Interview with the author.

of adaptability on the golf course was also apparent in Len Smith, who would play with just three clubs: a short-iron, a three-iron and a putter.[92])

The Demons themselves needed to adapt and pull something out of the bag when, in round 14 against Footscray at the Western Oval, they agonisingly crashed to their third defeat in four weeks. In muddy conditions, the Demons had led by five points before 'a wonderful, long, angle shot' by Alan Trusler proved the matchwinner with just seconds remaining.[93] The Demons had lost by one point and, yet again, they could blame their wayward kicking. Their inefficiency was never more evident than at quarter-time when they had kicked 1.10 (16) to the Bulldogs' 2.3 (15). At half-time, they trailed by 21 points. Smith revealed that he 'spoke very forcibly' to his players at the half-time break and insisted that they show 'greater concentration when kicking for goal'. This sparked an improvement, with the Demons kicking 7.6 in the second half, including 4.1 in the final term. Smith added: 'I am hoping that it is a sign that we have at least mended our ways in kicking for goal'.[94] In their three losses, the Demons had kicked an atrocious total of 20.50 – comprising 5.15 (45), 6.16 (52) and 9.19 (73) – while their opponents had slotted 28.25. It was a major concern, but it wasn't crisis point – the defeats had been to fellow top-four teams on their respective home grounds, by a combined total of 23 points.

Smith often told his players: 'Don't flirt with your form'; when you are playing well, don't relax; drive it for all it's worth.[95] But in kicking poorly, perhaps they had flirted with their form, and disaster. They were now level on points with both Collingwood and Geelong, and just a game clear of a lifting Footscray. Doubts now surfaced about whether they would actually make the finals. *The Football Record* speculated: 'Are the Demons safe? Have they gone into a slump?'[96]

In an interview with John Dunn from *The Herald*, Smith agreed that his side was in a slump of sorts, but reminded readers that the Demons were yet to field a full-strength side due to injury and illness. He also offered the following explanation for his side's recent performances:

> Our bad kicking at the goalfront and its adverse effect on the team has been the reason for our three defeats... It must be remedied. In the three games we have lost, we have had more shots than our opponents. To me, that indicates that our

---

[92] Bob Henderson, who played under Len Smith at Fitzroy. Interview with the author.
[93] *The Herald*, late July 1955.
[94] *The Herald*, late July 1955.
[95] Related by John Lord in an interview with the author.
[96] *The Football Record*, July 30, 1955.

approach to goal is sound, but that there is a lack of confidence in shooting for goal. This lack of confidence is like a disease. It's infectious and it spreads from one member to another. And it spreads also to the centres, defence and others further afield. The confidence of the whole side is upset. When players battle hard to get the ball to the forward lines and then see chances frittered away and all their good work gone for nothing, it must have an adverse effect on their play and on morale in general...

I think it is all due to the kicking. I won't listen to any of the talk which is circulating and which says that we have kicked points because our forwards have been caught, or harassed or bustled.

The majority of shots we have missed have been deliberate (set) ones. I think we can overcome this... The key to it is concentration...

Coupled with this has been a slight falling off in the standard of our play. Over the past few weeks we have not been going as well as earlier in the season. You could call it a slump, I suppose, although it is probably just a slight falling-off in form. It is very difficult for a team to hold top form throughout a season. I would go so far as to say that it is almost impossible. Two years ago, Geelong, after a long string of wins, found that they could not do it. They slumped at the wrong end of the season and ended up losing the premiership...

It could be a blessing in disguise if we can come back. We'll be freshened up and back at our top for the finals. We have as good a chance as any. (But) the opposition is all hard and has to be beaten.[97]

Although the Demons would continue to kick wildly at goal, their wastefulness would not cost them. Their sheer weight of scoring opportunities would overwhelm their opposition and they were not to lose another game for the season. They won the last four minor rounds, the most impressive being their 65-point massacre of Essendon at the MCG in round 16. The Bombers, who ultimately finished fourth, went into the game having won seven of their previous eight matches, yet they were made to appear 'completely innocuous' against the 'almost faultless' Demons.[98]

The only trouble Melbourne confronted in the last month of the home-and-away season was, surprisingly, in their round 17 match against middle-of-the-road Hawthorn at Glenferrie Oval. Ironically, this was in a game where the Demons had kicked accurately in the first half. They led by 32 points at quarter-time, and 35 at half-time (with a score of 11.3), but managed just 2.10 to the Hawks' 7.9

---

[97] *The Herald*, late July 1955.
[98] *The Football Record*, August 13, 1955.

in the second half to cling to a six-point victory. The Demons had 'started like racehorses… and finished like hacks'.[99] One of the biggest problems for Smith, and new centre half-back McGivern, was the Hawks' 198-centimetre forward Clayton 'Candles' Thompson.[100] McGivern said:

> 'Candles' Thompson seemed about nine feet tall – he was marking everything. The message came out from Norm: 'Try him from the back'. So I tried that, but that didn't work. The next message was: 'Try him from the side'. So I tried that, but that didn't work either. I started playing in front of him, but he was so tall he'd just lean over the top of me and take the mark. The next message from Norm was: 'Please yourself!'[101]

It mattered little as Melbourne recorded several milestones. The Demons finished on top of the VFL ladder for the first time since 1940; their 15-3 record was their best effort since 1939; they were the heaviest scoring team in the competition for the first time since 1941; and their percentage of 150.5 was to be the highest of any team coached by Norm Smith. Since 1931, only one team had achieved a higher percentage, and that was Essendon's 1950 premiership side, which tallied 162.2 percent.

Smith reflected on his four almost completed seasons at Melbourne and came to the conclusion that: 'Better things came quicker than we had anticipated. Our rise… was fast. It is no mean feat to come from last in 1951 and second last in 1953 to play off in the Grand Final for the 1954 premiership. I think some thought that our rise was too quick to be true and regarded it as a fluke. We have very effectively given lie to that this year'. He attributed the Demons' success to youthful enthusiasm, an evenness aided by that little bit of experience, which meant they did not rely upon any one strength, and the experience of hardened campaigners like Denis Cordner and Noel McMahen. Such was the Demons' thorough, all-round ability, Smith struggled to identify his team's greatest quality. 'It is very difficult to pinpoint,' he said. 'We have pace, marking ability and are strong physically. Above all, we have the determination and will to win, which is most important.'[102]

---

[99] *The Football Record*, August 13, 1955.
[100] Bill Stephen told the author of a Victorian team meeting before a state match against a South Australian side that boasted Thompson, who had been a sensation in Adelaide. Victorian coach Checker Hughes told Richmond wild man 'Mopsy' Fraser: 'Candles Thompson – one blow and he's out'.
[101] Geoff McGivern. Interview with the author.
[102] *The Herald*, late July 1955.

CHAMPIONS OF AUSTRALIA [1955]

Norm Smith had always pushed the boundaries of the laws of the game when it came to employing an unofficial, prohibited, team runner. Likewise, Hugh McPherson, his enthusiastic although discreet runner, pushed the boundaries of his role, which required him to masquerade as a trainer to avoid detection.

But on a number of occasions, umpires refused to accept McPherson's excuses for loitering on the field, and regularly approaching players with a few words and a gentle massage to a phantom sore spot. At times, umpires would stop games to order McPherson off the field. Alf Brown wrote in *The Herald*:

> Norm did not just dislike umpires; he hated some rules they administered. For years he complained that VFL rules precluded him from using a runner... In those days, coaches were not allowed on the ground, even at quarter-time. Teams just crossed over. Smith was right, of course. 'Why should I have to wait until half-time to correct something which becomes obvious early in the first quarter?!' he used to rant.[103]

It all came to a dramatic head in the mud at Footscray in round 14, 1955 – a game the Demons lost by a point. Melbourne rookie Freddie Webster – who was playing the last of his three VFL games that afternoon – twisted an ankle and was writhing in pain on the ground. McPherson recalled what happened next:

> Freddie went down not far from where we were on the bench and I was the nearest trainer to him, so I naturally rushed over to help him. While I was with Freddie, the Footscray crowd was roaring like hell because they knew I was the illegal team runner. The umpire, (Geoff) Robinson, stopped the game and told me: 'Get off the ground!'
> I said: 'No way. I'm attending an injured player'.
> He said: 'No you're not, Hughie; you're running messages'.
> I said: 'I'm not running bloody messages! This player is injured and I'm trying to *help* him! I can't just *leave* him here like this!'
> This went on back and forth for about three minutes. In the meantime, the game had come to a complete standstill. In the end, Robinson pleaded with me quietly: 'For God's sake, Hughie, will you just go off the ground and come back on after I get the game started up again?'

---

[103] *The Herald*, May 4, 1979.

I said: 'No way. I've got a job to do here.'

He said: 'So have I'.

Finally, another trainer came along and he helped me cart Freddie off the ground.

Soon after, the VFL held a meeting and they agreed to grant each coach an official runner to deliver messages to players, and they also allowed coaches to talk to their players on the field at quarter-time and three-quarter time, which had also never happened before. So Norm was able to force some changes that were good for the game. He was proven correct – runners are a big part of the game now.

As the runner – the first official runner in the league, I might add – I was given a blue armband with white stitching saying 'VFL'. I donated it to the football club for display. We also wore white uniforms in those days, nothing like the fluorescent yellow they wear now.[104]

Smith took advantage of the rule change, using McPherson up to 40 percent more when he became a legal, official runner. While McPherson ran 30 to 40 messages a game originally, he was suddenly delivering about 50. Smith also gave McPherson a licence to act upon his own critical observations.

Norm and I formed a great combination. He would say: 'Get out there and stay out there – you know what I want'. In closer games, and especially towards the end of quarters, he'd make me go to every backman and tell them: 'Tighten up. Don't give him an inch to create the play'. After a while I did that automatically because I knew what he would have wanted me to do. He trusted me to carry out his wishes, as we'd been mates for a long time. We'd worked together, played together, socialised together. I knew him better than most people. He allowed me to sit with him at all times. He didn't keep any secrets from me where football was concerned.[105]

And, in his official capacity, McPherson no longer had to be as subtle with the players as he had previously, which caused some anguish among the players. 'It was very hard to accept initially,' Clyde Laidlaw said. 'Although Hughie had been doing it previously, he was now allowed to do it more openly, and the message was often clearer and more aggressive. You'd be struggling along and you might make a mistake, and all of a sudden Hughie's up alongside you giving you an

---

[104] Hugh McPherson. Interview with the author.
[105] Hugh McPherson. Interview with the author.

instruction, or a dressing down. More or less, you'd tell Hughie: "Get out of my way!" Although the message was coming straight from Norm, you didn't respect Hughie's position at the start because it was a new thing and you weren't entirely comfortable with it.'[106]

Smith later explained: 'I often send a runner on to the ground to remind players of their mistakes so they will not repeat them. It's surprising how even the best players let little things slip their minds.'[107] Clearly, one of his best players was Barassi, and just as clearly, Barassi was also one of his most rebellious charges when it came to accepting messages from the runner. Barassi's excuse was: 'I was so focused on what was happening and what was about to happen out on the ground that sometimes messages from the runner would go in one ear and out the other. And sometimes my responses were very frank and to the point. I was in a mental zone where I was just so focused on the game, and the last thing I wanted was someone getting in my ear and distracting me. Having said that, when I coached later on, I came to understand the importance of the runner, and that while I wanted players with great determination and drive, it was crucial that every player accept the message and do everything in his power to carry out the coach's wishes'.[108] But this belated realisation didn't help McPherson, who recounted the following colourful exchange:

> Barassi could be a real problem for a runner. He was my main trouble at times. He was the only player who ever told me to tell Norm to get effed! – the most direct expression in the English language. He was also the last one to do it.
>
> At North Melbourne one day, Norm told me: 'Go and tell Ronny that if he doesn't do his job properly and lift the bloody side, you'll cart him off'.
>
> When I went out and told him, Ron said: 'You can go back and tell him he can get __!'
>
> I said: 'Right, Ron', and I headed straight for the bench as though I was about to tell Norm.
>
> Ronny came running after me, yelling: 'Don't tell him! Don't tell him!'
>
> When I got back to the bench, Norm said: 'What's going on?!'
>
> I said: 'She's all right mate'.
>
> I would never have dobbed Ron in. I just made him think I would, and it had the desired effect because, after that, nobody ever tried me again. I continued

---

[106] Clyde Laidlaw. Interview with the author.
[107] Craven, John (editor), *Football The Australian Way*, Lansdowne Press, 1969.
[108] Ron Barassi. Interview with the author.

to deliver the messages the same way as Norm spat them out – usually with fire. If I had told Norm what Ronny had said, he would have dragged him and torn strips off him, which wouldn't have been good for anyone.[109]

At times, though, Smith could see the humour in the responses of his players. Keith Carroll said: 'Hughie might come out with a message, or tell you something you didn't want to hear, and you might say: "Tell Smithy to get stuffed". After the game Norm would say: "I know what you told Hughie", and you'd be ready for a spray, but then he'd just laugh about it, which was a relief'.[110]

Despite the closeness between Smith and McPherson, they still clashed, at times heatedly. McPherson said:

> I made a mistake early in my running career. Norm wanted me to make six positional changes, but somehow I buggered it up. I think I put Geoff McGivern to centre half-back and someone else to centre half-forward when it should have been vice-versa. After I'd made the moves, something didn't feel right. As I was on my way back to the bench, I thought to myself: 'I've stuffed this up'. When I got back, I realised what I had done and I confessed to Norm.
>
> Ivor Warne-Smith said to Norm: 'Gee, that was a lot you gave the lad to do in the one hit'.
>
> Norm wasn't pleased about it but he took it OK. He said: 'If you had've lied to me and not admitted the mistake you made, you know what would have happened, don't you?'
>
> I said: 'Yes I do – I would've been in real trouble; that's why I told you'.
>
> But because I'd been honest about it, he let me off the hook. Norm only had time for people who told the truth, and 'bugger the rest'. He believed: 'If a person can't be trusted, what good are they to anyone?'
>
> As far as I can recall, I didn't make a mistake after that. And I don't think Norm ever gave me six messages at one time again either![111]

In his coaching notes, Smith referred to the lesson that emerged from this kind of situation as follows: 'Be careful when you make your decision to alter a team placing that your runner has the message correctly and that he understands what

---

[109] Hugh McPherson. Interview with the author.
[110] Keith Carroll. Interview with the author.
[111] Hugh McPherson. Interview with the author.

you want him to pass on. We have had instances where messages were either incorrectly given or received with results that were not so good'.[112]

Another dispute between coach and runner almost became a violent confrontation in the changerooms. They argued over the fitness of a player who had under-performed. McPherson said the player was injured, but Smith had been told otherwise, and warned McPherson: 'In future, keep your nose out of medical business'.

McPherson felt affronted. He said:

> I said: 'Norm, there's one thing you've always told me which I've always abided by: never tell a lie because you'll be found out. I object to you accusing me of lying'.
>
> He carried on again and I was so mad that I said: 'Look Norm, let's settle this outside.'
>
> Fancy challenging the coach to a fight!
>
> But Norm declined. He said: 'No, no, no. We're not doing that'.
>
> That night at the club dance, I felt a hand on my shoulder, followed by the words: 'How are you, cobber?' It was Norm. He said: 'How you goin, cob?'
>
> That was as close to an apology as he could give. Norm couldn't say sorry. He just couldn't do it. He'd worked out that I was telling the truth, and that someone else wasn't. The player in question didn't play the next week, and Norm never again took anybody's word against mine.
>
> Norm had very high principles and he couldn't stand being lied to. If he found out that someone had lied to him, he would take them to task, regardless of who they were or where they stood in the hierarchy of the club.[113]

McPherson remained as the Demons' runner until 1963, after which he continued to faithfully serve the club as a trainer until 1967.

ŶŶŶŶŶŶŶŶŶ

One of the notable individuals to play under Norm Smith was champion wingman Brian Dixon.

Strong-minded, opinionated and remaining passionately faithful to his beliefs, Dixon would, during the latter part of his playing days, start a long and distinguished

---

[112] Norm Smith's notes titled: 'My Theories and Practices For Fitness For Melbourne League Team', believed to have been written in 1959.

[113] Norm Smith's notes titled: 'My Theories and Practices For Fitness For Melbourne League Team', believed to have been written in 1959.

career in Victorian Parliament, which included terms as Minister for Youth, Sport and Recreation in successive Liberal goverments.

Even as a 19-year-old in 1955, in just his second season at Melbourne, Dixon displayed his penchant for independent thought. Unfortunately for him, it was to have disastrous consequences at the end of the season and lead to the most disappointing period of his career.

Dixon's father, Norman, an invalid pensioner with a debilitating spinal disease which caused paralysis, died when his son was 14. When Dixon joined the Demons from Melbourne High School as a 17-year-old in 1954, he came to look upon Norm Smith as 'sort of a father figure', as he did with other club leaders like Jim Cardwell and Bert Chadwick.[114]

Dixon broke into the Demon line-up in round five of his debut season and played eight senior matches for the year, including the Grand Final, when he was the 20th man. He made excellent progress on the wing in 1955, and was viewed by the Demons as a 'determined and valuable player'.[115]

Dixon, in turn, valued the influence of Smith, Chadwick and Cardwell. 'I had an enormous amount of respect for those three guys,' he said. 'And I more or less took what they said to me to be gospel. And where Norm was concerned, I was always very appreciative of him and was determined to do whatever he wanted me to do. But, on the other hand, I guess I always had my own view as to what was happening and I wasn't backward in coming forward with my views.'[116]

Dixon played the first 11 games of 1955 before spraining an ankle and missing two matches. 'When I came back, I struggled a bit,' he said.

But while his form had tapered, the major bone of contention was his role as captain-coach of the commerce faculty team at Melbourne University, which played on Wednesdays. Dixon revealed:

Norm told me: 'Look, I think you need to stop your university football'. In other words: 'You will stop now'.

I thought: 'Well, that's fair enough'.

The commerce faculty side was playing in the Grand Final, and when I turned up to coach the team that afternoon, the players had heard that I wasn't going to play, and they said we'd lose if I didn't play, because the opposition side had a VFL player - it was either (Richmond ruckman) Frank Dunin with the Ag Science team

---

[114] Brian Dixon. Interview with the author.
[115] Melbourne Football Club *Annual Report*, 1955.
[116] Brian Dixon. Interview with the author.

or (North Melbourne rover) Allen Aylett with Dentistry. I thought: 'Well, it means so much to these guys, and I've been captain-coach for the whole year, and there's probably no way that Norm will know I've played, so why not'.

The next day, the Thursday, one of the newspapers had Dixon best-on-ground in the premiership.

That night at training, Norm said: 'I told you not to play'.

I said: 'That's right, you did. But I played because the blokes wanted me to play'.

He said: 'OK, well, you're out'.

I was dropped and didn't play in the '55 finals series. I was an emergency. It was pretty tough, especially sitting there watching the Grand Final, instead of playing in it.

My form at the end of the year wasn't as good as it was earlier, but I was expecting to be selected for the finals. I came about eighth in the best and fairest, so it would seem to be a bit out of the ordinary. But Geoff Case, my replacement, could argue that he was picked on his merits and that I was dropped on my merits.[117]

Case was sympathetic to Dixon's plight. 'I was favoured by a bit of good fortune,' Case said. 'Dicko committed what Norm felt was a misdemeanour and to show who was boss, Norm left him out. It just so happened that I was fortunate enough to get the gig.' Smith, who used Case as a spare-parts/utility player, was a fan of his frenzied, manic style of play, and nicknamed him 'Mad Mick'. Case explained: 'I suppose I would tear in at all costs and attempt to do things that normal people probably wouldn't!'[118]

By dropping Dixon, Smith had done something that many other coaches wouldn't have done. However, even Dixon admitted the decision had some long-term benefits.

> It was a huge, disciplinary tactic, which, in my case, certainly worked because I never wanted to cross the line again. If Norm gave me an instruction, I did my best to carry it out. It made me all the more determined to make sure I was part of any more success we might have. A premiership with the commerce faculty is obviously a bit different from a Melbourne Football Club premiership.

---

[117] Brian Dixon. Interview with the author.
[118] Geoff Case. Interview with the author.

That incident always weighed heavily in my mind. I always feared that I might be dropped the next week, which was probably good for my football because I was always thinking: 'Hell, I've got to play well today or I'll be dropped next week'. So the fear aspect of coaching has some merit. If anything, it made me more determined to succeed. In fact, I was always sort of scared that next week would be my last week. That really kept me focused on trying to play good football. From that point of view it was a plus.

The only two guys who played in the six premierships (between 1955 and 64) were Bluey (Adams) and Ron (Barassi), and I think I would've played in the six had it not been for that incident.'[119]

※※※※※※※※※※

Norm Smith was understandably wary of the threat posed by Collingwood in the 1955 second semi-final. Although the Magpies were without their inspirational 1953 premiership skipper, Lou Richards, who had retired on the eve of the finals (after a 15-year career), they had won 12 of their previous 14 matches by an average of 29 points. And, of course, they had toppled the Demons in their most recent encounter at Victoria Park in round 11. Smith was very nervous before the game.

'Matches against Collingwood are never easy,' he said later. 'We have become traditional rivals. Both sides are unyielding and the matches always develop into bone-crushing affairs. The games always feature hard bumping, rugged duels. Sometimes it is unscientific, he-man struggles, at other times the football sparkles. No matter what position we hold on the ladder, there is an unusual tenseness when we meet the Magpies. I think that is the reason both sides ...(suffer) unexpected hidings the week after one of these clashes. That 1955 semi-final was no different and added to it was the tenseness of a final.'[120]

A good omen for Melbourne was that it would be the first time the two teams had met in a final since 1948, when the Demons won the preliminary final on the way to a remarkable premiership.

On an MCG quagmire worsened by persistent rain, Melbourne and Collingwood staged 'one of the most exciting football spectacles ever witnessed under such appalling conditions'.[121] Melbourne led narrowly all day, by no more than two

---

[119] Brian Dixon. Interview with the author.
[120] *Melbourne Truth* series, 1962.
[121] *The Football Record*, September 10, 1955.

straight kicks, except for a brief period in the third term when Collingwood stole the lead. The Demons were just seven points in front at three-quarter time – thanks largely to Stuart Spencer, who, in a phenomenal best-afield performance, had kicked five of their seven goals – but faced the worrying prospect of kicking into the breeze in the final term.

An early goal to Bob Johnson put Melbourne 13 points clear and it was enough for the Demons to hold on and win 'one of the greatest tests of endurance and stamina seen on a sporting field'.[122] One player who stood tall in the final term was defender McGivern, who defied the dreadful conditions to snare several saving overhead marks. McGivern opposed Ken Smale, the Magpie's leading goalkicker in 1955 with 47 majors, and kept him goalless. He said:

> After the game, Norm came up to me and said: 'Geoffrey' – he always called me Geoffrey; everyone else called me Geoff – 'that was wonderful. You kept him out of the game and you took those marks when we needed you. That was great'.
>
> He had that beautiful glint in his eye that you knew that deep down he was so grateful that we'd made it into the Grand Final.[123]

Publicly, Smith's simple appraisal of the victory was: 'We wore Collingwood down'.[124] Magpie coach Phonse Kyne told *The Sun* that although the Pies didn't get the points he was 'convinced' they had scored 'a moral victory', explaining that they had 'strained the Demons to the limit in the mud'. However, that same mud would likely prove pivotal in the fortnight ahead, according to *The Football Record*, which astutely observed that the result 'could well have decided the premiership chances of both teams', suggesting that the heavy ground and the 'gruelling nature of play' would take an enormous toll on the Magpies, while the Demons had a week's rest to prepare for the Grand Final.[125] And so it came to be.

Collingwood defeated Geelong by 12 points in the preliminary final to earn another shot at Melbourne in the Grand Final.

Smith was confident, and said so to Percy Taylor from *The Argus*. The mind games of the modern era clearly did not apply in 1955. Smith said:

> Melbourne will win the 1955 VFL premiership with speed, height and marking advantages, according to my summing up... Another reason is that we will be entering

---

[122] *The Football Record*, September 10, 1955.
[123] Geoff McGivern. Interview with the author.
[124] *Melbourne Truth* series, 1962.
[125] *The Football Record*, September 10, 1955.

this final fresher than Collingwood, which will be playing its third successive hard game. We know that from our experience last season... I can assure you it is difficult to win after playing three tough games in three weeks. I don't rate Collingwood as easy to toss. In fact, I'm sure they will make it hard. It should develop into a great game.

Wet ground or dry, I think we can beat them, because we are a proved all-weather team, with players able to adapt themselves to any conditions...

According to my estimate, Melbourne is the faster side, with the advantage that we have a few good "cruiserweight" men who will be able to outmatch the smaller type of players in the Magpie outfit. Those cruiserweights are good, safe marks, with dash and pace, and physically strong enough to cope with anything Collingwood can produce.

Collingwood defenders are among the toughest in the League, but I think our attackers can do better than in the last match two weeks ago... (We) should have a slight edge in the air, with some of our boys brilliant in that department. Even our rovers are good marks, and so are our half-forwards. Then, as a last stab, our height should give us an advantage in the ruck duels. With this array, I think I can be pardoned for suggesting that this should be *our* year.'[126]

In private, for the ears of his players only, Smith hatched a plan to run the Magpies ragged. He later told *The Argus*: 'Believing that Collingwood would be feeling the effects of two hard games in succession, we had planned to kick the ball as far as we could, to make the opposition stretch out'.[127]

Meanwhile, Phonse Kyne was playing mind games with the Demons. 'Melbourne has had a spell of two weeks,' Kyne said, 'and there is much more spring warmth in the air now than there was 14 days ago. This change from bracing cold to sunshine and warmth often finds a team out. It could easily tell to the disadvantage of the Demons.'[128] Also pushing the Collingwood angle was Lou Richards, who said, with typical bravado: 'There are two certainties today – and one is that Collingwood will win the 1955 VFL premiership. The other one is that the sun will rise this morning'.[129] Conversely, Richards' soon-to-be sidekick Jack Dyer held the opposite view, telling readers of *The Sun* that Melbourne was 'the greatest certainty to win a Grand Final for many years'.[130] But regardless of the result, the Grand Final was expected to be 'as tough as barbed wire'.[131]

---

[126] *The Argus*, Saturday, September 17, 1955.
[127] *The Argus*, Saturday, September 17, 1955.
[128] *The Argus*, Saturday, September 17, 1955.
[129] *The Argus*, Saturday, September 17, 1955.
[130] *The Sun*, Saturday, September 17, 1955.
[131] Percy Taylor, *The Argus*, Saturday, September 17, 1955.

A crowd of 88,053 people attended the Grand Final and, as expected 'the stands were decorated with more black-and-white emblems than red-and-blue'; however, 'it was all red and blue on the fence'.[132]

Field umpire Harry Beitzel, 'a popular choice', was 'cheered all the way to the players' dressing rooms before the game.[133] Once in there, Beitzel noticed 'a certain attitude' about the Melbourne players. 'They had a lot of young blokes in their side,' Beitzel said, 'but they had a real steeliness about them. Looking back, and an umpire probably shouldn't say this, but you just knew that they were going to be very difficult to beat.'[134] Smith said later: 'Imagine the atmosphere in the dressing rooms. We knew it was going to be hard; there was little between us in that semi-final'.[135]

Despite his outward confidence, Smith had been feeling the pressure all week – even more than normal, prompting Marj Smith to reveal in an interview with a newspaper reporter: 'I just couldn't stand the strain of another week like this... it's worse than spending a few days at the dentist!'[136]

The selection meeting was also as agonising as pulling teeth. The Demons surprisingly omitted Athol Webb in favour of Noel Clarke, despite the fact Clarke had not played a senior game since being injured more than two months earlier. 'After I got full movement of my arm back, I trained like a racehorse,' Clarke said. 'I was very lucky to get a game, and "Webby" was very *un*lucky. I didn't think I'd get in, especially after being out for so long. But Smithy would always keep you back after training for a few shots at goal and this particular night I was dobbing them from 50 and 60 yards, so I think that might have helped a bit.'[137]

The MCG was 'as hard as granite' and bathed in sunlight under a clear blue sky, 'the warmth tempered by a cool breeze which favoured Collingwood in the first term'.[138] Melbourne was by far the more inexperienced side – it had 10 players no older than 21, while the Magpies had just five – but Demon skipper Noel McMahen quickly came to share his coach's optimism. He said: 'Before the first bounce, I looked around and noticed that all of the Collingwood players seemed to only come up to our shoulders. We had a striking physical advantage all over the field. As is tradition, the umpire, Harry Beitzel, asked me if I was ready. I said: "I'm ready if they are".'[139]

---

[132] *The Argus*, Monday, September 19, 1955.
[133] Percy Beames, *The Age*, Monday, September 19, 1955.
[134] Harry Beitzel. Interview with the author.
[135] *Melbourne Truth* series, 1962.
[136] Contemporary newspaper report.
[137] Noel Clarke. Interview with the author.
[138] Percy Beames, *The Age*, Monday, September 19, 1955.
[139] Noel McMahen. Interview with the author.

McMahen sparked the first sensation of the afternoon. Early in the first quarter, Collingwood, kicking to the Punt Road end with the aid of a breeze, led 1.1 (7) to 0.1 (1), after Magpie superstar Bob Rose kicked the first goal of the match following a kick-in turnover. Shortly after, Rose went for a run and, a split-second after he kicked the ball, while he was still in the air, McMahen delivered 'a fierce, bone-shaking bump on the side',[140] sending Rose into 'a perfect nose-dive from a height of five feet',[141] and inciting 'a full-throated crescendo of indignation' from the Magpie army.[142] McMahen said Rose, the best Collingwood player he saw, only had himself to blame. 'Fancy taking the risk of bouncing the ball *twice* in the first quarter of a Grand Final, especially when you're the *best player*,' McMahen said. 'I couldn't believe my luck. You were always on the lookout to crunch a champion if the opportunity presented itself. He set himself up. You just don't do that – everything's red-hot, so it's asking for trouble.'[143]

Although most unbiased observers regarded it as a fair bump, umpire Beitzel awarded a downfield free kick to Collingwood, from which Murray Weideman kicked the Magpies' second goal. McMahen was as ropeable as the Collingwood fans. 'I screamed at Beitzel: "It shouldn't have been a free kick! I didn't use my bloody elbow – I bumped him perfectly!" Beitzel said: "Look at the outer (stand). They were all on their feet – I thought they were going to climb the fence and kill me". Beitzel had – for want of a better term – soiled his pants.'[144]

Beitzel – who gave, according to Grand Final umpire of 1951 and 1952 Harvey Jamieson, 'the best exhibition of umpiring I have ever seen'[145] – had a somewhat different recollection of the incident. 'Technically, it wasn't a free kick,' he conceded, 'but it's important for an umpire to take control of the match from the outset, particularly in a Grand Final, to let them know you won't take any funny business, so I blew the whistle and awarded a free kick. "Macca" turned to me and said: "Come on, H! What was that for?!" I said: "Don't worry about it, Macca. It's just a bit too early for the perfect bump".'[146]

It was a telling blow, as Rose was reduced to mere mortal status for the remainder of the match. Incensed Collingwood players tried to retaliate, and it appeared to be working when they had the only two goals on the board after 10 minutes, but their over-physical approach only served to drain their energy from them, and the fresher

---

[140] Percy Beames, *The Age*, Monday, September 19, 1955.
[141] *The Argus*, Monday, September 19, 1955.
[142] Percy Beames, *The Age*, Monday, September 19, 1955.
[143] Noel McMahen. Interview with the author.
[144] Noel McMahen. Interview with the author.
[145] *The Argus*, Monday, September 19, 1955.
[146] Harry Beitzel. Interview with the author.

Demons absorbed their best shots, responded with a few more of their own and took control. At the 19-minute mark, after a 'torrid, fiery session of non-stop, hard-hitting football',[147] the Demons finally registered their first goal through Clarke.

Melbourne led by a point at quarter-time and completely dominated the second quarter with the breeze. But while they restricted the Magpies to just three behinds for the term, they could manage just 1.7 from 10 shots at goal – 'a pathetically weak reward' for their efforts[148] – to lead by only 11 points at half-time. *The Sun's* Kevin Hogan wrote that 'the "goalpost gremlins" that have jangled the nerves and bewitched the feet of Melbourne forwards from start to finish of the season might have cost (it) the premiership'.[149]

Demon fans groaned in unison as the behind tally mounted, and Smith, while trying to convey an air of composure, was similarly churning inside. 'I couldn't sit still,' he said, 'and being on that bench watching the boys that day was 100 minutes of agony. You feel like jumping up and taking a kick yourself.'[150]

During the half-time interval, the McMahen/Rose clash, and the resultant Collingwood goal, was still playing on Smith's mind. While Checker Hughes quietly praised McMahen for his aggression, Smith gave him a rare rebuke of sorts. McMahen said:

> Smithy came over to me in the rooms, which was unusual. He didn't say: "Well done, keep it going" or anything like that; all he said was: "Don't get caught". That's all. It was one of very few comments he made to me before or during a match. He'd usually just leave me to my own devices, which I was quite happy with. Often with coaches, if they don't say anything to you that's a good thing, because if you do something wrong you'll hear all about it, especially with Norm. Perhaps he didn't feel he had to give me much advice. Maybe that's a compliment in itself. But this was the biggest game of our lives at the time and I think he was just making sure we kept things under control.[151]

After the break, Ian Ridley kicked one of his three goals for the afternoon to give the Demons a three-goal lead, which appeared more as Collingwood's 'nebulous' attack[152] had been goalless for more than two quarters. However, consecutive

---

[147] Percy Beames, *The Age*, Monday, September 19, 1955.
[148] Percy Beames, *The Age*, Monday, September 19, 1955.
[149] *The Sun*, Monday, September 19, 1955.
[150] *Melbourne Truth* series, 1962.
[151] Noel McMahen. Interview with the author.
[152] Hugh Buggy, *The Argus*, Monday, September 19, 1955.

goals to the Magpies brought them back to within seven points – 4.13 (37) to 4.6 (30) – and lifted their spirits enormously. Denis Cordner single-handedly kept Melbourne's advantage intact by repelling three Collingwood attacks, before the siren came as a welcome relief to the Demons. All afternoon, Smith had been 'almost sick with tension' as he watched the game from the bench.[153] Now his anxiety had reached its peak. 'I had almost eaten my fingers to the elbow by three-quarter time,' he said. 'Knowing what fanatics those Magpies can be, I was worried.'[154]

The coach's concern was well-founded. The Pies kicked their third successive goal early of the final term to reduce the margin to one point. The sides were 'locked together like a couple of straining wrestlers'.[155]

But eventually the Demons broke free, as their 'waves of solid bumping'[156] and planned long-kicking game, according to Smith, 'paid dividends' and had 'Collingwood's boys... scratching for a kick'.[157] In 'a smashing recoil' that struck the Magpies 'with the force of a battering ram',[158] Melbourne kicked away with four unanswered goals in the last 13 minutes.

But the drama didn't end there. In 'an extremely hard-hitting contest',[159] the hardest, and most unfortunate, hit of the afternoon was saved for the dying stages. And it even prompted some to question Smith's role in the incident and, moreover, his integrity.

With just a few minutes remaining, and Melbourne holding onto a 13-point lead (following goals to Bob McKenzie and Big Bob Johnson), Smith decided to give his 19th man, Frank 'Bluey' Adams – a 20-year-old he affectionately referred to as "Blue Boy" – the chance to absorb some of the on-field atmosphere. Geoff Case was the player designated for a well-earned rest. As was Smith's custom, he held Adams back until Case crossed the boundary line on the other side of the ground. Adams 'crouched down on the boundary line like a sprinter ready to take off when the gun goes'.[160] Smith recalled that he 'rocketed on to the field'.[161]

---

[153] Dyer, Jack and Brian Hansen, *Jack Dyer's The Greatest: The Most Sensational Players of the Century*, Brian Hansen Nominees, 1996.
[154] *Melbourne Truth* series, 1962.
[155] Hugh Buggy, *The Argus*, Monday, September 19, 1955.
[156] Hugh Buggy, *The Argus*, Monday, September 19, 1955.
[157] *The Argus*, Monday, September 19, 1955.
[158] Hugh Buggy, *The Argus*, Monday, September 19, 1955.
[159] Percy Beames, *The Age*, Monday, September 19, 1955.
[160] Fred Goldsmith, South Melbourne full-back and the 1955 Brownlow Medallist, *The Herald*, Monday, September 19, 1955.
[161] *Melbourne Truth* series, 1962.

CHAMPIONS OF AUSTRALIA [1955]

Star Collingwood wingman Des Healey[162] had just taken possession of the ball and, seeing acres of vacant territory between him and the forward pocket, he put his head down and took off, bouncing the ball as he went. But, said Beitzel – who was within metres of the Magpie – 'out of the blue came Bluey, like a bullet out of a gun, straight at him'.[163] The crowd 'waited for the elusive Healey's famous side-step',[164] but, Beitzel lamented, 'poor Dessy didn't even see him coming'.[165] Adams added ominously:

> When I rushed at Healey, I remembered that coach Norm Smith told us to always go straight at Collingwood players. Smith said it was useless to pull up two yards from them as they were so clever they would baulk and dodge around you.[166]

Adams intended to hit Healey hard, but legally, shoulder to shoulder. In the six seconds he had been on the ground, Adams had covered about 50 metres and said he was 'absolutely flat out' when he reached Healey.[167] 'Flat out' in Adams-speak was terrifyingly fast. He was running professionally, and well inside even time – he had a 9.3-second 100-yard dash to his credit – and was a finalist in both the Stawell Gift and the Bendigo 1000.

Smith had often told his players that when they ran at an opponent: 'Watch his eyes, not his feet. His eyes will tell you which way he'll swerve'. As Adams approached Healey, he watched the Magpie's eyes for a tell-tale sign. Healey didn't swerve. Adams recalled, with a shudder: 'We cannoned into each other – BANG! – and our heads clashed'.[168] Percy Beames wrote that 'it seemed an unnecessary act of vigor and/or courage by... Adams'.[169]

The crowd gasped – 'a tremendous but strangely hushed 'Oh'[170] – as Healey and Adams had 'the crash to end all crashes'.[171] The sickening THWACK! of the collision was heard by spectators in many parts of the stadium. Witnesses had never seen two players clash so heavily. Healey later said: 'It was like hitting a brick

---

[162] Healey, then 28, was in his eighth season at Collingwood and had been an All-Australian and premiership star in 1953, won Collingwood's best and fairest in 1955 and had been in the top three in the club award in four of the previous five seasons. He was rated by both Lou Richards and Phonse Kyne as Collingwood's greatest wingman.
[163] Harry Beitzel. Interview with the author.
[164] *The Argus*, Monday, September 19, 1955.
[165] Harry Beitzel. Interview with the author.
[166] Frank 'Bluey' Adams, *The Herald*, Tuesday September 20, 1955.
[167] Frank 'Bluey' Adams. Interview with the author.
[168] Frank 'Bluey' Adams. Interview with the author.
[169] Percy Beames, *The Age*, Monday, September 19, 1955.
[170] Kevin Hogan, *The Sun*, Monday, September 19, 1955.
[171] Ian Ridley, *Football Life* magazine, September 1973.

wall'.[172] The 'terrific impact' lifted both players into the air and 'they fell yards apart, unconscious'.[173] Healey was hospitalised after suffering a fractured skull, three breaks to his nose, bruising around the eyes, severe shock and concussion. He never played in the VFL again (after 143 games), explaining: 'I couldn't stand another blow like that one'. Adams was unmarked but concussed – in fact, he was unconscious for 45 minutes. On regaining consciousness, Adams had no idea where he was, saying: 'Don't take me off, Norm, my leg's all right!' It had been a serious accident, Adams said, 'but it could have been a lot worse.'[174] Smith observed that Adams had 'had the shortest Grand Final game ever'.[175]

No free kick was awarded and play continued unabated. Ian Ridley said: 'The ball spilled out and someone kicked it and I marked it and kicked the goal to seal the bloody premiership, but I don't think anybody realised it. No bastard cheered for my goal because all eyes were on Bluey and Healey sprawled out on the deck on the wing'.[176]

The collision sparked a dust-up in the middle of the ground and 'nearly started a conflagration'.[177] Collingwood supporters booed and heckled wildly. Those in the vicinity of the Melbourne bench abused Smith, while others hurled projectiles – bottles, fruit, etc. – towards the out-cold Adams as he was carried by four trainers to the dressingroom. Smith described the pandemonium:

> And didn't that Collingwood crowd howl. It was natural though - they had to have an outlet for that tension and disappointment which had built up during the game.
>
> If Bluey had not been unconscious, anything could have happened. I doubt if there has ever been an uglier crowd. Hundreds decided 'Bluey' had deliberately charged Des Healey to put him out of the game. The controversy raged for weeks. How ridiculous.
>
> Would a man race at another head-on, knock himself out, to put a man out of a game already won?... Bluey is not that sort of footballer.[178]

Some bitter Magpie fans even accused Smith of sending Adams onto the ground with instructions to flatten Healey. Beitzel was bewildered by this insinuation.

---

[172] Des Healey, *The Argus*, Monday, September 19, 1955.
[173] Kevin Hogan, *The Sun*, Monday, September 19, 1955.
[174] Frank 'Bluey' Adams. Interview with the author.
[175] *Melbourne Truth* series, 1962.
[176] Ian Ridley. Interview with the author.
[177] Percy Beames, *The Age*, Monday, September 19, 1955.
[178] *Melbourne Truth* series, 1962.

'What a sick joke that was,' he said. 'There's no way in the world Norm Smith would do such a thing. His standards of sportsmanship were too high – higher than the vast majority of people – for him to lower himself like that.'[179] Demon runner Hugh McPherson agreed:

> In all the speeches I heard Norm make, and I heard them all in the time I was at Melbourne, I never heard him ask a player to harm an opponent. He was different from Checker in that he didn't want them to purposely go out there to hurt players, but if it happened fairly and in a manner that didn't cost the team, he took no notice of it.[180]

The Healey injury left Collingwood one short for the last few minutes of the match, when Noel Clarke kicked his third goal to extend the Demons' lead to 28 points – 8.16 (64) to 5.6 (36).[181] 'When the siren blared,' Smith said, 'I felt like jumping for joy, for the boys' sake as well as my own... Some of the slaps on the back would have knocked a normal man over, but I felt (like) a giant that day.'[182] Indeed, although Lou Richards described the match as 'the worst (spectacle) of the final series', and Dick Reynolds added that it was 'not at all an attractive exhibition of our code', Smith could not have cared less. At the age of 39, he had achieved one of his greatest football ambitions: coaching his beloved Demons to a premiership. 'We took the flag... perhaps a little earlier than I had anticipated,' he said.[183] He was enormously proud of his players. 'The boys were magnificent,' he said. 'They never let up an inch.'[184] He reflected:

> As we were second last year, perhaps it is fitting that we should go one higher this year... The boys... showed tons of team spirit and lots of dash and pace. They finished on well, and, I think, most onlookers will say that we were the better team. But there's no doubt about this Collingwood side. It never gives up, and we had to fight all the way.[185]

---

[179] Harry Beitzel. Interview with the author.
[180] Hugh McPherson. Interview with the author.
[181] In 1955, Melbourne conceded a total of just 153 goals, at a remarkably miserly average of just 7.5 a game, while kicking 230 goals themselves at an average of 11.5 a game.
[182] *Melbourne Truth* series, 1962.
[183] *The Sun* series, 1967.
[184] *Melbourne Truth* series, 1962.
[185] *The Argus*, Monday, September 19, 1955.

Phonse Kyne congratulated the Demons, saying: 'Melbourne's physical strength was greater than ours, and that made the real difference between the two teams at the finish... Melbourne deserved to win'.[186] Dick Reynolds went further in his column in *The Argus*, declaring: 'With 17 wins in 20 matches, this Melbourne combination must take its place among the great premiership teams of the past... The Demons can confidently look forward to being a football power for several years'.[187] The victory certainly vindicated Smith's faith in youth. He said: 'We were ridiculed when we brought youngsters Barassi, Case, Adams and Williams into the team at 17 in 1953, and Dixon at 17 and Bob Johnson at 18 in 1954, but our youth policy paid off handsomely when they developed'.[188] On this point, Lou Richards later wrote: 'What (Smith) did now ranks as one of football's greatest achievements. They livened up their recruiting methods and... signed youngsters for the thirds who were to become famous in every football household'.[189]

The celebrations for Melbourne's first premiership in seven years – there were only three survivors from the 1948 premiership side (Noel McMahen, Denis Cordner and Bob McKenzie) – were understandably something to behold. Smith, who received a £75 ($150)[190] bonus from the club after the triumph, revealed: 'We were all like schoolboys that night'.[191] A 'hilarious' dinner was held in the Melbourne Cricket Club pavilion overlooking the MCG. Dessert was red and blue ice cream, which, 'strangely... tasted all right'.[192]

In his address to the gathering, Smith paid particular tribute to the efforts of his two veterans. He declared that his skipper, Noel McMahen, 'must go down as one of the greatest fighting captains ever to lead Melbourne', adding that McMahen had given him 'the most wonderful support any coach could expect from a captain'. To Denis Cordner, Smith said: 'I have always thought you one of the greatest players Melbourne has ever had. Tonight, I feel you are *the* greatest'.

He finished his speech with some prophetic words: 'It will get easier next year'. Ralph Lane took it to mean: 'We've broken through and done it once, and now we know we can do it, so let's capitalise on this successful period and win more premierships'.[193]

The Demons 'made history by taking the sacred cricket club bar by storm and conducted singing from the top of the bar counter. Captain Noel McMahen was the

---

[186] Phonse Kyne, *The Argus*, Monday, September 19, 1955.
[187] Dick Reynolds, *The Argus*, Monday, September 19, 1955.
[188] Craven, John (editor), *Football The Australian Way*, Lansdowne Press, 1969.
[189] Richards, Lou as told to Ian McDonald, *Boots And All*, Stanley Paul, 1963.
[190] In 1955, the average wage in Australia was about £11-a-week.
[191] *Melbourne Truth* series, 1962.
[192] Alf Brown, *The Herald*, Monday, September 19, 1955.
[193] Ralph Lane. Interview with the author.

first to jump up. Then followed coach Norm Smith, Ken Melville, Denis Cordner, and others'.[194]

Hugh McPherson also changed the lyrics of Collingwood's theme song, *Good Old Collingwood Forever*. 'When I sang this to Noel McMahen,' McPherson recalled, 'he loved it and soon had every Demon singing it.'[195] The altered lyrics were:

> Good Old Collingwood Forever
> They knew how to play the game
> Side by side they fell together
> To the might of the Demons' fame
>
> Hear the barrackers a' squealing
> Like their barrackers do
> For the premiership's a cakewalk
> For the good old Red and Blue

A fortnight later, in the battle for the unofficial title of the 'Champions of Australia', the Demons travelled to Adelaide to take on South Australian Football League premier Port Adelaide under sub-standard lights at Norwood Oval. The crowd capacity was about 18,500 people, but an estimated 23,000 crammed into the ground and the gates had to be closed well before the teams took the field. It was 'a thrilling and spectacular game'.[196] With a minute left, the scores were level and the ball was deep in Port Adelaide's forward line. John Beckwith recalled the frantic dying moments:

> I picked up the ball and looked up, thinking: 'What am I going to do?' The team rule was that we had to kick wide in the backline, and we did that religiously. But the game was tied and I saw a lone Melbourne player - 'Bluey' Adams - in the middle of the ground, so, instinctively, using some initiative, I kicked it in his direction. 'Bluey' ran on to it, had a couple of bounces and kicked a point (he kicked 0.4 for the night) and the bell rang, and we won by a point. We were premiers of Australia. I was thinking: 'God, I've broken the team rules'. But Norm never said a word. He certainly didn't even say good kick or anything like that.[197]

---

[194] Peter Banfield, *The Argus*, Monday, September 19, 1955.
[195] Hugh McPherson. Interview with the author.
[196] Melbourne Football Club *Annual Report*, 1955.
[197] John Beckwith. Interview with the author.

The conduct of the Melbourne players on the Adelaide trip was exemplary, prompting SAFL secretary Tom Hill to write, in a letter to the Melbourne Cricket Club: 'I would like to congratulate the Melbourne Football Club on the behaviour of its players, which, in my considerable experience of over 30 years of football in South Australia, has had no equal'.

Melbourne reinforced its great depth at all levels of competition by winning the McClelland Trophy for the first time (it was only the fifth year of its existence), and again the Demons pipped Collingwood, by 10 premiership points. As expected, Smith received the following glowing praise in Melbourne's annual report to members:

> When in 1952... your committee decided to seek the services of Norman Smith as coach, yet another step towards the premiership of 1955 was taken. In Norman, we obtained a coach of very considerable worth, his football background being outstanding... No better team player has ever worn his club's colours. All that remained to be proven was whether Norman Smith could impart the great football knowledge he possessed. In the four years that Norman has been coach, he has achieved the distinction of having his side play in two successive Grand Finals, and the greater joy of coaching a premiership in 1955...
>
> It is a tribute to him that the younger players absorb that club spirit and play with a determination for victory that brooks no opposition. The spirit that now rules at Melbourne is unsurpassed anywhere in the League, and the inspired coaching of Norman Smith has contributed greatly to achieve this end.

The Demons were in a position of strength, but club leaders refused to be satisfied. The annual report added: 'Despite our success this season and the youthfulness of nearly all members of the team, it certainly is not the intention of your club to rest on its laurels for next season. Recruiting has been going on from the very week following the... Grand Final, and there are many young players of outstanding promise to fully test our older players in the practice matches of 1956. We are determined that the club will not lose its high position in the leading four, and will be hoping that your team might emulate the performances of the 39-40 and 41 teams'.[198]

---

[198] Melbourne Football Club *Annual Report*, 1955.

In 1955, both Norm and Len Smith coached their first premiership teams, and in the process became the first brothers to lead VFL teams to flags in the same season.

In the under-19s Grand Final, Len guided Fitzroy to a 10-point victory over South Melbourne – 7.14 (56) to 7.4 (46). It was Fitzroy's first Grand Final appearance at any level since the club's seconds side finished runner-up in 1946. Although the competition operated for another 36 years, the Lions would win just one more premiership, in 1982. However, they would finish runner-up five times.

Len Smith's success was hard-earned. His side did not secure a spot in the final four until the final home-and-away round. But although it was the Lions' first-ever finals campaign in the thirds competition, and they faced the difficulty of coming from fourth, they went through the series undefeated.

The Fitzroy committee extended 'very hearty congratulations' to Len Smith and his team: 'This success is a belated reward to Len for the great work he has performed, and compensates for the narrow misses of the past few seasons... The manner in which the boys fought their way through to the Grand Final and their meritorious victory... did credit not only to each and every player but also to the Coach who brought them to such fine physical condition at the right end of the season. That the boys carried out the instructions received was also a tribute to the excellent discipline exercised by Len and his (team) manager, Arthur Ireland'.[199]

Frank Walsh from *The Sporting Globe* raved about Len Smith's oratory, which differed markedly in style from his brother's: 'To hear Len Smith address his team is a revelation. His talk is full of football knowledge, and his fatherly interest in the boys is very apparent. He always stresses that the lads play the game as it should be played without resorting to negative or unfair tactics. He is not the dynamic speaker that Norm is, but he gets there just the same by milder methods'.[200]

The Lions were excited by the prospect of what the coming seasons might bring. The annual report enthused: 'The great success achieved by our Third Eighteen is further proof that the fortunes of the Fitzroy Football Club are in the ascendancy and the future can now be viewed with optimism'.[201]

Len Smith almost achieved a rare coaching double that season – the other team under his guidance, Brunswick, was runner-up in the Sunday league.

---

[199] Fitzroy Football Club *Annual Report*, 1955.
[200] Frank Walsh, *The Sporting Globe*, late September, 1955.
[201] Fitzroy Football Club *Annual Report*, 1955.

14

THE FINEST MELBOURNE SIDE OF ALL

[1956]

Experts are unanimous that the best side in the Demons' era of domination was their 1956 combination. In that glory-drenched season, the Demons achieved what remains their greatest win-loss record in a premiership season – 18-2 – and cruised to back-to-back premierships.

Nothing could slow the Demon juggernaut – even the loss of their two most prolific forwards since Jack Mueller and Norm Smith. The pair in question was Bob McKenzie and Noel Clarke. Since McKenzie's debut in 1948, he had played 125 games and kicked 254 goals. Clarke was the next best contributor in this time, slotting 155 goals in 77 games. Although they played in the 1955 premiership side and would be missed, both had spent extended periods on the sidelines due to injury and the Demons had coped well in their absences. (In 1955, Clarke managed 24 goals in 10 games, while McKenzie played seven matches, including the last six, and kicked nine majors.)

Clarke – who kicked 3.3 in the Grand Final but felt he should have kicked more goals on Collingwood's best-afield full-back Jack Hamilton – spoke openly about his reasons for returning to Tasmania at the age of 25.

> The decoy full-forward thing was one of the reasons I left Melbourne. When I accepted a very good offer to come back to Tassie, I was recognised as a full-forward and everyone respected the fact that I could kick goals. The standard of football in Tassie obviously wasn't as high as the VFL, but at least I could play like I felt a full-forward should be allowed to play.

THE FINEST MELBOURNE SIDE OF ALL [1956]

I'd also been moved around the ground so much, gap-filling, and I was never allowed to consolidate in one position. I was very unsettled. I would have been quite happy just playing on a half-forward flank, but I played all over the place: in the centre, ruck-rover to Denis Cordner, on the wing, in forward line. I'd be looking at the paper each week just to see which position I'd play next.

But Norm often said: 'The club is bigger than the individual'. And it is. There are lows and highs in football and you've just got to accept them as part of the game, and think yourself lucky that you got a game.[1]

Clarke was adamant his differences with Smith did not extend beyond football. In fact, he regarded his coach 'a great bloke; a top man', and insisted they had been on very friendly terms off the field. Clarke said their mateship was cemented in 1954, when Smith approached him with an idea about an off-field venture.

I was a builder by trade and Smithy said to me: 'I'm going to build a holiday shack at Rosebud. How would you like to build it for me?' I jumped at the idea. I stayed down at Rosebud and built it for him. I'd drive to Melbourne for training twice a week. Norm was very conscious of not being seen to favour a player because they were doing something for him off the field. Training was part of the routine that we couldn't brush aside simply because I was building the coach's shack. I had to conform with all the rules to do with training, just like every other player. I understood that. The travel didn't worry me too much anyway because there wasn't the traffic they get today.

It was good to get to know each other outside of football, which not a lot of players and coaches do. We developed a very good relationship out of that. We were good mates. We got on well. He was happy enough with my workmanship. He wasn't real fastidious until it came to football. You could make mistakes elsewhere, but not on the football field![2]

Clarke ultimately regretted his decision to leave Melbourne. 'It was quite a mistake, really,' he said. 'At the age of only 25, you're just out of your nappies, aren't you? I should never have left. I could have played another three or four years at Melbourne.' He added that Smith would look him up whenever he had cause to

---

[1] Noel Clarke. Interview with the author.
[2] Noel Clarke. Interview with the author.

travel to Tasmania. 'You had to go out with him and bring your wife,' Clarke said. 'Norm was very, very soft-hearted in lots of ways.'[3]

Peter Smith explained:

> Dad always referred to his players as 'my boys'. That was a respectful thing to them; that they were like his boys. He admired them for their courage and determination and the type of people they were. It was never just about football, even though that's what had brought them all together. His attitude was: 'While you're here, you're my surrogate son and I'll treat you as such. I'll be hard on you – *extra* hard even – but I'll be fair with you'. He wasn't just interested in their football careers, but also their lives, their jobs, their families, and them being good people.[4]

In describing his affection for his players, Norm Smith said: 'I like to look upon them as my boys, and I hope that they look upon me more in a fatherly way and also as a mate'.[5] His attitude left a lasting impression on 19-year-old recruit John Lord. The teenager, who would in time become a regular senior player, vividly recalled the Demons' 1956 season launch – a black-tie affair held in the Long Room at the MCG.

> Speeches were the main fare of the evening. Mr Chadwick held your attention and respect, but the attendees were hanging out for Norm Smith's address. At this time I'd had little, if any, personal contact with Norm. As the room hushed for his address, I was totally stunned by his unexpected opening words. He basically said: 'Look at them' – indicating us players – 'I love them'. Those final three words were to stay with me forever, especially in our relationship as coach to player, and person to person. And the way he said it, those words were dripping with passion. He loved us, and in moments when he would berate you for a perceived failure or non-delivery, you knew he loved you, for in so many other ways he continued to demonstrate that to us all. He would passionately hug you after matches, win, lose or draw, and suffer with you, but he never took his mind off what was best for Melbourne.
>
> Norm had more of a love of success than a hate of losing. Love is positive; hate is negative. Love to do things; don't hate having to do something. I sometimes jokingly describe myself as 'the world's greatest lover'. That came back to the first speech I heard from the great Norm Smith.[6]

---

[3] Noel Clarke. Interview with the author.
[4] Peter Smith. Interview with the author.
[5] *Midweek Magazine*, August 1964
[6] John Lord. Interview with the author.

However, Smith's brand of affection could certainly be termed 'tough love'. Keith Carroll said: 'Norm would say he loved us but you had to wonder sometimes with the way he got stuck into us'.[7]

And he didn't 'love' every player.

During the pre-season of 1956, several players were shocked by the manner in which Smith sacked a particular young player. The player in question – who didn't want to be identified – was in his early twenties and yet to play a senior match for the Demons. During a training drill at the Old Scotch ground near the MCG, he delivered a superb stab-pass to a teammate who responded appreciatively: 'Beautiful!'

Smith was apparently the only person present who wasn't impressed. 'Too bloody slow!' he roared.

On hearing this criticism, the player cursed himself, but Smith thought it was directed at him.

'Did you swear at me?!' Smith demanded.

'No,' insisted the player. 'I swore at myself.'

A teammate tried to intervene, but Smith would have none of it. He pointed a rigid finger at the subject of his anger and said: 'Get off the ground. Get back to the rooms'.

Like most others present, the player knew it was pointless arguing with the coach because he simply couldn't win. He trudged back to the MCG dressing rooms and was subsequently cut from the Demons' list.

Sometime later, Ian Ridley asked Smith: 'Why did you sack him like that?'

'Well,' Smith explained, 'I wanted to make an example of him, just to let every player know what can happen to them if they don't do it my way. But always remember this: only sack those who aren't good enough. Never sack a player who can really play the bloody game.'[8]

The discarded player joined another VFL club and, later that season, kicked three goals in a match against Melbourne, before disappearing from the VFL scene. He recalled:

> They dropped me off the list and while it wasn't very pleasant, it was probably fair enough because, according to the club, I wasn't good enough. But it was a decision made by the selection committee, not just one man.
>
> But I had the greatest respect for Norm, both as a man and as a coach. While I might have been disappointed, and maybe a bit bitter because I'd gotten to know

---

[7] Keith Carroll. Interview with the author.
[8] Related by Ian Ridley in an interview with the author.

all the blokes at Melbourne, the bitterness didn't last long. In fact, Norm continued to be a mentor to me, even when I played on at another VFL club. On two or three occasions, I drove all the way to Norm's house on the other side of the city and sat down with him and drank coffee and listened to him talk. I learnt a lot from him.

One little thing I remember him saying was: 'Don't run after every ball like a fox-terrier dog'. And he used the example that if you're in a pack of players in the centre and the opposition full-back kicks out to one side, instead of running over there and clogging it up and being just another number in a pack, you might run to that wing because that's where the opposition will kick the ball if they win it at half-back'. Very logical but very smart.

Seventeen years later, I went to Norm's funeral. They're not the actions of a bitter man, are they? You don't do those things for someone you don't like. I really admired him.[9]

Over the years, there were other instances of Smith axing players during the pre-season. A country recruit got on the wrong side of the coach a few times in quick succession and was told: 'See the race over there? Well, you run right through it, and keep running, and don't bloody well come back!'[10]

Another time he understandably took a hard line with a gifted youngster. Sam Allica (who became Smith's runner in the early 1960s) recounted: 'This young fella had all the hallmarks of being anything: he was quick, a strong mark, a beautiful kick. He played in a practice match on the Saturday and the following Tuesday he didn't turn up to training on time. Someone said he was up in the bar. When he turned up on the Thursday, Norm read him the riot act. He gave him an ultimatum: "Either you train with us or you can pack your bags and don't come back because you'll be wasting our time!" He quit. A little later on we heard that he played for one of the university teams and he arrived for one of their finals in a terrible state, but he was best-on-ground that day. Norm would never have tolerated that, no matter how well he played'.[11]

▼▼▼▼▼▼▼▼▼

The Demons also lost some of their soul in terms of their training arrangements, which were haphazard at best in 1956. In this regard, it was 'a year of very

---

[9] Interview with the author. During the discussion, the player was adamant he did not want to be named in this book.
[10] Bill Stephen. Interview with the author.
[11] Sam Allica. Interview with the author.

THE FINEST MELBOURNE SIDE OF ALL [1956]

difficult conditions'.[12] With the MCG to be the centrepiece of the Melbourne Olympic Games, to commence in November, construction of the stadium had forced the Demons off their home ground. They changed into their training gear at the MCG, and would then walk through Yarra Park, and 'dodge through the traffic' on Batman Avenue, on their way to training at Olympic Park, which they would share with athletes priming themselves for the Olympics. The practice matches were played at both Olympic Park and the main oval at Xavier College. When the season started, training was held at the Albert Ground, where Smith and his teammates had been forced to go through their paces during World War II. As was the case back then, accommodation was poor, 'players were forced to change in separate rooms, and medical treatment of players suffered because of (a) lack of amenities'.[13] To compound matters, the lighting in the change rooms failed on their first night. But while these obstacles could have derailed a less committed playing group, these were merely minor inconveniences for the Demons in their journey to superstardom.

Although Smith feared that his largely young side would grow complacent, he needn't have worried. His Demons were hungry for more success. Geoff McGivern said: 'Everyone thought: "Well, we've won one flag; let's do it again and really capitalise on this". The young players had another season under their belts and they were growing in stature every week. If we'd lost the first few games, people would have thought: "Last year was just a flash in the pan". But that didn't happen, and we not only kept our form up, but we kept improving'.[14]

Even Smith admitted: 'We were in even better form in 1956'.[15] It was hard to argue. Although the Demons were now the target of any side looking for credibility (as Smith said, 'even when we met the lowly sides, to them it was a Grand Final'[16]), they won the first 13 games of 1955 to stretch their winning streak to a club record of 19 (since round 14 the previous year). They were third on the all-time list, and within striking distance of the 23 consecutive victories achieved by Geelong in 1952-53, and Collingwood's 20 wins in a row in 1928-29.[17]

The Demons had won their matches by an average of 29 points, and restricted the opposition to an average score of just 51. Twice against good opposition they had sewn up games by three-quarter time with remarkable scorelines: 10.15 (75)

---

[12] Melbourne Football Club annual report, 1956.
[13] Melbourne Football Club annual report, 1956.
[14] Geoff McGivern. Interview with the author.
[15] *Melbourne Truth* series, 1962.
[16] *Midweek Magazine*, August 1964.
[17] Melbourne's 19 straight wins is the fifth longest winning run in AFL history. Equal second with Collingwood are Essendon's 2000 side and the Brisbane Lions' 2001-02 combination.

to Carlton's 1.7 (13) at Princes Park in round two; and 13.14 (92) to Essendon's 1.11 (17) at the MCG in round nine.

The Demons' 13-0 start was made even more meritorious by the fact they had been forced to play each of the first four rounds away from home. The Demons finally returned to the MCG to unfurl their 1955 premiership flag in round five, when they hosted 1955 preliminary finalist Geelong in a top-of-the-table encounter. Terrible conditions – worsened by recent regrading of the MCG playing surface – contributed to a meagre, wayward scoreline: Melbourne 6.20 (56) to the Cats' 6.12 (48). Surprisingly, the Demons' major culprit was Stuart Spencer, who recorded what remains the equal worst scoring analysis in AFL history. Spencer kicked 0.11.[18] In total, he kicked 18 straight behinds over three matches! As Spencer explained:

> 'They had allowed the grass to grow to quite a long length to consolidate a good, lush finish for the Olympics. And, of course, it absolutely poured rain on the Friday night and Saturday. The ground was like a lake, and the ball was like a slippery eel. A lot of the behinds I kicked would have been soccered off the ground because extraordinary circumstances weather-wise made it impractical on many occasions to pick the ball up and do anything with any level of accuracy. Because of that, there weren't any major recriminations from Norm. But while he was telling me I'd wasted all these opportunities my teammates had set up for me, I reminded him that I'd kicked a winning score, because we'd won by eight points! As Norm used to say: "A win is a win is a win".'[19]

That night, Hugh McPherson tried to lift Spencer's spirits, informing him about a day when even Norm Smith, the great full-forward, had been similarly inaccurate. McPherson said: 'At the after-match dinner, Norm had another go at Stuey, but Stuey replied: "Is it true, Norm, that you once kicked 11 points in a match?" Norm looked straight at me and said: "Oh, you bugger. You told him, didn't you?"'[20]

A fortnight later, in the Grand Final rematch with Collingwood at the MCG, the Demons finally arrested, to a large extent, their problems with inaccuracy. At three-quarter time, the Demons trailed by eight points. To that point – six and three-quarter games into the season – Melbourne had tallied an appallingly

---

[18] Spencer shares this unflattering distinction with Richmond's Tom Allen, who, in his debut season as a 19-year-old, kicked 0.11 against North Melbourne at Punt Road in round 14, 1949.
[19] Stuart Spencer. Interview with the author.
[20] Hugh McPherson. Interview with the author. Norm Smith kicked 4.11 against North Melbourne at Arden Street in round seven, 1940.

wasteful 67.114 (516) – at just 37 percent accuracy. (Incidentally, their opposition had posted a combined 49.59 (353).) But their potent last quarter effort of 4.3 to 0.1 against the Magpies sparked both an 18-point win and a turning point in their conversion rate. For the remainder of the season, including this pivotal final term, the Demons kicked a far more respectable 156.178 (1126) – at 46.7 percent accuracy – to their opponents' 101.132 (738).

During the Demons' 13th successive win of the season – a 15-point victory over Carlton – Smith squeezed an extra few percent out of rover/goalsneak Ian Ridley. Ridley said:

> I copped a badly corked thigh in the second quarter and I could hardly walk. At half-time, Smithy said: 'We've got to work on you; you've got to get back on the field.'
> I said: 'Forget it, I can't walk'.
> They worked on me throughout the half-time break but in the end I told Smithy: 'I can't go'.
> He said: 'You're going back on, and that's all there is to it'.
> I repeated: 'I can't bloody walk'.
> He repeated: 'You're going back on!'
> He wasn't taking no for an answer, so I had no choice. I was very proppy but in the first couple of minutes of the third quarter I kicked the longest goal of my career! I ended up staying on for the rest of the game.[21]

Despite feeling sore, Ridley, like many of his teammates, felt increasingly confident. 'Whenever we ran out on to the ground in that era,' he said, 'we were so full of self-belief that it was never a case of: "Will we win?" It was a case of: "We'll win, all right, but how much will we win by?" If you could bottle that feeling, that belief, you'd never stop winning premierships. That was part of the reason we were so tough to beat. It was like we were riding this huge wave and crushing everything in our wake.'[22]

But not everything was as harmonious as the Demons would have liked. Midway through the 1956 season – no-one seemed to recall the exact match – Norm Smith had a very public fallout with his greatest mentor, 'Checker' Hughes. As Hughes usually did, he took a seat beside Smith on the bench, between the fence and the boundary line. At one point, Smith instructed runner Hugh McPherson to make

---

[21] Ian Ridley. Interview with the author.
[22] Ian Ridley. Interview with the author.

a particular move. But before McPherson took the field, Hughes 'put his nose in and added his two-bob's worth'.[23] Hughes said: 'If I were you, Norm, I wouldn't do that'. He had 'pressed... (his) opinion too hard',[24] but really it wouldn't have mattered how diplomatic he had been. He had challenged a decision Smith had made, and he had done it in front of two underlings – the runner and the 'shocked' 19th man, Keith Carroll[25] – not to mention any spectators within earshot. Such an act was tantamount to insubordination. Smith hated interference from anyone – even one of his most trusted, respected allies like Hughes. Smith reacted in the way he usually did when he felt suitably insulted. He 'exploded',[26] but in a manner that McPherson didn't find disrespectful.

'Checker,' Smith said through gritted teeth, 'you've had your day as a coach, but that day has been and gone. I'm the coach now. Now go and sit up in the grandstand.'

Alf Brown's account of the incident in *The Herald* portrayed a more abusive, bullying tone to Smith's outburst. Brown reported that Smith had actually roared: 'Get up in the grandstand where you belong, you old bastard!'[27]

Fifty years on, however, McPherson himself exploded when asked if Smith had used these stronger words attributed by Brown. 'Where the hell would Alf Brown get that from?!' he said. 'There was only Norm, Checker and I there. And Norm would never speak to Checker like that because he respected him too much.'[28]

Regardless, Checker, 'leaning heavily on his walking stick',[29] did as Smith had ordered – he 'stomped off... in high dudgeon',[30] and took a seat in the grandstand and 'did not rejoin Norm for a long time'.[31]

Until this point, there had been a feeling that while Smith was the coach, many of the Demons' strategies had been plotted by Hughes and Ivor Warne-Smith, from both of whom the coach had taken considerable counsel. And why wouldn't he have done so? Both gentlemen were, after all, among the game's more astute minds. But this incident on the sidelines had changed this perception, even among those in the Demons' inner sanctum. Even Ron Barassi marvelled that it took Smith four-and-a-half seasons, two Grand Final appearances and a premiership to

---

[23] Hugh McPherson. Interview with the author.
[24] Alf Brown, *The Herald*, May 4, 1979.
[25] Keith Carroll. Interview with the author.
[26] Alf Brown, *The Herald*, May 4, 1979.
[27] Alf Brown, *The Herald*, May 4, 1979.
[28] Hugh McPherson. Interview with the author.
[29] Alf Brown, *The Herald*, May 4, 1979.
[30] Sheedy, Kevin, with Warwick Hadfield, *The 500 Club*, News Custom Publishing, 2004.
[31] Alf Brown, *The Herald*, May 4, 1979.

finally be recognised as 'No. 1; the man in charge'. His 'blue' with Hughes, Barassi said, 'made people finally realise that the old supercoach in the background wasn't the one pulling the strings'.[32] Barassi recalled that the overwhelming feeling was: 'By golly, Smithy really is in charge'.[33]

Unfortunately, the incident had ramifications for the Smith-Hughes relationship. Hughes' son, Frank Hughes junior, revealed that the once unbreakable partnership had been fractured. 'There's no doubt that it had a negative affect on their relationship,' Hughes junior said. 'Regrettably, they didn't talk as much after that. It gradually became a water-under-the-bridge situation, but it was a pity that their relationship never quite got back to what it was. Dad never bore a grudge about it though.'[34]

From then on, Warne-Smith, the chairman of selectors, sat on the bench with Smith – along with McPherson and the two reserves players. 'A man of sound judgement' and 'one of the most charmingly unassuming people that one could wish to meet',[35] Warne-Smith was 'as quiet as a mouse'[36] and generally a silent observer of the game. He was also an excellent pacifier who could somewhat offset Smith's fire. But, according to Mark Warne-Smith – one of Ivor's grandsons – even this seemingly compatible arrangement had its moments of high tension, with the pair coming to blows in the lounge room of Warne-Smith's house in Mt Martha. Apparently, Warne-Smith had vehemently opposed Smith's plan to select a player who had blatantly broken a team rule the previous week.[37]

ȲȲȲȲȲȲȲȲ

Melbourne's 19-game hot streak ended against Footscray on a soft MCG surface in round 14. The Demons had lost just two games in 12 months – it was exactly a season ago to the round – and both defeats were at the hands of the Bulldogs. And, as had been the case in their previous clash at Footscray, the Demons' inaccuracy cost them the match and a shot at creating more history.

Melbourne fired two more scoring shots than the Bulldogs but lost – 7.17 (59) to 10.12 (72). The Demons, who lost explosive defender Don Williams during

---

[32] Ron Barassi. Interview with the author.
[33] Ron Barassi, in *The Champions: Conversations with Great Players and Coaches of Australian Football*, by Ben Collins, GSP, 2006.
[34] Frank Hughes junior. Interview with the author.
[35] Taylor, E.C.H., *100 Years of Football: The Story of the Melbourne FC 1858-1958*, Melbourne Football Club, 1957.
[36] Hugh McPherson. Interview with the author.
[37] Mark Warne-Smith. Interview with the author.

the match, hit the post four times. It was a defeat that, Smith said, 'dented our morale'.[38]

Smith's man-management hadn't been up to its usual standard. His stubborn insistence on Ian Ridley playing on the previous week with a badly corked thigh came back to haunt him. The normally lively Ridley – who had kicked a goal in each round and had a season tally of 28, just one behind Big Bob Johnson – was rendered largely immobile and went goalless for the only time that season. Ridley said: 'My thigh just about killed me – that and the fact I was playing on Wally Donald, who was a great back-pocket player. I hardly got a bloody kick. But that was pretty rare for Norm to get it wrong with an injury'.[39]

Smith was naturally disappointed that his side couldn't keep its unbeaten record intact, but later said: 'Defeat lifted us out of our lethargy'.[40] He still found positives in the loss, one of which was the performance of Geoff McGivern on Bulldogs' superstar Ted Whitten. McGivern said:

> Before the game, Norm had said to me: 'Here's your big chance today. You've got Whitten'.
> Whitten, of course, had given me a hiding in the 1954 Grand Final.
> I said: 'She'll be right, Norm'.
> Norm said: 'I know it will be. In fact, I'm *sure* it will be'.
> This was to be the only time I ever played on Whitten when I was centre half-back and he was centre half-forward, and I managed to do the job. After the game, even though we'd lost, Norm shook my hand and said: 'Thanks. Good show. You'd just about be square with him now, wouldn't you?' Norm would never go into volumes of words of praise. If he said: 'Good show', you knew you'd done well.[41]

McGivern said that while he and Smith had 'an interesting relationship' punctuated by the odd disagreement, he believed that Smith respected his matter-of-fact nature. 'I think Norm appreciated that he could ask me a question and I'd give him an honest answer,' McGivern said. 'There are a lot of people who will give the answer that they think their boss or their coach wants to hear, rather than expressing their true feelings, but that was never in my make-up, nor was it in Norm's.' An example of their relationship emerged in the lead-up to the 1956 finals series. McGivern said:

---

[38] *Melbourne Truth* series, 1962.
[39] Ian Ridley. Interview with the author.
[40] *Melbourne Truth* series, 1962.
[41] Geoff McGivern. Interview with the author.

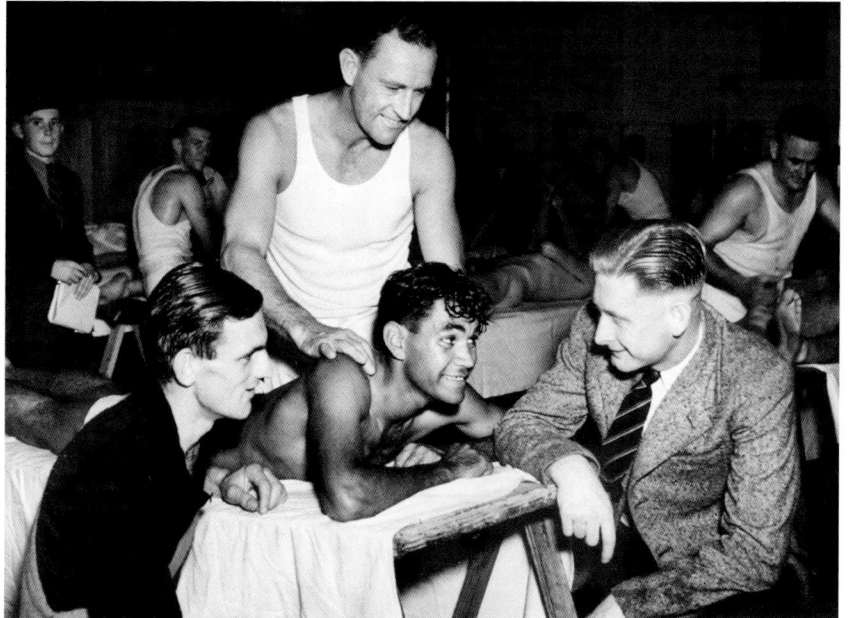

Smith returned to Melbourne as coach in 1952 after getting the job by a vote from La Fontaine. Here, he renews acquaintances with brilliant Aboriginal player Eddie Jackson. *(Private collection)*

Enjoying a cup of soup after training with *(from left)* Ron Barassi, Noel McMahen, Don Williams, Smith, Geoff McGivern and Peter Marquis. Smith had a complex relationship with his captain, McMahen, who revealed they shared 'mutual respect, but no great fondness'. *(Melbourne Football Club Collection)*

Smith congratulates his star pupil, Ron Barassi, on his first selection for the Victorian side in May 1956. The Smith-Barassi union was legendary. Smith had been a close friend of Barassi's late father, 1940 premiership teammate Ron senior, who was killed at Tobruk during World War II. Barassi junior lived with the Smiths from the age of 16 to 21, until he married in March 1957, when he was one of the biggest names in the game. Smith was hard on all of his players, but hardest on Barassi, and often targeted him in order to lift the side. They remain the only two men in AFL/VFL history to win 10 premierships as players and coaches. *(Herald & Weekly Times)*

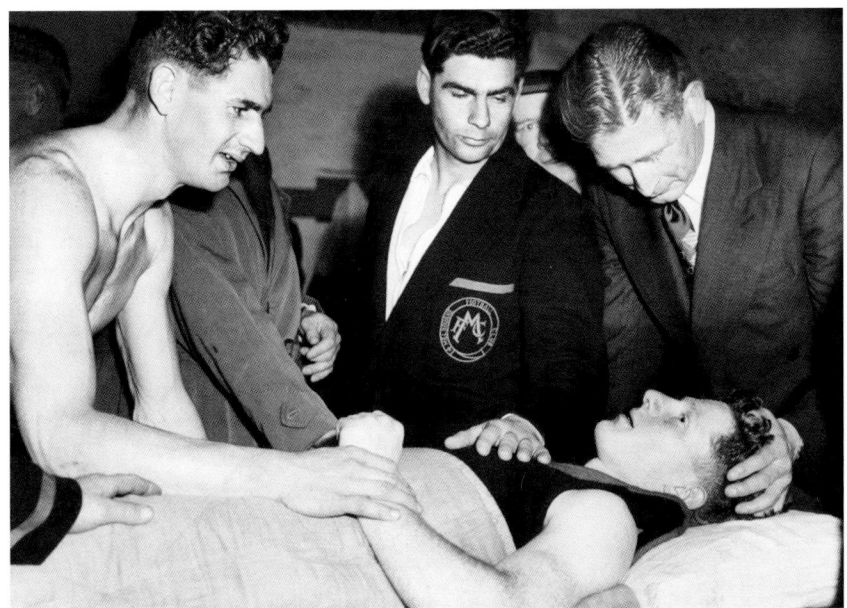

Skipper Noel McMahen (*left*), head trainer Jack McLoughlin and Smith inform a groggy Frank 'Bluey' Adams of the Demons' '55 triumph. Adams had played 'the shortest Grand Final ever' after colliding with, and KO'ing, Collingwood's Des Healey as he raced onto the field from the reserves bench. Amid accusations of deliberate violence, Smith asked: 'Would a man race at another head-on, knock himself out, to put a man out of a game already won?' *(Herald & Weekly Times)*

Norm and Marj Smith celebrate the 1955 premiership with players (from left to right) Don Williams, Clyde Laidlaw, Laurie Mithen, Noel McMahen, Ken Melville and their partners. Smith said he 'felt (like) a giant', and that night he and his team were 'all like schoolboys'. *(Private collection)*

The brains trust: (*from left*) Checker Hughes, Jim Cardwell (partially obscured), Smith and Ivor Warne-Smith monitoring play, with runner Hugh McPherson (*far right*). Midway through 1956, Hughes challenged a Smith move and the coach banished him to the grandstand. Hughes didn't rejoin Smith on the bench for some time. (*Hugh McPherson*)

Before her sons coached against each other for the first time on June 21, 1958, Ethel Smith said: 'I can only hope it's a draw'. Len won the first 'Battle of the Brothers' by 41 points. Ever gracious in defeat, Norm said: 'I knew he would cook something up for us'. In their nine encounters, Norm won four, Len won three and there were two draws. (*Norma Harmes*)

Smith was in his element during after-match get-togethers, when he would invariably hold court while others – like Melbourne's John Beckwith *(second from left)* and Fitzroy's Bill Stephen *(far right)* – picked his brain. Although he didn't drink until his 30s, Smith became a 'party animal' who was usually the last to leave club functions. *(Herald & Weekly Times)*

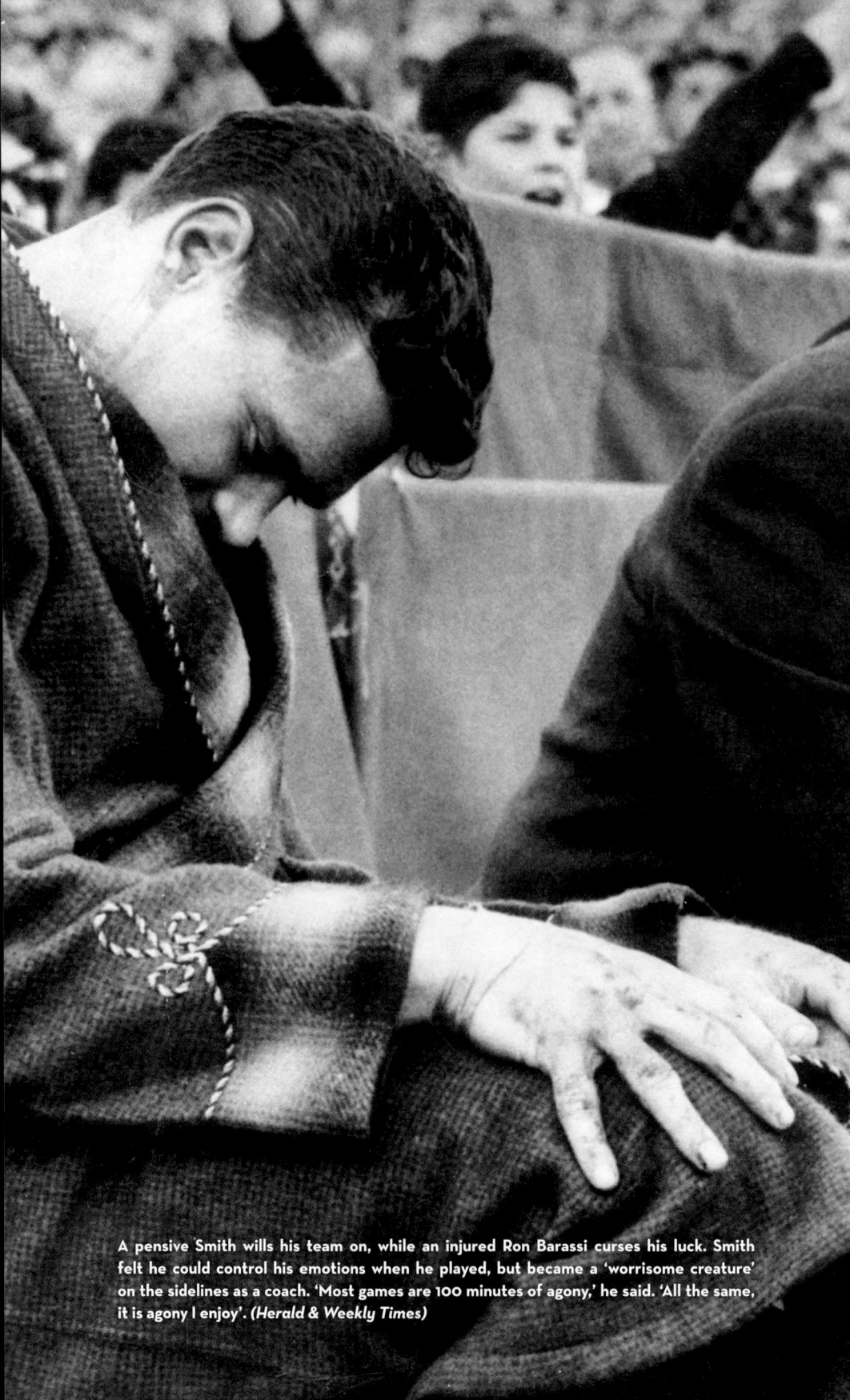

A pensive Smith wills his team on, while an injured Ron Barassi curses his luck. Smith felt he could control his emotions when he played, but became a 'worrisome creature' on the sidelines as a coach. 'Most games are 100 minutes of agony,' he said. 'All the same, it is agony I enjoy'. *(Herald & Weekly Times)*

In the dying seconds of the 1964 Grand Final against Collingwood, Smith vowed not to 'put on a show', but when the final siren sounded, in a rare show of public emotion, he leapt into the air. Checker Hughes (*left*) screamed: 'We won it!' Smith replied: 'My oath we've won it!' It was his sixth premiership as coach and was widely regarded as his greatest triumph. *(Courtesy of The Age archives)*

THE FINEST MELBOURNE SIDE OF ALL [1956]

We were in the showers after training one night and Norm asked me: 'Who would you put next to (centre half-forward) Clyde Laidlaw: Laurie Mithen or Geoff Case?'

I said: 'Casey's a half-back flanker. Mithen's the most gifted player in the side'.

Norm was quite taken aback. He said: 'Do you really think so?'

I said: 'Yeah, I think he is'.

He said: 'Oh'.

After we'd had our showers and got dressed, Norm came back over to me and said: 'Getting back to Mithen, do you really think he's the most gifted player here?'

I said: 'Yes, Norm, that's what I think'.

He said: 'Hmm, that's bloody interesting'.

I thought to myself: 'I've actually given him something to think about there. That doesn't often happen'.[42]

Mithen was a supremely gifted footballer, but he didn't always impress his coach. In fact, at times he infuriated him. Such was the case midway through the 1956 season, when Mithen and Peter Marquis were lucky to escape a precarious situation with their lives, let alone play football again. At the start of the snow season in June, Mithen and Marquis took their girlfriends to the snowfields of Mt Buller, but when the weather deteriorated rapidly they were caught in a blizzard. After being reported missing for 18 hours, the four were finally rescued and hospitalised, requiring treatment for frostbite to their hands and feet, shock and exposure. Smith was far from happy with his two young stars, who he felt had acted irresponsibly and endangered not only their own lives but those of their partners.

He also cracked down on another of his promising youngsters before Melbourne's round 17 clash with North Melbourne at the MCG. Smith was already on edge after the Demons had dropped their second game in three rounds – to Geelong in poor weather at Kardinia Park. The Demons had mustered just 3.8 by three-quarter time to trail the Cats by 13 points, before slamming on 5.0 to 3.1 in the final term to go down by just two points. It wasn't exactly cause for panic. The Demons were still clear ladder leaders and their two losses had been by a combined total of just 15 points.

For the match against the bottom-placed Kangaroos, Melbourne's selectors had chosen another product of Melbourne's thirds, 19-year-old Ian Thorogood, as an emergency. It was to be the first and last time Thorogood would be selected in this capacity for the season. He recalled:

---

[42] Geoff McGivern. Interview with the author.

I made the mistake of being about 10 minutes late to the MCG – I'd been caught up in traffic – and, boy, did Norm tear strips off me. The message that he imparted loud and clear was that even though I wasn't required to play, I could have been; and that an emergency was important because someone could have been ill or had a smash on the way to the ground, and I would have let the club down because I was late. Those were the days when the reserves played at the same time as the senior side but on the alternate ground, so I drove out to North Melbourne with my tail between my legs. But, importantly, I thought to myself: 'I'm never going to be late again'. And I don't think I ever was. It was a very good lesson.[43]

As expected, the Demons comfortably defeated the Kangaroos, who had won just three games for the season. But the 'Roos didn't go down without a fight. Melbourne was outscored in the middle quarters – 8.2 to 7.7 – and was just two goals clear at three-quarter time, before running away with the game with a 4.8 to 0.1 blast in the final term to win by 33 points.

The final home-and-away round featured what many correctly predicted to be a Grand Final preview – Melbourne versus Collingwood at Victoria Park. The Demons had lost their previous four matches at Magpie headquarters – their most recent win there had been back in 1951 – and the situation looked decidedly gloomy at quarter-time when they had registered just two scoring shots and trailed by three goals. But from that point on, the Demons' running game went into overdrive and they piled on 9.12 to 5.5 in the last three quarters to record a 13-point win.

The victory confirmed the Demons' second successive minor premiership – with their 16-2 record, they finished three games clear of Collingwood and Geelong and five games clear of fourth-placed Footscray – and it was also an important psychological victory. The Demons would face the Magpies again – in their next match a fortnight later – in the second semi-final at the MCG. Smith enthused that his side had produced 'top-class football – its best for at least six weeks'.[44]

The Demons' preparation for the finals had been near-perfect, but the same couldn't be said for their coach. In the lead-up to the second semi-final, Smith was bed-ridden with a bout of 'flu, which rendered him unable to take training on the Tuesday before the match. In his absence, the job was taken on by skipper Noel McMahen, who accepted the responsibility of training the Demons.

'Training was fairly basic in those days,' McMahen said. 'If the same thing happened today and the coach, for whatever reason, couldn't take training,

---

[43] Ian Thorogood. Interview with the author.
[44] *The Argus*, Monday August 20, 1956.

an assistant coach would take charge and it would be planned to the letter. But all we did back then was basically end-to-end and circle-work, so anyone could have done that. It was just about ensuring everyone trained to a standard, and by that stage we were ready to go.'[45]

As had been the case in their previous two meetings, Melbourne and Collingwood staged a mighty battle for the right to advance to the Grand Final. And, as had also been a common theme of their recent clashes, the Demons overwhelmed the Magpies late in the contest. Although they lost Geoff McGivern to a season-ending ankle injury at half-time, and trailed by a point at the last change, the Demons kicked 3.5 to 0.6 in the final term to win by 16 points – 11.14 (80) to 8.16 (64).

One of Melbourne's heroes was 19th man Jim 'Little Bull' Sandral, who charged into packs just as his nickname suggested. After the match, Sandral – whose instructions were simply: 'Go in. Get it. Kick it' – told *The Sun*: 'It was an education to sit beside Norm (in the first half) and have all the errors pointed out to me. I kept thinking that if I get the chance to take the field I just could not afford to make one mistake... (Then) after listening to Norm's pep-talk at half-time, I felt better than at any time of my football career'.[46]

Collingwood earned a return bout with Melbourne in the Grand Final after easily disposing of Footscray in the preliminary final. Smith told *The Sporting Globe*: 'We've beaten Collingwood five times in a row and I'm sure Saturday will be the sixth... It will be hard, but Melbourne will be in front at the finish'.[47]

🏆🏆🏆🏆🏆🏆🏆🏆🏆

The 1956 Grand Final attracted the best and worst of football fanaticism.

A massive crowd of 115,803 spectators – at the time, the biggest crowd to watch a football match in Australia – crammed into the reconstructed MCG and produced a cauldron-like atmosphere. During the reserves Grand Final – won by Melbourne – many spectators, including women, risked their lives by climbing onto the roofs of stands about 25 metres off the ground. As the crowd swelled, fans spilled over the fence, and then over the boundary line. Fearing a crowd crush, the Health Department ordered the gates closed more than an hour before the senior Grand Final was scheduled to start. This sparked chaos outside the stadium as thousands of angry supporters broke through the gates after fighting off police

---

[45] Noel McMahen. Interview with the author.
[46] *The Sun*, Tuesday September 4, 1956.
[47] *The Sporting Globe*, Wednesday September 12, 1956.

and ground attendants. Many people were knocked down in the stampede. Others climbed into the ground on ladders and even tree branches. Many others didn't get inside.

It was similarly impossible for visitors to gain entry to the Melbourne rooms before the match. A pensive Norm Smith 'chewed gum non-stop as he prowled around his boys, patting them on the back and giving them words of advice'.[48] Smith wanted his players to showcase their skills and produce their best football, but in his pre-match address he asked for one thing: raw commitment. Keith Carroll recalled:

> I'd walked around the tunnel to get into the back of the rooms and saw the ambulance was sitting outside the door. It's not the kind of thing you want to see before you play a football match. Then Norm demanded, as he always did, that we lay our bodies on the line. But I'll never forget his words: 'Some of you are going to get hurt today. If you're not prepared to get hurt, leave now!' You always go onto the field knowing you can get hurt, but it's not the kind of thing you want spelled out for you. I thought: 'Jeez, I hope it's not me'. But after half-time, (Collingwood centreman) Bill Twomey broke my nose and I had a ride in the ambulance to the Alfred Hospital.[49]

Melbourne conceded three of the first four goals to trail by 15 points late in the first quarter, but that was the end of the Magpie resistance. Smith later said: 'We were often headed in the early stages of matches. But the other side's game would deteriorate from sheer frustration, usually late in the second quarter'. The Magpies deteriorated under Melbourne's intense pressure much sooner than that. According to Alf Brown, 'the result was never in doubt after the first quarter'.[50] Remarkably, the Demons had the next 15 scoring shots. Their 'wretched' return was 4.11 – 'inexcusably bad kicking in perfect conditions'[51] – and their half-time lead of 20 points should have been at least double that margin, but Smith remained confident his side would eventually capitalise through sheer weight of opportunities.

Late in the third quarter, with the premiership in Melbourne's safe keeping, chairman of selectors Ivor Warne-Smith decided it was time to celebrate. As he often did when matches were sewn up, Warne-Smith felt the urge to mark the occasion with a nip of whisky, a bottle of which was routinely supplied by runner

---

[48] *The Argus*, Monday, September 17, 1956.
[49] Keith Carroll. Interview with the author.
[50] *The Herald*, Monday, September 17, 1956.
[51] Alf Brown, *The Herald*, Monday, September 17, 1956.

THE FINEST MELBOURNE SIDE OF ALL [1956]

Hugh McPherson and concealed in a towel and placed under the coach's bench. Warne-Smith gave Smith a gentle nudge and said: 'How about we open the bottle of whisky?'

The coach was having nothing of it. He later said: 'I'm never complacent about a result (because) anything can happen in football and you have not won until that siren blares'.[52] He responded accordingly to Warne-Smith's suggestion. 'No, no, no, Ivor!' he said dismissively. 'Not yet! It's too early for that!'

But midway through the last quarter, with Melbourne holding an unassailable lead, Smith – who was enjoying seeing his players 'toy with Collingwood'[53], and Magpie supporters file out of the ground – finally relented. He said: 'OK, Ivor,' he said, 'I think we're safe to open it now'.

Warne-Smith gave the nod to McPherson, who reached under the bench, only to find that the bottle had disappeared – it must have been stolen by one of the many spectators jammed in around them. Warne-Smith forgot all about what was left of the game and pleaded with the fans to give it back, claiming it belonged to the players. But apart from a few giggles and heckles, he received no response.

As was the case in the 1954 Grand Final, the over-flowing crowd caused havoc with the players. John Beckwith, one of the Demons' best with 17 kicks, five marks and four handballs, said: 'You had that thought as you were chasing the ball towards the boundary that you couldn't very well slow down because that's against the principles of Norm Smith. You had to run flat out at every ball... So you just kept going and fell into the crowd'.[54]

From about the 20-minute mark of the first term, Melbourne piled on 15.15 to Collingwood's 3.9 to win by 73 points – 17.19 (121) to 6.12 (48). In 'one of the most crushing displays of pace and power seen in a League Grand Final',[55] and one in which the Demons 'rose to new heights of greatness',[56] they had recorded the equal biggest win in Grand Final history, matching Essendon's effort against Carlton in 1949.[57] In doing so, the Demons became the only side to have beaten Collingwood four times in a season, and won their second successive McClelland Trophy, relegating Collingwood to second again.

---

[52] *The Sun* series, 1967.
[53] *Melbourne Truth* series, 1962.
[54] *Red and Blue* documentary, 2005.
[55] Kevin Hogan, *The Sun*, Monday, September 17, 1956.
[56] Percy Beames, *The Age*, Monday, September 17, 1956.
[57] Melbourne and Essendon are now equal seventh on the all-time list behind Geelong's 119-point massacre of Port Adelaide in the 2007 Grand Final, Hawthorn's 96-point belting of Melbourne in the 1988 Grand Final, the Hawks' 83-point drubbing of Essendon in 1983, Richmond's 81-point thumping of Collingwood in 1980, West Coast's 80-point hammering of Geelong in 1994, and Essendon's 78-point thrashing of Hawthorn in 1985.

Most of Smith's individual match-ups had worked. He had assigned Ken Melville the task of beating the brilliant Bill Twomey. It was something of a leap of faith as Melville had been 'playing without dash or confidence and was one of Melbourne's weakest players in the second semi-final'.[58] But his success was 'the most unexpected and telling blow struck against the Magpies' normally productive centreline'.[59] Along with Bluey Adams, who had the job on Collingwood's champion wingman Thorold Merrett, they 'greatly retarded the Magpie machine's main drive'.[60]

In defence, Peter Marquis had also kept Collingwood spearhead Ken Smale, an eight-goal hero in the preliminary final, to just one goal, while up forward Athol Webb answered Alf Brown's public criticism in the best way possible, by slotting 5.1 from 15 kicks. Best-afield was Stuart Spencer, who amassed 25 kicks, five marks, seven handballs and 5.4, while Barassi wasn't far behind with 19 kicks, six marks and 3.3.

Remarkably, the Demons now boasted 12 players no older than 22 who had appeared in at least two Grand Finals. Five of them – Adams, Barassi, Big Bob Johnson, Laurie Mithen and Don Williams – had played in all three.

After the match, Smith told *The Argus*:

> We won the premiership with long kicking and because our players showed great courage by going into packs for the ball all day. When I talk of courage, I don't mean that the players have to go around knocking opponents down. What I do mean is that I expect our players to be prepared to go in and get that ball in any circumstance. Never have they been instructed to "get" any opponent, but, rather, they have been asked to make the ball the objective all the time. The "tall timber" is expected to go for the marks, and the little fellows are to hover around and pick up the crumbs.
>
> Much has been said about our relief followers and rovers kicking most of our goals during the season. Well, what of it? When those chaps are off the ball, they are forwards, and, as such, isn't it their job to kick goals? After all, what does it matter who kicks the goal?! The ball comes toward goal because of the good work of players farther away, and the player in the best position to kick goals is the player who should be given that opportunity...
>
> The boys did a remarkable job. All 18 of them were in it all the time. This was a really satisfying premiership and I'm proud of them.[61]

---

[58] Kevin Hogan, *The Sun*, Monday, September 17, 1956.
[59] Kevin Hogan, *The Sun*, Monday, September 17, 1956.
[60] Former Geelong champion Lloyd Hagger, in his column in *The Sun*, Monday, September 17, 1956.
[61] *The Argus*, Monday, September 17, 1956.

THE FINEST MELBOURNE SIDE OF ALL [1956]

Amid the euphoria in the Melbourne changerooms, Collingwood coach Phonse Kyne and club president Syd Coventry (a boyhood idol of Norm Smith's) battled their way through the throng to congratulate the victors. Bluey Adams recalled:

> One of the first things I ever heard Norm say, and I heard him say it many times, was: 'Be a modest winner, and a gracious loser'. Once we got a bit of success, people from outside the club would say things like: 'Melbourne's arrogant. They're up themselves'. But that was so far from the truth it was laughable. I think that kind of sentiment was driven by jealousy. If Norm won he didn't crow, and if he lost he didn't whinge. And he instilled that in everyone at the club. He would say: 'Football is a great grounding for whatever you do in your later life. The way you react to the enjoyment of a win, or the despair of a loss, is important. Not everything is good, not everything is bad. It's the same in life as it is in sport'.[62]

During Smith's speech at the premiership dinner, he proposed a toast to his team, recognising their efforts with rare, lavish words of praise, referring to them as 'the great Melbourne side'. The players then sang *Happy Birthday* for Athol Webb and Geoff Case – both of whom had just turned 21 – and followed it up with a rendition of *The Girl That I Marry* for Ian Ridley, who had announced his engagement to his sweetheart, Judy Rogers.

Smith was so proud of his 'boys' he was almost overcome with emotion. With tears in his eyes, he told Edna Carroll, Keith's wife: 'I love Keith; I love them all'.[63]

Two other boys he loved – Peter Smith and Barassi – squabbled in the days following the premiership victory. Smith rang *The Herald's* Alf Brown and asked him to help 'restore order' in the Smith house. He explained: 'Young Pete pinched a *Herald* premiership poster from Ronny's room and stuck it on the front door of a Collingwood supporter down the street. Ronny is furious and is gunning for Pete. Can you get me another one?' An amused Brown promptly obliged and the dispute was settled.[64]

The Demons' Olympic year success didn't end there. They embarked on an end-of-season tour of Tasmania, South Australia and Western Australia, in what was believed to have been the first tour of its kind. Melbourne emerged undefeated, smashing Tasmania's North West Football Union combined team by 86 points

---

[62] Frank 'Bluey' Adams. Interview with the author.
[63] Edna Carroll. Interview with the author.
[64] *The Herald*, 1967.

before outlasting both SANFL premier Port Adelaide (10 points) and WAFL premier East Perth (11 points), to confirm their No. 1 status.

Indeed, many fans were even pondering if this Demons' side was as good as the club's 1939-41 sides. Smith's answer was: 'Yes and no. The present team is not so strong in attack as the side before the war, but is stronger in defence. There were more brilliant individuals in our winning sides before the war, yet this side works more as a team. After all, we've only lost five games in two seasons. This team might not have the names, but it has produced the goods. What better can you do than win the Grand Final by 12 goals?'[65]

Melbourne's committee enthusiastically praised Norm Smith for his influence on the club's winning mentality, stating: 'Norman... has been an outstanding success at Melbourne, but to those in close association with him it is not surprising, for his completely honest approach to players, but his stern but fair castigation of mistakes, his unerring appreciation of his own and opponents' weaknesses, his desire to coach for the success of the team alone, quite apart from any glorifying of his own part in that success, his sincerity in addressing the players, have all so won the support of the players that they are completely behind him in every respect... A very busy man engaged in running his own steadily developing business, Norman is not coaching for monetary reasons, and it is to be hoped that the club will have his services for many years ahead.'[66]

ŸŸŸŸŸŸŸŸŸ

After the Demons had won back-to-back flags, they were perhaps due for a loss. But few could have predicted they would suffer such a staggering, seemingly crippling loss of key personnel. At the end of the 1956, the Demons farewelled no fewer than six premiership stars – skipper Noel McMahen, Denis Cordner, Stuart Spencer, Geoff McGivern, Ken Melville and Ralph Lane. Among them were two captains, a vice-captain, 697 games' experience, numerous Victorian guernseys, and five best and fairest winners (all but Lane) who had, between them, claimed the previous seven club awards.

Smith acknowledged their contribution to the Demons' success. 'Everyone knows how much they have meant to Melbourne,' he said, 'and we are greatly indebted to them for the grand work they have done.'[67]

---

[65] *Adelaide Advertiser*, October 10, 1956.
[66] Melbourne Football Club annual report, 1956.
[67] *The Argus*, Monday, September 17, 1956.

During Cordner's farewell function the following July (before he set off for a four-month stint in London), this exchange took place between Smith and his revered ruckman:

> **Smith:** Denis was born too soon. He belongs to the jet age. The grounds weren't big enough for his drop-kicks. Like jet planes, they needed a lot of room before they could get off the ground! After last year's Grand Final, we gave captain Noel McMahen the football used in the match (and) there were two deep stop-marks across the top of it – that happened when Denis tried to drop-kick the ball!
>
> **Cordner:** When Norm first became coach, he took me aside and said: 'Your drop-kicking is awful. We'd better do something about it'. He gave me special drop-kicking tuition for three weeks. Everything I know about drop-kicking I owe to Norm Smith![68]

The circumstances of four other high-profile retirements – those of McMahen, Spencer, Melville and McGivern – are worthy of elaboration for the role and reactions of Norm Smith.

McMahen admitted: 'I'd played at Melbourne for 11 years, my legs were gone and I was finished. In the 1956 Grand Final, I was the only Melbourne player who was beaten by his opponent. I'd played at centre half-back on (Murray) Weideman. But what a way to go out – a 13-goal victory over Collingwood in a Grand Final in front of 116,000 people. It was Utopia'.[69] But within two hours of the final siren, the match committee, which included Norm Smith, ushered the soon-to-be 30-year-old McMahen into a small library off the Long Room. McMahen recalled:

> Jim Cardwell asked me: 'We want to know what you're going to do tonight.'
> I said: 'I'm going to announce my retirement; you know that.'
> Checker Hughes said: 'Well we don't want you to.'
> They said: 'We think you should give us another year to help the kids with your leadership and experience'.
> Harry Long (a selector) piped up and said: 'You owe it to us.'
> I said: 'I don't think I owe you anything at this stage. But I'm listening'.
> At one point, I asked Smithy: 'What do you think?'
> He said: 'Please your bloody self'.

---

[68] Newspaper report, July 1957.
[69] Noel McMahen. Interview with the author.

I asked Ivor Warne-Smith for his opinion and he said: 'Noel, I think it would be a shame if you played again. I think you've come to the end of your time as a League player and I'd hate to see you go out on a bad note'.

I said: 'Thanks for being honest, Ivor'.

Ivor protected me from any ego which might have swayed my decision. For a candid meeting like that to take place virtually straight after winning a premiership was wonderful – it showed the strength and diligence of the club.[70]

Despite the complexities of the coach-captain relationship, McMahen – who took up the coaching job at Bendigo league club Rochester – revealed two subsequent acts of generosity from Smith. 'Later on,' McMahen said, 'we wanted to raise some money at Rochester because it was only a little town and we had a lot of expenses. I originally asked (Jack) Dyer and (Lou) Richards to come up and do a sportsmen's night for us, but they wanted £250 each, which was enormous money in those days. But Smithy and 'Checker' drove the 90-odd miles (150 kilometres) up and did it for me for nothing.[71] Another time, Norm drove up to Rochester and dropped off some scooters for my kids.'[72]

The Demons' greatest loss at the end of 1956 was the logical successor to McMahen's captaincy, Stuart Spencer. Regarded by all at Melbourne as 'the best rover in Australia', Spencer, at 24, had won the previous two club best and fairest awards and been best-afield in the 1956 Grand Final, and an All-Australian the same year. Some believed that if he stayed he could have become Melbourne's greatest player of all time. But he left for family reasons – his wife Fay was heavily pregnant with their first child and wanted to be close to her family in Hobart. He said: 'Norm, Checker Hughes and Jimmy Cardwell said: "Give us another year, Stuey", and said if I changed my mind they could pretty well guarantee me the captaincy. Although it didn't seem like such a big deal I was going to Tassie, I would never have even contemplated it now. It's an enormous regret in our lives.'[73]

It was also a significant regret of Smith's. Fay Spencer revealed: 'At get-togethers in the years afterwards, Norm would say to me: "If it wasn't for you, we would have won our four premierships in a row". He wouldn't say it in a nasty way – it was a compliment to Stuey. Norm told me that so many times. That's how much Norm missed him'.[74]

---

[70] Noel McMahen. Interview with the author.
[71] Norm performed similar favours for a number of players throughout his coaching career.
[72] Noel McMahen. Interview with the author.
[73] Stuart Spencer. Interview with the author.
[74] Fay Spencer. Interview with the author. Stuart Spencer played a further 161 matches for Clarence, and won four best-and-fairests and another All-Australian selection in 1958. He was president of Melbourne Football Club from 1986 to 1991.

He would also miss the courage and steadying influence of his centreman, Ken Melville. A recently ordained minister with the Presbyterian Church, Melville, 25, had accepted an appointment in London. He said:

> People tried to convince me to play on, and some even argued with me, but Norm never pushed or tried to influence me one way or the other, because he accepted what I had chosen to do, and I appreciated that.
>
> Norm understood that players who had professional lives, or were preparing for professional life, had different concerns and demands from others and he understood that they would probably retire early from football.

Geoff McGivern, also 25, was another premature retiree. The talented key-position player had missed the 1956 premiership through an ankle injury suffered in the second semi-final. After the death of his father earlier in the year, and his marriage in November, he decided to hang up his boots to become a partner in his family's quarrying business. 'I could have played another four or five seasons of footy,' McGivern said, 'but it was too good a business opportunity to pass up. I knew what I wanted to do – play footy – but I also knew what I had to do.'[75]

The news was a bombshell. McGivern recalled:

> Norm said: 'You *can't* be finished. No, I won't accept that'.
>
> I said: 'Norm, you haven't got any choice. I'm not playing any more. I'm going into the business, and that's that'.
>
> He came out to see me at work (at Kilsyth) a couple of times and tried to talk me into going back and playing football. He said: 'You've still got so much to achieve with your football. You should've had a Victorian guernsey a couple of years ago, so you've still got to get that; you'll play 200 games easy; and we need you'.
>
> I said: 'But what I'm getting out of this in a financial sense is terrific'.
>
> A few years later, we were at a function and Norm told me: 'You made the right decision for yourself. I can't argue with that. But it still would have been nice to have you playing for us'.[76]

Smith had always respected, and been intrigued by, McGivern's occupation. Initially, though, he held grave concerns for his young star's welfare. McGivern said:

---

[75] Geoff McGivern. Interview with the author.
[76] Geoff McGivern. Interview with the author.

Norm asked me: 'What do you do in that quarry?'

I said: 'Drive a truck; get up on the face with a jackhammer...'

He said: 'You what? What do you do up there?'

I said: 'Bore holes and then blow it down'.

He said: 'Jesus!'

Norm actually lobbed out there one day to see for himself. He had a look and he nearly dropped dead! I was up on the face, about 50 feet (15.2 metres) up in the air, and on a ledge about two foot (61 centimetres) wide. He said: 'I can't look'. He also said: 'You don't do that on a Friday do you?'

He couldn't get over it. He'd often say ask me: 'So have you been doing anything stupid this week?' He respected what I did because he told me: 'I wouldn't have the courage to do that. It doesn't worry you?'

I said: 'No. It's just something I have to do as part of my job'.

Norm would say: 'You're pretty much a free spirit, aren't you Geoffrey?. Nothing perturbs you much, does it?'

I said: 'It's not worth it'.

He'd laugh and say: 'You're so laid-back that sometimes I wonder about you!'

Norm was always very appreciative of the fact I had a strong body. He said: 'That's the beauty of what you do for a living. It's like being in a gymnasium seven days a week'.[77]

Smith had a genuine soft spot for players who worked with their hands and weren't afraid to get them dirty. McGivern said: 'Norm reckoned the blokes who did manual work were a lot fitter, could go longer, and absorb punishment a little bit better than blokes who worked in offices'.[78]

Conversely, Smith was generally hard on white-collar workers, but particularly those who had come through the public school system. They were 'not really Norm's kind of people'.[79] Although the highly-educated Cordner brothers had been among some rare exceptions, Smith typically 'had no tolerance for public schoolboys'[80] and would taunt them with comments like: 'Don't be afraid to get your hands dirty'. He also became sensitive and impatient with those who suggested Melbourne was an exclusive club of public schoolboys, and that 'you have to wear an old school tie to get a game'.[81]

---

[77] Geoff McGivern. Interview with the author.
[78] Geoff McGivern. Interview with the author.
[79] Hugh McPherson. Interview with the author.
[80] John Lord. Interview with the author.
[81] Alf Brown, *The Herald*, 1958.

Carlton great Ken Hands, who became a firm friend of Smith's, revealed that he had once told him: 'These bloody academic bastards; they wouldn't know when to come in out of the rain. Give me a country kid any day; they've got more natural sense than the academics'.[82] Although he often used the term 'academic genius, common sense fool', he actually had more trouble adapting to their ways than vice-versa. Academics confused Smith, and some felt he didn't know how to speak or relate to them. He once wrote that team lectures on Thursday nights should never be allowed to become players' discussion nights. His reasoning was: 'If you allow the players to do the talking, then you might as well allow them to do the coaching also. I have to keep a close watch on this one at Melbourne, as I have a few Dip. Ed. blokes, and a few bachelors of Commerce, etc., and I couldn't keep up with them anyway. They would blind me with science, and probably blind themselves while they were at it!'[83]

Anyone who displayed pretensions to high society would be eyed with suspicion and perhaps taken down a peg or two. Tassie Johnson said:

> Norm didn't like the upper society. He'd worked with his hands all his life, so if you turned up with a tie on, he'd let you know about it. It was just something from his upbringing and his make-up. He liked people who got their hands dirty and he reckoned that they could try harder than other people. I was a fitter-and-turner-cum-engineer, which fitted in with what Norm liked ... initially. Later on, I was offered a job as a new car salesman, where the money was better, plus I got a new car, and Norm turned on me because I started to wear a suit and tie! He'd make the odd comment off the field. And you could feel it too. It wasn't an animosity thing; he just preferred his players to be tradesmen.[84]

On this issue, it appeared Smith was at the wrong club. With Melbourne Football Club perceived as an organisation rife with bluebloods and silvertails, Smith's desire for manual-labouring, working-class footballers from the bush seemed unrealistic. But the reality was much more to his liking. Clyde Laidlaw said: 'In that era, the whole public-schoolboys-at-Melbourne thing was a fallacy. They were very much in the minority and those who were there were first-rate fellas and footballers – the likes of Denis Cordner, Kenny Melville, Geoff Case and Geoff Tunbridge. The rest of us were from the country or had working-class backgrounds, which really

---

[82] Ken Hands. Interview with the author.
[83] Norm Smith's notes titled: 'My Theories and Practices For Fitness For Melbourne League Team', believed to have been written in 1959.
[84] Robert 'Tassie' Johnson. Interview with the author.

fitted in well with the kind of group Smith wanted. But once you got out on the ground, opposition players would say: "Come on boys, let's get into these public schoolboys!" I used to think: "What a joke that is".'[85]

John Lord agreed: 'Everyone talked about Melbourne being the bluebloods, but in my time (1956-65) I reckon we had more plumbers and builders playing for us than bloody Collingwood!'[86]

In 1965, Smith hit back at the consensus view that he was opposed to public schoolboys, explaining: 'Public school footballers are equally good, if not better, than the average school footballer. It must be pointed out, however, that they are not always capable of achieving the dedication of other players because often they are thinking of a profession. If they cannot afford to throw all their energy into League football, they might as well stick to the amateurs... A man must be honest about how much of himself he is prepared to put into the game'.[87] (And, according to Len Mann: 'Norm wasn't too keen on amateur footballers because they didn't play for money, so he didn't think they'd be as desperate as others. But he didn't hold a grudge against amateurs'.)[88]

However, there was a contradiction between Smith's beliefs and actions in relation to public schoolboys. He sent his own son to Melbourne Grammar, one of the city's most exclusive public schools. Over time, Smith had developed a certain amount of respect for the public schooling system through his friendship with the Cordners. Not long after Peter was born, Smith had told Don Cordner: 'Donald, I've known you and Ted for a long time, and you've got something that I'd like my son to have. Therefore, I'm sending him to Melbourne Grammar'.[89]

Cordner later reflected: 'That was one of the greatest compliments that I've ever had paid to me. I was very proud of that because when I first met Norm, he wouldn't have a bar of public schoolboys. He'd say: "Privilege, blah, blah", and so on. But along the way we had given him a different outlook. That was the point: that he probably realised that we weren't all stuffy people!'[90]

Others have explained that the decision to send Peter Smith to an elite public school was simply through a yearning to provide his only child – a shining light in his life – with the very best opportunities to succeed. However, Peter – who attended Melbourne Grammar from Grade 5 – wished he had completed his education at

---

[85] Clyde Laidlaw. Interview with the author.
[86] John Lord. Interview with the author.
[87] Newspaper report, 1965.
[88] Len Mann. Interview with the author.
[89] Don Cordner. Interview with the author.
[90] Don Cordner. Interview with the author.

a state school with his mates. He said: 'Don't get me wrong, I'm grateful that my parents did what they thought was best for me. But it was the worst decision we made as a family, because of the amount of money it cost Mum and Dad to put me through that school – we weren't rich by any stretch – and also for the fact I think I would have been better going to Coburg High School with people I knew. Generally speaking, we were different people from the kids I went to school with, who lived in upper-class areas and led different lifestyles from what we did'.[91]

In his senior years at school, he learned economics from Demons star Brian Dixon. There was some of the father in the son. 'Peter was a very intelligent student,' Dixon recalled. 'The methodical approach of his brain to the work that he had to cover was similar to Norm. However, it was a bit of a battle to get Pete to do all of his work. I never brought any of it up with Norm, though. I kept the two things quite separate, which was probably a wise move!'[92]

ŸŸŸŸŸŸŸŸŸ

Norm and Marj Smith were such a staunch combination, and Marj was so determined to help her husband achieve all his coaching ambitions that she happily agreed to lend a hand with recruiting. An example of this was the case of mature-age newcomer Geoff Tunbridge.

Melbourne, like several clubs, had been keen to secure the services of Tunbridge, 24, from Ballarat Football Club. With VFL clubs bound to abide by the Coulter Law, which ensured each player was paid equally, clubs had few options when it came to offering inducements to get their man. But Melbourne officials always had the advantage of being able to casually mention to a prospective recruit: 'If you join us, you'll play on the Melbourne Cricket Ground every second week, and you'll gain membership of the Melbourne Cricket Club'. In many ways, it was perhaps an unfair advantage. Combined with the Demons' no-expense-spared hospitality, Melbourne Football Club was an attractive proposition.

Tunbridge described part of the courting process:

> Melbourne invited my then-fiancée Judy and I down to the 1956 Grand Final. I found out later that Marj Smith and Mavis Cardwell had been summoned to go to the old Grey Smith Stand – at God knows what time they had to get there – to reserve a seat for 'Geoff Tunbridge's fiancée'. They wanted me to play for them, so

---

[91] Peter Smith. Interview with the author.
[92] Brian Dixon. Interview with the author.

it was a nice gesture. When we got there, Judy was taken one way by the ladies and I was taken the other by club officials. I had quite a good time and afterwards I asked Judy how she went. She didn't know much about footy, and she said: 'I was sitting with someone called Mrs Smith'. That had Norm's imprints all over it. He organised to make things nice for people, and make them feel important.[93]

The following weekend, when Smith could have been forgiven for wanting to bask in the afterglow of back-to-back premierships on the senior team's trip to Tasmania, he accompanied his recruiting officer, Ken Carlon, and selector Harry Long to watch Tunbridge play in the Ballarat Football League Grand Final. Tunbridge was the playing coach of Ballarat, which was defeated by Geelong West. That night, after some casual conversation over a few quiet ales, Tunbridge agreed to play with the Demons. He had been impressed with their approach. But he was to become further impressed by Smith's recollections of that day. Tunbridge said:

> The night of the Ballarat Grand Final, a mate of mine had had a few beers with Norm, Ken and I. A handful of years later, without ever seeing my mate in between, Norm saw him after a Melbourne game and said: 'Dick! I remember you from that day up in Ballarat'.
>
> My mate was in seventh heaven. He told me: 'Jesus, that's terrific. I'd only had a few words with Norm at a country do after a defeated Grand Final, yet he remembered me!'
>
> It astounded both of us. That's a power, a gift, that influential men have. And it also comes from paying attention to people and taking a genuine interest in them. It's hardly the act of a kind of arrogant egotist that some try to portray him as.[94]

Smith 'made a study of remembering people's names'.[95] He was a 'master' at it,[96] and had a 'remarkable recall for detail'.[97] His memory was described as 'phenomenal'[98] and 'unique'.[99]

Fay Spencer marvelled: 'Our eldest daughter Shelley was born six weeks after we arrived in Tasmania, so Smith never actually knew her, but whenever we saw him

---

[93] Geoff Tunbridge. Interview with the author.
[94] Geoff Tunbridge. Interview with the author.
[95] Clyde Laidlaw. Interview with the author.
[96] Clyde Laidlaw. Interview with the author.
[97] Fay Spencer. Interview with the author.
[98] Ron Barassi and Hugh McPherson. Interview with the author.
[99] Hassa Mann. Interview with the author.

he would say: "How's Shelley?" He always remembered her name, even though he only saw her very occasionally'.[100]

Hugh McPherson was equally astonished by an after-match experience.

> A bloke came to me and asked: 'Do you think I'd be able to talk with Norm Smith? I haven't seen him in years.'
>
> I said: 'Yes, but just wait a little while because he's with the press at the moment'.
>
> When Norm came out, I said: 'Norm, there's a man here to see you who hasn't seen you for a long time'.
>
> Norm said: 'Well bring him in'.
>
> Norm looked at him closely and said: 'Now wait a minute. I met you in such-and-such a town about 30 years ago. You're so-and-so!'
>
> He was spot-on, and the chap was beaming.[101]

He also used his 'gift' to advantage in his coaching, particularly in his analysis of player performances. After a match, he could – and usually did – tell each of his players what they had done right and wrong (with an emphasis on the wrong) 'and he could do that for every player on both teams, which was a remarkable feat'.[102] He could actually 'remember every game, or parts of it, better than any of the players who took part in it'.[103] John Beckwith said: 'Norm had the best memory I've ever struck of anyone. He was a genius at remembering what happened, and I think that was his biggest forte as a coach'. Hassa Mann added: 'Norm didn't have to watch a video replay of a match because his recollection of incidents was virtually flawless. It might have been 1964 and he'd say: "Back in '59 you did this". That would annoy some players, but you could never argue with him or question him because he was never wrong.[104]

Even in the early 1970s, Smith could recall matches from his playing days 30-odd years earlier and recount the exact scores – not just the totals, but the goals and behinds recorded by each side, after each quarter.[105]

---

[100] Fay Spencer. Interview with the author.
[101] Hugh McPherson. Interview with the author.
[102] John Beckwith. Interview with the author.
[103] Brian Dixon, in *High Mark: The Complete Book on Australian Football*, 1964.
[104] Hassa Mann. Interview with the author.
[105] Ricky Quade. Interview with the author.

Aside from his friendship with *The Herald's* chief football reporter Alf Brown, Smith had an often prickly relationship with the media. But in the mid-1950s he came to trust a young radio commentator by the name of Mike Williamson, who grew up in the same street as Marj Smith. Norm Smith went generally out of his way to accommodate Williamson for interviews on training nights and after matches on 3AW. He nicknamed him 'Fearless', because he believed Williamson was afraid of everything.

Williamson's calling 'debut' was the Richmond-Melbourne clash at Punt Road in round one. He recounted how Smith made him feel at ease. 'I was in awe of it all and nervous as anything,' said Williamson, 'and as I walked into the Melbourne rooms after the game, Norm called me over. He then called over Noel McMahen and said: "Noel, this is young Michael's first match. Take him around and introduce him to all of the players". That was a great privilege and a great help, because there wouldn't have been many media people who were treated like that.'

On another occasion a year or two later, Williamson entered the Melbourne rooms to interview Smith after he had already refused several other interview requests. When Williamson approached him, Smith said: 'All right then, Fearless. I'd better talk to you, otherwise you'll get the sulks'.

But even Williamson had trouble at times in trying to get a comment out of the coach. 'He could be bloody difficult,' Williamson said. 'I soon worked out when not to approach him. If I saw the lips drawn together tightly to make a thin white line, and the red hair was standing up, you either waited until the volcano erupted and subsided, or you just didn't go near him. You learnt that the hard way.'[106]

🏉🏉🏉🏉🏉🏉🏉🏉🏉

Len Smith once again guided Fitzroy's under-19s side to the Grand Final in 1956. But this time, however, he had to settle for second-best.

The Lions had been disadvantaged by a draw between two other finalists, which delayed the staging of the Grand Final by a week. On the big day, Len's lads were outclassed by South Melbourne – 8.6 (54) to 4.10 (34). Despite the disappointment, the Fitzroy committee remained 'well satisfied' with their runner-up billing, and extended its 'warmest thanks' to Len for 'keeping our colours to the fore'.[107] Len's reputation was rising. Six of his players were promoted for their senior VFL debuts in 1956.

---

[106] Mike Williamson. Interview with the author.
[107] Fitzroy Football Club *Annual Report*, 1956.

THE FINEST MELBOURNE SIDE OF ALL [1956]

About this time, Len Smith started formulating what were to become his famous football coaching notes. Ron Barassi, who at the time was a junior colleague of Len's at Miller's ropeworks, believed Len spent many of his lunchbreaks committing his philosophies to paper. Barassi provided the following fascinating insight:

> Whenever I walked past Len during his lunchbreak, he was always writing and poring over notes. One day he called me over and said: 'Ronny, what do you think would be the quickest goal from the centre bounce?'
> I said: 'About 20 seconds or something'.
> He said: 'No, no, no – try seven-and-a-half seconds'.
> I said: '*Seven-and-a-half seconds?*'
> He said: 'Well, think about it. Time starts the instant the umpire bounces the ball, then it's knocked by a ruckman to a rover running past at top speed, and he kicks it almost immediately he is balanced, long towards the goalsquare where the full-forward rises above the pack and, rather than marking it, he knocks it down to a crumber, who kicks the goal. That should take about seven-and-a-half seconds'.
> I said: 'Hmm, yeah, fair enough'.
> Then Len said: 'Do you realise that it's possible to kick 700 goals in a game?'
> It wasn't likely, but theoretically possible, and that's what Len was all about: the possibilities of playing attacking football. His believed that the ball should never be stationary; it should be in motion at all times.[108]

Len Smith also challenged conventional wisdom with another of his theories, as Barassi explained:

> Len was the first coach to tell his players: 'When you've got the ball, you should be thinking of attack – even if you're in the backline, you are in charge of the game because you have the ball. You are the most important person on the ground in that split-second.' He was also one of the first coaches to sum up the game as: 'Freeze-frame film of a football match and you will get one of three scenarios: either we've got the ball, they've got the ball, or it's neutral.' How simply put. He then went further than that by listing all the things that players should do in each of those three situations. It was basic, common sense logic, but no-one else had gone to those lengths before to produce a document that was basically a how-to manual on playing football.[109]

---

[108] Ron Barassi. Interview with the author.
[109] Ron Barassi. Interview with the author.

15

THE SECOND HAT-TRICK

[1957]

It seemed inconceivable, yet, at the same time, highly understandable that Melbourne – the VFL powerhouse which had won 40 of its previous 46 matches – was being dismissed as a likely 'also-ran' in the lead-up to the 1957 season. The youthful Demons had suffered a mass exodus of experienced players – household names – who had been crucial to their success, and the club's brains trust now faced the supreme, dual challenge of somehow replacing these players while remaining among the VFL's upper echelon. But even Norm Smith conceded: 'I knew I would have a hard battle on my hands to go anywhere near winning the flag'.[1]

He believed: 'In order to win premierships, each year you need to bring five regular senior players into the team because that'll cover injuries and give you a continual build-up of players to create depth and competition for spots'.[2] In 1956, Melbourne had the luxury of a settled line-up, using just 27 players (including only three debutants) – five fewer than Essendon, and five fewer than the Demons had used themselves the previous season. The VFL average was 36. But in their transitional 1957 season, these figures would increase dramatically – 36 players and 13 debutants – as the Demons searched for the right mix.

Before the campaign began, Melbourne's committee, while acknowledging the monumental task in front of it, was enthusiastic about the immediate future, stating: 'We feel that with the development of many juniors over the past few years, we can look forward with confidence to 1957. Our recruiting has been of such a nature that already we have signed many outstanding players who, together

---

[1] *Melbourne Truth* series, 1962.
[2] Barry Bourke. Interview with the author.

with recruits from our Second and Third Eighteens, will contest the places vacant on our training list for 1957, so we can anticipate some sparkling and vigorous practice matches in 1957 and another good year'.[3]

The Demons made a bold statement when they announced their on-field leaders. John Beckwith, 24, was appointed captain, with Ron Barassi, who had just turned 21 on February 27, awarded the vice-captaincy. It was the youngest leadership duo in the competition. The Beckwith appointment was no surprise – 'Becky' was one of the most crafty defenders in the game – but Barassi's promotion had been unexpected. Although Barassi was the Demons' best and most inspirational player, and appeared certain to one day captain Melbourne, some felt his rise to the deputy's role – ahead of several more experienced teammates – was premature.

Nonetheless, Melbourne had selected a leadership duo to be reckoned with: young, fit, strong, mature beyond their years, recognised champions who were greatly respected by the entire football fraternity. Both would relish their roles. It said much about the Smith approach: he and his fellow selectors would place their faith in the club's youth.

Despite Barassi's relative youth, he was maturing rapidly. Before the start of the season, Barassi had left the Smith house after marrying Nancy Kellett, a fellow Miller's ropeworks employee he had met in 1953. Barassi said: 'I did some of my courting in Norm's yellowy-cream coloured van. It was home-made and it looked like it too. My future father-in-law wasn't too impressed when I turned up!'

Barassi remained grateful for the four years he lived with the Smiths. He said: 'I was so very privileged to have spent such an important chapter of my life, my formative years, both as a footballer and a person, from being a young man into adulthood, with such upstanding people. It provided me with a great foundation for whatever life threw at me from that point on.'[4]

Smith admired the fact that Barassi didn't wait for life to throw things at him. He said: 'This drive, this desire to improve himself on and off the field was always there… As a young man, he invested £300 in a rotary hoe and became a landscape gardener in his spare time. Bear in mind he still had his regular job and was studying electrical engineering at night school at the same time. But he'd go out and work hard. He'd make lawns and, while I don't know if they all came up, it showed that he had the drive and the initiative to do things on his own'.[5]

---

[3] Melbourne Football Club *Annual Report*, 1956.
[4] Ron Barassi. Interview with the author.
[5] *The Sun* series, 1967.

While Barassi was an in-your-face personality – both on and off the field – Beckwith was more subtle in approach. The new skipper said:

> The main advice Norm gave me was: 'Be yourself, play your own game, and make sure you vote for whatever I vote for in selection!' His reasoning was: 'You should always vote with me because I'm the coach and I'd like to have the team I want. I'd rather succeed or fail on what I want'.
>
> I said: 'OK Norm'. I went along with him most of the time because it was Norm's team and he was a very clever judge of football, although we argued on a couple of occasions. I voted against him only two or three times but it didn't matter because he had the numbers anyway.
>
> Although there were only five of us voting, Ivor Warne-Smith's habit was to jump in early and declare what he wanted. He and Norm clashed a bit in selection meetings. I quickly learnt that unless I jumped in early and said: 'I reckon we should select so-and-so', I'd finish up with the casting vote. I was just the captain; I didn't want that pressure. But most of the time the team picked itself anyway, because we had a lot of good players playing well and usually we only squabbled over the 19th and 20th men. You had to pick versatile players because if you got an injury you had to fill it up somehow. We usually went for a big bloke and a little bloke.[6]

To have been a fly on the wall in such meetings would have been an enlightening experience, as four members of Melbourne's five-man selection committee – Smith, Beckwith, Warne-Smith and 'Checker' Hughes – had either captained or coached the club. The fifth selector, Harry Long, had been vice-captain in 1934.

Interestingly, Smith didn't select players on their best games; he selected them on their worst games.[7] The 'better' the worst game, the better chance a player had of being picked. The team would always be guaranteed a minimum level of output.

In the tense selection-table environment, Beckwith became closely acquainted with some of his coach's preferences. 'Norm liked having players turning inboard onto their natural foot,' he said. 'If blokes are turning outwards, you're almost invariably trying to kick goals from out near the boundary, so he was very smart with some of his positioning. He'd have Geoff Tunbridge, a left-footer, on the right half-forward flank so that when Geoff got the ball, he'd turn inboard and the ball would always be coming back into the corridor rather than being kicked wide. 'Big Bob' Johnson was a left-footer as well, so Norm played him

---

[6] John Beckwith. Interview with the author.
[7] Terry Gleeson. Interview with the author.

in the right forward pocket for the same reason. It always had the opposition under pressure.'[8]

Smith had identified another left-footer, Clyde Laidlaw, as a potential successor to the role of centreman, which was left vacant by the departure of Ken Melville. The other candidate was Laurie Mithen. The pair fiercely contested each other for the coveted role in the pre-season, before Smith told Laidlaw: 'You've done well, but I want Laurie to play in the centre. We'll keep you at centre half-forward'.[9]

Melbourne wasn't able to 'keep' Laidlaw at all. After working several dead-end jobs, the bullocking centre half-forward finally landed a job in his chosen field, as a dental technician, in Warracknabeal, 331 kilometres north-west of Melbourne. Laidlaw became the seventh player from the 1956 premiership side to leave the club. It would be only a temporary departure, but he would miss virtually the entire 1957 season.

The remaining vacancies in the Melbourne line-up were adequately filled. Denis Cordner's ruck spot was shared by the likes of Big Bob Johnson, newcomer Dick Fenton-Smith and Terry Gleeson; Stuart Spencer's roving role was alternated between Ian Ridley and Bluey Adams; Noel McMahen's position at half-back was taken by another hard man, Ian Thorogood; while John Lord replaced Geoff McGivern at centre half-back. 'Players just slotted in,' Bluey Adams said. Laidlaw, however, would remain a huge loss at centre half-forward.

Part of the reason the new players quickly found niches was the willingness of established players to welcome them into the fold. Fenton-Smith said: 'A lot of the players who came up into the senior side in 1957 were players who had been groomed from the junior ranks. Players like Dennis Jones, Thorogood, Lord, etc. They had a friendly *esprit de corps* that Geoff Tunbridge and I weren't in because we'd just arrived, but they made us feel enormously welcome. You felt part of the team right from the first practice game. The great atmosphere at Melbourne at the time oozed confidence and strength. We were a very close, happy family.'[10]

Ian Ridley attributes such attitudes to the influence of Norm Smith. 'Norm was a great gatherer of people,' Ridley said. 'He had a great skill in bringing new players to the club and making them feel at home, and also having the other players accept them. He bonded us tightly, which came from being together so much off the field. He felt that if you knew each other well and spent that time together, you'd automatically know what your mate would do out on the field, and you'd help each other without even thinking about it. It was a pretty sound philosophy'.[11]

---

[8] John Beckwith. Interview with the author.
[9] Clyde Laidlaw. Interview with the author.
[10] Dick Fenton-Smith. Interview with the author.
[11] Ian Ridley. Interview with the author.

YYYYYYYYY

The doomsayers appeared vindicated, and the Demon faithful's worst fears materialised, when the reigning premier suffered a shock round one defeat to Fitzroy (which had finished eighth in 1956) at the Brunswick Street Oval.

In a 'wildly exciting finish',[12] the Demons succumbed to the Bill Stephen-led Lions by three points. It was a monumental boilover. When the final siren sounded, Fitzroy fans 'ripped the roof off the old grandstand'[13] and chaired Stephen off.

In the rooms shortly afterwards, Smith made a speech, which 'brought the house down'.[14] His most memorable words were saved for Stephen. 'Little Bill... my apprentice,' Smith said with pride. 'Congratulations on beating the master'.[15]

Stephen, who regarded it as a moment of pride, later said: 'It wasn't an egotistical remark from Norm, because he would never seriously refer to himself as the master, or imply that he was superior. He would have said it laughing his head off'.[16]

But the loss was no laughing matter for the Demon coach. It merely confirmed in his – and everybody else's – mind the arduous journey ahead for the Demons if they were to seriously challenge for a hat-trick of premierships.

The situation became more dicey when Melbourne 'slumped' to a 4-3 record. Despite stirring wins over Collingwood (by eight points) and rising power Essendon (by 45 points), the Demons unexpectedly dropped matches to an improving Hawthorn (by 18 points at Glenferrie Oval, after being outscored 4.6 to just 1.3 in the second half) and middle-of-the-road Richmond (by two points, without Big Bob Johnson and after kicking 0.8 in the third term). Although Smith acknowledged that the stuttering start had only 'emphasised' his belief that the Demons faced a hard road to success, he enthused: 'Our new players were gaining experience and combining well'.[17]

Steadily, things started to click. The Demons regained confidence with a stirring victory over eventual finalist Carlton at Princes Park. The Demons had trailed by two points at the final change but stormed home with six goals to one to win by

---

[12] *The Football Record*, April 27, 1957.
[13] *The Football Record*, April 27, 1957.
[14] *The Football Record*, April 27, 1957.
[15] Hugh McPherson. Interview with the author.
[16] Bill Stephen. Interview with the author.
[17] *Melbourne Truth* series, 1962.

28 points. This sparked a five-game winning streak (by an average margin of 48 points), which restored the natural order – Melbourne was back on top.

The newcomers were making their mark and a host of established players like Athol Webb were enjoying career-best seasons. After 12 rounds, Webb had kicked 36 goals – not outlandish by anyone's standards, but certainly an impressive tally considering his selfless role in Smith's forward system. (The next best Demons were Barassi 19, Tunbridge 18, Fenton-Smith 16, Ridley 15, and Big Bob Johnson 12.) In the 10-goal drubbing of Geelong at the MCG in round nine, Webb had bagged a career-best 8.2 from 12 shots. He recalled an interesting observation Smith made about his on-field relationship with Geoff Tunbridge.

> One day Norm told me: 'Tunbridge is making you'.
>
> I said: 'Tunbridge?' I wasn't sure if I'd heard right because Geoff Tunbridge was a terrible kick. We called him 'Heinz 57 Varieties' because no-one knew where he was going to kick it! But Smithy said: 'Yeah, that's right – Tunbridge. No-one knows where it's going, but you're quick enough to get there first!'[18]

A newcomer who was making an impact in more ways than one was John Lord. After being best-afield and taking 20-plus marks in two reserves finals the previous season, Lord immediately became a key member of the Demon line-up at centre half-back. But he had the capacity to both frustrate and delight his coach. Lord recalled an exchange he had with Smith in the rooms before the round 10 win over North Melbourne at Arden Street.

> I was a bit short in the concentration department, and I didn't think much about a game before I got out onto the ground. All I needed to know was which way to kick. This particular day Norm had me on my own in a corner and was laying down the law on my lack of concentration and pre-match thought. As he was reaching his peak, he looked down and saw me pulling on *black* shorts. What a dopey thing to be doing! In those days, every club wore black shorts for home games and *white* shorts for away games.
>
> Norm blew up. He pointed at my shorts – 'Look at them! Look at them!'
>
> He stormed away and called for Jim Cardwell. He threw his hands in the air and said: 'It's no good! It's no good! I give up!'[19]

---

[18] Athol Webb. Interview with the author.
[19] John Lord. Interview with the author.

That afternoon, the entire Melbourne side appeared to lack concentration, with the Kangaroos leading by 13 points at the final change, before the Demons blew them away with an eight-goal to one last quarter to win by 31 points.

In round 12, the Demons exacted revenge on Fitzroy and Smith's 'little apprentice', Bill Stephen. At half-time in the MCG fixture, Melbourne led by 67 points – 15.7(97) to 4.6 (30) – and eventually cruised to an 84-point win. It probably wasn't the ideal preparation for the following round's tough encounter with Collingwood at Victoria Park. The Demons had a tough day – they were lucky to escape with a draw after Ian Ridley snapped truly in time-on – but perhaps none had it tougher than Dick Fenton-Smith. For several weeks, the former Ormond Amateurs ruckman was played at centre half-forward, with some success – he had performed well on St Kilda champion Neil Roberts in round five. Fenton-Smith said: 'The main thing Norm wanted from his forwards, especially big blokes like myself and 'Big Bob' Johnson, was to be in front because they'll give you a free kick sooner or later because they'll have to clamber over you'.[20] The Magpies clambered over Fenton-Smith's pride. He said:

> Little Ron Kingston played on me – he was six inches shorter than me – but he gave me a bath. I didn't touch the ball in the first three quarters. Early in the last quarter, Smithy took me off. Boy, did I feel humiliated. I had to walk from one end of the ground to the other, around the boundary, and they hit me with orange peel and Coca-Cola cans.
>
> Afterwards, Smithy came up to me in the rooms and I was sitting there and I'm sure I was bawling my eyes out in shame. But he put his arm around me and stuck a bottle of beer under my chin and a glass in my hand and said: 'Well, Dick, it wasn't a great day. That's three weeks'. That was the going penalty for a bad game. He was a stern disciplinarian. If you mucked something up, you could expect to get it between the eyes. And fair enough too.[21]

Smith was also wary of the Collingwood army. Hugh McPherson said:

> Before the game, Norm said that if we won he wouldn't go over to the Collingwood rooms, but if we lost he would. When the game ended as a draw, Norm asked me: 'What should we do, Hughie?'
>
> I said: 'We should still go into their rooms'.

---

[20] Dick Fenton-Smith. Interview with the author.
[21] Dick Fenton-Smith. Interview with the author.

We pushed through the crowd to get to Phonse Kyne and when we reached him, Norm put out his hand and said: 'Phonse, that was a good game'.

Phonse replied: 'Good game, be buggered! We were robbed!'

Phonse was filthy about it. Like most Collingwood people in the room, he thought they'd been hard-done-by with the umpiring. Norm couldn't stand that attitude. He believed that once the game was fought and decided, you should shake hands with the opposition and mix with them. So after he spoke briefly with Phonse, he thought it was a good time to leave, and so did I.[22]

About this time, Norm Smith made one of his most puzzling selections. Full-back Peter Marquis had represented Victoria with distinction against Western Australia in Perth. In his absence, Smith replaced him with half-back flanker Keith Carroll. When Marquis returned from interstate duties, he naturally assumed he would slot straight back into his usual position. But Smith surprised Marquis and perhaps the entire football fraternity by telling him: 'Keith Carroll did very well, and I like him as a full-back – he's a bit more mobile than you – so we'll start you on the bench'.[23] Marquis later quipped that it was 'not a bad kick in the pants for a bloke who was supposed to be the best full-back in Victoria!'[24] Marquis quickly resumed at full-back, but the issue was always a source of amusement for Marquis and Carroll. Carroll said: 'He would rubbish me about it. Every time he tore a thigh muscle, I'd say: "How is it?" And he'd say: "You don't care!"'[25]

The Demons faced another big test against an impressive Essendon at Windy Hill in round 14, and this time they conquered in controversial circumstances. With the Demons five points down and deep in attack with just seconds left in the match, Bomber rover Stan Booth was penalised for a deliberate out-of-bounds. From the resultant free kick, Athol Webb somehow threaded his third goal to give Melbourne a one-point win. In an amazingly even season, it was to be a crucial victory. From an Essendon standpoint, the uproar didn't end there. Although the media present and the umpiring fraternity believed that umpire Frank Schwab[26] had paid the correct decision, incensed Essendon fans were adamant Schwab had simply moved to appease Norm Smith. The Melbourne bench had been within close proximity to the incident, and Smith had jumped up and appealed for a free

---

[22] Hugh McPherson. Interview with the author.
[23] Clyde Laidlaw. Interview with the author.
[24] Hobbs, Greg, *125 Years of the Demons 1858-1983*, Progress Press Group, 1984.
[25] Keith Carroll. Interview with the author.
[26] Frank Schwab was a brother of subsequent AFL executive commissioner Alan Schwab, and the father of Hawthorn premiership player Peter Schwab.

kick. The 'violently hostile' crowd[27] hurled abuse and missiles at Schwab, who required a police escort to leave the ground.

Smith had his own problem with an umpire – Bill Barbour – in the round 16 game against St Kilda at the Junction Oval.[28] Smith later regarded the incident as 'one of my funniest memories', but conceded: 'I wasn't in a laughing mood when it happened, and I don't suppose Bill was too pleased either'.[29] Smith recalled:

> There was a dust-up right in front of the coach's box. I'd been troubled by indigestion all day, which didn't make my mood any better, and when I sprang to my feet I cracked my head a beauty on the roof of the box. Well, that finished things. I shouted to Barassi to go back to the centre and Peter Marquis to get to full-back. Then I roared to the umpire: 'And you bounce the so-and-so ball, Bill!'
> Bill was so upset... by all that was going on, he did bounce it too. Probably as a result, he was dropped next week.[30]

Smith respected certain umpires – 'In my time,' he said, 'Harry Beitzel, Allan Nash, Jack Irving and Jeff Crouch have been the tops... The virtue they all had in common was the low number of free kicks they awarded. They allowed the game to flow, and this is very important'[31] – but they generally weren't his favourite people. He disliked the 'dramatics' and 'histrionics' of some umpires and thought they should be 'less obtrusive'.[32]

Ian Ridley said: 'I think Norm was pretty typical of coaches at the time – they rarely thought they were getting a fair go. A common saying would be: "Bloody umpires!" Smithy thought they were hopeless. He was very rarely happy with them.'[33]

Terry Gleeson recalled:

> Norm reckoned: 'There should be a tunnel out to the middle and the umpire should come out through a chute and do his job and when the game was over he would just disappear down the tunnel'.

---

[27] *The Sun*, July 29, 1957.
[28] Melbourne won 6.13 (49) to St Kilda's paltry 1.5 (11), which remains the Saints' lowest score against the Demons. Amazingly, though, it is not among the 36 lowest scores in AFL history.
[29] *The Sun* series, 1967.
[30] *The Sun* series, 1967.
[31] *The Sun* series, 1967.
[32] Alf Brown, *The Herald*, 1958
[33] Ian Ridley. Interview with the author.

He absolutely despised it when he felt that umpires got carried away with themselves and thought they were as important as the players. He reckoned some umpires carried on as though the spectators had come to watch them perform instead of the players. Norm felt that they were only there to enforce the rules, nothing more. He progressively became more intolerant towards them.[34]

He didn't hide from the fact he had been prone to reacting aggressively towards the men in white, openly admitting: 'I ... had my share of blow-ups with umpires... These were heat-of-the-moment outbursts, something that happens when you're het up during a game... Most of my boundary outbursts at umpires have been caused by frustration and irritation over differing interpretations of the rules'.[35]

A typical Norm Smith response to what he viewed as a poor umpiring decision was: 'Give us a go! Just give us 50/50!' At one point, the Demons became so disillusioned with what they perceived as an umpiring bias against them that Smith asked umpire Alan Nash to talk to his players. Nash emphasised to the Demons: 'You're a lot faster than most teams and you tackle more, therefore you're going to make more mistakes with your tackling'. The Demons accepted the explanation, and Smith told his players in part-jest: 'If we've got the ball, we won't have to worry about tackling!'

But there were certain things he could not accept from the men in white. Ron Brophy, 'a real larrikin umpire',[36] once said that while Smith was vigorously disputing one of his decisions, he ran towards him and said: 'Get stuffed Smithy!'

This shocked and further angered Smith, who stood up and said: 'You can't say that! I'll have you reported!'[37]

A similar instance involved umpire Jack Irving. Smith was 'abusing Irving for all he was worth', and Irving responded by giving him the thumbs-up sign. Smith was indignant. 'I want him reported to the League! Umpires shouldn't do that!'[38]

There was also an occasion at an after-match gathering when he allowed his frustration with the umpiring fraternity boil over into a regrettable, although mildly humorous confrontation. Ian Ridley observed:

> Smithy was having trouble with an umpire and an umpires' advisor. Over drinks, they were having a ding-dong argument, and it became so heated that Norm leant

---

[34] Terry Gleeson. Interview with the author.
[35] *The Sun* series, 1967.
[36] Keith Carroll. Interview with the author.
[37] Keith Carroll. Interview with the author.
[38] *The Age*, July 30, 1973.

over, grabbed the umpires' coach by the nose – with fingers that were bent and twisted to buggery – and shook it quite vigorously. He said: 'Now you listen to me, you bastard!' Of course, that didn't exactly endear him to umpires after that![39]

On one occasion, Smith was so upset with the performance of a particular umpire that he wanted him barred from the after-match function. He told Jim Cardwell in no uncertain terms: 'Don't you dare let him in!'
Cardwell replied: 'You can't do that, Norm; he's an umpire'.
Smith threatened: 'Well if you let him in, I'll throw the bugger out!'
There were, however, umpires he treated with genuine warmth. One such umpire was Harry Beitzel, who had officiated in the 1955 Grand Final. Beitzel said:

> Norm Smith was one of the first coaches who gave me a big thrill as an umpire. In the rooms before a game in the early fifties, he told his players, while I was standing there: 'Don't ever argue with this umpire. Trust him, and don't waste your bloody time staging for free kicks because here's a bloke who's fair dinkum'.
>
> I never had any problems with Norm trying to influence me on how to umpire, aside from what you would call the odd robust debate, which is a healthy thing. In fact, I feel that Norm made it easy for umpires like me. Some of my umpiring colleagues were paying 60 or 70 free kicks, whereas I'd pay about 20 for the day. The reason was that he had instructed his players: 'Don't test this umpire. Don't try to put something over him because he'll take no notice of it. There's no home-ground in him as an umpire'.[40]

By this stage, various sections of the football fraternity were suggesting – as they had during Melbourne's golden years of 1939-41 – that the Demons had an unfair advantage in being able to play finals at their home ground. But Smith hit back, saying that such critics 'should remember that the ground to us is merely a place where we do hard work. The other sides must get a greater lift than we do in playing in the MCG atmosphere'. And, 'as for the crowd, it is usually anti-Melbourne round most of the outer'.[41]
The Demons appeared to have lost their air of invincibility anyway, suffering shock defeats to Hawthorn (by seven points) and the lowly South Melbourne (four

---

[39] Ian Ridley. Interview with the author.
[40] Harry Beitzel. Interview with the author.
[41] Newspaper report, 1965.

points) in rounds 15 and 17 respectively. The loss to the Hawks was of particular concern. The Demons had led by four points in time-on, but allowed the Hawks to kick two goals against the breeze and snatch victory. For the second time that season, the Demons had been toppled by Hawthorn, a potential opponent in the finals. But the loss to second-bottom South Melbourne at the Lake Oval was far worse. The Demons trailed by 18 points at half-time, and led by eight at the last change but were again over-run in the final term.

A 49-point win over Richmond in round 18 restored some faith, and sealed top spot on the ladder by one-and-a-half games. The Demons had won their third consecutive minor premiership, but this time with a moderate tally of 12 wins, six losses (by an average of eight points, with the biggest defeat being by 18 points) and a draw. In the 87 VFL seasons that have comprised at least 18 rounds, it is the worst record by a minor premier. Just seven games separated the Demons and bottom side Geelong.

The Demons prepared for the second semi-final clash with Essendon justifiably confident in the knowledge they had beaten the Bombers twice during the season. Their confidence was shared by the experts, who almost unanimously tipped the Demons to win. The Demons were on track when they led by seven points at quarter-time, but they, like everyone else, were in for 'one hell of a shock'.[42] The Bombers responded with a second term blast of 9.3 to 0.2 to open up a 48-point lead.

Roused by an impromptu rendition of *A Grand Old Flag* initiated by skipper John Beckwith during the interval, the Demons bombarded the goalfront, kicking 4.10 to 1.3 in the third term to slash the margin to 23 points. They continued to keep the Bomber defence under siege in the final term to reduce the deficit to just 10 points with 10 minutes left. An Essendon goal steadied the underdogs and they went on to record a special 16-point victory.

Melbourne would play a total of seven second semi-finals under Norm Smith, but this would be its only loss.

The attitude of the Demons before the match, and during the first half, had been a concern. At the time, Beckwith admitted that they had taken the Bombers lightly[43] – a fact of which their coach was acutely aware. Smith commented later: 'Perhaps we were a little over-confident'.[44]

Beckwith believed Smith contributed to the loss with a poor positional move.

---

[42] Ian Ridley. Interview with the author.
[43] John Beckwith, *The Sun*, September 20, 1957
[44] *Melbourne Truth* series, 1962.

Part of the reason we played so badly in the first half was that we didn't have players in the right spots. That was actually Norm's fault because he had an obsession with having a big centre-half forward. Earlier in the year, when we were due to play Hawthorn at Glenferrie Oval, Norm said at selection committee: "We've got to get a bigger centre-half forward". He decided he wanted to move Big Bob Johnson from the forward pocket and put him at centre-half forward. Bob played well, largely because Glenferrie Oval was such a small ground and play virtually had to be channelled through him. Smithy was also keen on having Bob at centre-half forward in the second semi. But it didn't work. Bob was a quick player against the ruckman but he wasn't quick against the centre-half back. We were also badly beaten in the ruck – Geoff Leek had a field day kicking three goals. Then Norm decided to put Bob back in the ruck and the pocket, and swing Trevor Johnson to centre-half forward and that worked much better. Trevor was a good workhorse, unobtrusive, very strong, played in front and had a good pair of hands.[45]

Although the second semi-final loss had been 'a huge kick up the backside'[46] for the Demons, Beckwith also regarded it as 'the best thing that ever happened because suddenly we had to regroup, (and) we weren't the favourites'.[47]

The Demons were, however, heavily favoured to defeat Hawthorn in the preliminary final – a game that showcased the tactical genius of Norm Smith. The Hawks held high hopes of making their first Grand Final after winning five of their previous six matches, including their first finals victory – by 23 points over Carlton in the first semi-final, a match played in driving hail.

In the committee room after training on the Thursday night, Smith conducted a memorable team meeting – his version of a 'council of war'. He later said: 'I had a few stern words with the boys that week. They had not played their best football (against Essendon) and I demanded they do better against Hawthorn – or else'.[48]

Smith enlightened – and incited – his players with Hawk coach Jack Hale's lowly opinion of them.

'Hale is saying that you're a pack of bloody jibs,' he said, challenging his team to explode the theory.[49]

---

[45] John Beckwith. Interview with the author.
[46] Ian Ridley. Interview with the author.
[47] John Beckwith, on the *Red and Blue* documentary.
[48] *Melbourne Truth* series, 1962.
[49] Keith Carroll. Interview with the author.

He then spoke of each player's specific role and revealed several tactics that ultimately went a long way towards sealing Hawthorn's fate. Much of Smith's pre-match planning was devised after gaining access, for the first time, to film of their loss to Hawthorn in round 15. A key focus of the film analysis – which took place in a little theatrette in Jolimont, just a couple of drop-kicks from the MCG – was finding a way to nullify Hawthorn's successful ruck strategy in which captain John Kennedy would wrestle the opposing ruckman and enable his ruck partner, the high-leaping Maurie Young, to punch the ball forward or take possession unopposed. Smith's counter ploy was to have tall defender Colin Wilson block Young or, at the very least, ensure he didn't monopolise ruck duels. This necessitated a positional move that shocked everyone. Barassi recalled:

> I got to the ground and Norm told me: 'You're opening up in the forward pocket, Ron.' I said: 'Oh, OK'. I was disappointed not to be starting on the ball, especially as there was no explanation. It was like I'd been demoted. But that wasn't the case. Norm was very open to change, even with a player like myself who was more or less a permanent fixture as a ruck-rover, and vice-captain in this cut-throat final.[50]

The result was that Kennedy – who had won a club record four best-and-fairest awards – had such little influence on the match that he was actually given Bronx cheers by his success-starved supporters, while Wilson was one of the Demons' best players. Of course, it helped Melbourne's cause when Kennedy broke his hand early in the match.

Smith had also identified Hawthorn half-forward flanker Graham Arthur as a major threat, and assigned Keith Carroll the task of stopping him. Carroll said:

> In the team talk, Norm told me: 'Graham Arthur makes a big swing around the pack, so if he's ahead of you, let him go, but cut across the back of the pack hard and you'll catch up with him on the other side as he's straightening up'. Well, you wouldn't believe it, in the first 30 seconds of the game the ball came out and Graham Arthur grabbed it and I let him swing around the pack and by that time I was running flat out around the other side and, just as he was about to kick, collected him with everything I had. He went down, but he jumped up and threw a couple of punches at me and I got a free kick. I'd corked his thigh. I mentioned it to him a few years ago and he said: 'I'm still limping!' That was Norm's genius.[51]

---

[50] Ron Barassi. Interview with the author.
[51] Keith Carroll. Interview with the author.

Smith's other memorable words of advice before the preliminary final were delivered to his two rovers, Bluey Adams and Ian Ridley, who changed in the forward pocket on quality Hawthorn defender Alf Hughes. That year, Hughes won Hawthorn's best-and-fairest and represented Victoria and had thrashed both Demon small men, not only depriving them of the ball as they alternated between him and roving duties, but continually winning the ball. Ridley was to start the preliminary final in a forward pocket and Smith told him: 'You played too close to goal last time; you've got to get 60 yards out, around the boundary, because you'll out-run him'. Meanwhile, he instructed Adams: 'When you're resting in the pocket, don't position yourself next to the goalsquare, position yourself on the boundary line, and you'll take Hughes right out of it'. Both ploys worked. Hughes 'couldn't get a sniff of it'[52] and the Melbourne rovers kicked five goals between them: Adams three and Ridley two.

Although the Hawks restricted Melbourne's use of a strong breeze in the early going, prompting Beckwith to fret: 'Oh god, we're in trouble here', the Demons exploded with seven goals to three against the wind in the second term en route to a 68-point demolition. The Demons kicked 22 goals, just their third tally of 20-plus for the season, and had eight multiple goalscorers. As Smith later observed: 'Hawthorn must have wondered what struck them'.[53]

▼▼▼▼▼▼▼▼

John Beckwith could hardly move, let alone run, yet Norm Smith and his fellow selectors were asking him to lead Melbourne in the 1957 Grand Final.

The Melbourne captain, who had been one of the Demons' few good players in the second semi-final loss, had torn a groin muscle during the preliminary final and left the field late in the game. In the days afterwards, Beckwith had barely managed to hobble. He had sought treatment from various 'faith healers' in the faint hope he might recover in time, but had written himself off as 'a hopeless case' and virtually resigned himself to watching the Grand Final from the sidelines.[54]

But to Smith and his selection committee, it was simply incomprehensible that their young side could enter a Grand Final without its inspirational skipper – a man who was rarely, if ever, beaten. They asked Beckwith to at least attempt to run a few laps on the Thursday night. Beckwith agreed, but thought it was pointless.

---

[52] Ian Ridley. Interview with the author.
[53] *Melbourne Truth* series, 1962.
[54] John Beckwith. Interview with the author.

He ran a few stop-start laps interrupted by bouts of intense pain, which reinforced his opinion that he was 'no chance'.[55] He was given a final, secret fitness test at 10am on game-day at the Albert Ground, under the eyes of the selectors and the club doctor, Dr Don Duffy. Bluey Adams was also under scrutiny with a knee injury.

For about 30 minutes, Beckwith and Adams were put through their paces and were asked to kick varying distances. Beckwith was 'pretty restricted' and almost ready to rule himself out. But his coach and doctor had other ideas.

'Look,' Smith told Beckwith, 'if you don't play, it'll be a huge psychological hit to the team.'

Dr Duffy added: 'If I give you pain-killing injections before the game and at half-time, I think you might get through the game.'

Beckwith nodded: 'OK'.

'Now Becky,' Smith said, 'you realise the consequences, don't you?'

Beckwith said: 'Well, I'm happy to give it a go if you are'.

Adams also scraped through the fitness test.

The Demons' injury problems, combined with their poor showing against the Bombers in their previous meeting, prompted as many experts to tip Essendon as tipped Melbourne. Smith sensed: 'Essendon were still feeling pretty chirpy and felt confident'. He planned to use their confidence, and his own side's recent humiliation, to the Demons' advantage. 'I gave the team a warm-up blast,' he said, 'reminding them of their blunderings in the previous game against Essendon.'[56] The effect was that the cockiness that had proved so detrimental to the Demons in the second semi-final had been replaced by an overwhelming resolve to make amends. They ran onto the field with 'minds like steel-traps'.[57]

Before the players took their positions in front of a near-capacity crowd of 100,324, the Bombers gathered around their retiring captain Bill Hutchison and gave him three cheers. The party-poopers would be the Demons, who had been stung into a frenzy by their loss to the Bombers a fortnight earlier. Smith later noted that his team 'went out as though they only had a few minutes to win the match'.[58] Barassi kicked the first goal within 16 seconds, and Melbourne, kicking into a breeze, raced to a 23-point lead by quarter-time. Smith believed: 'The result was never in doubt from then on'.[59]

---

[55] John Beckwith. Interview with the author.
[56] *Melbourne Truth* series, 1962.
[57] Ian Ridley. Interview with the author.
[58] *Melbourne Truth* series, 1962.
[59] *Melbourne Truth* series, 1962.

Although the Demons blazed six successive behinds in the second term, Barassi kicked four of Melbourne's nine first-half goals to take a 35-point advantage into half-time. But Smith was far from satisfied with his 20-year-old centre half-back, John Lord, appearing in just his second final. Lord recalled:

> I'd missed the second semi-final with a bruised heel, and carried it into the Grand Final and re-bruised it early on. I battled on until half-time hoping I could get some padding, or a needle, or some bloody thing to make it easier to run and jump on in the second half. I thought I'd been going OK though. I rushed in at half-time with a great relief and started reefing off my boot to get some treatment. I had my head down and Norm came up to me and blasted me: 'You're giving away too many free kicks!'
>
> With that, I burst out howling - *uncontrollable* howling - out of frustration, and a bit of pain, but feeling totally unappreciated for playing on with the bruise, which Norm would not have had any idea about. But if you have a key-position player howling his eyes out at half-time of a Grand Final and looking like he's going to completely cave in, maybe you have a problem. And we'd already lost a player *(Keith Carroll injured a thigh and was replaced by Ian Thorogood in the second quarter)*, so we couldn't afford to lose another.[60]

Typically, after Smith had delivered such a blast, he would walk past Cardwell and say: 'Now it's your turn, Jimmy. Go and pick up the pieces'.[61] They were a classic good-cop/bad-cop combination. Cardwell was 'Norm's greatest apologist'. He would almost habitually say: 'You know what Norm's like, boys. He only wants the best for you'.[62] And in the case of John Lord, this is exactly what happened. Cardwell, the great pacifier and rejuvenator of players' spirits, ushered Lord into the medical room to 'console and placate' him.[63] Lord continued:

> I was almost inconsolable and hurting and Jim came over to soothe the wounds. I was hostile, in a hysterical kind of way. I was determined that: 'There's no way that redheaded bastard is getting me off the ground!' I think Jim misheard me. He must have thought I'd said I *wanted* to come off the ground, because he said: 'I'll give you 10 shillings for every kick you get after half-time'. I didn't need that kind

---

[60] John Lord. Interview with the author.
[61] Ian Thorogood. Interview with the author.
[62] Frank 'Bluey' Adams. Interview with the author.
[63] John Lord. Interview with the author.

of incentive, but the offer was made nonetheless. I got back on the ground and played OK.[64]

'OK' translated to playing 'like a man possessed'.[65] And Lord continually reminded Cardwell of his financial obligation, signalling with his fingers how much he was owed. Hugh McPherson observed: 'Just shows what a bit of "bull psychology" can do'.[66] In the end, Cardwell handed over £6 to Lord. Smith was well satisfied, believing his spray had worked, but was upset to learn of Cardwell's offer. Smith thought: 'Did he do it for me, or for the money?'[67]

Lord admitted: 'I was a crier – I wore my heart on my sleeve – so Norm saw me as a big softy. Everything was forgiven, but I'm sure I frustrated him'.[68]

Regardless, Lord was among the Demons' top five players in a resounding 61-point win. Despite losing the free kick count 28-12, Melbourne had more than doubled Essendon's score – 17.14 (116) to 7.13 (55). When the siren sounded, Smith and Hugh McPherson, in a rare public display of joy, leapt off the bench in unison and threw their hands into the air. Melbourne had created history by becoming the first club to win three successive flags twice, and Norm Smith became – and remains – the only man to have been part of two hat-tricks. It was just the fourth instance of a premiership hat-trick in VFL history.[69]

Demon skipper Beckwith and Adams 'justified the risk taken and contributed to the team effort',[70] with Beckwith particularly prominent with 17 kicks and six marks. He became the Demons' sixth premiership captain and remained grateful to Smith, the selectors and Don Duffy for making it possible. Beckwith said: 'Norm took a big risk with me that day. If I'd played badly, or broken down, and we'd lost, his name would have been mud. He really stuck his neck out. I was lucky enough to captain my first premiership, but I wouldn't have done it if it hadn't been for Don Duffy's treatment and Norm's insistence. But it could easily have been the greatest shemozzle of all time. Thankfully, it didn't backfire on us.'[71]

---

[64] John Lord. Interview with the author.
[65] Hugh McPherson. Interview with the author.
[66] Hugh McPherson. Interview with the author.
[67] Hassa Mann in an interview with the author.
[68] John Lord. Interview with the author.
[69] Carlton won three premierships in a row in 1906-07-08; Collingwood won four on the trot in 1927-28-29-30, and Melbourne, of course, achieved the same distinction in 1939-40-41. Since Melbourne's 1955-56-57 triple treat, there has been just one such instance – the Brisbane Lions in 2001-02-03.
[70] Percy Beames, *The Age*, Monday September 23, 1957.
[71] John Beckwith. Interview with the author.

In *The Age*, Percy Beames predicted doom for rival clubs, at least in the short-term, with the Demons expected to improve further. 'Having lost the opportunity to pull Melbourne from its perch in its "vulnerable" season,' Beames wrote, 'other teams will find it even harder in the immediate future. It is not unreasonable to believe that greater strength than in 1955 and 1956 can be developed. If it is, there is no telling when Melbourne's premiership run will end.'[72]

Melbourne's premiership dinner at the MCG was 'a noisy, happy, anything-goes affair'[73] in which guests ate what was now traditional red-and-blue ice cream.

One of the first to make a speech was Ron Barassi. Barassi had produced what he always regarded as one of his greatest performances to be easily best-on-ground with 24 kicks, six marks, five handballs and 5.2. (It was only the second time Barassi had kicked five goals in a VFL match.) In his heart-felt address to the gathering, Barassi referred to Norm Smith as 'The Prince of Coaches', but quickly upgraded it to 'The King of Coaches'. The Melbourne vice-captain, remarkably still just 21, directed further praise Smith's way, announcing: 'I'm happy to be one of a team which has achieved something that will make your name go down in football history – the coach of three successive premiership winners'.[74]

When it was the coach's turn to respond, he 'seemed close to tears' and admitted he had actually cried immediately after the game.[75] He saved one of his biggest tributes for Don Duffy, saying: 'He's a terrific doctor; we owe a lot to him'. He also acknowledged his team's achievement, saying:

> We won the premiership not because we were a better side, but because we were a better combination. Everyone at Melbourne played a part. No one person has won a premiership for Melbourne. If it could be numbered, it probably would amount to 200 people. This effort will grow in stature as the years go on. In 10 or 15 years' time a player will say: 'I played in three successive Melbourne premiership sides'. And somebody will say: 'Which ones – 1939-'40-'41 or 1955-'56-'57?' No other club has ever won three in a row twice.[76]

The statistical similarity between Melbourne's 1939-41 and 1955-57 efforts was striking. They boasted almost identical win-loss-draw records. Checker Hughes' side posted 49 wins and 11 losses; Smith's had 49 wins, 11 losses and a draw.

---

[72] *The Age*, Monday September 23, 1957.
[73] Alf Brown, *The Herald*, Monday September 23, 1957.
[74] *The Herald*, Monday September 23, 1957.
[75] Alf Brown, *The Herald*, Monday September 23, 1957.
[76] *The Herald*, Monday September 23, 1957.

Both had also contested seven finals for six wins. And they won their Grand Finals easily: Hughes' team by an average of 40 points (comprising 53, 39 and 29-point margins); Smith's by an average of 54 points (by 28, 73 and 61 points).

The 1957 premiership confirmed Smith's status as a great coach. If there had been any scepticism over his coaching ability – a common, naive knock was: 'He should win flags; have a look at the players he's got' – it disappeared after he had triumphed over adversity. This most challenging of seasons – in which Smith had to rebuild after the Demons had lost their captain, their centre half-back, centre half-forward, centreman, ruckman and rover, in a time when positions meant far more – once and for all revealed his extraordinary coaching powers.

Melbourne's committee trumpeted its coach's talents: 'It is hard to conceive anybody challenging the record of this great personality… It does seem as if Norman could establish new figures in coaching records… as he is still quite a young man; certainly the spirit and determination to have the team produce its best on all occasions is burning stronger than ever with Norman… He has had his greatest triumph'.[77]

The first official Melbourne Football Club history was largely written in 1957 and published the following year. Written by E.C.H. 'Percy' Taylor, *The Story of the Melbourne Football Club* featured this description of Smith's achievements: 'Norman's success can be attributed to his honesty of purpose, his unbounded enthusiasm, and love for his old club, and his insistence on absolute fitness, with emphasis on team work as opposed to individualism. He coaches as he played, club first and foremost, both on and off the field. He demands of his charges the sacrifice of personal ambitions for the sake of the team, and they have responded in a remarkable manner. Success has been achieved as a natural corollary'.

YYYYYYYYY

Before the 1957 Grand Final, Norm Smith agreed to a friendly wager with Brian Dixon. The star wingman recalled:

> Norm said to me: '(Reg) Burgess is your man and you've got to beat him'. Burgess was a very important player for Essendon, but I thought I could do the job. I said, and I don't know why I said this: 'Well, if I beat him and we win, I want to coach the team and take training'. We were due to play in the night series at the Lake Oval (South Melbourne) on the Thursday night after the Grand Final, so we would train

---

[77] Melbourne Football Club *Annual Report*, 1957.

almost as normal during the week. To my surprise, Norm agreed to my suggestion. I beat Burgess and took training, and I had match practice, and I put Norm on Terry Gleeson. Norm was in his mid-40s and Terry was a big, strong ruckman. But to his credit, Norm did it without a complaint.[78]

Ian Thorogood recalled that neither the Melbourne players nor the club wanted to participate in the night series, but they had no other choice. In the first round of the knockout competition, an under-strength Melbourne took on Footscray (which had finished sixth, a game-and-a-half out of the final four). The Demons were still in a celebratory mood and lacked the 'extra oomph' from just five days earlier and unsurprisingly produced a poor performance. At half-time, a very measured Smith told his players: 'Look, you have nothing to prove here. You have proven yourselves the best team in the competition that counts. Just give it your best shot – win, lose or draw'. After the Demons were shock 26-point losers, Smith was far from upset. He said: 'Right, now we're going to have a bloody good time', and the premiership celebrations continued.[79]

Although Fitzroy's under-19s side didn't make the finals in 1957, Len Smith's coaching career was gaining serious momentum. He was considered, by his own committee, to have had no peer in the short history of the VFL under-19s.[80] By now, Len was also Fitzroy's chairman of selectors and a member of the club's committee. It made for a seven-day week of football. He would devote himself to the thirds on Monday and Wednesday nights and Saturday mornings; his senior selector's role took up Tuesday and Thursday night and Saturday afternoons; and he continued to coach Brunswick in the Sunday amateur league. Len Smith performed all these duties in addition to his full-time, responsible job as a foreman in charge of the maintenance engineering department at Miller's ropeworks.

There was no greater evidence of his coaching skills than the composition of Fitzroy's senior side, which lost to Collingwood by two points in round five. Of the 20 players who represented the Lions that day, 14 had progressed through thirds' teams coached by Len Smith. Of the 44 players on the training list, 22 had played with the thirds. They included eventual club greats Kevin Murray (who eventually

---

[78] Brian Dixon. Interview with the author.
[79] Ian Thorogood. Interview with the author.
[80] Fitzroy Football Club annual report, 1957.

played a club record 333 games, and won the 1969 Brownlow and nine best-and-fairests), Owen Abrahams, Wally Clark, Graham Campbell and Kevin Wright.

John Craven, a football writer with *The Herald*, uncovered Len Smith's 'shrewd, long-range plan' aimed at mass-producing senior VFL footballers. Craven revealed that each year Len Smith would select six of his most promising youngsters to play with the other side he coached, Sunday league club Brunswick, 'to gain experience against older players' and fast-track their development. Campbell, who had just established himself in Fitzroy's senior side at the age of 20, praised Len's belief in the Sunday league, saying: 'Playing with the amateurs kicked me along because you are up against former League and Association players as well as other young chaps. It is a lot rougher than League'.[81]

Fitzroy's under-19s side would certainly have had a rough season if it wasn't for the bonding abilities of Len Smith. With just six of his players boasting experience at under-19 level, he managed to recruit about 25 younger boys. Fitzroy's committee reported that 'the performance of the thirds under these circumstances was most noteworthy'. As the season had progressed, Len Smith had 'formed a team which... could be a strong contender for the 1958 premiership'.[82] However, Len wouldn't get the chance to win a second under-19s flag. Bigger challenges awaited him.

At the end of 1957, he was holidaying with wife Flo in Queensland when he was surprised by a phone call from Fitzroy secretary Ward Stuchbery. He was asked if he would like to be interviewed for Fitzroy's senior coaching job. He had no hesitation in cutting short his holiday to chase what had seemed a pipe-dream of becoming a VFL coach.

Bill Stephen had left Fitzroy to coach Yarrawonga in the Ovens and Murray Football League and the battling Lions were still without a coach after their two other leading candidates had withdrawn from the running. The job had initially been accepted by North Melbourne great Wally Carter, in a close decision over former Carlton star Bert Deacon. But Carter pulled out of the deal after experiencing 'too many complications' regarding his clearance. The Lions again approached Deacon, who refused to be their 'second choice'.[83]

In late November, the Lions were still without a coach. They looked within their own ranks and, on Monday December 2, 1957, appointed 45-year-old Len Smith as senior coach. The committee looked favourably upon his 'major success' with the thirds – many of whom had graduated to the senior team – and expressed the

---

[81] *The Herald*, 1957.
[82] Fitzroy Football Club *Annual Report*, 1957.
[83] Peter Bye, *The Sporting Globe*, November 1957.

wish that supporters would 'give Len their unstinted support, as it is obvious that his qualities as a coach are meritorious'.[84]

Norm Smith was one of the first people to congratulate his brother. Len Smith told Dave Andersen from *The Sporting Globe* that while Norm was happy about his appointment: 'He refused to lie down for me the first time we meet the Demons!'

The next day, reporters got the brothers together to discuss their unique situation as the only coaching brothers in VFL/AFL history. They warmly shook hands and smiled for the camera, and Norm Smith cheekily ruffled the hair of his unruffled elder brother. He said: 'We are all very excited at Len's appointment. Mum was overjoyed when I was talking to her this morning... I hope we meet Fitzroy early next season, so we can get an idea what they are like under Len's coaching'. To the amusement of those present, Len didn't share his brother's wish, saying: 'I want to get a few games under my belt before we have to face up to Melbourne'.

Len believed his new role would feel familiar. 'A lot of players who were under me in the thirds will be with the seniors next year,' he said. 'It will be a great help in moulding a good team. In fact, will be just like the thirds all over again!'

However, it wouldn't be an easy road. At Fitzroy's annual general meeting just eight days after Len Smith's appointment, a reform group led by former club secretary Bob Biddle announced plans to take over the club. They were unsuccessful, but former player Alan Fitcher, writing in *The Sporting Globe*, expressed his disgust: 'I deplore the... bitterness which has never been far from the surface at Fitzroy. I am jealous of clubs such as Collingwood and Melbourne, which go from year to year without internal quarrels being reflected in the team's performance. Strangely enough, both sides of the fence are Fitzroy-crazy, yet do not appear to realise their acting can only lead to trouble, which in turn keeps the Maroons struggling at the bottom of the list. How long will this state of affairs continue? It's been hampering the club for... years'.[85] Len Smith did his best to wade through the politics, telling *The Sporting Globe*: 'Once I have all these people right behind me, then my job will be a lot easier and results will come with much more speed'.

Although the Smith brothers were about to move in similar footballing circles, their personalities would remain 'poles apart';[86] 'like chalk and cheese'.[87] They shared a close, at times almost telepathic relationship, and affectionately referred to each other as 'Normy' and 'Lenny' – Len also called Norm 'Fatty' – but, as Peter Smith described, they were complete opposites: 'Len was quiet, whereas Norm was

---

[84] Fitzroy Football Club *Annual Report*, 1957.
[85] *The Sporting Globe*, December 11, 1957.
[86] Ken Emselle. Interview with the author.
[87] Norma Harmes. Interview with the author.

in your face. Norm drank; Len didn't.[88] Len smoked; Dad didn't. They were close, but didn't live in each other's pockets. They didn't have to. They had so much respect and love for each other they would have just accepted the fact they were different. To a certain extent, they probably revelled in their differences. But they had similar values. There was a right way and a wrong way of doing things. It's just that they had different ways of imparting the same message'.[89]

---

[88] Smith later lamented: 'Old Lenny didn't drink – he had no release'. (Source: John Townsend. Interview with the author.)
[89] Peter Smith. Interview with the author.

16

THE MOST BITTER DISAPPOINTMENT

[1958]

Norm Smith was always on the alert for the slightest sign of complacency in his players. With each success he became increasingly wary of any hint of a change in player attitudes – whether it be egotism, a feeling that success would simply come as a natural matter of course, or perhaps even a minor dropoff in competitive edge or killer instinct. Smith worked vigilantly to stamp these issues out as soon as he detected them. He felt they were insidious elements of human nature, that were always to the detriment of sporting teams, especially those striving to achieve even higher levels of performance.

To him, it was a crime against self and team to rest on former glories. New boundaries had to be explored to stay ahead of the baying pack. To this end, he would say quite bluntly to his players: 'One reason for our success is that I know everyone is born a little lazy, and at Melbourne you aren't allowed to practise that habit'.[1]

His radar for such attitudes was more finely tuned than ever in the lead-up to the start of the 1958 season. On the surface, Smith's hardline stance appeared both justified *and* paranoid. His Demons had won the previous three premierships, they hadn't lost any players and – from an outsider's big-picture perspective – barring an horrific run with injury and/or an astonishing uprising from another club, they would again be the front-runners in the race for the flag. Logic dictated that their only enemy could be themselves.

The question was: did they have the hunger to go all the way again? Although Melbourne had played in four consecutive Grand Finals, the composition of the

---
[1] Trevor Johnson, in a facsimile to the author.

THE MOST BITTER DISAPPOINTMENT [1958]

side had changed markedly and their best players were now those in their early to mid-20s. In 1958, the likes of John Beckwith and Peter Marquis would turn 26, Ian Ridley and Laurie Mithen would turn 24, Don Williams, Big Bob Johnson, Bluey Adams and Geoff Case would turn 23, while Ron Barassi and Brian Dixon would turn 22. This nucleus of Demons was yet to reach its individual and collective peak – most were still improving – so there appeared no reason why they couldn't maintain their No. 1 status. Indeed, any decline in output could only result from a decline in mental approach.

There was little doubt about the coach's intentions. He had become a success junkie: the more he achieved, the more he wanted to achieve. He was hellbent on winning a fourth successive flag, which would equal the record set by Collingwood from 1927-30. The record Smith had cheered and revered as a boy, he now viewed with green-eyed envy. Four years later, he vividly recalled the intensity of his motivations. 'I badly wanted to equal that Collingwood record,' he said.[2]

Accordingly, he wasn't about to let anything – or anyone – jeopardise the Demons' quest for immortality. Barassi said that under Norm Smith, 'premierships didn't go to your head. He'd been there himself and played in four premierships. He passed on the right instructions, hints, threats, whatever you want to call it'.[3]

That theory was tested early in the 1958 season, when Smith was reliably informed that 'seven or eight' of his young players would meet each Monday at the Baden Powell Hotel in Victoria Parade, Collingwood, for long boozy lunches. One of those present, Ian Thorogood, said: 'A few of us, as young guys, thought we'd made it in '57 when we played in a senior premiership, so we were quite intent on enjoying ourselves. It had been suggested, through a very staunch Melbourne supporter, that perhaps a few of us could catch up for lunch and a bit of fun together. Most of us worked in sales, so it was pretty easy for us to get away for extended lunches that stretched well into the afternoon and became a great day'.[4]

Unbeknown to this group of revellers, their coach had somehow found out about their rendezvous – 'either someone dobbed us in, or word got around about what we were doing', Thorogood speculated. In any case, Smith's reaction took the culprits by surprise. Thorogood recalled:

> Norm called a halt to training and said: 'Everyone can go in except for...', and he named each of the players concerned. He really gave it to us.

---

[2] *Melbourne Truth* series, 1962.
[3] Ron Barassi, *The AFL Record*, round 21, July 28-30, 2000.
[4] Ian Thorogood. Interview with the author.

He said: 'So you think you've made it? Well I'm here to tell you that you haven't! Even though you've played in a premiership! You can all be very easily replaced, one by one.'

Norm ranted and raved for about 15 minutes on the various do's and don'ts, and he said: 'If you still want to do it, that's fine, but you won't be here!'

Our heads were down like naughty schoolboys. At the end of his tirade, Norm said: 'And the *biggest* disappointment that I've got as coach, is that not one of you – *not one of you*! – had the guts to invite me... Now get off the bloody ground!'

It was a real reality jolt. Norm had gotten his message across in two ways. Firstly: 'Get your feet back on the ground', and secondly, the human part of it: 'Don't leave me out'.

Quite a few of us in that group went on to play for quite a few more years, and I have often wondered to myself, had Norm not known, and had he not taken that stand with us, would we still have had the success we ended up having? It's an interesting question.[5]

￼￼￼￼￼￼￼￼￼

Although Melbourne's coaching set-up under Norm Smith had brought enormous success, the coach himself was continually exploring ways to produce an even better football team.

Smith wanted to hire an assistant coach who could take a predominantly hands-on role while he himself devoted more time to specialised coaching. With this in mind, he identified his old mate Ron Baggott as an ideal candidate for such a role. Baggott – who had captain-coached VFA club Brunswick for three years in the late 1940s, and was a football commentator on the Kia-Ora Sports Parade on 3KZ – was a man Smith respected and trusted immensely, and who shared similar football philosophies.

Protocol dictated that Smith take his proposal through formal channels. He approached the Melbourne committee requesting the appointment of an assistant coach, and that he wished to offer the job to Baggott. The committee agreed to his request on both counts.

Smith's phone-call, and offer of the assistant coaching job, was 'the surprise of a lifetime' for Baggott.

'To think,' Baggott marvelled, 'that we'd grown up together as kids and become very close mates during our playing days, played in three premierships together,

---

[5] Ian Thorogood. Interview with the author.

and our families were close also, and here Smithy is, he's just coached Melbourne to a hat-trick of premierships and he's asking me – *me*! – to assist him. I don't think he needed much help! But, naturally, I was delighted to accept. Assistant coaches were more or less something new back then and I was grateful to Norm for the privilege to fill that role alongside him. It was a real eye-opener, too.'

Baggott initially felt out of his depth. 'At the age of 41 and not having touched a football for nine years, not to mention being somewhat overweight, I found the going pretty hard,' he said. But Smith encouraged him and seemed to enjoy his input. 'We never had any arguments,' Baggott said. 'He was the boss, and I was more than happy to do whatever he wanted.'

But Baggott recalled an occasion when Smith wasn't happy with his efforts.

> Norm was taking circle-work and he said to me: 'Hey Baggs, how about you take Big Bob for some goalkicking practice?'
>
> I said: 'OK, Norm, no problems'.
>
> So I took Big Bob up one end of the ground and had him taking shots at goal from 40 or 50 yards out. It only took a couple of minutes for Norm to come over in a huff and say: 'What do you think you're doing?!'
>
> I didn't know what he was on about. I said: 'I'm doing what you told me to do, Norm – I'm giving Bob Johnson some goalkicking practice'.
>
> He said: 'Oh yeah? And where do you think Bob Johnson kicks most of his goals from – how far out?'
>
> I said: 'About 25 yards out in the forward pocket'.
>
> Norm nodded his head and said: 'That's right. So what the bloody hell are you doing making him kick from that far out?!'
>
> He'd made his point. As usual, he was right. I sort of said: 'Righto boss'. I had no problem with that. That was Smithy: he wanted things done *exactly* the way he wanted it. He was a perfectionist. Fair enough too – it was his team.[6]

ŶŶŶŶŶŶŶŶŶ

Although Norm Smith was the undisputed No. 1 coach in the VFL – a fact reinforced by the Demons winning the first five games of 1958 – his elder brother was making more headlines... and for all the right reasons.

Len Smith had inherited a Fitzroy side that had finished second-bottom (11th) in 1957 – just half a game from being wooden-spooners – with a 6-12 record.

---

[6] Ron Baggott. Interview with the author.

In the previous four years, their record had been 23-48-1, finishing 11th, ninth, eighth and 11th respectively. They had made the finals just once in the previous 10 seasons. While supporters urged the Lions to embark on an extensive recruiting campaign, Len Smith stunned them with his decision to persevere with the same playing list. Part of his decision was forced upon him as Fitzroy's country recruiting was 'the poorest in the competition and no help at all to a coach'.[7] Understandably, Len wasn't making any big predictions. 'I'm not saying we are going to make the four this year or later,' he told *The Sporting Globe* during pre-season training. 'But, by heavens, I'll be hoping for it all the time'.

But hope was quickly replaced by optimism and expectation. And justifiably so. Fitzroy wasn't expected to beat an improved North Melbourne (coached by Wally Carter) in the season opener at Arden Street, but in what was believed to have been the hottest temperature ever for a VFL round – a stifling 29°C – the Lions turned up the heat on the Kangaroos and caused the sensation of the day, producing a record-breaking four-quarter avalanche of 23.21 (159) to just 5.9 (39).[8] After the match, an excited Fitzroy fan told Len: 'We'll have to call you "Killer" Smith'. Typically modest, Len replied quietly: 'It's still Len Smith – the same as it was last year when I was coaching the thirds'.

Despite the hype and Len Smith's preference to play down his side's performance, the fact was the Lions had vaulted straight to the top of the ladder... with a mammoth percentage of 407.69. They soon proved it was no fluke, winning six of their first seven matches to regain top spot by percentage from the Demons. But for some dubious umpiring decisions, which cost the Lions their round three match against a rejuvenated Collingwood at Victoria Park, they would have been undefeated and a game and considerable percentage clear of Melbourne.

Norm Smith was well aware of the increasing threat of his brother's combination, which was becoming known as the 'glamour team' of the competition. The football world gained an indication of his wariness of Fitzroy after a round four win which had kept the Demons at the head of the table. Immediately after the match, Smith had asked reporters whether Fitzroy had beaten Richmond. When told it had, by 57 points, he said: 'Len has done it again. He's mighty good, you know. We are glad to be on top, but we could just as easily be chasing Fitzroy with a percentage gap nearly as good as a win to make up'.[9]

---

[7] Ron Barassi, *The Australian*, Wednesday May 12, 1965.
[8] It was the Lions' third-biggest winning margin (eventually their fifth), and the highest score by a visiting team at Arden Street.
[9] *The Sun*, Monday, May 5, 1958.

THE MOST BITTER DISAPPOINTMENT [1958]

The Sun's scribe Kevin Hogan captured the public consensus when he wrote: 'Len (Smith), least known among League coaches when he took charge of the Lions this year, has in four weeks lifted his team – and himself – from football raggedness to riches'.[10]

Ken Hands told readers of *The Sporting Globe*:

> I was amazed at the new-look brand of football that Fitzroy turned on... It was hard to recognise this fast, systematic, play-on Fitzroy side as the hard-bumping, vigorous team that depended mostly on brawn in recent seasons. You couldn't have bettered their position play, backing up and their foot and hand passes... They made the most of their pace by kicking wide to the half-forward flanks. This kept their forward line open... (This) comes as a surprise when you realise that they've still got the same side as last season. Most of the credit for this improvement must go to the new coach, Len Smith.[11]

But Len wasn't getting carried away with his early success. He remained the same old Len Smith, renowned for – as his full-forward, Tony Ongarello, described it – 'his sincerity and kindness, his patience with kids... (He was) always quiet and earnest'.[12] Despite the fact he was a much-sought-after figure by newspaper reporters and photographers, each Friday Len would conduct coaching clinics for about 40 schoolboys – primary school boys one week and high school youths the next.

To the masses, Len Smith was an overnight sensation; despite the fact that all at Fitzroy had rated his abilities for some time. All, that is, except for Alan 'Butch' Gale. The new Lions skipper hadn't seen eye-to-eye with Norm Smith almost a decade earlier and he wasn't overly impressed with his brother, either... initially. Gale reflected:

> I resented him when he came along. I treated him with suspicion. He took over from a mate of mine – Bill Stephen – and I thought he was too soft, too sympathetic. I used to abuse players but he showed compassion.
>
> I used to drink and he didn't. He didn't join in with the boys in after-match socials. He didn't like many of the things I did.
>
> Once, when we were trailing our opponents at half-time, he said: 'Alan, you're captain – you've got to do something'.

---

[10] Kevin Hogan, *The Sun*, Monday, May 5, 1958.
[11] Ken Hands, *The Sporting Globe*, Saturday May 3, 1958.
[12] Tony Ongarello, *The Age*, May 14, 1971.

So I KO'd a bloke.

After the game he took me aside and said: 'Alan, I didn't mean something like *that*'.

We were almost exact opposites in every way. But he won me to his way of thinking in just four or five weeks.[13]

Gale became so impressed with Len Smith's leadership style that he also told *The Sporting Globe*: 'For years at Fitzroy there's been too many chiefs and too few Indians… (Now) there's only one man in control… and that's coach Len Smith'.

Fitzroy full-back Bob Henderson described Len as a thorough gentleman who was always very measured. But there was one thing in particular that caused him to momentarily lose his cool. 'If you yawned when Lenny was addressing you, oh gee, he would go crook,' Henderson said. 'Fair enough, too, because it was a sign that maybe you weren't concentrating on what he had to say. Apart from that, though, he never raised his voice above the normal pitch. He wasn't a ranter and raver; he didn't blast players or just treat you like a number – that wasn't his style. He was a terrific man-manager who gained great respect by treating us with respect.'[14]

Full-forward Tony Ongarello said Len Smith didn't need to use fire-and-brimstone to get his message across. 'He inspired but in a quiet kind of a way,' Ongarello said. 'In some ways he hardly ever had to be a disciplinarian – people seemed to do the right thing for him anyway.'[15]

Len Smith told *The Herald*, that three key elements had helped the Lions' rise: teamwork, comradeship and physical fitness. 'One of the things I have concentrated on,' he said, 'is getting the boys to know each other properly. I have done my best to get them to talk to each other all the time. When they are friends, they help each other more.'

The bonding started with developing tightly-knit groups within the team. Murray said: 'Len would get the players on each line – the full-backline, the half-backline, the centreline and so on – to train together. You'd do your laps together and other things together. Len was so good at organising people and building team spirit and understanding'.[16]

Len Smith organised semi-regular team meetings at his home the night before big matches. Unlike Norm Smith's single-speaker lectures, Len made it an open forum for players. One night, Butch Gale held the floor for 20 minutes. Len Smith's reasoning was: 'I like every player to understand the problems of all his teammates.

---

[13] Alan 'Butch' Gale, *The Age*, May 14, 1971.
[14] Bob Henderson. Interview with the author.
[15] Tony Ongarello, *The Age*, May 14, 1971.
[16] Kevin Murray. Interview with the author.

(Full-forward) Tony Ongarello should know what (full-back) Bob Henderson is trying to achieve, and vice-versa. That builds confidence and teamwork'.[17]

This Friday night initiative was well received. Murray told *The Sporting Globe*: 'Just to sit down for two hours and chat about a game rationally and quietly helps. It gives you something positive to think about, something that's still fresh in your mind the next afternoon'.

The players had little doubt about the merits of Len Smith's approach to the game, and quickly came to respect his demands for, among other things, effort, hardness, fast movement of the ball and smart play.

Henderson described Len Smith's demand for hardness:

> The No. 1 thing Lenny wanted us to do was have a go. His words still ring in my ears. He said: 'The hardest part of football is getting it. I don't want players who shirk the contest. All I want is triers. If you play your guts out and we get beaten by a better side, I can accept that. There's no disgrace in that. It's only a disgrace if you haven't given your absolute all. I don't want 90 percent, or 99 percent even – I want 110 percent. If you don't give your all, you'll be having a run in the seconds'.
>
> He had a passion about him that you could not resist. He was so passionate that you would willingly die for him.[18]

In Len Smith's mind, the fast ball movement and smartness became paramount as he was well aware that the Lions lacked key forward targets and marking followers, but that they had a relative abundance of little men. The instruction to move the ball quickly and continually was perhaps what set Len Smith apart and eventually led to his unofficial yet widely acknowledged title – subscribed to by the likes of Ron Barassi – of 'the father of modern football'. He is generally recognised as the man who created fast, play-on football, which became more prevalent in the 1970s and beyond. Len Smith implored his Lions to follow 'the momentum system'[19] – ie. 'keep the ball in motion, and move it as quickly as possible'.[20] This had always been Len Smith's ideal mode of play, but it was also tailored to the strengths and weaknesses of the players he had at his disposal at Fitzroy.

'Movement was the secret of our game,' Henderson said. 'It had to be, because we never had many big blokes. We had "Butch" Gale, who was a lion-heart and

---

[17] *The Sporting Globe*, 1958.
[18] Bob Henderson. Interview with the author.
[19] Alan 'Butch' Gale, *The Age*, May 14, 1971.
[20] Kevin Murray. Interview with the author.

a great player but weak overhead... We had to run the ball, otherwise we were sitting ducks. Lenny made us run and run... He also figured: "The longer you hold up, the bigger the opposition builds the hill in front of you".'[21]

To get over the 'hill', Len Smith preferred long kicks, specifically drop-kicks. He wasn't in favour of punts, reasoning that: 'The old drop-pass only goes so high and it's harder to stop because it travels from A to B a lot quicker'.[22] But while he emphasised that 'handball never takes the place of a kick',[23] he also encouraged his players to lower their vision and try to break up the play and get over the next line through a combination of handballs and short passes.

'Len Smith was probably more keen on handball than any other coach had ever been to that stage,' Henderson said. 'His idea was that: "If there's a chance to pass the ball, pass it; don't go over your teammate's head just to kick it an extra 30 yards. Let's use the free man, otherwise it's a waste of his effort getting free". But if we were under pressure, we had to go long.'[24]

Len Smith also devised a clever method of creating time and space for handball when it might otherwise have been fraught with danger. Murray explained: 'If you had a mark or free kick, regardless of where you were on the field, rather than going straight back from the mark, you were to go back quickly on an angle to give your teammate flying past for the handball the opportunity to get it when he was in the clear and not kicking the ball under pressure, which enabled him to direct the ball better. And you'd follow up your handball just in case it went astray or he fumbled it, and you could shepherd off for him if you were needed. Whereas if you just went straight back from the mark and handballed to a teammate, you'd risk your opponent on the mark tackling him. It was quite intelligent, creative play, and it worked a treat'.[25]

Some of the 'set-plays' Len Smith devised and explained on a blackboard – using code words to make positional changes – were even more successful. One codeword was 'Brunswick', and was referred to as 'The Brunswick Plan', which was a forward line switch of up to four players, involving the likes of Owen Abrahams, Wally Clarke and Kevin Wright, who simultaneously rotated through the attacking zone and midfield to baffle the opposition and create loose men within scoring range. Butch Gale explained: 'On that signal the forward pocket would move into the goalsquare, the full-forward went out towards centre half-forward, the centre

---

[21] Bob Henderson. Interview with the author.
[22] Bob Henderson. Interview with the author.
[23] Kevin Murray. Interview with the author.
[24] Bob Henderson. Interview with the author.
[25] Kevin Murray. Interview with the author.

THE MOST BITTER DISAPPOINTMENT [1958]

half-forward towards the centre. In a couple of seconds, we had a straight line of four men from (the) centre to the goal. That system was created to give Owen Abrahams extra room to kick goals. It confused others and allowed Abrahams to get a lot of goals… (Len) shocked some people with his positional changes. He once put tiny Wally Clark on big John Lord. It looked wrong. Len told us to pass the ball to Wally on the ground. It worked'.[26]

YYYYYYYYY

The much-anticipated 'Battle of the Brothers' – the first clash between Norm Smith's Demons and Len Smith's Lions – captured the imagination of the football public.

In the red-and-blue corner was the best coach in the VFL, and probably the land, in command of the greatest team in the country; while in the maroon-and-blue corner was the rookie senior coach who had taken charge of a poor side and magically transformed it into a premiership contender.

The match also loomed as a battle of contrasting styles, with the Lions to pit their play-on-at-all-costs style against Melbourne's strong-marking positional play and general machine-like approach.

It must have been a surreal scenario for both men, but perhaps more so Len Smith, who informed *The Herald*: 'Fitzroy is the only side I would like to see beat Melbourne… (because) I've been one of their most one-eyed barrackers at the finals in recent years'.[27]

Everyone, it seemed, apart from Demons fans, wanted a victory for Len Smith's Lions, who were clearly the underdogs for the round 11 encounter at Fitzroy's Brunswick Street Oval. Melbourne was atop the VFL ladder, two games clear of both Collingwood and Fitzroy, who were separated only by percentage.

The Demons had an imposing 9-1 record, but had been seriously challenged in half of their matches, five of their wins being by no more than 15 points. They had been forced to call on their supreme fighting abilities: in round four against Hawthorn at the MCG, they were down to 15 fit men but managed to stave off Hawthorn in a desperate last quarter into the breeze; the next week against Essendon at the MCG they faced a six-goal deficit late in the third term before slamming on 9.6 to 1.3 to win in fine style. Melbourne's only blemish had been a shock one-point loss to St Kilda in round six at the Junction Oval. But they had won their past four matches, the most recent being a last-gasp 11-point win

---

[26] Alan 'Butch' Gale, *The Age*, May 14, 1971.
[27] *The Herald*, 1958.

over Collingwood – in 'one of the most thrilling games that could be witnessed'[28] – in front of a record home-and-away crowd of 99,256 on the Queen's Birthday Monday at the MCG.

Fitzroy, meanwhile, had lost two of its previous three matches, sparking some speculation about whether they could sustain their form. Balancing the scales, though, was the Demons' patchy recent record at Brunswick Street (2-2) and the fact they been given just a five-day break since the Queen's Birthday match, in comparison to the Lions' seven.

In the days leading up to the match, the Smith brothers and their mother, Ethel, met a photographer and reporter from *The Herald* at the Brunswick Street Oval to discuss their unique contest. They posed for photos, one of which showed Ethel Smith, flanked by her smiling sons, facing her palms skyward like they were balancing scales, as though she was saying: 'Who will win? Who will I support? I can't decide'. She diplomatically told the reporter: 'I can only hope it's a draw'. On game day, the reporter spotted the two brothers talking and asked their opinion of the published photograph of them with their mother. One of them gratefully replied: 'We were glad for Mum's sake that it was such a good photo'.

Ethel Smith had been so anxious about the match that she arrived at the ground at 10.30am – some four hours before game-time. Norm Smith was also anxious, as Fitzroy player Graham Campbell recalled:

> Len spoke to us in the boardroom because there was only a temporary partition between us and the Melbourne players in the dressingroom. Len was very quietly spoken. When he came out of the boardroom he said: 'Listen to this boys', as his brother was berating the Melbourne players. 'How would you like to be coached like that?'[29]

Bob Henderson provided an example of the kind of speech Len Smith would have made before they embarked on their giant-killing quest:

> Before a big game like that, Len would have said, very calmly, something along the lines of: 'We've both got 18-a-side, so there's no advantage to either side. It's a pretty simple game. You've only got one man to look after. It's man-on-man and the better man will win. If we've got more better men than they have, we'll win. You're in the side because you're the best we've got. But that doesn't guarantee

---

[28] Melbourne Football Club *Annual Report*, 1958.
[29] Donald, Chris, *Fitzroy: For the Love of the Jumper*, Pennon Press, 2002.

THE MOST BITTER DISAPPOINTMENT [1958]

you a game next week. It all depends on what you do today. Nothing else matters, except what you do today'.[30]

Just a few hours later, Len Smith's Fitzroy side emerged as a genuine premiership threat; while, at the same time, Melbourne's campaign appeared to be in some jeopardy. There was no shame in losing to Fitzroy at Brunswick Street – the Lions would remain undefeated at home in 1958 – but the main concern was the magnitude of the loss. The Demons had led by four points at quarter-time, but were swamped in the remaining three quarters, adding just 3.9 to the Lions' 10.12 to go down by 41 points. It was Melbourne's heaviest defeat since the 1954 Grand Final. They had been beaten in all departments, not least of all in marks, taking just 37 to Fitzroy's 66.

As *The Sun* aptly summarised in its headline, 'Jaded Demons Blundered Into The Fitzroy Trap', Len Smith had outwitted his successful brother with a key positional move, swapping usual centre half-forward Keith Bromage with star half-forward flanker Owen Abrahams, the result being that Abrahams proved far too mobile for lumbering Demons centre half-back John Lord in a best-afield performance, while Bromage took defensive playmaker Don Williams out to the boundary line and out of the play. Kevin Murray believed: 'All Norm had to do was switch Lord and Williams and things might have been different'.[31] But Norm Smith had no intention of making such a move. Lord said:

> Owen gave me a thrashing, so embarrassingly that by the end of the day he was apologising and I just didn't know what to do. I thought the obvious thing to do was swap Don and I. At a much later date, I asked Norm why he didn't make the change. His comment was: 'You will be playing at centre half-back on Grand Final day, and a bit of bleeding wasn't going to hurt'.[32]

After the match, the brothers shook hands. Norm Smith raised a forced smile and told the gathering in the Fitzroy rooms: 'We know we can't win every game, but we certainly don't like being beaten. I've always had great respect and admiration for (my) brother. He is a coach who uses his brain and really thinks out his football. I knew he would cook something up for us'.[33]

Despite their shock defeat, the Melbourne players were pleasantly surprised by the humble approach of the Fitzroy players. Melbourne forward Clyde Laidlaw

---

[30] Bob Henderson. Interview with the author.
[31] Kevin Murray. Interview with the author.
[32] John Lord. Interview with the author.
[33] Contemporary newspaper report.

said: 'Whenever we played at Fitzroy and Len Smith was coaching, your direct opponent would invite you back to the rooms and he would look after you socially and introduce you to other blokes. That was all part of Len Smith's gentlemanly approach to the game'.[34]

In an interview in *The Sun*, Lions skipper Butch Gale compared the coaching methods of the Smiths: 'Both are master tacticians, and basically there is little difference in their methods of getting a side fit. Norm's main outlook is towards teamwork, (while) Len has a more personal approach'. Gale cheekily added: 'There's no argument about it after Saturday's result – Len has proved he is the better coach'. This point would be the subject of serious debate for decades to follow.

But Len Smith refused to take all the credit for Fitzroy's meteoric rise. Without any hint of false modesty, he paid tribute to his predecessor, Bill Stephen, who he felt had been unlucky not to reach the finals during his three-year reign, but who he believed had set a fine example for his players and built the foundations of the Lions' current success. Len Smith continued to use Stephen as a mentor, regularly writing letters to him asking for advice about player and team issues.

At this stage of the season, Fitzroy didn't have too many issues of concern, which was reflected in the reactions of supporters, whose collective passion had been reignited. Len Smith told *The Sun* his biggest thrill had been hearing supporters spell out F-I-T-Z-R-O-Y when the Lions kicked a goal. He marvelled: 'I (had) never heard that before in my life'. The Fitzroy faithful could easily have spelled out the name of its revered coach, according to Graham Campbell, who told *The Sporting Globe*: 'Len is fantastic. Words can't describe what we think of him. He has made us and Fitzroy. I'm proud to play under his leadership'.

Ongarello admired Len Smith's modesty and his ability to maintain a sense of balance in the roller-coaster world of VFL coaching. 'He didn't change much,' Ongarello said. 'He didn't become noticeably depressed in defeat or exuberant in victory. He contained his emotions… He was a very humble man. He didn't seek success for his own glory'. Ongarello agreed with Gale that Len Smith didn't often mix socially with his players – 'perhaps that was one of his faults, I'm not sure' – but he was never short of company when he did. 'He didn't set out to make friends,' Ongarello said. 'Friendships happened naturally because of his sincerity.'[35]

Always a deep forward-thinker, Len wasn't content with simply winning matches. He also wanted to bring about changes for the betterment of all involved

---

[34] Clyde Laidlaw. Interview with the author.
[35] Tony Ongarello, *The Age*, May 14, 1971.

THE MOST BITTER DISAPPOINTMENT [1958]

in the game. For one, he believed that reserves matches should be played as curtain-raisers to the seniors, if for no other reason than for the development of young players. 'As it is,' he explained, 'seconds players don't get an opportunity to watch the seniors in action or to hear the coach's address. If they did, it could make a lot of difference.'[36] His wish was granted the next season.

YYYYYYYYY

When the VFL was considering candidates to coach the Victorian team in the 1958 'centenary' carnival, two names emerged as front-runners – Dick Reynolds and Norm Smith.

There were few better-credentialled men for the job than Reynolds. The Essendon legend had played a League record 320 games, won three Brownlow Medals and been the Bombers' playing-coach in 10 Grand Finals for four premierships (in 1942, 1946, 1949 and 1950).

At a VFL meeting, some delegates campaigned for Reynolds to get the job, citing his Brownlow Medals as proof enough. But, as Alf Brown argued in *The Herald*: 'Reynolds was not even captain of Essendon when he won these (Brownlows). As a playing-coach of Essendon, Reynolds was successful. (But) since be became non-playing coach in 1951 Essendon have not won a premiership', whereas Smith had won three in this capacity. Brown continued: 'As Victoria wanted a non-playing coach, Smith's choice (selection) should have been automatic'. While the eventual vote was an overwhelming 15-6 in Smith's favour, Brown was adamant it 'should have been unanimous'.

As expected, Smith wasn't the only Demon to be selected for interstate duties at the carnival, which was to be held in Melbourne over 20 days from late June to mid-July. (No VFL matches were scheduled during this period.) He was joined in the Victorian side by five of his charges – John Beckwith, Ron Barassi, Laurie Mithen, Big Bob Johnson and Don Williams, although Beckwith had to withdraw through injury.

Victoria's official team leaders were the larger-than-life characters of Geelong star Bob Davis (captain) and Footscray champion Ted Whitten (vice-captain). Davis said of his impression of Smith:

> Norm was a very autocratic, domineering coach, and a pretty scary fella, even for experienced players like myself – and I'd played my whole career under Reg

---

[36] *The Herald*, 1958.

Hickey! He made you do things out of sheer fear. Don't dare deviate from his plan – or else'.[37]

The 'plan' worked superbly in the Vics' first three matches, with big wins over South Australia (by 118 points), the VFA (49 points) and Tasmania (102 points).

One young player Smith had 'a tremendous impact' on was South Melbourne's 19-year-old prodigy Bob Skilton.[38] The star rover was on his way to winning the first of his nine best-and-fairests with the Swans (he hadn't yet won any of his three Brownlows) and was making his debut for Victoria. He said: 'I was in awe of Norm Smith. To play with the likes of Whitten, Barassi, Nicholls, Murray, etc. was an absolute highlight, let alone to be coached by the man who had the best side and had the reputation as the best coach, was one of the highlights of my whole football career. To play with, and under, the best made you a better player. I was overawed'.[39]

Victoria met Western Australia in the series decider at the MCG on July 12. The Sandgropers had earlier been defeated by Tasmania, but they were a different team in the final, as Davis recalled:

> It was a close game – a lot closer than we thought it would be – and these damn West Australians just wouldn't go away. Teddy (Whitten) was playing at centre half-back and I was playing on a half-forward flank – the positions we'd made famous! Teddy came running up to me during a break in play in the last quarter and said: 'We have to do something here to put these Sandgropers to sleep. How about you go into the centre and I do the ruck-roving and we'll liven things up a bit?'
>
> I thought it sounded like a good idea, so we made those moves ourselves and they worked because we ended up winning quite comfortably.
>
> When we were walking off the ground, very proud abut earning the title of national champions, Teddy said: 'Gee, Bobby, I don't know how "Smithy" will react to what we just did' – because Smithy hated anyone making their own moves; he was the boss.
>
> As soon as we got into the changerooms, Smithy made a beeline for us. Teddy said to me: 'Look out, Bobby, here we go; we're in for it now'.
>
> But we were lucky because we were both reasonably street-smart. Smithy eyeballed us and said: 'Who made those moves?'

---

[37] Bob Davis. Interview with the author.
[38] *The Age*, Monday July 30, 1973.
[39] Bob Skilton. Interview with the author.

Teddy and I pointed at each other, and Norm's mood changed – all of a sudden he seemed quite happy. He said: 'Oh, so you did it, Bob?'

That was my cue to say: 'Yes I did, Norm'.

Norm patted me on the back and said: 'Very good moves. You showed great initiative just when we needed it. You won the game for us. Thanks so much for that'.

I said: 'No problems, Norm'.

Teddy was most upset because it was his idea and he hadn't got the credit for it. But we were very happy that Norm let us off the hook. I was happy to accept the credit alone, but I wasn't going to accept any blame alone![40]

The week before the national carnival began, Davis – who was later named captain of the 1958 All-Australian team – had been a target of Smith's attempts to nullify him. Before Melbourne took on Geelong at the MCG in round 13, Smith gave big John Lord the unenviable task of stopping 'The Geelong Flyer', who was to line up at centre half-forward. Lord said: 'It was probably a strange match-up because Bob was very fast, and I wasn't'. Lord said:

> Norm told me: 'I want you to play Bobby Davis from behind', which was a shock because with Bobby's advantage in speed you wouldn't want to give him a head-start. But it was going to be a pretty hard task to control Bobby if you played in front, behind, on top, wherever. Norm's reasoning was: 'You won't stop Bobby getting a lot of kicks because they'll all be looking for him, so let's just make sure he gets his kicks up near the centre of the ground. If he gets the ball in the centre, the rest of the forwards will also be out of their territory when they receive the ball. He'll be less likely to kick goals and so will the rest of them. Push him up the ground and just make sure he never gets between you and the goals'.
>
> Bobby Davis would have received all the best-on-ground votes issued that day – the Brownlow Medal, the media awards, Geelong's club votes, etc. He got a million kicks that went nowhere. I had very few possessions and there had been many a call from the stand to move me. But for one of the very few occasions in my career, I got the nod from Norm as Melbourne's best player. He actually acknowledged that I'd done exactly what he'd wanted. I was very proud of my efforts, although it was a lousy way to play footy.[41]

---

[40] Bob Davis. Interview with the author.
[41] John Lord. Interview with the author.

Norm Smith delivered some almighty sprays in his coaching career, but the granddaddy of them all was the one he gave Ron Barassi late in the 1958 season.

The Demons had just lost their round 16 clash with Essendon at Windy Hill by three points, after leading by 16 at three-quarter time.

On one of the few occasions in his career, Barassi had faltered under pressure. Twice in the dying stages, the Demon vice-captain had golden opportunities to snatch victory from the Bombers. But in both instances he had been penalised for holding the ball while attempting outlandish manoeuvres when disciplined, percentage play was required.

His second blunder was, in his coach's eyes, utterly unforgivable.

According to various people who saw it, Barassi had gained possession of the ball around the centre or wing, took between one and three bounces, and perhaps even 'handballed to himself' before attempting an extravagant baulk. What is not in dispute is that he had 'tried to beat the field' and was run down at half-forward.

This type of instance was neither a one-off in the match nor in the young superstar's career. It was one of Barassi's rare bad habits, and probably the only real chink in his armour. According to his teammates, Barassi 'thought he was the master of the baulk'[42] and at times 'over-did' it.[43] Bluey Adams revealed: 'There were two things that Barass loved but couldn't do very well: running with the ball, and baulking or swerving around the man on the mark. But he kept persisting with them, which made Smithy hopping mad. They were the only two facets of Ron's game that could be called a break in discipline.'[44]

Barassi himself confessed: 'There's no doubt that I sometimes tried to do too much with the ball. I'd usually get away with it – which probably just encouraged me to keep doing it – but occasionally I didn't. Norm knew my game so well that he would know what I was going to do, or try to do, before I did'.[45]

Smith found Barassi's baulking attempts so predictable, he would say to those beside him on the bench: 'Watch this: Ron will try to run past the man on the mark here'.[46]

---

[42] Frank 'Bluey' Adams. Interview with the author.
[43] John Beckwith. Interview with the author.
[44] Frank 'Bluey' Adams. Interview with the author.
[45] Ron Barassi. Interview with the author.
[46] Ron Barassi. Interview with the author.

THE MOST BITTER DISAPPOINTMENT [1958]

Although Barassi believed his mistakes resulted from 'over-confidence',[47] runner Hugh McPherson was slightly more forgiving. 'Ron had that much in his body to give that you couldn't stop him,' McPherson said. 'If three opposition players were in front of him, he thought he could beat the lot of them himself, instead of handballing to somebody and getting the ball clear. Norm tried to stop him from doing it – boy, did he try! – but Ron's endeavour was so overpowering that he kept it up. He just could not stop himself, and neither could anyone else, even someone as strong-willed as Norm.'[48]

For Smith, the double-whammy at Windy Hill was the final straw. The visitors' changerooms became charged with tension the moment Smith stormed in and began to berate Barassi. Some of his players, including captain Beckwith, had never seen their coach as wild with fury. 'Norm reduced Barass to tears that day,' Beckwith said. 'I felt sorry for Barass. Norm reckoned he'd been a selfish bugger; that as vice-captain he hadn't set the right example; and that if he'd handballed, we might have won the game. Did he degrade him! Norm could be very cutting when he wanted to.'[49]

Smith described his barrage as 'the greatest strip I have ever torn off a player'. He explained he had 'bawled Ron out' after 'Melbourne lost... mainly because Ron tried to run with the ball. He had been warned against this before the match. I know that blast hurt him, but I am a sticker (sic) for discipline and demand that I am obeyed'.[50] It was the worst of many blasts Smith fired at Barassi. Although he was hard on most of his players, Barassi was his 'favourite whipping-boy'.[51] Whenever Smith felt the Demons needed a lift, or a spray, he almost invariably needled, insulted or outright abused Barassi. Bluey Adams recalled:

> Norm would roast Barass unmercifully. Barass might make a minor mistake like staging for a free kick and I might make a *major* mistake like trying to mark when I should have punched and it costs us a goal, but Barass would be singled out. Norm would always pick on Barass first and the hardest. He was the scapegoat on numerous occasions.
>
> You'd walk up the race at half-time and the first thing you'd hear was Norm's voice: 'Jeeeeesus Ronny!' Norm would be standing there fuming and staring holes through Ron, and berating him.

---

[47] Ron Barassi. Interview with the author.
[48] Hugh McPherson. Interview with the author.
[49] John Beckwith. Interview with the author.
[50] *Melbourne Truth* series, 1962.
[51] Clyde Laidlaw. Interview with the author.

Everyone knew that deep down that Smithy and Barass loved each other, but because they were close, and just to make sure there wasn't even a hint of a perception of favouritism, Norm took it to the other extreme and almost victimised Barass. At times you'd be relieved and think: 'Phew! At least I'm off the hook'. But there were also occasions when I'd be thinking: 'This is grossly unfair'. I really felt for Barass at times.[52]

Barassi was Smith's weapon; not just one of the best players in the competition, but one who could produce his best when the stakes were highest, and find a way to conquer when the situation appeared hopeless. Smith knew Barassi could give more than others in terms of effort and performance; perhaps he also felt he could take more by way of abuse. Regardless, he knew how to push Barassi's buttons to achieve the desired result. At times, it was a case of the bigger the blast, the angrier the response, the better Barassi performed. Barassi said:

> After some of those bursts from Norm, I'd have steam coming out my ears and felt like I was going to explode, but I never back-chatted to Norm – that's not the done thing in a team environment; you're always best to just shut up and cop it. Aside from that, Norm would have gone absolutely bananas if I mouthed something back to him. But I'd virtually say to myself: 'I'll show you, you old bastard!' Then I'd go out and play the second half like a bloody man possessed. Later on, when you'd calmed down, after playing well in a winning side, you'd see the method in his madness. You'd realise that while you'd played the second half to spite Norm, you'd actually responded in the very manner Norm was hoping you would. The end had justified the means. Although, I must say, the 'means' was often quite mean![53]

Smith also believed: 'If they see me getting stuck into Ron first, and he's the best player, they'll all know they're lucky I'm not getting into them'.[54] However, the barrages became so commonplace that Barassi was seen as the buffer between Smith and the rest of the players and, according to John Lord, the message occasionally lost its impact. 'Sometimes when Barass was copping it,' Lord said, 'it was a bit like crying wolf once too often. You thought: "Barass is the sacrificial lamb again – we've heard all this before". We knew it was a bit artificial.'[55]

---

[52] Frank 'Bluey' Adams. Interview with the author.
[53] Ron Barassi. Interview with the author.
[54] Peter Smith. Interview with the author.
[55] John Lord. Interview with the author.

Amongst it all, though, there was the odd slice of humour – albeit unintentional – and the butt of the joke was Barassi. Keith Carroll said:

> At half-time one day, Norm had the 20 of us sweaty players crammed into the little property room, and he was standing in the middle, sweating and raining saliva all over us, the veins in his neck popping out, as he tried to fire us up. And then he said: 'Ronny, you're playing like a crab!'
> None of us knew what he meant.
> Then Norm said: 'Well, you've all seen a crab, haven't you?' Then he started moving like a crab, sideways across the room. Jeez it was funny. But you'd dare not laugh. A few of us put our heads down and tried our darndest not to laugh because Norm would have done his block.[56]

Smith's treatment of Barassi extended to marking him harshly in individual awards. Peter Smith said: 'Dad was on a panel on *The Tony Charlton Football Show* on Channel Nine and he had to give votes for their best player award. In this particular game, Ron was clearly best-on-ground and most people thought he was a shoe-in for the three votes, which would have won him the award, but Norm gave him only one or two votes, which meant Ron lost by a vote or something. It was another clear example of Norm not wanting to be seen to favour Ron'.

Poignantly, Peter Smith suggested that his father, on reflection, might have regretted the way he treated Barassi.

> If Dad was alive today, he'd probably say: 'Ron, I'm sorry; I was too hard on you'. Ron was a lot closer to Norm's feelings than any other player. He was virtually a son to him. I'm sure Norm loved Ron. But maybe he didn't show it to him.[57]

Ironically, Barassi later employed the same hard-nosed coaching methods with his champions as Smith had applied to him. And perhaps it was no coincidence that Barassi, like Smith, also enjoyed an ultra-successful coaching career.

Clyde Laidlaw was certain that it was Smith who moulded Barassi into the great he became. 'Barass had the raw ability, the strength of character, the enthusiasm and the devil in him,' Laidlaw said, 'but Norm polished it, drove him harder and further than he drove the rest of us, and brought it together for all to see. I think Barass has a lot to thank Norm for. Barass was fortunate that the stars were in

---

[56] Keith Carroll. Interview with the author.
[57] Peter Smith. Interview with the author.

alignment and that he was associated so closely with Norm Smith. Well, really, we were *all* fortunate'.[58]

🏆🏆🏆🏆🏆🏆🏆🏆🏆

After coaching against his mate Bill Stephen at Fitzroy one day in the mid-1950s, Norm Smith made what Stephen regarded as a startling revelation. As the pair discussed football in the after-match get-together at the Brunswick Street Oval, Smith shocked Stephen with his views on love and hate between players and coaches.

He told Stephen: 'I want my players to hate me'.

The remark didn't quite register with Stephen the first time. He couldn't believe his ears. But after a brief pause, he repeated: 'I want my players to *hate* me'. It was a powerful statement, and left a lasting impression on Stephen, who recalled:

> It might have been one of Norm's mad moments, but from the look in his eyes and the intensity with which he said it, I could tell he meant it. He reckoned: 'Only then will they give everything. If they love the coach, they won't, because he's probably too soft on them. My players can love me as much as they want, but that won't do anything for me. But if they hate me, they'll do everything for me because they'll be driven by hatred'.
>
> Years later, I heard one of Norm's former players speak disparagingly, almost with bitterness, about how hard he was, and I was immediately reminded of what Norm had told me. I thought: 'The man was a genius'.[59]

To Melbourne players, this would have explained everything; not least of all, why he drove them so mercilessly. Some of his players perhaps did hate him, if not completely then at least some of the time. Mention the phrase 'fair and just' to a Melbourne player of this era and it usually prompts a snigger. It originated on a post-season trip – some say in Perth, others say New Zealand – when a player had the following exchange with Smith:

> Player: There's no doubt about you, Norm; you're very fair and just.
> Smith: Gee, thanks.
> Player: Yeah, a *fair* bastard and *just* a prick!

---

[58] Clyde Laidlaw. Interview with the author.
[59] Bill Stephen. Interview with the author.

THE MOST BITTER DISAPPOINTMENT [1958]

This soon became a running joke, but Smith's reaction to it would vary depending on the manner and environment in which it was mentioned, and the individual responsible.

He openly admitted he was dictatorial disciplinarian – 'but... an honest one'[60] – who acknowledged that his approach had at times 'made life difficult' for himself and others. He said: 'I will rant and rave, I will bully, I will praise and plead... Sometimes it must be wearing on everybody, but as I say to the boys: "You may think I am pushing you too hard, but this is the way I work. If you win, you'll like me; if you lose, you'll hate me".' For this reason, he once even remarked that his nickname ought to have been 'Torture'.[61]

He later elaborated:

> I was tough with players. I was hard, I was demanding of them – you've got to be all these things or it's no good being in it. You can say I lacked tact and you could be right. I'm not even denying this. Personally, I don't think of my approach as (displaying a) lack of tact. Blunt, yes. But at the same time honest. Sure, I could have tried a different approach. I could have been loved by the players. But I wouldn't have been successful and neither would Melbourne.[62]

To illustrate his point, he cited the example of Knute Rockne, the legendary American football coach.[63]

> I remember reading a story in an American book once about a football coach at Notre Dame. His name was Hugh Devore. He must have been a fine bloke. The players loved him, they thought he was tremendous. So they promptly went out and lost six matches in a row for him... The same university (earlier) had a coach named Knute Rockne who lifted them. He was the most fantastic coach of the period over there. He was tough and he was ruthless and he got results. To me, the two theories speak for themselves.[64]

He also believed that his players, either immediately or eventually, came around to his way of thinking.

---

[60] *Midweek Magazine*, August 1964.
[61] *The Sun*, Saturday, July 31, 1965.
[62] *The Sun* series, 1967.
[63] Between 1918 and 1930, Knute Rockne established what was then a college football record winning percentage of 88.1 percent with the University of Notre Dame.
[64] *The Sun* series, 1967.

I think the boys themselves have a perfect understanding. They know that by being a disciplinarian I'm only doing it for their good and for the good of the team and the club in general... I know boys who have left here and gone to other clubs who will now say, 'You were hard. Things are relaxed here, but we would sooner be back'... In the long run they're appreciative of my efforts, just as I am appreciative of their efforts to change their ways... With some players you have these little clashes more frequently than with others, but after a year or two they are prepared to see it your way. This... is dictatorial. It tends again to the disciplinary side of it, but it is most essential. This is where a team is made.[65]

Generally, the Melbourne players felt their coach was hard – *very* hard; 'a real tough bastard'[66] – but fair. Past Demon great Percy Beames, who retained close contact with his old club while writing for *The Age*, went a little further in his description of his former teammate: 'He was tough, almost cruel, but scrupulously honest and fair'.[67] The fairness factor was an essential ingredient – without it, the logical sequence of events would have been for players to rebel, and even revolt, which would likely have spelled the end of Smith's long reign. But it never got to that, nor even threatened to. While individual players at times felt aggrieved, the overwhelming majority – happily or otherwise – conformed with their coach's demands.

The Smith style found an ally in the positive peer pressure that developed in a playing group so accustomed to, and expectant of, success – success that had been achieved Smith's way. It might well have been possible to achieve success with other methods, but the Melbourne players didn't have an alternative point of reference on this front – at least, not one that had been as successful – so they went with it, at times with grimacing reluctance, but ultimately, almost without fail, acknowledging that it got results.

Laurie Mithen, who had his share of tense moments with his coach, later reflected: 'It was a real education to play under him as a coach. He made the rules and he enforced them, and you can't ask for a straighter deal than that. It makes playing pretty easy when you know exactly where you're going and you accept what's said. And most of the players that I've played with down there were willing to do this and this is, I think, the reason for our success over the years; the fact that no matter whether you thought he was good or bad, or making mistakes or

---

[65] *Midweek Magazine*, August 1964.
[66] John Lord. Interview with the author.
[67] *The Age*, Monday July 30, 1973.

the best in the world, you still did what he said. And if players don't do this with a coach, no matter who he is, well you will not have success'.[68]

Clyde Laidlaw said: 'Just about every player I know who played under Norm Smith has a story to tell, and it was usually an abusive situation – and Norm was the one being abusive. Something would annoy him and that would be the trigger; he'd latch onto it and drive it for everything it was worth. Every player copped it somewhere along the line. He was like a schoolteacher who would tell you off in front of the whole class and make you feel very small, with the idea that it would teach you a lesson. That was one of Norm's teaching methods, to stand you up and toughen you up'.[69]

In this manner, Smith 'loved' his players more with each passing season. Keith Carroll explained that in Smith's early days as coach at Melbourne, 'he was one of the boys to a point, a bit of a joker, but as the years went by and we became more and more successful, he gradually got harder and harder'. However, Carroll understood the need for a tougher stance, saying: 'Well, it was getting harder every year because everyone was trying to knock Melbourne off – each week, it was like a Grand Final for the opposition – so Norm's way of dealing with that and staying at the top was by becoming tougher to try to draw even more out of us'.[70]

Although 'the penalty occasionally exceeded the misdemeanour or shortcoming', Smith's criticisms were 'generally warranted'[71] and 'needed to be said'.[72] Tassie Johnson said: 'Norm's verbal outbursts all made sense. If I'd been the target, I might initially have been angry or upset, but I always looked back on what he'd had to say and I'd think: "Yeah, well, I did do that. I deserved that".'[73]

Ian Thorogood added: 'If all of the players who played under Norm are fair dinkum, about 90 percent would say: "Yes, I was verbally abused, but I forgive him because I understood what he was on about". Even the players who cried after copping a burst, and there are a number of them – I saw about six cry. It was all about trying to get that player to do better, and it was the only way Norm knew to get them to do better, and Norm was never satisfied. There might only be two or three who never forgave him for using that method. They probably nearly got to the stage of leaving, but as far as I'm aware no-one actually did that'.[74]

---

[68] *The Tony Charlton Football Show*, Channel Nine, Sunday July 25, 1965.
[69] Clyde Laidlaw. Interview with the author.
[70] Keith Carroll. Interview with the author.
[71] Frank 'Bluey' Adams. Interview with the author.
[72] Bryan Kenneally. Interview with the author.
[73] Robert 'Tassie' Johnson. Interview with the author.
[74] Ian Thorogood. Interview with the author.

Smith had 'nothing against' players who cried. He said: 'I am a very sensitive man and I show my emotions, too... I'm (not) a fire-breather by inclination. On the contrary'.[75] However, Smith was also 'very careful to pick his mark' when it came to belittling a player. Bluey Adams said: 'If a mistake had been made by a young player who hadn't yet developed his confidence, Norm would go easier on him, whereas he'd really roast an older player for doing the same thing'.[76]

Noel Clarke, who left Melbourne because of the restrictions Smith placed on him as a forward, had a rounded view of his methods. 'He would only occasionally pat you on the back, but he would always tell you where you went wrong,' Clarke said. 'If you played well, he might say: "Well, you did a bit better today, but you'd want to keep it up. Don't forget to do this and this". Whatever you did was never good enough. It was just his nature. But I think that helps you in a lot of ways. At times, you can get too much praise and, if you're a young bloke, your head can blow up and you can start thinking you're better than you are. You've got to keep an even balance, and I think Norm did that, and perhaps went a little bit the other way.'[77]

Adams explained that, in the context of Smith's tirades, it was important to remember: 'A coach is working under incredible pressure, which can cause fluctuations in their moods. But a lot of us expect a coach to behave like a rational human being 24 hours a day, which is too much to expect, because human nature doesn't work like that with most people, and Norm wasn't immune to it either'.[78]

Smith behaved perhaps a little irrationally towards Ian Thorogood in the property room at half-time one day. A witness, Hugh McPherson, said:

> I was stretching and Thurra was puffing away on a cigarette when the door opened and in walked the redhead. He referred to something Thurra had or hadn't done in the first half. Norm said: 'What did you do such-and-such for?'
>
> Thurra replied to Smithy with the cigarette still hanging out the side of his mouth. Smithy didn't like that, so he went whack! He knocked the ciggie out of Thurra's gob. He did it so hard and fast that it looked like Christmas! Ash went everywhere.[79]

Thorogood added:

---

[75] *The Sun*, Saturday, July 31, 1965.
[76] Frank 'Bluey' Adams. Interview with the author.
[77] Noel Clarke. Interview with the author.
[78] Frank 'Bluey' Adams. Interview with the author.
[79] Hugh McPherson. Interview with the author.

THE MOST BITTER DISAPPOINTMENT [1958]

But this day I felt a bit of a windy-woosh, and I thought Norm was actually throwing a punch at me. But then I realised he wasn't trying to hit me but my cigarette, and he actually succeeded in knocking it out of my mouth. He was pretty pissed off.

But in all my years at Melbourne, I never saw Norm hit anyone. He never even laid a hand on his players – not once did he even shake one of them. Abuse? Yeah. But then, to his credit, he would try to pick up the pieces – or have Jim Cardwell do it for him.[80]

Thorogood believed there was a misconception of Norm Smith as a kind of sadist who enjoyed inflicting pain and misery on his players. 'Because of his stubbornness and his ruthlessness,' Thorogood said, 'Norm occasionally rubbed people the wrong way. To be honest, you wouldn't talk to anybody the way he spoke to some of our players. That's where certain individuals paint him as arrogant, selfish, insincere, etc. But I can't believe that there are people who say he was like that. It's not accurate at all. We saw the tyrant that kept our feet on the ground, and the father figure who picked us up when we were down. In life, it's an art to be at both ends of that scale.'[81]

Five former Demons interviewed for this book – John Beckwith, Ken Melville, Ian Ridley, Geoff Tunbridge and John Townsend – insisted they were never subjected to a Norm Smith blast. It must be said that each of these players was highly respected by Smith and if he had favourites, they would have been among them. As such, they would have given him little reason to take them to task.

Beckwith, the near-flawless defender, said: 'Norm never really criticised, or ever said I was doing anything wrong as a player. He gave me very simple instructions: "Get the ball first, Becky. Keep him on the boundary line", etc., and that was it. I got off pretty lightly'.[82]

Melville revealed that he found it difficult to reconcile the Norm Smith he occasionally reads about – the 'hard taskmaster and stern disciplinarian' – with the Norm Smith who coached him from 1952 to 1956. He said: 'The discipline side of him, I thought, was that he kept everything simple and straightforward, and we had to stick to that. The only time he rebuked me in any way was when I arrived late to a game. I was held up in traffic or something and he got quite upset about it. He told me that just wasn't on. But I accepted it because I think he was quite right in what he said'.[83]

---

[80] Ian Thorogood. Interview with the author.
[81] Ian Thorogood. Interview with the author.
[82] John Beckwith. Interview with the author.
[83] Ken Melville. Interview with the author.

Ridley was acutely aware of Smith's ability to 'nail a player to the wall' with a few well-chosen words. 'Smithy didn't pull any punches,' he said. 'He could land 'em pretty hard when he had to, but he wouldn't be trying to make a bloody fool of you, either. Any hard words he had to say would stay within the confines of the team and those four walls.' Ridley never had cause to question Smith's coaching methods. 'Smithy never embarrassed or humiliated me – in any shape or form – in my eight years under him,' he said. 'I think he realised I was trying my best and I was a team player. They were two of the things he wanted from his players'.[84]

Tunbridge explained: 'It was quite funny that while Norm had this reputation as a fearsome coach – and he gave Barass some awful bursts, and he had Lordy in tears – but he never told me off. Never even instructed me to do anything. He occasionally sent out a message with the runner to say: "Tunner, browse around". In other words, "leave your position and roam wherever you like to get a kick".' He also recalled: 'One time Eric Guy of St Kilda was getting heaps of kicks on me and the message came out from Hughie McPherson: "For Christ's sake, get on Guy and you might get a kick!" But that was about the extent of it'.[85]

Townsend said: 'Smithy never got stuck into me at all; never gave me a lecture individually. He got into the good blokes most of the time, so he probably thought I was doing as well as I could do with what I had'.[86]

Hassa Mann said that Smith's approach attracted enormous loyalty and respect from his players.

> Undoubtedly, Melbourne players played for Norm, rather than in spite of him. He evoked great loyalty and passion from us. He was the only person in my life who, if he said: 'I want you to run through that brick wall', I would do it, knowing I'd knock myself out, and I'd get up again and do it for him. I would do anything for Norm because I respected him so much, and I realised very early on that: 'If I'm going to experience success, it's going to be with Norm Smith. He would provide that opportunity'.[87]

Smith was also very hard on himself, and it could dictate his moods at home. Peter Smith recalled: 'When his teams lost he blamed himself; when they won he gave them (the players) all the credit'.[88]

---

[84] Ian Ridley. Interview with the author.
[85] Geoff Tunbridge. Interview with the author.
[86] John Townsend. Interview with the author.
[87] Hassa Mann. Interview with the author.
[88] *The Sporting Globe*, Saturday September 7, 1974.

THE MOST BITTER DISAPPOINTMENT [1958]

Melbourne was hurtling towards history. After losing to Fitzroy in round 11, the Demons had won six of their next seven matches – the single loss being by just three points to Essendon at Windy Hill – to win their fourth minor premiership in succession, with a record of 15-3, three games clear at the top of the ladder.

Adding to the culture of success that pervaded Melbourne Football Club, the Demons' performances at the three levels had won them their third McLelland Trophy in four years. Now their focus was squarely on making it four premierships from four attempts. No result is ever certain in sport, but the Demons were as close to sure things as there had ever been.

With a bit of luck, it could have been a Melbourne-Fitzroy/brother-vs-brother Grand Final. The Lions had regained second spot in round 14 when they trounced Collingwood by eight goals at Brunswick Street, but they soon received some shattering news. About a month before the finals, Len Smith suffered a heart attack. Fortunately, despite the seriousness of Len's condition, the attack wasn't severe enough to threaten his life. Doctors gave him the 'all-clear' to resume coaching duties a few weeks later. In Len's temporary absence, skipper Butch Gale became the stand-in playing coach, but Len resumed the role in the finals. When asked of Fitzroy's premiership aspirations, Gale told *The Sporting Globe*: 'I hope we can win the flag, if only for Len Smith's sake'.

With their coach sidelined, it's little wonder the rudderless Lions didn't produce their best. In fact, they reverted to their worst football, surrendering second spot after a dismal showing against the lowly Footscray at the Western Oval. After leading by 22 points at quarter-time, the Lions scraped together just 2.7 for the rest of the match while the Bulldogs piled on 20.11 to record a shock 90-point win. The Lions had the chance to take second position and the double-chance right until the last round, but they fell to Hawthorn by four points at Glenferrie Oval, and Collingwood relegated them to third by just 2.8 percent. This loss to the Hawks was to prove critical.

Fitzroy bowed out in the first week of the finals – but not without a fight. The Lions faced North Melbourne – which they had defeated by 120 and 31 points respectively during the minor rounds. However, minus injured stars Kevin Murray and Don Furness, Fitzroy was the side under pressure all afternoon. They trailed by 18 points at three-quarter-time but kicked four of the next five goals to take a two-point lead in time-on. With just seconds left, Fitzroy wingman Vin Williams was flattened by Allen Aylett on the defensive side of the centre. A groggy Williams had to be helped to his feet to take his free kick. A pass to Butch Gale at centre-half-forward was disallowed because Williams hadn't kicked over his mark. On his second attempt, Williams kicked towards Eddie Goodger in the muddy centre, but Goodger slipped, the ball was turned over and the Kangaroos slotted the winning goal with literally the last kick of the day. Most supporters slammed Williams for the two-point loss, but his coach refused to use him as the scapegoat. Len told Alf Brown:

> Williams was unlucky. His mistake was made in the last minute and everyone left the ground with it fresh in their memory. But every Fitzroy player made mistakes during the match. You can say all those mistakes contributed to our defeat. It's unfair to single Williams out and make him take all the blame.
>
> Instead of thinking about Fitzroy's defeat, I'm thinking about their near-win. I'm very proud of my boys and the way they fought back.
>
> Fitzroy had a good run all year but luck deserted us when we most needed it. We lost Murray and Furness and then it rained. I think we are faster than North; the heavy slippery ground did not suit us.
>
> But I think we had an excellent season – from second-last to the finals... We weren't disgraced and I didn't see anyone leaving the ground before the finish so the crowd must have been satisfied, too.[89]

Former Fitzroy star Alan Fitcher later wrote in *The Sporting Globe* that Len Smith had proved he 'was the wizard coach, able to make winning moves at the drop of a hat and cover weaknesses with a skill seldom seen before. He was the football genius; he made ordinary players champions'. Fitzroy's committee was also more than satisfied with Len's debut season, quickly moving to reappoint him for a further two years, until the end of the 1960 season. Norm Smith, too, was impressed with Len's 'attention to detail', his 'wonderful ability to find a way', and the fact 'he didn't worry much about... orthodox or pre-conceived ideas'.[90]

The overwhelming preconception of the football public, and perhaps many members of the other two remaining teams – Collingwood and North Melbourne – was that Melbourne would canter to the premiership. This view was merely reinforced by the Demons' 45-point drubbing of the Magpies in the second

---

[89] *The Herald*, Monday September 1, 1958.
[90] *The Age*, May 14, 1971.

semi-final. That they did it in the wet with such a comprehensive scoreline – 11.12 (78) to just 4.9 (33) – added to the inevitability. The Demons hadn't allowed Collingwood to operate with any system – each of the Magpies' goals had come from quick snaps out of packs.

'We'd absolutely thrashed them,' John Beckwith reflected. 'We looked invincible.'[91]

The problem was they starting to *think* they were invincible. All of which added to the tense demeanour of their coach.

Early in the landslide win, Norm Smith had been involved in a controversial clash with umpire Allan Nash. The ball had gone over the boundary line near where Smith was sitting on the coach's bench when Nash looked towards the bench and yelled: 'Chop it out! I am not going to put up with that sort of thing!'

Believing Nash had referred to him, Smith jumped up, stood on the boundary line, waved his finger menacingly at Nash and barked: 'Never mind about us! We can say what we like! You look after your umpiring and get on with the game!'

Both men quickly resumed their respective jobs, and after the match cleared things up over a chat. Nash had actually directed his comments at Hugh McPherson, who had apparently criticised his umpiring. The incident was written off as simply 'a misunderstanding'. However, it had threatened to spark chaos. Soon after Smith's outburst, a male spectator jumped the fence and ran 50 metres onto the field to abuse Nash, who pushed him away with both hands. Fortunately the man ceased his attack, but somehow he disappeared back into the crowd and eluded police.[92] One wonders what the consequences might have been for all involved – not least of all Smith – if Nash had been injured.

Collingwood, which had won just two of its previous six matches – their four losses being by an average of 29 points – regained some semblance of form when it defeated North Melbourne by 20 points in the preliminary final. The Magpies had been supreme for most of the afternoon, leading by more than 50 points until midway through the final term when the Kangaroos kicked five belated goals.

But the Magpies appeared to be just making up the numbers as most experts predicted a virtual replay of the second semi-final result. Melbourne hadn't been defeated by the Magpies since round 11, 1955, and that was in the confines of Victoria Park. The 10 head-to-head clashes since then had resulted in nine Melbourne wins and a draw. The Demons had triumphed in each of their previous nine encounters with the Magpies on the wide expanses of the MCG.

---

[91] John Beckwith. Interview with the author.
[92] *The Age*, Monday September 8, 1958.

Smith had been acutely aware of the possibility of his players becoming complacent and a month before their first final, had demanded at a Tuesday night training session: 'Right-oh, boys, the time has come. From now on, every game is a Grand Final. I want every man to get really stuck into his training tonight – and every night until we finish the season'.[93]

Despite what some Collingwood folk would have us believe with the benefit of hindsight, the realists among them didn't think they stood a chance, either. Even the Magpies' acting skipper, Murray Weideman, conceded: 'They were a much better side... Deep down in my own heart, I knew we couldn't beat them. There was no hope in the world of beating them'.[94]

But from the start of the day, there were signs that this would be no normal day, and that things would not necessarily go to plan.

Years later, Smith joked privately: 'It was Marj's fault we lost in '58'. I always wore a particular pair of green socks for big matches, but they were still wet – Marj hadn't dried them in time – so I had to settle for a pair of red socks. I didn't have my lucky charm – we were jinxed!'[95]

There was also a sensation that had nothing to do with actual play. The players' guernsey numbers had been unlawfully printed in *The Sun* – *The Football Record* held exclusive publishing rights – so the VFL forced both clubs to change their numbers. As a result, Ron Barassi, for example, swapped his now iconic No. 31 for No. 2. Soon it would appear that the sides had traded jumpers as well.

While Phonse Kyne revved up his Magpies with an inspirational address about protecting their proud record of four successive flags (from 1927-30), and ominously told them to leave the rough stuff to Weideman and Barry 'Hooker' Harrison, Smith issued a stern yet prophetic warning to his team. 'In the second semi-final,' he said, 'the Collingwood fellas reckon they nearly had us (sucked) in. Don't let it happen. Just remember what's at stake today.'[96]

In wet and heavy conditions, Melbourne got the jump-start, kicking the first three goals of the match, and five-to-two by quarter-time. The game appeared to be following a familiar pattern. No-one, not even the most parochial of Collingwood supporters, could have predicted what would happen in the next two quarters.

Weideman and Harrison (who had been given the job on Barassi) changed the complexion of the game with their ferociousness both on and off the ball. They sparked melees and many Demons, most notably Barassi and Laurie Mithen,

---

[93] *The Sun*, Wednesday August 6, 1958.
[94] Murray Weideman, on the *Red and Blue* documentary, 2005.
[95] Mike Williamson. Interview with the author.
[96] Geoff Tunbridge. Interview with the author.

shifted their focus from the ball to retribution. In the meantime, the Magpies began to play systematic football and stole a two-point lead by half-time. As Weideman walked up the players' race, his coach, Phonse Kyne, said, almost disbelievingly: 'Murray, whatever you're doing, just keep doing it.'[97]

While the Demons were rattled and beginning to doubt themselves under such a full-on physical assault, the Magpies, rank outsiders at best before the first bounce, were starting to believe they could actually achieve the impossible.

There was 'hell to pay' in the Melbourne rooms. Smith was so concerned about the scatterbrained approach of some of his players that he 'made them promise they wouldn't get involved in fights after half-time'.[98] He demanded greater discipline and sole focus on playing football, using words to the effect of: 'Don't get sucked in, boys. Don't let them drag you down'.[99]

He also had a crack at Keith Carroll, who recalled: 'I was playing on Brian Beers and he stayed right out on the boundary at half-forward. I kept saying to him: "Come into the game!" I left him and he kicked a goal, and Norm abused me at half-time. He said: "What the hell do you think you're doing out there?!" I said: "If I sit on him all day, Norm, I won't get a kick". But Norm said: "That'll suit me – stay on him and keep him out wide!" That simplified my role for the day, but it didn't make for any great enjoyment on my part'.[100]

For the Demons, anything resembling enjoyment evaporated in the third quarter as Collingwood piled on the misery, adding 5.3 to 0.2 to lead by 33 points at three-quarter time. In the second and third terms combined, the Magpies had outscored Melbourne 10.7 to 2.5.

With skirmishes breaking out all over the field, Barassi and Harrison were reported for striking each other, while Ian Ridley was dealt with severely by Bill Serong. Ridley said: 'Serong plastered my nose across my face and I felt like I was almost dead. But Norm's words were ringing in my head. I wasn't dead or knocked out, so I got up and walked off the ground. It took a lot of guts to do that – I was in a such a bad way that I can't remember much of that game – but that's the kind of thing you felt you had to do when Norm Smith was your coach'.[101]

The Demons finally got their game going in the final term. Amid the belated fightback, John Beckwith had a sudden burst of inspiration. 'I had this fantasy early in the last quarter,' Beckwith explained, 'that I could take off down the

---

[97] Murray Weideman. Interview with the author.
[98] Hugh McPherson. Interview with the author.
[99] Frank 'Bluey' Adams. Interview with the author.
[100] Keith Carroll. Interview with the author.
[101] Ian Ridley. Interview with the author.

ground, be a hero and kick a goal and win the game. But I thought: "Jeez no! Imagine what Norm would say if it doesn't come off and the ball rebounds and they seal the game". The consequences of it going wrong were enough to put me off attempting it. If I only had the guts to try it. After all, it couldn't have worked out any worse than it did.'[102]

Melbourne held Collingwood goalless in the last quarter but could mange just 2.4 themselves. It was a case of too little, too late, and they lost by 18 points in one of the greatest upsets in Grand Final history.

Against overwhelming odds, the Magpies had found something special and kept their proud record intact. The manner of Melbourne's capitulation was a subject of great anguish for Norm Smith. After all the years of simply copping the blows, 'turning the other cheek' and just being satisfied with winning the match, the Demons had lost their cool, lost the premiership and ultimately surrendered a loftier place in history.

Percy Beames believed that 'several Melbourne players became timid, while others were "baited" and lost their effectiveness because of Collingwood's fierce but well-applied vigour'.[103] The 'baited' Barassi admitted he had been 'sucked in'[104] and played 'a shocker',[105] but insisted he 'couldn't complain about Collingwood's tactics because, while they were rough and tough, they weren't dirty'.[106] Significantly, he revealed: 'Half of us wanted to fight and the other half squibbed it… or looked as though they squibbed it anyway… You can't ever succeed in a team game unless you're all doing the same sort of thing. I reckon if we'd been… united, we would have won because there's no doubt in my mind that we were the best team on the year'.[107]

Such statements counted for nothing, and Smith knew it. Most disappointingly, his players had done the very thing he preached against. Previously, he had watched with horror when one of his players belted an opponent in a cowardly manner. Smith had sacked the player with the words: 'We can't have that. One bad apple and the whole case is soured'. There was no more sour, bitter afternoon in Smith's career than the 1958 Grand Final.

After the match, as agony and despair gripped the Melbourne changerooms, Smith told Checker Hughes: 'Well, Checker, when Phonse Kyne comes in,

---

[102] John Beckwith. Interview with the author.
[103] *The Age*, September 26, 1960.
[104] *AFL Record*, round eight, May 16-18, 2003.
[105] Ron Barassi. Interview with the author.
[106] Collins, Ben, *The Champions: Conversations with Great Players and Coaches of Australian Football*, GSP, 2006.
[107] Ron Barassi, on the *Red and Blue* documentary, 2005.

THE MOST BITTER DISAPPOINTMENT [1958]

we've got to be very, very gracious'.[108] After waiting a short time for his coaching rival, Smith decided to make the first move – he walked through a door to the adjoining changerooms where the Collingwood side was celebrating its 13th premiership. Although he 'must have been bleeding to buggery',[109] he warmly congratulated the Magpies on their victory... in his own unique way.

A hush came over the Collingwood rooms as the unmistakeable figure of Norm Smith made his way through the throng of revellers. He stood up on a rub-down table and looked around the room, eyeballing as many people as he could.

'I *hate* you bastards!' he snarled, shocking many Magpies present. 'But, by God, I *admire* you!'

When the applause subsided, he added: 'Congratulations. You were the better team on the day. But we'll be back next year'. He then quietly made his way out of the room to confront his players.[110]

Although Smith's reaction to the defeat was variously described as being 'savage'[111] and 'very hostile'[112] for some time, he managed to remain 'very subdued'[113] and 'did well in the circumstances to conceal his emotions'[114] from his players on the night of the loss. In fact, he was 'at pains to console the players'.[115] 'Bluey' Adams said: 'He would've realised that we were as disappointed as he was, and that berating us wouldn't have served any purpose. He lived up to his own motto about being gracious in defeat'.[116]

Hugh McPherson knew Smith better than most, and, after the 1958 Grand Final, spent more time with him than most. He recalled:

> Norm was ropeable. Filthy. He couldn't believe his players could be so lacking in discipline and concentration in such a big game – a game where they could have achieved history. From a personal point of view, he was also a big believer in teams reflecting their coach – and he wasn't very happy with the reflection he saw that day. They had broken the promise they had made to him at half-time. That loss hurt Norm more than any other.

---

[108] Related by Melbourne stalwart Dudley Phillips in *The Grand Old Flag: The History of the Melbourne Football Club*, by Lynda Carroll, Hardie Grant, 1999.
[109] Garry Pearce. Interview with the author.
[110] Mike Williamson. Interview with the author. Williamson was in the room, conducting interviews for 3AW.
[111] John Beckwith. Interview with the author.
[112] Clyde Laidlaw. Interview with the author.
[113] Frank 'Bluey' Adams. Interview with the author.
[114] Clyde Laidlaw. Interview with the author.
[115] John Lord. Interview with the author.
[116] Frank 'Bluey' Adams. Interview with the author.

After the game, we sat down and he turned to me and said: 'Can you believe it, Hughie? Can you *believe* it?'

I said: 'No I can't, Norm. You've turned them into a wonderful team. For them to let you down the way they did, I know how you feel because I feel the same way'.

He said: 'Maybe one day they'll realise the opportunity they blew today'.[117]

At Melbourne's Grand Final dinner – where pre-made *1958 premiership* cake had to be struck off the menu[118] – Smith 'paid credit to Collingwood and admitted the Demons hadn't been good enough on the day'.[119] He also lifted the spirits of those present with a positive outlook for 1959 and beyond, declaring:

> To say I'm not disappointed would be wrong... Throughout the year, you have been the best side. At the end of the year, you are not the best side – Collingwood are. So you can start off next year from scratch. We will come back next year and come back fighting. Defeat acts as a spur to do better. We will do better, because we now realise we are not invincible. We fell down in some departments today, but I feel the lapse was only temporary. Four Melbourne premierships in a row will not be impossible in the future.[120]

Three-and-a-half years later, with the value of hindsight, he said: 'Whenever a new force has emerged in the League and appeared likely to equal or break the record, it has been Collingwood which has risen to break the run. I thought we had the record in our grasp... I think the threat to their record was one of the main reasons why they beat us... We were mad keen... I think the rivalry between the two clubs springs mainly from the fact that we had taken over from them as the power in the VFL. We were hot favourites... but I am always very uneasy against Collingwood. They really played hard that day and deserved their win. That was another of my greatest disappointments'.[121]

The loss was so traumatic for wingman Brian Dixon – who 'felt semi-responsible for the result' after being soundly beaten by Ken Turner – that he seriously considered retiring from VFL football. In the end, he 'hung in there'.[122] Not so Keith Carroll, who was inadvertently influenced by Smith to end his seven-season career. Carroll said:

---

[117] Hugh McPherson. Interview with the author.
[118] John Lord. Interview with the author.
[119] Frank 'Bluey' Adams. Interview with the author.
[120] *The Herald*, Monday September 22, 1958.
[121] *Melbourne Truth* series, 1962.
[122] Brian Dixon. Interview with the author.

Norm was a hard man, even when I retired. I actually retired because of him. I had a shocker in the '58 Grand Final, and in the summer I went down to the MCG to watch a cricket match, and Norm was there. He came over and said: 'How are you going, Keith? Are you getting fit?' I said: 'Yeah, I'm trying'. He said: 'Well you'd want to be fit enough to win the Brownlow this year, otherwise you won't be making it'. I'd had plenty of injuries by that stage, and I saw the writing on the wall, so I said: 'OK then, Norm, I'll give it away then'.

Carroll was immediately reminded of a comment Smith once made to him.

I asked him: 'Do you ever see any of the old players who were here when I first got here (in 1952)?' He said: 'No, and they probably wouldn't want to see me, either', because apart from the players that retired voluntarily, Norm had to end some careers, which is all part of coaching. But Norm and I weren't on bad terms.

When the (1959) season started, Norm got Jim Cardwell to ask me if I'd like to go back and play in the seconds. I said: 'Does Norm want me to come back?' Jim said: 'Yes'. That was unusual for Norm. I went down to the club and Norm said: 'Have you thought any more about what Jim said?' I said: 'What do you mean?' He said: 'Come back and play in the seconds and you might be a chance of getting back in the firsts'. I said: 'No, Norm, I've retired'. I would have been one of the only blokes who Norm asked to reconsider their retirement. In the end, Jim Cardwell got me down there to help them on match days. I basically sat on the bench with Norm for four years.[123]

---

[123] Keith Carroll. Interview with the author.

17

ORDER RESTORED

[1959]

Public humiliation affects people in different ways. Some meekly slink away from the spotlight, become virtual recluses and are never heard of again, while others at the opposite end of the scale – men like Norm Smith – accept their predicament, however reluctantly, and allow the agony, the guilt and the jibes to wash over them, and use it as a catalyst, a motivational tool, to get better and prove to the world just how good they truly are.

The 1958 Grand Final loss would continue to eat away at Norm Smith until he won another premiership – and probably well after that, too – but his ability to quickly regain his positive outlook, refocus his attention on the prize, and formulate new plans for success was never more evident than just weeks after the devastating defeat.

If the Melbourne players thought Smith was tough before the defeat to Collingwood, they were in for an even ruder awakening in the build-up to the 1959 season. From Smith's perspective, punishment wasn't the motivation – it was all about leaving nothing to chance in their preparation, with the aim that they might eventually earn some form of redemption.

Clyde Laidlaw recalled: 'After the 1958 debacle, Norm and the club got savage. Summer training was ordered. That wasn't the done thing back then. Prior to that, some players did it of their own volition but it was never made compulsory for a whole team. It was like the order came from an army general'.[1]

Melbourne rover Bluey Adams, who doubled as the Australian professional sprint champion, worked on the speed of about a dozen players at the Albert Ground, while another group completed strength training conducted by famous Austrian-born athletics coach Franz Stampfl. Both programs reaped rewards.

---

[1] Clyde Laidlaw. Interview with the author.

Then there was the bane of most footballers' lives: the compulsory, unavoidable hard yards of distance running, often in sweltering heat. One of Smith's favourite methods of getting miles into his players' legs was having them run time trials around the perimeter of the MCG stadium – up to five laps, with just a short break after each lap. Smith viewed it as an ideal running route because it was impossible for players to take shortcuts. The slog was an eye-opening experience for new recruit Hassa Mann, who vividly recalled the discipline Smith enforced during these sessions.

> It was as hot as Hades – 102 or 104 degrees (Fahrenheit, 39-40ºC) and there was a group of about eight of us, and we were halfway around and getting all buggered and upset. A couple of the senior players were saying: 'Bloody Smithy this, and bloody Smithy that. I'd like to see him do it'. As one guy was roasting Norm, from out of nowhere, who should appear in a doorway as we were running past – Norm. We sprinted the rest of the way and when we got there Norm was waiting for us. He must have cut across the oval or something, at a pretty good rate too for a bloke his age. He emphasised to all of the players: 'Pre-season training needs to be hard. If you don't train hard, you don't get results. You get out of it what you put into it'. He couldn't let our group get away without some form of punishment, so he said: 'For the group that just finished, you'd better do another one'.[2]

Another recruit, Tassie Johnson, said there were ways and means of rorting the system. 'As we got older, we got more cunning, and Norm knew damn well what was going on,' Johnson said. 'All the young blokes trying out for a spot on the list would zip around the outside of the MCG as fast as they could, but they then faced the problem of having to beat that time on their next run. But the old diehards would just plod around the first time, so they could improve upon it the next time. Norm would get stuck into us for that. He was right on to us.'[3]

Just so that everyone was clear on the ultimate objective, Smith laid it on the line. 'Last year was a lost year,' he said, 'but if ever the opportunity arises again when we play in a Grand Final – and we want it to be this year – there is no way in the world that we will lose it, nor should we lose it'.[4]

---

[2] Hassa Mann. Interview with the author.
[3] Robert 'Tassie' Johnson. Interview with the author.
[4] Hassa Mann. Interview with the author.

Nothing was going to stand between the Demons and glory, if Smith could help it. And that extended to his own life as well.

For the first time in several years, Smith had to make a significant decision regarding the way he divided his time, between work and football. His right-hand man for 16 years, reliable Russ Brown, whom Smith trusted implicitly, had moved on after accepting a job in the paint industry. 'Naturally, Norm didn't like it,' Brown said. 'But he had to accept it. I'd never worked anywhere else, so I wanted to experience life outside. I'd say Norm begrudgingly accepted it. He understood why, but he didn't want to lose me just the same.'[5]

With VFL football becoming more professional each year – although not yet at a level that could be even termed *semi*-professional – and coaches starting to explore different methods of training, and different schools of thought, the job increasingly demanded more time. For similar reasons, Jim Cardwell, who had operated his engineering business in the city, had in 1958 become the first full-time club secretary in the VFL.

Until now, Smith had knocked off work early on training nights, and often he would be down at the club by mid-afternoon discussing matters with Cardwell. But now something had to give. Smith already had another worker in his employ who was literally that – a man who would 'work like a Trojan' – but who wasn't business-minded enough to run the operation in the boss's absence[6]. In the short term at least, Smith spent a little more time than he would have liked picking up some of the slack left by Russ Brown. However, he could never fully replace Russ, and nor did he intend to by himself.

Smith had made sacrifices in his working life, and he expected his players to at least make some sacrifices in their own lives.

When the intra-club practice matches started, Smith clamped down harder than ever on players who had cricket commitments, which cut across pre-season football training and practice matches in the 'overlap' period. Even the exceptional case of Neil Crompton – who was an accomplished batsman in the Victorian side and a leading member of Melbourne's district cricket team – encountered difficulties on this front. Mercifully, Crompton, 21, was able to reach a compromise with Smith that allowed him to play in Melbourne's 1958/59 premiership side while satisfying most of his football requirements. It was a harsh stance, particularly considering Smith's cricketing background.

However, there was no such compromise for Clyde Laidlaw, who said:

---

[5] Russell Brown. Interview with the author.
[6] Russell Brown. Interview with the author.

> I was playing cricket in the eastern suburbs and we beat the top side in a semi-final and both myself and a teammate made hundreds. It was mentioned in *The Sun* because the other side had been undefeated until that game. We were doing pre-season football training at the time and Norm said: 'Do you play cricket, do you?' I said: 'Yes, I play out in the eastern suburbs'. He said: 'Well, practice matches start next week, so you won't be playing in the Grand Final'.
>
> Looking back, I should have stood up to him. I should've said: 'Look, it's only a practice game'. But Norm made it hard for Neil Crompton, so I felt I had to do as he demanded.[7]

Smith's one-in-all-in, no-excuses-accepted attitude also came to the fore during the four practice matches. New players, including two prized recruits – Hassa Mann and Tassie Johnson – weren't spared.

Mann was regarded as the recruit of the year after being chased by nine of the 12 VFL clubs. A country boy from Merbein via Rutherglen, he chose Melbourne because he wanted to play for the best. 'If I was good enough to play,' he said, 'I thought it would be easier playing for a top side than a bottom side.'[8] However, Mann's initiation with the Demons was anything but easy. He 'hardly got a touch' in the first three practice matches, prompting Jim Cardwell, the man who had recruited him to Demonland to say: 'Hassa, you are a bit of an embarrassment to me'.[9] Smith's response to Mann's poor form was typically unforgiving. Rather than try to ease the pressure on his boom recruit, he intensified the pressure by directly opposing Mann to 'Mad Mick' Case, who was told to 'test out' the youngster. Not only was Case tough and 'a bit callous',[10] but he was fast and very skilful, having represented Victoria the previous season.

Consciously or not, it was a courageous move by Smith, as Mann already had a contingency plan. 'If things didn't go as planned at Melbourne,' Mann said, 'I only had to stand out of footy for four weeks and then I could leave as a free agent because my Form Four would have expired. Geelong had offered me a new Ford, and Richmond had offered me a new Holden.'[11] Such was not required, as Mann kicked four goals and starred in the final practice match, thus proving in his own mind, and those of the Melbourne hierarchy, that he had what it took to make it with the Demons.

---

[7] Clyde Laidlaw. Interview with the author.
[8] Hassa Mann, *Inside Football*, August 13, 2003.
[9] Hassa Mann. Interview with the author.
[10] Hassa Mann. Interview with the author.
[11] Hassa Mann. Interview with the author.

The full-back position was also up for grabs after Peter Marquis had suffered a career-ending injury during the pre-season. Two contenders emerged – 'Tassie' Bob Johnson (from Tasmania, hence his nickname, which distinguished him from 'Big Bob' Johnson) and Bernie Massey (who had graduated from the under-19s). Johnson, 21, wasn't initially recruited for a key defensive post, but Smith gave him no other option. Johnson said:

> In the practice games, I wasn't going so well at centre half-forward and at half-time, Norm took me off and tried a couple of others there in my place. Then Peter Marquis got hurt and Norm said to me: 'Can you play full-back?' I said: 'Never tried it'. He said: 'Well, you better get back there and try your bloody hardest, because if you don't do any good there, you're back to Tasmania'. It was quite an ultimatum to cop first up, but I knew he meant it.[12]

Massey, Johnson's younger rival for the full-back role, recalled a 'funny' first meeting with Smith.

> My full name is Bernard, and that's all anyone had ever called me until I met Norm. He said: 'What's your nickname?' I said: 'I don't have one'. He said: 'Well, what do your mates call you?' I said: 'Bernard'. He must have thought my name was a bit too straight-laced or something, because he said: 'Well I can't be out on the field saying: "Kick the ball to me, Bernard". You've got to have a nickname... All right then, I'll call you Bernie'. Funnily enough, I'd never been called Bernie in my life.[13]

Although Massey admitted that Johnson was 'probably a better full-back' than he was at the time, he didn't do himself any favours. Sometime before the season started, Massey had agreed to be the best man at a cousin's wedding, not realising that it coincided with the season-opener. Massey stunned Smith and his fellow selectors when he informed them of his unavailability. He spent the entire season in the reserves, while 'Tassie' Johnson settled in well at full-back.

With this final piece of the jigsaw in place, Smith was entitled to be optimistic. He publicly expressed his supreme confidence that the Demons would bounce back with a vengeance in 1959. 'I'll get them back on top this season,' he declared. 'If I don't, then I'll deserve a blasting from every Melbourne fan.'[14] It was a belief,

---

[12] Robert 'Tassie' Johnson. Interview with the author.
[13] Bernie Massey. Interview with the author.
[14] *SPORT* magazine, March 1959.

and a personal challenge, built on the strongest of foundations: unprecedented levels of fitness and strength, big-game experience, the relative youth of the playing group (the average age was 23), and a burning desire to erase the hurt of '58.

During a noteworthy speech at Melbourne's pre-season dinner, Smith challenged his players: 'We must recapture the determination we had four years ago. We have become brittle. Because of greater love of club, greater determination on the field, Collingwood took the premiership off us. Nobody gave them a chance... Too often last year I had to tell players at half-time: "Fight! Show more courage and determination!" I can't put courage into a player; the player must have it'.[15]

The Demons started the season in fine style against Richmond at Punt Road. After leading by just two points at the last change, they powered home with the breeze, adding 6.5 to 0.1 to win by 47 points. It was the VFL debut of Hassa Mann, who recounted that while Smith did him no favours in the practice matches, he certainly 'looked after' him during the final quarter avalanche.

> I was picked as 19th man and came on with about five minutes left. Back then, players didn't have to go off through the bench; they could get off the ground wherever was closest. Smithy engineered my first kick. One of our players was diagonally opposite us on the other side of the ground and as the ball started coming towards us out of the Richmond backline, Norm yelled: 'Get him off! Get him off!' The player took two steps over the boundary line and Norm shoved me out on to the ground. I was all on my own and I immediately took a mark and passed to Barassi and he kicked a goal.[16]

Mann was demoted to the reserves in round two. After his first reserves match, Smith told him: 'Good players don't play in the reserves'; and: 'When good players are injured, they don't come back through the reserves'. Mann said this was typical of Smith's communication with players. 'If Norm knew you had the ability, you had to get it out,' he said. 'He'd help with a discussion, but he never seemed to have long discussions with players. Whatever he said to me was always meaningful. He never wasted words, and he never spoke for the sake of speaking. Norm didn't say a lot, but what he said was meaningful and with purpose.'[17] Mann proved the truth in Smith's words: he *was* a good player and, after being

---

[15] *The Herald*, Wednesday April 15, 1959
[16] Hassa Mann. Interview with the author.
[17] Hassa Mann. Interview with the author.

promoted to the seniors in round six (when he kicked five goals against Geelong in a win at Kardinia Park), he was not to play another reserves match in his distinguished career.

The Demons' reserves were now playing curtain-raisers to senior matches. But Smith said: '(Initially) I wouldn't go to their match. I'd get to the ground at about 1.20pm and be ready to go straight into action'. Later on, though, he would arrive early and watch the reserves, 'as I felt obligated to do. They get a kick out of knowing the senior coach is watching them, at least for the first half'.[18]

Smith's assistant coach, Ron Baggott, had taken over as coach of the reserves in 1959. This strong combination had a misunderstanding during a reserves match one day. Baggott recalled:

> Back then, the seconds would use the rooms in the outer (now the Southern Stand side) and the coach's bench was over there as well. This particular day we were being beaten and one of our players wasn't playing very well, so I moved him. Quick-smart, Smithy dispatched a trainer from the other side of the ground with a message, and I was told in no uncertain terms to return the player to his original position. Norm had told the trainer: 'You tell that so-and-so to put such-and-such back where I had him!' Norm must have had this particular player in mind for promotion to the firsts in a certain position, but he'd forgotten one thing – to inform me beforehand what he was thinking!
>
> After that, Norm stipulated exactly where he wanted me to play certain blokes, and the only moves I should make, but at times it was a real temptation to make moves when we were losing or we needed a lift because, as coach, my natural desire was to give the side the best chance of winning games. Norm's response was: 'I don't give a stuff about winning bloody reserves games. All I'm interested in is developing these boys into senior players'. It never became an argumentative thing between Norm and I – I understood where he was coming from.[19]

The continued development of Melbourne's list was obvious to all in the Grand Final rematch with Collingwood at the MCG in round two, with the Demons' four unanswered goals in the second term being the decisive factor in a 13-point win. Melbourne was 2-0, Collingwood 0-2 (which would soon become 0-5).

Although the Demons appeared to have bounced back well, they received a setback in 'Battle of the Brothers II' at Fitzroy in round three. Before the

---

[18] *The Sun* series, 1967.
[19] Ron Baggott. Interview with the author.

players even ran on to the field, Norm Smith had bad feelings about the match. Hugh McPherson said:

> There was something wrong with our boys and Norm could see it. He said to me: 'I think we're in trouble, Hughie.'
> I said: 'Why's that?'
> He said: 'Have a listen. What can you hear?'
> I said: 'Nothing'.
> Norm said: 'Nothing. That's exactly right – it's too damn quiet in here. There's not enough spirit in the room'.
> He was right, too – the room was dead. And try as Norm did to fire them up, it had no real effect. Norm was very upset with the attitude of the players that day, and he told them so. He warned them that they'd be slaughtered if they took that attitude out on the ground. If there was one thing Norm hated it was players without spirit. He felt: 'You can win without skill, but you can't win without spirit'.[20]

Len Smith thought he had received a bad omen himself in the lead-up to his second clash with his brother. During the week, he had taken up an invitation from their younger sister Marj to see her pet budgerigar. 'I have him talking now,' Marj enthused to Len. The budgie's first words to Len were: 'Come on the Demons!'[21]

Len Smith's fears were dispelled – and Norm's were realised – in the first half. The Demons were slaughtered. They trailed by 45 points at half-time. Young Lions fan Bill Atherton (now secretary of Fitzroy Football Club Ltd.) distinctly recalled the mood from both camps during the long interval. 'At half-time, a few of us stood at the back of the changerooms to hear what the coaches had to say,' Atherton said. 'We couldn't hear a word out of the Fitzroy rooms because Len Smith's style was to talk to each player one-on-one before giving a calm, considered address to the players as a group. But in the visitors' rooms, Norm Smith was going off his brain trying to fire them up. He must have been stripping paint off the walls. The contrast between the brothers was quite astounding.'[22]

Smith's efforts to energise his listless players made little impact, and by three-quarter time the margin had extended to 50 points. But his decision to swing centreman Laurie Mithen into attack sparked a Melbourne revival which produced

---

[20] Hugh McPherson. Interview with the author.
[21] *The Sun*, Monday May 11, 1959.
[22] Bill Atherton. Interview with the author.

seven unanswered goals – including 6.1 to Mithen – before the Lions sealed a 13-point victory with a late goal.[23]

While the Mithen switch had been a masterstroke, several others weren't so successful, attracting criticism from Lou Richards, who wrote in *The Sun*: 'I don't profess to be a tactician... but I can't for the life of me see what this new plan of Norm Smith's is supposed to do, apart from upsetting his own team. This idea of everyone "bobbing up" in positions in which they weren't picked, has whiskers on it'. Richards added that 'to play for Melbourne today, you have to be more versatile than Cilli Wang', the famous Austrian performance artist.[24]

One Demon who was as ferocious as ever against the Lions was Ron Barassi. But even his attitude – and misguided ferocity – had became an issue of great concern for Smith during the match. McPherson revealed:

> Ronny was trying hard but he was doing everything wrong, so Norm sent me out to take him off the ground. Although Ronny was playing terrible football, I was stunned that Norm wanted him off because he was the best player in the damn side. But my job wasn't to question Norm's moves; it was to carry them out, so out I went. I knew Ronny would take it badly, and he actually took it worse than expected. He just wouldn't come off. I went back to Norm and said: 'He refuses to come off'.
>
> Norm said: 'He what?! Well, he has to come off the ground! That's an order! Bloody well go out and tell him again!'
>
> I went out again and this time Ronny didn't even say a word; he virtually ignored Norm's order and continued to play. I went back to Norm again and said: 'He still won't come off'.
>
> Norm turned to (head trainer) Jack McLoughlin and said: 'Jack, you go out and bring him off. Tell him he's injured'.
>
> So Jack went out and brought Ron off. And didn't Norm give him a spray! Not only there and then on the bench, but later on in the rooms as well. He read him the riot act. He virtually said Ron was being selfish and that: 'When I give a message to be delivered, or make an order, I expect it to be obeyed. If you ever do anything like that again, I'll let you go'.

---

[23] Barrie Vagg related to the author an anecdote that Fitzroy centreman Don Furness had told him: Furness had been in good form the previous season (1958) and claimed to have had the better of Laurie Mithen in their battles in the centre, and was disappointed to have been overlooked for Mithen for selection in the Victorian side coached by Norm Smith that year. Some time later, Furness asked Smith (his former coach) why he hadn't been picked ahead of Mithen. His simple, indisputable explanation was: 'Donny, you'd never kick six goals in a quarter at full-forward'.

[24] *The Sun*, Monday May 11, 1959.

Norm didn't mean that last bit though. He never would have followed up on that threat. But it might have made Ronny think twice about testing it.[25]

Smith's powers of perception, which were so finely tuned before the loss at Fitzroy, enabled him to see things that many couldn't. Another example of this rare trait related to the seemingly inexplicable form slump of little dynamo Ian Ridley. Smith was becoming increasingly annoyed that Ridley was trailing his opponents, and tried to spark the little star with taunts like: 'What's up, Tiger – are you getting scared?!' But eventually he worked out the problem, and the solution. Ridley recalled:

> Smithy said: 'You're slowing down. You're not getting off the mark quick enough. I think you'd better get your eyes checked'.
> I said: 'What? My eyes are fine'.
> But he said: 'I'm telling you; you need to get your bloody eyes checked'.
> I did as he asked and, sure enough, I had a problem. I got fitted out with a pair of contact lenses, which improved my sight enormously. They helped me have my best season the next year, when I finished runner-up in the best and fairest, so I owe Smithy a fair bit for that, among other things.[26]

Smith also held strong perceptions of certain so-called advances in training, such as fitness programs that emphasised weight training. He had just introduced an element of it at Melbourne, but clubs like Essendon and Hawthorn were among the first to rigorously pursue both weight and circuit training, and Smith felt they were focusing too much on these areas. Before the Melbourne-Essendon clash in round eight, the Bombers were afforded the rare opportunity of training at the MCG and using the gymnasium. While watching the Essendon players pumping weights, one Demon remarked: 'Have a look at them; they'll kill us'. Smith's response was: 'Don't worry about them. You're not training to be a bodybuilders; you're training to be footballers'.[27] On game day, Melbourne did the killing. Ironically, the Demons' superior fitness proved decisive. After trailing by two points at quarter-time, Melbourne amassed 16.14 to 5.5 to record a stunning 73-point win.

Lou Richards later wrote that from 'about 1959 a number of clubs...(went) crazy over circuit training, but not Norm; being one of the old school, he stuck

---

[25] Hugh McPherson. Interview with the author.
[26] Ian Ridley. Interview with the author.
[27] Related by Bill Stephen in an interview with the author.

to the "Checker" Hughes type of coaching, and I don't think we can say he was wrong because his side kept on coming up again every year'.[28]

The victory over Essendon was the most impressive of a purple patch of seven successive wins (by an average of 45 points). The Demons were 10-2 – a game clear of second-placed Carlton. But during the hot streak, Smith never lost his hardness, as evidenced by his treatment of Neil Crompton. The Demons' 82-point win over North Melbourne at the MCG in round 11 was a watershed match in Crompton's fledgling career. With the team's two rovers, Ridley and Adams, sidelined with injury, Crompton shared the roving duties with Peter Brenchley. The 21-year-old had kicked just eight goals from his 13 games, but against the Kangaroos bagged a game-high 7.3. As he walked up the players' race after the match, no doubt proud of his efforts, Smith became the party-pooper.

'Well done,' Smith said. 'But you're not in the starting 18 next week'.

Crompton was understandably confused. 'But I've just kicked 7.3'.

'That doesn't matter,' Smith said. 'You'll be on the bench next week.'[29]

He was true to his word. Ridley and Adams returned to the side and Crompton started on the bench, as Melbourne recorded a 37-point win over Richmond.

Just when the Demons appeared to be cantering towards another premiership, they received a severe jolt to their senses. Over the next three weeks, they did not win a game. They dropped games to Collingwood (by three points at Victoria Park) and bottom side Footscray (which won just its second match, by nine points at the Western Oval) and drew with Fitzroy (at the MCG). Remarkably, it had been the third occasion the Smith brothers had matched wits and Norm Smith was still yet to enjoy a win against his brother.

Following the draw with the Lions, the Demons selectors dropped skipper John Beckwith. The champion defender had missed just two games in the previous four-and-a-half seasons. Beckwith revealed:

> I'd torn some thigh muscles in the '58 carnival and it lingered on into '59, and it contributed to my ordinary form early in the year. One selection night, Norm said something like: 'Becky, you're playing too negative back there; you've got to do something about it'.
>
> The next week (round 10) against North Melbourne on the MCG, I thought: 'Well if that's what he wants, I'll give it to him', so I took off and attacked, which I'd never done before, and I had an absolute field day. In fact, I had 29 kicks in the

---

[28] *Richards*, Lou with Ian McDonald, *Boots And All!*, Stanley Paul, 1963.
[29] Related by Clyde Laidlaw in an interview with the author.

back pocket, which I'd never done before either. I was even awarded a cup as Melbourne's best player. So Norm couldn't say anything at selection the following Thursday night.

But the week after at Fitzroy, I made a couple of mistakes and Kevin Wright kicked four goals on me, one of which went on the wrong side of the goalpost. So Smithy said: 'You're not right; they're kicking goals on you. I think you should go back to the seconds to find some form'.

I said: 'Oh, really? OK. If that's the way you feel, fair enough'.

Jimmy Cardwell announced that I'd volunteered to go back to find my form, which wasn't quite true but Jimmy was just trying to keep a lid on it.

We played at Footscray (in round 11) and I played in the centre in the seconds and had a pretty good day. The firsts had a dog of a day and got beaten. Norm was ropeable. Horrified.

At home on the Sunday night, I got a phone call from Rex Pullen from *The Sun*, and he said: 'How'd you go Becky?'

I said: 'I was reasonably happy. I got a few kicks'. Never said any more than that. Monday morning's *Sun* had three-inch headlines: BECKWITH SAYS HE WILL RETURN. So when I arrive at training on the Tuesday, Norm's waiting for me at the bottom of the stairs. He says: 'So you're picking the team now?'

I said: 'No. That's not what I said'.

But he was livid. There was no argument though. On the Thursday in selection, Norm said: 'Well, you've got your form back, Becky; you're in the side again'.[30]

Smith also threatened to drop Bluey Adams, who remembered: 'At a Thursday night team meeting, Norm would often go through every player starting with Becky in the back pocket and by the time he worked his way through to me in the forward pocket or roving, he'd run out of words. But not this time. When he got to me he said: "Checker Hughes didn't want you in the side, Harry Long didn't want you in the side, and I didn't want you in the side. But you're in because we had no-one else to bloody well pick!" It must have revved me up because I played well.'[31]

With a number of players nursing niggling injuries and general soreness, Smith shortened the length of a handful of training sessions, and it had the desired effect. A refreshed Melbourne won the last three rounds and struck a particularly telling blow in round 16 when it belted Carlton by 45 points at the MCG. The Demons – who finished minor premiers for the fifth year in a row, just half a game clear of the

---

[30] John Beckwith. Interview with the author.
[31] Frank 'Bluey' Adams. Interview with the author.

Blues – faced second-placed Carlton again in the second semi-final and the result was almost identical – a 44-point victory to Melbourne. They were so dominant that the combined totals of the two contests were Melbourne 24.29 (173) to Carlton 11.18 (84). Little wonder the Demons hoped the Blues would regroup to defeat Essendon in the preliminary final. It wasn't to be. The Bombers, who had been 4-6 after 10 rounds and scraped into fourth position – finishing just half-a-game clear of Fitzroy – pipped Carlton by seven points to advance to the Grand Final.

The Demons were heavily favoured to win another premiership, but Smith was wary, saying: 'Essendon must be a good side, playing with confidence, after their good performances in the past two-and-a-half months'. But he was also confident: 'The Bombers may be a young team, but so are we. (And) I think… (we) have greater experience and just as much pace as Essendon'.[32]

An injury concern for the Demons was Geoff Tunbridge, who recalled:

> I pulled a hamstring on the Tuesday before the Grand Final. I went up to Norm and said: 'Norm, I've pulled a bloody hamstring'.
>
> He said: 'Are you sure, Tunner?'
>
> I said: 'Yeah'.
>
> Norm said: 'Look, train a bit more and make certain'.
>
> So I did a bit more and went back to him and said: 'Yeah, Norm, I've stuffed it good and proper'.
>
> He said: 'Right, off you go then'.
>
> I went into the rooms where Jack McLoughlin, who was a genius of a masseur, examined my leg and gave it a gentle massage.
>
> Norm came in and said: 'What do you reckon, Jack?'
>
> Jack said: 'Well Norm, Tunner is a quick healer'.
>
> Norm said: 'OK'.
>
> I was treated by Jack every day between then and the Saturday, and then I had to have a fitness test at the Albert Ground on the morning of the Grand Final.
>
> When I arrived, there was Norm Smith, 'Checker' Hughes, Jimmy Cardwell, and a couple of selectors. I copped an injection, and Jimmy told me: 'Norm doesn't want to change the side because it might give the opposition a bit of a spur. So in this fitness test, don't run too hard; just go through the motions'.
>
> Someone was kicking the ball to me and I went about three-quarter pace and was picking it up and kicking it back. Norm and the others were a little bit away from us, kicking a ball among themselves. They weren't watching me at all!

---

[32] Contemporary newspaper report.

When we finished, Norm asked how it felt.

I said: 'It's all right, but I'm not terribly confident about it'.

He said: 'OK, you're in'.

I had another painkiller before the game and played the Grand Final with a torn hamstring and was absolutely useless. I could hardly run. But Norm was so adamant that he didn't want to bugger around with the side once it had been selected. I was quite surprised that he did that.[33]

First-year player Hassa Mann, who was the youngest player in the Melbourne side, gave the following insight into the mood of the Demons' changerooms, and the last-minute wisdom of Norm Smith, just moments before they ran out on to the MCG:

I was 18 and it was my first Grand Final. I looked around the rooms and guys like Barassi and Dixon and Adams – who had played in five Grand Finals to that stage – appeared nervous, probably because they got rolled in '58 after being red-hot favourites. And Big Bob Johnson had his usual nervous puke before the game. I thought: 'Hell! These guys have been there and done that and yet they're nervous and Big Bob's throwing up!'

I was just a little country kid sitting in the corner. Norm's walking around the rooms and I've got my head between my knees, doing my boots up, and taking a fair while doing it because I'm so nervous and thinking: 'He's getting closer'.

Norm came up to me, put his hand on my shoulder and said: 'Son, you may never, ever, get the opportunity to play in another Grand Final. Don't blow it'. That's all he said, then he walked away.

As I sat there, those words rang in my ears. They weren't words of assurance, but I felt empowered: that I had to perform, that I couldn't let the other 17 guys down, and that if I blew it I may not get another shot at it.

The next year he said exactly the same thing.

When I went to Perth and coached South Fremantle, we made the Grand Final in my second year (1970) and I told them the same thing. (South Fremantle defeated Perth by 43 points.)

Mann also shared the contents of a typical Norm Smith address before a Grand Final:

---

[33] Geoff Tunbridge. Interview with the author.

Norm would say: 'There are no prizes for coming second. The whole season hinges on this one result. The whole season is a waste of effort, a waste of time and sacrifices, if you don't win the big one. You don't lose Grand Finals'.

He would also say: 'Good players perform when it really counts'. Those kind of words certainly got the adrenalin pumping.[34]

The 103,506 fans were treated to a match that was played at a fast and furious pace – so fast in fact that Demon speedster Bluey Adams regarded it as being 10 percent faster than any other game he had experienced.[35] Essendon worried Melbourne with its pace and had established a 20-point advantage early in the second quarter – 4.6 (30) to 1.4 (10). The Bombers – whom Clyde Laidlaw described as 'a class side; more talented than we were'[36] – still led by two straight kicks late in third term. But just as the Demons did late in the second term, they kicked three majors in the last five minutes of the third to take a six-point lead by the last change. The Demons then exploded in the final term, playing 'smashing, full-blooded football'[37] and adding 6.3 to 1.2 to win by 37 points.

Alf Brown praised Smith's conservative yet effective approach in *The Herald*: 'Essendon worried Melbourne with their pace for the first three quarters, but stopped badly. It was a triumph for Melbourne's orthodox training methods over Essendon's casual track work and hard physical exercises. Melbourne won because they were fitter, more physically strong and had men who lifted their game when the pressure was on'.[38]

Barassi had produced another signature performance on football's biggest stage – 22 kicks, six marks, three handballs and 4.3, including three defining, half-chance goals in the space of seven minutes in the second quarter, just when the Demons were in danger of losing touch. Smith unashamedly praised Barassi, whose performances on Grand Final day 12 months apart could not have been more different. He felt the Demons were 'fortunate to win it' because they 'could have been three or four goals behind' at half-time.[39] Despite his fanatical focus on team, Smith believed that what followed proved that, 'of course, any team still relies at times upon individual efforts'.[40] He said 'it was *only* individual efforts such

---

[34] Hassa Mann. Interview with the author.
[35] Barassi, Ron and Peter McFarline, *Barassi: The Life Behind The Legend*, Simon & Schuster, 1995.
[36] Clyde Laidlaw. Interview with the author.
[37] *The Sun*, Monday September 28, 1959.
[38] *The Herald*, Saturday September 26, 1959.
[39] *The Sun*, Monday September 28, 1959.
[40] *Craven*, John (editor), *Football The Australian Way*, Lansdowne Press, 1969.

as those of Ron Barassi which kept us in the game',[41] thankful that 'timely goals' to both Barassi and Big Bob Johnson had given Melbourne 'a shot in the arm when the team was struggling'.[42]

Smith had shrewdly manipulated the ruck contests, rotating Johnson, John Lord and Dick Fenton-Smith to ensure a relatively fresh big man was on the ball at all times. He would tell his ruckmen: 'Ruck 'til your nose bleeds and then we'll move you'.[43] It had devastating effects. Johnson was particularly damaging, rucking most of the first half before having the luxury of spending the majority of the second half in attack. He finished with 18 kicks, five marks and 3.1.

Smith had also shown great faith in Dennis Jones to recover against star Bomber centre half-forward Ken Fraser. 'I played an ordinary first half,' Jones said. '(Smith) was probably on the verge of making the change, but decided to keep me there in the second half. I managed to keep Fraser quiet from then on.'[44] This was just one of many examples of Smith's enormous belief in the ability of his players. Hassa Mann said: 'He showed real faith in players. They'd selected players in certain positions and he gave them every opportunity to do the job. Just when a lot of coaches would have moved a player and perhaps even unbalanced their side a little because of it, Norm backed his player to eventually get back on at least level footing with their opponent. Players gain confidence from that.'[45]

Beckwith, the skipper who had been chastened by Smith just seven weeks earlier, was one of Melbourne's best, and received the honour of being the first VFL premiership captain to be presented – by the Governor of Victoria, Sir Dallas Brooks, and with Princess Alexandra in attendance – with a premiership cup. 'I had to go up into the middle of the crowd to be presented with the cup,' Beckwith said, 'and to stand there and hold the cup aloft like they do after the FA Cup soccer final at Wembley was a phenomenal feeling.'[46]

ϒϒϒϒϒϒϒϒϒ

Melbourne had repeated its remarkably durable effort of 1956 by using just 27 players – five fewer than Essendon, and 10 fewer than the VFL average. And, like in '56, just three Demons had made their debut, which was anything but a signof an

---

[41] *The Sun*, Monday September 28, 1959.
[42] *Craven*, John (editor), *Football The Australian Way*, Lansdowne Press, 1969.
[43] Terry Gleeson. Interview with the author.
[44] *The Sunday Herald Sun*, August 9, 1992
[45] Hassa Mann. Interview with the author.
[46] John Beckwith. Interview with the author.

old list. The heavy and successful blooding process of 1957 had continued to reap rewards, which, combined with the host of young veterans with multiple premierships to their names, would hold the club in good stead for some years to come.

As would the constant hunger of their coach to strive for even greater glory. Clyde Laidlaw said: 'Sure, we had a great side and a number of great players, and mostly great team players, but the main reason we got back in '59 was the attitude of Norm Smith. He prodded us and provoked us and also encouraged us to redeem ourselves and get back to where we should be – as premiers'.[47]

Smith was obsessed with keeping his side at the top. Hassa Mann said: 'It was almost like Norm's attitude was: "We set out to win the premiership, and we've won it; now let's worry about next year".'[48] Bluey Adams also recalled:

> The night of the 1959 premiership, at the celebration dinner, Norm got hold of me and said: 'Now, I've analysed where we're going wrong...'
>
> I couldn't believe my ears. I thought: 'Hold on, Smithy; three hours ago we won the flag – where could we possibly be going wrong?!'
>
> But he was adamant. He said: 'Next year, what I want you to do is take another group of players for sprint training over summer, because we really need these players to improve their pace'.
>
> The speed with which Norm prepared for the next season after winning a flag was astounding. He appreciated the flag, and enjoyed it, but he never rested on his laurels. As soon as it was won, he was already thinking about how we were going to stay on top. How we were going to find another edge, because other clubs were always trying to find ways to knock us off. He never sat back and thought: 'We've won the flag, we don't have to improve; we'll just get the same result with the same players next year'. He knew it didn't work like that. He was always full-on about the next challenge.[49]

ŸŸŸŸŸŸŸŸŸ

Many things happen in a football season, so a team's destiny is rarely, if ever, dictated by the outcome of one match – much less a last-second shot at goal. Even so, it was difficult for Fitzroy people to come to terms with the fact their team had missed the finals by half a game in 1959.

---

[47] Clyde Laidlaw. Interview with the author.
[48] Hassa Mann. Interview with the author.
[49] Frank 'Bluey' Adams. Interview with the author.

The two premiership points the Lions so despairingly rued were those that were awarded to Melbourne after their spectacular draw at the MCG in round 14. When Big Bob Johnson bagged his fifth goal late in the last quarter, the Demons had opened up a seemingly unassailable 12-point advantage. The Lions responded with two quick goals to level the scores, before a long shot by a Fitzroy player looked likely to score, but the ball bounced sideways, hit the behind post and was correctly deemed out of bounds. The siren sounded almost immediately to signal a draw. Any score would have won the Lions the match, and possibly earned them a spot in the finals – at the expense of Essendon, which had an inferior percentage.

Len Smith's second season as Fitzroy coach was expected to bring greater success than the Lions had enjoyed in 1958, and perhaps even result in the club's first premiership since 1944. But that was never realistically going to eventuate after the Lions had plummeted to 3-6 at the halfway mark of the season. They suffered several disappointing losses, but were particularly hurt by those to the battling Geelong (by 10 points) at Kardinia Park in round four, and St Kilda at the Junction Oval in round seven – the latter by just seven points after kicking 9.26 to 13.9. They were two of a series of close matches, which prompted Len to say: 'Much more of this and I'll look like a skewbald horse – red and white haired'.[50]

Although the Lions recovered to win seven-and-a-half of their last nine matches, and ultimately defeated three eventual finalists – Melbourne, Collingwood and Carlton – a record of 10-7-1 was generally regarded as a poor return.

However, the Fitzroy committee praised Len Smith's efforts: 'Len is to be commended on his knowledge of our great game, (and) his planning prior to a game, not only of his own players but also his analysis of the opposing players... His approaches individually to players prior to a game (are) worthy of mention. Len's sincerity of purpose has endeared him to the players, officials and supporters alike... Thank you Len from everyone at Fitzroy for two such memorable seasons, and may 1960 be even greater'.[51]

It would be. But in the meantime, the Lions didn't end 1959 completely empty-handed. While the top four teams fought out the finals series, the Lions proved they were the best of the also-rans by winning the night premiership. They defeated Richmond by 85 points and Geelong by 26 points in a semi-final before beating Hawthorn by five goals in the final. It was a small consolation in a character-building season.

---

[50] Contemporary newspaper report.
[51] Fitzroy Football Club *Annual Report*, 1959.

Len Smith also did his part in building the character of Ron Barassi. Although the Melbourne vice-captain was obviously an opposition player, the pair were close friends. 'Like Norm,' Barassi said, 'he... offered his help whenever I needed it.'[52] On one occasion, Len offered Barassi some strong advice when he made a serious error of judgement in a match against Fitzroy.

Barassi later claimed he had belted six or seven players in his career in retaliation. It was one of these acts of retaliation that raised Len Smith's ire. Barassi recalled:

> I once king-hit a player – and I've regretted it ever since. (Fitzroy centreman) Don Furness had a habit of raising his forearm when you tackled him. One day at Fitzroy, he got me in the throat, which really hurt. I could hardly bloody breathe. Two years later (in the late '50s), at Fitzroy again, Furness did exactly the same thing and this time he got me right on the nose... I was livid. I thought: 'Where is that prick?!' I snapped. It wouldn't have mattered if there was an umpire standing there right beside me – I wanted to kill him. It was the only time I ever did my block on the footy field – as distinct from just being angry. I took off after him and launched myself from about 10 yards away and downed him. The only reason I hit him from behind was that he had his back to me. I got up off the ground – he was still down (and was taken off in the hands of trainers) – and I started backing back to my position where I was resting in the forward pocket.
>
> When I got to centre half-forward, Kevin Murray evened up by decking me... Neither Kevin nor I was reported. When I got to work on the Monday morning, Len Smith, Fitzroy's coach, said: 'Ron, have you got a minute mate?'
>
> I thought: 'Bloody hell, I think I know what this'll be about'.
>
> In his lovely way, Len said: 'I know what happened on Saturday. I've spoken to Kevin (Murray) and I've got to say the same thing to you because what you did was not right'.
>
> I said: 'Len, you're right. I'm sorry about that. I absolutely lost it'.
>
> After about five minutes of discussion, I moved on and I thought: 'Who would be able to cop that – a blast from the opposition coach, at work, and on a Monday for Christ's sake?!'[53]

Although Norm Smith was also staunchly opposed to thuggery, his reaction to Barassi's behind-play king-hit was not recorded, and neither could Barassi

---

[52] *The Australian*, Wednesday May 12, 1965.
[53] Collins, Ben, *The Champions: Conversations with Great Players and Coaches of Australian Football*, GSP, 2006.

recall it. 'Norm mustn't have seen the incident,' Barassi asserted, 'because if he had, he certainly would have let me know all about it – in far more aggressive terms than Len put it. Donny Furness had been a visitor at Norm's house when he was coaching Fitzroy, and even though that wouldn't have really weighed into his thinking because all opposition players are the enemy out on the field, Norm wouldn't have accepted any excuse for my behaviour that day. He would certainly have heard about what had happened, but perhaps the two cagey old brothers discussed it with one another and because Len had seen it he was the one who decided to give me a little talking-to.'[54]

Len Smith also provided guidance for young opponents when he played cricket for Miller's ropeworks in the summer. Lions player Bob Henderson, a fine local cricketer himself, said: 'Later on in his playing days, Len would plonk himself behind the stumps and do a bit of wicket-keeping. Some of the opposition teams had kids playing for them who would fill in the numbers at the bottom of the batting order. Len would tell these kids: "There are some balls you shouldn't hit, so I'll tell you the ones you should let go". When the ball left the bowlers hand, he'd say to the kid: "Leave it". Even though they were social matches, fancy an opposition wicket-keeper, who are generally chirpy, antagonistic buggers at the best of times, helping opposition batsmen! But that's the kind of man Len was. He wanted to win, but he also wanted to help people improve'.[55]

---

[54] Ron Barassi. Interview with the author.
[55] Bob Henderson. Interview with the author.

18

'PUT THOSE SHOTGUNS AWAY!'

[1960]

Melbourne endured a significant loss of personnel before the 1960 season. Superstar half-back flanker Don Williams, 24, signed with WAFL club West Perth; decoy forward Athol Webb, also just 24, returned to his native Tasmania to captain-coach New Norfolk, while ruckman Dick Fenton-Smith retired from VFL football at the age of 27. Although this trio would be missed, the most significant loss – to the Demons as a whole, but in particular Norm Smith – was not a player. It was that of Ivor Warne-Smith. The Melbourne legend died from a heart attack at the age of 62 on March 4, 1960 – just six weeks before the start of the season. Not only had he been the Demons' chairman of selectors since 1949, but also a mentor and pacifier of Smith. Some believe that if Warne-Smith had remained in good health, the trouble that erupted between Smith and the committee in the mid-1960s would never have eventuated.

'Ivor was always a good backstop for Norm,' John Beckwith said. 'He was half the spirit of the whole thing.'[1]

After Warne-Smith's funeral, a group of former Melbourne players, including president Bert Chadwick and Noel McMahen, pondered the question: 'Who's going to take over Ivor's role?' McMahen recalled: 'Ivor had been such a levelling agent for Norm. We discussed it and were unanimous in picking out Denis Cordner, because Norm had such great respect for him'.[2] Cordner was sounded out and duly appointed the new chairman of selectors.

---

[1] John Beckwith. Interview with the author.
[2] Noel McMahen. Interview with the author.

That wasn't the only monumental change to the Demons' leadership structure. Not long before Warne-Smith's untimely end, John Beckwith was replaced as skipper by Ron Barassi. Beckwith later described how the decision was made, and Warne-Smith's role in it:

> At the start of pre-season training for 1960, I said to Jimmy Cardwell: 'I'm pretty sure I'm going to retire at the end of the year to go coaching'. Jimmy didn't argue about it, and neither did Norm or anyone else. It's not like Norm said: 'We want you to play on', which was in some ways disappointing because you like to think that you're needed or wanted. Within about a week, I got a phone call from Ivor Warne-Smith, who asked me to have lunch with him. We went up to the Flagstaff Hotel and sat down and Ivor said: 'Well now seeing you're going to retire at the end of the year, we think we should blood another captain, and we want Barass to be captain. We were hoping you would be vice-captain'.
> I said: 'I'm not happy about that, but if that's what you want, I'll do it'.
> So it all came about because I did the right thing and declared I was going to retire at the end of the year. If I hadn't have said anything, I presume I still would've been captain. But the club saw it as an opportunity to try someone early.[3]

The move was not immediately popular. Although Barassi had long been earmarked for the captaincy, some of his teammates – particularly those who were of a similar age, and had started out at a similar time – believed his ascent to the role had been premature, and took quite a deal of time to adjust to his leadership style. Barassi had always been upfront in his approach, and had never been afraid to speak his mind, but some of his teammates felt he had taken this personal trait to a disturbing extreme, to the extent that he was almost abusing his newly-bestowed power.

'It was a real shock to the system,' Clyde Laidlaw said. 'Becky was quite refined and would encourage you more than abuse you, whereas Barass, with his tremendous enthusiasm and vigour, would be hurling abuse at us at training and in games. It was quite dramatic and very challenging. There was a little bit of a feeling about that among the players – he was really angering a few of us. But Barass didn't care – he had a hide like a rhinoceros – and he kept driving us very hard.'[4]

Smith became aware as early as round two – when the Demons took on St Kilda at the Junction Oval – that his young skipper needed to modify his style. Laidlaw continued:

---

[3] John Beckwith. Interview with the author.
[4] Clyde Laidlaw. Interview with the author.

Barass was abusing me. He was screaming: 'Get out of there! Stop clogging up the ruck contests!'

I was playing on Neil Roberts and he said: 'Do you have to cop this all the time?'

I said: 'Yeah, we're copping it every week'.

Barass had a third go at me just before three-quarter time. I felt I needed to speak up on behalf of myself and a couple of other players, so I went back at him. People saw it – and more importantly Norm saw it – and it didn't look good.

When the siren went, Smithy called us over and said: 'What's going on here?!'

I said something like: 'He's abusing me and I can't take it any longer'.

Norm said: 'Ronny, you just worry about playing the game – leave the coaching to me! Got it?!'

Very fierce words.

Some time after the game, Barass and I were both brought in for a chat with Norm. Very early the next morning – the Sunday morning – there was a knock at my front door. It was Barass. We discussed what had happened and apologised to each other. It was smoother sailing after that. I suspect Norm instigated Barass' visit. I think it helped cement the team under his captaincy.[5]

Initial discontent soon became universal respect, as Barassi tamed his approach and became one of the great leaders in the competition – and, in time, one of the greatest in history. His combination with Norm Smith would also be hailed as one of the most formidable the game has seen. Theirs 'wasn't your normal coach-player relationship'. They were 'eventually almost equals – but Norm was more equal than Barass!'[6] Reflecting on the alliance in 1967, Smith said:

> The combination we had at Melbourne for years was ideal, with Ronny on the field and me on the bench. This is in no way a reflection on Hassa Mann's ability as captain because the case I'm talking about is rather special. Ronny thought the same way as I did and reacted in the same way. He had his moments of wildness, which perhaps I've got. It's something which drives people on... This fierce drive and enthusiasm on the field can be a valuable aid to a coach.[7]

One such benefit, Smith maintained, was Barassi's effect on umpires. 'It was argued he was getting umpires off-side,' Smith said. 'I doubt that. Most umpires

---

[5] Clyde Laidlaw. Interview with the author.
[6] Sam Allica. Interview with the author.
[7] *The Sun* series, 1967.

had great respect for Ron and when he raged it was usually with just cause. Umpires tried not to make mistakes when Ronny was around. They didn't fancy being dressed down or having mistakes highlighted, so they were prone to put the whistle away. I feel he did more good for his side by talking, pushing up and urging them on than any silent captain could do (simply) by the brilliance of his play.'[8]

Smith and Barassi were usually on the same wavelength, particularly when it came to discipline and effort. Richmond ruckman Neville Crowe described an incident – from Melbourne's 92-point demolition of the Tigers at the MCG in round six – which showed just how synchronised their minds could be: 'Near the finish ... a Demon was too casual, made a mistake and let us in for a rare goal. Then he laughed. Ron Barassi ... went berserk. He tore strips off the offender, shouting and swearing. I learned what dedication was all about. Then a message arrived from coach Norm Smith. It was delivered loudly and uncensored. I shuddered, especially at the part how they would both share the 'joke' after the game'.[9]

Although Barassi, as captain, was now a member of Melbourne's selection committee alongside Smith, and commanded great respect in his leadership role, he became even more of a target for his coach's outbursts. Hassa Mann said: 'Norm often had a go at Ron when he was the captain and the dynamo of the side, and the guy that probably always provided the spark. Norm would needle Ron, and was particularly demanding of him because he knew Ron had the ability to give something extra'.

Mann recalled an occasion when Smith actually questioned Barassi's courage:

> Norm was trying to extract something extra and he said: 'I'm not sure whether I saw it, Ron, but did you take a short step? I think you took a short step'.
>
> Fancy accusing Ron Barassi of taking a short step! It was like waving a red rag at a bull.
>
> Barass' eyes were popping out of his head and there was steam coming out his ears. When play resumed, Barass, in his inimitable way, with his teeth bared, made sure he cleaned someone up with a bone-crunching hip-and-shoulder right in front of Norm, and then glared at Norm. Apparently Norm had a wry grin on his face and turned to Checker and said: 'The message got through'.
>
> Norm would delight in getting a result from something he'd instigated with some choice words.[10]

---

[8] Dyer, Jack and Brian Hansen, *The Wild Men of Football*, Southdown Press, 1968.
[9] *The Sun*, Wednesday, July 19, 1989.
[10] Hassa Mann. Interview with the author.

In the Demons' 64-point win over South Melbourne at the MCG in round three, Smith chastised Barassi for losing his focus. Hugh McPherson said:

> Norm hated it when players got involved in things that distracted them from doing their job. When they did it, he came down on them like a ton of bricks, *especially* if it was Barassi. Against South Melbourne, Ken Boyd had sucked Barassi and Terry Gleeson in to the point that all they wanted to do was fight him. Norm was livid. He told me: 'Get out there and break them up, and tell them to play football!'
>
> Funnily enough, Gleeson escaped with a minor reprimand while Barassi copped it with both barrels. That kind of thing happened a number of times.[11]

But whatever tensions existed between the parties at various times, they translated it into wins – plenty of them. The Demons won their first three matches of the 1960 season by an average of 47 points. A minor speed-hump was a comprehensive drubbing at the hands of Collingwood in the mud at Victoria Park in round four. Melbourne led by three points at quarter-time but mustered just 1.3 in the last three quarters to lose by 36 points – 7.13 (55) to just 2.7 (19). It was Melbourne's lowest score in more than 40 years![12]

The next match, against Hawthorn at Glenferrie Oval, was the scene of one of the most regrettable incidents in Norm Smith's coaching career. It centred on Melbourne veteran Ian McLean, the 30-year-old wingman who had started at Melbourne in 1951, played in three premierships and finished third in the Demons' 1958 best and fairest award. After being named Melbourne's second-best player in the 1959 Grand Final – he amassed 20 kicks and five marks – McLean was suddenly out of favour with selectors and found himself dropped following the round four loss to Collingwood. He rang Jim Cardwell and said: 'Jim, I was going to give it away at the end of the year, but now that I've been dropped I don't want to fight my way back again. Now's as good a time as any to give it away'.

Cardwell – who regarded McLean as 'one of the gamest and most popular players ever to pull on a boot for the club'[13] – tried to talk him out of it, but McLean had made up his mind. Keith Carroll, a great mate of McLean's, was witness to an ugly confrontation in the visitors' changerooms at Hawthorn.

---

[11] Hugh McPherson. Interview with the author.
[12] In round 16, 1919, the winless Demons scored just 2.5 (17) while conceding 21.16 (142) to Fitzroy at the Brunswick Street Oval.
[13] Newspaper report, 1965.

Ian and I went into the rooms together, and it wasn't long before Norm came over and tore strips off Ian. He reckoned Ian wasn't prepared to play in the seconds, like it was beneath him or something.[14] Norm was quite rude to him, and humiliated him, in front of all these people. At one point, Norm turned to me and said: 'How many games did you play in the seconds?! You always came back (after being dropped)!'

I said: 'Leave me out of it, Norm; this has got nothing to do with me'.

Norm kept at him and after copping all this, Ian eventually said: 'Thanks very much for those remarks, Norm', and he just walked out.

I don't think Ian ever got over that. Neither did Norm, because he was quite upset at Ian's funeral (less than five years later in early 1965). He went over to Joan, Ian's widow, and said: 'Do you think Ian ever forgave me?'

'Of course he did,' Joan said. 'He never held onto things like that.'

That showed that while Norm could be hurtful, he could also be compassionate.[15]

There was, however, little for Smith to regret in terms of performance. The match and subsequent 20-point victory at Hawthorn sparked a sequence of 11 straight wins (by an average of 34 points). It was, and remains, the second-longest winning streak in Melbourne's history. It was also the third stretch of 10 or more consecutive wins since 1955. The Demons were also 14-1 – their equal best start to a season, matching their effort in 1956.

Such was the evenness of the Melbourne side, and the magnitude of the task for opposing sides, that Lou Richards actually bemoaned the difficulty of choosing the best Melbourne player in any given game. Richards wrote in *The Sun*: 'For one period in a match, you might spot six Melbourne players who are starring. Then they will fade and six others will start dominating'.

After smashing Collingwood by 46 points in round 15 – when they stormed home with 7.8 to 2.2 in the final term – the Demons dropped away dramatically. They lost their last three home-and-away games: the nine-point loss to Hawthorn at the MCG in round 16 was their first in a minor round game at the MCG in three years (which had also been against the Hawks, in round 15, 1957); an eight-point loss to bottom side Richmond at Punt Road in round 17; and a 13-point loss to Essendon in the final round after leading by 10 points at the last change. It was the Demons' worst losing streak since their dismal

---

[14] When dropping a player, Norm often told him: 'I spent more than two seasons in the seconds. A few games there won't hurt you'. (Source: Alf Brown, *The Herald*, 1958.)

[15] Keith Carroll. Interview with the author.

1953 season. It was also the first time they had lost consecutive matches since 1955.

Although the Demons were missing some key players during this period – namely Big Bob Johnson (for two matches), and Clyde Laidlaw, Terry Gleeson, Alan Rowarth and Dennis Jones, who each missed one match apiece – critics understandably began to downgrade Melbourne's premiership chances.

Smith lamented the difficulty of keeping players motivated when they have nothing to gain. 'My boys had no incentive in those last three games,' he told *Truth*. 'Irrespective of the result, we couldn't lose the double chance, and this fact seemed to take the edge off their keenness.'

On August 20, the night of the loss to the Tigers, Melbourne Football Club held its second annual players' revue before a capacity audience at Melbourne Town Hall. The souvenir program contained a message from Norm Smith to Demons fans, which said: 'For our part, we will do all we can to make this year as successful and as entertaining for you supporters as any you have enjoyed in the past'. The program also featured a photograph of Smith's face, superimposed onto the face of a fox. The accompanying text said: 'The newspaper boys, with reverent respect, have called him the "Old Fox of Footy", the "Planner of doom to opposing sides", the "Originator of decoy forward play", the "Father of power football". Very complimentary and very true. To us, he is our friend, our teacher – a master of his art… enterprising, imaginative, absolutely dedicated. To us, he is Norm Smith, Chief Architect of our power and success'.

Norm Smith's unofficial nickname – 'The Red Fox'[16] – was created by defender Ian Thorogood on an end-of-season trip on the Gold Coast in the late 1950s:

> I was sharing a room with Dennis Jones and Peter Brenchley and one afternoon, after we'd had a pretty good lunch, there was a knock at the door.
>
> 'Brench' said: 'Who is it?"
>
> The reply was: 'Open up, it's Norm'.
>
> We didn't believe he was who he said he was, so Brench said: 'This door's not opening for anyone'.
>
> The voice became more agitated: 'Open the bloody door – it's Norm Smith!'
>
> I said: 'Hell, is that you, Red Fox?'
>
> Norm put his shoulder to the door and it nearly came of its hinges. He burst in and wrestled all three of us, and it bloody hurt too; we were bruised.

---

[16] Smith was already referred to in the press as 'The Demon Dictator', 'The Melbourne Martinet' and simply 'Smithy'.

Norm then gave us a dressing down in a joking sort of way – 'None of you will ever refer to me as The Red Fox ever again!'

Then he said: 'Let's go down to the bar and join everyone else for a drink'.

The Red Fox nickname stuck with us – not that we would ever say it to Norm's face. We thought we'd gotten to know Norm pretty well and we thought: 'We should have a nickname for him – "Smithy" doesn't quite fit the bill'. Why The Red Fox? The 'red' part is self-explanatory, and with his planning, he was a fox.[17]

It appeared Smith would need every ounce of his guile to get the Demons back on track for the finals. Despite their form slump, the Demons were minor premiers for a record sixth successive season – eclipsing Collingwood's five between 1926 and 1930. However, they were to face the form team of the competition – Len Smith's Fitzroy – in the second semi-final.

The Lions had finished second on the VFL ladder, level on points with the Demons, with 14 wins and four losses. It was just the second time the Lions had finished the minor rounds in the top two since 1923; and just the fourth time the club had won at least 14 home-and-away matches in a season. Only percentage separated the two teams – Melbourne's 143.1 percent easily outstripping Fitzroy's 112.5. After sitting middle-of-the table at 5-4, the Lions won their last nine matches (by an average of 24 points) to secure the double chance. It was roundly acknowledged as a stunning achievement, and most of the plaudits went to Len Smith. The Fitzroy committee responded by reappointing Len as coach for a further two years – until the end of the 1962 season.

Lou Richards later wrote: 'Len has been the mandrake of coaches. He may not be the prince of coaches, but he was certainly a magician the way he handled his players... He has pulled more switches than a SEC powerhouse'.[18]

Fitzroy president Mr Les Phelan agreed. In a long speech in front of the media, in which he extolled the virtues of the Lions coach as a coach and as a man, Phelan concluded his talk with: 'We think we have the best coach in the League. He has done wonders for our club, and we think there is nobody to compare with him. And here he is ... Norm Smith!' It was an embarrassing *faux pas*, but Len took it in good humour and actually laughed more than most.

There was no greater admirer of Len Smith's coaching than his brother. In fact, Norm Smith regarded Len as a better coach than himself. He said that Len 'never won a VFL premiership because he didn't have the players. He got Fitzroy into the

---

[17] Ian Thorogood. Interview with the author.
[18] Richards, Lou with Ian McDonald, *Boots And All!*, Stanley Paul, 1963.

finals… with practically nothing'.[19] To highlight the importance for coaches to use their imagination and 'look beyond the accepted principles of the game', Norm often cited 'the achievements of Len Smith with a mediocre Fitzroy combination'.[20] He added: 'Len was a fine coach. He had a wonderful football brain and there were few men who knew more about the game'.[21] Perhaps the greatest compliment Norm Smith bestowed upon his brother emerged in general football conversation. Even when he himself was perhaps regarded as the pre-eminent expert on football, Norm Smith would often, without any false modesty, defer to his brother by starting sentences with: 'Well, Lenny reckons…' or: 'Len says…'

Peter Smith said: 'Norm had so much respect for Len's coaching ability because he never had the cattle so to speak, so he had to find ways around that to beat more talented sides. It was either that or bounce around the lower rungs of the ladder. But Len's sides were never like that. Norm regarded Len as a great thinker, and probably the best tactician in the game'.[22]

Even Melbourne players were lavish in their praise of Len Smith's coaching ability, and while they generally rated Norm Smith the greatest coach of all time, many believed Len Smith was in the same realm of greatness. John Lord, who had been a victim of Len Smith's forward tactics, revealed: 'While I can only see Norm Smith as the greatest of coaches, anybody who says that brother Len was as good, or better, I don't dismiss. Fitzroy's sides of those years should never have made the finals, but Len got them there through his brilliant thinking. Only an excellent coach could have done what he did'.[23] Barassi speculated: 'I believe Len was a better coach of lesser players, but Norm was a better coach of better players. But it's not something you could prove either way'.[24]

Although the Smith brothers generally agreed on most football topics – or at least held similar views – they were, however, diametrically opposed on a couple of major issues.

In accepting part of the blame for the game not being the spectacle he felt it was in the 1930s, Norm Smith explained: 'Of course, there were other factors too – the no-dropping-the-ball rule, no frees for kicks out of bounds and the increased tempo of the play-on game all contributed – but there's no doubt I didn't help by putting great emphasis on defensive football. I was out to win matches and

---

[19] *Allsport Weekly*, August 2, 1973.
[20] *The Age*, Wednesday June 19, 1968.
[21] *The Sun* series, 1967.
[22] Peter Smith. Interview with the author.
[23] John Lord. Interview with the author.
[24] Ron Barassi. Interview with the author.

I proved this was one way, an important way, of doing it. This was one of the rare things my brother Len and I differed over in our football thinking... It was his theory that football must be an attacking game all the way. That as long as you kept kicking goals you must win matches'.[25]

The Smiths also clashed, quite vehemently, on another major football issue in the late 1950s and early 1960s – the controversial form of handball known as the 'flick-pass'. Len Smith taught his players to hit the ball with an open hand, which proved quicker and easier to distribute, and enabled them to move the ball with great speed. Kevin Murray said: 'The flick-pass made us a lot quicker. Blokes like Owen Abrahams, Wally Clarke and Kevin Wright were great exponents of it – the ball would leave their hands in the blink of an eye'.[26]

It was not a revolutionary tactic. It had been used in phases throughout football history, in accordance with changes to the rules. It had been permitted until 1925, when the VFL amended its definition of a legal handball to state that the ball had to be punched with a clenched fist, not just struck. The old rule was reinstated in 1934, and during that pre-season even Checker Hughes instructed the Demons, including the Smith brothers, on the correct use of the flick-pass.[27]

The rule (in 1934) stated: 'A player may handball by holding the ball in one hand and hitting it with the other'. Significantly, there was no stipulation that the ball had to be hit with a clenched fist.

Len Smith popularised the flick-pass with his Fitzroy sides and was adamant that, executed correctly, it was a legal handball; while Norm Smith was just as bullish that it did not constitute a legal handball; that it was, in fact, a throw; and, furthermore, was the result of rule-tampering and was against the spirit of the game. 'The flick-pass was the rule that was given all sorts of interpretations,' Norm Smith said. 'My brother Len didn't help things here, of course... He had the flick down to such a fine art that I'm sure some umpires didn't know what was going on half the time.'[28] He was also credited with saying: 'It's cheating, and making good players out of ordinary players'.[29] However, it is doubtful he would use such strong language to describe any of Len's actions, or question his integrity in any way.

---

[25] *The Sun* series, 1967. An outspoken critic of Norm Smith's was Jack Dyer, who held him mostly responsible for the perceived decline in standards since the 1930s. Dyer believed that in response to Melbourne's lack of a full-forward, Smith had developed a scrambling, congested, negative style of play, which had resulted in an ugly spectacle he termed 'frustration football' or 'footbrawl'.
[26] Kevin Murray. Interview with the author.
[27] *The Herald*, April 1934.
[28] *The Sun* series, 1967.
[29] Dyer, Jack and Brian Hansen, *Jack Dyer's The Greatest: The Most Sensational Players of the Century*, Brian Hansen Nominees, 1996.

Other critics termed it 'flipball', 'flickball', 'whizball' and 'throwball', and Fitzroy people were understandably insulted by any insinuation of foul play. Bob Henderson insisted: 'It was known as the flick-pass but it wasn't a flick. We were taught that if you put the ball on one hand and you hit the ball with the other, whether it be with a closed fist or an open hand, it was a legal handball... Len got us to slap behind the ball with an open hand. He had us practising it all the time'.[30]

Debate raged. Initially at least, most umpires deemed the flick-pass legal. However, when Fitzroy used it to devastating effect in 1960, controversy reached fever pitch.

Before the Melbourne-Fitzroy second semi-final, former Collingwood star Bill Twomey supported the Lions' methods, writing in *The Sporting Globe*: 'I don't consider that Fitzroy's handball is suspect. It's just that the Lions have mastered the art. Many of the "throwing" taunts against them have been started by other clubs whose teamwork and attempts at handball can only be classed as clumsy... I feel the standard will improve if more sides follow the Lions' lead'.

The flick-pass was a key ingredient in the Lions' much-vaunted running game, which they planned to unleash against the Demons in the second semi. The most recent meeting between the teams had finally resulted in Norm Smith's first win over his brother. It had taken him four attempts, after their previous three encounters had produced two Fitzroy wins and a draw. But this time, in round nine, the Demons pounded Fitzroy by 42 points and, in the process, recorded their first victory at the Brunswick Street Oval in four years. Afterwards, Len revealed that, win or lose, he had been receiving critical letters from an anonymous Fitzroy supporter. After the loss to Melbourne, the writer's theme was that a good big team will always beat a good little team. Len Smith's typically diplomatic response was: 'I couldn't agree with him more. But perhaps he will tell me where I can get some more good big players!' It was this very weakness the Demons would attempt to expose.

September 10, 1960 marked the only occasion brothers have coached opposing sides in a VFL/AFL final. Success-starved Fitzroy supporters were hopeful it would be momentous for another reason: that the Lions would use it as a springboard to reach their first Grand Final since 1944 – the year they won their only premiership since 1922. The Lions had played at the MCG just twice in the previous three seasons, with their most recent match there being their draw with Melbourne in round 14 the previous season (1959).

---

[30] Bob Henderson. Interview with the author.

On form, though, they appeared a big chance: they had won their past nine matches, while the Demons had lost their past three. Fitzroy skipper 'Butch' Gale was adamant his side deserved hot favouritism, telling *Truth*: 'Our form is just too good. That's all there is about it... If this were a horse race instead of a football match, we would be 3/1 on favourites'. But his coach was more circumspect. Len Smith told *Truth*: 'Melbourne has played in the last six Grand Finals, and they are on their own ground, so you see how hard it is... I expect to meet a six goals better Melbourne side than the one downed by Essendon... I am definite about one aspect of the match – every Fitzroy supporter will get top value from the team we send out to represent us... Although I am not prepared to say we will win, I do say we can win'.

Norm Smith was, as always, 'quietly confident', but didn't 'underestimate the ability of Fitzroy'. He said: 'Three defeats in a row is not a happy omen to carry into the finals, but I am sure the incentive of a place in the Grand Final will spur my boys on to greater heights... A big trump card in our favour is experience in finals series... This is a tremendous advantage, as many experienced players are overawed, momentarily, by the big occasion and crowd in their first appearance in the finals'.[31]

Some Lions players certainly had a novel way of relaxing before the big game. The previous week, Len Smith accepted an offer from a barber (the father of a thirds player) to wash his players' hair before the final-round match against St Kilda. While it would have been hard to imagine his brother endorsing such a thing, Len Smith was pleased with the results. 'It seemed to freshen up the players,' he said. A few players followed the same pre-match routine before the semi-final. Jack Dunn from *The Sun* wrote that 'there could be a new cry at the MCG on Saturday – "Come on the Shampoo Kids".'

While Ethel Smith would barrack for the side that was losing,[32] a predominantly pro-Fitzroy crowd attended the MCG to support the sentimental favourite. However, it was blatantly obvious by quarter-time – when Melbourne led by 16 points after kicking into a strong breeze at the city end – that the expected epic struggle would deteriorate into a huge anti-climax. The Lions appeared lethargic and overawed; the Demons confident and decisive. Kevin Hogan informed readers of *The Sun*: 'If coach Norman Smith had trained his players for the Stawell Gift, they couldn't have been more alert and faster into stride'.[33]

---

[31] *Melbourne Truth*, September 1960.
[32] *The Sun*.
[33] *The Sun*, Monday September 12, 1960.

Melbourne restricted Fitzroy to just two goals by the 15-minute mark of the last quarter, by which stage the Demons were more than 11 goals clear. So many Lions fans had vacated the stadium that Alf Brown observed in *The Herald*: 'Never have I seen so many thousands leave a game so early in the last quarter'. Lou Richards had also witnessed something unique, informing readers of *The Sun*: 'I've watched and played football for a long time… but I've never seen a more determined and ruthless team than Melbourne was on Saturday'. Fitzroy kicked two belated goals to reduce the final margin to 62 points – 14.18 (102) to 4.16 (40). Richards added that the Lions could be thankful for umpire Frank Schwab, who awarded them 31 free kicks to Melbourne's 11. Richards declared: 'If he hadn't given them such a fair go, the Lions may not have scored!'

Remarkably, the Demons had, for the third successive year, held their second semi-final opponent to just four goals, and Fitzroy's scoring effort was the best of the three. The combined totals of these finals were 36.45 (251) to 12.38 (110).

After the game, Norm and Len Smith warmly shook hands just inside the fence.

Melbourne had qualified for a record seventh successive Grand Final appearance, surpassing the six achieved by both Collingwood (1925-30) and Essendon (1946-51). Norm Smith told reporters: 'We clicked today… It was overall evenness that won it'. However, he did express slight concern that he would have 'preferred a four or five-goal win', to give his players a more hard-fought contest before having a weekend's rest.

A shattered Len Smith would have preferred to have simply been competitive. 'I can take a licking,' he told *The Herald*, 'but I hate to see people walking out on me. I am greatly upset that Fitzroy's showing was so poor that the crowd should walk out on us. But I don't blame them.'

He made no excuses. 'Every team has an occasional "off" day, and we had our birthday of "off" days against Melbourne,' he said. 'We were beaten by a side that would have walloped any team in the League by four goals – and that includes Fitzroy playing at its best… Only seven of our team played anything like the brand of football that helped us win nine games on end.'[34] Describing it as 'the worst position I have ever been in',[35] Len Smith took solace in the fact that his side couldn't play any worse than it had against the Demons.

Len Smith was determined that his players would prove 'that good men can take a beating and come back fighting'[36] against Collingwood in the preliminary final.

---

[34] *Melbourne Truth*, September 1960.
[35] *The Sun*, September 1960.
[36] *The Herald*, September 1960.

They did, but it wasn't enough. In one of the most exciting finals of the era, the Lions led by eight points at the last change but were beaten by five points. They had bowed out of the finals in straight sets, and were yet to win a final in three attempts under Len Smith, but the coach expressed his pride, saying: 'I bet no-one walked out on us today'.

Fitzroy's committee was similarly proud of Len, announcing: 'Len Smith, for the past three seasons… has put the word "value" into the Fitzroy Football Club. His knowledge of the game and training methods has earned him the title of one of the shrewdest and most tactical coaches in the League today. Sincerity of purpose has endeared him to supporters and players alike. This was demonstrated when he apologised to the public through the press and radio for a poor showing against Melbourne in the second semi-final and promised them that the Lions would redeem themselves in the final against Collingwood. This was done.'[37]

Len Smith was held in such high regard that he was the subject of a tribute poem, *Ode to the Mighty Smithy*, which read in part:

> On the hallowed Fitzroy ground,
> The mighty Smithy stands,
> Speaking to the Fitzroy lads,
> Who form a happy band.
>
> He talks to them sincerely
> And always understands;
> It is this wonderful attribute
> That makes him oh! So grand.
>
> He never roasts a player
> Who isn't going well,
> Instead he gives them wisdom
> That he alone can tell.[38]

Although the Demons were short-priced favourites for the flag, they planned to do some redeeming of their own. They appeared certainties, but they needed only recall the unforseen happenings of two years earlier to remain grounded. Norm Smith certainly grounded backman Dennis Jones. After playing most of the

---

[37] Fitzroy Football Club *Annual Report*, 1960.
[38] Private collection of Norma Harmes, a daughter of Len Smith.

season in the seniors, Jones – who described Norm as 'the hardest, most ruthless coach I have seen, but... also a genius'[39] – was left out of the Demons' line-up for the Grand Final against Collingwood. Jones was devastated. Jim Cardwell was consoling a tearful Jones in his office when Smith walked in.

'What's wrong with him?' Smith asked Cardwell.

'He's crying because he has been left out of the side,' said Cardwell. 'Say something to him, Norm.'

'I don't speak to children,' Smith said dismissively as he left the room, only increasing Jones' pain.

Later that night, Cardwell told Smith: 'You were pretty hard on Jones'.

Smith's response took Cardwell by surprise.

'I had to get out of the room, Jimmy,' Smith explained. 'I was almost ready to cry with him.'[40]

Cardwell later offered the following reasoning for Smith's actions: 'Inwardly, Norm had a gentle heart. He felt every hurt his players suffered, but he would never let on to his players. He never let them see the other side of him in case they thought he was soft'.[41]

ŸŸŸŸŸŸŸŸŸ

The man in the best position to predict the outcome of the 1960 Grand Final was Len Smith, who had coached against both competing teams in the preceding fortnight. When asked for his tip, Len replied with a definitive: 'Melbourne for mine'. He added: 'Norm is my brother so naturally I'm saying he's the best coach in the League. Anyway his record proves it'.[42] Smith would confirm this widely acknowledged status in the most emphatic fashion possible.

Many Demon fans weren't so convinced before the match. Everything appeared eerily – ominously – identical to that disastrous Grand Final day in 1958. The Demons were again raging favourites and they were up against the same opponent (Collingwood) who would surely apply the same provocative tactics, at the same ground (the MCG), and in the same conditions (wet and miserable). Melbourne's line-up featured 10 survivors from the '58 Grand Final, while Collingwood had 13.

As the Melbourne players made their way to the changerooms, their fans overwhelmed them with well-meaning advice like: 'Remember what happened two

---

[39] *Sunday Herald Sun*, August 9, 1992.
[40] *The Age*, July 30, 1973.
[41] *The Age*, July 30, 1973.
[42] *The Sporting Globe*, September 1960.

years ago', 'Just play the ball', 'Don't get sucked in', 'Don't be cocky like you were last time'. But the Demons didn't need to be reminded.

Barassi, who was leading the Demons in a Grand Final for the first time, gave a spine-tingling insight into the mindset of the Melbourne players: 'Norm didn't even mention '58 in his pre-match address. He didn't have to. We were just so disciplined and focused and so hell-bent on gaining vengeance that the atmosphere in the rooms was electric. Our players were looking through people. There was nothing on our minds except how we were going to play that day. I've never seen a team more determined than we were that day. It didn't matter what Collingwood did to us – they could have hit us with baseball bats – and we wouldn't have retaliated. We were going to play football and nothing else. Of course, that was a credit to Norm that we were able to approach the game in such a manner, but as players we also had great pride in our performance'.[43]

John Lord recalled the gist of Smith's pre-match address:

> He told us there three reasons for us to win: win for the supporters, who had stuck with us through thick and thin; win for the people who kept us going: the committee, the trainers and other staff; and win for ourselves, because of all the hard work we'd put in all year to put ourselves in this position. And then Norm nearly had a few of us with tears in our eyes when he said: 'And if that's not good enough, do it for me'.[44]

Barassi was the classic example of the Demon approach. Early in the match, Collingwood captain and chief hardman Murray Weideman – who had been so devastating with his physicality in the 1958 Grand Final – punched the ball and Barassi's face simultaneously in the same motion. The force of the blow was to give Barassi a tingle in his upper-lip that lasted 20 years. But he didn't retaliate. He merely looked at 'The Weed' and played on.[45]

An indication of Smith's confidence was his decision to release half-back flanker Ian Thorogood from his usual close-checking role for the first and only time in his six-year career. Thorogood said: 'I was pleasantly surprised that the time Norm chose to use me that way was in, of all games, a Grand Final. His instructions were along the lines of: "Just go out there and attack the ball. Help 'Lordy' beside you and 'Dicko' in front of you and let's see what you can do".'[46]

---

[43] Ron Barassi. Interview with the author.
[44] John Lord. Interview with the author.
[45] Ron Barassi. Interview with the author.
[46] Ian Thorogood. Interview with the author.

However buoyed the Magpies were by the conditions, they quickly floundered. The game was over by quarter-time, with Melbourne establishing a commanding lead – 4.3 (27) to 0.0 (0). The Demons 'made a tragedy out of the premiership battle'.[47] Lou Richards wrote in *The Sun* that the Demons had made Collingwood look like 'arthritic tortoises', and marvelled: 'There've been some massacres down the ages – Custer's last stand, St Valentine's day... But September 24, 1960, will go down as the day Norm Smith and his boys composed a new song: *Slaughter on Brunton Avenue*'.[48]

Melbourne's domination was such that they boasted 10 players who amassed at least 15 kicks, while Collingwood had just three, as the Demons recorded a premiership victory which, Melbourne great Percy Beames trumpeted, 'could be classed the most satisfying, if not the best, in the club's history'.[49]

Melbourne won by 48 points, but the margin was probably the equivalent of more than 100 points in dry conditions. Most impressively, the Demons had won by eight goals after kicking just eight goals themselves. The scoreline was: Melbourne 8.14 (62) to Collingwood's 2.2 (14). Of the Magpies, Beames wrote that 'it could even be argued that they were lucky to finish with that total',[50] as both Collingwood goals had an element of good fortune about them. In the second quarter, 'Tassie' Johnson dropped a mark in the goalsquare, allowing Magpie ruckman Ray Gabelich to toe-poke an easy goal; while John Henderson's goal from about 45 metres in the third quarter was heavily disputed by the Demons, who were adamant Johnson had touched it on the goal-line.

Even in the midst of one of the most comprehensive victories in Grand Final history, Norm Smith couldn't relax. Such was his intent to humiliate the Magpies – especially after their own humiliating defeat at Collingwood back in round four – that he felt his team should have kept them to a single-figure total. Hugh McPherson recalled: 'Norm was furious that the boys let Collingwood get two goals. He thought we were so much better than Collingwood that day that they shouldn't have even got the ball to the goalsquare, let alone kick a damn goal'.[51]

If Smith had his way, the Demons would have kept Collingwood to the lowest score in a Grand Final. Instead, they posted the second-worst total, and the lowest in 33 years, since Richmond had managed just 1.7 (13) against Collingwood in the

---

[47] Percy Beames, *The Age*, Monday, September 26, 1960.
[48] *The Sun*, Monday, September 26, 1960.
[49] *The Age*, Monday, September 26, 1960.
[50] *The Age*, Monday, September 26, 1960.
[51] Hugh McPherson. Interview with the author.

1927 Grand Final. It was a fitting end for the much-loved John Beckwith: as an integral part of a miserly defence at its miserly best.[52]

In the two biggest matches of the 1960 finals series, the Demons had held their opponents to an astonishingly low, combined tally of just 6.16 (52), while totalling 22.32 (164) themselves. Lou Richards echoed the sentiments of many, announcing: 'This is the greatest football machine I've ever seen in my life'.

Norm Smith fed the media a clichéd explanation for the Demons' success – 'Our win was the result of a great team effort. It was a case of 18 players all playing their part' – but it was true. Meanwhile, Collingwood coach Phonse Kyne conceded that while the Magpies had not produced their 'real form', only an outstanding side would have challenged Melbourne on the day.

The after-match celebrations were strangely subdued, according to *The Herald's* Alf Brown, who was in attendance.

'Melbourne's Grand Final dinner,' Brown wrote, 'was not the riotous affair you would expect from a club that had just overwhelmed its bitter rivals, Collingwood... Last year Melbourne's celebrations were quiet. I thought it was because Collingwood had not been their Grand Final victims. This year was just as quiet – and Collingwood *were* the victims. Perhaps it is because Melbourne have become accustomed to winning premierships. But there is nothing complacent about Melbourne. There couldn't be with fiery Norm Smith as coach... Players had just settled down to dinner when a large bundle of *Heralds* was distributed among them. Food was forgotten... as players and officials read about their triumph. It was an extraordinary scene. Every player had his head buried in a *Herald*. (The) only sound was the ruffling of the pages. It was more like the reading room of a big library than a dining room where a premiership dinner was under way. A stranger suddenly entering the room would never have guessed all these studious young men were celebrating a great victory.'[53]

The mood livened up during a pianist's rendition of *Champagne Charlie* – Norm Smith's favourite song – and was further heightened by the premiership cup's mouth-to-mouth journey around the room. With premiership posters adorning the walls and dinner tables containing pre-made serviettes with the words: 'VFL Premiers, 1960', the scene was set for one of the more memorable public addresses

---

[52] The Demons' triumph was the best Grand Final win of all time in terms of 'percentage' – their 442.86 percent easily outweighing the effort of Geelong's 2007 side, which, although it recorded the greatest winning margin in a Grand Final of 119 points against Port Adelaide, posted a percentage of 370.45. The next best is Hawthorn's 271.43 percent against Melbourne in 1988.

[53] *The Herald*, Monday September 26, 1960.

of the coach's life. But the gathering of players, officials and guests could not have expected him to start with a scathing broadside aimed at critics within the Demons' ranks. He said:

> This has not been my happiest year at Melbourne. Many people in this room have to put away their shotguns for another year. These critics are within the football club itself. There are too many people in the club who claim to know a great deal about football - more than anyone else - but they do nothing about it except criticise. Today, I have given those critics my answer. We have done the job and we have done it well. I am being frank as I always am. I have had this choked up inside of me for a long time. It's easy to criticise the selection committee. We might argue keenly among ourselves behind closed doors, but when the team is finally selected we accept it without question. I ask that next year the critics within the club do the same: accept the teams that are selected to play and stop criticising. Put those shotguns away. Hang them up on the wall.[54]

He then proposed a toast to his side: 'They are the greatest band of players any coach could have the privilege of coaching'.

Amid great applause and adulation, he recognised the contributions of others. To ruckman Terry Gleeson, who missed the finals with a broken leg, he said: 'We haven't forgotten you, Terry. You helped us get into the finals... You're a great trier, an honest player who battles and battles, and a fine team man. You even trained on a cracked leg to try to get on to the reserves' bench for the finals'.

Of Jim Cardwell, he said: 'He calms me down when I want to have a go and, with talent scout Ken Carlon, has signed many fine players'. And turning to Checker Hughes, he said: 'What Melbourne owes to you no-one will ever know. You gave Melbourne a transfusion. Since you came to Melbourne they have never been weak. If I live to the year 2000, I will still sing your praises'.

In the meantime, the football world sang the praises of Norm Smith, who had presided over what remains the most dominant six-year dynasty by any club in VFL/AFL history. Between 1955 and 1960, the Demons won an unprecedented five premierships – their Grand Final victories being by an average of 49 points. In 121 matches in this period, they recorded 96 wins, 23 losses by an average of 12 points,[55] and two draws, and produced 39 premiership players.

---

[54] This is a combination of the transcripts that appeared in both *The Age* and *The Herald* on Monday September 26, 1960.
[55] Ten of the 12 clubs defeated Melbourne between 1955 and 1960, with Collingwood triumphing four times and each of Essendon, Hawthorn, Footscray and Fitzroy winning three.

At the age of just 44, Smith had become the youngest five-time premiership coach in VFL history. The three other men to have coached at least five premiership sides were comfortably older: Jock McHale (Collingwood) was 46, Jack Worrall (Carlton/Essendon) was 52 and 'Checker' Hughes was 54.

Many believed Smith would have had six flags if the Demons had won in 1958. But others, conscious of fluctuations in desire and commitment, took a more conservative view.

John Lord said: 'Would we have won premierships in '59 and '60 if we had we won in '58? Some people think we would have won six in a row, but it might have worked the other way as well – that might have been the end of the era because the hunger mightn't have been there. Maybe losing in '58 motivated us to win in '59 and '60. We'll never know either way'.[56]

Bluey Adams had a similar theory: 'If we won in '58, we might've thought: "We've won four in a row, we've equalled the record, there's not much else to achieve", and then lost the spark to win in '59 and '60. In '57, we talked about how we wanted to achieve a hat-trick; then the next year we wanted to equal the record. They give you incentive and drive you on, but it's a big effort to keep the same intense attitude over a long period and, although Smithy did everything in his power to keep us up there, in the end it probably wears you down'.[57]

---

[56] John Lord. Interview with the author.
[57] Frank 'Bluey' Adams. Interview with the author.

19

THE PARTY ANIMAL

Footballers have long observed the code that 'what happens on the trip, stays on the trip'. However, poor behaviour on end-of-season jaunts certainly didn't go unpunished at Melbourne Football Club.

Before Melbourne players and officials left on these much-anticipated getaways, the 'godfathers' of the touring party – Norm Smith and Checker Hughes – would lecture the group on the standards of behaviour expected. The general message would be: 'Let's have a great time together but don't for one second forget that you are representing the Melbourne Football Club. If your conduct affects this great club's reputation in any way we will have no hesitation in sending you straight home, where you might face further consequences.'

Keith Carroll recalled: 'It was always a pretty decent lecture, and it left no doubt in anyone's mind what they could and couldn't get away with. You were put on notice and you'd be pretty silly to step outside the guidelines.'[1]

John Lord added: 'We were indoctrinated with Norm's standards of living, and they were as high – if not higher – than what he demanded from us in a football sense.'[2]

There was even a strict dress code. Lord said: 'You could dress casually during the day, but when we all met up for dinner at night we had to wear a jacket, shirt

---

[1] Keith Carroll. Interview with the author.
[2] John Lord. Interview with the author.

and tie.[3] Those dinners kept everyone together, and ensured no group went off on its own. It also helped the quieter blokes mix better.'[4]

Mixing with women – especially for players who were married or had girlfriends – was strictly forbidden. Quite apart from the fact that any such dalliances would threaten the unity of the group, Smith was more concerned from a moral standpoint. Barassi said: 'Norm didn't go to church, but he was a moralist, and very ethical. He would frown upon any married bloke who even looked at another woman.'[5] If a player seemed in danger of straying, Smith would lecture him on the importance of remaining faithful.

Smith was an excellent example in this regard. Although he was 'a passionate man' who 'had a lot of love in his system',[6] he 'wasn't interested in any other women'[7] – 'the only woman for him' was Marj,[8] who he 'clearly adored'[9] and to whom he remained 'absolutely faithful'.[10] Smith was so tough on his players because he wanted them to be 'straight down the line, upstanding citizens'.[11]

On the trip to Perth at the end of 1955, Smith blasted Keith Carroll, a married man he'd mistakenly believed had breached this moral code. Carroll recalled:

> I looked up some family over there and I met up with a female cousin, and she just happened to be really attractive. I took her back to our hotel for lunch. I saw Norm walk past the door of the dining room, and he came back for another look. I had a fair idea of what he was thinking, but it was all innocent.
>
> That night Norm said: 'Keith, you know how I feel about married blokes playing up with women.'
>
> I said: 'Oh, Norm, that girl you saw me with at lunch was–'
>
> He cut me off: 'I don't want to know about it!'
>
> He went on and on and I didn't get a chance to explain myself. He was wrong, but he was only trying to protect us all.[12]

---

[3] Norm Smith never relaxed these standards, even in the early 1970s when he went on end-of-season trips with his South Melbourne side. Swans player Wayne Walsh told the author: 'Norm hated players wearing thongs in a bar. He told (Brian) 'Wrecker' Leahy (the former Melbourne player and then Swans recruiting officer) several times to put some shoes on. Wrecker ignored him, so Norm stomped on Wrecker's foot and almost broke one of his toes'.
[4] John Lord. Interview with the author.
[5] Ron Barassi. Interview with the author.
[6] Tassie Johnson. Interview with the author.
[7] Clyde Laidlaw. Interview with the author.
[8] Tassie Johnson. Interview with the author.
[9] Clyde Laidlaw. Interview with the author.
[10] Ron Barassi. Interview with the author.
[11] Geoff Case. Interview with the author.
[12] Keith Carroll. Interview with the author.

Smith was all about protecting his 'boys', especially in unfamiliar environments. After beating SANFL premier Port Adelaide in a 'Champions of Australia' match in the mid-'50s, the players secretly arranged to attend a party without Smith's knowledge. Geoff Tunbridge recalled:

> Most of the players had drifted off to the party, but a few of us hadn't left yet and Norm came in and quite sternly said: 'Righto, where have they gone?'
> I said: 'I'm sorry, Norm, but we're not meant to tell you.'
> He said: 'Bugger that – out with it!'
> Eventually we very reluctantly told him the venue of the party – reluctantly because we didn't want to incur the ire of our teammates and spoil the night for everyone. I jumped in a cab with Norm and Checker and we went there. Norm didn't have a go at any of the players; he just mingled with everyone.
> He cared about the players and he was always worried about us. That was a terrific trait of his. He was just concerned that things would get out of hand, so he wanted to be there to make sure everything was under control.[13]

Smith also instilled in his players the need to look out for each other. Tunbridge referred to the aftermath of a pre-season match in Launceston, Tasmania, where the Demons played Carlton: 'We saw a Carlton player who was drunk in the gutter. None of his mates were there so we picked him up and helped him. That type of thing never happened at Melbourne Footy Club because we were always a tight-knit group, were always kept together and were always taught to keep an eye out for each other. And that largely came down to the influence of Norm Smith. He was the boss, but he was also a very caring father figure. I genuinely loved the man.'[14]

Smith also did his best to encourage intermingling the between various social groups within the Demons' touring party. John Lord said: 'I'd say there were three types: the "city-ites" were down the back of the bus playing cards, the drinkers were in the middle, and the country boys like me were up the front looking out the window. Norm was a drinker but he'd always be with us, the country yokels, and he'd make sure everyone was involved.'[15]

The trips were so well planned that officials even gave deep thought to which players roomed with each other. Len Mann said: 'You don't know a bloke until you room with him on a trip, and we were made to swap our room-mates quite

---

[13] Geoff Tunbridge. Interview with the author.
[14] Geoff Tunbridge. Interview with the author.
[15] John Lord. Interview with the author.

regularly. It was a conscious ploy to get everyone to know each other better. For instance, we might room with blokes who we wouldn't normally mix with. There are always blokes you naturally get along with better than others, but through little things like that we all got along pretty well.'[16]

While on such trips, Smith often shouted rounds of drinks and meals for his players; so often in fact that some believe he probably spent more money on football than he actually made out of the game. 'Norm wouldn't have made a zac out of footy,' Barassi said. 'There wasn't big money to be made out of footy anyway, but whatever he did make he virtually gave it all back because of his giving nature'.[17] Bluey Adams agreed: 'Norm spent a lot of dough on the boys on footy trips – he probably spent most of his earnings from the season.'[18]

Money had never meant much to Smith (aside, of course, from his younger days during the Depression and the war). He was never wealthy by any means, but that didn't stop him from helping friends who had fallen on hard times, including former teammates, for whom he often 'made arrangements' to provide financial support for accommodation, medical bills, school fees, etc.

During a footy trip in Surfers Paradise, Smith signalled his intention to spend quite a deal more money than usual. While dining with his players at a restaurant, he complained, a little too loudly, 'My steak is too tough.' The insulted manager told Smith he'd had too much to drink and ordered him to leave the premises after he had finished his meal. Smith became agitated. '*Finish* my meal?' he said. 'I can't even *eat* the damn thing!' He then claimed to have the solution to the misunderstanding, boasting: 'I tell you what, Mr Proprietor: I'll buy this damn restaurant!' Hugh McPherson recalled: 'After it all calmed down, Norm realised he didn't even have enough money on him to pay for his meal, let alone buy the restaurant. He actually had to *borrow* money to pay for his feed. They should have served him humble pie!'[19]

Despite the traditionally boozy nature of these gatherings, Smith never lost sight of the bigger picture. According to Clyde Laidlaw: 'Norm was always coaching – even on players' trips. Whether you were on a train or in a hotel room, he could pull you aside and say: "I think you can improve in this department." It was a very relaxed situation, so you'd be able to ask him questions and discuss it with him. It was a very positive, two-way thing and

---

[16] Len Mann. Interview with the author.
[17] Ron Barassi. Interview with the author.
[18] Frank 'Bluey' Adams. Interview with the author.
[19] Hugh McPherson. Interview with the author.

part of the ongoing teaching process.'[20]

But Smith could still drop his guard on occasions and be 'one of the boys'. Sam Allica said: 'We were having a beautiful dinner and being feted in this magnificent dining area at the top of the Broadbeach Hotel, when the lift comes up and out pops (South Melbourne champion) Bobby Skilton and about four of his South mates, and they're singing the Swans theme song. Norm jumped up and marched them over to the table, arm in arm, singing their song with them. He arranged for them to have meals and they stayed with us the night. It was terrific.'[21]

Smith was so accommodating that he would open up his house to strangers. Peter Smith said: 'Up at Surfers Paradise one year, Dad befriended three young blokes over a few beers and told them that if they were ever in Melbourne that they were welcome to come to our place at Rosebud. Sure enough, sometime later the three of them turned up and stayed for a few days. That was the sort of guy Dad was – he'd talk to anyone. He reckoned you could learn something from anyone. But he didn't like it when people wanted to go on and on and on.'[22]

※※※※※※※※

The Smiths' holiday house in Hayes Avenue, Rosebud – built by former Demon full-forward Noel Clarke in 1954 – became a haven for Smith away from the pressures of coaching, and not just in the summer months. Occasionally after matches, Norm, Marj and young Peter would get in the family car at 8.30pm and drive to Rosebud, and not return until Monday morning.

Peter Smith said: 'Mum and Dad liked to get away. It probably helped Dad put the stress of coaching behind him and spend some real quality time with Mum and I. He was a great father, but I never had enough of him. I had to share him with everybody else. So I treasured the times we got away together.'[23]

The Smiths also spent a great deal of time with George and Marj Lenne, staunch Demons club people who had a block of land nearby. George Lenne had played 21 games for Melbourne alongside Smith in 1941-42 and 1945 (his career was interrupted by war service) and was the reserves team manager from 1955-69 (a role which often required him to report to Smith and the selection committee) and a Board member from 1970-74. Meanwhile, Marj Lenne was on the ladies' social committee.

The Smiths and Lennes became extremely close and Marj Lenne would describe

---

[20] Clyde Laidlaw. Interview with the author.
[21] Sam Allica. Interview with the author.
[22] Peter Smith. Interview with the author.
[23] Peter Smith. Interview with the author.

Norm Smith as a 'generous gentleman'. She recalled him asking them several times: 'When are you going to build on that block of yours?' They would reply: 'When we can.' Smith would say: 'I'll lend you the money.' But the Lennes 'couldn't let him do that'.[24]

Smith also helped an opposition footballer he happened to come across in Rosebud's main street. The player was so drunk and dishevelled that he had even urinated in his own trousers. Smith was disgusted, but he took the player back to Hayes Avenue to clean him up. He also took the opportunity to strongly advise the miscreant to take better care of himself. 'You can't get around looking like *that*,' Smith told him. 'Have a bit of respect for yourself. Clean up your act, son.' Smith then sent him on his way, hoping his words might have some effect.[25]

Marj Smith was similarly of strong principles. On one occasion she 'put her foot down' with a Melbourne player who took along his new girlfriend to stay with him at the Smiths' holiday house. Mrs Smith wasn't about to have any 'funny business' between an unmarried couple under her roof, so she made the young couple sleep in separate beds.[26]

During summer, the Smiths' weekender became 'a football camping ground'[27] for players and officials of all clubs. The 'never-ending stream calling in for a beer and a yarn'[28] included some of the biggest names in the game – Bob Skilton, Polly Farmer, Reg Hickey, John Coleman, Ken Hands... and their families. Coleman and Hands were frequent guests.

Peter Smith said: 'It was unique because it was a regular social gathering between three VFL coaches and their families. In those days, Ken Hands was coaching Carlton (1959-64) and Coleman was coaching Essendon (1961-67). Dad respected those blokes and enjoyed their company immensely. They'd play tennis on the court Dad built and then sit under the trees in the driveway and have a few beers. We'd have a barbecue or some chicken sandwiches that Mum would make. Dad loved entertaining, and loved having people over. He loved socialising with football people and talking footy. I was lucky enough as a kid to sit there and listen to them and other football identities.'[29]

Hands recalled that football discussions with Smith often developed into robust debates. 'Norm was always very forceful in his argument,' Hands said. 'But he

---

[24] Marj Lenne. Interview with the author.
[25] Marj Lenne. Interview with the author.
[26] Margaret Clay. Interview with the author.
[27] Peter Smith. Interview with the author.
[28] Ron Carter, *The Age*, July 30, 1973.
[29] Peter Smith. Interview with the author.

was rational about it too. You'd always listen to what he had to say, even if you strongly disagreed with him, because it was always well thought out, and always had substance.'[30]

From the early 1960s, Smith and Hands were co-panellists on *The Tony Charlton Football Show*, which screened on Channel Nine from noon to 2pm on Sundays. Charlton said: 'I approached Norm directly about being part of the show and he readily agreed; he said he would like to do it.'[31] It was something of a media coup. Before then, Smith's television and radio appearances had been, by choice, rare at best. Only once previously had he agreed to appear on television, and the only time his voice was heard on radio was when the odd recording was made in the changerooms after matches or at training sessions. But despite his lack of experience in front of the camera, Smith took charge, and displayed what was later described as a 'rare capacity to glean information from other coaches when they didn't even know they were giving it to him'.[32] Smith's role on the program was, principally, to interview the coaches. Charlton said: 'When Norm spoke, people listened.'[33] And, it seems, when others spoke, Smith listened even more intently.

Hands remembered:

> Norm was pretty much the compere, the senior panellist. Most of the other blokes on the panel were current coaches and Norm tried to get information out of everyone, but no-one would tell him anything because they knew he would use anything you said to his advantage. He clearly asked certain questions purely for his own benefit, while portraying himself as someone who was just trying to keep the viewers at home well-informed. It was very cunning. He was always probing. He did the same thing down at Rosebud, but it was more relaxed then.[34]

A witness to one such conversation at Rosebud was Mike Williamson, who recalled:

> Ken Hands was asking Norm all these questions about coaching and Norm was free and easy with the knowledge he passed on. Towards the end of the night, Ken said: 'Thanks very much, Norm. Your help has been invaluable.'
> Norm said: 'Well Ken, let me tell you this: all the advice I've given you, use it

---

[30] Ken Hands. Interview with the author.
[31] Tony Charlton. Interview with the author.
[32] Brian Bourke, South Melbourne president from 1967 to 1970. Interview with the author.
[33] Tony Charlton. Interview with the author.
[34] Ken Hands. Interview with the author.

against everybody else but don't use it against me, because there are a few things I've kept up my sleeve. I've got a counter to everything I've told you.'[35]

The Smiths – widely regarded as 'terrific hosts'[36] – threw an annual New Year's Eve party attended by as many as 100 family, friends and football people. It was 'the best night of the year, with a lot of singing, dancing, jokes and tall stories'.[37] The Smiths loved entertaining so much that they saved $20 a week to cater for visitors over the festive season.[38] To ensure no-one went thirsty Smith would provide a trailer-load of 20 dozen long-neck bottles of beer, supplied at mates' rates by his old Demon pal and publican Shane McGrath. On a rare occasion when Marj and the ladies didn't prepare food, young Peter was sent to the local fish shop with an order for 40 hamburgers and a mountain of chips.[39]

Although it was the middle of cricket season, football was always high on the agenda, as Hassa Mann remembered:

> I had this special rapport with Norm where, invariably, at some stage in the night I'd be seated on the couch with him, oblivious to the tens of other people who were there, and we'd just talk footy. He'd mention things that the team would have to do, and special challenges that he would give certain players that year. We would talk about new roles that he would try out with me. He'd say: 'This year I want you to try this and do this to become a better player.' He was very much of the view that no matter what you'd achieved in your career, you could always improve. He didn't like it when players thought they'd made it and could just continue on as they had, without trying to add something new to their repertoire.[40]

Smith particularly liked entertaining his players at Rosebud because, as he once told George Lenne: 'There's a lot of room out here, there aren't any neighbours nearby, so they can go for their life and make as much noise as they like without any worry of getting into trouble.'[41] In turn, the players loved spending time with their coach away from the football environment. They loved seeing 'the other side of Norm Smith: gentle, loveable, jovial, warm'.[42]

---

[35] Mike Williamson. Interview with the author.
[36] Barry Bourke. Interview with the author.
[37] Hugh McPherson. Interview with the author.
[38] Marj Lenne. Interview with the author.
[39] Peter Smith. Interview with the author.
[40] Hassa Mann. Interview with the author.
[41] George Lenne. Interview with the author.
[42] Barry Bourke. Interview with the author.

But he was the same fierce, competitive beast on his gravel-cum-asphalt tennis court. Smith's edict was: 'If you play anything, play to win. Never insult your opponent by not trying, even in a social match.'[43]

Ken Hands said: 'The doubles combinations would be John (Coleman) and I against Norm and (Fred) Fanning. Norm was getting a bit older and slower by that stage – and Fanning certainly wasn't very quick either – but Norm lived for a contest. Our wives would drink tea and watch. Heaven knows what they thought of these silly, middle-aged fellas busting a gut over a social game of tennis.'[44]

TV presenter Mike Williamson had a particularly confronting experience when, after a few obligatory drinks, he partnered Smith against Brian Dixon and Ron Barassi.

> When it was Norm's turn to serve, he said: 'Fearless, get right up on the net.'
> I said: 'Norm, I don't like being right up on the net; I like to *advance* to the net.'
> 'Do as you're told, Fearless!'
> We had this ongoing argument while Norm was serving.
> Barass deliberately aimed a return of serve right between my eyes. I ducked and put my racquet up to protect myself and the ball hit the frame of the racquet and flew out of court.
> Well, I've never heard such a tirade!
> 'You gutless mongrel!' Norm roared. 'No wonder you're called Fearless – you've got no bloody guts! You wouldn't get a game with my team, you weak bastard!'
> When he paused for breath, I threw my racquet down and said: 'Now listen. I'm your guest here. Don't you ever bloody well speak to me like that! I'm not a dog and I'm not one of your damn players, and I wouldn't play tennis with you again if it was the last thing on earth!'
> Then I stormed off the court. Norm jogged over and grabbed me and said, quite calmly: 'Fearless, if you can't control your temper, you shouldn't play sport.'
> I thought: 'Hang on a minute; *you're* the one with the hot temper who gave me this almighty dressing down in the first place – I think *you've* got the anger management issues!'[45]

---

[43] Related by John Lord in an interview with the author.
[44] Ken Hands. Interview with the author.
[45] Mike Williamson. Interview with the author.

Norm Smith much preferred to socialise away from the prying eyes of the public. Once his fame was established, Smith only ever set foot in a pub when he was with a group of people.

Peter Smith recalled: 'In all the years at Rosebud, Dad would have gone to the pub only twice. Away from footy, he was a private bloke. If he ever went to a pub, he'd want to spend time with his mates, but he just couldn't get any peace because there were always people coming up to him and wanting to talk football. He tried to give people a fair go but he got so tired of being pestered that he just couldn't be bothered with it.'[46]

Bill Stephen said: 'Like many figures in the public eye, Norm was pretty guarded when people approached him to talk. He'd generally go to places where he could be a bit protected from the public. One night a woman was driving him mad because she was trying to bail him up to talk about football. Finally, Norm said: "Woman, I'll give you *one minute*." He talked to her for a minute and then he left her and that ended it.'[47]

Peter Smith found it difficult to convince his father to even play a round of golf, for instance, and 'do a lot of the things that fathers and sons do'.[48] However, Smith played a lot of backyard sport with his talented son, who said:

> Dad never kicked the footy with me out in the street – he would have been mobbed because there were 75 kids in our street – but he often had a kick with me in our backyard in Shedden Street (Pascoe Vale). It was just fun, nothing serious.
>
> In the summer, we'd play cricket on the concrete across the back of the house. Dad would bowl at me for hours. We'd use these hard, plastic cricket balls that would swing and skid off the concrete; and when they got roughed up he'd bowl leg-breaks.
>
> Then when we moved to Bell Street (also in Pascoe Vale, in 1962), we had a tennis court in our backyard where we'd play tennis, footy and cricket. Len (Smith) would also teach me things. He and Dad coached me out on that court. Looking back, not many kids would have been fortunate enough to have such highly qualified skills coaches! But to me they were always just Dad and Len. There were also other big names popping over.
>
> Dad never pushed me with my sport. He just encouraged me to enjoy it and do the best I could. There was certainly no pressure to play or pursue it at a high level.[49]

---

[46] Peter Smith. Interview with the author.
[47] Bill Stephen. Interview with the author.
[48] Peter Smith. Interview with the author.
[49] Peter Smith. Interview with the author.

Smith also enjoyed taking his wife and son for Sunday picnics on the banks of Deep Creek at Konagaderra Springs – a quiet, then-rural spot near Mickleham, north of Melbourne. Peter Smith said: 'There was virtually nothing there – a creek, a bridge over the water, a few trees, some grass down by the bank, and just a little general store – but it was nice for the three of us to go there for some peace and quiet together out in the fresh air. We did that a few times a year.'[50]

Norm Smith helped initiate a much bigger annual picnic – between the two oldest Australian Football clubs: Melbourne and Geelong. These fondly recalled functions were held for more than a decade, from the mid-1950s to the late 1960s – almost the length of Smith's time as Melbourne coach – and were held on a Sunday in February at the picturesque Maddingley Park in Bacchus Marsh, a nominal halfway point between the two cities. Many of those in attendance played social tennis and contested athletic events.

The Demon-Cat connection was forged by their legendary coaches – Smith and Reg Hickey – who, by 1960, shared 13 premierships (nine to Smith, four to Hickey) as players and coaches. They also shared many similarities in character and, not surprisingly, formed a strong friendship.

Melbourne stars Clyde Laidlaw and John Lord, both of whom trained under Hickey in their early days before joining Melbourne, regard themselves as extremely lucky to have come under the influence of both coaching doyens. Laidlaw observed that the pair had 'the same tough, gruff persona, no punches were withheld, and there was no nonsense';[51] Lord recalled them being 'interested in you both as a footballer and as a person';[52] while 'Bluey' Adams regarded them as 'the two greatest men I have met'.[53]

Geelong champion Bob Davis believed they were kindred spirits.

'Hick' and Smithy were both clean-living, straight-talking fellas, very strong on their values and very similar in their decision-making, and they both liked a beer, so it's no real surprise they got on like a house on fire.

After a game, if a player from either of their sides had a blue with an opposition player or an argument with the umpire, they'd get the two fellas together to shake hands and smooth things over to make sure there were no hard feelings.[54]

At the picnics, Smith and Hickey were in their element, talking football over a few beers with their extended footballing families. Hugh McPherson added:

---

[50] Peter Smith. Interview with the author.
[51] Clyde Laidlaw. Interview with the author.
[52] John Lord. Interview with the author.
[53] *Barassi: The Life Behind The Legend*, 1995.
[54] Bob Davis. Interview with the author.

They'd rib each other about who was the best coach but not in the way that you might think. They'd be saying to each other, 'You're a better coach than I am,' and all that kind of baloney. They went back a long way – they'd played against each other, and played *on* each other as direct opponents – and they had some very funny banter going at times. They'd also talk seriously about football matters and that would be very interesting. You felt very privileged to be in their company, and they kept it going until late in the night. They were special times with special men.'[55]

---

[55] Hugh McPherson. Interview with the author.

20

THE END OF AN ERA

[1961]

Many people who knew Norm Smith never saw him outwardly express emotions of love or grief. Although he wore his heart on his sleeve, he was generally quite stoic... at least in front of others. But early in 1961, it was clear that he was a devastated man. His runner and mate, Hugh McPherson, had been diagnosed with testicular cancer and given just six months to live.

In March – just a month before Smith was to lead the Demons into their most challenging season in some time – McPherson underwent an operation to remove the cancer. It appeared successful, but cancer being the insidious disease it is, no-one could be certain. McPherson's condition improved so rapidly that he was back as the Melbourne runner in late April, while still receiving treatment at the Peter MacCallum Cancer Institute. McPherson said:

> It put the fear of God into Norm. He thought: 'The bugger's going to drop dead on me'. An old saying comes to mind – 'You don't know what you've got 'til it's gone'. And that's the way Norm was acting towards me. He came to me and said: 'Here, I want you to have this'.
>
> He handed me £30 – his pay for appearing on *The Tony Charlton Football Show*. I said: 'What's this for?'
>
> Norm said: 'I know you need it'.
>
> I said: 'I don't, Norm; I'm OK'.
>
> He said: 'Will you please take it, Hughie? I insist'.
>
> I said: 'If it'll make you happy, I'll take it'.

He said: 'Nothing will make me happy, except you getting your health back. I'm just letting you know I'm here to help you'.

You could see that the whole thing had knocked him around quite a bit. There was pain in his eyes. It wasn't a bad thing that he felt like that, though, because he took it a bit easier on me when I started running for him again! Well, at the start anyway.

And then when the players were all set to go to New Zealand on the end-of-season trip, Norm said: 'Hughie's not the best, so I think we should take him on the trip'. He paid all my expenses. He didn't let me pay a damn cent!^[1]

Smith also helped – unknowingly – his friend Mike Williamson to attract a strong panel for the season-opening episode of *Football Inquest*. The popular Channel Seven program had planned a coaches' night. Williamson explained:

All the other coaches – Ken Hands, Bob Davis, John Coleman, etc. – would say: 'If you can get Norm Smith in, I'll be in it'.

Then Norm would say to me: 'I don't know, Fearless. If Len will do it, I might'.

Marj told me: 'If you can sway their mother, they'll never disappoint her'.

It was a cloak-and-dagger job. I went to their mother, who was affectionately known as 'Nanna'. I said: 'Nanna, wouldn't it be nice to see the boys on television together?' She thought that was a great idea. And Marj was in her ear about it.

On the Sunday before the start of the season, it became a ritual that we'd have lunch at Nanna's place. This particular time Nanna said to Norm and Len: 'I'm looking forward to seeing you both on Mike Williamson's show next week'.

They had to do it then. Later, Len laughed and said: 'Well done, Fearless!'

Norm's reaction wasn't as complimentary, but he still said it with a half-grin: 'Fearless, one day you'll go too far'.[2]

While other clubs were hoping Melbourne wouldn't go too far in 1961, Norm Smith certainly didn't appear concerned by talk of a possible slump. 'I don't think we will,' he asserted on the eve of the first round. 'I think we will notch our second hat-trick of premierships in seven years.'[3]

Despite his confidence, he did however acknowledge the threat of 'a new force' – Hawthorn – which had taken fitness to another level with its circuit training and

---

[1] Hugh McPherson. Interview with the author.
[2] Mike Williamson. Interview with the author.
[3] *Melbourne Truth*, Saturday March 25, 1961.

early-morning sessions. 'The "Aunt Sally" of so many years (is) now a definite power,' Smith wrote, impressed by the Hawks' 1960 effort to lift from 0-5 to 11-7 and within just percentage of a finals' berth. 'Last season,' he continued, 'I felt that Hawthorn were becoming more mature than it had ever been in the past... (and) that (coach) John Kennedy was infusing a new spirit into the club, a spirit that will take Hawthorn a long way. We have this spirit at Melbourne. It embraces loyalty to the team, to the coach and to teammates. It is the spirit essential for success. Give me a mediocre player with team spirit before a football champion with none.'[4] Smith's assessment of the Hawks would prove correct. In 1961, 'Kennedy's Commandos' would give the Demons more trouble than any other side had for many years.

Kennedy, who had always been an ardent listener to Smith's philosophies during after-match get-togethers, realised that the only way his side could hope to compete with the likes of Melbourne was to be supremely fit. He said: 'Melbourne had the blueprint for success if you like, and because they'd been so successful for so long they hadn't needed to change the blueprint. They were skilful, fit and tough. We often pushed them at Hawthorn but they always seemed to break away from us at the end. The reason for that wasn't their skill level – they were simply bigger-bodied and stronger, and would keep thrashing in for the ball and working us over physically and eventually the knocks would take their toll on us and they'd run over the top of us. We had to try to reverse that trend, and the only way to do it was through sheer hard work, and perhaps setting some new kind of benchmark in the area of strength and fitness. We wanted to get our side fitter than it had ever been – and hopefully even fitter than any other team – and then play the game in a non-stop way to make our fitness a telling factor'.[5]

Kennedy also explained how his theories on fitness differed from those of the Demon coach he so admired: 'Norm Smith once told me: "You not only have to get the players fit, but football fit". He wasn't as taken with circuit training as he was with having players fit for what was required on a Saturday. At the same time, we felt circuit training benefited our players, so we pursued that hoping it might give us an advantage over sides like Melbourne, or at least get us on level terms with them'.[6]

The Hawks' quest to challenge Melbourne for the premiership appeared even more difficult when Smith announced that the Demons' pre-season form had been

---

[4] *Melbourne Truth*, Saturday March 25, 1961.
[5] John Kennedy. Interview with the author.
[6] John Kennedy. Interview with the author.

'first-class',[7] which was confirmed by their 29-point win over Fitzroy in a low-scoring match at Brunswick Street in round one. A round two meeting with the Hawks proved telling. Melbourne kicked poorly all afternoon and the Hawks beat them at their own game, by 32 points, after displaying what Smith hailed as 'the best form I have ever seen from a Hawthorn side'.[8]

The Demons slipped to 2-2 after suffering a three-point defeat to another improving team, St Kilda. But just when the critics were circling, the Demons returned to their brilliant best, winning their next seven matches by an average of 48 points. The spark for the form explosion was a superb second-half performance at Geelong in round five. After trailing the Cats at half-time – 1.7 (13) to 1.9 (15) – the Demons piled on 16.11 to 6.4 to win by 65 points. After eight rounds, the Demons were on top of the ladder and looking invincible once again. Hawthorn was two games behind in eighth place.

Lou Richards was so confident of a Melbourne win over Len Smith's Fitzroy at the MCG in round 13 that he wrote in *The Sun*: 'In the interest of the game, what about introducing the handicap system – either start the Demons off seven goals behind scratch or make them wear boxing gloves and divers' boots'. Richards was way off the mark. In atrocious conditions, Melbourne and Fitzroy staged their second draw in the space of two years – 6.8 (44) apiece.

A debutant in this period was Brian 'Doc' Roet, a medical student and former University Blacks player. Roet spent the first three rounds in the reserves, which didn't impress his mother, who told him: 'You tell that Mr Smith that you haven't left the University amateurs to play with the seconds'. Roet took his mother's advice literally, and approached Smith at training and said: 'My mum says–', before his incredulous coach cut him off and 'blew his stack'.[9]

But that was nothing compared to Smith's reaction to Brian Dixon on his return from the national carnival in Brisbane. Dixon had starred for Victoria (which had been coached by Len Smith) and became the first Melbourne player to win the Tassie Medal, awarded to the best player in the carnival. Dixon recalled:

> Norm had always instructed me to stay within my zone on the wing – don't go too far forward or too far back. So it was quite refreshing to go away to the carnival and have Len Smith give me a lot of freedom. Len more or less told me: 'Brian, go wherever you want to go'.

---

[7] *Melbourne Truth*, April 15, 1961.
[8] *Melbourne Truth*, April 29, 1961.
[9] Related by John Lord in an interview with the author.

I came back and told this story to Norm, who was totally unimpressed with the fact I enjoyed playing with all this freedom. He accused me of being selfish, and that I had to do exactly what he said and not tell him anything about his brother's coaching techniques because what Len had done with me would have absolutely no bearing on how Norm would use me.

The worst repercussion of that episode took place when on our end-of-season trip in New Zealand. Norm, Checker Hughes and Shane McGrath got hold of me at about 1am – after we'd all been drinking – and reduced me to tears by telling me how selfish I was and I should understand that everything I did had to be for the team. That was tough to take, and came as a real shock to me, because from my point of view, everything I did *was* for the team. Shane McGrath was the main talker on that occasion, but he and Norm were very close, and it was obvious to me that Norm had decided I should be punished for what I'd said about playing under Len. I felt totally unworthy and, for the next three or four days, I wondered what my future as a footballer at the Melbourne Football Club would be.

During the carnival, I also felt Len was a lot softer and more encouraging, whereas Norm was very, very disciplined, and you felt you were doing it for Norm out of this sort of love/fear relationship. I sort of loved Norm, but I sort of feared him as well. I don't have any regrets, though, having spent 14 years under Norm, because he probably got the best out of me.[10]

Norm Smith was closely linked with the leadership of the Victorian side – not only was Len coach, but Barassi was captain (just the second Demon to lead a Victorian carnival side after Bert Chadwick in 1927). Smith hadn't been considered for the state coaching job because a VFL rule stipulated that anyone who had previously coached Victoria was ineligible. On this basis, Ken Hands (Carlton), Phonse Kyne (Collingwood) and Des Rowe (Richmond) were also ruled out. Len Smith then became the logical choice. However, he originally declined the job after Fitzroy had lost the first four games. 'In the circumstances,' Len explained, 'it would not be right for me to take the state job… I think it would be an embarrassment'. But Fitzroy then won four consecutive games and the selectors changed Len's mind.

Barassi was impressed with Len's ability to quickly build team spirit. 'His methods and manner soon made short work of inter-club rivalries,' Barassi said.[11] Even greater praise came from Essendon's champion centreman, Jack Clarke,

---

[10] Brian Dixon. Interview with the author.
[11] *The Australian*, Wednesday May 12, 1965.

who had earned All-Australian selection after playing under Norm Smith in the 1958 carnival. Clarke declared: 'Len was by far the best of the state team coaches I played under. He was no great orator but there was a wealth of knowledge in what he said and he didn't squander his breath on emotional appeals. You might enjoy a good stage show twice or even three times, but if you had to watch it week after week, month after month, you'd go insane'.[12]

Victoria easily accounted for both Tasmania (by 61 points) and South Australia (58 points) before suffering a shock nine-point loss to Western Australia, which cost the Vics the title by just 1.1 percent. Barassi said: 'It was no fault of his (Len's)'.[13] Len made no excuses, and praised WA as deserving winners, but suggested the VFL put more time into preparation for future carnivals to combat increasingly strong WA and SA sides, which had trained together for months.

The VFL's strongest club, Melbourne, also appeared in serious danger of losing its lofty status. After the draw with Fitzroy, the Demons had lost three successive matches – to Hawthorn (18 points) and St Kilda (11 points), both for a second time that season, and Essendon (nine points) – and in each instance had trailed all day. A contributing factor was the absence of players like Barassi, Adams, Dixon, Ridley, Case, Thorogood, Gleeson and Lenn Mann. With three rounds remaining, the Demons were still in second place, but were now vulnerable, with Geelong level with them on points and sixth-placed Fitzroy just a game behind.

North Melbourne coach Wally Carter wrote in his weekly column in *The Truth*: 'MEMO SPORTING EDITOR, *TRUTH*: Please book extra press box seat at this year's finals for *Truth's* football writers. The seat should be booked in the name of Mr Football himself, Norman Smith. Mark my words, there is no certainty that Norman will rate a seat on the bench inside the playing arena during this year's finals... Let's face it. Melbourne are in more trouble than West Berlin'.[14]

Norm Smith was very conscious of the need to regain form. 'We must pull out of our slump,' he said, 'as a loss now could push us out of the four.'[15] The situation became dire against Geelong at the MCG. The Demons, who hadn't won a match for 42 days, trailed by 11 points at half-time and two points at the last change, but managed to scrape home by two points.

---

[12] Contemporary newspaper report.
[13] *The Australian*, Wednesday May 12, 1965.
[14] *Melbourne Truth*, August 12, 1961.
[15] *Melbourne Truth*, August 12, 1961.

They then finished off the home-and-away season with wins over tough opponents – top-four side Footscray (40 points) and Carlton (one point). The Demons had recorded a 12-5-1 record and finished second, and missed out on the minor premiership (to Hawthorn, by a game-and-a-half) for the first time since 1954, but at least they had made the finals. It was a strange final four, with the other three teams – Hawthorn, St Kilda and Footscray – having claimed just one premiership between them (Footscray in 1954).

Although the Demons had lost their past three matches against Hawthorn (including their past two at the MCG), and the Hawks were in red-hot form after winning 10 consecutive matches, Smith appeared undaunted by the prospect of facing them in the second semi-final. 'I think we can topple the Hawks from their perch,' he said. 'Knowing the tradition down at Melbourne, I feel that the importance of this match will bring out the best in our men.'[16]

Midway through the second term, Smith's optimism seemed vindicated with Melbourne leading 7.3 (45) to 3.1 (19). A hat-trick of premierships beckoned. But then the game changed. The turning point was the seemingly premeditated felling of Laurie Mithen 60 metres off the ball. Fights broke out all over the field and the Demons lost their focus and the match, conceding nine of the next 13 goals to go down by seven points in what many believed was the Grand Final preview. Remarkably, the Hawks had beaten Melbourne for the third time in the season to advance to their first Grand Final. To make matters worse, Smith also had a fiery exchange with Hugh McPherson, who recalled:

> Norm sent me out to Laurie Mithen on at least five separate occasions to tell him to pick up his man, Brendan Edwards. Every time Norm saw Edwards, Laurie was a mile away from him. Norm didn't want to give Edwards any room because he was in terrific form. The ball came out to the boundary right in front of us and here's Mithen, in a pack of players, but where's Edwards? He's about 50 yards away, and on his own, in the centre. Norm was furious. He roared at me to once again, for the umpteenth time: 'Get out there and tell Mithen to pick up Edwards!'
>
> I said: 'Well there he is; tell him your bloody self!'
>
> Norm glared at me and said: 'You're sacked! Get that armband off and give it to (head trainer) Jack McLoughlin!'
>
> I threw the armband on the ground. Norm told Jack to put it on. Jack said: 'I don't need an armband to go out there. Everybody knows who I am'.

---

[16] *Melbourne Truth*, Saturday September 9, 1961.

Norm said: 'Well I'd like you to put it on.' In other words: 'Put the bloody thing on right now!' But Jack again refused.

Five minutes later, Norm told me: 'Put that bloody armband back on!'

I did that and then Norm sent me out with more messages to give players. Not another word was spoken about the incident and I was still the runner.[17]

Although the Demons were expected to comfortably dispose of Footscray in the preliminary final, they were never in the contest. Ten minutes into the last quarter, the Bulldogs led by nine goals, and eventually won by 27 points. The football community was in shock. The mighty Demons had been dethroned.[18] They had failed to make the Grand Final for the first time in eight years. Inconceivably, they had bowed out of the finals in straight sets. In hindsight, their form had been well below par. All they had to show for their last nine games was three wins and a draw. It was the end of an era, and Smith knew it. In the players' race after the game, he semi-choked Jim Cardwell by the tie and demanded: 'Get me some players with guts!' Mavis Cardwell recalled:

> Afterwards, Norm went up to Jim with a couple of bottles of beer and said "I shouldn't have done that. You shouldn't have let me do that". But that wasn't Jim's style – he wouldn't argue with anybody. Norm did his lolly lots of times, but he didn't do it for nothing – he had a cause when he did it. But once he was annoyed, he couldn't hold it back, whereas Jim could conceal it. If someone said something Jim didn't like, he might say 'You know better than that', and just walk away. Jim was a great diplomat and a calming influence, and that's how he and Norm got on. If they had both been like Norm, they'd have killed each other![19]

The incident with Cardwell was uncharacteristic of Smith's overall demeanour after the loss to the Bulldogs. In the Melbourne rooms, he told his players: 'For eight years you have built up a great record and you have been terrific winners. Now you have been beaten by a better side, but I don't want you to whinge about it; I want you to go in there and be good losers'.[20]

The Melbourne committee reported with pride: 'One of the features of the season was the manner in which the side and our coach faced up to defeat after such

---

[17] Hugh McPherson. Interview with the author.
[18] In the 1961 Grand Final, Hawthorn defeated Footscray by 43 points. Brendan Edwards was best afield.
[19] Mavis Cardwell. Interview with the author.
[20] Related by Geoff Tunbridge in an interview with the author.

a magnificent run. It might well be imagined that at its conclusion some unhappiness would be shown. However, such was not the case. In particular, the sporting way in which… Norm Smith accepted defeat was favourably commented on by all. This splendid coach gained as many friends in defeat as those he enjoyed in victory'.

▼▼▼▼▼▼▼▼▼

If competition had been tough for the Demons in 1961, it wasn't going to get any easier in the short-term following the loss of their best big man (Big Bob Johnson) and their best small man (Ian Ridley). Both could be damaging on the ball and in attack, where they had supplied almost 500 goals between them over the previous eight seasons. Johnson, 27, accepted the captain-coaching job at WAFL club East Fremantle, which he took to four successive Grand Finals and a premiership (in 1965). Johnson later revealed he left purely for monetary reasons. He said: 'I'm now sorry I went because Smithy got us together socially and he got a lot of the club (spirit) into us and we were successful because of Norm Smith'.[21] The retirement of Ridley, also 27, was an entirely different matter, because he had been determined to play on. Ridley said:

> About six weeks before the finals, my bloody knee collapsed on me and I was in incredible pain. I'd stretched a ligament in the side of my knee and missed a few games because of it. But Smithy and the selection committee decided to play me in the finals, which was a great show of respect to me. I probably shouldn't have played – I had to go off at three-quarter time.
> At the end of the season, I said to Norm: 'I'll go and see a specialist.'
> He said: 'You don't need to; you're buggered.'
> I said: 'Hang on. I don't know about that.'
> He said: 'No, you're buggered.'
> I insisted: 'I want to get it checked out.'
> He said: 'All right then, go for your life.'
> I got it checked out and went back to Norm and he said: 'How did you go?'
> I said: 'I'm buggered'.
> He knew I was gone. He had that sense. It was a great disappointment to me because I was runner-up in the best-and-fairest only the year before, in a premiership year. It just shows your career can finish a whole lot quicker than

---

[21] *Red and Blue* documentary, 2005.

you think. An applicable saying of Norm's was: 'Play every game like it's your last'. It's a very common saying nowadays but I hadn't heard it until I heard Smithy say it. He was 'the man', and I was just so privileged to have played under him.[22]

🏆🏆🏆🏆🏆🏆🏆🏆🏆

While captain-coach Ted Whitten and his Footscray side continued to employ the flick-pass with stunning results in the 1961 finals series, Fitzroy players and officials became embittered by what they felt was a gross double-standard. Not only were the Bulldogs using the very weapon the Lions had been virtually forced to abandon due to inconsistent umpiring interpretations, but they occupied the place in the final four that the Lions felt should have been theirs.

Fitzroy secretary Ward Stuchbery even went as far as saying that the flick-pass debacle had cost the Lions a spot in the finals. The Lions missed the final four, and possibly even third spot, by just half a game. Regardless of the validity of their grievances regarding the adjudication of their brand of handball, the Lions could also blame themselves. Just when they appeared set to make a serious assault on the premiership following an impressive 1960 season, they lost the first four rounds (by an average of 23 points). And then, perhaps more damningly, after recording nine wins, two losses and a draw from their next 12 games, and poised to secure a spot in the four with their two remaining fixtures against the two bottom sides in the offing, they stumbled again. A 12-point loss to bottom side North in round 17 actually flattered the Lions after they had trailed by about six goals for most of the day. A belated 103-point spanking of 11th-placed South Melbourne meant nothing with Footscray and St Kilda winning on the same day.

The Lions had finished in the top five in each of Len Smith's four seasons as coach. But they had contested just two finals series, and missed the other two by just half a game (according to some, by just 'a kick' in both instances). It had been an admirable performance by a team lacking size, marking power and stars. Len' Smith's senior coaching record stood at 75 matches, 46 wins, 27 losses and two draws, at an impressive success rate of 61.33 percent. But hard-nosed Fitzroy folk, like Len himself, felt they could have done better.

The flick-pass debate had hung like a cloud over their heads and ultimately dictated that they revert back to the more traditional, cumbersome, style of handball.

---

[22] Ian Ridley. Interview with the author. Ridley later filled many off-field roles at Melbourne, including senior coach (1971-73), board member (1975-85) and club president (1992-96), and was also a VFL director, state selector and a member of the VFL/AFL tribunal.

The Lions couldn't help but think: 'What if?' Len refused to look backward, but at the time he was understandably disillusioned. He cited the example of Australian Test cricketer Ian Meckiff, whose career ended after he was called for 'chucking' in the First Test against South Africa at the Gabba in December 1963. Len believed it was only after Meckiff started having success that he was labelled a 'chucker'; before that, when he wasn't taking many wickets, there hadn't been a problem. And he believed it had been a similar story with Fitzroy's handball.

Exacerbating Len Smith's frustration and confusion, a conference between league delegates and the umpires' board found the flick-pass kept the game flowing and made for a better spectacle. After the Lions' seven-point loss to Geelong in round 10 – a loss that broke a five-match winning streak – Len spoke his mind on the subject: 'If Fitzroy is to make the four, we must be allowed to play our own style of football, using our own style of handball. Am I to give up years of practice and hard work because of umpires' different interpretations of our handpassing? If so, I'm gone. Fitzroy will be forced to either cut it out, or play according to each umpire's interpretation. But all umpires obtain their interpretations of the rule from their coach, Mr Harry Clayton, who has verified this season that our style of handpass is quite correct... Yet two umpires... disagreed... The penalising of my players... is upsetting to them as it creates doubt in their minds. The VFL must alter the present rule and make it clear that the ball must be punched, or allow us to carry on with our style of passing, which is quite legitimate under the present rule. I have been coaching for more than 15 years and have always taught this style of handpass... but I don't know what to do if umpires continue to penalise it'.[23]

Alf Brown backed Len Smith, commenting in *The Herald*: 'Wouldn't it be wonderful if some day we could watch a game of football umpired according to the rules and not to a set of interpretations known only to a select group of people?... The definition of handball in the rule book is: 'Handball is clearly holding the ball with one hand and hitting it with the other hand'. Surely that's clear enough. There is nothing in the rule about punching the ball. So why that rule, and others equally straight-forward, should have to be interpreted baffles me'.[24]

In the end, Len took the only option he felt was available to him – he instructed his players not to use the flick-pass. Kevin Murray said: 'Sometimes our players made it look like a throw, and they were getting penalised for it, when that might not have actually been the case, so we stopped doing it altogether. It just wasn't worth giving away so many free kicks. They're hard enough to get at the best of

---

[23] *The Sun*, June 26, 1961.
[24] *The Herald*, June 29, 1961.

times without giving them away. Len was obviously disappointed with the way the rule was umpired, and disappointed he had to abandon what was a very dangerous weapon, but, like everything else, he accepted it, reluctantly, and moved on'.[25]

The flick-pass was eventually outlawed in 1965 and the handball law was amended to ensure the ball was struck with a clenched fist. Norm Smith had been a pivotal figure in the rule change. Whitten maintained that Smith had done the game a disservice for using his considerable influence to stamp the flick-pass out of the game for good. Before the pass was outlawed, Whitten had said: 'I admire Norman Smith as a successful League coach, shrewd tactician and good judge, but I can't understand his reasoning for being against teams using the flick-pass. Norm… has had the players and success where he possibly doesn't need the flick-pass. Len… and myself… have been battling to get top-class players all around the ground and are trying something new to bring success to our clubs, and are being criticised… Do we have to please our players, our committee (who pay us for coaching), our supporters (who keep the game going and want success), or do we have to please Norm Smith?'[26]

Although Len was disappointed about the demise of the flick-pass, he believed: 'The ruling is for the good of the game generally, and has simplified the handball interpretation for players, umpires and spectators alike. I was, of course, very happy with the flick-pass, as it helped to open up the game… However, the new, revised law is not a backward move, as it places an emphasis on the increased skill of learning to handball both hands. I, for one, could never handball with my left hand – instead I used the flick-pass. So now all youngsters must be taught to use their left hand as well as their right, to handball with the clenched fist.'[27]

Len Smith was also influencing the next generation of supercoaches. One of his keenest admirers was St Kilda's young coach Allan Jeans. In his first season, as a 27-year-old – believed to be the youngest non-playing coach in VFL/AFL history – Jeans had guided the Saints to third spot, before being eliminated by Footscray in the first semi-final. After the match, Jeans received a letter from Len Smith which read: 'Commiserations are no bloody good to a losing coach, as no matter what I say about St Kilda's wonderful effort in the semi, you yourself are still stuck with the disappointment of losing and will be stuck with it until you settle down again… May I suggest that when you do settle down, don't look for any excuses, Alan (sic), look for the reasons and then become determined to

---

[25] Kevin Murray. Interview with the author.
[26] Contemporary newspaper report.
[27] Contemporary newspaper report.

correct the weaknesses, both in yourself and in your team, so you can go one better next year'.

Jeans said he took two major lessons out of Len's wisdom: 'If something goes wrong, analyse yourself first because you might be the problem'; and: 'Before you try to understand others, you've got to understand yourself'[28] – both of which were to prove helpful in his long and illustrious coaching career.

---

[28] Allan Jeans. Interview with the author.

21

JUST OFF THE PACE

[1962]

In the pre-season practice matches of 1962, Norm Smith performed his almost customary in-house humiliation of one of his players, but few could have predicted the carefully selected target would have been skipper Ron Barassi, and that it would ignite such a powder-keg reaction.

Smith had been grinding an axe for Barassi and looking for an opportunity to cut him down to size, since about 5pm on Saturday September 16 the previous year. Following Melbourne's disastrous defeat to Footscray in the preliminary final, Barassi had, as was customary, gone into the Bulldogs rooms to congratulate victorious captain-coach Ted Whitten and his team on making just their second Grand Final. Barassi and Whitten were two of the best players and biggest personalities in the game and virtually shared the title of 'Mr Football'. Barassi – who won had his first club best and fairest award in 1961 – recalled:

> The Footscray people were so happy they were turning cartwheels, and they received me very well. 'EJ' (Whitten) was standing on a rubdown table, so I joined him up there and shook his hand and congratulated him and the Footscray boys. I also made the remark to EJ, in front of everyone: 'The title of Mr Football is yours today!' We often joked about that so-called title over the years. So, being a gracious loser, as Norm had taught us, I surrendered it to EJ that day. It got a laugh and there was a bit of banter about it, but I didn't think anything else of it. But I later found out that it had annoyed Norm. He never tolerated any behaviour that could have been perceived in any way as being big-headed or arrogant. If he sniffed it, he would bring the player – or players – crashing back to earth with a real thud. I certainly found that out.[1]

---

[1] Ron Barassi. Interview with the author.

For once, Smith didn't immediately give Barassi the tongue-lashing he felt he deserved. Such an act would have been forgotten by the start of the 1962 and therefore would have served no purpose other than putting the skipper back in his place. Instead, he stewed on it over summer and planned to use it to the team's advantage. After such an unexpectedly poor finish to their 1961 finals campaign, there could be no cause for complacency in the Demons camp anyway, but Smith wouldn't take any chances. He would burst Barassi's inflated opinion of himself at the first available opportunity in the pre-season, in the hope it would strike a cord among his players and provoke them into reproducing their best football.

The moment came at half-time of an intra-club practice match. Smith snarled: 'And you think you can lay claim to being Mr Football?! You're not Mr Football! You're just playing like someone who thinks he's Mr bloody Football! It has obviously gone to your head because you are playing very selfish football!'[2]

Smith had struck the rawest of nerves. 'Norm generally knew which buttons to press with me,' Barassi said, 'but that was the wrong buzzer.' Barassi was 'absolutely bloody wild about it – as wild as I'd ever been'. In fact, if Smith had been a teammate or someone else, Barassi would have been 'tempted to belt him'. But he settled on a more calculated, but no less spiteful reaction. He thought: 'All right then, if you think I'm selfish now, I'll show you bloody selfish'. He played the second half in a manner he had never done before: he refused to acknowledge he had an opponent, and tried to do everything himself. He was surprised that Smith didn't take him to task about his petulant display.

When Barassi got home, he was 'still steaming'[3] and he 'stewed and stewed' over Smith's blast.[4] He felt the best course of action to prevent a repeat performance by the coach was to write a letter to Denis Cordner, Melbourne's chairman of selectors. The letter effectively said:

> Dear Denis,
>
> On Saturday the senior coach, Norm Smith, humiliated me in front of all of my teammates by referring to me as a selfish player.
>
> How the senior coach could possibly arrive at such a conclusion is completely beyond me. I have examined my handball statistics and they show that I have been the most prolific handballer for Melbourne for the past three seasons.

---

[2] Ron Barassi. Interview with the author.
[3] Ron Barassi. Interview with the author.
[4] Barassi, Ron and Peter McFarline, *Barassi: The Life Behind The Legend*, Simon & Schuster, 1995.

> While I know it is absolutely against team discipline, I am putting you on notice that if ever the coach publicly accuses me of selfishness again I will – regardless of when or where it takes place – have it out with him on the spot. I realise this is the wrong thing to do but I will not tolerate it.
>
> I trust you will use your good sense to prevail this upon the senior coach.
>
> Yours sincerely,
> Ron Barassi[5]

The mere fact that Barassi – like his coach, a stickler for discipline – had threatened to 'have it out' with Smith irrespective of the circumstances was telling. 'You can have it out with the coach,' Barassi explained, 'but never at training or during a match because there isn't the time… It shows how furious I was that I was prepared to break it in this case.'[6]

Before sending the letter to Cordner, Barassi thought it best to do Smith the courtesy of allowing him to read it first and inform him of his intentions. Norm and Marj Smith read it. According to Barassi, 'Norm wasn't upset; he played it cool and was very considered about it, probably because he knew he'd said the wrong thing'. The pair 'thrashed it out'[7] and, at one stage during an emotional heart-to-heart chat which lasted a few hours, both Marj and Barassi were in tears. Smith managed to suppress any emotions he felt.

Barassi said: 'I just knew I wasn't a selfish player. I might have been a lot of things, but I certainly wasn't selfish. I actually prided myself on being quite the opposite – sel*fless*. I said to Norm: "Do you know I've actually had the most handballs in the club?" His response to that was: "Yes, but a lot of those handballs you gave and received back". There was a lot of to-ing and fro-ing. Norm obviously wanted to resolve the issue, but he wasn't about to buckle at the knees and plead forgiveness – that wasn't his style'.[8]

At the end of the crisis meeting, Smith said to Barassi: 'Well what do you plan to do with that letter now? Why don't you drive out to see Denis now?'

Barassi drove the 40-odd kilometres across town to Cordner's firm in Croydon. He later suspected that, while he was on his way, Smith had telephoned Cordner to prepare him for his livid visitor. 'Norm would have told Denis: "Ronny is on his

---

[5] Ron Barassi. Interview with the author.
[6] Barassi, Ron and Peter McFarline, *Barassi: The Life Behind The Legend*, Simon & Schuster, 1995.
[7] Ron Barassi. Interview with the author.
[8] Ron Barassi. Interview with the author.

way over to see you. He's got this letter and he's pretty upset, so hear him out and calm him down and everything will be OK".'⁹

Cordner did exactly that, and told Barassi: 'Oh well, you have had a chat with Norm. Nothing else is going to happen from now on. Just get on with the game'.¹⁰ This seemed to satisy Barassi, who tore up the letter and agreed to take the issue no further. But he had made his point, and the whole episode was never mentioned again… and Smith never again referred to Barassi as selfish. Barassi joked: 'He referred to me as other things instead!'

YYYYYYYYY

Smith questioned the wisdom of Hawthorn's training regime after the reigning premier had lost the Grand Final rematch with Footscray by 33 points at the Western Oval. In the process, he enlightened readers with some of his own philosophy. 'What caused the Hawks' dismal flop?' he asked. 'They were slow, sluggish and looked second-rate. There is no doubt that physically the Hawks are the fittest team in the league. In fact, I say they are too fit. I believe they are overtrained. There is more to playing League football than having stamina. Players driven too hard at training will leave their form on the track. Too much hard training flattens players. Circuit training is John Kennedy's baby – most other coaches scoff at it. But last year Kennedy had the last laugh. It was he alone who lifted the Hawks to their great premiership win. No side could stand up to their physical strength. But they had a goal then – something to lift them above the ordinary – their first premiership. Players cannot stand up to that sort of training year after year.'¹¹

The training workload Smith set his players was working superbly at the start of the season. The Demons won their first six matches (by an average of 32 points) to sit atop the ladder, 33.6 percent clear of Essendon, which was also undefeated.

A debutant during this period was pacy half-forward Barrie Vagg. The teenager from Shepparton played the first five games before being dropped. He later admitted he hadn't been ready for League football. Regardless, he was still worried about his form, so he approached Smith for advice. The response was typically curt.

---

⁹ Ron Barassi. Interview with the author.
¹⁰ *Barassi*, Ron and Peter McFarline, *Barassi: The Life Behind The Legend*, Simon & Schuster, 1995.
¹¹ *Melbourne Truth* series, 1962. That season, Hawthorn recorded just five wins and finished ninth. It was the biggest fall of any premiership side. The Hawks have since been 'overtaken' by two clubs: the Adelaide Crows, which tumbled from premiers in 1997-98 to 13th in 1999; and Essendon, which plummeted from a flag in 1993 to 10th the next season.

Smith barked: 'Get more bloody kicks!'

The coach then 'just walked off' and left Vagg to absorb his stinging rebuke. Vagg 'momentarily lost respect' for his coach. He felt a coach should be approachable, particularly when a young player was asking for help. But he quickly came to understand that Smith's method for getting the best out of players was to 'have a crack at them, even if it meant being scathing at times'. But in hindsight, Vagg – who eventually did get more kicks and, in fact, became renowned as an excellent kick on either foot – said: 'I'm glad Norm was the way he was. He helped open my eyes up to the world. You're a bit sheltered living in the country, but he taught me that you have to fight for yourself and take the good with the bad'.

Smith was also critical of what Vagg's perceived casual approach. The coach would demand: 'For Christ's sake, "Vaggy", have a bloody go!' Vagg recalled: 'I think I looked a bit laconic and he probably thought I was a bit soft. I wasn't as hard at the ball as he wanted. I wish I'd been more aggressive, but it just wasn't in my nature. I didn't have the body for it, either. In the social rooms, Norm spoke to my brother, who is a bigger-boned fella. Norm told him: "I wish your brother had your physique". I wish I had too'.[12]

▼▼▼▼▼▼▼▼▼

Despite losing three of their four matches between rounds seven and 10 – to take their record to 7-3 – the Demons steadied to win seven of their last eight matches. Their only loss had been by 16 points to a quality Geelong side at the MCG in round 13. Although Melbourne had finished the minor rounds with an imposing 14-4 record – statistically better than its premiership years of 1957 and 1959, and the equal of 1960 – it was only enough to give the Demons third spot, behind Essendon (16-2) and Geelong (14-4, but with a 13.5 percent advantage).

The Demons entered the first semi-final – their first such final since 1954 – with great confidence. Their opponent, Carlton, had finished a game and considerable percentage behind them. Crucially, the Demons had gained a massive psychological advantage over the Blues when they hammered them by 35 points in the final home-and-away round at the MCG – 11.9 (75) to 5.10 (40).

After an even first half, the Demons broke away with a 5.5-to-3.2 third term to lead by 14 points at the last change. However, injuries to proven finals performers and a poor umpiring decision cost them dearly. John Lord had been forced off

---

[12] Barrie Vagg. Interview with the author.

the ground with injury in the first quarter, while Barassi was severely afflicted by a groin problem and hobbled off midway through the final term. After adding just one behind to Carlton's 2.5, Melbourne was two points behind. With about 30 seconds remaining, the Demons mounted one last challenge.

A quick succession of handballs resulted in 'Bluey' Adams sending a long ball to the advantage of Geoff Tunbridge, who had his opponent, Carlton defender Graeme Anderson, out-positioned about 20 metres out from goal. 'A player of my experience should have moved toward and marked,' Tunbridge admitted, 'but I made the mistake of waiting for it.'[13] Tunbridge dropped the chest mark – which would have given him a shot at goal from just 20 metres, almost directly in front – but could also have received a free kick after Anderson crashed into him from behind. The ball spilled to the ground and Laurie Mithen gathered the loose ball and goaled from point-blank range. The Demons should have been in front by four points. However, umpire Frank Schwab – an experienced whistle-blower who was voted *The Sporting Globe's* umpire of the year in 1962 – inexplicably called the ball back for the first of two ball-ups in the dying seconds, before the siren sounded to signal a two-point win to Carlton. It also signalled the first time in 10 seasons that Melbourne hadn't progressed beyond the first week of the finals.

Tunbridge was taken aback by Smith's reaction to his blunder:

> As I came off the ground, at the top of the race were Denis Cordner and Norm Smith. I said to Norm: 'Norm, I'm sorry, I should've taken that mark'.
>
> I wasn't much of a kick for goal, and Norm said, almost jovially: 'That's all right, Tunner. It would have meant we would've lost by *one* point!'
>
> Denis Cordner went a further and said: 'No, Norm, it'd be the same result!'
>
> For someone who was as competitive as Norm to be able to joke about it and not berate me for a bad mistake was a sign of the man. It was first-class. He was a great bloke. He never had a harsh word for me.[14]

It was to be Tunbridge's last act in a VFL match. The then 30-year-old was part of an illustrious group of eight Melbourne players to retire at the end of 1962. The others were Laurie Mithen (28), Clyde Laidlaw (aged 28), Ian Thorogood (26), Geoff Case (26), Terry Gleeson (28), Trevor Johnson (27) and Dennis Jones (25).

---

[13] Geoff Tunbridge. Interview with the author.
[14] Geoff Tunbridge. Interview with the author.

Smith occasionally warned his players: 'Time's running out, boys. You'd better make the most of it while it lasts'. As is often the case, some players thought it was a melodramatic statement. 'You instantly dismiss it because you think it's never going to end,' Case said. 'But all of a sudden she's all over.' Case's dreaded moment came when Smith approached him and said: 'You'll have to lift your game a bit; you're slipping'. Although Case acknowledged that his motivation was starting to wane because he was supporting a young family, it still gave him 'a kick in the tail'. He said: 'I thought: "I'll show the bastard I'm not finished". But unfortunately, "the bastard" was right, as he so often was'.[15]

However, Smith didn't see Thorogood's departure coming, and tried to convince him to stay. Thorogood recounted their exchange:

> I lived in Waverley and they wanted me to coach them (in the VFA), so I went to explain it to Norm in the committee room at Melbourne. His initial reaction was: 'There's the door'. But then he calmed down and said: 'Tell me why'.
>
> I said: 'Well, Norm, the challenge has gone out of it. I've played in four Grand Finals and I don't think I can contribute a great deal more. Coaching in the VFA is a new challenge'.
>
> Norm said: 'Challenge?! There are challenges here at this club that you haven't even bloody considered'.
>
> I said: 'What are the challenges then? Tell me'.
>
> He said: 'I'll give you three points of view: first of all, Ronny won't be here forever and you have the qualities to captain the side; secondly, you've only played 93 games, so you need seven to have your name up on the honour board; and thirdly, you haven't played interstate football. Think about those three things'. Then he leant across the table and said: 'But I will not - and don't think I will - make up your mind for you. But if you decide to go, you've got my full support, and if you need any help you know where I live and you know my phone number'.
>
> Even though I was still only 26, I'd been through the mill, and numbers of games didn't mean much to me, so I pulled the pin.
>
> At Waverley - and with Norm's constant guidance in background - we went from second bottom in second division to beating Port Melbourne in a first division Grand Final inside four years. Norm was one of the first on the phone with all these words of praise, followed by: 'Why didn't you do this? Why didn't you do that?' He was always very keen to help.[16]

---

[15] Geoff Case. Interview with the author.
[16] Ian Thorogood. Interview with the author.

Smith certainly helped Gleeson's decision to retire. 'In my last year,' Gleeson said, 'I had a fairly senior job, and I arrived late for training one night and my secretary had left a message for me to call her. I went straight into the secretary's room to ring her and Norm blew the hell out of me. He said: "You're here for footy, not work!" It was becoming too difficult to combine the two, so I retired.'

He did persuade Gleeson to continue his involvement with the club in a different, more meaningful capacity. Gleeson said: 'Norm suggested to me: "Why don't you go on the committee?" There was a certain part of Melbourne's culture that Norm didn't like – the top-of-the-town people who associated with the club – and I think he felt that having someone like myself on the committee might help to balance things a little. I stood for election and got on, and it was probably only because Norm had advised me to do it that it came about'.[17]

Tunbridge probably best summed up the impact Smith had on the lives of his players: 'It's hard to pinpoint the influence Norm Smith had on me, but it was profound. He was such an honest and strong man, which encouraged you, in turn, to be honest in what you did. He took defeat on the chin, even though you knew he was boiling underneath. That in itself is a great value system to have. He was a mixture: a guy who was voluble, didactic, irascible and argumentative, but also very gentle at the same time. It was that mixture that was very appealing to me. Norm was a very strong figure in my life. Still is. Whenever I see his face in a picture, I think great things, and feel great feelings'.[18]

A man who was perversely 'feeling great feelings' in the wake of Melbourne's second successive unsuccessful finals campaign was renowned athletics coach Percy Cerutty. The eccentric Cerutty was famous for devising a revolutionary fitness regime that included miles of hard running up and down sand dunes on the Mornington Peninsula – a regime that had driven Herb Elliot to Olympic gold in Rome in 1960. Cerutty wrote to Smith at the end of 1961 and offered his services, for a fee, believing that with the benefit of his training schedule in pre-season, the Demons would again be premiers. Smith 'politely declined' Cerutty's offer, and when the 1962 season ended in another finals failure, he received another letter from Cerutty, who basically said: 'Hah-ha told you so. You might have won the premiership if you had let me train your players'.[19]

---

[17] Terry Gleeson. Interview with the author.
[18] Geoff Tunbridge. Interview with the author.
[19] Related by Peter Smith in an interview with the author.

Bert Chadwick stepped down as Melbourne president at the end of the 1962 season after 13 years in the job. Although Chadwick and Norm Smith had endured their share of friction, there was great mutual respect between the pair.

In Melbourne's annual report, Chadwick expressed a general view that such robust debate had been beneficial for the club. 'In a vigorous and progressive football club,' Chadwick explained, 'there is plenty of scope for differing views on various matters, our club being no exception. However, our various opinions have been coordinated while maintaining our personal respect and regard for each other, and I am sure this healthy state of affairs will always prevail at Melbourne.'[20] It didn't. Although Chadwick's departure was perhaps a relief for Smith in one way – in that he would likely have more chance of getting his own way with someone who wasn't as strong-minded – it would also be cause for concern in another.

Chadwick's replacement was Dr Don Duffy – the club doctor for the previous 12 seasons and a committee member for the past four. Another of Melbourne Football Club's war heroes after serving with distinction in World War II, Duffy was a man of good intentions, generally regarded highly both as a medical practitioner and as a person – common descriptions included 'great bloke', 'charming' and 'lovely man'. However, he would also be found to be severely lacking in football knowledge – a common lament being 'he wasn't a football person' – and, most unfortunate of all, 'clearly out of his depth' in his early years as club president. These drawbacks – which became particularly magnified when compared with Chadwick's vast acumen – would become more apparent in 1965, when he and his committee collided head-on with Norm Smith. In the short-term, though, there would be no such problems.

Len Smith could not make the same boast. Len had encountered such terrible trouble with the Fitzroy committee that he resigned as coach at the end of 1962. The problems began months before the season even started. In January, Len was seething when he was informed that Oliver 'Buller' Hornsby would continue in his role as a member of the Lions' selection committee. More than a decade earlier, Hornsby had been the chief agitator against Norm Smith, and he had been doing

[20] Melbourne Football Club *Annual Report*, 1962.

the same thing with the calmer Smith brother, stubbornly standing against Len on many selection issues. Hornsby and other selectors, who harboured 'petty jealousies', had actually insisted on sitting with Len during games and making decisions. It was an arrangement that Len knew couldn't continue; that 'one man must be in control after the team has been picked'.[21] Seeing more obstruction ahead, Len immediately tendered his resignation. The committee refused to accept his resignation and conducted a new election for selectors. Hornsby and another antagonist, Norman Hillard, bowed to committee pressure and did not seek re-nomination, although both retained their positions on the Lions committee.

Len's cause wasn't helped by the retirements of stars 'Butch' Gale and Kevin Wright. The Lions could ill afford to lose Gale, one of their rare big men.

Fitzroy lost their first three matches, each to good sides – Essendon (37 points), Footscray (68 points) and St Kilda (38 points) – but the jungle drums were already beating, for both Len and his players.

Len staunchly defended his players against claims that they were 'squibs' – ie. they weren't attacking the ball hard enough. Generally speaking, he believed: 'There are no cowards in League football. Any man who is game enough to pull on a football guernsey and run out before thousands of people is not afraid'.[22] Now, with his own men being questioned for their lack of courage, he was adamant: 'I won't blast them. They are not squibs. The boys are as game and determined as any other players. What we lack is confidence. We started badly and now we have reached rock-bottom. We have the players to make up a good winning team, but you cannot win without confidence. Confidence is infectious. It spreads through an entire side, and so does the lack of it. If you lack confidence, you create hesitation, and when you hesitate you are lost'.[23]

Len and his supporters were also fending off claims about his supposedly diminishing coaching abilities. *The Sporting Globe's* Alan Fitcher, a Fitzroy star of the Depression era, spoke with Len in the rooms after an early-season loss and made the following observation: 'I did not ask him to talk, as I know he loved Fitzroy too much to reveal anything that would add coals to the smouldering fire. Even so, I got the impression that he had been through the wringer and had taken a mental thrashing. I also felt he was a lonely man, and was almost washed up… Yes, Len Smith has his critics at Fitzroy… (But) they should be told quite candidly that they have one of the top coaches in Australia, and if he goes the bottom will fall out of the club'.

---

[21] Norm Smith, *The Age*, Wednesday June 19, 1968.
[22] *The Herald*, 1967.
[23] *Melbourne Truth*, May 5, 1962.

Fitcher's words would prove prophetic.

Another key to the so-called 'pin-pricking war'[24] against Len Smith was his unauthorised appearance on *The Tony Charlton Football Show* on May 6, the day after the Lions' third successive loss. The Fitzroy committee had refused permission for Len to appear on the 'losing coaches' segment of the program because it considered it embarrassing and 'not in the best interests of the club'. However, Len defied the ban because he felt he should honour his agreement with Channel Nine. Before Len appeared on the program, Norm Smith said: 'I think this is a case of gross pettiness by the Fitzroy club'. Mercifully, the Lions committee backed down on punishing Len. But it drove a deeper wedge between the coach and certain committee members.

Len's major saving grace was the unwavering support of his players. 'The loyalty and cooperation given to me by the players is, and always has been, 100 percent,' he said. Reinforcing this view, the players passed a vote of confidence in their coach. However, they, like Len, had little confidence in certain club officials.

Norm Smith kept a close eye on developments, and remained in close contact with Len throughout the saga, but eventually couldn't contain his disgust. On *The Tony Charlton Football Show*, he said: 'I'm not speaking as Melbourne coach, but as a former one at Fitzroy and who has been similarly treated. The same thing that's happening now, happened to me. Len has told me he's being left like a shag on a rock by the committee and doesn't know where to go or whom to turn (to) for support in this crisis… Only the players support Len. It is a dreadful state of affairs… Len has been a great success and deserves a better go than he is getting. If it hadn't been for Len Smith, Fitzroy would not have risen above eighth or ninth place during his coaching years'. Fitzroy president Les Phelan responded angrily to the comments, saying: 'I am amazed that a League coach should try to interfere with the management of another club'.

Following further uproar among the Fitzroy committee, Len clarified his stance in a written statement, which said, in part: 'It is true that I said in a moment of stress that I have been left like a shag on a rock. I now realise the embarrassment that has been caused to my friends on committee and desire to withdraw that statement and apologise to them for my action.' However, 'Buller' Hornsby didn't escape criticism, with Len writing: 'I have every confidence in, and have received every cooperation from the president, secretary, selection committee and all members of the committee except Mr O. Hornsby'.

---

[24] Coined by *Melbourne Truth*'s sports editor Brian Hansen.

Although little was going right for the Lions, they suddenly began to show some encouraging signs on the field. Sitting on the bottom of the VFL ladder at 0-3, they responded by winning four of their next five matches to square the ledger at 4-4. They were eighth – two games and almost 40 percent out of the four – but back in stride. Their round eight win over Melbourne appeared to cement their resurrection. The Demons had been three goals clear midway through the third term, before Fitzroy slammed on six goals with the breeze to lead by 12 points at the last change. Melbourne kept squandering opportunities in the final term against the economical Lions, the result being a chalk-and-cheese scoreline: 12.4 (76) to 9.20 (74).

The win gave Fitzroy the remarkable distinction of being the best-performed club against Melbourne between 1958 and 1962. In eight encounters with the Demons in that period, the Lions posted three wins, three losses and two ties. The next best clubs were both Essendon and Hawthorn, who each had 4-5 records against Melbourne. At the same time, both Collingwood and Carlton were 3-8.

The Fitzroy resurrection was short-lived. The effect of friction between their coach and committee – which only intensified throughout the season – eventually contributed to a dramatic plunge down the ladder. The Lions lost nine of their last 10 matches to finish 5-13 and 10th – their worst effort since 1957.

The season couldn't end soon enough for Len Smith. On September 6 – less than a fortnight after the Lions' final match of the season – he submitted his resignation. In addition to the off-field turbulence, there was the physical toll. Len, then 50, admitted: 'I am too old. At most I could have put in one more year, and if I felt as tired as I did at the end of this season I might not have lasted the distance'. In a letter to Fitzroy secretary Ward Stuchbery, a firm friend, Len expressed his disappointment with several aspects of the club and the treatment he had received.

> It is most obvious that team-building must take place in the next two or three years and then maintained constantly. I feel that a younger man is needed for this most difficult job and he will need the fullest support and loyalty of every member of the committee... Unfortunately, I believe that this most necessary support and loyalty has not and would not be available to me. I am fully aware that both Mr Hornsby and Mr Hillard have been criticizing my coaching methods, such criticism being typical of them. Although I expected such criticism from them, it has added to the mental strain involved in coaching a League team.
>
> I am also most disappointed that recruiting was not carried out during the year to assist the 2nd and 3rd eighteen coaches...

I find now that the physical effort required of a coach is getting beyond me, so please accept this decision as final.

My deepest thanks go to you, Ward, for wonderful friendship and assistance and I assure you that I will retain forever wonderful memories of many happy and lasting associations formed in the club with officials, players and staff.

Stuchbery's written reply expressed 'sincere appreciation' to Len for the 'four wonderful and happy years' he had devoted to the club, and mentioned that Len's letter of resignation had been 'read and accepted with regret' by the committee. Stuchbery added: 'Full credit must be given you for our success... However, one felt that success often brings complacency on the part of officials and in this case is indicative'.

In *The Sporting Globe*, Alan Fitcher described Len's departure as a tragedy for the Lions. 'He was expected to build a skyscraper out of old, second-hand timber,' Fitcher said. 'No wonder he found the task beyond him.'

Inconceivably, the actions of certain committeemen had forced the resignation of the man who would, 39 years later, be named as the coach of Fitzroy's 'Team of the Century'. It was a sad end to Len Smith's 23-year association with Fitzroy – nine as a player, nine as coach of the thirds, and five as senior coach. His senior coaching record, although tarnished by a poor showing in his final year, was: 93 matches, 51 wins, 40 losses, two draws, and a success rate of 56 percent.

Despite the angst, Len reaffirmed his love of Fitzroy. 'I wish the club nothing but the best,' he told *Truth*, 'and I have the deepest regard for the other committeemen and my successor, Kevin Murray.'

Murray was a champion who had just won the fifth of an equal record nine best-and-fairest awards, but he was just 24 and hadn't even captained the Lions when he was appointed captain-coach.

The Lions' stocks plummeted in Len's absence. They won just one game in the next two seasons, and just 14 of their next 110 games – a strike rate of just 12.72 percent. They would not make the finals again until 1979. Such was 'the curse of Len Smith'.

22

'WE SHOULD HAVE WON THE FLAG'

[1963]

With Laurie Mithen accepting the coaching job at VFA club Port Melbourne, the Demons needed to appoint a new vice-captain for the 1963 season. The leading candidates to become Ron Barassi's deputy were two of his best mates, 'Bluey' Adams and Brian Dixon. Norm Smith wanted Adams. Others wanted Dixon. It was a close call.

New committee member Terry Gleeson recalled:

> I arrived late to the meeting and Norm asked me: 'Who would you have as vice-captain – Dicko or Bluey?'
> I started to say: "Dicko possibly, but I wouldn't give it to either of them because you ought to give it to a younger bloke', and I was going to mention Hassa Mann, but Norm caught me half-stream while I was trying to explain it – he could do that at times – and he was pissed off with me. Dicko was appointed vice-captain, much to Norm's annoyance, and he blamed me for it![1]

The Demons had only themselves to blame for an uncharacteristically poor start to the season that had many pundits predicting the end of Melbourne as a force. Since winning the premiership in 1960, the Demons had finished third and fourth, and the downward trend appeared to be continuing when they slumped to 3-4. Each of their losses had been away from the MCG, including those to ninth-placed Collingwood (48 points) and 11th-placed South Melbourne (four points).

---
[1] Terry Gleeson. Interview with the author.

'WE SHOULD HAVE WON THE FLAG' [1963]

A round eight clash with the super Geelong side at the MCG loomed as a must win encounter for the Demons to stay in touch with the top four. Melbourne trailed by four points at quarter-time, but in an amazing turnaround, kicked 9.8 to 1.9 in the final three quarters to record a morale-boosting 47-point win. The best player afield that day was centreman Hassa Mann, the Demons' 1962 best-and-fairest winner who had continued on in a rich vein of form. But Smith wasn't entirely satisfied with his young star's performance. Just before half-time, Mann missed a goal he should have kicked, which would have almost buried the Cats. Instead, for all Melbourne's domination, they led by just 20 points – 5.11 (41) to 3.3 (21). Mann recounted the biggest 'bake' he ever received from his coach:

> I'd made a mistake, but I was playing as well as I'd ever played, so I didn't expect to cop it too much. How wrong could I have been? Norm pinned me to the wall like only he could. He said: 'By missing that opportunity, you've let your teammates down! It could cost us the game!'
>
> I'd had two opponents to that stage and then I finished up having another two opponents in the second half, and I was picked as the best player on the ground. But I was so upset with Norm that after playing so well and making only one mistake I'd copped the whole half-time address. I was still spitting chips when I came off the ground. As I was walking up the race, Norm grabbed me by the ear and, with that resin in his voice, said: 'I want to see you. Now'. I threw my hands up in the air. Norm repeated: 'Now!' I knew I was in for another burst.
>
> I followed him into the coach's room. He said: 'So you didn't like the roast you got at halftime?'
>
> I said: 'No I bloody didn't. I can take a roast from anyone, but that wasn't fair'.
>
> He said: 'At half-time you were easily the best man on the ground'.
>
> I said: 'I thought I was playing pretty well'.
>
> He said: 'You had two opponents up until half-time and you killed them both'.
>
> I said: 'I thought I was playing pretty well'.
>
> He said: 'After half-time, when you got the ball you were kicking my head'.
>
> I said: 'And I hope it bloody hurt.'
>
> He then said: 'You had two more opponents throughout the game, you led from the front and you were the best man on the ground by a street'.
>
> I said: 'I thought I played fairly well'.
>
> Norm then said: 'Well, Hassa, when I was roasting you for making one mistake, just think, mate, how the other 17 players felt'.
>
> I said under my breath: 'You bastard! You got me again!'

Although the other players didn't cop the roast themselves, they were on notice. It would've helped them lift their games. Norm was before his time as a coach. His use of psychology to get a result was just exceptional.[2]

The win over Geelong was the start of a run of 10 wins in 11 matches (by an average of 52 points). The Demons were the heaviest scoring team in the competition by almost 200 points and had the biggest percentage. Some of their triumphs were vintage performances. In round 11, the Demons held Ted Whitten's Footscray to just three goals – the Bulldogs' worst performance in 38 years – and kept St Kilda to just five goals in a 59 point win at the MCG the following week. A fortnight later, they belted reigning premier Essendon by 51 points at the MCG.

The Demons were in super touch, and becoming increasingly confident about winning another premiership, but there were still people who wanted to disturb their momentum. Sam Allica, the Melbourne trainer, told of an unusual confrontation between the coach and a dissenter one night after training at the MCG:

Norm and I were coming down from the players' room and it was pitch black – all the lights were out in the coliseum. When we got to the last landing before the concourse, there was a bloke standing on his own in the corner. It was all a bit strange. I thought: 'What's this about?'

The bloke said: 'Mr Smith, can I have a word with you?'

Smithy said: 'Yes, all right', and moved over to the chap.

Next minute, the bloke went flying off the top of the stairs – he might have touched one halfway down! He landed on his hands and knees. I don't know how it came about: whether Norm pushed him, which I don't think he would've done; or if he tried to hook his fingers around the bloke's nose like he occasionally did and you felt like your bloody nose was going to come off; or if the bloke fell over as he tried to back pedal away. In any case, the bugger pooped himself and took off, and Norm and I continued on our way.

I didn't ask him about it because I thought: 'If he wants to tell me, he'll tell me'.

Norm said: 'Do you know what that fella wanted? He was telling me that a couple of my boys were down at a hotel drinking beer. I tell you what: if my boys don't know how to behave themselves, I can't teach them when I'm not there.'

Whatever the fella's reasons were for approaching Norm – whether it was out of genuine concern for the team, or jealousy, or just to big note himself to the best coach in the business – I don't know. But it was a stupid idea.

---

[2] Hassa Mann. Interview with the author.

'WE SHOULD HAVE WON THE FLAG' [1963]

The next Thursday night, on Smithy's insistence, the whole club – all the men and their wives – had dinner at the same pub halfway down Punt Road hill on the left-hand side. We took over the whole dining area, and it was a great night.

It was perhaps to prove a point that just because his players were at a pub didn't mean they were drinking maniac soup.[3]

Smith also schooled other coaches in ways to create a successful environment. After Melbourne thrashed St Kilda at the MCG in round 12, he went out of his way to help Saints coach Allan Jeans. Hugh McPherson recalled:

We were having a drink after the game and Norm said to me: 'Look at Allan Jeans on his own over there'. Nobody seemed interested in Allan. His team was at the crossroads, and he cut a very lonely figure. Norm told me: 'Ask Allan to come over to our table; I'd like to talk with him'.

I brought Allan over.

Norm said: 'So things aren't going too well, Allan?'

Allan said: 'No, they're not'.

So Norm gave Allan some ideas on how he could turn it around. Norm explained the guts of his own coaching methods and how, every Thursday night, he would get his players together in the dining room at the MCG to talk about the upcoming match, and how we'd put on fathers' nights and so forth – nights that really brought everyone even closer together. After that chat with Norm, Allan somehow got everything together at St Kilda and then everyone wanted to talk to him.[4]

Jeans felt privileged to have the opportunity to pick the Smith brain.

Norm always wanted to have a drink with you after the game. We'd talk, not so much about football, but what your problems were and how you were going. He was a real man's man, and I just loved being in his company.

I got to know both Norm and Lenny quite well. We'd be on *World of Sport* on Channel Seven together, sometimes we had to go to Channel Nine as well, so that gave me the opportunity to talk to them. I think they took pity on me and were so kind to me because I was only 27 when I started coaching, and I was coaching St Kilda, which hadn't won a premiership to that stage.

---

[3] Sam Allica. Interview with the author.
[4] Hugh McPherson. Interview with the author.

Learning from great coaches like them was crucial because we didn't have coaching courses or the coaches' association back then like they have now. We had crash courses, where we were just thrown in the deep end and had to learn on the job and from other coaches.

Their encouragement was important. We trained at the MCG one night and I didn't know Norm was watching, but one Sunday at Channel Nine he said to me: 'You train your players very well'. I prided myself on that, but those few words from Norm gave me the confidence that I was on the right track. Little things like that from experienced campaigners help a young coach.

Norm and Len were my type of blokes. I'd have loved to have played footy under them. That's the highest compliment you can pay another coach.[5]

St Kilda won its next six games by an average margin of 64 points to climb to fourth on the ladder and set up a first semi-final clash with third-placed Melbourne; a battle between the master (Smith) and the apprentice (Jeans). This time the master was the man under pressure.

The Demons had lost just one game since June 1 on their way to a 13-5 record, but they were to face the success-starved Saints without Ron Barassi. The Melbourne skipper had been controversially suspended for the entire finals series after being found guilty of a dubious striking charge against Richmond at Punt Road in round 17. Barassi and several teammates maintained that he had collected Tigers captain Roger Dean across the chest, but Dean was just as adamant he had been struck in the face. The incident, which whipped the Richmond crowd into a frenzy, had taken place near the Melbourne bench. Smith had tried valiantly to get Barassi out of the vicinity until the angst subsided, and perhaps even enable him to escape being reported. Barassi said:

The runner told me: 'Go off the ball', but in all the commotion I thought he said: 'Go *for* the ball', so I just brushed him off. There were a couple more boundary throw-ins in the same area and the crowd was becoming more unruly. The runner came out twice more with the same message, and by this time I was wild because I thought the coach thought I wasn't going for the ball; that I was going for the man instead. I said: 'I *was* going for the bloody ball!' I'd got my wires crossed. I finally went *off* the ball, but it was too late. I was reported and got four weeks.[6]

---

[5] Allan Jeans. Interview with the author.
[6] Ron Barassi. Interview with the author.

'WE SHOULD HAVE WON THE FLAG' [1963]

Before his suspension, Barassi had described the current Melbourne side as the best he had played in.[7] However, to say the Demons would miss Barassi in the finals would be a gross understatement. They didn't seem to initially when they led St Kilda by five goals at three-quarter-time of the first semi-final, but they lacked his leadership in the final term when they were under siege. The Demons were outgunned 4.8 to 1.3 but scraped home by seven points.

Melbourne then lacked Barassi's vigour, and Brian Dixon's prolific ball-winning, in the preliminary final against a typically physical Hawthorn, going down by nine points. It was another tense afternoon for Smith, who wrongly criticised teenage centre half-forward Ray Groom during one of the intervals. Groom recalled:

> I was chasing the ball out on the flank and I knocked it in front of me and I was grabbed and it looked as though I was holding the ball, so a free kick was awarded against us at a critical moment. Norm was fuming, and he really let me have it. But a couple of days later, after he'd seen some footage of it from a different angle, he apologised to me. He said: 'Sorry I had a go at you. I saw it on TV and I realised I got it wrong. It didn't happen the way I thought it did'. It wasn't a big deal apology but it was rare, and I appreciated it.[8]

It's hard to believe that Barassi and Dixon wouldn't have been able to reverse the result to give the Demons a shot at eventual premier Geelong, which they had hammered at the MCG in round eight, and had beaten in nine of their previous 10 clashes. That year, the Cats had been trained in pre-season by athletics guru Percy Cerutty.

Smith was as disappointed as he had ever been. Bluey Adams said: 'Norm was convinced that we would have won the flag had it not been for Roger Dean's play-acting, which got Barass suspended, and also if we'd had Dixon. Things had gone against us at the wrong time'.[9] Barassi agreed, saying that Smith was 'not alone' in his attitude. 'It sounds very arrogant,' Barassi said, 'but we *knew* we were a better side (than Geelong). We'd thrashed them... Geelong, at that period in time, always used to beat Hawthorn... They played Hawthorn in the last match of the season to get in the finals. They played Hawthorn... (in their) next game two weeks later in the second semi-final... (and) they win... They play Hawthorn again (in the Grand Final), so they played... their favourite side

---

[7] Related by Harry Beitzel in *Footy Fan* magazine, September 1963.
[8] Ray Groom. Interview with the author.
[9] Frank 'Bluey' Adams. Interview with the author.

three times in a row in five weeks, so we didn't take any notice of them winning the premiership'.[10]

Smith and Barassi were presented with an opportunity to prove their point, to some extent, when Geelong agreed to play the Demons in two exhibition matches in America – less than a month after the Cats had won the premiership. It was to be the first expedition of its kind by Australian football clubs.

From the outset, it was never going to be the usual end-of-season jaunt. The Demons, driven by their fanatical coach, were determined to win everything, including the race to arrive in America. The Cats had publicly stated they would become the first Australian Football team in the US, and had as much emblazoned on the pockets of their blazers. Geelong officials were angry to discover the Melbourne touring party waiting to greet them at Honolulu airport.

Any hopes the Melbourne players had of relaxing on famous Waikiki Beach were soon quashed. The odds were stacked against a Melbourne victory. Smith realised: 'We were half recruits and half experienced players, opposed to almost the same side which won the flag'.[11] He was so 'obsessed' with winning, and regaining lost pride, and 'proving' the Demons were the best side in the competition – even 9000 kilometres away from home – he trained them hard and enforced strict curfews. Players had to be in bed by midnight on Wednesday night, by 11pm on Thursday, and by 10pm on Friday, match eve. Smith reminded some players of their own father when he sent them to their sleeping quarters with the comment: 'Righto, fellas, off to bed'. The curfews were in place for all but two of the 15 nights. John Lord said: 'To my knowledge, no-one broke the curfew. I don't think anyone would've been game to, because we all knew we would've been sent straight home'.[12]

The first game was played at Honolulu Stadium, a square-shaped, all-purpose arena that had hosted gridiron, baseball (including superstars Babe Ruth and Joe DiMaggio), athletics (Jesse Owens), stock-car racing, concerts (Elvis Presley, 1957) and the odd evangelical experience (Billy Graham, 1958).

Barassi was so revved up by Smith's pre-match address, and the fact he had missed the finals, that he deliberately flattened Geelong's superstar ruckman Graham 'Polly' Farmer, who had been best-afield in the Grand Final just three weeks earlier. Although commentator Tony Charlton observed that 'the Yanks knew nothing about the game and those who turned up watched on in some bewilderment',[13]

---

[10] *Red and Blue* documentary, 2005.
[11] *Melbourne Truth*, Saturday November 2, 1963.
[12] John Lord. Interview with the author.
[13] Tony Charlton. Interview with the author.

the Demons wouldn't have cared if the game had been played in front of two camels in the middle of the Sahara Desert. Pride was on the line and the Demons followed their skipper's lead and won the game by 12 points.

The battle lines were drawn.

While Smith was pleased about the result, he noted that the match had been 'unusually torrid', and with umpire Harry Beitzel not having the power to report players, he was concerned about the potential for unchecked violence in the second and final match in San Francisco. He and Geelong coach Bob Davis took Beitzel aside for a chat about how he should perhaps umpire the match. Smith said later: 'I felt that if he ignored obvious free kicks, the players infringed against would retaliate... I didn't want this game in front of Americans to be a schemozzle, nor did I want it to be a cream puff'. But despite their best attempts and intentions, Smith lamented, the game 'still turned into a brutal affair'.[14]

Geelong snapped out of their premiership malaise and played for keeps at San Francisco's Golden Gate Park. In an ugly, spiteful match, Beitzel's plea for players to 'cut it out, fellas' fell on deaf ears. The teams fought like rarely before, prompting Bluey Adams to describe it as 'the roughest game I ever played in. In reality, the stakes weren't that high, but they certainly rose in that game. Blokes seemed to be playing, and fighting, for their lives'.[15]

Friendships were forgotten during the two hours of mayhem. The previous night, Smith had chatted with Geelong full-forward Doug Wade and defender John Devine. Discussion turned to rough play and Smith told Wade that he would be a far better player if he controlled his temper and didn't fight so much. The next day, Melbourne full-back Bernie Massey split open one of Wade's lips – which required surgery – and an incensed Wade bellowed at Smith: 'Look at my bloody mouth! You spent all night with me; why don't you talk to your own players?!'[16]

Smith wanted to do just that, and he wanted Davis to do the same. He recalled: 'At one stage, I ran 50 yards onto the ground and I tried to catch Bob Davis' eye. I hoped that we could stop the game temporarily and each of us tell our players to concentrate on football and not to step outside the rules'.[17] This didn't eventuate, but Melbourne was proud to win the fights and the football – this time by just five points. The series clean-sweep was a minor consolation, but at least both club and personal pride was back intact.

---

[14] *Melbourne Truth*, Saturday November 2, 1963.
[15] Frank 'Bluey' Adams. Interview with the author.
[16] Ron Carter, *The Age*, July 30, 1973.
[17] *Melbourne Truth*, Saturday November 2, 1963.

The two team buses pulled up alongside each other as they were about to leave the stadium. Adams recalled:

> There was still plenty of tension and ill-feeling simmering between us, and we started giving the Geelong boys the raspberry and gesturing: 'Up your jumper', and: 'We stuck it up you!' With that, Norm immediately stood up and said: 'Can it! Cut it out!' He then gave us a lecture on being modest in victory. It was a footy trip and we were overseas but he felt that was unacceptable behaviour regardless of the circumstances. That spoke volumes for Norm's high standards of integrity.[18]

In the Melbourne committee's 'desire to express its appreciation and thanks' to its coach, it took what it regarded as 'the unusual step' of reappointing him for a further three years – until the end of the 1966 season. In arriving at the decision, the committee described it 'more as a gesture to him' than motivated by a 'hope that he will achieve any more than he has over the last 10 years'. The committee added: 'It has become evident that over the latter years Norm has enlarged his great knowledge of football and football administration', and that it was 'proud to have his association with the young men of our club'.[19]

▼▼▼▼▼▼▼▼▼

Although Len Smith had been physically and mentally exhausted after a traumatic final season at Fitzroy in 1962, he soon jumped back on the coaching merry-go-round. Shortly after relinquishing his role at Fitzroy, he was approached by the VFA's Lions, Coburg. After several weeks of negotiation – during which Coburg secretary Jack Jones revealed: 'Our offer to Smith ranks with any ever made to a VFA coach'[20] – Len Smith agreed to coach them in 1963.

Modest as ever, he said: 'I felt honoured to be appointed coach of Coburg, for after all, I've been a long time in the game. It was great personal satisfaction that a senior team wanted me'. Although he had coached Victoria in 1961, he added that it wasn't demeaning to drop back to VFA level; that he felt he was 'coming home' to the VFA after a 26-year hiatus.[21]

Before he coached his new club for the first time, Len Smith had attended Fitzroy's opening-round clash with Carlton at the Brunswick Street Oval, and

---

[18] Frank 'Bluey' Adams. Interview with the author.
[19] Melbourne Football Club annual report, 1963.
[20] *The Sun*, late 1963.
[21] *The Sporting Globe*.

'WE SHOULD HAVE WON THE FLAG' [1963]

entered the Lions' changerooms pre-match to wish his successor, Kevin Murray, and his players the best of luck.

Len had actually inherited a Coburg side that was similar to Fitzroy in that it lacked tall players, so he decided to introduced the same, fast, play-on style. The flick-pass became a feature of Coburg's play in the VFA's 16-a-side competition. Coburg had finished third the previous year; Len had them second for some time, and they they finished the minor rounds in third – a game off top spot – and they lost the first semi-final to finish fourth. The Coburg hierarchy felt that the club was on the cusp of a premiership. The Lions' annual report stated: 'Len Smith proved... the reputation he won at Fitzroy was no myth. He quietly took charge of the team and won the respect of each player... The players learned quickly, but unfortunately time passed too quickly and the season finished before the lesson was complete... We are proud that this quiet gentleman was connected with our club'.

It was a case of 'would have' because Len was successfully courted by Richmond in the latter part of the season.[22] After Essendon champion Jack Clarke remained at Bomberland and Collingwood great Bob Rose got the Collingwood job, the Tigers chased Len Smith, who eventually accepted a deal worth about £35-a-week, plus incentives. Len would only agree to a one-year appointment, so that they could part ways if either he or the club was dissatisfied with the arrangement.

Legendary Tigers secretary Graeme Richmond had been the most pivotal person in getting Len to Punt Road. Years later, the Tiger official was asked to reveal the best thing he had done in football and his answer was simply: 'Sign Len Smith'.

Len replaced club great Des Rowe – whom he had known since childhood – and took charge of a club that hadn't made the finals since 1947, hadn't finished higher than seventh since 1955, and had won just 21 games in the previous five seasons.

Alf Brown wrote positively of Len's appointment in *The Herald*: 'One of Richmond's problems is that for years they have been living in the shadow of Jack Dyer... (and) have tried to bump their way to success, and skill has been forgotten. Smith will change this with his slick brand of handball, which helped lift Fitzroy'. The Richmond committee couldn't contain its excitement: 'We feel we have a man who will carry on the great traditions of the former coaches of the club... The Smith brothers... have established a reputation for football know-how which has become almost a legend in their own time'.[23] Meanwhile, Lou Richards observed

---

[22] *The Leader* reported Len Smith's remark that he had been associated with the Gorillas and Lions (Fitzroy) and now that he was with the Tigers he 'just can't seem to get out of the jungle!'
[23] Richmond Football Club *Annual Report*, 1963.

that: 'Any side that gains a "recruit" like Len Smith must improve, so the Tigers can be a better outfit – if they listen to the Old Master'.[24]

Len foreshadowed a slight modification in Richmond's game plan. 'The only apparent difference between Richmond and the other two clubs (Fitzroy and Coburg),' he said, 'is that Richmond have more big men. I would not want a big man to play the same type of game as a small man, but the basic play-on principle will still be there. You can't tell 18 men with different ability, technique and football brains to do the same thing'.[25]

Len performed one of his first acts as Richmond coach at the end of the 1963 season. He gave a motivational talk to the Tigers' under-19s side – at the invitation of their coach, former Coburg star Ray 'Slug' Jordon, then aged 26 – before they played in the first semi-final. When he had finished his lecture, Len then happily answered numerous questions that were fired at him by the enthralled youngsters, who felt privileged to have the new senior coach take such an interest in them. Unfortunately, the Tiger cubs were severely hampered by injuries and lost the semi-final by two points to Geelong.

Len was officially welcomed to the club at the annual general meeting in February 1964. In front of 600 members at Richmond Town Hall, Len said: 'We must have mutual respect and feeling and friendship, unselfishness and hard work. It is a challenge to each Richmond player in his mind and body for the club to rise up the ladder. I won't promise results. But I do promise you members fit players who will play with a plan and who will improve.'[26]

New president Ray Dunn assured all present, and Len included: '(The) Richmond committee will back Len Smith to the full'. Len had heard such assurances before, and they had proved empty promises, but there seemed something different about Richmond. Everybody was working together.

---

[24] *The Sun*, April 14, 1964.
[25] Contemporary newspaper report.
[26] Contemporary newspaper report.

23

THE GREATEST PREMIERSHIP

[1964]

After three consecutive finals misfires, people were beginning to doubt, with some justification, whether the Smith charm had worn off at Demonland. Smith himself was concerned that 'complacency had crept up on our club',[1] particularly at committee level, and that his players were in danger of developing an unhealthy acceptance of defeat. He decided that if the Demons were to progress, and again become a premiership side, he would have to shake these harmful elements from the collective mindsets of players and officials.

Urgency was required. Three of Melbourne's most experienced, and perhaps best, players – Ron Barassi, Bluey Adams and Brian Dixon – were entering the twilight of their distinguished careers, and therefore any planned success would have to be achieved almost immediately. This, in addition to the triple finals 'failures', made Norm Smith hungrier than ever before.

He had decided that 1964 was *the* year. Although he had always thrown every last muscle fibre of energy into coaching the Demons, he was about to give even more to the job. Perhaps more than any coach had ever done previously.

When he was awarded a three-year extension, Smith also received a significant pay-rise, in the order of £500 – to boost his coaching salary to £1500 a year. Later in the season, he spoke of his attitude towards being paid to coach. 'I never like to think of it in terms of payment,' he said. 'It has never been discussed by me... I'm lucky, I'm with a good club. There have been rises for different services that I've rendered. I have not asked for them. The club

---

[1] Melbourne Football Club *Annual Report*, 1964.

has been happy to pay me, and I'm very happy with the way things have worked out'.[2]

The pay-rise was a win-win for both parties. The Demons would be well compensated for their outlay. Instead of using the extra money for pure financial gain, Smith virtually re-invested it back into Melbourne Football Club.

He had long harboured a dream to devote most, if not all, his time to coaching. It was becoming more difficult to combine the demands of business and coaching – ever-increasing demands when it came to football. Rather than spread himself thin and perform both roles moderately – which was certain to cause inner conflict for the perfectionist Smith – he logically wanted to succeed in both areas. But football remained his greatest passion, and, courtesy of the pay increase from the Demons, he could finally pursue his perfect-world scenario of becoming a full-time coach.

The first and most critical part of his plan was to hire someone he could trust to manage his pram parts business. The first person he approached was his cousin Russ Brown, who had worked in the paint industry for the previous five years. Dangling the more responsible role and a wage of about £15-a-week, he was able to entice Brown to return to his employ. 'From that point,' Brown said, 'Norm just oversaw the business and looked after the finances. He still had two or three other fellas working for him, and he gradually came to work less and less. He might spend only a couple of hours a day in the factory – if that. And it was like that for the rest of his coaching days.'[3]

The effect of this altered timetable was that Smith had more energy and ideas to throw into resurrecting the Demons as a power. 'I'm thinking football with my soup, and I'm still thinking it with my coffee,' he said.[4] Many Melbourne players, especially those who had played for several seasons, had not thought it possible that Norm Smith could be more driven, more manic, in his quest for success. But from the outset of pre-season training, some players noticed an even greater intensity about their coach. Brian Dixon said: 'Norm trained us longer and had more meetings, and everything went up a notch – the standards, the expectations. We felt we should have won the flag in each of 1961, 1962 and 1963, so 1964 was built up as the year that we would return to our glory days. There was a really concerted effort to win the flag in 1964. Everything was geared towards achieving that goal, and no effort would be spared to get there'.[5]

---

[2] *Midweek Magazine*, August 1964.
[3] Russell Brown. Interview with the author.
[4] *The Sun*, Saturday July 31, 1965.
[5] Brian Dixon. Interview with the author.

Bluey Adams felt that, more than ever before, Smith directed most of his 'forceful encouragement' at his older players. 'Norm pushed the experienced players – Barassi, Dixon and myself – very hard throughout 1964,' Adams said. 'He drove us all the time – "You can do better! Work harder! You've let us down! Pick yourself up! Blah, blah, blah!" It was hard work copping it night after night at training, but I had utter faith and trust in Smithy and his methods, so you just did it.'[6]

The Demons had retained virtually the same playing list as 1963, and were strengthened by the return of brilliant half-back flanker-cum-centreman Don Williams after a five-year absence.[7] The return of such a prodigal son wasn't as smooth as one might expect. With some ill-feeling still lingering over Williams' angry exit west after being named on the bench in the 1959 premiership side, Melbourne officials initially tried to organise another country coaching job. However, Williams was so determined to make up for lost time at VFL level that eventually Smith relented.

Hugh McPherson said: 'Donny asked if he could try out again, but rather than say yes immediately, Norm told him: "If you prove yourself, I'll give you a chance". Norm knew it was a formality, but he wanted Donny to know that just because he had been a great player for the club in the past, it didn't mean he was going to automatically walk back into the side and be a great player again'.[8]

▼▼▼▼▼▼▼▼▼

On the eve of what would have been his first official match as coach of Richmond, Len Smith suffered his second serious heart attack. He had actually endured a minor heart attack during the final pre-season training session on the Thursday night, but had stoically, foolishly, kept his pain to himself and not sought a medical examination. He went to work as usual the next day and it was there that he collapsed after being gripped by a more severe attack. He was rushed to Sacred Heart Hospital in Moreland, where doctors told him he would need to rest for six weeks and limit his activities for 12 months.

Although Len had endured his first heart attack five-and-a-half years earlier, it was a massive shock to the wider football community. Norm Smith was a daily visitor to his brother's bedside.

---

[6] Frank 'Bluey' Adams. Interview with the author.
[7] Williams represented WAFL club West Perth with distinction and in 1961 was a member of the West Australian team that defeated Victoria for the state carnival. In 1963, he coached Victorian country side Sale.
[8] Hugh McPherson. Interview with the author.

Len must have been concerned about his own mortality, but – outwardly at least – all he worried about was that he had let the Tigers down. His health problems had flared at a most inopportune time for both parties. Len had started a rebuilding process he no longer felt he was physically capable of carrying out 18 months earlier at Fitzroy. Although there was little doubt the Tigers were significantly more advanced than the Lions, the task still required considerable energy. Len knew Fitzroy inside and out; but by his own admission he had started at Richmond as 'a complete stranger',[9] unfamiliar with many of the individual quirks of the players, and the general dynamics of the club. While he wanted to implement certain ideals – the Tigers committee had actually asked him if he could develop his play-on style of game[10] – his first season would largely be a suck-it-and-see experience, after which bigger decisions would be made on the playing list, and his own methods.

The enormity of his task was highlighted during the first training session. While standing in the centre of a circle of 20 players and firing handballs and receiving them back, 'often he just shook his head with disgust as players took seconds to return the ball'. He told his players their handball skills were 'really woeful. There's not enough follow-through'. After training, he told Jack Dunn from *The Sun*: 'I'll fix all that. They will be different within a week or so'.[11]

Len also insisted on players using loud, clear voices to instruct and direct teammates. He made an early example of a young player who failed to obey this guideline. The player made perfect position to accept a handball from Len, but the handball never came because he had not called out loud enough. His punishment was to do a 50-metre sprint. Very quickly he had his players making a lot of noise on the training track. An interested onlooker at one of their sessions was Checker Hughes, who was amazed by the change of atmosphere at his old club. Hughes marvelled: 'The Richmond players were like magpies – not Collingwood, but the bird – they were so enthusiastic they wouldn't stop squawking throughout the whole session. Len must be having a great positive influence'.[12] He was. Roger Dean, who would later captain the Tigers, later admitted: 'Most of us thought we knew everything about football but we really didn't until Len Smith came along'.[13]

Ambitious Richmond supporters were commonly saying: 'It will be our own fault if we miss out (on the finals) this season, because we have the best coach in

---

[9] *The Herald*.
[10] *The Herald*.
[11] *The Sun*, Friday February 28, 1964.
[12] Related by Frank Hughes junior in an interview with the author.
[13] Contemporary newspaper report.

the League'. But Len took a more conservative view. He aimed at nine wins, and earmarked the 1966 season – his third season, if he should retain his position – as the coming of age of the Tigers. 'That's when I expect Richmond to be pushing the top teams,' he said. '(Then) I hope the team will be experienced and stabilised.'[14]

An incident in the Tigers' first practice match threatened to destabilise their 1964 campaign. Len had pigeon-holed emerging centreman Bill Barrot as a half-forward flanker, which the headstrong Barrot took as an insult. When he lined up there in a practice match at Hamilton, he staged a protest. 'I stood there with my hands folded in the first quarter,' he recalled, 'and the ball went between my feet and I wouldn't move.' At quarter-time, Len told his players: 'One bloke's not trying'. With that, Barrot ripped his jumper off in disgust and threw it at Len. Barrot was banned from training for a week and also survived a players' vote to remain at the club.[15] He was to become a superstar centreman for the Tigers.

Despite this disturbance, Len believed he had 'made progress' in the pre-season, particularly in relation to introducing play-on football,[16] and felt he was 'just on the point of succeeding in that task' when he was struck down by heart problems.[17]

Len spent 19 days in hospital, during which he was sincerely touched by the level of support afforded him, which included many letters and visits by Richmond players and officials. He said: 'I have built up friendships in weeks which might have taken years in normal circumstances'. He was most touched by members of the Tigers cheersquad who presented him gifts, including a toy tiger. 'I wished I could have jumped out of bed and gone straight down to Richmond I was so moved,' he said.[18]

In Len's absence, his assistant and reserves coach, Dick Harris,[19] was appointed acting senior coach, while Jack Titus – another club great – took over Harris's original roles. When 52-year-old Harris was appointed the night before the season-opener, he said: 'All I want tomorrow is for Richmond to win for Len's sake'. The Tigers didn't – they lost to Footscray by five goals at the Western Oval – but the sentiment was genuine.

Almost daily, Len had long telephone discussions with Harris, during which they dissected every matter relating to the Tiger cause. He was so impressed with

---

[14] Contemporary newspaper report.
[15] Bartlett, Rhett, *Richmond Football Club: A Century of League Football*, GSP, 2007.
[16] *The Herald*.
[17] *Footy Fan*, June 27, 1964.
[18] *The Herald*.
[19] Dick 'Hungry' Harris kicked 548 goals in 196 games for Richmond from 1934-44. He also kicked 30 goals in eight interstate matches.

the manner in which his support crew of Harris, Titus and Jordon carried out his wishes that he maintained: 'Richmond really have four coaches'.[20]

Len's family understandably didn't want him to return to coaching – after all, both heart attacks had been during times of great strain and expectation: before his first finals series in 1958, and now before his first match in charge of Richmond – but such was Len's passion for the game and his new club that his family members eventually resigned themselves to the inevitable. A disturbed Brian Hansen wrote in *Truth*: 'Richmond are prepared to gamble on Smith, and Smith is prepared to gamble on his health. And I don't like the odds. This is one case where the individual should be bigger than the game. Because his health, and possibly his life, are at stake... They (Richmond) intend to do everything to minimise the strain on their coach... But I still doubt whether Smith is the type of man who could take his football quietly. Although mild-mannered, he becomes terribly keyed up. Coaching a League side imposes a tremendous strain on the nervous system and Len Smith cannot make himself immune to it'.

Len had his first official contact with his players since his illness when he gave them a talk at his house the night before the round five match against St Kilda. The Saints had comfortably defeated Melbourne the previous week, but the Tigers found another gear and pulled off a surprise seven-point win – their third in a row after starting the season with two losses.

Len didn't attend a match until round six, when he ignored doctor's orders by watching from the bench. A fortnight later, he was cleared to resume coaching. Although he acknowledged that Harris and Titus had performed 'a great job' in his absence, he was proved correct in saying 'the loss of eight weeks was a big hurdle to overcome for the team'.[21] By that stage, the Tigers were 3-5 – three games out of the top four.

ㄚㄚㄚㄚㄚㄚㄚㄚㄚ

The Demon doomsayers were nodding their heads knowingly and boasting 'I told you so' after just four rounds of the 1964 season. The Demons were 2-2 and had been less than impressive. They were playing like a spent force.

But Norm Smith quickly rallied his troops, and Melbourne immediately embarked on one of its famous sprees – 11 successive wins by an average of 40 points – to take top spot by round 12. But the spree wasn't without its share of drama.

---

[20] Contemporary newspaper report.
[21] *The Herald*.

Smith and Checker Hughes had another dispute on the bench – and it came about in similar circumstances, and had similar results, to the one they had famously waged eight years earlier. In a five-point win over Hawthorn at the MCG in round six, Hughes – the Demons' chairman of selectors – suggested strapping 17-year-old debutant Maurie Bartlett be moved to centre half-forward. Smith disagreed. Hughes 'kept pushing and pushing', and eventually the coach snapped: 'Checker, if you're going to keep harping on about it, you can go inside'. Rather than argue the point further, Hughes got up and walked off. In the changerooms immediately after the match, Smith approached Hughes and said: 'Checker, how about you go into the trainers' room and talk to them about being alert out on the ground. I think they'd really benefit from your wisdom'. Hughes agreed, and all was forgiven.[22]

Young full-forward Barry Bourke found forgiveness hard to come by during the round seven clash with Footscray at the MCG. Bourke had enjoyed a terrific debut season in 1963 after graduating from the under-19s, kicking 48 goals in 19 matches as a leading, decoy-type forward. Coming into the Bulldogs match, he had kicked 10 goals in the first six games. At half-time, the Demons led by just five points and Bourke was being soundly beaten by star full-back David Darcy. Bourke said:

> I'd hardly had a kick, hadn't kicked a goal, and had been caught behind a few times. Norm gave me the biggest roast of all time. His main message was: 'You have to play in front!' If you didn't play the game Norm's way, look out.
>
> We ended up winning the game and I kicked five goals in the second half. After the match, I was taking my boots off and Norm, as he usually did after a game, walked around with Checker Hughes and talked to players. When he got to me, he said: 'How many did you get?'
>
> 'I got five, Norm.'
>
> Norm turned to Checker and said: 'The bastard got five', and he walked away. He'd been annoyed with me at half-time and, just because I'd kicked a few in the second half, there was no way he was going to pat me on the back. But he got the message through – I wasn't going to be caught behind again.[23]

Smith was even harder on talented forward/on-baller Ray Groom. The Tasmanian import desperately wanted to visit his then girlfriend (now wife) Gillian and family early one week, which meant he would miss a Tuesday night training session.

---

[22] Sam Allica. Interview with the author.
[23] Barry Bourke. Interview with the author.

Groom explained the situation to Jim Cardwell, who said: 'So you'll be back for Thursday. That's fine'. Groom believed he had been granted permission. He was sadly mistaken. When he arrived at training on the Thursday, Smith summoned him. 'Hey, you come here,' he barked, before blasting the 19-year-old.

Groom said: 'Hang on, I spoke to Jim Cardwell'.

Smith wouldn't accept his excuse.

'No!' he roared. 'You don't speak to Jim; you speak to me! I'm the coach! You had no right to go back to Tasmania without seeing me first about missing training! If you do it again, it'll be the end of you at this club!'

Groom recalled: 'I thought that was harsh. I naturally expected that Jim would have told Norm. Jim didn't say to me: "Go and see Norm". But I had enormous respect for Norm. He was a mentor of mine'.[24]

Midway through the season, Smith again coached Victoria with great success. In the first of two matches against South Australia at the Adelaide Oval, he led the Vics to a 32-point win. The only downside was that state duties had forced him to miss the round eight game against Fitzroy at Brunswick Street. His stand-in replacement was the injured Barassi, who was the non-playing coach for the day. Unusually, Smith didn't give Barassi any express instructions on how to coach the side, probably because of the poor opposition – Fitzroy was in the middle of a winless season. The Demons did as expected and won by 67 points.

A fortnight later, Victoria met Western Australia at the MCG. Smith was involved in a bitter selection dispute. He wanted Ted Whitten (Footscray) and Graham Arthur (Hawthorn) – both proven champions, and leaders of their respective teams – in the side, but found it difficult to get his own way. Smith described Whitten as 'a player I've got tremendous admiration for... He was one of the first blokes I wanted in my side'. The problem was that Whitten, even by Smith's reckoning, 'hadn't gone too well' against SA, and his three fellow selectors 'weren't too keen on playing him' against WA. But when Essendon's champion centre half-forward Ken Fraser was forced to withdraw, Smith was adamant: 'I wanted Teddy at centre half-forward. Well, I pestered the selectors until they agreed, just to get me off their backs. But I didn't let up then'. He was determined to play Arthur on a flank beside Whitten. 'That was an even

---

[24] Ray Groom. Interview with the author.

harder battle,' he said. 'But I finally got my way. And didn't my argument pay off'. Whitten kicked four goals and, according to Smith, 'took the WA boys apart', while Arthur 'wasn't far behind him as best man on the ground' as the Vics won by 112 points. Smith said of the two stars: 'I've got the highest regard for both of these players. Everyone knows they're marvellous footballers. But to me, what is more important is that they're tremendous team men, completely unselfish, and give you wonderful loyalty. No coach could ask for more.' [25]

Another notable in the Victorian line-up that day was South Melbourne superstar Bob Skilton, who had already won two of his three Brownlow Medals and five of his nine best-and-fairests. But reputations counted for nothing, as Melbourne star Hassa Mann – who was also in the Victorian side – recalled: 'Smithy loved interstate football, and he was very serious about winning, so the same rules that applied to us at Melbourne applied to the champions who played under him in the Victorian side. Norm treated everyone as an equal. Irrespective of who you were – even if you were Skilton, Whitten or Barassi – you had to toe the line, and you would cop Norm's wrath if you deserved it. Norm demonstrated this in a very strong manner on this particular day'.

Smith had asked the players to gather at the ground by a specific time for a team meeting. A hush came over the room when vice-captain Bob Skilton and fellow rover Ian Law (Hawthorn) arrived about five minutes late. (Mann later told Skilton: 'Fifteen minutes early is late at Melbourne!'[26]) Mann continued:

> If looks could kill! Norm verbally pinned Bobby to the wall, basically saying that as a senior Victorian player and a leader of the side, he had let down his teammates and the state of Victoria. As he copped this barrage, Bobby was shrinking before our eyes. Ian Law was hardly mentioned because Bobby was one of the keys. Norm let it be known, in front of the whole team, that Bobby may not be in the starting 18. This really hit Bobby hard, and it made us all sit up and take notice because here was an all-time great being absolutely berated. I've never seen a guy take so long to do his shoelaces up as Bobby did that day. He was in complete shock. He still didn't know if he was playing or not because Norm was giving him the cold treatment. Bobby was still sitting there like a little schoolboy in the corner with the dunce's hat on when Norm addressed the team again just before we were due to run out onto the ground.[27]

---

[25] *The Sun* series, 1967.
[26] Bob Skilton. Interview with the author.
[27] Hassa Mann. Interview with the author.

Smith told Skilton: 'I can't drop one of you without dropping the other. I've only got (Billy) Goggin (to rove)'. In other words, if the Vics had two other players to fill the roving duties, both Skilton and Law would have been dropped.[28]

He gave Skilton one last warning: 'You'd better hope you play bloody well!'

After gaining the last-minute reprieve, Skilton 'stood to his full 5'7" (171cms), his chest expanded, and he ran onto the ground like a man possessed, and he played a fantastic game.'[29]

After the match, Smith put an arm around Skilton. 'Well, Skilts,' he said, 'you've copped it sweet and you've shoved it up me. Let's go and have a drink together'.

Skilton later reflected: 'I could tell that although I was a South Melbourne player, Smithy was genuinely happy that what he had wanted to happen had happened. But at the time, you don't like copping it. But by that stage at least I'd already seen Barassi and Whitten cop it in state sides'.[30]

During after-match drinks, Smith asked the MCC to supply a round of complimentary drinks for players and officials from both teams, but his request was rejected. He then reached into his pocket and produced a cheque – his payment for coaching that day – and put it over the bar to shout everyone himself.[31]

That day, he had also shattered a myth – that he had an intimate knowledge of the tricky, swirling winds at the MCG. Victorian skipper Kevin Murray had asked him which way he should kick if he won the toss. Murray was surprised when Smith replied: 'I wouldn't have any idea'. He later explained: 'I am supposed to know all about the wind-pockets at the MCG, but I don't think anyone does… The winds at the MCG are unpredictable'.[32]

It mattered nought. Smith was now undefeated in six games as coach of Victoria. Furthermore, his state sides had amassed a total of 974 points and conceded just 362 points – at the staggering percentage of 269.06.

Smith's run of landslide victories continued when the Demons took on his brother's Richmond side in round 10. The Tigers hadn't beaten Melbourne at the MCG during Norm Smith's reign and it was obvious from the outset that they weren't to have any joy this time either. In what was to remain the biggest winning margin in Norm Smith's coaching career, the Demons powered away to a 113-point victory – 23.18 (156) to 6.7 (43).

---

[28] Bob Skilton. Interview with the author.
[29] Hassa Mann. Interview with the author.
[30] Bob Skilton. Interview with the author.
[31] Stan Rule. Interview with the author.
[32] Newspaper report, 1965.

THE GREATEST PREMIERSHIP [1964]

A fortnight later, Melbourne took top spot from Geelong after defeating the Cats by 21 points at Kardinia Park. That day, Smith almost sacked his new runner, Sam Allica.[33] The pint-sized Allica, a former state championship wrestler, was unlucky to run foul of Smith after a mix-up with Barassi involving the removal of a player from the field. Allica said:

> John Devine ran through (Brian) 'Wrecker' Leahy and Wrecker had to go off. In the meantime, Norm told me to run the reserve player, Tony Anderson, around the ground to warm him up. I got our property steward, old (Les) 'Pepper' Green,[34] to take off with him around the ground, while I ran across to get Wrecker to go off on the other side of the ground, where the reserve player would be.
>
> Unbeknown to us, Ronny had told Wrecker: 'Run straight off', which meant Wrecker was running off on the wrong side of the ground. When I got back to the bench, the old man (Norm) was sitting there and looking daggers at me. After the match, he was still looking daggers.
>
> After I'd collected the blankets and rugs from the bench and got to the rooms, 'Pepper' Green was waiting for me. 'Pepper' was a nervy type after being a POW in Changi. He was frantic: 'Don't come in! Don't come in!'
>
> I said: 'I have to come in'.
>
> When I got in there, Norm was waiting for me. He had Ronny with him. He said to us: 'What the bloody hell do you think you're doing?! Do you think you're the coach of Melbourne Football Club?!'
>
> We tried to explain to him what had happened but he didn't want to hear it. Ronny was half-defending me but he was terrified to oppose the old fella too much. Smithy gave us a real blast and when he'd had enough of this he said to Ronny: 'You and Sammy can get on the bloody bus and go home with the seconds!'

Allica's quick wit was well suited to the role of a VFL runner, especially when he had to be the conduit between headstrong men like Smith and Barassi. On one occasion when Allica delivered Barassi a message from Smith, Barassi's snarled a well-worn Anglo-Saxon, two-word response. Allica told Barassi: 'I'm only paid to take the messages out, not to take them back!' Allica said: 'If I had taken that back to Norm – boy, oh boy! – the human volcano would have erupted!'

---

[33] Allica had taken over the running job from Hugh McPherson, who relinquished the role after 10 years to become a trainer.
[34] Norm gave Green the nickname 'Salt 'n Pepper' because 'he was in everything'.

But Allica also gained an insight into the closeness and like-mindedness of Smith and Barassi:

> Quite often, Norm would tell me: 'Sammy, go out and tell such-and-such... Actually don't worry about it; Ronny's talking to him now'. That's how much trust Norm placed in Ron. They had their differences, but in many ways they were like two peas in a pod. They were deadly serious about their footy, and deadly serious about winning and doing things the right way.

However, Allica recounted the story of a match at Footscray when Smith 'played funny buggers'. Each time Allica entered the field, Bulldogs captain-coach Ted Whitten had his reserves coach, Billy Findlay, run out alongside Allica to listen to his messages. Findlay (who had been a star rover/goalsneak with North Melbourne and represented Victoria in the 1940s) revelled in his sneaky role. Allica recalled:

> Findlay came out of the era where giving someone an ankle-tap was accepted, and he even had a bit of a kick at me. I ran him along the boundary to our coach's box and when we got there I gave him a little bump and he took a tumble. Norm was there with his claw and he grabbed him by the nose and said: 'What's wrong with you Bill, you silly old bugger?!'
>
> Norm got me to run a message to Bob Johnson. With Findlay listening in, I said: 'The Footscray runner is a silly bugger'.
>
> 'Big Bob' didn't know what to think.[35]

There were other humorous moments. On the tour of the United States, Smith had learnt some military lingo and began to inject it into his addresses in 1964. One day, John Lord was playing poorly, 'didn't let the fact that he was big, slow and cumbersome stop him from trying to go for a run at every opportunity', and was caught several times. Smith told Allica: 'Tell "Lordy" that battleships have a turning circle of three miles, so can he please try something else!'[36]

There was nothing to laugh about after the Demons' round 16 clash with Essendon at the MCG. After leading by 31 points midway through third term – 7.6 (48) to 2.5 (17) – the Demons were held scoreless for the rest of the match while the Bombers added 4.9 to win by two points.

---

[35] Sam Allica. Interview with the author.
[36] Sam Allica. Interview with the author.

The round 17 encounter with Hawthorn proved crucial to Melbourne's premiership campaign. The Demons were on top of the ladder, but just a game separated them from the fifth-placed Hawks.

Club	W	L	D	%	Pts
Melbourne	**13**	**4**	**-**	**147.7**	**52**
Geelong	12	4	1	133.2	50
Essendon	12	4	1	130.2	50
Hawthorn	12	4	-	127.4	48
Collingwood	11	5	1	121.0	46

Melbourne had to win to be assured of a spot in the finals. A win would also give them the double-chance and a vital week off to rest a number of injured players.

One of the key factors in the result was Smith's decision to finally accede to Brian Dixon's perennial suggestion to swing him to the opposite wing. Sam Allica recalled: 'Every time I went to the team meeting on a Thursday night, the same thing happened. Norm would say his bit and then he would invite the players to discuss the match, and that's when Dicko would pipe up: "Norm, I believe that if I…" Norm would cut him off immediately by saying: "Brian, I know what you're going to ask me. Sit down because you are *not* going to play on the other wing". Everyone would laugh, and it became a bit of a running joke.'[37] Dixon explained: ' I felt that if I was left-foot-in instead of left-foot-out like I always was, that I would be able to bring the ball down the corridor and into the goalsquare, rather than around the wing and into the forward pocket. Occasionally he would put me on the other wing, but he preferred me to be left-foot-out'.[38]

When the Demons had their backs to the wall against the Hawks, Smith granted Dixon his wish – to telling effect. On a heavier-than-usual Glenferrie Oval, where Hawthorn had been undefeated all season, the home side led by 16 points at the last change after adding 3.5 to 0.2 in the third term. Smith reinforced to his players that both the reward for victory (the double chance) and the punishment for defeat (potentially missing the finals) were great. He also switched Dixon and blasted Hassa Mann, who later confessed: 'I deserved it – I hadn't fired too many shots in the first three quarters. I had to do something'.[39]

---

[37] Sam Allica. Interview with the author. Norm also joked privately: 'Dicko came to me once and showed me 17 different ways we could get the ball out of the centre, and all of them ended with Dicko kicking a goal!'
[38] Brian Dixon. Interview with the author.
[39] Hassa Mann. Interview with the author.

The Demons dominated the final term with the breeze – thanks largely to an inspired Dixon, who kicked a goal, assisted in two others and created several other opportunities – but they were still trailing narrowly deep into time-on. Enter Hassa Mann. With a minute left and Melbourne down by two points, Mann gathered the ball in the forward pocket and from the boundary line, about 25 metres out, threaded a freakish goal. Mann described it as 'more good luck than good management'; teammates went further and said he had 'kicked it out of his backside'. Regardless, it helped set up the Demons for a serious assault on the premiership.

Melbourne lost its final round match against Footscray by 40 points at the Western Oval, which prompted many people at the time and since to say that the Demons would have finished fifth, and traded places with Hawthorn (which missed the finals by half a game) if Mann's impossible shot at goal went astray at Glenferrie Oval. But it wasn't as simple as that. If the Demons had in fact lost to the Hawks, they would have travelled to Footscray with their season on the line and would surely have produced a more desperate performance. As it was, the pressure was off because they couldn't lose the double chance, which might explain the general lack of urgency in their play against the Bulldogs.

The Demons actually finished on top to win their first minor premiership since 1960 – and their seventh in 10 seasons. The ladder standings at the end of the home-and-away season were:

Club	W	L	D	%	Pts
Melbourne	**14**	**4**	**-**	**138.1**	**56**
Collingwood	13	4	1	133.2	54
Essendon	13	4	1	130.2	54
Geelong	13	4	1	127.4	54
Hawthorn	13	5	-	121.0	52

🏆🏆🏆🏆🏆🏆🏆🏆🏆🏆

After beating Hawthorn and sealing another finals berth, the Demons let their hair down in the Hawks' social club. At the centre of festivities, as always, was Norm Smith, who was perhaps more relieved than anyone about the events of that afternoon. He knew how lucky the Demons had been; he also knew that Hassa Mann's freak goal had them in pole position in a very open race for the flag. Now was the time to celebrate a memorable victory, and dream of greater celebrations in the weeks to come.

THE GREATEST PREMIERSHIP [1964]

Late in the night, though, he forgot about celebrating and started intimidating. At one point he turned his attention to young reporter Greg Hobbs, who had covered the game for *The Age*. Hobbs had started his journalistic career with *The Herald* in 1957 and hadn't enjoyed the most cordial relationship with Smith. 'For a cub reporter,' he recalled, 'going to see Norm Smith was like going to see the headmaster at school. You'd almost get a state of the nation address. Norm didn't like the press much, but he liked Alf Brown. He trusted Alf. Everyone did. I was just a bloody kid as far as Norm and Jim Cardwell were concerned.'

Those were the days before clubs had media managers to cater for the needs of news outlets, which created the odd problem for reporters. At training sessions, for instance, the less-than-ideal procedure was for Hobbs to ask the coach: 'Can we borrow a couple of players to get some photos?'

When Smith was the coach in question, often he would respond with comments like: 'Oh Christ! I'm here to train footballers; I can't be worrying about you press bastards! Why should we help you anyway – all you do is bloody rubbish us!'

Against this backdrop, Hobbs crossed paths with Smith in the Hawthorn social club. Hobbs later said:

> There were jugs of beer everywhere and everyone was half-pissed and carrying on. Norm was holding court and big-noting himself and threatening people. Somehow I got involved with him, and he wanted to knock my block off too. I'd had a fair crack at the booze, so I had the courage up. Norm was saying he was gonna do this and gonna do that, and I said: 'Bullshit! I'll knock your bloody head off!'
>
> It got to the stage where we virtually had to be separated.
>
> Marj (Smith) was sitting at a table crying. But nothing eventuated. In the end, Norm put his arm around me and shook my hand and said: 'I admire you for standing up to me. You're not a bad bloke after all'.
>
> You wouldn't believe it, but from that moment I became one of Norm's mates around the traps. Whenever I went to Melbourne training, he'd say: 'Oh, how are you going?'
>
> I even ended up going to his funeral. It was a far cry from my early years as a reporter, when I wouldn't have attended his funeral even if it was held on my nature-strip. He was a fiery bastard, and a complex character, but I admired him after that. It became a pleasure dealing with him because he'd accepted me. But I almost had to have a bloody fight with him to gain that acceptance.[40]

---

[40] Greg Hobbs. Interview with the author.

Melbourne's 1948 premiership player Stan Rule had just secured a job as a talent scout for St Kilda. Within 24 hours, his phone rang. The terse voice at the other end said: 'Why are you going to St Kilda? You're my mate; you should be at Melbourne'.

Rule quickly realised he was speaking to Norm Smith, and said: 'But, Norm, I haven't been back to Melbourne since the '48 flag'.

'I don't care,' Smith said. 'Call Jeansy and tell him you're very sorry but you're now working for Melbourne.'

Rule did exactly that.

The first recruit he brought to Smith's attention was a skinny but talented 18-year-old on-baller named Stan Alves. Rule recalled:

> One training night just before the finals in 1964, I took 'Alvesy' down to Melbourne. I told Smithy: 'I've got a young fella here who will make your side next year'.
>
> Well, you should have heard Smithy!
>
> 'We're the top side, and hopefully on the way to winning a premiership, and you're telling me this skinny little kid is going to make the side?! Come on, Stan; I'm a coach, not a bloody miracle worker!'
>
> I said: 'He'll make it, all right. He's got all the ability in the world.'
>
> Smithy said: 'We're the top side!'
>
> I said: 'Yeah, but you bloody fluked it. If Hassa Mann hadn't kicked that goal, you wouldn't have even made the bloody finals!'
>
> Norm tried to brush me off and walk away, and I knew I had to get his attention, so I said: 'You didn't hear the bugle in '39 and you're not hearing it now!'
>
> That got his attention all right. He glared at me. Very few people could talk to Norm like that and get away with it, and I only just got away with it. He said: 'All right! I'll talk to him!'
>
> He took Alvesy into a little room. They came out about 45 minutes later and Norm told me: 'That kid knows where he's going; I'll take him'.
>
> If I didn't offend Norm and come on so strong with him, he wouldn't have taken Alvesy and it might have been a great career down the gurgler.[41]

But Alves' future at the Demons was far from sealed. Two weeks before the 1964 Grand Final, the youngster signed with the Demons and was then invited to

---

[41] Stan Rule. Interview with the author.

train that night. About 20 minutes into the session, Smith summoned Alves into the centre of the MCG.

'What's your name again, son?'

Alves reminded him.

'Well, young Alves,' Smith said, 'there are two things that stand out. The first is that you can do every kick in the book but you can't do any of them right. Secondly, you are running around like a headless chook and you're stuffing up training. We're on a mission. We've got a premiership to win. I'd like to wish you all the best, wherever it is, but it won't be here!'

Alves had been signed and then dismissed in less than an hour. He made the analogy that 'it was like an apprentice jockey winning the Melbourne Cup at his first attempt and then being disqualified for life after losing the race on protest'.[42] A devastated Alves cried all the way home on the train, believing 'all my dreams had now finished'.[43]

After 48 hours of soul-searching, Alves mustered his courage and returned to the MCG for training. No-one was more surprised to see him than Smith. Alves said: 'Norm Smith walked past, looked at me, and shook his head. At training, I didn't get a touch. No-one would kick it to me'.[44] Alves resigned himself to the fact he had given it his best shot and failed.

The next morning at work, Alves received an unexpected phone call from Smith, who wanted to know why he had returned after being given his marching orders.

Although extremely nervous, Alves responded with a question of his own. 'I know, Mr Smith, that you're a great coach,' he said. 'I know Melbourne is a great team, but how can you possibly tell after only 20 minutes if someone has the ability to play League football?'

There was a short pause.

'Well, Stan,' Smith said, 'what are you doing for lunch?'

Smith picked up Alves from work, handed him a sandwich and drove to the banks of the Yarra River for a one-on-one talk. Alves recalled:

> I listened intently as he outlined his thoughts about the future of the Melbourne Football Club. I was a small wingman and in his opinion the time of the small wingman had passed. He was now looking for tall and athletic players to pay in that position and I simply did not fit the bill. I didn't reply but I was thinking: 'How

---

[42] Alves, Stan with Col Davies, *Sacked Coach*, Crown Content, 2002.
[43] *The Sunday Age*, November 22, 1998.
[44] *The Sunday Age*, November 22, 1998.

many times do I really need to hear this?' Collingwood had knocked me back... Richmond... St Kilda... and now this.

But as we were about to leave, he then said, totally unexpectedly: 'HOWEVER!'

My ears pricked up... It was undoubtedly the most important 'however' I would ever hear.

'Never let it be said,' he pointedly emphasised, 'that Norm Smith denied somebody with such an obvious passion the opportunity to play League football.'

It was again made patently clear I was far from ready. I was told I'd been enrolled in a city gym run by a bloke called Stan Nicholes, who had helped train some of the most illustrious names in Australian sport (including tennis legends Rod Laver and Margaret Court). My challenge, he (Norm) told me, was to put on a stone (6.35kgs)... before the start of pre-season training. If I succeeded, I would be allowed to play in the practice games, otherwise all bets were off.[45]

Alves added the required weight and made his senior debut in round seven the next year. He eventually played 227 games for Melbourne, won two best-and-fairests and captained the club (from 1973-76), before playing in a premiership under Ron Barassi at North Melbourne in 1977. The lesson stayed with him when he coached St Kilda from 1994-98. During his final season a an AFL coach, Alves reflected: 'When I look at some of my players, and obviously I'll get exasperated at times and think: "This guy is hopeless", then I go back to 1964 when a person told me that I might have been hopeless too'.[46]

ÏÏÏÏÏÏÏÏÏ

Norm Smith also gave some career-altering advice to an opponent – Geelong full-forward Doug Wade. The 22-year-old had tried out at Melbourne in 1960 and actually bagged six goals in a practice match, before following the wishes of his parents and joining the Cats. Wade had won Geelong's goalkicking in his first three seasons, and had headed the VFL goalkicking in 1962 with a tally of 68 majors, but since undergoing knee surgery had struggled to regain form, and was languishing in the reserves when the Cats played Melbourne.

---

[45] Alves, Stan with Col Davies, *Sacked Coach*, Crown Content, 2002.
[46] The *Sports Factor* program on ABC Radio National, September 11, 1998.

Wade recalled being approached by Smith in the rooms after the senior match: 'Norm gave me a long chat. He told me: "You're too good to be playing in the seconds. This is what you should be doing, and need to be doing to get back". He also gave me a series of notes about confidence from his brother Len. I never looked back after that – it turned my football career around. Norm was a fantastic man, and I owe him a lot for that'.[47]

Len Smith's coaching notes, which included a pamphlet containing his 10 'golden rules', were fast gaining a reputation for helping players and coaches at various levels of the game. When their existence was revealed in *The Sun* at the start of 1964, Len received about 100 requests for copies. It was impractical to reply to everybody, so Len made a rule that they would only be circulated to former Richmond and Fitzroy players. However, there was the exception of Melbourne players, and others, Norm Smith passed them on to. Norm was always conscious of Len receiving due credit for his musings, and ensured the notes were accompanied by the label: 'These notes were compiled by Len Smith, a man who dedicated his life to football'.

🏆🏆🏆🏆🏆🏆🏆🏆🏆

Melbourne had qualified for its 11th successive finals series under Norm Smith. In the same period, the next most regular finalists were Collingwood, Essendon and Geelong, each of whom contested six finals series.

Smith said his players would enter the second semi-final against old foe Collingwood 'physically fit' but that 'psychologically, the problem is bigger. The best way to prepare them is to talk to the boys and make them realise the importance of what lies ahead. I think that we have down here the type of boy who is able to receive and react favourably to the psychological approach... All boys are of different temperaments, but I think that you can prepare them and I believe this mental approach to football is more important now than it was pre-war'.[48]

In the lead-up to the finals, Smith unleashed one of the most scathing psychological ploys of his coaching career. It centred around a seemingly minor indiscretion he had witnessed in the Melbourne changerooms after training one night – an indiscretion that had left him fuming. Smith was showering, while his oldest player (Bluey Adams) and one of his youngest players (20-year-old Frank

---

[47] Doug Wade. Interview with the author. When Wade retired at the end of the 1975 season, he had kicked a total of 1057 goals in 267 matches for Geelong and North Melbourne.
[48] *Midweek Magazine*, August 1964.

Davis) bathed separately in the two big tubs. In walked Brian Dixon, who sat in the tub occupied by Adams, who was one of his closest mates.

Dixon said: 'Norm saw what I'd done and he felt I should have got in the tub with Frank Davis instead, because he was a young player who had only recently come into the senior side and could have done with some encouragement from an experienced player. And he told me so in no uncertain terms. He also told me that I wouldn't be in the team that Saturday, which I was very upset about. After I got dressed and calmed down, I went and saw Jimmy Cardwell and told him what had happened and said that I hoped wiser counsel would prevail, which it did, and I played that week'.[49]

Although Dixon believed the matter to be over, and his lesson learned, and Adams didn't give it another thought because he had done nothing wrong, it remained embedded like a thorn in Smith's brain. He chose Melbourne's pre-finals dinner, on the Tuesday night before the September action started, as the appropriate setting to air his anger. Smith was introduced to noisy applause from the 400 guests, but the room quickly fell silent as he launched into a tirade of criticism against two of his highest-profile players. Adams recalled:

> Norm said words to the effect of: 'Two players have let the Melbourne Football Club down to an extent that no player who had ever appeared in the Melbourne guernsey had ever let the club down before... If we had players to replace them, they wouldn't be in the team. The two players I'm referring to are Frank Adams and Brian Dixon.'
>
> I'd eaten my meal and was onto the sweets and I sort of said: 'What did he say?'
>
> Norm went on to say: 'They don't assist the younger players, and they don't live up to the standards that have been set by players X, Y, Z'.
>
> I was dumbfounded as to how he could arrive at such a conclusion, and what I'd done to deserve a public burst. I was more shocked than angry. But I thought: 'Now's not the time to ask Norm what it's all about. I'm out of here'.
>
> As I got up, Dicko got up and we both walked out.
>
> Dicko said: 'What do you think?'
>
> I said: 'This is too big a distraction for me at this stage. I don't want to know about it; I'm out of here'.[50]

---

[49] Brian Dixon. Interview with the author.
[50] Frank 'Bluey' Adams. Interview with the author.

THE GREATEST PREMIERSHIP [1964]

The second semi-final confrontation between Melbourne and Collingwood was expected to be one of the truly great finals between the old enemies. Bob Rose's Magpies hadn't been beaten since round 10, and their only clash with Melbourne, in round nine at the MCG, had resulted in just a 10-point loss. The Demons were completely overwhelmed early. Midway through the first quarter, Collingwood led – 2.2 (14) to Melbourne's 0.0. But equally as inexplicable as the Demons' lack of presence was the utter deterioration of the Magpies. In the last three-and-a-half quarters, Melbourne annihilated Collingwood, piling on 19.20 (134) to just 4.7 (31). The Demons won by 89 points – then the greatest winning margin in a final.[51]

Smith tempered talk of the Demon demolition, saying that while he was pleased with the way his side had recovered after a sluggish start, 'the form of the two teams... must be discounted after half-time. A team on top can do no wrong'.[52]

The Demons weren't the super side they appeared. Although they were blessed with champions like Barassi, Dixon and Mann, and boasted a strong defence and a multi-pronged attack (with nine players eventually contributing 14 or more goals) – they had the most points for and the second-least against – they amazed many people simply by being minor premiers, let alone dominating the second semi-final in a manner reminiscent of their halcyon era. On paper, the Melbourne line-up appeared deficient in several areas. They were not regarded as a particularly pacy or classy side, and they had just one ruckman – Graham Wise.

Recommended to the Demons by the Victorian Premier, Sir Henry Bolte, Wise had played just three senior matches before the start of the 1964 season. But, according to Alf Brown, Smith transformed the 21-year-old from 'an ordinary player' into one who 'could ruck unchanged for a whole game'.[53] Sam Allica said: 'Wise rucked "Lone Ranger" for the whole year. Although he wasn't the most talented player, and he was a very quiet fella, he had great strength of character – and Norm loved that about him. Norm loved players with skill, but he'd take the bloke with character every time'.[54]

Smith didn't expect Wise to win many possessions or even many hit-outs, but he expected him to contest fiercely and at the very least negate the usually

---

[51] The Demons' mark, which surpassed Carlton's 88-point win over Collingwood in the 1931 first semi-final, stood for five years until it was eclipsed by Richmond, which pounded Geelong by 118 points in the 1969 first semi-final. The current record margin is 133 points, created by Essendon against Collingwood in the 1984 preliminary final. Melbourne's effort stands equal 12th (to the end of the 2007 finals series).
[52] *Melbourne Truth*, Saturday September, 19, 1964.
[53] *The Herald*, Monday July 30, 1973.
[54] Sam Allica. Interview with the author.

bigger opposition ruckman, and the lion-hearted youngster didn't let him down. To compensate for this perceived weakness, Smith 'had ruck-rovers in Barassi and Brian Kenneally cruising the packs like destroyers around a battleship'.[55]

Barassi explained: 'We were well managed and well-coached, and we really had a go, and (if you do that) you're going to have a chance no matter if you're... not as strong as one would like to be here or there'.[56]

Smith also provided the solution to another obstacle before the Grand Final against Collingwood.[57] Allica said:

> Norm told me that every year they'd made the Grand Final they'd never been stopped from using their own changerooms. But in '64 we lost the toss for the choice of rooms and Collingwood decided to use our rooms and we had to use the Richmond rooms.
>
> On the Thursday night, the whole club was sitting in the Richmond rooms and Norm was talking to them and giving them a gee-up. Normally it would be only the players there but on special occasions Norm liked to have the whole club there.
>
> Jimmy Cardwell came in and said: 'We've lost the toss and they won't change'.
>
> Norm always thought very quickly on his feet, and this was no exception. Rather than wasting time complaining about it, which might have also rubbed off on the players - which Norm never did anyhow - he decided on a positive course of action. He told Jimmy to get hold of the builder who did a bit of work for us from time to time and 'see what he can do for us between now and Saturday about putting up a coach's room'.
>
> Norm's idea was to make an unfamiliar room seem more familiar. It also served a practical purpose because it enabled him to talk to just the players without anybody else around, away from committeemen, past players and other people.
>
> By the time they got the timber and sheeting, they probably didn't start building the coach's room until 1am Friday morning. But they finished it on the Friday afternoon and gave it a rough coat of paint. There were a couple of long benches in there and so on, but it was pretty basic - no linings or anything. You could imagine a Sheedy doing something like that. Good coaches just seem to know where to turn, and what to do, in any given situation.[58]

---

[55] Alf Brown, *The Herald*, 1979.
[56] *Red and Blue* documentary, 2005.
[57] The Magpies had defeated Geelong by four points in the preliminary final.
[58] Sam Allica. Interview with the author.

Smith also knew that Collingwood would be a far tougher proposition than it was in the second semi-final, when the Magpies had almost seemed to surrender as the Demons reduced the match to little more than a training run. But the ghosts of 1958 still haunted many Melbourne people, the coach included. Just five members of the Demons' 1958 Grand Final side were still playing, but revenge remained a strong motivating force.

Smith wrote in *Truth*: 'There is no doubt about Collingwood. When they look their weakest, that is when they fight their hardest. There will be no complacency in the Melbourne camp in spite of our big win in the semi-final – 1958 is still fresh in our memories... A team with the fighting Collingwood qualities must be respected and they are worthy Grand Finalists... If Collingwood beat us, there will be no excuses'.[59]

On the morning of Saturday September 26, 1964, Norm Smith awoke at 7am in a slightly disorientated state. What day is it? What's on today?

'My thoughts were in turmoil,' he said later. 'Something important was nagging at my brain... and then it struck. The Grand Final! This was the big one – the flag I wanted more than any I had ever chased.'[60]

Even he was surprised by his anxiety, admitting that 'after 11 successive years in the finals, you'd expect a coach to be immune to the pangs of worry that make you almost physically ill. But there it was again – that awful sinking feeling hit the pit of my stomach and I was gripped with tension'.

As had become his usual pre-match routine, Smith remained in bed while Marj prepared his breakfast and brought it to him. He preferred to be alone with his thoughts, and he kept those thoughts to himself. Communication was kept to a minimum. He didn't speak unless he had to. He believed that 'doubts or fears of defeat must be stifled', and plenty of doubts were circulating through his mind. 'Melbourne versus Collingwood,' he pondered, and the memory of past experiences told him that 'this was to be a tough one', because 'you never have those Magpies beaten until the final siren'.

Marj and Peter Smith knew not to discuss the game with him, or between themselves in his presence. Smith conceded: 'They are probably afraid I am a bit too much of a grump'. The reasoning behind his silent treatment theory was that

---

[59] *Melbourne Truth*, Saturday, September 19, 1964.
[60] *Melbourne Truth*, Saturday, September 26, 1964.

if he could conceal his emotions, particularly the negative ones, and maintain an air of assurance and control, he would find it easier to 'work the same with the players'.

Work was also part of the Saturday morning process. But this time Smith had no intention of working – he drove to his factory in North Coburg for no reason other than it was 'a footy day habit'. This was just one of a number of his idiosyncrasies and superstitions – he referred to them as 'my little quirks' – which he followed on Grand Final day 1964. They also included donning the same pair of old, 'just about worn-out' shoes, and the same suit he had worn to every match. 'I guess I feel they can bring me luck,' he said.

According to most tipsters, the Demons wouldn't need much luck – they were easily the better side and would win comfortably. But this made Smith uncomfortable. 'I am never very happy when the majority of experts tip Melbourne to win,' he said. 'It is good ammunition for a rival coach and I knew I would have to crush all feeling of complacency out of my players.'

The morning seemed to drag on, and Smith's stomach hadn't improved much, and it was affecting his appetite. Just before 11am, he forced himself to eat an early lunch of steak. A sizeable meal was required to sustain him throughout a draining day and what he was to describe as 'the biggest match of my career'.

When the Smiths arrived at the MCG, they battled their way through a heaving throng of supporters –102,469 people would cram into the stadium that day. Once inside, Smith, 'as quickly as possible', reached 'the sanctuary of the Members' Reserve'. There he watched the end of the under-19s Grand Final, which the Demons won by 14 points over Collingwood. It was a good omen.

The first of his players he saw was Tassie Johnson. Smith sensed Johnson was tense, but he hardly reassured his big back-pocket. 'Hello, Tassie. Feeling edgy?' he asked. He later recalled that 'it wasn't a particularly stirring remark'.[61]

More of his players arrived and he engaged in casual conversation, and although he found it impossible to properly digest all the small talk as tactics flooded through his brain, at least his anxiety eased slightly. But soon he became concerned that his more relaxed attitude might negatively impact on his players, by diluting the healthy tension footballers are meant to feel before a big match.

At 1.30pm – 50 minutes before the first bounce – Smith left the players and went to 'a little hideaway' where he could be relatively alone and again 'whip' himself back to 'the peak of tension'. He studied the notes he had compiled for his pre-match address and other more individualised instructions.

---

[61] *Melbourne Truth*, Saturday September 19, 1964.

Smith reads the infamous letter – delivered by courier on Friday July 23, 1965 – that informed him of the Melbourne committee's decision to sack him. At the time, the Demons had a 9-3 record, but the issue related to long-standing off-field friction between Smith and club officials. It remains arguably the most controversial episode in AFL/VFL history. *(Herald & Weekly Times)*

(Left) The day after the sacking, Norm and Marj Smith disguise their grief during their first winter Saturday without football in decades. They listened to a radio broadcast of Melbourne's loss to North Melbourne, while fielding phone calls from media outlets desperate to gain exclusive rights to his story. The next day, Smith honoured his contract with Channel Nine by appearing on *The Tony Charlton Football Show* and, in one of the most riveting hours of football television imaginable, didn't hold anything back. *(Herald & Weekly Times)*

(Above) Just four days after the sacking, and just two days after both Smith and the Melbourne committee had declared their irreconcilable differences, the master coach was reinstated. The dramatic reversal was orchestrated by Trevor Rapke, a County Court judge, Demons' fan and 'a real Norm Smith man'. Although Smith and Demon president Don Duffy tried to portray an image of unity, an immovable wedge had been placed between them. *(Herald & Weekly Times)*

Norm and Marj congratulate their son Peter on being selected to make his debut for Melbourne in round three, 1966. Although Peter didn't find Norm overbearing, he was treated equally as hard as other players. Norm once forced Peter to have a haircut at half-time after his Beatles-style mop-top kept getting in his eyes. Peter played 23 games for Melbourne and 15 under Ron Barassi at Carlton. He was 'nothing like his father in looks and outlook', and was 'more like Marj – easier-going, and not as prone to explode'. *(Peter Smith)*

After a year out of football – during which he strengthened his philosophies on leadership by reading about the likes of Winston Churchill and American gridiron coach Vince Lombardi – Smith couldn't resist a return to coaching. In late 1968, he accepted the job at the battling South Melbourne. *(Herald & Weekly Times)*

In 1970, Smith's second season with the Swans, he produced one of his finest coaching efforts, lifting an average South side to its first finals series since the 'Bloodbath' Grand Final of 1945. The Swans lost the first semi-final to St Kilda, but Smith's legend was enhanced. With his health waning, he did it with a revolutionary coaching set-up, with assistant coach Ian Thorogood doing the heavy, hands-on work at training. *(Herald & Weekly Times)*

Smith's last two season at South Melbourne produced just five wins, as it became a struggle just to remain competitive. The coach's focus was also diverted from strictly football matters, with much of his time spent arguing with committeemen on the sidelines, leading to another acrimonious departure at the end of 1972. *(Private collection)*

Smith had accepted the role of chairman of selectors at North Melbourne and was starting to spend more time with his family when he was diagnosed with an inoperable brain tumour. He died at home, five months later on July 29, 1973. His funeral was attended by more than 800 mourners. *(Peter Smith)*

When he joined his players in the changerooms, he was alarmed to discover that he had never been more tense. Still afflicted by 'that sinking feeling in the stomach', he 'paced nervously backwards and forwards, stopping players as random thoughts occurred to him. He later said:

> All the time I was getting more and more on edge, and I could see it was affecting some of the players in the same fashion.
>
> To Crompton, I said: '"Frog", you have had a great year. You haven't given away many goals and you have hardly given away a free kick. Don't let today be the day'.
>
> I went to Tony Anderson: 'You are watching (David) Norman. Be careful of the rover changeover. They will do it when you least expect it'.
>
> Back to Crompton: 'Watch for the rover changeover. When it's on, make sure you talk to your players. Know what they are doing'.
>
> Then to Don Williams: 'Remember how you played against (John) Henderson last time. You played wide early, (but) you did better when you got in closer'.
>
> To... (Graeme) Jacobs I said: 'You have a shorter opponent at centre half-forward today in (John) Mahon. You have been inclined to jump early for your marks against ruckmen. Today, back your judgment'.[62]

He then crammed his players into the medical room, which was about 'as big as a telephone box'. He used a psychological tactic – real or imagined – that he hoped would strike a nerve and ensure his side didn't take the Magpies lightly. 'I've heard a rumour,' he said, 'that some of you blokes don't think we can win. Well, anybody who thinks that, put your hand up now and we'll get someone to replace you'.

Predictably, no hands were raised. But voices were. The Demons began to fire up the way the coach had wanted them to. Young Frank Davis later said: 'I didn't think any of the players even thought that way. I just reckon Norm was trying to rev us up so that we didn't think we were just gong to go out there and do it as easy as we'd done in the second semi'.[63]

Smith again disappeared to his 'hideout' where he 'reconstructed' his address and 'whipped up a bit more fury'. He later maintained: 'Do not think this building up of tension is an act to trick the crowd and players. A coach must burn with the same fervour as his players if he is to raise them to any heights'.

---

[62] *Melbourne Truth*, Saturday September 26, 1964.
[63] Frank Davis. Interview with the author.

Smith's 'vital, last, eight-minute address',[64] contained words along the lines of: 'This is the most important day of your lives. All of your football earlier in the year is forgotten. History will judge you on your game today. The side with the fierce desire to get the ball first will win the premiership'. He also 'warned of complacency' and how it 'destroyed the club' in 1958, when Melbourne was defeated by its rival for this flag – Collingwood.

For all that, he wasn't entirely happy with the emotion he evoked from his players: 'To be a good coach you have to be somewhat of a hypnotist… I studied the expressions on their faces. I could see by the intentness of Barassi and Williams I was through to them. Expressions on other players' faces I knew well, and I knew they were in the right frame of mind. But there were other faces, expressionless faces. I couldn't gauge whether I had them or not and I was a bit perturbed'.[65]

His emotions fluctuated rapidly, and to extremes. As the ball hit the turf at the opening bounce, his immediate thought was: 'In two hours it will be all over. Thank goodness'. That thought – which he later dismissed as 'strange' and slightly washed-out' – was momentary. From that point on, tension constantly mounted within him.

When Bluey Adams broke free, only to have it called back after a free kick had been awarded against Tassie Johnson, Smith was furious. 'I did not see what Tassie did,' he admitted, 'but I was annoyed he should infringe when Bluey had the ball in the clear.'[66]

Then when Collingwood's Terry Waters marked in attack, Smith 'couldn't see him kicking the goal from the boundary against that tricky wind', but his 'heart sank' as Waters somehow kicked truly to post the first goal. He observed: 'The Magpies were away to a flying start, and the agony was on. Would they get a break?' Despite his penchant for fearing the worst, he added: 'I never really believe we will be beaten, but it is agonising when it looks as though you can be'.[67]

When John Lord had a shot at goal and the ball sailed out of bounds, Smith lamented that it was 'an opportunity wasted, and you cannot waste opportunities in Grand Finals'. But he was thankful, however, when John Townsend 'made amends with a beautiful snap' to level the scores.

Smith said his 'hopes soared' in the second quarter when the Demons slammed on three successive goals to lead by that margin midway through the term.

---

[64] *Melbourne Truth*, Saturday September 19, 1964.
[65] *Melbourne Truth*, Saturday, September 19, 1964.
[66] *Melbourne Truth*, Saturday, September 19, 1964.
[67] *Melbourne Truth*, Saturday, September 19, 1964.

He was inspired by the tough approach of his players. 'Tassie Johnson was hit hard,' Smith grimaced. '(But) I knew he would get up and go on with the game. He knows football is a game for hard knocks.'[68]

The Demon coach was soon 'in the depths of despair' as Collingwood hit back with three goals of its own late in the second term to hit the front. In a low-scoring game, Smith was concerned with the ease in which the Magpies had been able to score. He fretted: 'I was praying for the half-time siren before they could widen the gap'. When the siren came, the Demons trailed by two points – 5.7 (37) to Collingwood's 5.9 (39).

Barassi was a major concern. 'During the first half,' Smith said, 'I was worried about... Barassi's inability to lift his game. I kept sending the runner out to needle him and urge him to lift... I know Ron reacts violently. He might abuse the trainer, but he also takes it out on the opposition. (But) all to no avail. He could not get firing. He seemed leg-weary.'

During the half-time break, Smith levelled a similar allegation, among others, at his entire team. He was as acid-tongued as he had ever been. 'I will not repeat the things I said to the players at half-time,' he said. 'I said some very hard words (because) I knew we had a fight on our hands (and) I was worried... I was most caustic with the players. I tried to sting their pride.'[69] But no matter how ferociously he abused his players, and what insults spewed from his mouth, he sensed it had fallen on deaf ears. 'I was perturbed,' he said later. He felt he wasn't 'getting through to them', but that 'it is hard to tell when players set their faces' to conceal their feelings.

The Demons, though, produced the desired response in terms of effort, if not in conversion, in the third term. 'We had the play but could not put the score on the board,' Smith said. 'I was starting to think Collingwood would have the scoring end in the final quarter.'

Although the Demons kicked 2.3 to 0.2 for the term to lead by 11 points at three-quarter-time, Smith remained 'very worried'. He had expected the Magpies to be exhausted by this stage, and nervously observed that while they had played 'hard and tenaciously, they were not slowing up'.

Smith felt that while an 11-point advantage was 'a handy lead' in such a 'slogging, low-scoring game', his team could ill-afford to relax. 'It might not be enough,' he emphasised to his players. 'Guts alone will decide this premiership.'

The last quarter – one of the most dramatic in Grand Final history – had everything: guts, heroes and the odd villain on either side. Smith later announced:

---

[68] *Melbourne Truth*, Saturday, September 19, 1964.
[69] *Melbourne Truth*, Saturday September 19, 1964.

'That last quarter is the most agonising I have experienced in football. What a quarter.'[70] Meanwhile, Barassi – who lifted himself somewhat in the second half to finish with 17 kicks and seven handballs – rated it 'the most high-pressure quarter of my playing career'.[71]

Melbourne attacked fiercely in the opening minutes of the final term, but managed just three successive behinds – to John Townsend, Barassi and Bryan Kenneally – to stretch the margin to 14 points when a goal or two would probably have sealed the premiership. Smith was particularly 'disturbed' when the goal umpire ruled Townsend's attempt at his fourth goal a point. 'John and many others believed it was a goal,' he said. 'Still, the umpire's decision is final. But it was a vital decision.'[72]

Shortly afterwards, Magpie star Des Tuddenham slashed the deficit to eight points. A stalemate developed and there weren't any goals kicked for the next 12 minutes. 'We held on and held on,' Smith said, 'and my heart was in my mouth.'

At the 17-minute mark, Collingwood skipper Ray Gabelich wrenched the ball out of a boundary throw-in and kicked a goal and suddenly the Demons were just three points clear.

Then, at the 23-minute mark – with just five minutes remaining – Smith was 'horrified' at the 'lack of discipline in the Melbourne side' that enabled Gabelich – the slow, lumbering ruckman – to receive the ball about 40 metres from goal (not the 60 or 70 that is often quoted), and about 20 metres clear of the nearest Demon, and with no-one between him and the goal. Smith was 'praying' Gabelich would have a shot shortly after taking possession. 'Gabbo' didn't. Instead, he took four agonisingly erratic bounces, each time regathering the ball, and each time with Smith willing the ball to 'run away' from him.[73] To simultaneous roars and groans, Gabelich – whose run was described by Lou Richards as being slower than a glacier[74] – slammed the ball through from the goalsquare. It was, Smith conceded, 'a great captain's effort, but I was in no mood for praise'.[75] The fact was that Gabelich, in his 131 previous matches, had mustered just 19 goals, yet he had just kicked two consecutive majors in the space of six minutes late in the last quarter of tight, low-scoring Grand Final. More importantly, he had put Collingwood two points in front.

---

[70] *Melbourne Truth*, Saturday September 26, 1964.
[71] Ron Barassi. Interview with the author.
[72] *Melbourne Truth*, Saturday September 26, 1964.
[73] *Melbourne Truth*, Saturday September 26, 1964.
[74] *The Sun*, Monday, September 21, 1964.
[75] *The Sun*, Monday, September 21, 1964.

Gabelich's direct opponent, 'Tassie' Johnson, later confessed: 'I caused Gabbo's run. Smithy didn't know that the time and he asked the question and I said: "Well, I went in to bump Tuddenham and he sidestepped me and kicked it out". Norm accepted that for the time being until he saw a replay later on. He said: "I see what you mean now", and he went to argue then and there about it. "Why didn't you grab him? Why didn't you do this?" I said: "It was just a decision I made at the time, Norm, and it obviously didn't work'.[76]

Although proud that his side continued to show 'plenty of guts', Smith felt the premiership may have slipped from Melbourne's grasp. Before the next centre bounce, a television camera focused on Smith and Checker Hughes sitting on the bench. Channel Nine football commentator Ian Cleland observed: 'Norm Smith, the man without the hat, is the coach, a worried coach, of the Melbourne side'.

Smith's spirits rose when Hassa Mann claimed one of the few big marks of his career – and his 10th for the day. After slotting the miracle goal at the death at Hawthorn, a shot from about 20 metres out, virtually directly in front, and with his 24th kick, should have posed no problems for the Demon sharpshooter. Smith thought: 'I know he'll score (a goal) and put us in front'.[77] Mann himself thought: 'You beauty, I'm going to make a hero of myself again here by kicking the goal that wins us the premiership'. But, as he freely admitted, he quickly went from hero to zero: 'I can imagine Smithy thinking: "This'll be a goal". I went back and made the mistake of taking longer than I should've and, for some reason, as I started to come in, the pressure got to me and my legs went to jelly. In the end, I was lucky to make the distance and scrape in for a point. I'd missed an absolute sitter. I just wanted to dig a hole for myself to hide in. Within a matter of seconds, I almost convinced myself that when the siren went I was going to walk out of the ground with the crowd. I felt so guilty that I wasn't going to go back into the rooms; it would have been too painful. After being the hero a few weeks earlier, I was suddenly the villain'.[78]

Smith had conceded defeat. 'Our final hope was gone,' he said.[79] Mann had kicked 1.3, but he wasn't the only wasteful Demon. Barassi and Barrie Vagg had nine shots between them and failed to kick a single goal. In fact, they failed to even register a score with four shots. It would take a defender to save them.

Following Mann's unforgivable miss, the Collingwood kick-out landed in the hands of best-afield Brian Dixon, who marked unopposed after Magpie star Kevin Rose just as unforgivably failed to create an aerial contest. Dixon sent his 23rd

---

[76] Robert 'Tassie' Johnson. Interview with the author.
[77] *Melbourne Truth*, Saturday September 26, 1964.
[78] Hassa Mann. Interview with the author.
[79] *Melbourne Truth*, Saturday September 26, 1964.

kick, a typically wobbly punt, to the 'hot-spot' 20 metres out from the Melbourne goal, where Barassi flew for the mark, and the ball spilled to the front of the pack where – surprise of all surprises – back-pocket Neil Crompton gathered the ball and, off one step, let fly with a punt kick – which Barassi described as 'the sweetest, truest, most glorious kick of the whole darn season'[80] – and it sailed through for a goal. It was Crompton's first goal in 59 games – since round seven, 1960![81]

The Demons were back in front by four points deep in time-on.

'I couldn't believe my eyes,' Smith said. 'I didn't know whether to abuse him for his lack of discipline or to cry on his shoulder. (But) I'm glad he did use his initiative. There are times when a player has to – and without him we would not have won'.[82] That was Smith's measured, public front; he would vent his true feelings to Crompton after the match, and for some time after that.

There was no escaping the fact Crompton had defied his coach's express orders. The general rule for Demon defenders was they could follow their opponent as far as the centre. But following Gabelich's second goal, Collingwood coach Bob Rose threw both of his rovers onto the ball in an effort to defend their lead, which freed Crompton, who did as he was told and stopped at the centreline. In these desperate circumstances, Smith sent Allica out to tell Crompton: 'Don't go past centre half-forward, and pick up the other rover when he comes out'.[83]

Soon after, with Allica on the field running messages, Smith summoned Hugh McPherson, who recalled the coach being so 'frantic' about Crompton being 'sucked too far down the ground' that he feared the Magpies would clear the ball and kick a match-sealing goal. Smith bellowed to McPherson: 'Get out there and tell "Crommo" to drop back to the centre! What the hell's he doing down there?!' By the time McPherson got out there, Crompton had goaled.[84] If Crompton was meant to be in the centre, he was up to 60 metres out of position. Even if he was supposed to be at centre half-forward, he was at least 30 metres at fault.

In the meantime, though, there was still 2 mins. 41 secs. for the Demons to negotiate. Smith didn't dwell on the bittersweet frustration he felt towards Crompton. Immediately following the goal, he almost duplicated Rose's tactic by moving Barry Bourke from full-forward to defence. Bourke, who had struggled all day, marvelled: 'Norm was so tactically sharp that before the ball had even been

---

[80] *The Sun*, Monday, September 21, 1964.
[81] Brief footage of the dying stages of the 1964 Grand Final can be seen on YouTube – au.youtube.com/watch?v=K7EuMkjbmzU
[82] *Melbourne Truth*, Saturday September 26, 1964.
[83] Sam Allica. Interview with the author.
[84] Hugh McPherson. Interview with the author.

bounced in the centre, the runner had been sent out to me and I was on my way to the backline'. The switch had instant results. Soon after Crompton's match-winning goal, and with the Demons under siege as the Magpies launched three forward thrusts, Bourke took a goal-saving pack-mark in the defensive goalsquare. That night, clearly proud of Bourke's efforts – and perhaps his own foresight – Smith would refer to Bourke as 'my little back-pocket player'.[85]

In the midst of this desperate battle for the 1964 flag, and the siren only seconds away, Smith suddenly – strangely – became self-conscious. He had noticed that newspaper photographers had 'moved in', with their lenses poised to capture his reaction to the result. He thought: 'They are waiting for you to put on a show, Norm'. He was determined not to humour them, recalling: 'I steeled myself and resolved that no matter which way the game went, I would keep control'. It must have been difficult to do so when, with just nine seconds remaining, Collingwood full-forward Ian Graham gathered the ball and perhaps should have received a free kick just 40 metres out, directly in front of goal, after copping a head-high bump from Bourke. When the siren sounded to signal a famous Melbourne victory, Smith gave in to his raw emotions:

> I found myself leaping in the air and yelling to Checker Hughes: 'We won it! We have won it!'
> Checker replied: 'My oath we've won it!'...
> Never again do I want to experience such a day of agony.[86]

As Smith stood on the dais for the presentation of the premiership cup, he spared a thought for his brave opponents. 'I felt pangs of sympathy for Bobby Rose and his players,' he said. 'They had been worthy opponents. And fully deserved victory. I did not want my players to show too much elation.' (As a player and coach, Smith contested five Grand Finals against Collingwood and won four of them, one as a player and three as a coach.) He then reflected on his own coaching performance: 'Midway through the season, I told my players I would spare nothing and nobody to get this premiership. If they didn't like it, they would be replaced. I've had many quarrels and been ruthless. At times I have been ashamed of the things I have done. After the victory, I apologised to the players and thanked them for their tremendous support. I am sure now when they think back, they will realise my ferocity was worth the reward'.[87]

---

[85] Barry Bourke. Interview with the author.
[86] *Melbourne Truth*, Saturday September 26, 1964.
[87] *Melbourne Truth*, Saturday September 26, 1964.

In the changerooms, at least six of our players were weeping with relief. 'Dicko was the worst,' said Allica. 'He'd run his little backside off.'[88]

Smith also became emotional when his brother walked into the rooms. The pair 'smiled at each other from ear to ear', shook hands and warmly embraced. Len told Norm: 'Fatty, that's your greatest premiership ever'.

He raised his eyebrows slightly. 'Why do you say that, Lenny?'

'Well, you didn't have a bloody side,' Len said. 'For instance, you've got one ruckman, Wise, who's only had about three kicks for the year, but you got him to perform the role you wanted out of him.'[89]

Checker Hughes agreed, later saying: 'We weren't big enough, we weren't fast enough, we weren't good enough, but Norm talked the players and himself into believing that we could win'.[90] Barassi added: 'We were nowhere near as formidable a side as we had been in the past, and I think we won the 1964 premiership largely because of Norm's coaching, which was probably worth a few extra players, and extra goals, to us'.[91] John Townsend agreed: 'There were better sides than us, but no side was better managed than we were'.[92]

There had also been an element of luck that even the coach acknowledged. Peter Smith said: 'Dad always felt they'd stolen the flag in '64. He thought they'd been very lucky just to make the finals because they were just one of five teams who were fairly equal. And they'd fluked wins in two crucial games – the one at Hawthorn, and then the Grand Final – on both occasions with the last goal of the day. Dad was only too aware that things could have turned out a lot differently. But he also thought they were as deserving of the premiership as any other side in it, and that maybe it was a payback flag for '58'.[93]

But even in victory, Smith wasn't completely satisfied. With a deadpan expression, he reminded Mann of his blunder. 'Thank goodness Crompton can kick straight,' Smith said, before walking away with a wry grin.[94]

Crompton wasn't allowed to forget his magnificent 'mistake' either. Although his teammates never seriously questioned Crompton about his actions – on the contrary, they actually felt indebted to him – Smith would never congratulate Crompton. He remained steadfast in his conviction that – win, lose or draw –

---

[88] Sam Allica. Interview with the author.
[89] Related by Hugh McPherson in an interview with the author.
[90] Checker Hughes' speech at Norm Smith's testimonial dinner at Melbourne Town Hall on December 20, 1967. Recorded in *Trident Monthly*, April 1968.
[91] Ron Barassi. Interview with the author.
[92] John Townsend. Interview with the author.
[93] Peter Smith. Interview with the author.
[94] Hassa Mann. Interview with the author.

it was a sin to break a team rule, regardless of the circumstances; even if the act in question resulted in a premiership. Hugh McPherson said: 'The rest of us thought Crommo was a hero, and he was, but Norm treated him like a villain. Norm was like an angry dog with a bone – he just wouldn't let it go'.

He initially gave Crompton a brief, controlled rebuke in the changerooms. Other players weren't sure if it was serious or in jest, but they suspected the latter.

'You shouldn't have been *up* there,' Smith growled at Crompton. 'What were you *doing* there?'

It was a rhetorical question – no explanation was going to satisfy the coach.

McPherson said: 'We couldn't believe that Norm paid out on Crommo. Norm never forgave Crommo for that. There was none of this: "Well done, son, you've won us the premiership". Norm was happy and relieved to have won, but disappointed with the way it happened'.

Smith gave Crompton a particularly hard time on a trip to Adelaide the week after the Grand Final. McPherson recalled:

> Norm was still getting stuck into Crommo - not in a joking way, and not in a very nice way. He was deadly serious, and it was getting a bit uncomfortable.
>
> I said to him: 'Oh, let up, Norm; I think he's got the message'.
>
> Norm took me aside and said: 'But it hurts inside, Hughie... Remember '58, when they all promised me they wouldn't go out there and fight? And what the hell happened? They were out there five minutes and they were punching up again. No, Crommo went against what I said and I don't give a damn if he kicked the winning goal. It's about the principle of the thing. Winning is important - it's damn important - but it's not as important as sticking to solid principles. If you deviate from the principles, you deteriorate quickly'.
>
> Even if Norm and Crommo were both alive today, I reckon Norm would still have a little dig at him about it - and mean it. Most coaches would have swept it under the carpet and all would have been forgiven, but not with Norm. He was one out of the box. Never met anyone else like him.[95]

On the night of Melbourne's premiership win, Brian Dixon approached his coach for a serious talk, and an explanation.

'Norm,' Dixon said, 'I just want to clear up something with you. Why did you attack Bluey and myself at the pre-finals dinner? We're two of the most experienced players at the club, and I felt the way you treated us was most unkind. You embarrassed us.'

---

[95] Hugh McPherson. Interview with the author.

Smith replied with a question of his own.

'Dicko,' he said, 'who were our two best players over the finals series?'

'Bluey and myself.'

'Well there you go,' Smith nodded, 'you've just answered your own question.'

He walked off and left his star to ponder the possibility that his coach had actually goaded the pair into producing their best football.

Adams – who retired after the 1964 Grand Final, and, along with Barassi, joined Collingwood's Collier brothers as the only players to win six premierships[96] – had his own theory on Smith's motivations for the pre-finals outburst:

> I think Norm had been desperate to rev us up and he was struggling to find something, so he latched onto this relatively minor thing regarding young Frank Davis having a bath on his own. By that stage, Melbourne as a team was graphing down, so Norm probably felt he had to pull any rotten caper he could.
>
> He also picked his mark. He knew we wouldn't drop our bundles and cry. He knew we'd hit back harder, and that's the exact response he wanted. I mean, I was trying really hard, but then I had that extra bit of venom: 'I'll show that bastard!'
>
> I never even spoke to Norm about it.
>
> All Norm said was: 'It was worth it to win a flag'. But he didn't go on with it. There was no explanation. Nothing else mattered at that stage.[97]

Despite his success that day, Smith was certainly in no mood to be trifled with on that premiership evening. Talent scout Stan Rule had pre-arranged to take a promising young footballer to meet the coach at the Grand Final dinner at 8pm. Smith had suggested the time and place. Rule said: 'It sounds like a strange time to meet, but Smithy believed a player could get no better introduction to a club than on the night of a premiership, because the club portrays itself in its best light. There's the success, the good times, everyone's talking about how good the club is, how good the coach and committee are, and everyone's happy and friendly. He said: "Just get him down here, Stan! A kid would be mad not to want to come down here and play with us after soaking up a night like that".'

Not everyone was friendly, but Smith quickly 'fixed it'. Rule said:

---

[96] Hawthorn's Michael Tuck, the AFL's games record-holder, holds the record with seven premierships (from 1976-91). Also, of the 21 players to have won at least five premierships, eight of them played under Norm Smith at Melbourne. Aside from Barassi and Adams, the six Demons with five flags were John Beckwith, Brian Dixon, Big Bob Johnson, Laurie Mithen, Ian Ridley and Don Williams.

[97] Frank 'Bluey' Adams. Interview with the author.

I told the bloke on the gate: 'I have an appointment to see Norm Smith and Jim Cardwell about this young lad'.

He said: 'You haven't got a ticket, so I'm not letting you in'.

I said: 'Well we'll just wait here then'.

Not long after, Smithy comes along and says: 'What's the problem?'

I said: 'I've just been knocked back at the gate because I haven't got a ticket'.

Norm said to the gateman: 'Open the gate and let them in'.

The fella said: 'I'm sorry, I can't'.

Smithy said: 'Stan and the kid are coming in!'

Smithy ripped the gate open – he nearly ripped it off – and then he slammed it – BANG! – and broke the bloke's hand. That was that.

Norm was great with the kid. On one of the biggest nights of his coaching career, when everyone wanted to talk to him, he took time to talk to the kid, and took a real interest in him. How many other premiership coaches would have done that? He was unique.[98]

Smith had also entered new territory by becoming the first man to win 10 premierships: four as a player and six as a coach. (He also figured in two reserves flags.) In 1977, this record would be equalled, fittingly, by Ron Barassi, although in reverse order: six as a player, four as coach. In creating this remarkable record, Smith had surpassed Jock McHale's nine flags (including eight as coach), and also moved past both Checker Hughes and Jack Worrall, and into second place behind McHale, on the premiership coaches' ladder.

Barassi said of this achievement: 'I know coaches can't win premierships without good players, and during Melbourne's great years we had many great players. Norm's greatness lay in his being able to make all these players keep their noses to the grindstone, year in, year out. Without him, we would have certainly won two premierships, we may have won three, but he won six'.[99]

Melbourne's annual report trumpeted: 'We are indeed fortunate to have a man of his ability... He stands without comparison as the Number One Coach in Australian Football today'.

In 11 successive seasons of finals action from 1954-64, Norm Smith had guided the Demons in 221 matches for 165 wins, 53 losses and 3 draws – at the astonishing success rate of 74.66 percent. They had also won 16 of their 23 finals – with an

---

[98] Stan Rule. Interview with the author.
[99] Ron Barassi's speech at Norm Smith's testimonial dinner at Melbourne Town Hall on December 20, 1967. Recorded in *Trident Monthly*, April 1968.

average winning margin of 40 points and (barring the 51-point loss to Footscray in the 1954 Grand Final) an average loss of just 13 points.

In his excellent book, *Immortals: football people and the evolution of Australian Rules*, Lionel Frost noted: 'The magnitude of Norm Smith's contribution to Melbourne can be illustrated by the following point: Melbourne's first hundred years... produced only two flags in the 70 seasons that Smith was not involved as a player or coach; in the 30 seasons in which Smith was actively involved with the club, it won 10 flags'.[100]

As this striking statistic reveals, the Demons' run of premierships came to an abrupt end after 1964, and their tally has not been added to since. However, before 1964 was over, they managed to enjoy another slice of success when they travelled to Adelaide to take on SANFL premier South Adelaide. In a hard-fought encounter under lights at Norwood Oval, Melbourne won by 11 points. South Adelaide coach Neil Kerley – who became a football legend in his own right – vividly remembered having the 'rare privilege of picking Norm Smith's brain'. The morning after the match, Smith visited Kerley at the hotel he owned and the pair discussed football for 'about two-and-a-half hours'. Kerley recalled: 'Norm did most of the talking; I did most of the listening. I fired all sorts of questions at him and he gladly obliged. Time with great men like Norm Smith is precious and I made the most of it. He was very strong on discipline and teamwork, and he kept talking about the importance of 'the first give' – that players bust their guts to get into a position to receive and if you keep ignoring them eventually they won't give you that option; they'll stop running, and if that happens you're stuffed. So the discipline and the teamwork and the first give were all interlinked – if you fell down in one of those areas, you'd fall down in all areas. It was a very enlightening experience, and I was able to use some of what Norm said successfully in my coaching career'.[101]

ŸŸŸŸŸŸŸŸŸ

A month before the 1964 finals series, Len Smith approached Ron Barassi with a startling proposal.

'Ronny,' Len began, 'I would like you to seriously consider coming to Richmond as captain-coach.'

Barassi was understandably taken aback.

---

[100] Frost, Lionel, *Immortals: football people and the evolution of Australian Rules*, John Wiley & Sons, 2005.
[101] Neil Kerley. Interview with the author.

'I can't do that; *you're* the coach of Richmond,' he said.

Len said: 'With the way my health is, it's becoming a bit too difficult for me to be the head coach. A younger man such as yourself would be ideal. But I don't plan to step aside completely; I'm proposing that I become your *assistant* coach. That way, you can look after things on the field, and I can look after things off the field, and we can work together to bring some success to Richmond.'[102]

After he overcame his initial shock, Barassi – who had harboured coaching ambitions for some time – became very interested in making the move across Jolimont Park. Barassi was in awe of Len's selflessness. 'What man would voluntarily step aside... to put the interests of his club before his own coaching career?' he marvelled. 'It was a real example of the depth and quality of Len Smith – the football coach, the man.'[103]

Len had endured a tough debut season at Richmond. In addition to – and perhaps as a result of – his health issues, the Tigers hadn't performed as well as he had expected. After being 3-2, they won just three more matches (all in the space of four rounds). Although they had finished ninth, their tally of six wins – three wins short of Len's pre-season aim – had been the club's best performance in six years.

Len said that while the Tigers had 'done nothing outstanding',[104] he believed they had progressed, 'mainly in team spirit, which is the basis of any club'. Furthermore, they had developed an attitude more conducive to achieving success. 'This year,' Len explained, 'Richmond developed a will to win – and when they were beaten, it hurt. For instead of... expecting defeat, they expected to win'.

As for Len's self-analysis, he felt he had 'only got into the run of things in the last six weeks of the season'.[105] He had also 'taken stock'[106] of the Tigers situation, assessed the playing list and realised that hard decisions needed to be made on many careers. (By the start of the 1965 season, he axed 26 of their 47 players.)

Len had made it clear to Tigers president Ray Dunn and secretary Graeme Richmond that the club needed at least one established star to accelerate its rise up the ladder. The perfect candidate was Barassi. Len told the Tiger officials of his idea to lure the Melbourne skipper to Richmond as captain-coach. They gave Len the go-ahead. After Len's initial approach, the president and secretary became involved in official, though still preliminary, talks with Barassi, who became increasingly keen on the prospect of making the switch to Punt Road.

---

[102] Ron Barassi. Interview with the author.
[103] *The Australian*, Wednesday May 12, 1965.
[104] *The Sporting Globe*, 1964.
[105] *The Herald*.
[106] *The Sporting Globe*.

The problem for the Tigers was they were negotiating with Melbourne Cricket Club about becoming co-tenants with the Demons at the MCG. Dunn soon abandoned the pursuit of Barassi because he was concerned that it would jeopardise their move, which would provide the Tigers with a financial windfall and secure the club's future.

When this was announced publicly, Richmond great Jack Dyer expressed his relief, saying that a Barassi-Smith coaching combination probably would not have worked anyway. 'I am glad Ron Barassi is not going to Richmond,' Dyer wrote in *Truth*. 'He would have brought about a pretty ticklish situation... I don't see how Len Smith could have successfully coached the side with Barassi without causing some friction along the line. They appear to me to be two different types.'[107]

Disappointed but not crestfallen about the Barassi backdown, Len set about enacting the next part of his blueprint for success: recruiting and developing a superior breed of footballers. 'As a coach I have always wanted big, fast men,' Len revealed. 'I prefer six-foot (183cm) flankers, even wingmen, to smaller men, but they must have pace.' The man who would prove pivotal in recruiting footballers of such rare athleticism to accede to Len's requirements was Graeme Richmond. The Tigers secretary attacked his job with zeal because he believed in Len's plan. In the club's annual report, Richmond enthused: 'Brighter days are ahead. The tremendous potential of our players, supplemented by an influx of good recruits, will be exploited to the fullest by the coaching genius of Len Smith'.

Ruckman Neville Crowe (later Richmond president from 1987-93), who in 1964 won the second of his three Tiger best-and-fairest awards, described some of Len's genius: 'I learnt more in one season with Len Smith than I learnt with anyone else I ever worked with. He was just a mastermind! ... He showed us such a lot in a scientific manner for those days ... what a ball can do when it's in transition from being kicked; how quickly a man can get from player A to player B while the ball is in the air. (Before then) you never thought about it, that someone could run 50 yards while the ball was being kicked in the air'.[108]

But even in his reverence of Len's coaching powers, Graeme Richmond disagreed with Len on one aspect of football – physicality. The Tiger secretary believed in brutality – fair or foul – while Len felt compelled to play fair or not at all. Before an important match against Footscray, Richmond told Len they needed to send a player onto the field with the specific instruction to 'knock out Johnny Schultz', the Bulldogs' champion ruckman and 1960 Brownlow Medallist.

---

[107] *Melbourne Truth*, Saturday October 3, 1964.
[108] Bartlett, Rhett, *Richmond Football Club: A Century of League Football*, GSP, 2007.

'What?!' said Len. 'Knock him out?! Johnny Schultz played under me in the state side – he's a lovely bloke. You can't touch him.'

Richmond thought: 'Christ, what have we got here? We're in this to win football matches any way we bloody can, not to be nice people'.[109]

Three years later, a rugged youngster from VFA club Prahran named Kevin Sheedy fell foul of Len's beliefs on this front. Sheedy (who went on to play in three premierships with Richmond and coach Essendon to four flags) flattened an opponent in a practice match, prompting Len, then a selector, to tell the youngster he didn't think he should 'play like that'. The effect on Sheedy? 'I think I just did the same thing from then on (but) with a bit more decorum.'[110]

Len was also man enough to concede his own failings. He initially didn't rate John Northey, the will-o-the-wisp half-forward flanker who had debuted in 1963. But once Northey had established himself in the senior side, Len told him: 'I never thought you'd make a league footballer'. But, as Northey recalled, Len was 'prepared, as we all should be, to admit our mistakes to our players'.[111]

Although the plan to lure Barassi to Richmond had been unsuccessful, the superstar's coaching aspirations continued to gather momentum. He was soon approached by Carlton, and thus began one of the most controversial and talked-about sagas in football history.

Norm Smith was – both directly and indirectly – a key figure in the decision-making process. As Barassi considered his future, he had a number of lengthy, emotional discussions with his coach and mentor. They met in several places, including the Smith house in Pascoe Vale, the holiday home in Rosebud and even in Smith's car in the MCG carpark.

Smith had increasingly come to see Barassi as coaching material. Two years earlier, when asked of Barassi's coaching potential, he said: 'He has the ingredients for success. He loves football, he's a good talker and he can inspire players. But he can be a bit of a hot-head. Who knows what pattern his coaching will follow. If it is my style, he will be a mixture of Bull Adams, Checker Hughes, myself and whatever other coaches I have pinched ideas from. And he'll toss in a few ideas of his own'.[112]

---

[109] Wayne Walsh, Richmond and South Melbourne player. Interview with the author.
[110] *The Sunday Herald*, April 22, 1990.
[111] *The Sunday Herald*, April 22, 1990.
[112] *Melbourne Truth* series, 1962.

In return, Barassi believed that his coaching education had been fast-tracked by his close association with the Smith brothers, but in particular Norm Smith, who he said had virtually 'trained' him for a mentoring role.[113]

From the time Barassi had settled into the captaincy, many Melbourne people had taken for granted that his first – and hopefully last – coaching job would be at Demonland. Melbourne appeared to have the best succession plan in the VFL. It seemed logical – and almost inevitable – that Barassi would finish his playing career at Melbourne sometime in the mid to late '60s, by which time he would be ready to make the transition to coaching and Norm Smith would be ready to relinquish that role and assume another leadership position within the club. That assumption was now in tatters.

Smith was so desperate to keep Barassi at Melbourne that he offered to surrender the coaching position to him. But it wasn't the coach's decision to make. He could certainly step down as coach, but the decision about his replacement would be made by the Melbourne committee. Barassi later admitted he was 'very touched' by the gesture.[114] 'It was a fairly unusual situation,' he said. 'First Len had offered to stand aside for me at Richmond, and here Norm was, offering to do the same thing – just after winning his sixth premiership in 10 years! All this for an untried coach! But it showed that both men were wholly and solely concerned with what was best for the club – their own interests didn't even come into the equation. Although it must be said that in this case, the best thing for their clubs was to have them coaching, not me. I wasn't a better option than either of them.'[115]

Smith lamented that Barassi 'wasn't particularly interested' in his offer, and rejected it immediately. He said: 'I know one reason he wouldn't consider it was out of loyalty to me. He said it was my job and the last thing he wanted to do was take it from me before I was ready to give it up.'[116] But ultimately, it wouldn't have mattered how Barassi responded, because the committee refused to entertain the idea of Norm Smith vacating his position. It certainly would have been strange if the club had agreed to Smith's proposal, given his record and the fact that Barassi was untried, albeit perhaps the most credentialed untried coach of all. He was, after all, a virtual playing-coach.

---

[113] *The AFL Record*, May 16-18, 2003.
[114] Collins, Ben, *The Champions: Conversations with Great Players and Coaches of Australian Football*, GSP, 2006.
[115] Ron Barassi. Interview with the author.
[116] *The Sun* series, 1967.

THE GREATEST PREMIERSHIP [1964]

The last weeks of 1964 was an agonising period for Barassi, who described it as 'one of the hardest decisions I've ever made in my life'.[117] He changed his mind several times in as many weeks because he just couldn't bring himself to leave his beloved Demons – the emotional pull was too great. On the other hand, he knew he had a golden opportunity to begin his coaching career at Carlton, one of the most well-supported and parochial clubs in the VFL, and he had been offered a small fortune to do it – £3000-a-season for three seasons, and a £10,000 loan that he ultimately put towards buying a partition company – the kind of money he would never have received at Melbourne.

The clincher for Barassi was a conversation he had with a mate, who asked him: 'If you stay at Melbourne, you'll probably be coach one day, won't you?'

Barassi nodded. 'Possibly.'

'What'll happen to Norm?'

'Hopefully he'll be my chairman of selectors,' Barassi said.

His mate made a valid point. 'You know what'll happen then; whatever success Melbourne has, they'll say it was all due to the old fox in the background.'

Barassi thought: 'Bloody hell, that's right!' Not only did it make sense from a human nature perspective, but it actually mirrored the early part of Smith's coaching career at Melbourne, when Checker Hughes was the 'old fox' in the background. It also reminded Barassi of the sad fallout between Smith and Hughes on the bench in 1956. Barassi said: 'I saw that happen with my own two eyes and I didn't want it to happen to Norm and I because we had so much history together. So I decided: "I'll get out so I can see if I'm a good coach in my own right. That way, if I succeed it's mine, and if I fail it's mine'."[118]

Smith had told Barassi: 'My only condition is that I want to be told personally by you that you have signed. I don't want to read it in the papers (first)'. When Barassi had decided to take the Carlton job, he made his way to Rosebud where the Smiths were enjoying their Christmas holidays. Smith recalled: 'It was typical of the boy that he drove 40 or 50 miles down there to tell me his final decision rather than let me read about it'. During another thorough discussion, Barassi's strong sense of pride shone through. Smith recalled: '(He) wanted to prove he could stand on his own feet, away from my influence, (and) the Carlton job was just the sort of challenge that appealed to him'.

---

[117] *The AFL Record*, July 28-30, 2000.
[118] Collins, Ben, *The Champions: Conversations with Great Players and Coaches of Australian Football*, GSP, 2006.

Smith was impressed with the high expectations Barassi had placed on himself. 'He said to me at the time that his ambition was to do as well as I had done as a coach,' Smith said. 'Remember that we had just won a premiership... and won six flags. But that was the sort of target he set himself to achieve to be a success'.[119]

Once Smith was convinced there was no possible chance of Barassi remaining at Melbourne, he pledged his unreserved support of his move. But Barassi could not have known the level of support Smith would demonstrate, or the lengths he would be willing to go for him... or that he would be criticised and questioned about his motives for providing such staunch support.

Barassi still needed to obtain a clearance from the Demons. Melbourne committeemen were divided on whether they should grant Barassi his wish. The debate was heated and prolonged, and caused a bitter row between Smith and Checker Hughes.[120] Smith was the strongest advocate for clearing Barassi; Hughes was the most vocal in opposing it. Both made impassioned pleas stating their case before the committee. Smith later explained: 'The people who voiced their opposition were only right – he would be a tremendous loss... But in my case, I knew more about his background than anyone else. I knew what he had given to the club. He had played 204 games and shown the club tremendous loyalty'.[121] He also believed 'it was time for (Barassi)... to look after himself' and his young family financially,[122] realising that 'if he had stayed on at Melbourne, he could not have earned a quarter of what he would make at Carlton'.[123] And finally, he felt it was pointless to oppose the clearance because Barassi would have won it on appeal.[124]

The Melbourne committee granted Barassi's clearance by the barest margin – seven votes to five. The football world spun on its axis. Club loyalty, long considered paramount, had seemingly been discarded in favour of personal ambition. Rarely, if ever, before or since, had a player so closely-entwined with the history of a football club defected in such circumstances. Never had it taken place so publicly, or with such a backlash from supporters. Smith defended Barassi, saying: 'People have condemned him for doing what he did. But they must remember he was one of the many members of the club responsible for our great success around this period. He was due for some reward'.[125]

---

[119] *The Sun* series, 1967.
[120] Alf Brown, *The Herald*, Saturday, July 24, 1965.
[121] *The Sun* series, 1967.
[122] *Melbourne Truth*, Saturday, July 31, 1965.
[123] *The Sun* series, 1967.
[124] *Melbourne Truth*, Saturday, July 31, 1965.
[125] *The Sun* series, 1967.

The coach himself was also a subject of condemnation, along with conspiracy theories and innuendo. He had been so strong in his support of Barassi's move to Carlton that malicious rumours soon circulated that he had acted out a charade, and manipulated the situation to his own advantage. It was suggested that he had campaigned for Barassi's clearance with the sole aim of removing the greatest threat to his coaching job. Barassi dismissed such talk as 'the biggest load of codswallop of all time, and a bloody insult. Norm was not like that at all'.[126]

Peter Smith was similarly adamant: 'Dad didn't have any ulterior motives or hidden agendas. What did he have to be protective of? Dad's attitude was: "I don't have to protect myself. I'm the coach and I've coached six premierships in the past 10 years. What do I need to be worried about?" He was at his peak as a coach – he wasn't in any danger of anyone taking his job off him'.[127]

Norm Smith was bewildered by the speculation. 'To say I would sacrifice a champion and such an admirable man as Ron Barassi for my personal security is a terrible accusation,' he said. 'Yet this was suggested to me by a committeeman... It could be thought, he said, that my support for Barassi was purely one of self-protection. It seems they do not remember that my wife Marj and I raised Ron Barassi as our son from the time he was 16. I admire, respect and treasure our friendship. I was acting only in his best interests'.[128]

This almost slanderous allegation was utterly baseless, and had already been proven so by Smith's offer to vacate the coaching position for his protégé. Smith had done everything in his power to try to keep Barassi, but once Barassi had made up his mind he then did everything in his power to help him.

Barassi left Melbourne with the unspoken understanding that he would return as coach... one day. Some Demons felt that the original succession plan would still be fulfilled: that Barassi would coach Carlton for two, three, maybe even four seasons, and take over when Norm Smith retired.

In the meantime, Barassi spoke of his relationship with Smith: 'We've never been closer... He's a great man; he's offered to help me in any way coaching-wise, (with) any problems... He knows the trouble about leaving a club that he had had a lot of association with and (then) going to a new one. Any way he can help me, well, he will'.[129]

---

[126] Collins, Ben, *The Champions: Conversations with Great Players and Coaches of Australian Football*, GSP, 2006.
[127] Peter Smith. Interview with the author.
[128] *Melbourne Truth*, Saturday July 31, 1965.
[129] Channel Seven, early 1965.

Smith and Barassi were both condemned after this controversial transfer became official, but the biggest loser was Melbourne Football Club. The Demons have not won a premiership since Barassi left. But, inconceivably, worse was to come just seven months later, when the Demons and Norm Smith would endure perhaps the most traumatic period of their respective lives.

🏆🏆🏆🏆🏆🏆🏆🏆

In the summer of 1964/65, Norm Smith (then aged 49) captained Melbourne Football Club's cricket team in a series of social matches held at the Albert Ground on Wednesday afternoons.

In a game against 'The 29 Club', or 'The 29-ers' – a club for hit-and-giggle players within Melbourne Cricket Club – Smith fronted up against his old premiership captain and now committeeman Don Cordner. It was Cordner's first match in 10 years, so when he walked out to bat – after Smith had taken a wicket – Smith gathered his team around him and said: 'This is Don Cordner's first game in a long time, so let's give him a chance out here'.

Cordner recalled: 'I reckon Norm had me LBW first ball. He jumped up in the air and went: "Uh-", but didn't appeal, so I couldn't be given out. I then realised what Norm was up to. I said in a loud voice: "Thank you very much!" I went on to make about 40, and thoroughly enjoyed myself, and it was because of Norm's willingness to give me a chance'.[130]

Rarely again would relations be so cordial between the coach and a committeeman.

---

[130] Don Cordner. Interview with the author.

24

CALM BEFORE THE STORM

[1965]

In the wake of Ron Barassi's departure, Melbourne was left with the decision of appointing a new captain. Hassa Mann, then 24, appeared the logical choice after serving as Barassi's deputy in 1964, but the Demons also had to consider whether the honour should be bestowed upon a more experienced player.

One man who felt ready to fill the void was Brian Dixon. The champion wingman had been vice-captain in 1963 but had lost the title to Mann without explanation. In June 1964, Dixon (then 28) was elected as the Liberal MP for the state seat of St Kilda,[1] but his new role did not affect his football as he was clearly Melbourne's best player in the 1964 final series. Dixon decided to put his name forward as a candidate for the captaincy. 'Even though I was in parliament,' Dixon said, 'I thought it was not unreasonable that I be considered as a replacement for Ron.'[2]

Only months earlier, Dixon had written: 'Under Norm Smith, football has become an absorbing study to me, a great source of satisfaction and pleasure... To me, he is a great man, a man of integrity, modesty and genuine love of his players, combined with a paradoxical hate and ruthlessness to anything against the team's interest... Ideally, a coach must always love his players. Norman Smith owes much of his success to this quality, so elusive in others'.[3]

Armed with this knowledge, Dixon and his first wife, Marie, visited the Smiths at Rosebud in January 1965. Over a meal, Dixon broached the subject

---

[1] Brian Dixon held the St Kilda seat until 1982. Under Rupert Hamer's regime, Dixon also held various portfolios including Youth, Sport and Recreation; Social Welfare; Housing; and Employment and Training.
[2] Brian Dixon. Interview with the author.
[3] Pollard, Jack (editor), *High Mark: The Complete Book on Australian Football*, Murray, 1964.

of the captaincy. 'Seeing Ron has left,' he told Smith, 'I believe I have reasonable credentials to be the captain, and I hope you will seriously consider me for it.'[4]

Smith didn't need to be reminded of Dixon's credentials – he had enormous respect for his playing ability. The previous year, both Norm and Len Smith had rated Dixon with Collingwood's Thorold Merrett as the best of the post-war wingers; and, furthermore, that he 'would not suffer by comparison with any giant of the past'.[5]

But, Dixon conceded, Smith 'wasn't very impressed' with the suggestion.

He told Dixon: 'You won't be captain, Brian. We're going for a younger man'.

Dixon, in turn, wasn't impressed. He left shortly after, his pride considerably dented. Dixon wasn't even appointed *vice*-captain. That honour went to Bryan Kenneally, soon to turn 23. Dixon said: 'I was naturally disappointed, but I certainly didn't harbour any ill feeling over it. And it certainly didn't affect my football'.[6]

Although Mann became the youngest skipper in the VFL at the time – he was eight months younger than Essendon's Ken Fraser – he was seemingly as prepared as anyone to take on the job. He had played finals in each of his first six seasons, was a three-time premiership player, had won back-to-back best-and-fairest awards in 1962-63, had represented Victoria and was regarded as a big-game performer. However, he was not made aware of the decision to appoint him until late in the practice match period. Mann said:

> I was given no indication that I would be captain. I thought I was a big chance but, just like anyone else, I had to prove myself again by performing in the practice games. But that was Norm – he was always big on making you earn your stripes, and then he would take pleasure in telling you: 'You've earnt this'. He basically told me: 'You've been appointed captain. The club has given a lot of thought about you as a person and as a player, and we feel the best thing you can do as captain is to continue to be a consistent team player and lead from the front'.

Mann was one of Smith's greatest supporters. He explained that he accepted his coach's word as gospel:

> Like Barass, I was an unashamed disciple of Norm's. I would have been labelled as 'a Norm Smith man', and I had no problem with that, because any success

---

[4] Brian Dixon. Interview with the author.
[5] *Pollard*, Jack (editor), *High Mark: The Complete Book on Australian Football*, Murray, 1964.
[6] Brian Dixon. Interview with the author.

I had in football and business I attribute to Norm. I achieved more than my ability warranted and I credit Norm with dragging that out of me.

He taught me more than football; he taught me about life. Norm felt that you came to the football club as a player and you left as a better player and, more importantly, a better person. The principles and fundamentals he taught me as a footballer are the principles of life. I applied those principles – honesty, hard work, ethics, etc. – to my own life. Norm Smith was the greatest influence on me, and was the person who, for good or bad, made me who I am today.[7]

Mann replaced Barassi in other ways, too. He became the coach's favourite whipping boy on the training track and during addresses. Young Stan Alves was shocked by the ferocity of some of Smith's attacks on his skipper. Alves recalled:

> He was incredibly hard on Hassa Mann, often without justification. This... really upset me and I told Hassa that if he didn't say something I would. It was then that I was let into one of the club's best-kept secrets. 'Don't even think about it,' Hassa said, 'he's told me he's gonna get stuck into me. Not because I've done anything wrong, but he knows if he gets into some of the other players they'll drop their bundle.'[8]

One such attack on Mann jeopardised the recruitment of a talented youngster. At half-time one day, Smith was berating his skipper: 'You weak-gutted bastard! Get that jumper off and show these blokes your yellow belly and the yellow streak down your back!'

When Smith had finished and had calmed down, recruiter Stan Rule approached him and introduced him to the youngster. 'Norm,' Rule said, 'I'd like you to meet this young man with me who has plenty of football ability and he's interested in playing with Melbourne. I thought I'd just bring him down here so he can see what happens. Also, as a matter of interest, his father is a reverend.'

Smith's eyes 'nearly popped out of his head'.

'Why didn't you tell me before?!' Smith exclaimed.

'I didn't have time,' Rule said, 'because you were going off your rocker.'

Smith quietly turned to Rule and said: 'I've already got one strike against me because I'm not a believer; now He might strike me down where I bloody stand!'[9]

---

[7] Hassa Mann. Interview with the author.
[8] Alves, Stan with Col Davies, *Sacked Coach*, Crown Content, 2002.
[9] Stan Rule. Interview with the author.

On another occasion, Smith attracted the attention of the law with his strong language. During the practice match period leading up to the 1965 season, Smith decided to trial a couple of innovations. Sam Allica recalled:

> Norm had the idea that he wanted to watch the game from an elevated position in the stands. A lot of people have taken credit for it over the years, but Norm was the first one. The next logical step was finding a way to communicate down to the bench. Norm decided: 'We'll use walkie-talkies.'
>
> The cricket club gave him permission to use a box in the stand (at the MCG), and he decided to trial it in a practice match. George De Morton was the middle man between Smithy and I on the bench – he'd take Norm's message and relay it to me. We also had Hughie McPherson sitting on a bench on the other wing with a walkie-talkie. It wasn't long into the game when around came a policeman. He asked George: 'Are you using walkie-talkies?'
>
> George said: 'Yes we are, officer. What's the problem?'
>
> The officer said: 'Well, if you keep using them someone's going to jail'.
>
> I think he was just winding us up. But George pooped himself; he said: 'What? What do you mean? We can't go to jail for that can we?'
>
> The officer said: 'Every taxi that comes within about 200 metres of this ground can hear everything you say, and some of the language isn't very complimentary'.
>
> That nipped that idea in the bud until they improved communications.[10]

Smith wasn't the first man to experiment with technology in football. In fact, he wasn't even the first man in his family to do it. Four years earlier, Len Smith had actually tried something far more radical. With the help of sound technicians at Channel Seven, Len tested a communication system similar to what is used in American football. During a training session at Fitzroy, Len's voice was transmitted from a microphone to a small earpiece taped to a player's ear. However, the idea didn't progress beyond novelty value because it was deemed impractical.

The Smith brothers faced each other in round one, 1965, when co-tenants Richmond and Melbourne clashed at the MCG. The Tigers had not beaten Melbourne at the MCG since 1951, but Norm Smith's pre-season declaration to his players that the 1965 season would be 'a year of challenge to every player on the list'[11] appeared accurate, with their six-point win hardly impressive. A relieved

---

[10] Sam Allica. Interview with the author.
[11] Melbourne Football Club program for second practice match, 1965.

CALM BEFORE THE STORM [1965]

Norm Smith conceded: 'We were lucky to win'.[12] It was to be the last 'battle of the brothers', with Norm finally gaining the upper-hand after seven years – he had four wins (by an average of 35 points), three losses (ave. 19 points) and two draws.

A fortnight later – after just three rounds – Len Smith's coaching career came to an abrupt halt. On Tuesday May 4, he conducted the Tigers' training session and attended a selection committee meeting until 10.30pm. Shortly after arriving home, he suffered his third heart attack. He was admitted to Sacred Heart Hospital in Moreland (near Coburg) and spent some weeks recovering.

The Herald's Alf Brown lamented: 'Richmond will miss Smith tremendously. Although they have not won a game this year, they have done well against three strong sides in Melbourne, Collingwood and St Kilda. Under Smith, and on the MCG, they have become a drawcard'.

That week, the Tigers dedicated their performance to their fallen coach – and with club legend Jack Titus standing in as caretaker coach – delivered on some of their promise against eventual premier Essendon at Windy Hill. Len had smuggled a transistor radio into his room so he could listen to the match. But by half-time in the broadcast, with Richmond leading by nine points, a nurse – mindful of the need for Len to rest completely without any source of stress during his convalescence – confiscated the radio. Len again broke the rules by getting out of his bed and arguing that there could be nothing worse for his ailing heart than the suspense of not knowing whether his Tigers had gone on with the job. He need not have worried, however, as the Tigers controlled the second half and won by 24 points. Len told friends that the win was the best tonic for his health.[13]

One of Len's many visitors was new Carlton coach Ron Barassi, who stated publicly: 'Unfortunately for football, it looks as though Len is finished as a coach… He is too good a man to be out of football, and… if Richmond is foolish enough to let him go, I would turn Carlton inside out to get him there in some capacity'.[14]

On doctor's orders, Len resigned as Richmond coach in May 1965. When he was well enough, he joined the Tigers selection committee and gave the odd lecture to players. He couldn't stay away from the game. 'Football is my life,' he said.

🏆🏆🏆🏆🏆🏆🏆🏆🏆

---

[12] Contemporary newspaper report.
[13] Ron Barassi, *The Australian*, Wednesday May 12, 1965.
[14] *The Australian*, Wednesday May 12, 1965.

Len Smith's last significant act as a coach was to blood a jockey-sized 18-year-old named Kevin Bartlett in round three. He informed Bartlett of his promotion by simply saying: 'This week you will be 19th man'.

Bartlett took it to mean he would be the 19th man in the reserves.

Surprised at the youngster's lack of enthusiasm, Len asked: 'Aren't you happy?'

Bartlett explained that he felt his form in the previous two reserves games had warranted another game in the starting 18.

'No, no,' Len reassured him. 'You're 19th man for the *seniors*.'[15]

Bartlett played a little over a quarter on debut – in an 11-point loss to St Kilda at Punt Road – but impressed his coach. After the match, Len asked Saints' coach Allan Jeans: 'What did you think of that skinny little kid of mine?'

'He's quick,' Jeans said, 'but I haven't seen enough of him yet.'

'Don't you worry about him, Allan,' Len said with near certainty. 'He'll be a great player'.[16] And so he was.[17]

'Sadly,' Bartlett recalled, 'my very first game was Len Smith's last game.'[18]

Unbeknown to Norm Smith, his coaching career at Melbourne was coming towards its own end, although it wouldn't become apparent for some weeks.

As he had often done in the past, Smith drew the attention of his players to photographs of Melbourne premiership teams and said: 'Forget about them. What matters is the space at the end – we've got to fill those too'.[19]

The Demons appeared to be on their way to do just that when they stormed to their best start to a season since 1956. They won their first eight games to be the outright league leader – a game clear of Geelong, two games clear of St Kilda, and three clear of eventual premier Essendon and Carlton. Wins over Collingwood (their 20th over the Magpies in their previous 25 encounters) and the previously undefeated Cats were meritorious, as was their eighth successive victory – over the Barassi-led Carlton at Princes Park. The Blues had won just five matches for the entire 1964 season. Barassi had lifted them to five wins after just seven rounds, and had beaten Essendon, Geelong and Collingwood.

---

[15] Bartlett, Rhett, *Richmond Football Club: A Century of League Football*, GSP, 2007.
[16] Allan Jeans. Interview with the author.
[17] Kevin Bartlett went on to play a then VFL record 403 games and kick 778 goals for Richmond between 1965 and 1983. He is an official Legend of Australian Football.
[18] Bartlett, Rhett, *Richmond Football Club: A Century of League Football*, GSP, 2007.
[19] *The Sun*, Saturday July 31, 1965.

Percy Beames previewed the Carlton-Melbourne clash in *The Age*: 'It is the first meeting of the pupil with the master... Melbourne's pride would be hurt and Smith's prestige lowered if Barassi came out... to lead Carlton to victory over undefeated Melbourne. As far as Barassi and Smith are concerned, the next six days will be something like the week before a Grand Final. Everything possible will be done by each coach to get the maximum of effort, thought, courage, determination, physical fitness and team effort out of every player chosen for the game'.[20]

Smith also tried to play mind games with Barassi, who said:

'Norm had gone through the same thing himself at Fitzroy, and I'd seen first-hand how cut up he was by the prospect of playing against his mates from his old club. So he had an advantage: he knew how I would be feeling, and how emotionally tough it would be. It would have been hard enough just coaching against them, but playing as well was even tougher. Norm milked it for all it was worth, too, to make sure I was as nervous as hell. The bloody umpire had to go in twice to tell them to come out. They took so long that the umpy could almost have started the game without them. I didn't know what to do. I'd revved up the players, and revved myself up, and yet we had to bloody wait. It was excruciating. I thought: "You bloody cunning old fox! I know what you're up to!" It had the desired effect, though'.[21]

Before the match, Smith had been informed that a supporter had offered to give the Demons £50 for each goal Melbourne won by. Smith declined the offer because he didn't want his players to feel they were playing for any special monetary reward. They didn't really need any incentive anyway. He had told his players something along the lines of: 'As much as we love Ronny, he's playing with the opposition, so don't give him any concessions. Treat him as you would any other opposition player'.[22] He had also hatched a plan to limit the effectiveness of both Barassi and gun ruckman John Nicholls. Smith assigned Bryan Kenneally the task of stopping Barassi, while Graham Wise was to fiercely contest Nicholls and other on-ballers were to ensure the Blues big man's taps didn't reach Barassi or rover Adrian Gallagher. It worked a treat. Although Barassi gathered 'about three possessions in the first 90 seconds' and thought: 'I'm in for a big day here', he 'hardly got a kick after that'.[23] In fact, Barassi performed 'like a nervous recruit',

---

[20] *The Age*, May 31, 1965.
[21] Ron Barassi. Interview with the author.
[22] John Lord in an interview with the author.
[23] Ron Barassi. Interview with the author.

and that he had 'made more mistakes than he had in all his previous games this season'.[24]

Barassi reflected: 'Norm won the first battle between us, but there would be others where my side had the upper-hand'. (Barassi won nine of his next 10 head-to-head encounters with Norm Smith. It must be said, though, that Barassi was in charge of clearly superior sides.) Barassi regretted that he never sought advice from Smith about coaching. 'I wanted to show that I could work things out for myself,' he said. 'It was probably wrong, and a bit too proud on my part, because there were times when I didn't know how to handle something and probably needed advice. Norm certainly would have given me some if I needed it. He was an open book, just as Len was. I don't know if I would have been as giving as they were.'[25]

Beames observed: 'The important thing for Melbourne... was that it proved something it believed at the start of the season – that it could operate at a premiership level without Barassi... The unbeaten Demons deserve to be the top team in the League, both in prestige and position, and their chances of playing off in another Grand Final are second to none'.[26]

Barassi's iconic No. 31 guernsey had also been reallocated. Smith had always been excited by the potential of Ray Groom. In the youngster's first stint at Melbourne, he had had played in the Demons' fourths and thirds, before the death of his father lured him back to Tasmania at the age of 16. Smith had spoken to Groom's mother and said: 'I'd quite like to look after Ray. He could come and board with us'. The kind offer was not taken up, but it was nonetheless noted by Groom. Now, with Groom a strapping 20-year-old and a seeming heir apparent to Barassi's role in the Melbourne side, Smith offered him Barassi's number. 'I wasn't quite sure if I really wanted it,' Groom reflected. 'I'd played for two years and was quite proud of my number 15 guernsey. But I felt it was an honour, a privilege and a thrill to be asked by Norm, especially considering his close relationship with Ron.'[27]

---

[24] Percy Beames, *The Age*, Monday June 7, 1965.
[25] Ron Barassi. Interview with the author.
[26] *The Age*, Monday June 7, 1965.
[27] Ray Groom. Interview with the author. Groom later enjoyed a distinguished political career with the Liberal Party. He was the Federal Member for Braddon between 1975 and 1984, and Premier of Tasmania from 1992 to 1996. He said of Norm Smith: 'He's one of the great men I've come across in my life. You learn a lot of things from a man like Norm. For instance, when you're faced with tough times, you just have to hang in there and keep going. He never gave in, which is an important lesson in life'. When asked to ponder what kind of politician Smith might have made, Groom said: 'I don't think a career in politics would have suited Norm. It wouldn't have been his scene. He had very black and white views on things, which you can't always afford to have in public life. You need to compromise a bit, but he wasn't one to compromise'.

CALM BEFORE THE STORM [1965]

The Demons had won five of their eight matches by no more than eight points, and boasted just the fifth-best percentage in the competition, which indicated that their lofty status was perhaps inaccurate – a belief fully endorsed by Smith himself – but no-one could have predicted the dramatic decline that would follow. Unbelievably, the Demons would win just two of their remaining 10 matches and miss the finals for the first time in 12 years.

Smith still appeared to be at the top of his game. Former Demon full-back Peter Marquis, who travelled from Tasmania to watch Melbourne's round five victory over a strong Geelong at Kardinia Park, raved about Smith's inspiring oratory. 'Norm's speech at half-time was the best I've ever heard,' he said. 'Age hasn't mellowed Norm. His blistering speech... was 200 percent better than anything I've heard before.' It had a physical effect on Smith, too, with Demon officials later revealing that he was 'white and shaking' after delivering the speech.[28]

The rot started the week after the win at Carlton. In front of 72,000 people on the Queen's Birthday weekend, St Kilda belted Melbourne by 61 points at the MCG, with the second-half scoreline reading 10.8 to just 3.3. It was Melbourne's first 10-goal loss in Smith's reign, and the Demons biggest defeat since round nine 1951. While Saints coach Allan Jeans remarked: 'That was the day I knew I had a good side',[29] it also represented – in retrospect – the fall of a football empire. After further losses to Essendon and Richmond – it was their first loss to the Tigers (now coached by Titus) at the MCG in 14 years – in the next three weeks, the Demons had suddenly 'slumped' to 9-3. All three defeats had been at their MCG fortress.

All the while, other forces were at play, which destabilised the once rock-solid administration and, in turn, impacted on the players. In the days following the loss to Richmond, the Demons' on-field deterioration paled into insignificance when the club's off-field problems – between Norm Smith and the committee – exploded into the public forum. It would be the second aggressively debated furore to engulf the traditionally staid, scandal-free Melbourne Football Club in the space of just eight months. Although Barassi's exit had caused many to predict the Demons' downfall, the firestorm that erupted following the sacking of Norm Smith – with its allegations of back-biting, jealousy, pettiness, deceit, disloyalty, betrayal, and more – would seal their doom.

---

[28] Contemporary newspaper report.
[29] Allan Jeans. Interview with the author.

25

SACKED

[1965]

Norm Smith had always experienced problems with Melbourne's committee.[1] Privately, he often expressed his long-held view that 'the best football committee has three members, with two away sick'. Generally, though, during his time at Melbourne, any rough seas would be deftly negotiated with a minimum of fuss, and with all parties retaining their dignity. If Smith had an issue with something or someone, he would state his case – often quite strongly – to the person or people concerned and either a resolution would be reached or, at the very least, the friction would be smoothed. This process owed much to the honesty and diplomacy of both parties – the diplomacy usually being supplied by the likes of Jim Cardwell – and was a credit to the Demons' administrative strength, headed by worldly chairman Bert Chadwick. But since Chadwick's retirement in 1962, the leadership dynamics had changed and Smith believed the committee led by Don Duffy lacked the strength of the previous regime.

He often quarrelled with the committee because, as Ron Barassi once put it, 'people did not have the ability to match his drive and capacity for work'.[2] Smith had been concerned for several years that the committee was becoming soft, complacent and lazy. He took aside both Duffy and Cardwell and 'spoke to them as friends', warning: 'The club is slipping'.[3] But he also believed that his well-meaning warnings were being ignored – and, worse, were regarded as efforts to undermine their authority. He 'felt like he was beating his head against a brick wall',[4] and it became increasingly difficult for him to stop his frustration from boiling to the surface. He thought: 'Everybody can see it happening but the fools

---

[1] Norm Smith, *Melbourne Truth*, Saturday July 31, 1965.
[2] *Melbourne Truth*, August 1973.
[3] *The Tony Charlton Football Show*, Channel Nine, Sunday July 25, 1965.
[4] Hugh McPherson. Interview with the author.

who run it!'[5] He voiced his criticisms – strongly – telling certain committeemen he thought they were weak. And more than once around the bar, he had even referred to the committee as 'weak bastards'.

Even Ron Barassi believed that the committee had been 'spoiled' by success and 'had caught the fat cats' disease'.[6]

A major cause of Smith's discontent was the distinct lack of quality recruiting in recent seasons. Admittedly, the Demons had reasons for not being as active on this front. For most of the 1950s, they had been blessed with a seemingly endless stream of gun youngsters who had formed the backbone of the Demon dynasty. The highest of standards had been set – and almost expected – and this was to prove impossible to sustain. Adding to the difficulty, the Demons had, in the early 1960s, lost a handful of these young veterans to premature retirement.

Then there was perhaps the most significant issue of all in the Demons' diminishing recruiting power: buying players – or, more accurately in their case – their *refusal* to buy players. Melbourne's stance was driven by two issues: its ethics, and the club's financial arrangement with Melbourne Cricket Club. The football club's official title was Melbourne Cricket Club Football Club. Apart from being a mouthful, it meant it was merely the football section of the cricket club, the MCC – the umbrella organisation that also boasted cricket, tennis, baseball, hockey, lacrosse and rifle-shooting clubs. Although the football club raked in the vast majority of revenue, the MCC controlled the purse strings. Such had been the case in the previous 76 years of the football club's existence. (It had been absorbed by the MCC in 1889 after falling into financial strife.)

The MCC also strictly adhered to the long-standing Coulter Law, which restricted player payments. Meanwhile, to Smith's chagrin, other clubs found a way around this law and secured the services of big-name interstate players like Darrel Baldock (St Kilda) and Graham 'Polly' Farmer (Geelong). Smith understood the principle behind the club's conservative stance – and broadly agreed with it, believing: 'You can't buy team pride with a cheque book' – but he feared the worst for the long-term survival of his club unless a compromise was struck. He believed that: 'While we were winning premierships, it wasn't an issue. But it's a different ball game now that money has entered the game. Unless the MCC change their attitude and allow the football club to buy players, we won't have the best players, we won't win premierships and the Melbourne Football Club could go out of existence'.[7]

---

[5] *The Tony Charlton Football Show*.
[6] Barassi, Ron and Peter McFarline, *Barassi: The Life Behind The Legend*, Simon & Schuster, 1995.
[7] Related by Ian Ridley in an interview with the author.

With the goalposts shifting in regard to recruiting, Smith did not feel the same effort was being applied in this area at a time when the Demons actually needed to devote more energy than ever to the task of attracting talented youngsters. He believed the club had become 'lax' in this department. 'Tension has built up,' he said, 'and I think I may have got irritable because the responsibility has been to extract more from players of less brilliance... players of slightly lesser ability have had to carry the burden. It was obvious we were in for a tough time.'[8]

He harboured such fears at the end of the successful 1964 season. Hugh McPherson said:

> At the end of '64, Norm said to me: 'I'm getting rid of a few players, Hughie, and I'd like to get your opinion.' He told me, and I agreed with his plans. He then said: 'The problem is I want to bring in some new players but I'm getting no help whatsoever from the committee. They're not out there looking for players for me. They haven't got off their backsides and done anything because they've had it too good for too long. They're bloody complacent.'
>
> There was a bit of venom about the way he spoke. If he could coach and never have to deal with a committee, he would have done it.[9]

Smith later emphasised the importance of mutual respect between a coach and the club secretary, who was charged with recruiting duties. He believed that: 'Unless there's a happy relationship between these two people, the club has no hope of succeeding'.[10] Unfortunately for the Demons, this once great partnership was deteriorating. Talent scout Stan Rule recalled a surprising conversation he had with Cardwell at the 1964 premiership celebrations:

> Jim took me over to a corner and said: 'You're one of the only blokes in this club who can walk up to Norm and say what you want to say to him. I want you to talk to him for me.'
>
> I said: 'Have you two had a blue or something?'
>
> He said: 'He's being very difficult to deal with. He won't listen to me. He won't talk to me in the office. He won't do this and he won't do that.'
>
> I said: 'What would you want me to say to him - that he has to talk to you?'

---

[8] *The Sun*, Saturday July 31, 1965.
[9] Hugh McPherson. Interview with the author.
[10] *The Sun*, Saturday July 31, 1965.

'Yes, that's exactly what I want you to do. I know the relationship between you and Norm – you can say anything to him, but I can't. I need your help.'

I said: 'Smithy won't think much of me if I go to him to back you up. It's your responsibility to get Smithy in a room, one on one, and lock the bloody door and get him to listen to you.'

He told me that's what he'd do. I don't know what effect it had though.'[11]

Cardwell believed Smith should have retired after winning the '64 flag. 'We pinched that premiership,' he said. 'Norm could have been chairman of selectors, president, or anything with the club. But he told me: "I will coach until I die".'[12]

Barassi revealed that Smith's disputes with the committee had put him off coaching in the early 1960s. 'Norm Smith is the best coach in Australia,' he mused, 'yet here he is being hassled constantly by the committee. Bugger coaching. Who would want to be a coach?'[13]

Relations between the two parties became so strained that, at the end of 1964, Smith had actually considered resigning and pursuing another VFL coaching position. In fact, if Barassi had rejected the Carlton offer, Smith would likely have offered himself to the Blues. He had friends at Princes Park, including selector Jack Wrout and former coach Ken Hands, and would have been well suited to the more working-class environment. Terry Gleeson, who was then a Melbourne committeeman, recalled: 'Norm told me that he didn't want to cut in on Barass, but if Barass knocked the Carlton job back, he would've seriously considered it. He'd almost had enough of Melbourne. There was a snobbish part of the club that Norm didn't like. To be fair to some of those Melbourne people, I think there was a barrier that was put up on both sides. Norm had generally tolerated it all fairly well, but over time he became less tolerant.'[14]

Journalist Greg Hobbs, then with *The Age*, later pondered: 'Imagine if Norm Smith had coached Carlton when George Harris had been president! Both were great blokes, but they were also two of the most heavy-handed people you could come across. It would've been interesting to see how they would have got on. I reckon they wouldn't have existed together, because they would've had a bust-up just about every time they saw each other.'[15]

---

[11] Stan Rule. Interview with the author.
[12] Jim Cardwell, *The Sun*, Friday August 20, 1982.
[13] Collins, Ben, *The Champions: Conversations with Great Players and Coaches of Australian Football*, GSP, 2006.
[14] Terry Gleeson. Interview with the author.
[15] Greg Hobbs. Interview with the author.

Smith's support of Barassi's transfer to Carlton continued to spark angry exchanges with some committeemen. He reiterated: 'I was not going to stand in his (Barassi's) way, (but) there were people down there who were prepared to stand in the way; people who fought me bitterly; people who I thought had forgotten the whole thing, but never did they forget it. They were always ready to knock and shoot on every possible occasion.'[16]

The biggest – and ultimately irreparable – blow-up between coach and committee flared after Smith's mouth got him into trouble on August 1, 1964. The Demons had defeated St Kilda by 18 points in a low-scoring game at the MCG in round 15 – and recorded their 11th successive victory – but Smith was far from pleased. He was adamant his side had received a raw deal from umpire Don Blew.[17] During an after-match interview with radio station 3AW, Smith publicly criticised Blew's performance. Many people wrongly believed that he had called Blew 'a cheat'. In truth, he said the umpire had been 'subconsciously biased towards the underdog'. In other words, he believed that while Blew had awarded free kicks he honestly felt were correct, he had favoured the underdog (the Saints) in the vast majority of the 50/50 decisions. Most Melbourne players held a similar opinion. Barassi said:

> 'We all felt Norm was right in what he said: that umpires had been favouring opposition clubs and giving us the rough end of the stick because we'd been steamrolling everybody. Norm didn't usually worry too much about it – if he did, he concealed his thoughts quite well. He believed it wasn't good coaching or playing policy to worry about things like that – it was just an excuse for failure. Just win the bloody ball and take the umpires out of the equation. But eventually it must have worn him down and Don Blew happened to be the umpire in the wrong place at the wrong time.'[18]

Harry Beitzel, who later became the VFL's director of umpiring, said:

> 'It wouldn't have been only Donny Blew who was biased towards the underdog – most of us at some stage would have been guilty of that. In the majority of cases, statistics would confirm that the home side would get more free kicks, and in the case of underdogs, they would always get more free kicks, particularly near the end of the game when they had no chance of winning. Call it a failing, call it

---

[16] *The Tony Charlton Football Show*, Channel Nine, Sunday July 25, 1965.
[17] Blew's brother Russell played 125 games with Essendon between 1960 and 1968, and played in Victorian sides under Norm Smith.
[18] Ron Barassi. Interview with the author.

what you like, but it's also human nature, and umpires are only bloody human. They aren't robots. As much as you're there to be fair and impartial, who wants to be hooted all day? Umpires are like anybody else – they hate being criticised."[19]

Smith's critical remarks had not gone live to air on 3AW. Cardwell had listened to a recording of the interview and gave permission for it to be broadcast. When it hit the airwaves that night – and was replayed on the station the next day – a chain of events was set in motion that would result in perhaps the greatest controversy in football history.

Don Blew heard the interview and was understandably upset. The umpires' board was also up in arms. Blew, who at the time was 26 years old and in just his second season as a VFL umpire, described the reaction:

> It was spoken about among the umpires and we were quite annoyed about it. No umpire is going to be biased. We decided: 'We want an apology', so we sent Norm Smith a letter demanding one. That's all we wanted; for him to say something like: 'The way it came out was not the way it was meant. It was a poor choice of words. I didn't mean to say he was barracking for the other side. I apologise'. If he did that, it would've been over with. These days, the AFL would fine the coach thousands of dollars, so an apology is a lot short of that. But Norm Smith wouldn't budge.[20]

It soon became clear that Smith had no intention of apologising to Blew. Typically, he struggled to apologise (in words anyway) to his closest friends, so an umpire had little or no chance, particularly when he believed he was right. As a result, senior umpiring officials encouraged Blew to pursue legal action. In March 1965, the umpire issued a writ against both Norm Smith and 3AW for broadcasting comments he believed had damaged his reputation. Blew sought a trial before a judge and jury.

Smith engaged the services of solicitor Ray Dunn – who was also the president of Richmond Football Club. He also sought the support – including that of a financial nature – of the Melbourne committee. His initial private discussions with committeemen proved fruitless – and agitating. Smith was told he would struggle to get the committee to agree to foot the bill for his legal expenses. This made Smith so 'wild'[21] that he again began to consider his coaching future.

---

[19] Harry Beitzel. Interview with the author.
[20] Don Blew. Interview with the author.
[21] Hugh McPherson. Interview with the author.

He decided to make an official request, in writing, for total committee support. On Tuesday June 29, 1965 – just three days after the Demons' second successive loss (in round 10) – Smith wrote a letter to Jim Cardwell which stated:

> In a conversation last Monday with (VFL president) Sir Kenneth Luke and (VFL secretary) Eric McCutchan, I was surprised to hear that Don Blew intended to continue with the writ he has taken out against me.
>
> In view of this development, I would now ask the committee of the Melbourne Football Club for a definite decision in writing as to whether they will wholeheartedly support me in this action or not.
>
> I think I am entitled to this support because the committee expects loyalty from myself and all its players, which has always been forthcoming; so much so we are entitled to loyalty and support at all times from them.
>
> If I fail to receive the wholehearted support of the MFC committee in this matter, I can only take this as a vote of no-confidence in myself as coach and also yourself Jim, as you heard the tape before it went on the air.
>
> Therefore, if you cannot support me I must convey to you my decision not to seek reappointment next year or in future years.[22]

The letter was read at a special committee meeting that night. (Checker Hughes and Terry Gleeson were not in attendance.) The minutes of the meeting state: 'It was unanimously resolved that full moral and wholehearted support be given re coach Norman Smith's request, but the Melbourne Football Club cannot indemnify him against any loss as a result of this action. However, the committee reiterates that it or a sub-committee is prepared to meet him to discuss this matter further if he so desires'. The sub-committee, if required, would comprise Duffy, Cardwell, Don Cordner, Shane McGrath and Tom Trumble. The committee also resolved to 'ask the VFL if it is in its opinion proper, in view of the pending legal action for umpire D. Blew to officiate at matches at which the Melbourne Football Club is engaged'.[23] (The VFL refused this request.) Two days later, Smith received Cardwell's reply, which contained each of the above points.

Terry Gleeson added: 'The committee's view was: "Norm's a big man, he knows the ways of the world, and what you can and can't say; he got himself into it, he

---

[22] *Melbourne Truth*, Saturday July 31, 1965.
[23] Melbourne Football Club, Minutes of Committee Meetings, courtesy of the Melbourne Cricket Club Library.

acted alone, so he should sort it out alone". But Norm got angry about that, and it was something that continued to fester within him.'[24]

Smith found the committee's decision completely unacceptable. Little over a month later – and just days after he was sacked – Smith said, quite pointedly: 'I place loyalty very high in my demands'; and he quoted the famous Australian General, Sir John Monash: 'I don't care a damn for your loyalty when you think I am right; the time I want it is when you think I am wrong'.[25] Most agreed that Smith had been wrong in the Blew case, and even though he stood by his aired comments, he privately acknowledged that he had been 'perhaps a little foolish' to state them publicly.[26] But that didn't excuse, in his mind, the committee's token support for him. He was incensed, later saying: 'It riled and rankled that the club would not stand behind me financially, yet offered to stand behind me morally.'[27]

Smith did not believe in boasting – he didn't need to – but by way of partly justifying his stance, he offered: 'I'd given the club 29 years' service and helped in 10 premierships'.[28] He told close friends: 'If they think I've done anything for Melbourne, and helped the club in *any* way – why don't they do something for me to help me out of this?'[29]

Barassi was coaching Carlton at the time, but still held strong views on Smith's treatment. 'Norm may have been wrong to publicly bag an umpire,' Barassi conceded, 'but the club should have backed him because of all the success he'd brought the club, and been involved in over the previous 30 years. With that kind of service, you back people. End of story. The committee should have said: "Norm, we feel you made a mistake, and please don't let it ever happen or you'll be on your own, but we will back you this time". Surely he'd earned a few Brownie points!'[30]

Although Duffy and fellow committeeman Les Millis approached Smith with personal pledges to provide financial support in the Blew case, he politely declined their offers. To Smith, it was a matter of principle. 'This is not what I wanted,' he said later. 'I wanted the club to display loyalty, and this they did not do.'[31] The very thought repulsed Smith. 'It was unacceptable to me,' he said, 'that I could work with men who wouldn't back me. Men who would expect me to get the utmost

---

[24] Terry Gleeson. Interview with the author.
[25] *The Sun*, Saturday July 31, 1965.
[26] Related by Hugh McPherson in an interview with the author.
[27] *Melbourne Truth*, Saturday July 31, 1965.
[28] *Melbourne Truth*, Saturday July 31, 1965.
[29] Related by Hugh McPherson in an interview with the author.
[30] Ron Barassi. Interview with the author.
[31] *Melbourne Truth*, Saturday July 31, 1965.

from the players, and demand from the players the loyalty and support, and, at the other end of the line, weren't prepared to give me their support.'[32]

Smith's disdain for the committee as a whole, and some of its members individually, intensified. He found he 'could not tolerate them', and developed a virtual *us-versus-them* mentality in his dealings with club officials. He stopped going to the Committee Room for drinks, and even snubbed the social functions he usually revelled in; or if he did attend, he was only there briefly, and hardly, if at all, spoke to committeemen. He admitted: 'I was frankly intolerant... (and) I became uncooperative to a certain extent, but not to the detriment of the team'.[33]

Don Cordner, who had joined the committee the previous year, held 'great affection and respect' for his former teammate, but even he was not blind to Smith's change in demeanour. Cordner harboured 'great regret that Norman so immersed himself in the win-at-all-costs attitude... that he lost some of his own pleasant personality and that in his many, often heated, clashes of temperament with other personalities he himself did not escape unscathed'.[34]

Other friends had also noticed Smith's increasingly agitated state. *The Herald's* Alf Brown wrote that he 'has become so tense that he seems to be sitting on a barrel of gunpowder which the slightest spark... will explode'.[35]

Just a week later, Smith explained: 'What many people have failed to realise is that behind this explosive element in my temperament is tension. I explode because of that tension. And it has become more acute with Melbourne struggling in recent weeks. Undoubtedly, I have been more difficult and I know I cause tempers to fray.'[36] (After winning the first eight matches, the Demons had lost three of their next four games.)

Ian Ridley, who had returned to Melbourne as the assistant secretary in 1965 – 'What a year to come back!' he exclaimed – was shocked by the vicious sniping he witnessed behind closed doors:

> Norm was becoming disrespectful to committeemen, and committeemen were becoming disrespectful to Norm. I saw them get nasty in selection meetings. There were also personal things said between Smithy and (committeeman) Charles Loughrey that would have been best left unsaid. It went both ways too. For instance, Loughrey taunted Norm with: 'Why didn't you go to the war?' That was a very hurtful thing to say, and it made Norm blow his stack.

---

[32] *The Tony Charlton Football Show*, Sunday July 25, 1965.
[33] *Melbourne Truth*, Saturday July 31, 1965.
[34] Don Cordner's personal memoirs.
[35] *The Herald*, Saturday July 24, 1965.
[36] *Melbourne Truth*, Saturday July 31, 1965.

As assistant secretary, I was talking to Loughrey in the rooms one night. After he walked away, Smithy came over – he was fuming – and he picked me up by the elbows and shook me like a doll, and said: 'Don't you let me see you speak to that bastard in these dressingrooms again!'

Trust seemed to get worse and worse. There was never any problem between Norm and I, though.[37]

Don Cordner lamented that a number of committee members had gone to 'great lengths' to try to 'reach some understanding' with Smith, but 'unfortunately their efforts did not meet any reciprocal softening of attitude'.[38] He revealed:

When the committee would try to work with Norm, he would say words to the effect of: 'Get lost! I don't need you to tell me what to do!'

Personally, I didn't have anything to do with Norm during that period, and I'm glad I didn't. I didn't say: 'Look Norm, let's talk this through'. On reflection, perhaps I might have been the best bloke to try, considering my playing history with Norm. But I would have failed. When he had his mind made up, you couldn't say or do anything to sway him. He was a really nice gentleman – I don't recall us ever having an argument or a fight – but he turned out to be his own worst enemy.

One prominent Melbourne personality who did try to placate Smith was Bert Chadwick. Cordner said: 'Bert Chadwick always prided himself on the fact that he could negotiate with anyone, and he decided that he would get on-side with Norm Smith. But he came back to me and said: "Smith is impossible".'[39]

Cordner also claimed that 'on several occasions when speaking to the players, Smith criticised – either directly or by inference – the committee and its activities'.[40] One such instance was believed to have taken place in early July, shortly after his plea for committee support had been rejected. Around the same time, a rumour had circulated that Smith would leave Melbourne to coach Richmond. Ever since Len Smith had become ill and announced his retirement as coach – and particularly with caretaker coach Jack Titus declaring that he would relinquish the role at the end of the season – Norm Smith had been linked to the Richmond job. In light of the problems he was enduring at Melbourne, Len had actually tried to persuade him to make the move to Punt Road, where Len was a selector, for 1966.

---

[37] Ian Ridley. Interview with the author.
[38] Don Cordner's personal memoirs.
[39] Don Cordner. Interview with the author.
[40] Don Cordner's personal memoirs.

'Listen boy,' came Smith's curt reply. 'While I'm coaching Melbourne, don't you talk to me about any other club.' Len was disappointed, but immensely proud of Smith's 'loyalty (and) his dedication to the one club'.[41]

But, mindful of what his players might have been thinking after hearing the rumour, he tackled the issue head-on. At a players' meeting after training one night, he asked the players if they had heard rumours that he would be leaving Melbourne to coach Richmond. One player said: 'Yes'.

Smith responded: 'I want to tell you this: I have not discussed anything with Richmond... I'm here to coach Melbourne, and while I'm coaching Melbourne that's my job.'[42] He told them to put the thought out of their minds, and assured them: 'I'm Melbourne through and through, as I always have been'.[43]

To reinforce his point, he recalled when, midway through 1951, Jim Cardwell had approached him about returning to coach his beloved Melbourne. Smith had told Cardwell not to talk to him about it until the end of the season because he had to be loyal to his Fitzroy players.[44]

However, he did inform them – and this is the part that the committee vigorously objected to – of some of the contents of his recent letter to the committee. He recalled: 'I told them it was true that I had given the committee a letter stating that if I did not receive their support I would not coach the team next year, and I intended to carry this out if the support did not come. This was a simple statement of fact. I was not critical of the club and I did not want the players to listen to half-baked rumours. It was an off-the-cuff assessment of how things stood, purely to clear the air so we could get on with our football.'[45]

Nonetheless, it incurred the wrath of the committee, and was recorded as another strike against his name.

Around the same time, perhaps over this, or a related issue, Smith had a violent argument with an official. Weeks later, he admitted: 'I almost came to blows with a social committeeman. I was in the wrong and I regret it. We've made up since.'[46]

Although most players were blissfully unaware of the heightening tensions between coach and committee, Don Williams (now deceased) later said: 'It lessened his concentration when coaching; it filtered through to the team midway through the season. Often the usually punctual Smith would be late out for training –

---

[41] *The Tony Charlton Football Show.*
[42] *The Tony Charlton Football Show.*
[43] *Melbourne Truth*, Saturday July 31, 1965.
[44] *The Tony Charlton Football Show.*
[45] *Melbourne Truth*, Saturday July 31, 1965.
[46] *Melbourne Truth*, Saturday July 31, 1965.

he had been arguing with the committee. Sometimes he would be called off the track to confront officials.'[47]

This accumulation of events, escalating as they were in their frequency and intensity, prompted the committee to decide that Smith was out of order, and perhaps even out of control. The stern disciplinarian needed to be disciplined, maybe punished... and perhaps even sacked.

On Wednesday July 21 – just four days after Melbourne had lost to Richmond to drop to third spot on the ladder with a 9-3 record – Smith received a phone call from Jim Cardwell. The conversation was unusually formal. Cardwell told Smith he was required to attend a full committee meeting at 5pm that night. It was extremely short notice. But more than that, it was a curious development. Smith asked if he had been requested or ordered to attend. Cardwell said he had been ordered; and added that he was 'not at liberty to discuss it further', which Smith thought was 'strange', because in previous years he and Cardwell had freely 'discussed the most intimate club matters'. Confused, and with his suspicions aroused, Smith decided to call other members of the committee to find out what he could. He called the president, Don Duffy. Again he was informed that the matter could not be discussed before the meeting. 'Finally,' he recalled, 'I phoned my old coach and friend Checker Hughes – and got the same reply. I knew there was trouble brewing, but I didn't anticipate the heartbreaks ahead.'[48]

Smith's heart was already aching and breaking. No longer could he tolerate what he perceived to be a cocktail of interference, jealousy, complacency and weakness. His initial intention was to resign. He consulted his brother – the man who knew him better than anyone; the more level-headed of the two; an outsider with an intimate knowledge of simmering tensions between coach and committee.

Norm told Len: 'I think I'll offer my resignation.'

'Don't be a fool,' said Len. 'You owe it to the boys to keep coaching.'

Len's rational approach prevailed upon his brother, who changed his mind. He would stick it out and cop whatever came his way.

Len also appealed to Norm to maintain his composure at the meeting.

Len instructed: 'Eat humble pie.'[49]

Norm heeded his brother's advice.

Just days later he came to the conclusion: 'I was to be sacked on that Wednesday night – I was almost sure of this'. Although he had mentally 'conditioned' himself

---

[47] Batchelder, Alf, *Pavilions In The Park*, by, Australian Scholarly Publishing, 2005.
[48] *Melbourne Truth*, Saturday July 31, 1965.
[49] *The Tony Charlton Football Show*.

for the worst – that he could be sacked that night – he believed, and hoped, it was a 'clear-the-air meeting' in which both sides could air their grievances and come to a compromise that appeased both parties. 'The meeting did not strike me as a witch-hunt,' he recalled. 'In fact, with the tension and strain around the club, I felt that a meeting to clear the air was a sound idea.'[50]

Len's advice was timely, but Norm was not prepared for the allegations levelled at him. He had expected his hot temper to have been the focus of discussion, and would have openly admitted that while he believed his fiery nature had probably 'played a part in the great success of the club', it had also been a shortcoming in his dealings with club officials. He later reflected: 'I'm not going to spare myself or paint a saintly picture. I blew my top on many occasions... I've argued with committeemen and selectors. I've walked out in anger from a few of their meetings... I've said many things I've regretted. But these are traits I've had... throughout my football life. (But) these were not the things discussed at that vital meeting.'[51]

The committee's accusations took a completely different form. During the discussion, in which Smith recalled 'a few people had their say', he was surprised to be informed there were reports of him being disloyal, and criticising the committee in front of his players. He was ordered to stop speaking against the committee; promise loyalty to the committee; and cooperate with his fellow selectors.

After being caught off-guard himself, Smith turned the tables on his inquisitors. Although he felt 'a natural tendency to explode over the allegations' – and he was conscious of others expecting him to do just that – he showed uncharacteristic restraint. He recalled: 'I remained calm, gave my assurances and acceded to their demands'.[52] He had eaten humble pie, about which he later remarked: 'Oh, it's got an awful taste'. In the process, he believed he had 'tricked' the committee by not losing his cool and giving the committee 'the opportunity' he later felt they were probing for to sack him.[53] He also told the gathering that he did not want to leave the club halfway through the season.[54] He was not going to make the committee's job easy by simply resigning. If he was to be ousted, they would be forced to sack him – a massive undertaking, considering he was a six-time premiership coach.

One of the rare occasions in the meeting that Smith showed some semblance of opposition to the committee was when he told Duffy: 'You went to a public

---

[50] *Melbourne Truth*, Saturday July 31, 1965.
[51] *Melbourne Truth*, Saturday July 31, 1965.
[52] *Melbourne Truth*, Saturday July 31, 1965.
[53] *The Tony Charlton Football Show*.
[54] *Melbourne Truth*, Saturday July 31, 1965.

school; I went to a state school. But they still spelt principle the same way. And it's the principle for which I am fighting... If you haven't got principle, you haven't got anything. And I've got principle, and I'll fight for this principle 'til the day I die'.[55]

One of the main conditions stipulated at meeting was for Smith to address the players and declare his support for the committee. Just when this declaration was to be made became one of two major points of contention in the sacking of Norm Smith. Committee members expected him to take the first opportunity to fulfil this requirement – that being at training the following night. But Smith believed that no deadline had been specified. Regardless of what was said and meant at the meeting, the official wording of this condition demanded Smith 'to inform the players of your fullest support of the committee and its conduct of the club's affairs'. Smith was right – no specific time had been stipulated. However, vindication on this point would come as a belated and cold comfort for the coach, who, unbeknown to him, still had his head on the chopping block.

Smith asked Cardwell to provide him with a written copy of his instructions. This was not forthcoming on the night – if it had been, it might have saved a lot of embarrassment.

When he was excused from the meeting, he must have felt like a death-row prisoner who had gained a reprieve. He said later: 'I left thinking everything had been settled... I was led to believe it had all blown over... I was greatly relieved. A great load had dropped from my mind, and I thought the storm was over'.[56]

How wrong could he have been?

When Smith left, debate continued among committeemen. Cordner was not present at the meeting, but later revealed that 'a resolution was passed stating that, if the occasion arose, Smith would never be sacked until he had been given an opportunity to resign'.[57] This was to be another telling decision.

Ian Ridley – who was busy taking notes as the minutes' secretary – felt decidedly uncomfortable as the future of his former coach, a man he admired tremendously, was discussed. 'It was a unsavoury situation,' he said. 'I was thinking: "Who's for Norm and who's against him?"'[58]

That question would be answered in less than 48 hours.

---

[55] *The Tony Charlton Football Show.*
[56] *Melbourne Truth*, Saturday July 31, 1965.
[57] Don Cordner's personal memoirs.
[58] Ian Ridley. Interview with the author.

On the Thursday morning, Smith received a telephone call from Ian Ridley. It was not an official call; Ridley had contacted Smith as a friend. He wanted to check that his old coach – the man he rated as one of the three greatest influences on his life – was, in the cold, hard light of day, at least broadly satisfied with what had transpired at the committee meeting the night before.

Ridley should have known better than to question his old mentor's ability to cope with adversity.

'Tiddles,' Smith said matter-of-factly (using a nickname disliked by Ridley, who believed it made him 'sound like a bloody tom-cat'), 'this is a championship fight. And championship fights go 15 rounds. The first round was last night, and they think they won. But there's still 14 to go, and I'm gonna come out punching and give those bastards all I've got.'[59]

That night, in the changerooms before training, Jim Cardwell, as requested, gave Smith a typed copy of his instructions from the committee. He immediately placed the piece of paper in his shirt pocket and went about preparing for the training session. He did not have time to read it and give its contents the due consideration they deserved. He would read it later, at home, away from the vibrant chatter and unceasing distractions of changerooms occupied by 40 players. Anyway, there were more pressing matters at hand. It was a big night for the Demons – a much-needed tune-up before what Smith regarded as 'a vital and dangerous game'[60] against North Melbourne at their new home ground, the Coburg City Oval. Smith had inspected the playing surface of the ground two days earlier and knew the boggy conditions would reduce the match to a sheer battle of wills.[61]

Little more than an hour later emerged the second major point of conjecture – and gross misunderstanding – in the coach/committee dispute. It centred around the contents of a 15-minute address Smith delivered to the players on the MCG after training. Smith's version of what he said – a version supported by Hassa Mann and other players present – was:

> I said to the players: 'No-one wants to become disgruntled if they didn't get a game... Look, we fight, everybody fights. We have fights in (the) selection committee and we... argue, but when we finish, we all shut that door, and it's left behind that door, (and) we come out as mates... Not one of you players

---

[59] Ian Ridley. Interview with the author.
[60] *Melbourne Truth*, Saturday July 31, 1965.
[61] Norm Smith, in an interview with Tony Charlton on Channel Nine on the evening of Tuesday July 27, 1965.

SACKED [1965]

know whether I'm with you or against you, and that's the way I've always been... That is the way I operate... This is what makes our club the great club it is'.

Now, if they're words spoken against anybody, I fail to see it. I was supporting them and telling them what made it great.[62]

As they walked off the ground, two players were approached and questioned by committeemen. John Lord was one, and the other was widely rumoured to have been Brian Dixon, although Dixon strenuously denied this. Lord had sensed 'a strange tension' at training that night, but could not put his finger on its source. It got stranger when he was confronted by Cardwell. Lord recalled:

> Jimmy asked me something like: 'Did Norm say such-and-such to the players?'
> I just said: 'No, he didn't say anything about that'.
> I had no idea that Norm had apparently been expected to say something in support of the committee. Off-field politics didn't register with me – I just had a 'let's-play-footy' attitude – so I wasn't interested anyhow. In my vagueness, maybe I hadn't paid enough attention to what Norm had said – which wasn't the first time that had happened – and maybe he said it and I was thinking of something else. Or maybe I just should have told Jimmy: 'Yes, he did say it', and things might have been different. The ramifications were sad and unfortunate. All that out of responding to a simple question that I didn't place much importance on.
> I'd never have purposely done anything to hurt Norm. I loved Norm and I loved Marj, and I believe he and Marj loved me.[63]

Cardwell immediately called a players' meeting. Officially, there were two items on the agenda: providing directions to the Coburg ground, and discussing plans for the end-of-season trip. However, there was a third, more important item Cardwell expected Smith to raise: his pledge of support for the committee. But Smith was totally oblivious to this expectation. After Cardwell had completed his duties, he turned to Duffy and asked: 'Would you like to say something, Don?'

Duffy declined.

Cardwell then asked Smith: 'Would you like to say something about a certain matter?'

Smith thought it an unusual question, as he had just spent 15 minutes talking to his players, witnessed by Cardwell and other officials. He didn't know what Cardwell was 'getting at'.

---

[62] *The Tony Charlton Football Show*.
[63] John Lord. Interview with the author.

'No,' he replied. 'I don't want to say anything, Jim. I've already spoken to the players on the field.'

When the players left the room, Smith asked Cardwell: 'What did you mean by that?'

'Well,' said Cardwell, 'that was an opportunity to tell them that you were supporting the committee'.

'Ohhh!' Smith groaned. 'Well I didn't realise this. You didn't tell me. No-one's told me. I'll do it at my convenience, in my own time.'

Such decisions had always been left to Smith's discretion as the coach, and he was comfortable that the levels of success and discipline at Melbourne over the previous decade had 'justified that policy'.[64] Besides, the committee had not stipulated when the statement had to be made. Smith certainly had not decided when, or how, he would address the players over the matter. He had not had much time to think it over – after all, it had been just 24 hours since the committee had verbally made its demands… and less than two hours since Cardwell had handed him their written confirmation. Smith certainly did not realise that the committee was also demanding urgent action.

He would have waited until after the match against North Melbourne to satisfy the committee's wish. He said later: 'There was nothing about such a statement to embarrass or shame me… It was a matter of timing, (and) I did not want to jar them before the match… It would have been easy for me to make it at the players' meeting. Simply: "There has been a certain amount of friction in the club, but I want to assure you I have complete confidence in the committee and they have my full support". Possibly a statement like that might have helped me get a lift out of them. Who knows? But I made no attempt to evade the issue. In telling Jim Cardwell I had spoken to the players, I had no intent to mislead him. What would have been the purpose?'[65]

After the players' meeting, Smith felt comfortable enough again to mingle in the committee room and have a few social drinks. He found it 'a cordial gathering'. Then he attended the selection meeting. 'I felt the pressure was gone,' he said. 'Everybody was happy… (It was) a harmonious selection meeting.'[66]

He went home that night and finally read the contents of Cardwell's note. Not even then, after carefully absorbing each word, did he believe he had contravened any of the committee's guidelines, or committed any wrong.

---

[64] *Melbourne Truth*, Saturday July 31, 1965.
[65] *Melbourne Truth*, Saturday July 31, 1965.
[66] *Melbourne Truth*, Saturday July 31, 1965.

Yet again, he had either misinterpreted the situation, or he had been shielded from the true feelings of officials around him. In the eyes of both Cardwell and Duffy, the inescapable truth was that Smith had been presented with two opportunities to reaffirm his allegiance to the committee, and he had elected to ignore both. In doing so, he had shown a blatant disregard, and disrespect, for the authority of the committee. The chairman and secretary felt they had no other option but to arrange a special sitting of the committee and strongly recommend the most drastic action possible: that their greatest coach be sacked.

♟♟♟♟♟♟♟♟♟

On Friday morning, Smith was pleasantly surprised to receive a letter from committeeman Don Cordner, who congratulated him on his conduct at what Smith referred to as his 'humble pie night'. The letter, which reinforced Smith's belief that all was well, stated:

> Dear Norman
>
> I had nothing but admiration for you yesterday in your rather difficult interview with the committee, and by the end of the session you had gone up in my estimation.
>
> I must congratulate you on a grand exhibition of tolerance and cooperation in the club's interests.
>
> Despite your doubts, the men at the committee table are all supporters of yours. Some, of course, are more critical and volatile than others, but basically they're all behind you – nobody more so than myself.
>
> I told several of them I intended writing to you, and some of them may have done the same.
>
> May I again express my congratulations and good wishes.

However, the majority of the committeeman's colleagues were anything but complimentary of Smith's conduct. At a hastily-convened meeting on Friday July 23 – which Smith was neither notified about, nor invited to attend – the committee sat in judgement of its coach.

Cardwell's testimony was most damning. Terry Gleeson recalled:

> Jimmy was the one who told the committee words to the effect that: 'One of the players has told me that Norm Smith has criticised the committee in front of all of the players. We just can't have this going on. We must take action'.

Jimmy had been very close to Norm, and he was the secretary, which is like a general manager now, and a general manager has to be on everyone's side. So when he came to us with that, it held a lot of weight.

We had no option but to sack him. In a sense, it was a cut-and-dried case.

I probably had as much reason to support Norm as anyone. But I buried the emotions I felt for the man and took an objective view of the facts. And the fact was you can't have a coach bagging the committee in front of all the players.[67]

Two committeemen – 'Checker' Hughes and Cordner – spoke 'at considerable length' against sacking Smith.[68] Hughes pleaded with his colleagues, stating that 'it wasn't fair – in fact, it was almost cruel – to sack a man who had given the club such wonderful service over a long period of time, and who had been largely responsible for so much of our success'.[69] Cordner recorded in his personal memoirs:

> My objections to the sacking were not so much on the grounds of what Smith had or had not done, but were based on these quite incontrovertible facts: 1) Haste was unnecessary; 2) The previous resolution not to sack him without first giving him an opportunity to resign; 3) The quite impossible position the Melbourne team would find itself in without a coach the next day in the match against North Melbourne; 4) The quite unnecessary and unpleasant furore that would explode immediately; 5) If Smith were to be dismissed, it would be much more dignified, more practical, less traumatic and much quieter merely not to reappoint him the following summer, but to call for applications.

Cordner recalled that only Hughes, Shane McGrath and himself had voted against the sacking. (Colin McLean was absent.) A 9-3 vote (the club claimed it had been unanimous) sealed Smith's fate. When the verdict was confirmed, Cordner immediately announced that he would 'consider very carefully' whether or not he would resign from the committee over the issue. He later said: 'I have always regretted that I did not do so there and then'.[70]

Ridley, the junior member of the committee who was not entitled to vote, struggled to perform his role as the minutes' secretary. 'I was in a state of shock,' he said. 'You didn't know it was going to happen until it actually happened.

---

[67] Related by Terry Gleeson in an interview with the author.
[68] Don Cordner. Interview with the author.
[69] Related by Ian Ridley in an interview with the author.
[70] Don Cordner's personal memoirs.

SACKED [1965]

It was surreal. I was sitting there and listening to the debate that was going on around me – it was a pretty one-sided affair – when I really should have been paying closer attention to taking notes. I often wonder why I didn't take notes. It was almost like it was something you didn't want to know about; didn't want to record. Probably the less that's known the better, because it was one of the worst times in the history of the club.'[71]

The notes Ridley did take eventually took the following form: 'After due discussion, it was resolved that the services of coach Norman Smith be dispensed with forthwith and that a letter be sent advising him of the decision. It was (also) resolved that an appreciation of Mr Norman Smith's services to the Melbourne Football Club as coach be acknowledged'.[72]

Once the monumental decision had been made, a general mood of 'excited relief' came over the room.[73] But anxiety levels quickly rose again. Ridley remembered:

> There was actually more discussion about how they should tell Norm than there was in making the initial decision to sack him. No-one was game enough to do it in person, face-to-face, probably because they thought he would go berserk. No-one put their hand up for what was going to be an extremely unenviable job of telling a bloke who'd coached the club for the previous 14 years and won six flags that his time was over.
>
> In their wisdom, they took the easy way out. They decided to write him a letter and send it to him by courier.

Cardwell later revealed that the mode of dismissal had been Duffy's idea. He had 'wanted a neutral person to make the delivery to Norm's home'.[74]

The meeting closed at 6.40pm. The dismissal notice was drafted and approved and, as Ridley recalled, 'a female courier turned up, picked up the letter and took it to Smithy's place. Then we just battened down the hatches and waited for the news to break'.[75]

ϒϒϒϒϒϒϒϒϒ

---

[71] Ian Ridley. Interview with the author.
[72] Melbourne Football Club, Minutes of Committee Meetings, courtesy of the Melbourne Cricket Club Library.
[73] Ian Ridley. Interview with the author.
[74] *The Sun*, Friday August 20, 1982.
[75] Ian Ridley. Interview with the author.

Norm and Marj Smith had originally planned to attend Melbourne Football Club's dinner-dance after the game against North Melbourne at Coburg. Marj had bought a new dress and a matching pair of shoes. But after the accusations that were laid against him on the Wednesday night, Norm turned sour on the idea. Nonetheless, he was in good spirits. Marj later observed: 'On the Friday, I've never seen Norm so relaxed and so happy, thinking that everything was finished'.[76]

Demons' ruckman Graham Wise was staying with the Smiths, as he usually did on a Friday night. The three had debated which movie to watch on television that night. Smith then observed his Friday night ritual of telephoning Hassa Mann for a 10-15 minute chat about the match the next day. It had been raining for days and the Coburg ground – which had been dubbed 'The Everglades' – was sure to be a quagmire, so Smith told Mann how the side would need to play to adapt to the conditions. Their conversation was interrupted by the sound of the doorbell ringing. Smith told his skipper: 'I've got to go; there's someone at the door. I'll see you tomorrow'.[77]

It was about 8pm – an unusual time for someone to visit the Smith house on a Friday night. Marj answered the door first. She was confronted by a woman – a courier. 'There's a courier here, Norm,' she sang out. 'And she's got a letter for you.' The courier handed Smith an envelope bearing a Melbourne Football Club letterhead. He thought: 'What the hell could this be at eight o'clock on a Friday night?' He didn't have the slightest idea of what its contents might be. He tore open the envelope. It was written by Jim Cardwell on behalf of the committee and stated grimly:

> I have been requested by my committee to remind you of the matters discussed with you at its meeting with you on Wednesday last, the 21st, at which you advised the committee that you intended to resign at the end of the present season. At that meeting, you undertook:
>
> a) To cease speaking against the committee or its members and to loyally support the committee in its conduct of the club's affairs.
> b) To cooperate to the fullest extent with other members of the match committee in the coaching of players and the selection of the teams.
> c) To inform the players of your fullest support of the committee and its conduct of the club's affairs.

---

[76] *The Tony Charlton Football Show.*
[77] Hassa Mann. Interview with the author.

These undertakings were accepted by the committee in good faith and with the sincere hope that the normal, happy relations, which have existed within the club for a considerable period, would be restored.

The committee members were amazed when they discovered that on the very next night, Thursday the 22nd of this month, you not only expressed to the players your dissatisfaction with the selection committee but when asked by the secretary at a meeting of the players in the committee room to comply with the third undertaking, you told him a deliberate lie when you stated that you had already informed the players on the field.

Obviously you do not intend to honour your word and the committee is not prepared to allow your disruptive tactics to continue, and your appointment as coach is cancelled as from this day.

It is most unfortunate that your long and valued association with the club should have to end in this way but drastic steps must be taken to prevent any further disruption of the club's activities.

Before he even had time to fully digest the letter's contents, he called Mann again. It was only a couple of minutes since their initial phone call had ended. Smith didn't reintroduce himself; he simply said: 'Forget what we were just talking about; you'll have to do it all yourself. I've just been sacked'.

Mann didn't recognise the distressed voice at the other end of the line. He thought it was a prank caller. 'What are you talking about?!' Mann demanded.

'I've just been sacked… I've been sacked.'

Mann still couldn't make out the voice, and was about to hang up. He said: 'Get off the phone, you silly bastard, and stop bothering me.'

Smith finally convinced him.

'Hassa, it's me – Norm,' he pleaded. 'I'm serious. I've just been sacked.'

Mann later reflected: 'I hadn't initially recognised Norm's voice because it was trembling, and he was crying and all choked up, and I'd never heard him like that before. Then the enormity of what he was telling me – the fact he had been sacked – just hit me like a ton of bricks, and I had tears streaming down my face. It was like a death in the family'.[78]

Mann told Smith: 'Hang up. I'm coming over'.

In the meantime, Marj Smith had read the dismissal notice. Just two days later she said: 'I don't think if I lived to be a hundred I'll ever be able to

---

[78] Hassa Mann. Interview with the author.

work out, or explain to anyone, how I felt when Norm passed that letter over to me.'⁷⁹

Smith called his brother, who quickly came over with his wife Flo to comfort the couple. By the time Mann arrived with wife Glenys, both Smith couples needed comforting. Mann recalled:

> We were greeted at the door by Norm and Marj, who were both crying their eyes out, and Len and his wife were crying theirs out. It was the Friday night before a big game, and we were sitting in the lounge room just staring at each other in disbelief. I thought: 'How in hell could this happen?' Little was said. It was the first time I'd seen Norm stuck for words. Marj was a real sad case, too - we all were. I left about 2am and got home feeling absolutely terrible.⁸⁰

Smith was not only upset for himself. It hurt him to see Marj so 'deeply distressed'. That night, rather than just mope around in despair, Marj decided to be proactive. She 'phoned as many Melbourne players as she could' – as many as 16 of them – to ask if Norm had criticised the committee in front of them. Their answers varied from 'no', and 'ridiculous', to: 'If anything, he praised them'.⁸¹

Although he was understandably not in his most communicative mood that night, Smith brooded over his rawest emotions and explosive rebuttals, which in the days afterwards he would ensure found their way into the public domain.

Smith was well aware of the fickle nature of coaching. In fact, he believed: 'It is like in the jungle – one animal eats another animal, but life goes on, the species continues'.⁸² But this was something else entirely. After surviving the Wednesday night meeting, he had believed it was business as usual. 'I didn't even know it was in the air,' he said. He was 'sick with shock' over the way his sacking had been handled, and felt he had been maltreated on a number of fronts.

Firstly, he was offended that he had not been asked to appear at the meeting at which his position was 'cancelled'. He had not even been taken aside by an official. He declared: 'I firmly believe that I have been gravely wronged in being tried on hearsay and in being convicted without a chance to utter a word in my defence.'⁸³

Some people (including, as previously mentioned, Don Cordner) believed Smith should have at least been given the opportunity to resign first. In doing so, although

---

⁷⁹ *The Tony Charlton Football Show.*
⁸⁰ Hassa Mann. Interview with the author.
⁸¹ *Melbourne Truth*, Saturday July 31, 1965.
⁸² *The Sun*, Saturday July 31, 1965.
⁸³ *Melbourne Truth*, Saturday July 31, 1965.

their differences of opinion with Smith would have remained, the committee would have shown him some semblance of respect by allowing him to leave gracefully with his – and their – dignity intact. Although Smith's initial reaction to being ordered to attend the Wednesday meeting was to resign, his attitude had since hardened into an *I'm-not-backing-down-no-matter-what* mentality. 'I'd sooner be sacked than resign,' he said,[84] adding that he 'would not take the easy way out'.[85]

Smith was also devastated by the disrespectful and gutless manner in which the news was delivered. For a man who prided himself on looking the world straight in the eye, on making tough decisions and telling it like it was – man-to-man – there was no honour in this. It was probably the cruellest, deepest cut of all. The insensitivity of it all beggared belief, and completely bewildered Smith. 'What a way it came!' he cried. 'I guarantee I'm the first coach to be dismissed in such and off-hand fashion', via 'a blunt and personally slanderous letter' delivered by a complete stranger.[86]

The reasons stated for the dismissal also provoked an inevitably angry response from Smith, who disdainfully referred to the allegations as 'a complete and utter fabrication'. He believed that in questioning his honesty and integrity, the committee itself had 'created two lies'[87] – the first regarding what he had said to the players after training (with the evidence accepted by Cardwell being second-hand, and, in John Lord's case, of only a vague nature); and secondly that he had lied to Cardwell when asked if he had told the players of his support of the committee. Smith was outraged that he had been 'called a liar and accused of disruptive tactics'.[88] His denials were charged with furious indignation. 'One allegation was I told a deliberate lie,' he said, flabbergasted. 'Anyone who knows me knows I wouldn't lie. I'd sooner fight than lie... *I don't lie*.'[89] He added: 'There is no intent on my part to whitewash myself. I know my weaknesses and limitations. There have been times when I have done the wrong thing. There have even been times when I have been ashamed of things I have done. But I am not a hypocrite or liar.'[90]

Len Smith backed his brother's claims, saying he was 'so extremely proud' of Norm for his 'way of living' and his football achievements.[91] 'He's never done a dishonest thing in his life,' he said. 'I would believe him before anyone else.'[92]

---

[84] *The Tony Charlton Football Show.*
[85] *Melbourne Truth*, Saturday July 31, 1965.
[86] *Melbourne Truth*, Saturday July 31, 1965.
[87] *The Tony Charlton Football Show.*
[88] *Melbourne Truth*, Saturday July 31, 1965.
[89] *The Tony Charlton Football Show.*
[90] *Melbourne Truth*, Saturday July 31, 1965.
[91] *The Tony Charlton Football Show.*
[92] *The Herald*, Saturday July 24, 1965.

As for employing disruptive tactics against the committee, and related questions over his loyalty to the club, Norm Smith was similarly dismissive. 'That is completely against my principles,' he said. 'I have been for Melbourne – first, last and always.' Smith openly admitted he had been 'hurt... deeply hurt'. In fact, he said, 'this sacking, and the unfeeling way in which it was executed, is the greatest hurt I have suffered in a lifetime'.[93]

The news spread rapidly, and was met with sheer disbelief. When journalist Jack Dunn rang his editor at *The Sun* and informed him of the sacking, the response was: 'Norm Smith sacked tonight? Are you drunk?'[94] Meanwhile, over at *The Age*, young reporter Greg Hobbs recalled: 'The newspaper for Saturday morning was almost in place. When the Smith news came through, newspaper bosses were running in all directions. It was as if World War III was erupting!'[95]

☆☆☆☆☆☆☆☆☆

The football public awoke to news that shook it to its very core. The earth-shattering truth was confirmed by news-stand posters which screamed: NORM SMITH SACKED (*The Sun*, the morning paper) and, later, WHY DEMONS SACKED SMITH (*The Herald*, the afternoon). In *The Herald*, Alf Brown outlined the deterioration of relations between Smith and Melbourne officials, writing that Smith had 'made bad friends' on the committee over the Barassi and Blew issues.

Given the unparalleled success achieved by the Smith-Demons combination, such bitterness behind the scenes appeared inconceivable.

This was the man who, just 10 months earlier, had guided Melbourne to his – and perhaps the club's – greatest triumph. The man who had taken the Demons to 11 consecutive finals series, eight Grand Finals and six premierships. The man who was presiding over a team with a 9-3 record and seemingly with strong claims towards launching its almost perennial tilt at the premiership. The man who, since 1954, had coached Melbourne in 232 games for 173 wins, 56 losses and three draws, at the staggering success rate of 74.57 percent.[96] Yet he had been given his marching orders.

---

[93] *Melbourne Truth*, Saturday July 31, 1965.
[94] *The Sun*, Friday August 20, 1982.
[95] Hobbs, Greg, *125 Years of the Demons 1858-1983*, Progress Press Group, 1984.
[96] Norm Smith had already achieved all the accolades that would, in 1996, result in his selection as the coach of the AFL's Team of the Century – ahead of Collingwood patriarch Jock McHale, who coached the Magpies to a record 17 Grand Finals for a record eight premierships over a record 38-season reign.

SACKED [1965]

The public uproar was loud and angry. The general feeling was that regardless of the problems that had surfaced behind closed doors, surely if anyone could claim credit points it was Norm Smith. That his head could have been on the chopping block was simply unthinkable – to all, it seemed, except the committee of Melbourne Football Club.

The pandemonium – commonly described at the time as a 'hue and cry' – was perhaps most aptly described by Jack Dyer, who observed in *Truth*: 'If the poster had said nuclear war had broken out, it couldn't have caused a bigger stir'.

So haphazard was the committee's handling of the affair that one Melbourne senior player did not know about the sacking until *The Herald*'s reporter John Stevens broke the news to him over the telephone on the Saturday morning. Frank Davis said: 'I got a phone call from an official and was told what had happened, and advised not to do this and not to do that, and not to get involved in any way. Five minutes later I got a call from Hassa and he said we would be getting involved. I was just a teenage kid who wanted to play footy. It was all a bit of a blur.'[97]

Mann had contacted all players that morning to inform them of developments and arrange for them to have a players' meeting. He recalled: 'It was a crisis situation, so I felt it was important that we get together as a team to discuss what had happened and how we were going to approach things. My role as captain was to try to galvanise the team to put it out of their minds and get on with a game of footy. But it was bloody useless. What do you say? In retrospect, it was a nothing meeting.'[98]

Players and staff were also ordered to attend a compulsory meeting at the MCG at 10.30am (just four hours before the start of the match against North Melbourne), where Don Duffy explained, only in broad terms, why Smith had been sacked. He said it had been a unanimous decision, and one that had been forced upon the committee after Smith's repeated criticism of club officials. Duffy implied that Smith was power-hungry; that he was 'a dictator who was not seen as a servant of the club because he saw himself *as* the club';[99] that he 'wanted to control too many people, and that he'd gotten too big for himself and had overstepped the mark'.[100]

Duffy then sternly warned the players against becoming politically involved in the issue. Vice-captain Bryan Kenneally, who, like many others at the club at the time, believed the sacking would never have eventuated if Bert Chadwick had still

---

[97] Frank Davis. Interview with the author.
[98] Hassa Mann. Interview with the author.
[99] Hassa Mann. Interview with the author.
[100] Robert 'Tassie' Johnson. Interview with the author.

been in charge, remembered: 'Don Duffy threatened to discipline us if we didn't toe the line. He made it very clear that there would be consequences for players who spoke out of turn and became politically involved. He wanted us to pull our heads in, sit in the background and just play football. That annoyed me to some degree. When you've played your guts out for Norm for years, it was difficult to take any other side of the argument than Norm's.'[101]

Duffy then went even further, and completely overstepped the bounds of his own position, according to Mann:

> In those days, the captains appeared every Sunday on *World of Sport* on Channel Seven. But Don Duffy came up to me and said: 'You are not to appear on *World of Sport* tomorrow, and you are not to publicly discuss the committee's decision, or take sides in the matter.'
>
> I thought: 'That stinks', so I defied him.
>
> I said: 'Don, I *will* be appearing on *World of Sport* tomorrow; I *will* be discussing what's happened, and I *will* be advising that I am fully supportive of Norm Smith'.
>
> Don Duffy repeated his warning: 'You will *not* appear, and you will *not* discuss. If you do, your captaincy will be in jeopardy'.
>
> Again, my response was: 'Don, I will. And if it means I'm not captain next week, so be it'.[102]

That day, however, Duffy saw fit to tell *The Sun*: 'Norm Smith's services were dispensed with last night as the culmination of a long and painful business over the last few weeks'.[103]

Following the crisis meeting at the MCG, a number of players were confused and upset, which in turn exploded into anger. At some point, they considered staging a player revolt in defiance of the committee's decision. The question was raised: 'Should we play?' Suddenly, there was a possibility that the players would boycott the match against North Melbourne. The players were 'up in arms', and a number of them 'would've been quite happy not to play'.[104]

Cardwell was conscious of this prospect very early on. He telephoned seconds' team manager George Lenne and said: 'Make sure all your players are there today; we might need to call on them because some of the senior players mightn't turn up

---

[101] Bryan Kenneally. Interview with the author.
[102] Hassa Mann. Interview with the author.
[103] *The Sun*, Monday July 26, 1965.
[104] Hassa Mann. Interview with the author.

out of protest'.[105] Cardwell also arranged for both Brian Dixon and Ian Ridley to talk the players into taking the field. Dixon said he was approached 'as the most senior player', and because Mann's 'very, very close' relationship with Smith might influence proceedings. He recalled: 'I did as the committee requested, and simply reinforced the message that the club is bigger than the man, no matter how big the man is, and we all have to knuckle down'.[106]

Ridley was chosen to address the players because he 'had a foot in both camps' – as a former teammate of some of the players, and a committee member, albeit a junior one. Ridley felt 'there was no doubt that when I walked into the room, the chances of them changing their minds and playing were very limited'. He told them: 'Hang on; you just can't do this. You have an obligation to represent the club, whether you like it or not, no matter what happens. Players should never get involved in politics at football clubs, even though this is something that directly affects you. You are players. Your responsibility is to play'.[107]

Thankfully, a strike was averted, after Mann came to the conclusion: 'Norm would've expected us to play, and he would've expected us to win'. Mann later reflected: 'Deep down, it would never have happened – we were always going to play. It just showed how strongly we felt as a group about the treatment that had been meted out to Norm'.[108]

One player who was particularly distraught was John Lord, who revealed:

> I thought: 'Bloody hell! Have I had something to do with this?!' Even though I wasn't to know what had been happening behind the scenes, I had awful thoughts – a guilty conscience – for 10 or 20 years, believing I had something to do with getting Norm sacked. But I had nothing to do with it; I was innocent in the whole thing.[109]

Dixon's role in the sacking has long been the subject of speculation. However, he was adamant he did not lobby for Smith's removal:

> I was absolutely stunned when the sacking took place and I certainly had nothing to do with saying anything to anyone about whether or not Norm should or shouldn't be the coach. I didn't know anything about it; I was oblivious to it all. I only know what other people tell me. I've got absolutely nothing to hide about

---

[105] George Lenne. Interview with the author.
[106] Brian Dixon. Interview with the author.
[107] Ian Ridley. Interview with the author.
[108] Hassa Mann. Interview with the author.
[109] John Lord. Interview with the author.

that. I had no problem with him remaining as coach. I certainly wasn't part of any movement to unseat Norm.

I mean, this is 1965, I'm a Member of Parliament, fully immersed in my political activities, apart from my football of course. I'd played one of my best games just a couple of weeks earlier against Hawthorn - I took 19 marks or something. I certainly wasn't unhappy with the way the team was being operated. I can't imagine why people would think that I was in some way involved in trying to scuttle Norman because that's not true. And in any case, the committee would make its mind up as to what it wanted to do.

Norm and I always had a very civil relationship. He was a very, very significant person in my life. He certainly taught me a lot about self-discipline and external discipline, and I'm grateful to him for that.[110]

The Demons would try to retain some of the discipline Smith had instilled by appointing his mentor, Checker Hughes, as his short-term replacement. That afternoon, Hughes, at the age of 71 years and five months, became – and remains – the oldest coach in VFL/AFL history. By that stage, however, Hughes (who had relinquished his position as chairman of selectors at the start of the season) was 'way past it as a coach'.[111] As it was impractical for a man of Hughes' age and limited mobility to conduct training, the committee enlisted the services of Bluey Adams, who had been coaching Melbourne's fourths (under-17s). Adams, who had retired at the end of the previous season, was to train the players, under direction from Hughes and the match committee.

Against this hostile backdrop, the Demons journeyed to Coburg to take on the Kangaroos. Before the match, both Cardwell and Hughes 'made it very clear' to a writer from *The Sporting Globe* that they 'didn't want to cast any doubt on their admiration and appreciation for Norm Smith as a coach and a man'. And, they said, 'that went for the rest of the committee'.[112]

Hassa Mann described the atmosphere in the visitors' changerooms:

> The mood among the players and in the rooms before the game was one of disbelief, of shock. Players had glazed looks in their eyes, like they were wondering: 'Where's Norm?' It was almost a funeral-type atmosphere – certainly not what you wanted before a game of league football. It was the kind of atmosphere where

---

[110] Brian Dixon. Interview with the author.
[111] Ian Ridley. Interview with the author.
[112] *The Sporting Globe*, Saturday July 24, 1965.

you didn't even want to talk to your best mate in the team – you didn't feel like talking to anyone. If you mentioned Norm Smith's name, you felt the eyes of committeemen glaring at you. We were expected to just accept it and carry on as though nothing had happened. But our spiritual leader, the man that we held in such esteem, wasn't there. It would have been completely different if, for example, Norm had been sick and we knew he was going to be there the next week. But he was out – for all intents and purposes, never to be seen again.

Checker addressed us before the game, but I can't remember a word he said, and that's no disrespect to Checker – it was all just a blur.[113]

The sacking 'hung over the ground like a shroud',[114] and the spectre of Norm Smith also loomed large in the North Melbourne changerooms. Kangaroos coach Alan Killigrew – famously known as 'Killa' and 'The Hot Gospeller', the latter for his fire-and-brimstone style – told his players: 'This trouble over Norm Smith is the biggest bombshell since Pearl Harbor. What can you expect from Melbourne about it? You can bet Norm instilled into his chaps that the club is greater than the individual and they'll do a little bit extra today. OK, so North is bigger than the individual and you, too, must pull a little bit more out of the bag'.[115]

It's little wonder then that the Kangaroos performed so well and the Demons so poorly. As the Melbourne team ran onto the field, supporters urged them to: 'Play for Norm! Play for Norm!'[116] But playing football was the last thing most of them wanted to do. They didn't even feel like being there, let alone putting their bodies on the line for their mates... and for a club that had the previous night so contemptuously axed a man who had been a second father to many of them.

The Demons encountered a North Melbourne side that had entered the match with a 2-10 record – seven games behind Melbourne – and had lost each of its five home games at Coburg that year. The Demons had not been beaten by the Kangaroos in more than 12 years, but that did not stop them from suffering a 21-point loss that day, and tumbling out of the four to sixth. Some spectators aired a conspiracy theory that the Melbourne players had staged a protest by simply not trying. Such wild accusations were way off the mark. The Demons had tried... it's just that their hearts were not in the contest. In 'six inches of mud'[117] – conditions where heart beats skill every time – the more fancied Demons were doomed to defeat.

---

[113] Hassa Mann. Interview with the author.
[114] Russ Properjohn, *The Sun*, Monday July 26, 1965.
[115] *The Sporting Globe*, Saturday July 24, 1965.
[116] *The Herald*, Monday July 26, 1965.
[117] Bryan Kenneally. Interview with the author.

John Lord observed: 'From a playing point of view, the damage it caused was immediate. The Coburg ground was, at best, a sub-standard slush-heap. We weren't beaten by a better side – I am trying to be gracious in defeat here! – but by a side that could play better in those conditions and without any shock announcements'.[118]

After the match, committeemen attempted to impose restrictions on the players, ordering them not to visit Smith's house (which was little over a kilometre west on Bell Street) and reminding them that attendance at the dinner-dance at the MCG was compulsory. The players were told to 'basically disassociate themselves' from Smith. The normally mild-mannered Mann reacted angrily.

'You can't do that,' snapped the skipper. 'Don't expect me to even listen to what you are saying if that's the line you're going to push. I'm going back to Norm's place, and that's that. And anyone else who wants to do the same should be free to do it without fear of recriminations.'[119]

Cardwell had also gathered the trainers immediately after the match and, with tears in his eyes, informed them: 'The committee has ordered me to tell you gentlemen that you are not to go to Norm Smith's house tonight'.

Hugh McPherson was disgusted.

'Jimmy,' McPherson said, 'the damn committee doesn't have the power to make such a demand.'

Cardwell: 'I'm just doing as I'm told, Hughie'.

'Well, Jim,' McPherson said, 'Norm's my mate and I'm not about to abandon him in his time of need. Please accept my resignation.'[120]

Not only did the Melbourne trainers attend a gathering at Smith's house (along with the vast majority of players) but they also presented the Smiths with a watch each, as a token of their sympathy and appreciation.

For the first time since he could remember, Smith had not spent a winter Saturday at a football ground. Instead, he and Marj drank tea and coffee, and Marj smoked cigarettes, as they listened to the match on radio. It was, Smith lamented, 'the first time for 31 years that I've had to listen to something that I love'. It was 'not very easy to take',[121] particularly in light of the result, which 'terribly disappointed' him.[122]

But they did not suffer their disappointment alone. Friends from Melbourne and other clubs gathered around them for a night that was described by some as a

---

[118] John Lord. Interview with the author.
[119] Hassa Mann. Interview with the author.
[120] Hugh McPherson. Interview with the author.
[121] *The Tony Charlton Football Show.*
[122] *Melbourne Truth*, Saturday July 31, 1965.

wake and others as a party. In any case, it went late into the night. Marj recalled: 'We had so many people in and out of the house – we weren't lonely'.[123]

McPherson found it difficult to see Smith in such a distressed state, recalling: 'He was very upset. It was like his heart had been ripped out of his chest'.[124]

Mann admired the strength and selflessness Smith displayed just 24 hours after receiving the shock of his life:

> A lot of people wanted to talk to Norm and sympathise with him, but what do you say? But he was still the same Norm Smith. His attitude was: 'Forget about me. This is life, and life goes on. The football club will still go on – it'll still be around in the year 2000. You guys have got a job to do, you're representing the Melbourne Football Club and you've got to perform. You're sitting near the top of the ladder – go out and win another one'.
>
> All he wanted to do was talk about the club because the club was his life. Norm could be critical of individuals, but he could never, *ever*, be critical of the footy club. It provided him with a career, it made him as a person, and he couldn't say anything adverse about the footy club.
>
> It was hard to hear him say: 'Forget me' – it doesn't work that way. We couldn't *forget* him. In fact, I would have been there until 10 or 11 o'clock and went straight home afterwards. I didn't want to go back to the club because all some people would want to do is talk about it, and that was the last thing I wanted to do.[125]

Len Smith spoke about it that night. He was briefly interviewed by Channel Nine from his brother's loungeroom. Len was adamant: 'The allegations made against him are false... and I'm sure they'll be proved wrong in the end... There's not a word I can think of to express my opinion about it all'.[126]

ŶŶŶŶŶŶŶŶŶ

Not all of Melbourne's committeemen were blacklisted by Norm Smith. In fact, he had remained on friendly terms with some of the men who had voted to sack him. Smith had received a telephone call from Terry Gleeson, who admitted to voting in favour of sacking him, and although Gleeson did not back away from the decision, he offered Smith an apology.

---

[123] *The Tony Charlton Football Show.*
[124] Hugh McPherson. Interview with the author.
[125] Hassa Mann. Interview with the author.
[126] *The Tony Charlton Football Show.*

'I understand,' said Smith. 'I don't blame you. It's some of those other bastards that I've got a problem with.'[127]

He had also remained in close contact with Ian Ridley. On the Saturday morning, he telephoned Ridley and 'summoned' him.

'Come over tomorrow morning,' he told Ridley. 'I want to see you.'

Ridley thought: 'I'm the only member of the committee who didn't have a vote, so I'm probably the only one he'd want to speak to'. He recalled: 'I suspect that Norm wanted to his suck my guts for information, but he got one hell of a shock with what I told him'.[128]

Ridley and his wife Judith were 'quite nervous' as they travelled to the Smith house. But when pressed by Smith, Ridley said: 'You were in the wrong, Norm. You brought it upon yourself. With the way you've been behaving and your lack of respect for committeemen, you deserved to be sacked. You more or less asked for it. You gave them a reason to do it. What else could you expect the committee to do?'

Judith Ridley recalled: 'Ian didn't say it in a nasty or aggressive way. He said it in a reasonable, very matter-of-fact way. Norm was probably a little surprised with what Ian said to him, and he obviously didn't agree with it, but he listened and accepted it. Norm was fairly subdued – he certainly didn't rant and rave. He obviously respected Ian's opinion – if he didn't, he wouldn't have asked us to go out there in the first place. There certainly wasn't any animosity between them'.[129]

☥☥☥☥☥☥☥☥☥

On Saturday, as the football world digested the news of his dismissal, Smith had fended off numerous telephone calls from newspapers, radio and television stations, each desperate for him to tell his story exclusively. Each time, the response was: 'No comment'.

Although he had permitted a visit from his *Herald* friend Alf Brown that day, he had told the doyen reporter he did not want to comment just yet because he needed time to absorb the whole situation in his own mind. Brown observed: 'He was most upset, but he had his feelings well under control'.[130]

Channel Seven offered Smith £1000 ($2000) – a massive sum considering the Demons were paying him £1500 ($3000) a season – but he immediately rejected

---

[127] Terry Gleeson. Interview with the author.
[128] Ian Ridley. Interview with the author.
[129] Judith Ridley. Interview with the author.
[130] *The Herald*, Saturday July 24, 1965.

it. It was a simple matter of principle and loyalty. He was contractually bound to Channel Nine, and specifically *The Tony Charlton Football Show*, and Charlton was also a close friend, so if he were to air his thoughts on the controversy, it would be on Nine.

Charlton recalled that Smith 'didn't take much coaxing' to agree to appear on the show. He said: 'Norm kept his word to me. He just said: "I'll do it". I know that he was approached and offered a large sum of money by the Seven network – as he should have been. After all, this was *the* football story. But Norm kept his powder dry, so to speak, until our Sunday sports show. I admired him enormously for doing so, because it was a hell of a time for him. He remained true to the qualities of honesty and integrity that I already knew he possessed'.[131]

Charlton's popular program was assured its place in Australian television history on Sunday July 25, 1965, when Norm Smith used it as his forum to respond to the sacking. What followed was one of the most riveting and powerful hours of 'footy TV' imaginable.[132]

In many ways, it was a difficult decision for Smith to agree to speak out. He regarded the public airing of dirty linen as cancerous. He preferred to keep problems in-house. So the idea of revealing his rawest, innermost feelings about such a sensitive issue on television – in front of a massive viewing audience – would normally have struck him as a self-demeaning way for a man of his standing to conduct himself. He would have given serious consideration to observing what is commonly referred to as a dignified silence – aside from, of course, articulating some choice words to those responsible for his predicament – and simply let his record, the public, and the overwhelming majority of Demons supporters speak for him. But in this instance his core values of honesty and integrity had been questioned, so different rules applied. As his old mate Bill Stephen observed: 'Honesty was everything to Norm – he prided himself on it – so to have doubt cast over his honesty made him wild, and he wouldn't rest until the truth came out and he was proven correct. And pity those who crossed him'.[133]

Smith believed that the gloves were off; that he had been pushed beyond all reasonable limits of tolerance (as, no doubt, the committee had also), and treated with such contempt, that he felt duty-bound to expose the truth – his truth. He felt it was important that Melbourne supporters, and the wider football community, know what was going on at his club.

---

[131] Tony Charlton. Interview with the author.
[132] A short video clip of this controversial episode of The Tony Charlton Football Show appears on YouTube – *au.youtube.com/watch?v=6XZJRuj5z6w*
[133] Bill Stephen. Interview with the author.

'I don't feel I am being disloyal to the club in speaking (out),' he explained to Charlton. 'My loyalty is to the club, and not to individuals. And I believe it is in the best interests of the club that the true story should be told... The full, true story has to be told somewhere.'[134]

His approach was to lash out in the most upfront way he knew. If it brought about some positive action, and some back-pedalling, from the Melbourne committee, well and good, if the status quo remained, at least he had enlightened people to his perspective on the drama so that they could make up their own minds.

Many fans who tuned in to *The Tony Charlton Football Show* at lunchtime that Sunday were eager to devour any insight Smith was prepared to offer just 40 hours after his dismissal. But with his reputation for giving little away publicly – he had always been wary of supplying opposition coaches with 'ammunition' – the expectation was that he might speak briefly and only in general terms about his battles with the committee; at best, he might cryptically allude to few specific problems. But few could have predicted the stinging vitriol and emotional torment – and the stunning counter-allegations – that would spew forth like molten lava from the mouth of football's Mr Ruthless.

Charlton and his crew were understandably excited about the telecast. This, after all, would be one of the sporting scoops of the century. 'It was an amateurish production compared to modern standards,' Charlton later reflected, 'but for its time, I suppose it was quite engaging and dramatic.'[135] Such a modest, understated appraisal did little justice to a captivating program – good judges like experienced sports broadcaster and writer Stephen Phillips unashamedly regard it as 'the most amazing hour of television you'll ever see' – in which the sacking saga was covered in detail from virtually every conceivable newsworthy angle.

Titled 'The Norm Smith Story', the program opened with melodramatic, foreboding music and a sombre introduction from host Charlton, who announced the focus of the show as he pondered the key questions to viewers: 'What's this all about? How did it start? How could such a thing have possibly happened?... And why has this decision had such a widespread effect on this community? Why, indeed, has it created nothing less than a furore? Well, we will try to answer those questions, and those in between, in this special sports show on a monumental football decision'.

Although the program had a funereal tone, it did not take long for the fireworks to start. Smith generally appeared composed and calculated, but there were times

---

[134] *Melbourne Truth*, Saturday July 31, 1965.
[135] Tony Charlton. Interview with the author.

when he spoke through clenched teeth, and snarled, and others where he seemed to choke back tears.

The frequent use of close-ups in the camera work also added to the drama, with the lens zooming in on Smith as he let loose the pain and fury from within. Charlton later said: 'It was a surreal experience to interview Norm that day. There was great tension about it, and the explosive nature of this amazing story meant the atmosphere was just electric in the studio'.[136]

Truth's television critic, 'Veritas', later wrote: 'I would conservatively estimate that more than a million viewers were more hushed at 12 noon... than they are even at 11 o'clock on Armistice Day'.[137]

After Smith had revealed part of his story, and blasted the committee in the process, Charlton asked him: 'You don't feel you are being unreasonable in (making) comments of that kind?'

'Unreasonable?' he barked. 'I reckon I'm being *very* reasonable. I feel like saying a lot more.' He then started down the barrel of the camera and personally addressed the committee: 'And I say this to the 12 guilty men... sit back... and you just watch it'.

He implied that a kind of tall poppy syndrome might also have been partly responsible for the row. 'I think there (were)... two images of Melbourne that certain people wanted to destroy: in one sense it was Ronny, and then I think the other sense it's me... I can't understand it, Tony. I think it's jealousy. I looked at *The Sun* yesterday and I saw there I was "controversial", "master tactician", but at the end of it, it had another word – "successful". And I think with success brings jealousy. And I know that there are a lot of jealous men, but I could just shake them off, shrug my shoulders and ignore them, and it was this ignoring of people down at Melbourne that made the whole thing blow up'.

When Charlton speculated that perhaps the committee had taken the view that the club was bigger than the individual, Smith fired back:

> The club has *always* been bigger than the individual... But it's also bigger than 12 men who sit around a table. They don't own it! They're only delegated by the members, by myself, a member of the Melbourne Cricket Club, to run the club... for the best interests of the supporters. But they just go their own way... Surely this Melbourne Football Club committee are going to be big enough to offer me an apology. (But) it won't be forthcoming because they're not men enough.

---

[136] Tony Charlton. Interview with the author.
[137] *Melbourne Truth*, Saturday July 31, 1965.

In response to the accusation of disloyalty, Smith said: 'I have spoken to members of committee and told them that they were weak... (But) I didn't consider this to be disloyal. I didn't speak about them outside'. Neither did he try to conceal his own failings, prompting laughter with: 'I was a naughty boy at some selection committees – I got quite argumentative. Yeah, I know, you can't understand it, but... I did'. However, he revealed he had 'seen other things go on' which he could have reported to the committee. 'I've seen a committeeman come there and get drunk and go to sleep at selection committee,' Smith revealed. '(But) I don't go back and report it. You (don't) tittle-tattle. We're a football club, we're not a girls' school! ... I did the wrong thing at times, but other people did the wrong thing too.'

Smith was particularly upset by the fact a player had seemingly lied to committeemen about the content of his address to the players at training, and then the committee's willingness to accept the player's word over that of others. '*No player can say it*!' Smith asserted. 'Because it's a complete and utter lie. And there is someone lying in the club.'

Duffy and Cardwell declined an invitation for the committee to appear on the program, either in person or via a filmed interview. Unlike Smith, the committee resolved to keep a dignified silence – although there was nothing dignified about the fallout of their decision, or the manner in which it was carried out. However, Duffy conceded to demand by making a recorded audio statement, which said in part: 'The Melbourne football committee deeply regrets the step it found necessary to take... I must say that this decision was unanimous. Both the club and Norman Smith have personal dignity and feelings, which a public debate would not help and would possibly harm, and it's for this reason it was felt we should not indulge in such an action. Norman Smith's long and loyal service to the club over many years is acknowledged and this is something which made the whole decision a very difficult one to make... (But) the committee is quite sure that it made the right decision'. The statement clearly bemused the Smiths. As the recording was aired, a strained-looking Marj Smith (who had accompanied her husband into the studio) raised her eyebrows slightly for a split-second as she and Smith exchanged glances across the room.

Marj also consented to a rare interview with Charlton. It wasn't a token appearance either. Marj, whom Smith described as 'a solid ally in this crisis',[138] felt strongly about the unjust nature of her husband's sacking and was determined to express her feelings. With the words MRS. NORM SMITH appearing on the

---

[138] *Melbourne Truth*, Saturday July 31, 1965.

screen, Marj said: 'I know Norm, at times, is argumentative. I know he clashes with committeemen. But Norm is an honest man. I've never known Norm to tell a lie ever, and... until he dies, (he) will be able to walk with his head up. But there's people at Melbourne (who are) going to have to walk with their head down. If their head's up, you can look straight into their eyes (and) there's going to be a most peculiar look there because there's something wrong'.

Others agreed there was something amiss. Three Melbourne players – captain Hassa Mann, vice-captain Bryan Kenneally and star rover John Townsend – arrived in the studio of their own volition to offer their views and refute allegations. Reflecting on his appearance alongside his two leaders, Townsend said: 'It was probably none of our bloody business, but we thought that whatever had happened was bullshit and we wanted to show our support for Smithy. He was No.1. He was the man as far as coaches went. He virtually ran the Melbourne Football Club himself. He ran selection, the medical centre, everything. We thought he was as good as it gets, and no-one else came close to him in his time. Norm was the bloke who'd made me any sort of a footballer. I came under his influence straight from school. You felt lucky just to come in contact with the man, so probably the least we could do was show our support'.[139]

Another voluntary guest was Ron Barassi, who appeared visibly shaken by Smith's demise. Barassi said:

> I've come to... back up my friend Norm. Unfortunately... I'm with another club and I perhaps can't say as much as I would like - the program's not long enough anyway! But I would say one thing: everyone knows it's a tragedy... but the thing that I feel is mostly unjust is the allegations that the club have made on Norm Smith's character, which I feel is wrong, and I can't understand any committee coming to this decision... after knowing the man the way they have...
>
> I've admired Norm very much as a man and I feel that Melbourne owe a tremendous amount of their success to him. They've won six premierships in 10 years, and I'd doubt if they would've won more than two or three without him...
>
> What success I've had has been mostly due to the fact that I've improved as a player and Norm has been instrumental in this, but also due to the fact that I've been with successful teams and this is where Norm has been the leading hand. He's made successful teams possible (and) I've been part of them... I'm grateful to him... He's been like a father to me.

---

[139] John Townsend. Interview with the author.

Smith's fellow panellists then had their say, and offered strong character testimony. Magpie great Phonse Kyne said: 'I can't find words adequate enough to express my deepest expression of gratitude to a great fella... It's Norm Smith the man that I want to talk about. He's a straight-shooter. His hand of friendship is always there for you.' Former Carlton coach Ken Hands, who had resigned in acrimonious circumstances at the end of 1964, said: 'He's a man... and he doesn't know how to lie... I've had an experience, too, similar to Norm, and I'd say this: there's one thing you cannot beat and that's lies. And if lies go on, and you haven't got a chance to defend yourself, you are gone for sure'. Retired Hawthorn star Brendan Edwards said Smith's dismissal was 'like taking a pilot out of an aeroplane while it's in the air'. Another analogy came from ex-umpire and commentator Ian Cleland. 'Looking at it from a business point of view,' Cleland explained, 'if I've got a good manager at a plant... and he is a successful man... and he's paying us a 15 or 20 percent dividend, would I get rid of that man? I would listen to his reasons and I would reason with him. I don't want to go down and only be paid 2.5 percent. I would stick where the success is.'

Perhaps the most glowing reference came from Jack Mueller, who was interviewed for the program. 'I would say,' Mueller began, 'that this is one of the greatest calamities that ever happened at Melbourne... I don't think we'll be able to replace Smithy at Melbourne for many, many years... He's a colossal man.'

This colossal man, once his version of events had been told, appeared only concerned about the future of Melbourne Football Club. When Charlton stated 'this will split the club wide open', Smith bristled with passion for the Demons. 'This, Tony, could *make* the club,' Smith declared. 'It'll split the club if it's allowed to continue, but if they approach it the right way, it could make it. This is a time when you find your friends and from disharmony like this, when people get together, this is when you get strength, and this is a way the Melbourne club can get strength, by getting men there of substance with the right principles.'

He urged Melbourne supporters to band together to oust the committee. He said, 'The repercussions I'd like it to have is that every Melbourne Football Club supporter and every Melbourne Cricket Club supporter registers a protest in the strongest terms at the way it's been handled. Get rid of these blokes! That's the only way the club will progress.'

It was also the only way Smith would consider coaching the Demons again. 'There's only one way I'd ever go back to Melbourne: if those men ever offer themselves for election,' he said. 'They've never stood for an election. If they offer themselves for election; if they've got the courage of their convictions, they'll do this... But I don't think they will. They sit back and they're snug and they don't even approach me. They do it behind my back, everything that's done down there. Why? They're things I don't do'.

As for his own immediate future, and the potential of a switch to Richmond, he insisted: 'I'm Melbourne at this stage, Tony. I'm Melbourne. To talk about anything like that would be against these principles that I mentioned. I am Melbourne, and I am Melbourne through and through'.

After the show, St Kilda coach Allan Jeans expressed his commiserations. Smith had always liked Jeans. 'Stay,' Smith said, 'and I'll tell you what happened.'

Jeans took him up on his offer. They had a few beers at Nine before going to Shane McGrath's pub in North Melbourne, where they spent the afternoon and the early evening. Smith was presumably attempting to drown his sorrows, but talking about the situation was also therapeutic. He and Jeans also had a bit of a laugh when Mary McGrath criticised her husband for 'sacking his best mate'. (McGrath had actually voted against sacking Smith.)

When night fell, Smith asked Jeans if he would like to go back to his house for some of Marj's home cooking.

'No,' said Jeans, 'I think I've had enough for the day.'[140]

Smith had, too. It had been a big day, and a big weekend.

♈♈♈♈♈♈♈♈♈

Tony Charlton's long-held regret was that he invited the Smiths back to the Nine studios for a private screening of his much-publicised program. Charlton thought he was doing the right thing, as a matter of courtesy, but he became remorseful soon after the tape started rolling.

The program had been a huge success. It had provoked enormous public reaction and debate, and had attracted almost blanket newspaper coverage the next day (*The Sun* devoted its opening three pages to the drama; editors at *The Age* decided it warranted both the front and back pages), with the result being that Nine had 'scooped the sweet cream off the biggest cup of news coffee in Australian Rules modern history'.[141] Charlton decided 'it would be a good idea that everybody who was involved in it ought to sit back and have a look at it'.

Charlton explained:

---

[140] Allan Jeans. Interview with the author.
[141] *Melbourne Truth*, Saturday July 31, 1965.

> Norm sat there watching it with Marj, and although neither of them passed any comment, I felt it upset them and made them uncomfortable. I felt I put him through something I didn't need to. I thought: 'Maybe it would have been better had I not done that'. It was done unwittingly because I was young and hadn't thought it through. I had been thinking solely from an entertainment perspective rather than the human element, and the deep emotions it dredged up.
>
> I've always felt that the whole sacking saga led to the heart problems Norm later experienced, so to think that you had perhaps added to that trauma - even in only a very small way - certainly was a sobering realisation.[142]

Although the Melbourne committee's reaction to Smith's television outburst was, publicly, one of great disappointment – and, privately, one of horror – it still refused to be goaded into a slanging match with its former coach. Jim Cardwell expressed great pity that Smith felt he had to speak out in such a manner. 'We are genuinely sorry,' Cardwell said, 'that Norman and his wife Marjorie should have had to suffer such an emotional experience as they did during that long interview.'

However, Duffy unwittingly fanned the flames of the debate when he expressed the view that the issue was 'something between the club and Smith' and that neither Smith nor the public needed to be told everything. 'The club is disturbed by the bias of some of the statements made by Norman Smith,' Duffy said of the television appearance. 'But we still do not want to indulge in any criticism of him. It is obvious that there was more behind Smith's dismissal than appeared in the letter to him. We could have said a lot more'.[143]

This refusal to divulge the full details of the sacking provoked more confusion from Smith, 'I want to know why I was sacked,' he said. 'It bewilders me that Dr Duffy should say there were more reasons than those in the letter for my dismissal.' It also raised the question in his mind of why he was sacked on the Friday night and not the Wednesday. 'I did nothing from that Wednesday night meeting to Friday to incur the sack,' he said. 'So surely they should have brought all the allegations before me on the Wednesday night.'[144]

ŸŸŸŸŸŸŸŸŸŸ

---

[142] Tony Charlton. Interview with the author.
[143] *The Sun*, Monday July 26, 1965.
[144] *Melbourne Truth*, Saturday July 31, 1965.

SACKED [1965]

Ron Barassi was so upset about Smith's sacking that he raced around to Jim Cardwell's house to confront the Melbourne secretary.

Such an act was not undertaken lightly by Barassi, who regarded Cardwell as 'a marvellous man and a tremendous administrator'. "In fact," he said, 'I don't think Melbourne would have been as great without him'.[145] But Barassi also knew that the Demons could not have achieved success without Norm Smith, and just could not fathom how he could have been cast aside.

When Cardwell answered the door, the Melbourne-superstar-cum-Carlton-coach was glowering at him. 'I want a word with you!' Barassi demanded. 'I want to give you a piece of my bloody mind!'

Barassi cannot recall exactly what he said once he was invited inside – 'I think I was too blind with fury to remember,' he recalled – but he has no doubt that 'Jimmy got the message'.[146]

One theory was that Barassi threatened that unless Smith received an apology and was reinstated, he (Barassi) would never have anything more to do with the club, much less return to coach the Demons one day. Barassi did not dismiss the theory. 'That seems to resemble my mood at the time,' he said. 'I was absolutely furious. It was one of the worst times in my football life. I should never have gotten involved. It had nothing to do with me – I was at another club. But I felt compelled to say something. It makes me wonder how I would have reacted had I actually still been captain of Melbourne. I would have been right in the middle of it, and my reaction might have got me sacked too!'[147]

As it was, Barassi's reaction was explosive enough. Cardwell, who was on the verge of tears after receiving a frightful blast, told Barassi a player had informed him that Smith had criticised the committee on the Thursday night. Cardwell's wife Mavis later gave an insight into the ruckus caused by Barassi's outburst, revealing to *The Herald's* Alf Brown: 'It was a terrible scene. Jim was greatly upset; Ron was raging and stamping around the house and the Barassi children in the car outside never stopped tooting the horn. The neighbours came into the street to see what it was all about.'[148]

Jim Cardwell died in 1996, but Mavis Cardwell reflected:

> Norm was a tremendous man, very caring, very generous, and because Jim was such a loyal friend of Norm's he would never talk about the sacking.

---

[145] *The AFL Record*, May 16-18, 2003.
[146] Ron Barassi. Interview with the author.
[147] Ron Barassi. Interview with the author.
[148] *The Herald*, 1979.

> We were all terribly sad when Norm was sacked. None of us wanted him to be sacked. It rocked the whole club. It rocked Jim too – he didn't get over that. But it didn't spoil the friendship – we were still very good friends with Norm and Marj.
>
> It was an argument in the club, and it should have remained in the club. It was a case of nobody being able to say sorry. It should never have gotten out like it did. It was a simple thing, but sometimes simple things become big things because neither side will back down. Norm never backed down. You couldn't get a stronger-willed or more determined man – that's why he was such a great coach.
>
> Reporters tried to speak to Jim and I about it ever since, but we would never say anything to blemish Norm's name. He was too good a man for that.
>
> No-one ever came up to me and said anything against Norm. If they had've, I'd have knocked their head off... figuratively speaking of course.[149]

Although Smith felt like taking some scalps, he expressed his best wishes to his replacement, Bluey Adams. 'I wish Bluey Adams well,' Smith said. 'He has been brought up in a successful premiership team, and I am sure he can carry on with the job I left unfinished.'[150]

He also implored the Melbourne players to rise above the off-field problems. He said: 'I want them to think of Melbourne... I still feel they can make the finals. I dearly want them to. I will get a tremendous thrill if they go on and win. My heart is with them. I appeal to the players to give everything to the game, and to get behind the coaches. They have a big task but they are a tremendous bunch of young fellows and I'm proud of them. I know they can do the job, and they will have no keener supporter than myself. My relationship with the boys is happy – as coach and pupils, and also in friendship'.[151]

Smith had not even considered his own future. When asked what his plans were, he replied: 'Everybody seems to know where I'm headed but myself'.[152] After unsuccessfully trying to quash persistent rumours that he was a certainty to coach Richmond in 1966, he was also forced to dismiss talk of a possible move interstate after being approached by clubs in South Australia. He had no interest in moving interstate to pursue coaching. 'I'm a Victorian through and through,' he said.[153]

---

[149] Mavis Cardwell. Interview with the author.
[150] *Melbourne Truth*, Saturday July 31, 1965.
[151] *Melbourne Truth*, Saturday July 31, 1965.
[152] *Melbourne Truth*, Saturday July 31, 1965.
[153] *The Tony Charlton Football Show*.

SACKED [1965]

Furthermore, he had not even made up his mind to coach again. 'I don't even know if I will go back to football,' he said.[154]

The Richmond rumour continued to gather steam, and was given more momentum when Duffy opened the path for the Tigers to formally approach Smith. 'Seeing that we dispensed with his services,' Duffy said, 'we certainly would not have the right to put restrictions on him.'[155]

If Smith went to Richmond, 'he would not change grounds, just dressing-rooms'.[156] The Tigers were excited by the prospect. When asked how the Richmond players would feel if Norm Smith moved to Punt Road, full-back Fred Swift enthused: 'We would probably win the premiership for the next 20 years. With the two Smiths at Richmond we would have all the brains in the business'.[157]

With gentle persuasion from his brother, Smith might well have agreed to negotiate with Richmond. But it never got that far. Other plans were afoot to pave the way for him to return to Melbourne.

ȲȲȲȲȲȲȲȲȲ

Norm Smith had supporters in high places. Trevor Rapke, a renowned County Court Judge, was an MCC member, a passionate Demons supporter and 'a real Norm Smith man'.[158] Rapke regarded Smith as a coaching genius, and made it his business to get to the MCG early to secure seats behind the Melbourne bench, so he and his young sons, who were decked out in Demons gear, could watch the master in action from close quarters.

'Colourful, strong, fair and fearless',[159] Rapke also boasted 'an innate ability to smell a rat' in his court, and was 'absolutely horrified' by the Melbourne committee's treatment of Smith.[160] He felt compelled to act, to introduce some sanity to the madness, and was uniquely positioned to influence both parties, and perhaps even broker a reconciliation between club and coach.

After careful consideration, Rapke enlisted the expertise of two other eminent men – Audley Gillespie-Jones, a barrister and former Fitzroy and Melbourne player who was teammate of Smith briefly in 1935 and remained one of his oldest friends; and Alex Gray, Melbourne's secretary in 1948-49.

---

[154] *Melbourne Truth*, Saturday July 31, 1965.
[155] *The Sun*, Monday July 26, 1965.
[156] Alf Brown, *The Herald*, Saturday July 24, 1965.
[157] *The Herald*, Tuesday July 27, 1965.
[158] Hugh McPherson. Interview with the author.
[159] County Court Chief Judge Desmond Whelan, eulogy at Trevor Rapke's funeral in January 1978.
[160] Brian Bourke. Interview with the author.

Gillespie-Jones made the initial contact with Smith on the Monday (July 26), and that night drove him to Rapke's house where they talked until after midnight. Smith later admitted: 'I wasn't sure of my attitude when the first approaches were made to me... to see if there could be a reconciliation'.[161] Rapke, who was six years Smith's senior, used all of his powers of persuasion to talk him into 'a more conciliatory frame of mind'.[162] The talks continued the next day and eventually Smith agreed to allow the high-powered trio to work towards healing the rift on his behalf. Smith explained: 'A group, along with hundreds of supporters, asked me if I would reconsider. And I felt, because of their support and loyalty, that I must make myself available... I felt I owed it to... the many people who stood behind me in the crisis'.[163]

He knew only too well he had to prove he was willing to compromise with the committee if he was to have any chance of returning to what he and many others believed was his rightful position as coach of Melbourne. 'There (were) plenty of hard words spoken on both sides at the time,' he later reflected. 'Possibly there were faults on both sides, too. I know I certainly wasn't blameless.'[164]

Rapke also understood the importance of keeping the reconciliation bid secret, which meant enlisting the help of, and confiding in, Alf Brown, the city's best football news-hound. Rapke summoned Brown to his chambers, which were above the dock where Ned Kelly was sentenced to death in 1880. Late that Tuesday afternoon, Rapke outlined his 'Get Norm Smith Back' campaign, before darting back to court, where he was hearing a rape case. At regular intervals, Rapke adjourned the case to scurry to his chambers, 'gown swishing and wig bobbing', for a progress report.[165] Gray and Gillespie-Jones telephoned most of the Melbourne committeemen and were 'surprised and delighted at the mood of reconciliation they encountered',[166] and kept Smith updated on developments at home.

However, Brown was uncomfortable. 'Our mission was to get Norm Smith reinstated at Melbourne,' he later wrote. '(But) I was unhappy. I was there because I was a friend of Smith. But also I was a reporter and here was a story I could not write. I had given my word that I would not write anything until Melbourne agreed to reinstate Smith. A premature disclosure of plans might have blown it.'[167]

---

[161] *Melbourne Truth*, Saturday July 31, 1965.
[162] Alf Brown, *The Herald*, Wednesday July 28, 1965.
[163] *Melbourne Truth*, Saturday July 31, 1965.
[164] *The Sun* series, 1967.
[165] *The Herald*, May 4, 1979.
[166] Alf Brown, *The Herald*, Wednesday July 28, 1965.
[167] *The Herald*, May 4, 1979.

SACKED [1965]

Gray and Gillespie-Jones arranged to meet Duffy at The Tavern at the MCG at 5.15pm. By 6pm, Duffy still had not turned up, by which time the mediators' hopes of reconciliation had grown more forlorn by the minute. Gillespie-Jones walked around to the football clubrooms where he was informed by Cardwell that Duffy had been delayed at a monthly Melbourne Cricket Club meeting. When Duffy eventually arrived at the meeting point – about an hour late – Gillespie-Jones went straight to the crux of the matter.

'Is the door still open?' he asked.

Duffy replied: 'Yes'.

After further discussion, Gillespie-Jones drove to the Smith house to fill them in on the state of play and arrange a meeting between Smith and the committee. Gillespie-Jones later called the club. The phone was answered by Don Cordner, who was told: 'Norm had agreed to meet the committee. He is in a most receptive mood. What is the mood of the committee?'

Cordner went away, came back and said the committee was 'most amenable' to such a proposition.

Gillespie-Jones 'could almost see Dr Cordner smiling over the phone'.[168]

That was at 8.25pm. Smith and Gillespie-Jones met the committee at the MCG just before 9pm. Ian Ridley met them in the foyer and they spoke briefly. Ridley recalled: 'Norm appeared tense but happy enough. He could have been stepping into a bit of a hornets' nest, but you just hoped it all didn't flare up again'.[169]

They were greeted by the two doctors – Duffy and Cordner. Gillespie-Jones said afterwards: 'Our reception was magnificent. Committeemen showed great sympathy, tact and understanding... and the meeting was a huge success.' During a two-and-a-half hour discussion – which Smith said was accompanied by 'tremendous tension' but had been conducted in a 'manly and commonsense fashion'[170] – both parties, perhaps realising how their words and actions had been misconstrued, came to an understanding. Another consideration for the committee had been the hostile backlash from supporters. The club had received irate phone calls and letters, and a notice of motion from a member calling for the resignation of the entire committee. Smith had received numerous letters, hundreds of visitors and about 1000 phone calls of support. The phone virtually had not stopped ringing in the Smith house.

That Tuesday evening, after 11pm, the committee made its second monumental decision in the space of just 100 hours. Norm Smith was reinstated as the coach of

---

[168] *The Herald*, Wednesday July 28, 1965.
[169] Ian Ridley. Interview with the author.
[170] *Melbourne Truth*, Saturday July 31, 1965.

Melbourne. Smith was adamant: 'Nobody had to eat humble pie for me to rejoin Melbourne. My job as coach was offered back to me after talks. I wanted it, and I took it'.[171]

After the dramatic reconciliation, Smith and Duffy agreed to a joint, late-night interview with Tony Charlton on Channel Nine. Smith reassured Demons fans: 'The way this matter has been handled tonight, it's been handled to the satisfaction of myself, and I'm sure it's been handled to the satisfaction of the committee... I felt rather relieved and I thought: "Well, if they are prepared to meet me, I am prepared to meet them halfway – or even more than halfway".' In reality, both parties had gone more than halfway, and completed virtual 180-degree changes in attitude to bring about the reinstatement. Smith had said he would only return to Melbourne if its committee members offered themselves for election; likewise, Duffy had been adamant the committee had made the correct decision and would not change it.

From the debris that had been scattered so indiscriminately over the previous four days, Smith enthused: 'I think we will see Melbourne more united than ever... I am very happy to be back at Melbourne and look out: we are going on to better things. Essendon might be the form team at the moment, but it mightn't be in a month.'[172] It was more a hope than likelihood. But such spin-doctoring was entirely necessary on Smith's behalf after his warts and all exposé on *The Tony Charlton Football Show* just two days earlier. For the benefit of all parties, it was important to present a positive, united public front... even if it was just a charade. Perhaps continuing this theme, Duffy said he was 'very pleased' to announce that 'the difficulties have been resolved' and that Smith was back as coach. The reconciled president and coach were photographed by *The Sun* smiling broadly and shaking hands. All appeared forgiven, even if all participants to the affair regretfully understood it could never be forgotten.

Smith revealed it was the first time he had relaxed in a week, and the same could be said for his loyal wife. Smith, who described Marj as his 'staunchest ally', was well aware that recent events had shaken her and had even altered her appearance. But now, to his eyes at least, Marj had turned back the clock. '(She) is looking like a teenager... She looks marvellous again,' he boasted admiringly.[173]

Each of the Melbourne players asked for comment by *The Herald* were also ecstatic about their coach's return. Don Williams said: 'It's the best news

---

[171] *Melbourne Truth*, Saturday July 31, 1965.
[172] *The Sun*, Wednesday July 28, 1965.
[173] *Melbourne Truth*, Saturday July 31, 1965.

I've heard for years'; Tassie Johnson hailed it as 'a thrill'; while Hassa Mann said: 'It's tremendous to know he's back... Personally I feel something was missing in the short period Smith was away from the club... It's a pleasing shock – much more pleasing than the one I got on Friday night!'[174]

Smith told *Truth* of his intention to make himself available for the Melbourne coaching position for 1966. He also declared with a sense of finality: 'Now is the time to close ranks and get on with the game'.[175]

It was never going to be that simple. The football public was confused. *The Herald* tapped into popular opinion when it questioned the decision-making process of the committee, noting: 'Now, out of all this sea of bitterness, all is sweet and light again. The only people not enlightened are the public. Many of them must feel they have seen an extraordinary new demonstration in making mountains out of molehills'.[176]

Cardwell fuelled more bewilderment by overdoing the public relations campaign. The Demons secretary announced, a little too dreamily: 'Everything in the garden is lovely'.[177] In truth, the 'garden' was dying, and no amount of nurturing would ever return it to full bloom.

The four days between Smith's sacking and reinstatement may as well have been four months for the almost terminal damage it caused the Demons. There had been irreparable breaking of trust. Indeed, as Don Williams later remarked, 'something had died within the club',[178] and things would never be the same. From a team perspective, they would deteriorate faster than anyone could have imagined. The 'Grand Old Flag' had started to fade, and fray.

ŸŸŸŸŸŸŸŸ

Earlier that Tuesday night, Bluey Adams did his club duty, arduous as it was in the circumstances, when he took the Demons for their first – and ultimately only – post-Norm Smith training session. Before the session started, Checker Hughes addressed the players and mentioned Smith's name only once – when he implored them to continue on 'from where Norm Smith left off'.[179]

Adams recalled the eeriness of that experience:

---

[174] *The Herald*, Wednesday July 28, 1965.
[175] *Melbourne Truth*, Saturday July 31, 1965.
[176] *The Herald*, Wednesday July 28, 1965.
[177] *The Sun*, Wednesday July 28, 1965.
[178] Batchelder, Alf, *Pavilions In The Park*, Australian Scholarly Publishing, 2005.
[179] *The Sun*, Wednesday July 28, 1965.

I went into the dressingroom and the property steward, Les Green, took me over to Norm's locker and said: 'There you go'.

I looked at him and said: 'No way. I'm not putting my gear in Smithy's locker'.

I didn't know if he was trying to set me up.

I took training – which consisted of kick-to-kick and lots of circle work – and thought the atmosphere wasn't too bad. People tend to get on with things in times of crisis. But as soon as training finished, everyone just evacuated. I thought: 'I have never seen the Melbourne dressing-rooms clear so quickly in all my life'. It was understandable because it was an uncomfortable time for a lot of players.

We heard Norm was coming back to meet with the committee that night, and that's when he was reinstated. So I only looked after the side for one night and then Norm was back. Funnily enough, no-one told me I wouldn't be needed again. Not a word was said, which was a bit of an oversight. I still haven't been sacked![180]

Smith resumed his coaching duties on the Thursday. He brought the players together and, to reinforce the perception that he and the committee had 'kissed and made up', he got Hassa Mann to run over to the fence and invite Duffy onto the training track. Smith addressed the players for five minutes, followed by Duffy. Both pledged harmony and unity, and the players applauded both talks. As the players ran a lap, coach and chairman walked off the ground together in full view of – and perhaps stage-managed for the benefit of – reporters and photographers who were in attendance.

There was, however, another hurdle for Smith and the committee to overcome. As part of Smith's contractual obligations with *Truth* newspaper, he gave a lengthy interview to Brian Hansen, and the result was a three-page, first-person story, which was virtually the print version of his much-talked-about television appearance. The story appeared on the very day he returned to the club as coach. In his book, *The Awful Truth*, Hansen recalled:

> It was soon after noon on edition day. *Truth* was bubbling with excitement at the enormity of Norm's attack on the club. It would sell tens of thousands of extra papers. My phone rang. It was Norm Smith.
>
> 'Thank God I've got you,' Norm said. 'You've got to pull that story out. They've just given me my job back.'
>
> He was just in time, but I didn't let him know it... (But) to pull the story at that late stage would have created havoc. The story covered three full pages and

---

[180] Frank 'Bluey' Adams. Interview with the author.

I didn't have a thing to fill them with... and we had already printed all the posters and placed a fortune in radio and television advertisements...'

'You're too late - the paper is running.'

All I heard was: 'I'm dead!'

His phone dropped back into the cradle and I thought I heard a choking sob...

When Smithy rang me with his column a few days later, I asked him about Melbourne's reaction to his story.

'They weren't happy,' he laughed. 'I told them I tried to pull it out, but said, on reflection, "I only spoke the truth". And, privately, I'm bloody glad I said it. It's now on the record. Having given me the job back, they can't change their minds again.'[181]

Smith was not particularly concerned what the committee thought, anyway, outside where its actions affected his job as coach. He confided in Sam Allica: 'I don't really care what happens in relation to the committee side of things; all I care about is getting my 20 players out on the ground on a Saturday'.[182]

Nonetheless, the *Truth* story, combined with all that had occurred over the previous 10 days, made him uneasy when he attended his comeback match against Fitzroy at the MCG. The Demons defeated the Bill Stephen-coached Lions by two points – after managing just 2.5 to 5.8 in the second half – to improve their record to 10-4. That night the Demons were holding a function to celebrate Brian Dixon's 200th game. But in light of recent events, Norm and Marj Smith, to an extent, felt like outcasts, so they approached Bill and Betty Stephen straight after the match and 'begged' them to accompany them for dinner at the club. 'I don't think they felt very comfortable there after all that had happened,' Betty Stephen recalled.[183]

Dixon also felt slightly alienated by his coach, later revealing: 'Norm let me know that he knew that I'd been the person who had asked the players to make sure they all gave their best for the Melbourne Football Club in his absence. I felt under a fair bit of pressure as a result of that circumstance'.[184]

There is little doubt that circumstances largely contributed to a disastrous finish to the 1965 season. On his return, Smith had harboured great expectations. He told *The Sun*: 'There was an American gridiron coach who was said to be aggressive in every activity. Even when he was mowing the grass, he attacked it as though it was growing against him. That's how we must approach the winning of this

---

[181] Hansen, Brian, *The Awful Truth*, Brian Hansen Publications, 2004.
[182] Sam Allica. Interview with the author.
[183] Betty Stephen. Interview with the author.
[184] Brian Dixon. Interview with the author.

premiership'.[185] His optimism proved misguided. The Demons lost their last four games – three of them by at least 34 points – to finish seventh, two games and 36.7 percent out of the final four. Melbourne had missed the finals for the first time in 12 years, and would not play in September for another 22 years.

Smith later insisted that off-field dramas had played no role in the Demons' fall from grace. When his coaching career at Melbourne had ended, he said: 'It was wrong to blame the so-called "row" for our decline ... Melbourne was on the wane before the row. While the blow-up didn't help matters, it didn't make a lot of difference, either. We had cleared Barassi before the season started and you can imagine what sort of a loss that was. Also, Bluey Adams had retired and then "Doc" Roet left for overseas halfway through the season.[186] What people overlooked was that in several of the games we won we scraped through by a matter of points. Since then, we have not done particularly well, but the row... had nothing to do with our fortunes'.[187]

In Melbourne's annual report, the committee admitted some fault, but tried to present a veneer of harmony. 'It was a great credit to all parties concerned that this intolerable position was soon rectified and Norm was quickly reappointed,' the annual report stated. 'The rights and wrongs of the committee and the coach are not important at this moment, the important fact is that these differences have been resolved and that the club is functioning again.'[188]

In one of his rare public comments abut the controversy, Cardwell said: 'Certainly it was the most dramatic thing I have ever known in football. There were faults on both sides. At that time, Norm and I used to run the club... It was a tragedy the whole thing happened... I would not want to defend anybody or cast reflections on anyone. To point the bone at anybody would be wrong'. However, he said that Smith was prone to 'temperamental outbursts'.[189]

Although the committee conceded it had been an 'unhappy year' – which, it regretted, had been 'a new experience' at a club that 'boasted proudly of its freedom from misunderstandings, such as these'[190] – it would not publicly concede

---

[185] *The Sun*, Saturday July 31, 1965.
[186] Before Roet left to went to work in hospitals in Hong Kong and then London, he made the following controversial comments to a print journalist: '(Smith) is an excellent coach – tyrannical at times. I think he could do without his power to curb players off the field. I'm referring to incidents such as ordering haircuts and the shaving off of moustaches'. Smith's response was to praise Roet, saying: 'I tried to recall an opponent who has outclassed "The Doc" and I can't... This is the biggest compliment I can pay him... He will be very hard to replace'.
[187] *The Sun* series, 1967.
[188] Melbourne Football Club annual report, 1965.
[189] *The Sun*, Friday August 20, 1982.
[190] Melbourne Football Club annual report, 1965.

the fact it was actually an unhappy club. Stan Alves later wrote: 'Players were bitterly disappointed. It was not as though we didn't try. We did, but when it really mattered out there, we just couldn't produce. It's often been said that a house divided against itself cannot stand... When there are constant rumblings in the boardroom, it's almost inevitable the wheels will start to fall off'.[191]

Smith was 'always looking over his shoulder... aware that he didn't have full support'.[192] At times during team addresses, he would also take thinly-veiled swipes at committeemen standing behind him, making comments like: 'Some people would have you believe this, but...'[193]

Hassa Mann felt that tensions simmered for the remainder of Smith's reign as coach. 'There always appeared to be feeling of "us and them",' Mann said. 'You'd always feel the tension between a group of committeemen standing over one side of the room, while Norm was on the other side of the room with the players. It was a sort of disjointed atmosphere. How can you expect it to be harmonious when the men who were responsible for the whole, sad episode – the biggest single issue that has affected the Melbourne Football Club – are standing over there and still in charge of the running of the club? It just doesn't work that way'.[194]

The furore had affected Smith's whole being, and every facet of his life. The manager of his business, Russ Brown, said: 'I could see it hit him hard. In all the years I'd worked with him and knew him, I'd never seen him dwell on anything, and here he was suddenly showing real strain. It was really upsetting for people who knew and respected him. It really kicked the guts out of him. I reckon the whole thing killed him in the end. To me, he was never the same man after that.'[195]

But some things remained the same – namely Smith's enforcement of discipline, and willingness to make tough decisions.

John Lord had announced he would retire from the VFL at the end of the season to coach in a country league. After playing 132 games from 1957-65, Lord was dropped to the seconds for his last game at Melbourne. Lord recalled: 'It really hurt me. But that was Norm. He figured: "You're not going to be here next year, so why should you take the place of a player who might benefit from the experience and develop into a good player for the club?" I wouldn't have done it, most other people wouldn't have done it either, but he did it, and I understood. It was the truth. That's probably what made Norm different. He was forward-

---

[191] Alves, Stan with Col Davies, *Sacked Coach*, Crown Content, 2002.
[192] Hassa Mann. Interview with the author.
[193] Ken Emselle. Interview with the author.
[194] Hassa Mann. Interview with the author.
[195] Russell Brown. Interview with the author.

thinking and he didn't side-step anything, even a sensitive issue of a player's retirement. I also attributed it to the fact that Norm loved success, his team and his club so much that giving me the opportunity of finishing in the seniors came a distant second'.[196]

Stan Alves' debut season had also finished poorly. After breaking into the Melbourne side in round seven, Alves had played the last 11 games of the season, but was named on the bench in the last two rounds, even though he felt he should have been in the starting 18. On the Demons' end-of-season trip to Western Australia, they lost to Big Bob Johnson's East Fremantle by four points at Subiaco Oval. (It was the first defeat by a touring Melbourne side under Norm Smith.) Soon after setting off on their long train journey home, Sam Allica told 19-year-old Alves that Smith wanted a word with him in his private compartment. The 'word' turned into a 90-minute blast. Alves recalled:

> I had no idea what it was about. We got there and the big fellow told Sam to close the door and let nobody in. In less than no time, he had reduced me to tears. He told me there had been nothing wrong with my form and that I'd been dropped because I was a little man with a big head. I was strutting around thinking I was better than everyone else.
>
> On the trip over to Rottnest Island, players and officials were lined up and he said I had just come along and pushed right in front of them. There were hard-working people who had been around this club for years... and he said I had treated them little better than dirt. Never before or since has anyone spoken to me like that... (But) the big fellow was absolutely correct. He made it clear that if he ever saw me showing disrespect to anyone around the club again, my days at Melbourne were finished. There would be no second warnings. I would pack my bag that night.
>
> 'If you want to stay,' he said, 'you will show respect to everyone around the club. Nobody is ever better than you, and you are no better than anyone else.'[197]

During the same Perth trip, the Smiths celebrated their 25th wedding anniversary. The only problem was they were apart at the time. A party attended by family and friends was held at the Smith house, and Smith made numerous phone calls to Marj throughout the evening, becoming more emotional with each call as he drank with players and officials at a Perth hotel. 'He felt guilty about it, and he felt he was

---

[196] John Lord. Interview with the author.
[197] Alves, Stan with Col Davies, *Sacked Coach*, Crown Content, 2002.

really missing out on the party,' said family friend Marj Lenne.[198] Smith made up for it on other occasions, though, like when he threw a surprise birthday party for Marj at Fred Fanning's pub in Bacchus Marsh. Margaret Clay recalled: 'We were all hiding in the room. Norm had arranged it all and Marj knew nothing about it. He did some lovely things for her'.[199]

Smith also did some surprisingly generous things for others who would not have expected to be afforded such generosity. At the end of the 1965 season, the Smiths hosted a function at their house for all VFL umpires. An invitation was even extended to umpire Don Blew – the man who had indirectly and unwittingly been the catalyst for a sequence of events that led to Smith's sacking, and still had a libel writ hanging over Smith's head.

Blew rang his solicitor for advice. 'What should I do?' he asked. 'Should I go to the do at Norm Smith's house or should I stay away?'

The solicitor said: 'There's nothing wrong with going, as long as you don't discuss the case'.

Blew attended the Smith house and later reported that Smith did not – not outwardly at least – bear any ill-feeling towards him. 'Everything was fine,' Blew said. 'I was just treated like anybody else.'

Blew umpired in the VFL until the end of 1967, when he moved to Tasmania. In the meantime, the pending legal action 'just rolled on' and eventually 'fizzled out' when Blew decided not to pursue it any further. 'From the time the writ action was lodged,' Blew said, 'I didn't feel any pressure or malice from Melbourne or Norm Smith. I wasn't treated any differently, and I had no problems with Norm.'[200]

ŸŸŸŸŸŸŸŸŸ

When St Kilda qualified for the 1965 Grand Final after defeating Collingwood by a point in the second semi-final, Saints coach Allan Jeans sought advice from the highest living authority when it came to coaching premierships – Norm Smith.

'You've been in 'em,' Jeans told Smith, 'and you've been there and done that. How do I go about it? It's been 52 years since St Kilda made a Grand Final, so there's no bastard around to tell me what to do.'

---

[198] Marj Lenne, wife of George Lenne, who was a close friend of Norm Smith's. Interview with the author.
[199] Margaret Clay. Interview with the author.
[200] Don Blew. Interview with the author.

Smith replied: 'You're better off having a chat with Lenny – he's the smart one, and he's a better thinker than I am'.[201]

About the same time, Len Smith had written the following letter to Jeans, the result of which would have a profound effect on the St Kilda coach's approach.

> Dear Allan,
>
> Now that Richmond and Melbourne can't make it I have become a St Kilda supporter for this year's premiership.
>
> Good luck mate.
>
> If I can help in any way, on a purely personal basis between just the two of us, let me know and it would be my pleasure.
>
> I remember you saying that you were finding it hard to think of new things to talk about at your players' meeting and I have jotted down in an exercise book (at) home here quite a few points that I have used at lectures and players' meetings and it is at your disposal if you think it will help give you new ideas.
>
> Please don't feel obliged that you must accept this offer, Allan, because I will understand, but if you think it can help let know.
>
> Regardless, good luck for 1965. You have earned the right to be on top.
>
> Yours sincerely,
> Len Smith.

Jeans took up Len's offer in Grand Final week, catching a train to his home in Essendon. Although the information Jeans gleaned did not inspire the Saints to victory (they lost to Essendon by 35 points), he found it an invaluable experience.

Jeans recalled: 'Len pulled out his exercise book of notes and I was particularly interested in his theories on confidence and the mental aspect of the game. I used those notes throughout my coaching career, and added some of my own ideas to them along the way.'[202]

Len also felt that Richmond needed another coach to add to his ideas to bring the Tigers the success he believed they were capable of achieving, and sustaining. That individual was identified as former Richmond back-pocket Tom Hafey, who had guided Shepparton to the previous three premierships in the Goulburn Valley

---

[201] Allan Jeans. Interview with the author.
[202] Allan Jeans. Interview with the author.

SACKED [1965]

League and had built a reputation as an uncompromising coach. He appealed as a man with the energy and passion to take the Tigers to the next level.

The Tigers had just enjoyed their most successful season since 1954, winning 10 matches and finishing fifth – two games outside the final four. At the club's annual general meeting at Richmond Town Hall in December 1965, Len Smith warned the Tigers against becoming complacent. 'This is the only thing likely to stop Richmond going on and on,' he said.

26

SEVERED TIES

[1966-68]

Norm Smith had long warned Melbourne officials that the club was slipping, but not even he could have envisaged the speed and extent of the fall. After sitting on top of the VFL ladder, a game clear of all comers, after the eighth round of 1965, the Demons won just five of their next 28 matches.

Early in 1966, Smith reflected briefly on the tumultuous off-field events of the previous season, telling *The Herald*: 'Our morale fell to an all-time low last year, but there is no use crying over spilt milk'. In reality, the milk had gone bad, and curdled. The 1966 season was the Demons' worst effort since 1953 (Smith's second year as the Melbourne coach). They opened the season with six straight losses (by an average of 43 points), which, combined with the four defeats at the end of 1965, burdened Smith with 10 successive losses – the worst losing streak of his career to that point.

The Demons won three of their next seven games, with the high point being their first win of the season, a 34-point victory over reigning premier and eventual preliminary finalist Essendon in round seven.

Melbourne's new assistant coach, John Beckwith (who had returned to Melbourne after coaching Colac in the Hampden league), felt sorry for the coach as he battled to rebuild a weak playing list. 'Norm didn't have much to work with,' he said. 'He tried a lot of players, and we had a basis of a reasonable side, but we had far too many gaps.'[1]

Stan Alves later wrote that things quickly went 'from bad to worse' following the turbulence of 1965. 'We still had some very good players,' he noted, 'but the bubbling enthusiasm and confidence, which had been so evident on my first training night (in 1964), now lay in ruins.'[2]

---

[1] John Beckwith. Interview with the author.
[2] Alves, Stan with Col Davies, *Sacked Coach*, Crown Content, 2002.

If there was one thing Smith couldn't stand, it was a lack of enthusiasm. He once said: 'You can't teach a player dedication and you can't give him enthusiasm, and without these qualities, you don't get a great footballer'.[3] He also subscribed to the theory of one of his idols, superstar American football coach Vince Lombardi, who believed: 'If a player isn't fired with enthusiasm, he should be fired with enthusiasm'.[4] He also spruiked a variation of this which went: 'Enthusiasm is infectious, and so is the absence of it'. Perhaps for this reason, and the simple fact that some players simply weren't good enough, there was a lot of hiring and firing at Melbourne in 1966. In their desperation to ascertain which players had a future at the club, the Demons tried 46 players, which represented a massive turnover of stock.[5] The Demons also blooded 22 debutants – the most in a season at Melbourne since 1919 when the club returned to football after World War I.

One such youngster was none other than Smith's son Peter. The Smiths' only child, according to family friend George Lenne, had developed into a man who 'was nothing like his father. Norm and Peter were completely different – in looks and outlook. Peter was more like Marj – easier-going, and not as prone to explode'.[6]

Like his father, Peter was a full-forward – in fact, he had been since under-9s at Melbourne Grammar School – and was schooled by his father in the art of forward play, including the Smith approach to goal. Peter had enjoyed some success – he had kicked 20 goals in seven games for Melbourne Grammar in 1964 and was 'among the best players in public schools football in 1964 and 1965'.[7] The father had set high standards for the son. He would watch him play for the Grammar and, while he never interfered with the coach, afterwards he would assess Peter's performance. 'Dad found fault with my football as much as he praised me,' Peter said later. 'At home after a match he would point out my mistakes.'[8]

Peter originally earned a place on Melbourne's supplementary list, but was promoted to the senior list after amassing 40-odd disposals as a ruck-rover in

---

[3] *The Sun* series, 1967.
[4] Peter Smith told the author: 'Dad read a lot and quoted people like (Sir Winston) Churchill and gridiron coaches like (Vince) Lombardi (Green Bay Packers 1959-69) and (Knute) Rockne. He took an interest in what was going on elsewhere, not just what was happening in his own backyard, in his own club, in his competition, in his own sport, or even in his own country. He looked for other things that might help'.
[5] This was equal to the club record (the war-depleted Demons had used 46 players in 1944) and the most in the competition since South Melbourne had matched it in 1954. Since then, this figure has been equalled by five clubs (including the South Melbourne side coached by Norm Smith in 1971), and bettered only by St Kilda in 1980, when the Saints used 47 players. The record is 53, by St Kilda in 1920.
[6] George Lenne. Interview with the author.
[7] *The Sporting Globe*, Saturday September 7, 1974.
[8] *The Sporting Globe*, Saturday September 7, 1974.

the final practice match of 1966. After such a performance, no-one could claim the coach's 18-year-old son had been the beneficiary of favouritism. Quite the contrary. While Peter insisted he never felt the pressure of expectation that one would normally associate with being the son of a sporting legend, he believed his name might have actually worked against him when it came to selection. 'If it was a 50-50 situation between me and another bloke, the other bloke would have got the nod,' he said. 'And that's fair enough, too. Dad couldn't be perceived to be playing any favourites, and I understood that'.

One of the first minor issues Peter confronted was how to address his father at the club and on the training track. He recalled: 'I found it hard to start with because I didn't know what to call him. You can't call out: "Dad!" I ended up just calling him Norm like everyone else. I'd never called him Norm in my life. But he understood all that. It's what I had to do. Everyone knew that I was the coach's son, but you have to draw a line somewhere'.[9]

Although Smith treated Peter just like any other player, he didn't overburden his son with advice on how to play the game. He offered advice in other ways. In the days before Peter made his VFL debut in round three against Richmond (where his Uncle Len was a selector) at the MCG, Smith handed him a copy of Len's coaching notes. 'Rather than him laying down the law,' Peter explained, 'he did it in a more subtle way by giving me something to read, which told me what I should have been thinking about anyway.'[10]

On the morning of the match, Smith didn't want to worry Peter with too much football talk; instead he briefly advised him on how he was expected to play his role as a follower, before leaving the youngster to his own devices.

That afternoon, Peter – wearing the No.4 jumper that had been made famous by his father, and which had just been vacated by the retired John Lord – was flattened twice and struggled against Richmond. He had just one kick in the first half but improved as the game wore on and finished with nine kicks and two handballs. A nevertheless proud Smith said: 'That's better than I did. I only got four kicks in my first league game in 1935'.[11]

While Peter didn't find his father overbearing when he played under him, he said: 'We still had some blues. Actually, I'll rephrase that: Dad would have a go at me. It was one-way. But it wasn't personal; it was heat-of-the-moment stuff, and I accepted everything. Once the game was over, everything was back to normal'.[12]

---

[9] Peter Smith. Interview with the author.
[10] Peter Smith. Interview with the author.
[11] Contemporary newspaper report.
[12] Peter Smith. Interview with the author.

Smith couldn't hide his fatherly pride in one match. Sam Allica recalled:

> Peter got the ball just forward of the wing and took off on a run and they were closing in on him and he got down towards the forward pocket, on the boundary line, and he had a shot - and Peter was a magnificent kick, like his old man - and it went as straight as an arrow through for a goal. Norm's reaction was priceless. He was laughing and he said: 'Oh-hoh! What a magnificent goal!'
>
> Norm was rapt and for those few seconds he let his guard down and acted like a typical father who was just so happy that his son had done something special. It was pure pride. It was one of the rare occasions I saw Norm get that excited.[13]

On another occasion, Smith got 'all worked up' about his son for other reasons. Peter Smith recalled with a laugh:

> I started the game looking like a Beatle, with a mop-top hairstyle that was all the rage at the time. But Dad felt that when I went for the ball I was too preoccupied with flicking my hair out of my eyes. It was a distraction that had to go. Dad made me have a haircut at half-time. He threw me over to the barber - Arthur McKnight, who actually did cut The Beatles' hair at the Southern Cross (Hotel in 1964). Dad told Arthur: 'Cut his hair!' At half-time of a senior match, you're not going to argue with the coach if you know what's good for you, so the locks came off and I was sent out after half-time a slightly different looking bloke, with hair that was, in Dad's mind, far more presentable and, more importantly, not a distraction.[14]

Other players suffered similar fates, as Smith strove to protect the club's image – which he said was 'very important to everyone down at Melbourne'[15] – against 'unruly' hairstyles influenced by the likes of The Beatles and The Rolling Stones after the explosion of rock n' roll. Smith's philosophy was: 'Once they put on a Melbourne uniform, they are not representing themselves, they are representing the club'. He also firmly believed: 'You should always look like a footballer – even if you're not one'.[16] Fortunately, he said, most of his charges conformed and accepted it as 'part and parcel of being League players'. Smith wasn't completely against his players cultivating long hair, but he asked that they observe a strict condition that

---

[13] Sam Allica. Interview with the author.
[14] Peter Smith. Interview with the author.
[15] *The Sun* series, 1967.
[16] Ian Ridley. Interview with the author.

they 'at least keep themselves well groomed'.[17] He asserted: 'We don't send out our players with dirty boots or holes in their socks, and we don't want them going out looking like girls either, so we make sure their hair is a reasonable length'.[18]

Smith recounted a time he told a player to have his hair cut: 'There was nothing sissy about this bloke – he was a strong, fearless player. But he looked damned untidy and that didn't help Melbourne's image. He was inclined to argue about it. So I said: "It's 1.20pm now. Have your hair trimmed by 1.30 or you can pack up and go home; you'll be out of the side". He had it trimmed. He knew I meant what I said'.[19]

He also enforced a 'clean-shaven upper-lip' policy, as another Demons hard man, Bernie Massey, discovered. During a weekend off, Massey let his facial hair grow on the snowfields. When he returned, he shaved, but kept his moustache. Smith confronted him about it at training on the Tuesday night.

'What's the moustache about?' he demanded. 'What are you trying to prove?'

'Nothing,' replied Massey. 'I just thought I'd leave it on.'

Although Smith had made it clear that he didn't like the 'mo', Massey insisted he wasn't actually told to remove it.[20]

Unbeknown to Massey, Smith raised the issue of his moustache in a conference with the selection committee, who collectively decided 'it wasn't in the best interests of the club'.[21] The overriding fear was that it would spark an incident that would have severe consequences for the Demons. Smith explained: 'We were due to play North Melbourne on the Saturday (and) Alan Killigrew was North coach at the time, and you can just imagine what "Killa" would have done with that sort of ammunition. He would have had his blokes primed up to have a shot at Bernie and in no time (he) would have taken a swing at someone. Then Neil Crompton would have rushed in to back up Bernie and I could have ended up with two good players reported and perhaps out for several weeks. And believe me, no piece of fungus on some footballer's top lip is worth all that trouble, so it simply had to come off'.[22]

But, as Smith described, Massey 'became stubborn about it',[23] and arrived at the Thursday night session with an extra two days' growth to his top lip. Massey recalled that Smith 'had steam coming out of all his orifices'.[24]

---

[17] *Midweek Magazine*, August 1964.
[18] *The Sun* series, 1967.
[19] *The Sun* series, 1967.
[20] Bernie Massey. Interview with the author.
[21] *Midweek Magazine*, August 1964.
[22] *The Sun* series, 1967.
[23] *Midweek Magazine*, August 1964.
[24] Bernie Massey. Interview with the author.

'Are you trying to make a bloody fool out of me?!' Smith growled.

'No'.

'Well get the bloody thing off!' Smith ordered. 'If I had someone else to play full-back, I'd play him there.' He then explained the potential for suspensions.

After the session, some trainers told Massey: 'I think you'd better shave it off'.

'I'll be buggered if I will,' Massey responded.

Eventually he did as he was told, and later reflected: 'All that commotion over a bloody moustache. Just a year or two later everyone had long hair and beards!'[25]

Smith hated gimmicks of all kinds, which he felt were unnecessary. He even took exception to players wearing moulded-sole football boots – as opposed to those that required longer stops. Before a match at Essendon in 1963, Ron Barassi put on a pair of *adidas* boots that had been imported from Germany. Smith spotted them just as the Demons were about to run out onto the ground. He said: 'What the bloody hell are they?!' Barassi reckoned Smith would have made him remove them if it hadn't been so close to the start of the game. 'We won and I played all right so it wasn't an issue after that,' he said.[26] Later, when Smith coached South Melbourne, he needled Bob Skilton for wearing low-cut, soft-toe, Adidas soccer boots. The Swans legend said: 'Smithy hated them – he called them slippers!'[27]

🏆🏆🏆🏆🏆🏆🏆🏆🏆

The 1966 season highlighted some of the best and worst of Norm Smith's coaching. Although the results didn't show it in 1966, Smith had, on the whole, coached brilliantly. Assistant coach John Beckwith marvelled at his mentor's ability to manipulate match-ups and inspire solid performances from less talented players.

'No-one made many moves back in those days,' Beckwith explained, 'but Norm could shuffle players into different positions and gain an advantage, or counteract and put the clamps on good players on the opposition. It was a really enlightening experience for someone like myself who was just learning the coaching caper.'[28]

Smith's wisdom also had an enormous influence on players, like Stan Alves, who later coached League football. Alves – who Smith called 'Mick' – gave a stunning example of how Smith was on a higher plane of consciousness:

---

[25] Bernie Massey. Interview with the author.
[26] Collins, Ben, *The Champions: Conversations with Great Players and Coaches of Australian Football*, GSP, 2006.
[27] Collins, Ben, *The Champions: Conversations with Great Players and Coaches of Australian Football*, GSP, 2006.
[28] John Beckwith. Interview with the author.

> There was a boundary throw-in right in front of Norm... I heard the big fellow's voice shouting: 'Mick! Mick!' I looked up and saw him waving his hands, pointing for me to move into the forward line. I moved forward five metres, 20 metres, 15 metres and then he signalled me to stop. Guess what? The ball was thrown in, the ruckmen went up and it's knocked straight to where I was standing. I spun around, ran hard – BANG! – and kicked a goal. To this very day, I don't know why he did that, but to me it said here was a man who obviously had a mystical knowledge of the game... From that time on, I never doubted Norm.[29]

However, Beckwith observed, Smith developed 'strange obsessions' with some players. One that came to mind was boom teenage recruit Graham Osborne.

> Our recruiting officer, Ken Carlon, brought Graham Osborne down to the club and said: 'This is the best country player I've ever seen.' That pricked Norm's ears up; he said: 'Oh, is he?' Osborne was 6'2" (188cms) and he could run. Norm said: 'We'll put him at half-back'.
>
> He played reasonably well in his first few games but then his form dropped. In selection, Norm says to me: 'Becky, you're going to get Graham Osborne's form back in the seconds'.
>
> I picked him centre half-forward to get him in the play. We played Essendon at Essendon and just before half-time the game was going down the gurgler. We weren't playing very well and Osborne couldn't get a kick. We had another half-forward named *Ken* Osborne, so I swapped them over. Soon after, Ian Ridley tells me: 'Norm says: "Get Osborne in the game!"'
>
> I knew what he was talking about but I said: 'Which bloody Osborne?!'
>
> So 'Tiger' (Ridley) had to go all the way back up to Norm, and by this stage Ken Osborne's kicked a couple of goals and we're back in the game. Tiger comes and says 'GRAHAM Osborne!'
>
> I tried him in nearly every position on the field but he only had six kicks for the game. At the next selection meeting, Norm says: 'Well, I can't wait for Graham Osborne to find form; I want him back in the firsts'.
>
> It was a strange decision, but he was obsessed with making a player of him.[30]

---

[29] Alves, Stan with Col Davies, *Sacked Coach*, Crown Content, 2002.
[30] John Beckwith. Interview with the author. Graham Osborne played 146 games and kicked 61 goals for Melbourne between 1966 and 1977.

SEVERED TIES [1966-68]

Smith acted upon a common coaching obsession in the round 15 match at South Melbourne, when he gave Stan Alves the worst dressing down of his career. Indeed, it was the kind of blast all footballers dread. Alves later explained that he had set himself for a marking attempt but had hesitated when a teammate called 'leave it', and the Swans cleared the ball. At half-time, with the Demons trailing, Smith was on the warpath. In front of the entire team, he told Alves that he had had a chance to put his body on the line but had pulled out.

There was a pause, which brought complete silence. Alves then tried to defend himself, but Smith cut him off. 'No "Mick",' he said, 'you squibbed it. Unless you can overcome that, you'll never ever go on.'[31]

At the same venue about a month later, he blasted his runner, Sam Allica, after a misunderstanding in a night series match. Allica explained:

> Peter (Smith) was at full-forward and Ross Dillon was at centre half-forward, and Norm told me to swap them around. I did that, and I also had a message for someone on the wing. As I was running back past Peter on the way to the bench, he asked me: 'Where am I supposed to be?'
>
> I said: 'Centre half-forward.'
>
> And Rossy said: 'Wally just came out and moved us back to where we were.'
>
> Wally White was a trainer. I didn't know what was going on – the boys had gotten mixed messages – so I ran back to the bench. If Norm thought you'd stuffed up, it was like poking a finger in his eye. He expected everything to be spot-on. He said to me in a gruff voice: 'Do you think you're the coach of Melbourne?!'
>
> I said: 'No. I only did what you told me to do, Norman.'
>
> He said: 'Well who changed them back?!'
>
> I didn't want to dob in Wally, so I said: 'The two boys can tell you'.
>
> Norm said: 'Give Wally the armband and bloody well get inside!'
>
> I went into the rooms, had a shower, got changed and resigned myself to the fact that I'd just been sacked. When Norm came in after the game, he looked at me and said: 'Are you still here? Well at least you've got the courage to face me.'
>
> What he didn't know was I was only hanging around because I didn't know where (my wife) Roma was, and I couldn't go anywhere until the game had finished. I was reinstated immediately.[32]

ϒϒϒϒϒϒϒϒϒ

---

[31] Alves, Stan with Col Davies, *Sacked Coach*, Crown Content, 2002.
[32] Sam Allica. Interview with the author.

The 1966 season was the final year of Len Smith's intended three-year plan for Richmond to reach the finals, and for most of the season his prediction looked like becoming reality. After 14 rounds, the Tigers (coached by Tom Hafey) had stormed to an imposing 11-2-1 record and were on top of the ladder for the first time in 15 years. However, consecutive losses meant they tumbled to fifth and they missed the finals by half-a-game. No other side in history had won 13-and-a-half games and missed the finals.

'We were stiff,' was selector Len Smith's understatement.[33]

If it hadn't been for Len's health problems, which necessitated the instalment of caretaker coaches for much of the 1964 and 1965 seasons, and robbed the players of continuity in coaching, the Tigers might have already achieved Len's ambitious goal.

New coach Hafey had impressed all with his direct playing style and insistence on discipline, but Len certainly wasn't forgotten in the Tigers' rise. Geelong great Bob Davis, who stepped down as Cats coach at the end of 1965, wrote in *The Herald*: 'Len Smith (is), in my book, the smartest coach I've seen in 18 years of League football'.[34]

Len also took great pleasure in Allan Jeans' effort to guide St Kilda to its first premiership (by a point over Collingwood). After watching the thriller from a seat just a few rows behind the St Kilda coaching bench, Len felt moved to write to Jeans. His letter said, in part:

> I am not ashamed to admit that I had to use my hanky after the final siren, so glad was I that Alan (sic) Jeans and St Kilda had made the grade ... I went home a happy man knowing how happy you would be ... I guess you must know by now how much you have earned the respect of everyone connected with our great game.

ᵞᵞᵞᵞᵞᵞᵞᵞᵞ

Before he had even turned 50, Norm Smith already felt as though he was 'getting a little old' for coaching.[35] After 18 seasons in the caper, he questioned whether he still had the motivation to continue on.

Although he was well aware that coaching had taken an increasing physical and mental toll in recent years, he had always lived for football. But this hadn't been

---

[33] *The Herald*, May 1967.
[34] *The Herald*, 1966.
[35] *The Sun* series, 1967.

the case in recent times. He first suspected that perhaps his passion was waning when he realised he wasn't thinking about the game as much during the week. No longer did football occupy virtually his every waking thought; no longer did he think about football in his sleep, or feel that familiar pang of excitement when he woke up on the morning of a match; and no longer was he tense and edgy as game-time approached. Where once he would simply arrive at the ground at 1.20pm and go straight into rev-up mode, he had for several years felt obliged to watch the first half of the reserves match, but found he was 'getting very relaxed' – too relaxed – watching the curtain-raiser, and would have to find a quiet spot to get himself into the right frame of mind.[36]

Perhaps it had something to do with the Demons' dwindling fortunes. Perhaps he had simply lost his drive and was in dire need of a well-earned break from the game he had devoted his life to. Whatever the case, many players attested to the fact that Smith never outwardly appeared to lack his trademark intensity or his passion for perfection. A newcomer who quickly discovered this was Tasmanian recruit Max Walker, who later played Test cricket for Australia.

In January 1967, Walker and Peter Smith were playing cricket together in Melbourne's first eleven side.[37] They played a match against Essendon at Windy Hill in which Peter hooked a match-winning boundary off the last ball of the day. It had been pre-arranged that Walker would stay at the Smith house, so after consuming their fill of celebratory drinks, Peter and Walker eventually made their way home about midnight.

They stumbled inside the door and were confronted by a worried Marj, who hadn't been able to sleep as she waited for the boys to arrive home safely. Now that they were, she went back to bed where Smith was fast asleep. Peter decided he would give her a kiss goodnight, but all hell broke loose when he fell across the bed and accidentally kneed Smith in the groin. Smith groaned like a wounded bull. Walker, who swayed in the doorway, grimaced as he mused: 'What a way to be woken up'.[38]

By now, the atmosphere in the room was 'electric'.

Marj turned to Walker and asked: 'You boys have been drinking, haven't you?!'

---

[36] *The Sun* series, 1967.

[37] When Peter Smith made his first eleven debut for Melbourne in the 1965-66 season, Norm told a reporter: 'Whether he shows out better at cricket or football is up to him. All I will encourage him to do is keep playing sport'.

[38] *How to Hypnotise Chooks and Other Great Yarns*, by Max Walker, Gary Sparke Publications, 1987.

'Yes,' Walker admitted, 'just a little'.

The next morning, the two young men nursed hangovers and feelings of guilt. Marj gave them another blast in the kitchen as they drank tea. Walker later recalled: 'You wouldn't reckon a woman doing a small amount of washing up could make so much noise'.[39]

The lads decided they would try to duck out the back door, but Smith caught up with them first.

'Another cup of tea, Max?' Smith asked with surprising politeness considering the previous night's events.

'No thanks, Norm,' Walker said as he tried to follow Peter out.

'Max,' Smith said, a little firmer. 'Sit down and have another cup of tea.'[40]

Walker takes up the story:

> I was frozen because I had heard some of those vivid stories of Norm Smith verbally ripping strips of flesh from many of his senior players... As I pulled up the chair my eyes focused on the red and white fleck laminex table top... The next 20 minutes or so were quite revealing... (Norm) described my obligations to the Melbourne Football Club, my parents and most of all, myself... He set about philosophising about the pros and cons of drinking so clearly, that as I look back on my entire sporting career, both football and cricket, this was the most important moment in my life. It was at this point that I decided not to have another drink. *(Walker didn't have another alcoholic drink for six years - until he toured the West Indies with the Australian Test side in 1973.)* His parting words on the subject were, 'We will not discuss this topic again. You're big enough and ugly enough to make up your own mind'... The moral of the story is, if you want to be successful at anything, you must first assess the cost and just how badly you want to be successful. Unfortunately, you can't be one of the boys every night of the week and a talented athlete on weekends. The scales will never balance. Fortunately for me, I ran into Norm Smith at the right time in my life. I thank him... for pointing me in the right direction.[41]

To complete the lesson, Smith then challenged Walker to a game on his backyard tennis court. 'At 50-plus years of age,' Walker marvelled, 'yes, Norm Smith proved too hot for me to handle. Down I went – 6-1, 6-1, 6-0.'[42] Little wonder Walker

---

[39] *How to Hypnotise Chooks and Other Great Yarns*, by Max Walker, 1987.
[40] Peter Smith. Interview with the author.
[41] *How to Hypnotise Chooks and Other Great Yarns*, by Max Walker, 1987.
[42] *How to Hypnotise Chooks and Other Great Yarns*, by Max Walker, 1987.

came to describe Smith as 'one of the greatest men that I ever met, (who) had a huge impact on who I've become'.[43]

Smith also didn't mince his words when Ken Emselle – the son of his old mate Richie – breached a team rule before the round one match against North Melbourne at Arden Street. Emselle taught at Moe High School during the week and was allowed to train with Moe on a Thursday night rather than making another 268-kilometre round trip. Smith usually wanted his players at the ground by 1.30pm for a 2.15pm start. But one day, unbeknown to Emselle, he had arranged a team meeting for 12.45pm instead. When Emselle arrived, Smith snarled: 'Where the bloody hell have you been?!'

'W-w-what?' Emselle stuttered. 'I didn't know.'

'You should have known!' Smith boomed. 'It was your business to find out!'

From then on, Emselle always confirmed arrangements with a phone call.[44]

The Demons won that game (by five points) and, despite a 33-point loss to Geelong in round two, regained credibility with a two-point win over reigning premier St Kilda at Moorabbin in round three. Two losses followed, including a devastating one-point defeat at Footscray. Bulldog half-forward Don McKenzie was the hero, sneaking onto the ground undetected around the boundary, marking over Tassie Johnson and kicking the winning goal. Smith channelled his anger at Johnson, his new vice-captain.[45] Over a few beers afterwards, he asked him: 'Why didn't you see him?'

'Because I was too busy watching the ball,' said Johnson, who was backed up by his fellow backmen. A 'pretty full-on' argument ensued for about an hour, and Johnson maintained: 'We just didn't know that he was coming around there, we didn't see him, so good luck to them; they beat us that time'.

At 6am the next morning, Johnson was woken by a phone call. It was Smith. 'As vice-captain,' he said, 'never go on the side of the boys against me.'

'All right, Norm,' said Johnson, 'but I still didn't see McKenzie.'

'That's not the point,' said Smith. 'You should have backed me up and gone crook at the other players.'

Johnson later recalled: 'Norm felt that the captain and vice-captain should almost be clones of him, and should always support his methods, whatever they

---

[43] *Talking Heads*, ABC TV, February 19, 2007.
[44] Ken Emselle. Interview with the author.
[45] Johnson replaced Bryan Kenneally as vice-captain. Kenneally recalled in an interview with the author: 'Norm was always straight with you. Before it was announced, or anyone else said anything, Norm came up to me and said: "We're not going to reappoint you as vice-captain; we're going to go with Tassie". That was Norm: he wouldn't hide behind anything or anyone'.

may be. He felt it was important to show a united front in the regard. I understood where he was coming from, but he took a dislike to me at times for going against him with different things, and he would abuse the way I played because he knew I could lift myself.'[46]

Smith also put pressure on his skipper, Hassa Mann. The star centreman/half-forward was easily Melbourne's leading goalkicker with 22 goals in the opening eight rounds, by which time his side had improved to a 4-4 record. But when the Demons took on South Melbourne at the MCG in round nine, Smith knew that someone had to limit the effectiveness of its superstar, Bob Skilton. He gave the job to Mann, telling him: 'I've got a special role for you today. I want you to play on Skilton all day. If he's in the back pocket, you're right there with him'.

The two leaders roved for the entire game without a spell – unbeknown to Mann, Skilton had been instructed to stop Mann! – but Mann still managed to bag a career-best haul of seven goals. After the game, Smith praised his captain: 'That was one of your better performances'.

Mann later said: 'I was elated that Norm was elated. He loved setting challenges for players and seeing them succeed at those challenges, particularly if it meant they had to play an unfamiliar role. To him, that was a feather in his cap that he was able to get a player to perform to his wishes, and in a manner that perhaps the player hadn't performed before'.[47]

The elation was short-lived. Just when Smith believed his 'team-building' process was reaping due rewards,[48] the Demons went from the respectability of 5-4 to winning just one of their next six matches.

Around this period, a rumour circulated that the coach had fallen out with Brian Dixon. He later debunked this rumour, saying: 'All that happened was "Dicko" was finding it hard to fit in his training and his Parliamentary commitments. I pointed out I wasn't interested in him as a Member of Parliament, only as a footballer. I told him he was expected to fulfil his commitments as a footballer in exactly the same was as all other players at Melbourne'.[49]

Smith's actual comment to Dixon was: 'I don't care if you're a Member of Parliament or the damn Prime Minister, this is what you must do'. However, he awarded praise where it was due, adding: 'It's to Brian's credit that he knuckled down, got stuck into his training and was playing as well as ever'.[50]

---

[46] Robert 'Tassie' Johnson. Interview with the author.
[47] Hassa Mann. Interview with the author.
[48] *The Sun* series, 1967.
[49] *The Sun* series, 1967.
[50] *The Sun* series, 1967.

A common retort of Smith's in a typically feisty debate with Dixon was: 'You're MP and I'm MC (merit certificate)'. Such comments embarrassed Dixon, but the wingman recalled: 'We always got through our little irritations, and I think that there was genuine affection between us. I certainly really admired and loved Norm'.[51] In fact, there was even a humorous element to their verbal sparring. One day at Carlton, Dixon was crunched by Blues strongman John Nicholls and his shorts fell off. A trainer came out with a replacement pair, but Dixon didn't have time to put them on because the ball kept following him. In the meantime, he ran around Princes Park in his jock-strap, or 'scrotum support'. After the game, Smith joked: 'There goes the first MLA to bare his arse on the Carlton football ground!'[52]

Dixon reflected: 'Norm and I had a lot of lighter moments. He was a very significant person in my life, and I was a strong believer in a lot of the things that Norm espoused. He always preached that integrity was critical to success. He essentially wanted us to win on our merits. He didn't want to win by committing acts that were in any way untoward. That's something I've tried to take with me wherever I've gone in my life'.[53]

ΥΥΥΥΥΥΥΥΥ

In a cruel twist of fate, Len Smith died just two months before Richmond won the 1967 premiership.

Len suffered another heart attack and died in Sacred Heart Hospital, Moreland, on the afternoon of Sunday July 23, 1967. Although he had endured recurring heart problems over the previous nine years, his passing at the age of just 55 still came as a terrible shock.

Smith was devastated. He also had the heart-wrenching task of telling his mother the bad news. Ethel Smith, then 81, did not take it well. She was 'a wreck', and a doctor had to be called to sedate her. Smith wasn't much better. Peter Smith said: 'The day Len died was the only time I saw Dad cry. That night, Mum went to stay with Flo, Len's wife, and Dad and I slept together in a double-bed. He cried. He was grieving and upset, because Len was a huge loss. He'd lost his only brother. It shattered Dad, and I don't think he ever got over it'. Tears also welled in Peter Smith's eyes as he said: 'Len was like a father to me. He was a special person'.[54]

---

[51] Brian Dixon. Interview with the author.
[52] Brian Dixon. Interview with the author.
[53] Brian Dixon. Interview with the author.
[54] Peter Smith. Interview with the author.

Among the numerous death notices placed in newspapers in the days after, was the following:

SMITH – Leonard Victor.
The most loved and respected brother of Norm, brother-in-law of Marj and dearly loved uncle of Peter. In our memories forever.

Smith also comforted Flo in her grief, insisting that he pay for the funeral. 'If it was the other way round,' he said, 'I know Lenny would pay for mine.' Len's second daughter, Norma Harmes, recalled: 'It was a wonderful gesture by Uncle Norm. There wasn't a lot of money around but Mum would have been able to afford it. But Uncle Norm never hesitated, which was quite touching'.[55]

Another poignant reminder of this emotional time is contained in Norma Harmes' scrapbook. One of her sons, either eight-year-old Stephen or seven-year-old Wayne (the future Carlton star), wrote in grey-lead pencil: 'Yesterday My mother went to the Hospitel to see my poper. He was all right. She went at night time and wen she came back she tolled me that he was ded'. Wayne later said: 'I vividly remember the night when Mum and Dad were asked to go into hospital to see my grandfather. We stayed with the neighbours and even though I was very young, I knew what was happening. I said to my brother: "Pop's not coming out". Unfortunately I was right'.[56]

About 1000 people attended the service at Sleight's Funeral Home in St Kilda Road. To accommodate the throng of mourners, police were forced to cordon off parts of busy St Kilda Road and Park Street, and later provided an escort to the crematorium at Fawkner Cemetery.

In life, Len had been a peacemaker who remained friends with both of his siblings – even though brother Norm and sister Marj themselves did not communicate with each other. The sad irony was that Len's death brought Smith and his sister together for the first time in about 25 years.[57]

Smith was also moved to talk passionately about Len in an address to the Melbourne players at training that week. Again, he broke down in tears.[58]

The tributes flowed for Len Smith. Richmond president Ray Dunn said he had been 'a great inspiration' whose death had been 'a terrific blow to Richmond and football in general'. Former Fitzroy captain Alan 'Butch' Gale told *The Sporting*

---

[55] Norma Harmes. Interview with the author.
[56] Wayne Harmes. Interview with the author.
[57] Peter Smith. Interview with the author.
[58] Peter Smith. Interview with the author.

Globe: 'He was one of the finest men I've met in sport, and if I wanted my boys taught football he would have been the first man I'd go to'. One of the most eloquent tributes was provided by ex-umpire Harry Beitzel, who wrote in *Footy Week* magazine:

> Football lost one of its greatest gentlemen, thinkers and lovers of our game in the sad passing of Len Smith. Len was always doing or saying something constructive for the good of the game and the players. Quiet, unobtrusive, analytical but a fantastic tactician and teacher, Len was welcome everywhere... To have known him was an honour; to count him as a friend a privilege; to have the chance of talking football with him an education.

Len had also 'educated' two of his grandsons. (He had left behind six grandchildren.) Although Stephen and Wayne Harmes would have dearly loved to have spent a lot more time with their 'Pop', they at least stole a few treasured moments. Norma Harmes recalled: 'Dad would stand in the centre of the lawn in the backyard and the boys had to run round and he would handball to them as they ran around. They would have to say: "Pass, Poppa, pass". If they didn't say his name, he wouldn't pass to them. He told them: "The reason you have to use the name is to stop players from other teams saying: 'Pass', and you giving the ball to him".'[59]

Wayne Harmes shared some of his childhood recollections:

> As a six-year-old, I carried Len's bags into training a few times. That was a great thrill because I was a mad Richmond supporter and I got to see my hero, Roger Dean...
>
> When Mum and Dad were going out, they'd drop us off at my grandparents' place and as soon as we'd finished dinner, Len would disappear downstairs into his rumpus room, where he had a battlefield with little toy soldiers set up on his pool table. He came up with his match-ups, and planned his moves, and did a lot of his thinking down there. As kids, we weren't allowed down there much, but I can remember standing at the bottom of the stairs and peering around the corner and wondering what the hell he was doing. He was playing with his little soldiers. He was a footy nut. Any spare moment he had he'd go down there.
>
> I'd beg my parents to take me around there on Thursday nights when, at times, the Richmond players would meet there...

---

[59] Norma Harmes. Interview with the author.

He tried to teach me to mark a footy. He'd wind his clothesline up to a certain height and then hang me off it and when he said: 'Let go', I'd let go and he'd throw a footy at me. I was basically up and down until I kept catching it. Every time I dropped it, I'd be back up there again. It helped my coordination and ball-handling...

Even then, I was a footy fanatic, but because I was so young I didn't realise at the time the level of input and influence both Norm and Len had on the game. I'd grown up with it and it was nothing unusual to me, but as you get older and do some homework you're just so proud that you're related to these blokes.

Even then, I could tell they had different personalities. Norm always scared me. When we'd knock at the door, it was answered by what I looked upon as a huge man. I was scared to ask him anything - even though we were related - because he seemed to have this aura about him, whereas probably Len didn't. One was the dictator, the other was the educator.[60]

As fate would have it, the two league clubs Len had coached - Richmond and Fitzroy - met at the Brunswick Street Oval the Saturday after his death. As a mark of respect for a man who had left such indelible imprints at both clubs, a minute's silence was observed after a rendition of *The Last Post*. The battling Lions found something extra against a superb Tiger combination, and led by two points at the last change, only to go down by nine points. For the Tigers, it was the second of a run of six successive victories that culminated in their finishing on top of the VFL ladder, and then winning their first premiership in 24 years.

Earlier in the season, Len had enthused in *The Herald*: 'Richmond for premiers? A lot of people will not have it, but I am sure of one thing - the Tigers are not far off it. This is the best League side with which I have been connected, and I have been around the League scene for a long time. I handled some good Fitzroy sides, but none of them had the same premiership potential as Richmond have this year'. Len said Richmond's improvement since the end of 1964 had been the result of a combination of factors: the recruiting work of Graeme Richmond, 'foresighted' president Ray Dunn, 'continuity of coaching methods, and a capable committee'.[61]

In his terrific book, *Immortals: Football people and the evolution of Australian Rules*, Lionel Frost best summed up Len's influence on a Tiger dynasty that produced four premierships in eight years.

---

[60] Wayne Harmes. Interview with the author.
[61] *The Herald*, June 1967.

Of course, there is no way of knowing whether Len Smith, had he lived longer, would have had the same success at Richmond as Tommy Hafey did. Among Richmond people of that era, opinion is divided: on one hand, there are those who argue, as Graeme Richmond did, that Len 'set the whole philosophy, the whole style of game, gave us fresh thoughts and just regenerated a rundown Richmond Football Club'; on the other hand, Kevin Bartlett points out that Richmond under Len would have played a very different style of game from the physical, aggressive, long-kicking style they played under Tommy...

It is taking nothing away from Tommy Hafey to say that Len Smith's influence lived on at Richmond long after he died. Tommy took many of Len's core ideas, married them with his own and produced a playing style that in many ways was different from the style that Len used... Len's ideas were powerful enough to be reshaped and re-created in a different context, and yet still remain recognisable. Tommy Hafey certainly deserves his status as one of the great figures in football history, but in his coaching the presence, even the ghost, of Len Smith can be detected. Tommy called the shots, but Len certainly remained an invisible part of the coaching panel.[62]

In August 1974, just a month before the Tigers claimed their fourth flag under Hafey, prominent Tigers still felt a debt of gratitude to Len. Superstar captain Royce Hart wrote in *The Australian*: 'One regret I have is that Len is not alive to see his dream come true... No single person has done so much to improve Australian Rules, yet Len Smith has not been given the public recognition he deserves because he did not seek publicity... When watching this year's finals series, let's give a thought to the man who has moulded the modern style of football and made it such an attractive game'.[63]

Norm Smith also unwittingly had an influence on the Tigers' success. Hafey adopted the hard running and long-kicking style of play that had been so successful at Melbourne, explaining: 'The opposition knew what we were going to do, but they still had to beat us at it. That was the way Norm Smith won six premierships in a 10-year period, and I felt that style had so much common sense about it'.[64]

---

[62] Frost, Lionel, *Immortals: football people and the evolution of Australian Rules*, John Wiley & Sons, 2005.
[63] *The Australian*, August 29, 1974.
[64] Tom Hafey. Interview with the author.

Little more than a month before Len Smith died, he gave Smith a disturbing yet prophetic warning. Smith had confided in his brother that he was 'becoming more and more flattened by matches'. Len's response shocked him. Although Len had at times ignored medical opinion himself because 'he loved football as much as life itself', he told Smith he 'should give serious thought to quitting'. Marj also wanted him to retire. Their pleas had some impact on Smith, who later said: 'The decision (to retire) was in the back of my mind but I kept it there'.[65]

The issue was thrust to the forefront of his mind barely a fortnight later, when Hassa Mann stole victory with a last-gasp goal against North Melbourne at the MCG in round 12. For Smith, this 'tremendous struggle' ensured it all 'came to a head'. Since 1960, he had felt increasing pressure to succeed, and had found that 'the struggle' had become harder. But never had he felt so 'drawn out and tense' after a match as he did this day at the MCG. He asked himself: 'How long can I keep it up?' He knew the end wasn't too far away, later explaining: 'There was no question of taking things easier. I knew I wasn't built that way and that my own temperament made me drive myself'.[66]

Len's death underlined a worrying history of heart disease. Their father had died from a heart attack at the age of 58, Len had suffered the same fate at 55, and now Smith, at 51, was approaching the critical age bracket.

Smith soon had his first major heart scare. Whether it was due to the cumulative pressure of coaching, the stress of his brother's death less than a fortnight earlier, or genetics that made his heart a time-bomb, Smith too collapsed with a heart attack. The first sign that all was not well was at training on the night of Tuesday August 1 when he was short of breath. He asked John Beckwith to take charge of training as he left the field and consulted the Melbourne club doctor. The next day Smith underwent a cardiograph, and other tests, and was initially told his heart was in good condition. However, on the Saturday morning – just hours before the Demons were to play Carlton at Princes Park – he was told he would have to enter hospital for more tests.

In the meantime, however, he felt well enough to coach Melbourne. At half-time, the Demons were going well – they trailed the much-vaunted Blues by eight points. But Smith wasn't going so well. As he and Beckwith walked down the grandstand steps into the changeroom, he groaned and clutched his chest.

'I'm not feeling too good – I've got a pain over the heart,' he told a concerned Beckwith. 'You take over, Becky.'[67]

---

[65] *Melbourne Truth*, 1967.
[66] *Melbourne Truth*, 1967.
[67] John Beckwith. Interview with the author.

Smith was taken straight to Sacred Heart Hospital, where it was revealed he had a minor heart condition. Despite his disappointment that his two-week spell in hospital was the longest he had been 'laid up' in an unbroken 33-year football career, he was thankful that his condition had been detected before a more 'serious situation' developed.[68] Among the hundreds of get-well cards was one signed: 'From a Magpie supporter'. Smith joked: 'That's really something for an old Demon to treasure as he goes out of the game'.[69]

And he *was* going out of the game. Doctors strongly advised him not to return to coaching because it was too stressful for a man in his condition. He kept 'putting off' the decision to retire, but later revealed that he eventually came to the conclusion: 'The pressure on League coaches has increased enormously in recent years. I reckon it's strictly a job for young, fit, keen blokes who can take worry in their stride... There is not the slightest doubt that my recent illness was caused by the strain and tension, which seems an unavoidable part of coaching'. Worried that his condition might have 'developed into something much more serious' if he had not 'slowed down', he retired from coaching on September 12 – two weeks after the Demons' season had finished.[70]

He had made the momentous decision 'suddenly', without further consultation with anyone, not even Marj. 'It's the way I like to make up my mind,' he said. Soon after, he said that while he felt his condition was improving by the day, he never had 'those lingering regrets' that sometimes cause men to reverse their decisions. He added: 'I don't expect to have any yearning to coach again... There will be no comeback... That is my final decision no matter how much my health improves. I have no regrets'. A minor regret, though, was that he didn't finish his coaching career at Melbourne on a more successful note. 'But,' he conceded, 'had I made the finals with Melbourne, undoubtedly that stubborn streak would have driven me on to go that step further.' He said he would stand aside with 'a memory chest of bitter disappointments, and moments of extreme elation and achievement'. He also offered the following self-assessment: 'I have been labelled as an iron-willed disciplinarian. I don't wear that brand proudly. I prefer people to think of me as a person who believed in teamwork (and) the support of your fellow man, and put it into practice. I believe that most of the players I coached think of me with respect and not as a tyrant. I like to think that'.[71]

---

[68] *Melbourne Truth*, 1967.
[69] *The Sun* series, 1967.
[70] *The Sun* series, 1967. Melbourne finished seventh with eight wins and 10 losses.
[71] *Melbourne Truth*, 1967.

Peter Smith made an interesting observation about the potential causes for the heart problems experienced by his father and his uncle. He said: 'Len kept most of his emotions bottled up inside, which might have added to his stress levels, and that might have contributed to his death. But the opposite might have been the case with Norm – he would explode and maybe that contributed to his problems. Maybe neither of them found that healthy balance'.[72]

Norm Smith was regarded as a grand old man of football, yet he had retired from coaching at the age of just 51. During the 2007 season, five coaches were older than Smith was when he called it quits: Denis Pagan (Carlton, 59), Kevin Sheedy (Essendon, 59), Leigh Matthews (Brisbane, 56), Mick Malthouse (Collingwood, 54), Neil Craig (Adelaide 52),

Smith was also forced to make other sacrifices. A semi-regular squash player for much of his adult life, he formed the opinion: 'I'd better give it up, otherwise I might drop dead on the bloody squash court!'[73] But despite his genuine fear of suffering a similar fate to both his brother and his father, he didn't broadcast his feelings. 'Norm never complained,' said Russ Brown. 'He obeyed doctor's orders and took Wafarin tablets, but not once did he say: "Poor me". He wasn't a whinger – he'd prefer to suffer in silence than burden anyone else with his problems.'[74]

On November 20, 1967, the Norman Smith Complimentary Dinner (the chief organiser of which was former Demon secretary Percy Page – the man who recruited Smith 34 years earlier) was held at Melbourne Town Hall. Speeches were made by the likes of Don Duffy (who sat beside Smith at the head table), Ron Barassi and Checker Hughes, who told the 450 people present that the real test of one's friendship towards another is 'to know the other's faults, yet still love him'.[75]

In response, Smith thanked the club, the players, and opponents who had attended, and expressed particular appreciation of Marj for her support throughout his career. Just weeks earlier he had told *The Sun*: 'It goes without saying that I couldn't have stayed in the game so long without the wholehearted support of my wife, Marj. I was a very fortunate man to have a wife who was not only keen on the game but also so understanding. Her loyalty and encouragement have helped my career immeasurably'.[76]

---

[72] Peter Smith. Interview with the author.
[73] Russell Brown. Interview with the author.
[74] Russell Brown. Interview with the author.
[75] *Trident Monthly* (a newsletter produced by a Melbourne supporters' group), April 1968.
[76] *The Sun* series, 1967. Norm was always very protective of Marj. To exemplify this point, Sam Allica told the author of an occasion when the Smiths stopped at a petrol station on their way to a match. The attendant made an unpleasant remark to Marj, and an enraged Norm 'leant out the window and grabbed the bloke by the nose' and said: 'Now you listen here! You will not speak to my wife like that!'

While Duffy presented him with a cheque for $2000 (decimal currency had been introduced in Australia the previous year), Smith received another begrudging tribute from a Magpie fan: a $1 bill with an attached note stating: 'I'm a Collingwood supporter. (Expletive) Norm Smith. Enclosed find one dollar'.[77]

Four weeks later, on Monday December 18, 1967 – just a day after Australian Prime Minister Harold Holt disappeared in the sea off Portsea – the Demons farewelled Smith with a testimonial function at the MCG. The chief organiser of the evening, Tridents supporters' group president David Bickart told the gathering: 'Melbourne supporters should realise that you no longer, as a player or coach, belong to us. You now belong to the history of the game, and it is to the historians of the future that we must look for the final appraisal of your worth to football. We can, however, be confident that they will always acknowledge that special greatness that, I feel, is exclusively yours... For all that you and Marj have done for Melbourne and for all the pleasure you have given to so many Melbourne supporters over such a long period, thank you very much indeed'.[78]

This time Smith was presented with a floral sheaf and a cheque for $2009.67 (the amount that had been raised by the Tridents). He wrote a letter of gratitude to Bickhart, in which he stated: 'Just a brief note to say "thank you" to yourself, David, and to members of the MFC Tridents for organising the Norman Smith Testimonial. The amount raised was quite beyond my expectations... Please convey my thanks to the many people who contributed'.[79]

▼▼▼▼▼▼▼▼▼

The rocky relationship between Norm Smith and Melbourne Football Club encountered another problem in the summer of 1967-68. This time, however, it proved insurmountable and resulted in Smith severing all ties with the club.

Although he had just ended his coaching career, he didn't want to step out of football completely. 'I've been in the game more than 30 years,' he said, 'and I love it too much to get right out. It's part of my life.'

In fact, he was enthusiastic about taking on a role on the committee. And he planned to assist a Demon resurrection. 'At 52 I'm starting the third phase of my football career,' he said. 'The prospect excites me. Now I'll have the chance to

---

[77] *Trident Monthly*, April 1968.
[78] *Trident Monthly*.
[79] *Trident Monthly*.

put something back into the game as an administrator. I'll be taking it easy for about 12 months, but I see myself filling a recruiting role, perhaps lecturing to country coaches'.[80]

In his recent dealings with the committee, Smith felt more comfortable than he had for several years. He was certainly unaware that any residual tension existed, telling *The Sun*: 'Every member of the committee is a personal friend of mine, and while we've had our arguments about football matters since, it hasn't stopped us working together and getting on with the job. As far as I'm concerned, there are no grudges being held at Melbourne now'.[81]

At a meeting on September 21, 1967, the committee discussed Smith's written request to continue with the club as a committeeman. It was recommended that Duffy and Cordner – both medical doctors – discuss Smith's illness with him and 'if after this discussion Norman is still desirous of a committee appointment, he be approved'. (At the same meeting, Smith's name would have no doubt been mentioned as the committee resolved that new coach Beckwith 'be advised of restrictions re television and paper contracts'.) At a committee meeting a month later (October 23) it was noted that Smith was co-opted to the committee 'without the power to vote'.[82] He was simply a voice. That would do for the time being until he could become a full member of the committee following the December election.

While Smith's ascension to the committee was regarded as a mere formality, it soon became clear that he would face stiff, bitter opposition. History said it would be a tough ask. Denis Cordner had been the only man since the war to stand for election on the committee to oust a sitting member – and that was back in 1956.[83] But this was no ordinary candidate.

Smith submitted an informal vote because he didn't want it said that he had tried to oust any specific committee member.

However, his bid was blocked when a group of four committeemen formed a ticket and placed Smith last on their how-to-vote cards. He finished third-last in the ballot – just ahead of two other unsuccessful candidates: Brian Dixon and recruiting officer Ken Carlon.

---

[80] *The Sun* series, 1967.
[81] *The Sun* series, 1967.
[82] Melbourne Football Club, Minutes of Committee Meetings, courtesy of the Melbourne Cricket Club Library.
[83] Don Cordner. Interview with the author.

MFC Committee Election

December 1967

Colin McLean	351
'Checker' Hughes	341
Arthur King	312
Charles Loughrey	309
Terry Gleeson	301
Norman King	281
Harry Long	278
Ivan Porter	259
Norm Smith	**163**
Brian Dixon	147
Ken Carlon	122

Dixon's disappointment at being overlooked was overridden by his surprise at Smith's defeat. The Demon veteran said he was 'very sorry' for his former coach after the 'magnificent service he had given to the club'.

Smith didn't accept the result as easily. For him, this was the final insult. The election meeting – which Smith believed had deteriorated into a farce – became an ugly scene. He had always prided himself on being gracious in defeat, but this time he didn't feel his opponents had played fairly. He told some committeemen exactly what he thought of their actions. When a reporter asked him for a comment, he merely responded: 'It makes you think, doesn't it?' Flanked by his wife and son, Smith stormed out, bitterly disillusioned, never to return. Peter Smith recalled:

> 'Dad was angry at the four blokes who blocked him, and Mum and I were angry, too. He deserved better treatment than that. You've got to wonder why they did it. When it came to footy, no-one at the club knew more about the game than Dad did. Surely any club would want his expertise around the place helping to make some of the important decisions about the club's future. But I suspect those blokes were thinking more about their own positions than what was good for the club. They were probably also thinking that Dad would shake them up a bit too much. He'd "keep the bastards honest" all right! Maybe some of them felt it would have been a bit too much for them to handle'.[84]

---

[84] Peter Smith. Interview with the author.

At a committee meeting on December 5, Col McLean raised the possibility of again co-opting Smith to their ranks. But the minutes of the meeting bluntly stated: 'no action taken'. This time, though, it would have been too late for a reconciliation anyway. No amount of back-pedalling would get Norm Smith back this time. Just as clearly, some powerful people at Melbourne didn't want him there, either, at least not on the committee.

Peter Smith left the Demons as a player. When he walked out of the MCG following the shock election result, he vowed: 'I'll never play here again'. At the time, he told Alf Brown from *The Herald*: 'I would not like to continue to play at Melbourne with the same committee and with the same state of affairs existing'. Peter Smith had played 23 games and kicked 18 goals for Melbourne. He joined Barassi at Carlton, where he played a further 15 games in the three seasons, winning the Blues' best clubman award in 1969, and kicking 13 goals in a reserves match in his final season there in 1970. 'I was no superman,' Peter admitted. 'I was lucky to play 38 games. Actually, I was lucky to play *any* games.' He said he had 'some success'[85] in the VFA. He played for both Port Melbourne and Coburg, and excelled for the latter. In 1974, he thrilled Coburg fans by kicking 121 goals in a second division premiership side, including 12 in the second semi-final and eight in the Grand Final. He followed up with 82 goals in first division the next year.

In the meantime, Melbourne floundered. Norm Smith had known for some time that the Demons were going downhill, and when he left the club for good he confided in Hugh McPherson (who also retired as a trainer in 1967): 'It will be many, many years before Melbourne will play in the finals again, let alone become a force'. McPherson didn't view it as 'sour grapes' on Smith's behalf. 'He was just expressing his opinion, which, as usual, proved correct,' he said.[86]

⛀⛀⛀⛀⛀⛀⛀⛀⛀

For all the heroics Ron Barassi had performed in a Melbourne jumper, the day he made Norm Smith most proud was when he led Carlton in the 1967 preliminary final. The now injury-prone Barassi was in the twilight of his glittering career – it was his 243rd game – but he was arguably the Blues' best in a 29-point loss to Geelong. Smith marvelled at his capacity to battle adversity.

---

[85] Peter Smith. Interview with the author.
[86] Hugh McPherson. Interview with the author.

'In the final stages,' Smith said, 'he could kick the ball only 45 yards. He had willed his body beyond ordinary physical endurance, but he refused to quit. I've always had a great regard for Ron's character, his will to win and his determination. But it has never been higher than it was that day at the MCG.'[87]

Smith was confident that Barassi would continue to be an inspirational leader, and become 'a fine coach', when retired as a player. 'There have been others who have been great coaches by setting an example on the field, but have not succeeded later (as a non-playing coach),' he said. 'But I don't believe this will happen with Ron. He's a very deep thinker and I feel a very good tactical coach. And he is very demanding. They say I'm tough, but I think he'll be a lot more ruthless.'[88]

The following season – during Smith's year off – Barassi was to enter his first Grand Final as a coach (non-playing). He approached his mentor and asked him to speak to his players about a week before the match. Smith told Barassi to bring the players to his house. Although it must have been a strange experience for Smith to be invited into Carlton's inner sanctum after calling it the enemy for so many years, it was an unforgettably electric experience for the Carlton players. Young star Robert Walls, then just 18, was and remains the best mate of Peter Smith. Walls had been at the Smith house many times and 'came to know Norm as a father, rather than just the great coach'. He observed that while he and Peter 'got up to mischief as young blokes do', Peter showed the 'utmost respect' for his parents, who, in turn, 'absolutely idolised each other'. Despite his personal experiences with the Smiths, Walls was as enthralled by Norm Smith's pep-talk as any other Carlton player present at Bell Street.

> Norm was such an imposing man. He had so much presence. Back then they didn't use the word charisma, but if anyone had it, it was Norm Smith. He spoke to us as a group about playing in Grand Finals and preparation and so on. The thing that stood out to me was when he said: 'When you run down and the race and onto the ground, there will be a mighty roar from 100,000 people. But don't be overawed or intimidated by the occasion, and don't put your head down and think: "Jesus! Where am I? What's going on here?" Hold your head up high, look into every grandstand and soak up the atmosphere. Embrace it. Enjoy it. Run near the boundary line and look into the crowd. Puff your chest out and feel good about yourself, and believe that you are about to show everyone just how good you are'.

---

[87] *The Sun* series, 1967.
[88] *The Sun* series, 1967.

I did as Norm said for every Grand Final I played in, and ever major game in fact. It was certainly great advice, and I later passed it on to players I coached.[89]

Not surprisingly, the Blues won the flag, defeating Essendon by just three points in a low-scoring Grand Final in which they mustered just 1.6 after half-time. Barassi's evolution from superstar player to superstar coach was complete.

🏆🏆🏆🏆🏆🏆🏆🏆🏆

Very early in his short-lived retirement, the football fire still burned inside Norm Smith. 'I'm not going to sit at home rotting away,' he resolved. 'Football has been my life for nearly 40 years.'[90]

After sitting out the 1968 season, he began to 'miss the smell of liniment' and was 'itching' to coach again.[91] He faced a sobering paradox: coaching truly made him feel alive, yet it could also kill him. But he knew it wasn't a decision he could make alone. That would be selfish and pig-headed. He had loved ones to consider. He would need to consult Marj and Peter, and hopefully gain their approval, before he could seriously consider making a comeback.

In spring 1968, not long after speaking to the Carlton players – an experience which no doubt reinforced his desire to coach again – Smith drove Marj and Peter up to Mayfield, a suburb of Newcastle, to visit their friends, Dick and Betty Hingston. Dick Hingston had been a teammate of Smith's in Melbourne's 1939 and 1940 premiership sides. They all sat down to discuss whether he should return to football.

Although Peter Smith later said that his father had 'probably been driving Mum mad at home' during his lay-off, Marj was mainly concerned about the effect coaching might have on his health. This was despite the fact Smith had taken steps to improve his physical condition, by running laps of his tennis court or swimming each morning. But Peter was more positive about a return to football, telling his father: 'If you want to coach, do it'.[92]

He *did* want to, and now he would await an opportunity.

---

[89] Robert Walls. Interview with the author.
[90] Reproduced in *Inside Football*, August 4, 1973.
[91] Peter Smith. Interview with the author.
[92] Peter Smith. Interview with the author.

27

THE SAVIOUR OF SOUTH MELBOURNE

[1969-72]

South Melbourne had just started its hunt for a new coach. At the end of the 1968 season, the Swans had sacked Allan Miller after two unsuccessful seasons, and quickly set about finding a replacement.

It wasn't exactly a sought-after position – and hadn't been for a considerable time. Miller's initial appointment was a classic example of the Swans' inability to attract either an experienced coach or an untried star player with solid credentials. In the absence of standout candidates, South had been forced to settle for Miller, who, although he was an inspiring speaker, hadn't played VFL football and had been plucked from the relative obscurity of coaching the Swans' under-19s side.

The South Melbourne coaching job had become a poisoned chalice. The Swans were enduring the most barren period of their history. They hadn't finished above eighth for 16 years (since Norm Smith's first season as coach of Melbourne in 1952), and hadn't made the finals since they lost the infamous 'Bloodbath' Grand Final of 1945. In the subsequent 23 years, 10 men had coached the Swans. Among them were such notables as legendary key-position player Laurie Nash, three Brownlow Medallists in Herbie Matthews, Ron Clegg and Bob Skilton, former star Bill Faul, Melbourne's dual premiership captain Noel McMahen, and Essendon's 1946 premiership hero Gordon 'Whoppa' Lane. But for various reasons – including a lack of resources, playing depth, discipline and team focus, and an unhealthy emphasis on being the best social club – each of these men had failed to take the team into September. Indeed, since 1945 the Swans had been the worst performed club in the competition – by a considerable margin. Every other club had contested at least two finals' series.

Skilton explained why the Swans had underachieved for so long:

> There's no doubt we were not professional enough. Maybe South was even less professional than most of the other clubs in my time as a player (from 1956). We didn't have a great deal of on-field success... but we always lived in hope that next year was going to be it. Sometimes we got sucked in by the team doing well in the post-season night series when some players tried to redeem things a bit.
>
> When we had some talent, we didn't have good administration and so on. You need a blend of everything. One without the other isn't much good. We just couldn't put everything together at the same time.
>
> But we never considered ourselves to be at the arse-end of the competition. We weren't a great footy side, but we had the best social club. Our 'pleasant Sunday mornings', where supporters would mingle with players and training staff over a few beers for relaxation after the Saturday game, were almost legendary. In fact, some people regarded those mornings as important as the match itself. It was a way of unwinding when, really, the players should have been doing recovery exercises and starting to prepare their bodies for the following week. But we didn't know about all that back then; we were only part-timers.[1]

The Swans had also been hindered by off-field problems. Committee room brawls, divisive factions and shambolic leadership struggles had punctuated much of their past... that is, until the very recent past, when most, if not all, of the turbulence had been quelled by the club's no-nonsense president Brian Bourke. An eminent criminal barrister with a burgeoning practice, Bourke had reluctantly bowed to pressure applied by a group of committeemen and agreed to take on the presidency in 1967. Bourke wasn't a man to be trifled with – only the previous year he and Philip Opas QC had defended Ronald Ryan, who became the last man executed in Australia – and he soon streamlined the club's administrative structure and processes and had the off-field operation running smoother than many could remember.

Bourke knew the time had arrived to hunt a well-credentialled coach, and he was determined to rectify the coaching situation quickly because he didn't want any 'leaks about problems' at the Lake Oval. The same day Miller was sacked, Bourke sent his new secretary, Noel Brady, on a fact-finding mission. 'I don't know Norm Smith,' Bourke told Brady, 'but ring him up and get his ideas on who he'd appoint as coach if he was in our position.'

---

[1] Bob Skilton, in an unpublished interview with Jim Main, in late 2005. Main was researching a book on the Swans' 2005 premiership titled *Shake Down The Thunder* (GSP Books, 2005).

THE SAVOUR OF SOUTH MELBOURNE [1969-72]

The eager Brady, 26, rang Smith and then visited him at home, and spent a couple of hours discussing the South Melbourne job. Brady gained the distinct impression: 'I think he's interested in the job himself. I reckon we might be able to get him'.

Bourke recalled:

> Noel rang me either that afternoon or the next morning and said: 'If you come out to Norm's house now, you might get a surprise'.
>
> A surprise?! It was way beyond my wildest dreams!
>
> So I went out to Norm's house, and I told him: 'This is our position. I've got a big legal practice, so I don't want to be buggerising around with the running of the football club'.
>
> Norm said: 'Well, if you agree to certain conditions I'll tell you about – and they're not onerous conditions, but they're because of my health – I'll coach you. I can't get out on the ground now like I used to, and like all the other coaches do these days. But if you get Ian Thorogood to be my assistant, Clyde Laidlaw to coach the seconds, and Donny Williams to coach the thirds, I'll coach them for you'.
>
> He wanted to put together a coaching panel, which was fairly revolutionary for those days, but is almost par for the course now. It was brought upon by his health and inability to do that hard physical work himself, but nonetheless was ahead of its time.
>
> That did it for me. My attitude was: 'Well, you're the man'.
>
> I said: 'So, Norm, what's the money situation?'
>
> He said: 'You're not a money man are you?'
>
> 'No, I'm not interested in money.'
>
> He said: 'I'll coach South for $2500-a-year'.
>
> I said: 'I don't like agreements'.
>
> He said: 'We'll just shake hands'.
>
> The deal was done within about 20 minutes of me arriving. I'd had no idea Norm was interested in coaching again, so it was a complete fluke that we got him.[2]

But not every South Melbourne person was happy with the appointment. The unhappy ones weren't afraid to express their views. Bourke said:

> Someone on the (South Melbourne) Cricket Club committee said to me: 'Do you realise what you're doing?'

---

[2] Brian Bourke. Interview with the author.

I said: 'What do you mean?'

He said: 'Appointing him'.

I said: 'Hell, as far as I know he's the best bloody coach who's ever coached footballers'.

He said: 'You'll have trouble with him'.

I said: 'Well I'll be dealing with him. He'll look after the football side and I'll run the outfit in the committee room. I don't anticipate any trouble'.

And I never had any trouble with Norm. Certainly nothing of any consequence. We became the closest of friends. Whenever I went out to Courts in Coburg and Broadmeadows, I'd always stop for lunch with Norm and Marj.[3]

There was also some minor opposition to the considerable Melbourne influence on the coaching panel. Although the newcomers had brought with them experience, success and know-how, some of the older, dyed-in-the-wool South Melbourne people – who were protective of the Swans 'battling, fighting, backstreet' image – objected to the presence of so many former Demons. They felt as though they were being taken over by the toffs and in the process the Swans would lose some of their own unique identity.

However, they had gained a supercoach who was also willing to dig into his own pocket to help the club. This trait came to the fore about a month after the Smith appointment, when the committee arranged for him to meet the men who poured money into the Swans, including pantyhose king Leon Worth and heart surgeon Aubrey Pitt. Bourke made a brief speech, basically saying: 'Now that we've got Norm here, we've got to raise some money'.

Smith was the first man in the room to make a donation. 'I'll kick in $500,' he announced. This gesture promptly had the other gentleman reaching into their pockets and pledging even larger sums. That day alone the Swans raised about $8000, which was probably the equivalent of about $50,000 today.[4]

The only significant demand Smith made upon the club's finances was the construction of a players' room at the Swans' Lake Oval headquarters (which were largely dilapidated, and a far cry from the plush facilities at the MCG). He felt it was important for the players to be able to socialise together, before or after training, away from the rest of the club people. Bourke and Brady, with the approval of the committee, had agreed to throw their full support behind Smith, and so a players' room, complete with a pool table, was quickly built on top of the shower block.

---

[3] Brian Bourke. Interview with the author.
[4] Brian Bourke. Interview with the author.

THE SAVOUR OF SOUTH MELBOURNE [1969-72]

Smith also placed demands on his players well before pre-season training even started. He didn't even spare his captain, club icon Bob Skilton, who had just won his third Brownlow Medal in 1968. Skilton was ecstatic that he would get the opportunity to play under Norm Smith on a weekly basis.[5] But Smith wasn't exactly rapt with Skilton the first time they met publicly after the announcement.

Bourke had been keen to capitalise on Smith's appointment. He told Brady to call the annual general meeting. Brady reminded Bourke that the club's constitution stipulated that a specified amount of notice had to be given. Bourke replied: 'Bugger the constitution. Just call the meeting and get them there. It'll be great publicity for the club'. The meeting was fixed for 8pm at the South Melbourne Town Hall. Bourke spoke first, telling the gathering: 'The purpose of this meeting is to introduce you to Norm Smith, and to let you meet him. So without further ado, here's Norm'.

Bourke recalled what happened next:

> Norm got up, and he was a bit taken aback. Even though he was so good with people, he still had a streak of shyness. He'd been talking for 10 minutes when Bobby Skilton arrived. The people started cheering - he was the greatest. He walked up to Norm, shook his hand. Here they were, the two great men - the superstar and the messiah - who were going to save the club from oblivion. 'Skilts' then went to take a seat.
>
> Norm said: 'Bobby. I'm the coach here now. Never be late to another function at South Melbourne. Understand?'
>
> Immediately, he'd set the standard and laid down the law, that no matter who you were you had to toe the line. Norm always took on the tall poppies.[6]

The next morning, Smith unleashed his wrath on two other senior players – John Rantall and Paul Harrison – who had failed to attend the meeting. Rantall and Harrison lived together – along with an old schoolmate of Rantall's named Sandy Grant – above a grocery store in Punt Road, and were notorious for throwing wild parties that stretched into the wee hours. They wouldn't even curb their nocturnal activities the night before matches. One night the bath they had packed with booze and ice overflowed, and the water leaked through the floor and ruined most of the

---

[5] Skilton could easily have played his career under Norm Smith at Melbourne. He later explained: 'As a kid, I hated South Melbourne. If you lived in Port Melbourne, you hated South. I put in clearance applications to go to Melbourne, but they were knocked back, so I had to play with South'. (Source: *Red and Blue* documentary.)
[6] Brian Bourke. Interview with the author.

groceries below.[7] Such irresponsible behaviour disgusted Smith. The morning after the annual general meeting, he literally gave the trio a wake-up call. He arrived unannounced on their doorstep after they had hosted another huge shindig, this time for Rantall's birthday. Sandy Grant takes up the story:

> There was a bang at the door. I didn't get up immediately, but I eventually opened the door in my jocks. I'd never met Norm before then, so I made a great first impression!
> Norm said: 'Are Rantall and Harrison in here?'
> I said: 'Yeah'.
> Norm started to push in, so I said: 'Ah, do you want to see them?'
> He said: 'Yeah, as a matter of fact I do. You must be Sandy. I've heard you've got a big mouth. Keep it shut while I'm here'.
> 'Mopsy' (Rantall) and 'Harro' were coiled up in their beds recovering, but Norm got them out and gave them an absolute spray for about 50 minutes. He basically told them they were wasting their ability, and that if they didn't want to apply themselves they might as well give the game away.
> I was giggling to myself in the next room. But not even I escaped without a reprimand. Norm walked out and I was pretending to clean up - the place was a pig-sty - and he stopped and said: 'Why don't you go back to university? You're wasting your life. Just get back there and make something of yourself'. Then he just walked out. I'd been sleeping on the couch for about six months and bumming around doing casual jobs - not really doing much at all.
> By this stage it was after 11 o'clock, so we sat around and looked at each other like stunned mullets for about five minutes, had showers and then thought: 'Well, we've got to think about this'. We had to go to a place where we could think clearly, so we went to the pub for a counter-lunch! At the end of that discussion, 'Harro' said: 'Footy's just a game. I'll just go on doing what I'm doing'.
> But Smithy had a far more positive effect on 'Mopsy' (Rantall) and I. That was the day 'Mopsy' committed himself to becoming the best player he could be.[8]

Smith did various similar things to jolt the Swans players out of what he perceived was their lethargy, and casual attitude to their training. Soon after his arrival he scheduled a compulsory 6am training session. *The Herald's* Alf Brown later

---

[7] John Rantall. Interview with the author.
[8] Sandy Grant. Interview with the author. Rantall, then 25, went on to play a then club record 260 games for South Melbourne from 1963-72 and 1976-79, and in between became a member of the first North Melbourne premiership team (in 1975), coached by Ron Barassi. Overall, he played a then League record of 336 games.

revealed that he suspected it was a ploy to 'show the players who was boss rather than an early bid to get them fit'. Smith didn't need an excuse to make an example of some, but one player made the mistake of sleeping-in on that first morning. He was guaranteed a stern rebuke. Smith 'stormed to his flat, hammered on the door and pulled him, startled and sleepy, out of bed and down to the ground'.[9] If players refused to heed the message, they would have it forced down their throats.

Smith continued his crusade to get the most out of Rantall and Harrison. During his opening address to the players on the first pre-season training night, He said: 'I don't know many of you yet, but I certainly know two blokes: Paul Harrison and John Rantall. Although they've been around a while, I don't know them for their football prowess; I know who they are because they're always the last to leave the cricket club bar. I'm here to tell you two boys that that's going to cease'.[10]

Both players were shocked. But this was just the start of Smith's campaign to instil discipline into them and the club as a whole, which he later said had 'a shocking set-up' when he started there.[11] Every training night for the first two months, Smith gave the pair extra fitness work on top of the hard, slogging sessions they had completed with their teammates; sessions which often included 'a lake run' around adjoining Albert Park Lake. Rantall said: 'The challenge was thrown out immediately to myself and "Harro". He flogged the arses off us. It rocked us a bit because we'd both been at the club for six years. But I was virtually going nowhere, and at that stage I couldn't see it'.

Rantall insisted:

> If I hadn't come across Smithy, I reckon I might have played only 130-140 games and then disappeared. I've got him to thank for turning my whole life around – not just football. I was burning the candle at both ends and I had this opportunity with my football and I wasn't respecting it, but Norm taught me that respect. He was the one that was tough on me and made me knuckle down, and I don't think I ever would've sorted myself out without his guidance.
>
> My mother died when I was 21 and that contributed to me going down the wrong path. Norm and Marj came along as parental figures.
>
> It wasn't just football that Norm taught us. He might have come across as a hard man, and he was, but he just cared about people so much that he wanted to put them on the right path.[12]

---

[9] *The Herald*, March 1969.
[10] John Rantall. Interview with the author.
[11] *Newsday*, Thursday October 2, 1969.
[12] John Rantall. Interview with the author.

Significantly, his mate, Sandy Grant, also heeded Smith's advice – he returned to university. He reflected: 'I'd been half thinking about it, but you need a kick in the backside when you're a young bloke. It was the right advice at the right time'. Months later, Grant ran into Smith at The George Hotel in South Melbourne.

'You're back at university I hear,' he said.

'Yeah, I am,' Grant replied. 'Thanks for that.'

Smith shook his head. 'It was your decision,' he said. 'I just gave you the idea'.

Grant – who went on to senior management roles in superannuation companies like the Colonial Group, Industry Fund Services and Cbus – never forgot Smith's influence on him.

'There was something about the bloke,' he said. 'People talk about the aura of Norm Smith. Even my wife Anne, who isn't into footy at all, was just so taken with him; she said: "I see what they mean". There was just something about his personality and the way he carried himself that you just regarded him highly. It wasn't domineering, but it was next-door to that. He was a leader, *and a dynamic person.*'[13]

Smith wasn't as dynamic when it came to coaching. He had to control his emotions for the sake of his health. Clyde Laidlaw said: 'Norm wasn't allowed to get upset, which must have been difficult for him because he had a history of doing just that'.[14]

Smith consciously took on more of a supervisory role, while Thorogood and the other coaches did the hands-on, physical trackwork under his direction. This arrangement caused many to conclude that Smith and Thorogood were joint coaches. Ron Casey mentioned it on *World of Sport*, putting to Thorogood: 'I suppose that Norm makes the bullets and you fire them.'

Thorogood replied: 'Anybody who knows Norm Smith knows that he doesn't need anybody to fire his bullets'.

Thorogood later explained:

> The days of Norm stripping into footy gear and physically getting involved in drills were gone, but he was very much an active observer on the sidelines. He wanted to spend more time with players individually than collectively.
>
> We would talk nearly every day and, in particular, we would meet for an hour before training to discuss how we should approach that night's session, what he wanted done and what he wanted emphasised. Then he would stand on

---

[13] Sandy Grant. Interview with the author.
[14] Clyde Laidlaw. Interview with the author.

the sidelines while we trained. But as he saw fit, he would call players over to the boundary.

Norm had me doing most of the talking to the players, although there were occasions where he said: 'I'm going to have a say'. He was still the coach, but that's just the way he felt it should be approached.[15]

Skilton said that most of the players had no problems with the coaching set-up, but revealed that a minority loathed it. 'In some respects, the players hated Smithy watching from the sidelines and sitting up in the stand,' he said. 'Usually, when the coach was out on the ground you always knew where he was, and if blokes wanted to loaf a bit they could when the coach's back is turned; and they could hide at the back of the line. Most blokes love training, but there are some who will get out of it if they can. But from Norm's vantage point, he could pick them out. Some nights he'd come down breathing fire.'[16]

Smith's new coaching stint didn't begin well. The practice match period was a farce. Smith said: 'We did not even have enough players to hold two practice matches on one afternoon. That's hard to believe but it's true. I can tell you it won't happen again'.[17] In a practice match against another club – Port Adelaide at Alberton Oval – a disaster took place. Skilton snapped an Achilles tendon and missed the entire season.

The Swans then lost their first five games by an average of 28 points. Admittedly, they had played three powerhouses in eventual finalists Richmond (premier), Carlton (runner-up) and Geelong (third), but the fact was the Swans were second-bottom, just 6.5 percent clear of Melbourne.

Smith said later: 'I knew very little about South when I went there. A lot of players – particularly the older ones – got their positions too easily. There was not enough pressure on them'.[18]

Off the field, according to Bourke, it was a case of 'what culture?' He said: 'There was nothing to South as a club. Bobby Skilton had kept the bloody club alive. I told Norm once: "I reckon the apathy's in the mortar. It's holding this bloody building up". He took that on board to try to change it. In a sense, he did change it, but it was an Herculean task. I don't think there was much culture at South, but he tried to inject some. There was a lack of direction, but I think Norm gave the club direction. But to take the club to the point where it was a very

---

[15] Ian Thorogood. Interview with the author.
[16] Bob Skilton. Interview with the author
[17] *Newsday*, Thursday October 2, 1969.
[18] *Newsday*, Thursday October 2, 1969.

successful club in terms of winning premierships, it would have taken a very long time. But I reckon if we got Norm down there when he was 40 instead of 50-odd, anything might have happened because we had a number of Brownlow Medallists and champions in the 50s and 60s'.[19]

However, Smith was impressed with the passion and pain displayed by some of his players during this barren stretch. On one occasion, the Swans were trailing at half-time and young talent Peter Bedford (who would win the Swans' best-and-fairest in Smith's first three seasons at the club) was so frustrated with what had transpired that he punched a hole in a door inside the changerooms. Bedford recalled: 'Although Norm didn't say anything at the time, I think he was quite rapt in that because I was feeling the same frustration that he was, because we weren't doing what we should have been doing'.[20]

There was a time, though, when Smith wasn't entirely happy with Bedford... even if he quickly realised his anger was unwarranted. The star centreman/rover had received a heavy knock in the first half and spent most of the half-time break in the medical room with an ice-pack on his head. The doctor's instruction was: 'Leave it on your ear'. Bedford was doing that during Smith's half-time address, but the problem was he was on the wrong side of Smith, who could see he was holding something to his ear, but didn't know exactly what. Smith's immediate reaction was: 'Bedford! You're not listening to a race are you?!'

Bedford, horrified by the implication, quickly revealed the ice-pack and said: 'No, Norm, no'.

Smith relented: 'That's all right then', and continued with his address.[21]

After losses, Smith felt it was more important than ever to keep the players together, and lift their spirits. Occasionally he would take them to a pub on a Monday night for this purpose. 'His capacity to lift them was amazing,' Bourke said.[22]

The George Hotel was a regular hangout for South Melbourne people on Saturday nights, and Smith settled into this scene very quickly. Rantall said: 'When you had a beer with Smithy and listened to him talk about football, he really made you feel a part of the conversation. You might just be one insignificant person in the group, but he made you feel as though he was talking to you. That's a gift not many people have. I think that's why he could motivate you to produce your best'.[23]

---

[19] Brian Bourke. Interview with the author.
[20] Peter Bedford. Interview with the author.
[21] Peter Bedford. Interview with the author.
[22] Brian Bourke. Interview with the author.
[23] John Rantall. Interview with the author.

Smith was still the same social animal – often the last to leave. As usual, even in this atmosphere, he was still the coach. As players slowly filtered out of The George and left for home, Smith would warn them: 'Don't be late for training'. Rantall said: 'You could play up, as long as you did what he asked. Some players tried to take the piss out of him over a few beers late at night, thinking he wouldn't remember because he'd had a few. But on the Tuesday night, we'd finish training and he'd just call them into the centre and say: "I've got a bit of extra work for you, boys". You quickly learnt not to take him on because he never forgot'.[24]

However, Skilton revealed a contradiction in Smith's approach. Although 'everything was either black or white', with 'nothing in-between – and you daren't go in-between' – he could still be 'inconsistent', or 'unpredictable'. Following the odd late-night, alcohol-fuelled clash with players, 'sometimes it was forgotten and other times it wasn't' when they all fronted for the Sunday morning recovery session. No-one ever quite knew what the aftermath would be. Skilton said: 'Sometimes blokes would turn up to Sunday morning training and think all would be forgotten, but it wouldn't be. We got to the stage where we thought Smithy had a tape-recorder in his brain because you wouldn't even remember what was said, but he would. The next day he might say: "So you think so-and-so shouldn't get a game?" And then there were times when things had become so heated that you were sure it would be carried on the next morning, but there wasn't even a mention of it'. It all added to the 'fear factor' Smith waged on the players, who 'were all petrified of him, even if you were the captain'.[25]

On Sunday mornings, Smith would 'never show any after-effects of hangover from the night before', and would in fact 'come up like a new penny' and be 'as bright as a button'.[26] He also had a phenomenal recall of everything that had been said and done the previous night.

Two young players who found this out the hard way were Ricky Quade and Neville 'Nifty' Miller[27]. The Swans had played Fos Williams's Port Adelaide in a practice match in Adelaide. The Swans were slaughtered and Smith was furious. The team was scheduled to fly back to Melbourne the next day, but Smith decided they would return home immediately. He then laid down law: 'We're training tomorrow morning at 10 o'clock. No-one is to drink tonight, either on the plane or when we get home'.

---

[24] John Rantall. Interview with the author.
[25] Bob Skilton. Interview with the author.
[26] Peter Bedford. Interview with the author.
[27] Ricky Quade started with the Swans in 1970, captained the club from 1977-79, coached the club from 1982-84 and later served the Swans as the chairman of selectors and a director, while Neville Miller is the father of Melbourne player Brad Miller.

Quade recalled:

'Nifty' (Miller) and I thought: 'Bugger that'. When we got home, being young and stupid, we went out for a night on the town. 'Nifty' and I lived at The George Hotel, along with a few other players. The problem was that Norm always drank at The George, and when we got back around midnight, Norm and Marj were still there, having a drink with the owners, John and Shirley Burton, and some others. We had to walk past the bar. Norm saw us and called us over. We knew we were sprung.

'Nifty' said: 'I'll buy you a beer, Norm'.

Norm said: 'That's fine'.

We had a beer, and then 'Nifty' said: 'You're not a bad old prick after all', and he kissed Norm, but he seemed to take that OK.

The next morning 'Nifty' and I were hungover, and we had to do full-on match practice for about two hours. Everyone was buggered. Norm said: 'Right, that's enough... Ricky and "Nifty", just stay here'.

He made us do 400s, not together, but in opposite directions. The last bloke back had to do another one. After about the third 400, 'Nifty' spewed, and then I spewed.

Norm called us over and gave us a lecture. 'You must do as I say! If I tell you not to drink, don't bloody drink! If I see either of you drink in the next month, you won't be in the team... By the way, "Nifty" – never, ever kiss me in front of my wife again'.

Norm had been pretty pissed that night, and we thought he would have forgotten about it.[28]

On another occasion, Smith singled out Miller in front of his teammates on a Sunday morning. 'Nifty,' Smith began, 'in the toilet at the George at 1.30 this morning, you asked me why you weren't getting a regular game. That wasn't the time or the place, but this is'. Smith then went through the reasons, in detail, as to why Miller wasn't getting a game.[29]

Smith also hadn't forgotten how to memorise people's names. After enlisting Hugh McPherson as his team manager, he introduced McPherson to virtually everyone at the club, from the president to the boot-studder. McPherson marvelled: 'Nobody needed to tell Norm who they were or what they did around the place – he already knew everybody in that short period of time. That showed the respect

---

[28] Ricky Quade. Interview with the author.
[29] Peter Bedford. Interview with the author.

he had for people, and of course his amazing memory for details that most of us would forget'.[30]

ŸŸŸŸŸŸŸŸŸ

Although the Swans were 0-5, Norm Smith hadn't forgotten how to win. He guided his new club to three wins from the next four matches to climb to ninth.

In an interview with *Football Life*, Smith revealed how much he loved coaching again: 'I didn't mind just watching – or I didn't think I minded – but something was missing and I never realised how much until I took over at South. In fact it's quite true to say I was stagnating'. He also continued to describe himself as a disciplinarian, dogmatic and determined, adding: 'Just tell me one successful man who hasn't had those attributes. I don't want to be loved, (but) I do want to be admired and respected'.

The Swans' enormous respect for their coach was apparent during their round nine clash with his old club at the MCG. Bourke recalled:

> I was invited to an MCC pre-match luncheon, during which several people connected with the MCC questioned my judgement for appointing Norm. One of them even ruffled my hair. I looked at him and said: 'What the hell are you doing?'
>
> He said: 'Haven't you got any grey hairs yet, looking after that bastard?'
>
> I knew Norm would be sensitive about it, so I asked him: 'Do you mind if I just say a few words to the players?'
>
> He said that was OK. So I addressed them for a couple of minutes and told them how humiliating it was, not to me, but to Smithy. It upset us that he'd done a power of work for their club to make them a superpower, and this was how they treated him in return. Their bitterness was astounding. But we got Norm and we loved him. He revitalised the whole club.[31]

The Swans responded angrily to the fighting words of their 'visibly shaken' president,[32] producing a first-quarter blast of 8.1 (49) to 3.5 (23). The Demons fought back to be within 13 points by three-quarter-time but, with Smith 'cajoling' his players from the boundary line in his old plastic raincoat – his voice booming out: 'Don't let it slip!'[33] – the Swans again ran away to win by 25 points.

---

[30] Hugh McPherson. Interview with the author.
[31] Brian Bourke. Interview with the author.
[32] Peter Bedford. Interview with the author.
[33] Peter Bedford. Interview with the author.

Smith's build-up to encounters with Melbourne was always intense. Rantall described an incident after a later loss to the Demons at the MCG:

> Smithy hated getting beaten by Melbourne, because there was still all that unresolved tension. After this particular loss, I had to go to a family do, so I went up to Smithy and told him why I wouldn't be at training the next morning.
>
> He said: 'Yep, fair enough, Mopsy. I'll tell you what you should do. Get in your car and go for a nice, leisurely drive. Keep heading down the highway and when you get down to Point Nepean, on the right you'll see a lovely scenic view....'
>
> I'm thinking: 'This is great; Smithy's really relating to me here'.
>
> Then he said: 'Go round the corner and you'll come up onto this cliff, AND THROW YOUR BLOODY SELF OFF IT!'[34]

Rantall became one of Smith's favourite players. In fact, Smith awarded him the captaincy in Skilton's extended absence. But one of his worst pupils was star centre half-forward Graeme John (an AFL Commissioner since 2000, and managing director of Australia Post since 1993). John – who had joined South Melbourne from East Perth in 1964 – had initially been excited by the prospect of playing under Smith, and had actually sent his new coach a congratulatory telegram when he first got the job. But their relationship quickly deteriorated once training started. Smith and John, then 26, suffered a personality clash that was to have unfortunate consequences for the Swans. Ian Thorogood revealed:

> 'Graeme was seen as a crucial player in the future of the club, but he wouldn't train properly, which was completely at odds with Norm's philosophy that training was like a performance, where you had to attack the ball like you would under match conditions. But Graeme had it in his mind that he would do it his way, which was to move around the ground at a leisurely stroll, take a mark, receive a handball, have a nice kick and maybe sing out to somebody'.[35]

It all came to a head during a training session after the Swans had recorded their fourth win in round 12. Thorogood recalled:

> Norm stormed out onto the ground and tore Graeme to pieces. Graeme just walked off the ground and never came back. At a players' meeting later on, Norm

---

[34] John Rantall. Interview with the author.
[35] Ian Thorogood. Interview with the author.

said that in all his years of coaching, nobody had ever walked off the ground, at any time, whether it be a match or training.

Norm, Clyde Laidlaw and myself had a good talk about it and we all knew that we had to get Graeme back. Norm said to me: 'It's your job. You negotiate with him to get him back'.

I went to Graeme's office where he was sales manager for TNT in West Melbourne. I think he wanted to come back, but his attitude was: 'Why am I talking to you when it was Norm who started this?'

In Graeme's eyes, it wasn't he himself who started it, even though he didn't train properly. After many discussions that came to this same conclusion, I finally went back to Norm and said: 'Norm, the *only person* who is going to get Graeme John back is you. And *you* are going to need to, somehow or other, apologise'.

Norm blew up.

He said: 'I'm telling you, "Thurra", there is no way in the world that I'm going to apologise or even talk to Graeme John. He is a required player at the South Melbourne Football Club. Either he comes back of his own accord and starts to knuckle down the way I want him to, or that's the end of Graeme John in football'.

And that's the way it turned out. Norm didn't apologise, and Graeme didn't come back. It was tragic for all of us. We lost a really good player. But that didn't mean he could do what he liked. Everyone realised then that if you didn't toe the line your head would be on the chopping block.[36]

For his part, John asserted: 'There is some semblance of truth in it, but I resent any implication that I retired because I couldn't handle the training. I never had a heated conversation with Norm Smith about training. The fact was that at the end of '68 I'd undergone major shoulder and knee surgery, so I was already questioning in my own mind whether I was physically capable of continuing. I did have a disagreement with Smith, but it had nothing to do with training and remained unresolved'.[37]

However, there were exceptions. With a distinct lack of height at his disposal, Smith lured star ruckman Fred Way back to South Melbourne. In a stop-start career, Way had played for the Swans in 1964 and again in 1966 before returning to his trucking business and country living. Smith drew him back to South with the promise that he would have to train just once a week at the Lake Oval. He even

---

[36] Ian Thorogood. Interview with the author.
[37] Graeme John. Interview with the author.

accommodated Way at his Pascoe Vale home on Friday nights. The big man played some great football over the next few seasons, but on one match eve Smith was horrified to walk in on him soaking in the bath. He said: 'You can't have a hot bath the night before a game – it'll take all the energy out of you!'[38]

On one memorable occasion, Smith was lenient to another player who also travelled long distances to train. Ernie Hug, a ruckman/defender who joined the Swans from Collingwood in 1971, lived on his family's sprawling farm at Heyfield and, like Way, was only required to train once a week. He often made the journey in his parents' Rolls-Royce. One Tuesday night after a particularly dismal loss, Smith lambasted the players and then said: 'Everyone is going to run a lap of the lake'.

Hug said: 'What?'

'Everyone will run a lap of the lake,' he repeated, 'for their poor performance on Saturday.'

Hug shook his head. 'I haven't driven 200 k's to run around a bloody lake – I've got lakes all over the property.'

It was a gutsy stand, but it paid off – Hug didn't have to do the lake run.[39]

After losing Graeme John, the Swans promptly lost their next four matches by an average of 48 points – again, three of the defeats were to Richmond, Carlton and Geelong – to slump to 4-12. The Swans did, however, finish the season strongly, winning three of their last four games (it was now a 20-round season) to finish ninth (just a game clear of 11th-placed Footscray).

Smith, who said he was happy at South Melbourne, described it as merely a 'fair' performance in 'an assessment year'. He explained: 'We could have won more games if Bob Skilton and (South Australian recruit) John Murphy had been available.[40] But I'm a realist. I have only scratched the surface at South and there is a fair bit of hard work to be done... I think you will see improvement in the team next year... South did as well as could be expected with the material available... I think the club is now on the right track'.[41]

But even the most ardent South Melbourne fanatic could not have foreseen the season that was to follow.

---

[38] Brian Bourke. Interview with the author.
[39] Wayne Walsh. Interview with the author.
[40] Murphy was forced to sit out of football for a year to gain a clearance from SANFL club Sturt.
[41] *Newsday*, Thursday October 2, 1969.

Bob Skilton made his long-awaited return in 1970, to finally provide the Swans with their much-anticipated leadership combination – their greatest player, allied with the game's greatest coach. Although both were past their best in a physical sense, they were as sharp mentally as they had ever been.

Bedford marvelled: 'We had two great leaders. There was Norm, whose coaching record spoke for itself, and Bobby Skilton, whose playing record also spoke for itself. We were in excellent hands'.[42]

But it was a hard road back for Skilton. After spending 14 weeks with his leg in plaster and 16 weeks on crutches, and missing the entire 1969 season, he had needed to shed about 20 kilograms when pre-season training started. The coach didn't exactly nurse his captain back to full fitness, either. He confided in Hugh McPherson: 'How am I meant to coach a triple Brownlow Medallist?'

McPherson replied: 'Just the same as you would coach a new recruit. You're the boss; do as you see fit'.[43]

He saw fit to drive Skilton as hard as any other player, if not harder. He didn't make any concessions for his skipper. Skilton feared he 'might never play again', and on at least two occasions resigned himself to the fact: 'That's it; that's the finish'. His Achilles just 'didn't seem to be responding' to the pre-season trackwork. But one night, he recalled, 'everything loosened up and all the adhesions broke loose', and he steadily regained confidence in it.[44] However, Smith forced him to complete every session just like everyone else. On one occasion, Skilton's Achilles felt too tender to train. He told Smith: 'I can't do it; I can't train'. Smith blasted him. Skilton later reflected: 'I went out and did it, but it didn't help me the next Saturday'.[45]

The Swans suffered a major setback in their round one loss to Melbourne at the Lake Oval. Adding injury to the insult of the 25-point defeat at the hands of the Demons (the Swans had beaten them on both occasions in 1969), boom recruit Ricky Quade suffered a knee injury that required a full reconstruction. Quade echoed the sentiments of many South Melbourne people when he said that 'as great as Norm Smith was as a coach, I think he

---

[42] Peter Bedford. Interview with the author.
[43] Hugh McPherson. Interview with the author.
[44] Collins, Ben, *The Champions: Conversations with Great Players and Coaches of Australian Football*, GSP, 2006.
[45] Bob Skilton. Interview with the author.

was an even better man'. Quade's claim was strongly supported by several personal experiences, one of which was the way Smith treated him following his knee injury at the age of 19. Quade said: 'I was like a guinea pig – I was one of the first blokes to receive a knee reconstruction. The surgeon said I had less than a 50/50 chance to play again. Most coaches would have given up on me, but Norm was fantastic. Before we played Collingwood in a big game, he told me: "Wear a tie and a coat and you can come and sit on the bench with me, and you might learn something about the game". That was a great experience. He kept me involved in the club when it could easily have been the end of my career'.

Smith believed Quade had the ability to be an all-time great. After a practice match, he had told reporters Quade could become the next Barassi in the ruck-roving role. (The expectations were so high thereafter that Quade reflected: 'It was the only thing I was crook on Norm for!') However, the Swans initially had trouble keeping Quade. After just a month of pre-season training, the teenager from the Riverina area of New South Wales became desperately homesick. He missed his large family and the country life. He had told Smith: 'I hate Melbourne. I want to go home'. He didn't gain much sympathy. After telling Quade he wanted him to stay, he concluded with: 'You make up your mind: either you stay here and be in a big pool, or you can go home and be king of the kids'. The ultimatum worked. Quade stayed.

Smith was also conscious of providing Quade with some semblance of the family atmosphere he so dearly missed. To this end, he quickly made arrangements with experienced South Australian recruit John Murphy. Quade recalled: 'John Murphy had been a star for Sturt[46] and was a great role model. He was the straightest guy I've met: never smoke or drank, and he went to Mass every Sunday. Norm always made sure I went to "Murph's" place for a Sunday roast, to ensure I was mixing with the right people, who had good family values'.[47]

Smith was all about his players continually learning and developing, not just in football but in their general lives. Quade said: 'You could sit around and talk to him for hours. It was like sitting on your grandfather's knee. He was such a wise man in the ways of the world. He believed that you had to have something outside footy. In those days, everyone did work anyway, but if you didn't have a job, Norm was onto you and it was very hard to get a game. Even if you had a job but it was

---

[46] John Murphy played 205 games for Sturt in two stints from 1962-68 and 1974-76.
[47] Rick Quade. Interview with the author.

a dead-end job, Norm would push you to better yourself. The first thing he'd ask you was: "How's your job going? What are you doing? Where is it leading to?" His attitude was: "Idle body, idle mind". He kept you on the straight and narrow.'[48]

Further to this point, Smith created a variation of a quote from Phillips Brooks (1835-93), the prominent American clergyman and author. Smith wrote in his coaching notes:

> Sad is the day for any man when he becomes absolutely satisfied with the life he is living, the thoughts he is thinking and the deeds he is doing; where there ceases to be forever beating in his mind a desire to do something larger and better.

Ricky Quade's injury was one of the few mishaps endured by the Swans in 1970. After being 1-2 following disappointing losses to 1969 wooden-spooner Melbourne and a tumbling Essendon, which would plummet to 11th in 1970, the Swans went on a winning spree that reminded old-timers of their glory years in the early to mid-1930s. They won 10 of their next 12 matches, to improve their record to 11-4, which, when combined with their encouraging finish to the previous season, meant they had won 14 of their previous 19 games. The Swans were second – just percentage off top spot, occupied by Collingwood. Their fans – many of whom had 'come out of the woodwork'[49] – could scarcely believe it, particularly as they recorded a succession of wins over the likes of reigning premier Richmond, runner-up Carlton, a rising St Kilda and perennial finalist Collingwood.

The victory over Barassi-coached Carlton at the Lake Oval was a defining moment. It signalled the Swans had arrived as a genuine top four side. After defeating both the Tigers and Saints in the previous fortnight, Smith was intent on claiming his biggest scalp yet – the second-placed Blues. But first he was an interested onlooker in the reserves curtain-raiser, in which his son Peter was playing for Carlton. At one point, Peter, by his own admission, 'did something untoward to a South player', but was shocked almost beyond belief when his father sent the Swans' reserves runner out to tell him to 'pull his head in'. Peter recalled:

---

[48] Rick Quade. Interview with the author.
[49] Brian Bourke. Interview with the author.

'I thought that was pretty harsh, even though Dad might have been right'.[50]

Smith was also right with every move and match-up that afternoon. Bedford said: 'Norm was the catalyst – we were all in awe of him. That was one of a few games that season where we were under a fair bit of pressure. We won the toss and kicked against the wind and we were down 0.1 to their 5.1. But we turned a 30-point deficit into a 77-point win'. In the last three-and-a-half quarters, the Swans outscored Carlton 23.11 (149) to just 5.12 (42) to record a remarkable win against the side that would famously take out that season's premiership.

The injured Quade observed from the sidelines that the Swans had completed the demolition through their slick use of the ball. 'We didn't have any big marking forwards,' Quade said. 'Russell Cook was our centre half-forward and he was only 6'1" (185cms), so Norm introduced a style of play that had us playing on at every opportunity and moving the ball by hand. We were certainly encouraged to handball and run the ball more. It brought terrific results and helped change the way the game was played. Norm was ahead of his time. It's interesting to note that Barass has been credited with introducing the handball game in the 1970 Grand Final, but I reckon he might have learnt something that day against his old mentor.'[51]

It also helped that the Swans were not only fit but fresh. Wayne Walsh, who had been recruited from Richmond, said: 'After we lost the first game to Melbourne, it really upset Norm so he flogged us mercilessly on the track. We then somehow fell over the line in the second game and immediately Norm changed his whole attitude to the way we prepared. We trained a lot lighter and we didn't get any injuries and we probably played to our full potential'.[52]

The team spirit Smith had fostered was another crucial factor in the Swans' rise. 'We'd have crawled over broken glass for Norm,' said Bedford, 'and I think that's what we did in 1970. We just gelled so well as a group, and that was attributed

---

[50] Peter Smith. Interview with the author. Shortly after Carlton's loss to South Melbourne in the seniors, Barassi threatened to axe Peter Smith from the Blues' reserves side for a perceived breach of discipline. At the time, adidas had started supplying VFL players with assorted apparel in their club colours (no logos). Norm Smith had been given a tracksuit (red pants with white stripes, and a white top with red stripes) and so had Peter (navy blue with white stripes). Smith didn't like the colours – he preferred to wear navy blue – so he and Peter swapped. When Peter arrived at training in the red-and-white tracksuit, Barassi exploded, but eventually relented. Peter recalled: 'If Percy Jones had worn it, it wouldn't have mattered. It was only because Dad was coaching South – and probably also because South had thrashed Carlton – that he came down hard on me'. Incidentally, Norm Smith preferred navy blue polo shirts, and once refused to wear a pale blue shirt Marj bought for him. Smith could be just as particular about his food. For some variety one night, Marj cooked a fruit curry. Smith took one look at it and pushed it away and said disdainfully: 'If I'd wanted a fruit salad, I'd have asked for one'.

[51] Rick Quade. Interview with the author.

[52] Wayne Walsh. Interview with the author.

almost solely to the way Smithy managed the group. He ruled with an iron fist, but he developed a very strong, almost unbreakable bond between the players.'[53]

The following week, though, the Swans came crashing back to reality when they played terribly against winless bottom side Hawthorn at Glenferrie Oval. Although the Hawks weren't as bad as they had shown – after all, five of their seven losses had been by no more than 11 points – it didn't excuse the Swans for a pathetic first half, which resulted in a 49-point deficit, and an eventual 62-point defeat.

The Swans regained momentum by winning six of their next seven games – their only loss being by two points to Bill Stephen's Fitzroy at Brunswick Street after having eight more scoring shots. A one-point win over top side Collingwood at the Lake Oval – a Queen's Birthday encounter on a Monday – was another red-letter day. The game appeared over when Collingwood opened up a 19-point advantage shortly before time-on in the final term. However, the Swans slammed through three quick goals to take the slenderest of leads. This was all too much for the mass of Swans supporters, who flooded onto the field and mobbed the players after mistakenly believing they had heard the final siren, with police on horseback required to push the crowd back over the fence. When order was restored, Smith packed the backline with extra players in an attempt to defend the lead, but it didn't stop Magpie champion Peter McKenna from marking... a split-second after the siren.

The euphoria of this victory was soon replaced by doubt as the Swans dropped their next three matches – it must be said, to quality opponents in Richmond (by 14 points at home), St Kilda (20 points, at Moorabbin) and Carlton (four points, via a last-gasp goal to Syd Jackson, at Princes Park). The Swans were suddenly fourth, with just a one percent advantage over fifth-placed Geelong.

With their hold on a top-four berth slipping, a home clash with Hawthorn (which had won eight of its previous 11 matches) in round 19 loomed as a must-win encounter for the Swans. There was enormous pressure on Smith to lift his players, and added pressure to deliver an even more impassioned pre-match address than normal. Brian Bourke, with his legal contacts, often entertained judges at South Melbourne, and this particular Saturday was to have the company of three Supreme Court judges, including the Chief Justice, Sir Henry Winneke. Bourke asked Smith: 'Would it be OK if I bring these three judges into the rooms to hear your pre-match address?'

'That'll be all right,' replied Smith. 'As long as you understand the procedure: that when I'm talking to the players, you have to stand over in the corner.'

---

[53] Peter Bedford. Interview with the author.

Bourke thought to himself: 'These are three of the most high-powered judges in Victoria and we're going to tell them to hide in a corner!'[54]

However, it would be worth such an inconvenience, as Smith was about to show once and for all that he possessed – as *The Sun's* Barrie Bretland once described – 'a power to communicate that put him in the Billy Graham class'.[55] Bourke recalled:

> Norm started his address with: 'During the week, I took out the Bible and read *The Sermon on the Mount*' – and that's what he based his address on. Probably 15 of the 20 players wouldn't have even heard of *The Sermon on the Mount* but the way he explained it to them made it entirely relevant to what they were trying to achieve in that particular football match.
>
> As we were walking over to our seats in the cricket club stand, I said to Henry Winneke: 'So, what did you think of that?'
>
> Henry said: 'I wouldn't have believed it unless I heard it'.
>
> It was just amazing.
>
> After the game, I got Norm to come over and have a drink with them and he was the life of the bloody party. Norm was so relaxed, pleasant and comfortable in any company, and he could hold a conversation with anyone on almost any topic. He had wider interests. He was a much more profound man than the average footy coach in that he could talk to all kinds of people. He had some independence and knowledge of the outside world. He also had a sort of mystique about him, which I haven't seen in other coaches. He was in an area all of his own.[56]

That match against the Hawks was also memorable for a blast Smith delivered to Skilton. The Swans skipper had been playing his best game since his return from injury, but that didn't protect him from a brutal spray. Just before half-time, Skilton had taken a mark next to the behind post. He was on the proverbial 'impossible angle'. Normally, the legendarily double-sided Skilton would have simply run around to open up the goalface and had a shot with his non-preferred right foot. But at the forefront of his mind was his coach's belief that 'if you can, you should always use your natural foot'. Under this philosophy, Skilton decided to use a left-foot banana kick. It hit the post, and the Swans entered the rooms at half-time with a 19-point lead. Although his side had just produced a six-goal to three second term, Smith was on the warpath. He felt they should have been further in front,

---

[54] Brian Bourke. Interview with the author.
[55] *The Sun*, Monday July 30, 1973.
[56] Brian Bourke. Interview with the author.

and that they had let Hawthorn off the hook. Squarely in his sights was Skilton. The little champ recalled:

> Smithy ripped me to pieces. Part of what he said was: 'Never played in a final, and you don't deserve to! You're nothing but a rotten little liar!'
>
> It seemed like he went on at me for 10 minutes, but it was probably only 30 seconds. I sat there thinking: 'I'll show you, you bastard'.

Skilton produced an even better second half to complete what some described as one of his best performance in years. More importantly, it ensured the Swans kept the Hawks at bay in a vital 19-point win. He continued:

> After the game, I still felt it was unfair, but before I could find Smithy, I felt an arm around my shoulder, and I looked up and it was him, and he said: 'It worked, didn't it?'
>
> He had that happy knack of having you eating out of his hand again. As the old saying goes: 'Two kicks in the bum, one pat on the back'.
>
> The same day that he ripped you to pieces and you hated him, that night he'd want to know: 'How's the family?' etc. All of a sudden, he had you back on side. He took a genuine interest in you as a person, and what you did with your life outside football.[57]

On another occasion, Smith singled Skilton out for perhaps an even more personally scathing attack, which included the barb: 'Skilton, they warned me when I came here that the club revolves around you'.[58] In many ways it had, but it wasn't any of Skilton's doing. He couldn't do any more than play brilliant, courageous football, and it wasn't his fault he was rewarded with equal record tallies of Brownlow Medals and best-and-fairest awards. Smith knew this, so it was surely a case of employing his old abuse-the-best-player tactic.

Wayne Walsh recalled: 'Norm gave Bobby a fearful pay that day, and I was terribly embarrassed for Bobby. I wouldn't have taken it myself. Norm always bragged that he didn't want leading goalkickers or Brownlow Medallists in his side. I think he was right on that count, unless you get a super player, who, irrespective of how good the team is, is just so much better than his teammates. But Bobby was past his prime when Norm coached him, so it was pretty harsh. Norm could be

---

[57] Bob Skilton. Interview with the author.
[58] Wayne Walsh. Interview with the author.

really cutting. Another time he told a player he had a big yellow streak down his back. Talk about belittling someone!'[59]

Bedford was taken with Smith's rare ability to literally lift players: 'He was a brilliant speaker. Before he was even halfway through his speech, we'd be standing upright. That was the impact he'd have on us. He was like a general leading the troops into battle. You'd certainly like to follow Norm into battle'.[60]

After conquering Hawthorn, an even more crucial contest beckoned: fellow finals aspirant Geelong at Kardinia Park in a virtual mini-final in round 20.[61] With three rounds to go, the Swans were just a game and 5.2 percent clear of the Cats. Adding to the tension, the Swans were without Skilton and ruckman Fred Way, and hadn't won at Geelong for 12 years. They started the game accordingly, trailing by 23 points at quarter-time. While the Cats' faithful cheered in approval, Smith was so disgusted with the efforts of his players that he told Ian Thorogood: 'I'm not going out there. Why should I go out there and say anything to them after THAT?! Thurra, you go out there and say what you like'.

Thorogood recalled:

> Norm had really put me on the spot. As I was walking over to the huddle, I was racking my brain for what I should say. I said: 'Silence! Stand still and listen! Norm said: "The applause is for them, not you".'
>
> Norm hadn't said that but I had to come up with something. Then I said: 'Trainers, piss off. No-one needs a drink or a rub because no-one's done anything'.
>
> Then I walked off – after being out there all of about 30 seconds. When I got back to Norm, he said: 'Why are you back here so quickly? What the bloody hell did you say?'
>
> I told him and he said: 'Oh! You needed to say more than *that*!' And he went through the things I should've said.
>
> But it made no difference because the whole game changed anyway. But I don't accept any credit for that. I'm sure they were motivated to some extent by Norm's disgust.[62]

In the last three quarters, South Melbourne added 10.11 to 5.11 to record a gutsy seven-point win, despite incurring a couple more injuries during the match. Luck played a part, too. Of course, that was the day a late shot at goal from Cats

---

[59] Wayne Walsh. Interview with the author.
[60] Peter Bedford. Interview with the author.
[61] There were now 22 rounds in the VFL season.
[62] Ian Thorogood. Interview with the author.

star Doug Wade slewed off the side of his boot after it had been struck by an apple thrown by a Swans supporter.[63]

No such luck was required the following week, though, when South defeated Fitzroy by 19 points. It was the Swans' 14th win – more than they had recorded in the previous two years combined. More importantly, they had achieved what many had thought impossible – they had qualified for the finals for the first time in 25 years, thus ending the second-longest finals drought (behind Hawthorn's 32 years from inception in 1925 to 1957). Skilton, who was elated that he had persisted through his Achilles problems, summed up both the mood of the Swans, and the role Smith had played in their leap from mediocrity:

> After we beat Fitzroy in the second-last game of the year, we couldn't drop out of the four regardless of what happened the following week. I don't think I've ever felt better sitting in the bath afterwards. There was no pain – it was fantastic.
>
> I've never had any doubt that Norm Smith was the inspiration to get us over the line. He moulded the team and built a team spirit that we'd never had in my time at the club.
>
> You need a bit of luck, and we had that. Things ran for us that year. We hardly had any injuries, and we managed to win some real crunch games. The difference was Smithy. He probably got 130 percent out of us.[64]

Quade hailed Smith's performance as one of the greatest coaching efforts in his time in football[65]; Rantall hailed it '*the* greatest' he had witnessed.[66] *Inside Football* commented that most critics viewed Smith's achievement as 'practically the equal of his feats at Melbourne'. The general consensus was that with the exception of Peter Bedford and perhaps a couple of others, the side that Smith took to the top four was ranked somewhere between the eighth and 10th in the VFL on talent. Rantall marvelled: 'I just don't believe that any coach other than Norm Smith could have got our ordinary side up like that. It was genius. He did it through sheer respect – we respected him so much we would have done anything for him'.[67]

Although the Swans had were just a game and 1.3 percent behind second-placed Carlton, they had only a slim chance of trading places with the Blues and securing the double-chance. Lowly Melbourne (which would finish 10th) would need to

---

[63] As unbelievable as this sounds, it is a true story.
[64] Bob Skilton. Interview with the author.
[65] Rick Quade. Interview with the author.
[66] John Rantall. Interview with the author.
[67] John Rantall. Interview with the author.

upset Carlton, while the Swans would need to defeat Collingwood, which was two games clear at the head of the ladder, at Victoria Park. Although the Demons seriously challenged the Blues, the Swans were destroyed in the third term – the Magpie avalanche producing 12.3 to 1.2 in a 96-point drubbing. Although they entered the finals with just three wins from their previous seven games, they gained belief from the fact they had beaten every team in the competition.

🏆🏆🏆🏆🏆🏆🏆🏆🏆

Norm Smith was typecast in an unfamiliar role when the Swans faced St Kilda in the first semi-final: not only was his side the underdog, but it was also the sentimental favourite of the football public.

Hawthorn superstar Peter Hudson, in his column in *The Sun*, acknowledged the mammoth task before the Swans but also warned the Saints to be wary of any side coached by Norm Smith, particularly in September. Hudson wrote that apart from Bedford, 'South's other great trump is its coach, Norm Smith, who has sat on the MCG's coach's bench so often he must have worn a groove in it. There's nothing Smithy doesn't know about finals and the MCG, and it's doubtful if he has faced a greater challenge than that before him today'.[68]

Although aware of the significance of the day for South Melbourne people, Smith was conscious of staying in their usual match-day routine. Secretary Noel Brady asked him: 'Norm, do you want the rooms decorated?'

'No,' replied Smith. 'Just keep everything like a normal match. We don't want any fanfare that might distract the boys.'[69]

But with a massive crowd of 104,239, there was plenty to distract even the most focused veteran in the Swans' line-up. Skilton, finally playing his first final in a career dating back to 1956, was struck by the crowd noise. The roar at the first bounce was the loudest he'd ever heard; a roar that was both 'uplifting and unnerving' at the same time.[70] He later said: 'I don't think my mind was on the football at that particular moment',[71] adding: 'I can understand why players fumble for those first few minutes'. Skilton didn't have any problems handling the ball that day – he gathered a team-high 20 kicks to be one of the Swans' best players – but some of his teammates did, early in the game.

---

[68] *The Sun*, Saturday September 5, 1970.
[69] Noel Brady. Interview with the author.
[70] Bob Skilton. Interview with the author.
[71] Collins, Ben, *The Champions: Conversations with Great Players and Coaches of Australian Football*, GSP, 2006.

THE SAVOUR OF SOUTH MELBOURNE [1969-72]

St Kilda dominated the first term, kicking 6.1 (37) to 2.5 (17), and it appeared the match would deteriorate into an anti-climactic fizzer. But the Swans then produced one of their best quarters of the season – a sizzling second-term burst of 7.3 to 3.2 – to take a five-point lead by half-time. Thorogood later said: 'We all felt pretty good about the fact we were in front because I think that, in our hearts, we didn't feel we should have been there. Although we were faster than St Kilda, we were much smaller'.[72]

After the interval, the Swans should have extended their lead, as Skilton recalled: 'We attacked for the first 10 minutes of the third quarter but we just couldn't capitalise, and then St Kilda took it down the other end and kicked a goal. We'd worked so hard, and had all the play before that, but we weren't good enough to make them pay, and, boy, did they make us pay after that'.[73]

The Saints' big men took control of the match with their marking strength and crushed the Swans in the second half – 13.8 to 4.4 – to eventually win by 53 points.

The Swans had probably run their race before the finals had even started. The final round loss to the Magpies, written off by many as an aberration, had perhaps provided an accurate gauge of their form after all.

Skilton said: 'St Kilda whipped us for the simple fact they were a better side than what we were. But to win enough games to make the finals and then play in front of 104,000 people was absolutely wonderful. And for that great experience, we all owe a lot to Smithy'.[74]

Smith was typically gracious in defeat, telling *The Sun*: 'I am sorry and disappointed for South Melbourne supporters, but deep down I am tremendously proud of the efforts of the players. We all realise we had limitations, but the boys played to the best of their ability. No coach can ask for any more. Full credit to Allan (Jeans) and his boys – they were worthy of getting into the preliminary final'.[75]

The dream was over. It had been a magnificent effort, but ultimately class and a lack of size had told against the Swans. Thorogood later mused about the loss of a player who had both of these qualities. 'I often wonder,' he said, 'if we still had Graeme John, in the right frame of mind, how much further we might have gone. Unfortunately, that's something we'll never know.'[76]

---

[72] Ian Thorogood. Interview with the author.
[73] Bob Skilton. Interview with the author.
[74] Bob Skilton. Interview with the author.
[75] *The Sun*, Monday September 7, 1970
[76] Ian Thorogood. Interview with the author.

In 1970, Peter Bedford became just the second player (after Allan Ruthven at Fitzroy 20 years earlier) to win a Brownlow Medal under Norm Smith. The then 23-year-old became one of Smith's all-time favourite players. He privately declared on several occasions: 'Pound for pound, Peter Bedford is the best player I've coached'.

The respect went both ways. Bedford credited Smith with improving his approach to the game. 'Smithy played an enormous part in my winning the Brownlow,' he said. 'He provided that attitude, and that sense of endeavour and determination, to just persevere. A lot of us benefited from Norm instilling that into us.'

Rantall recalled selection committee meetings when Smith would say: 'Pete's being tagged and they're belting him around – we've got to take the pressure off him'. He decided to employ a merry-go-round midfield system that would enable Bedford to be shifted around the field – to a wing, a flank, a pocket – to shake close-checking opponents.[77] Not only did the ploy ease the young champion through the tough stuff, but it made him a more damaging player. In addition to amassing high numbers of possessions, he kicked 50 goals in the 23 matches. Bedford said: 'That system certainly helped us on-ballers. It freed you up a bit, and in those days you tended to have just the one opponent for the day, so they would follow you and you could really get an advantage'.

When Bedford was announced the winner of the Brownlow Medal,[78] Smith acknowledged it in typical fashion. 'Norm was never one to go over the top with praise,' Bedford said, 'but he quietly congratulated me on the award. He didn't treat me any differently after it – he always demanded the absolute best from you, so nothing changed there.'[79]

Over the years, it seemed, something had changed in Smith's treatment of footballers who also played a high standard of cricket. Bedford had been a cricketing prodigy, first representing the prestigious Melbourne Cricket Club at the age of just 16, and making his Sheffield Shield debut for Victoria as a 19-year-old in the summer of 1966-67. Bedford reflected: 'One thing that really endeared me to Smithy was the way he allowed me to combine cricket and football. As late as February, he'd let me have cricket training with Melbourne at the Albert Ground,

---

[77] John Rantall. Interview with the author.
[78] The 1970 Brownlow Medal count was the first to be televised.
[79] Peter Bedford. Interview with the author.

and then shoot across to South for footy training on the same night. And with Melbourne having very good sides and invariably being in the finals, I'd often come into a footy season after having played just one practice match. But Smith was of the opinion that one complemented the other. He was totally supportive of me playing cricket. He even came to watch some games of district cricket, and it was fantastic to have that support from him. His willingness to do that for me made me more determined to repay him as well as I could on the footy field'.[80]

Another star Smith continued to have a significant influence upon was Rantall. Standing just 183 centimetres (six feet) tall, Rantall had been a half-back flanker for most of his career to that point, but suddenly he was being thrown the biggest assignments in the game. He recalled: 'Smithy played me at full-back, centre-half back – wherever the opposition's No.1 forward played. Superstars like Hudson, McKenna, Wade, Jesaulenko: there wouldn't be one of the great forwards in the '70s that I didn't play on. I was generally a lot smaller too, but Norm had the faith in me to throw these roles at me each week. That added to my longevity in the game because I continued to get those roles when I went to North Melbourne later on (1973-75). But I wouldn't have been able to do it if it hadn't have been for Norm. He would mentally prepare you for it each week. He'd been a great forward himself, so he knew intimately what was required of a backman to stop players like that. That level of faith brings out the best in you. He made me believe I could do it'.[81]

☘☘☘☘☘☘☘☘☘

Norm Smith was paid the ultimate compliment in the days leading up to the 1970 Grand Final. Both opposing coaches – Ron Barassi (Carton) and Bob Rose (Collingwood) – visited him at home during the week to pick his brain on how to approach the match.[82] It wasn't as though Barassi and Rose – two of football's most prominent men – hadn't faced such big occasions before. Rose had been a Magpie premiership player in 1953 and had coached the club to narrow Grand Final losses in 1964 and 1966; Barassi's superb playing history had already been complemented with two Grand Finals as a coach, including a premiership in 1963. Although Smith respected both men immensely, his natural loyalty to Barassi had him firmly in the Blues' corner.

---

[80] Peter Bedford. Interview with the author.
[81] John Rantall. Interview with the author.
[82] Brian Bourke. Interview with the author.

On the morning of the match, Smith attended North Melbourne Football Club's annual Grand Final Breakfast, then held at the Southern Cross Hotel. On this occasion, he received the club's 'Football Personality of the Year' award. He made a brief, well-received speech in which he made mention of the contribution made to Melbourne's success in the 1939-41 period by Johnny Lewis, the old Shinboner star who had crossed to the Demons.

As had been the case for several years, Smith arranged to watch the Grand Final with Checker Hughes, former Demons' star Geoff Tunbridge and George De Morton (Melbourne's amenities officer), who would supply ham sandwiches and coffee. The quartet would sit just below the coaches' boxes.

At half-time, with the premiership seemingly decided with Collingwood 44 points in front, the Magpie hierarchy walked down past Smith on their way to the rooms and a couple of officials commented: 'We're going well here, Norm. We'll run away with this one'. But after the brilliant Carlton fightback, which resulted in the greatest turnaround in Grand Final history, no Collingwood official had the courage to even acknowledge Smith on their way down to the rooms. Smith was quietly amused. 'Couldn't have happen to a nicer side,' he said.[83]

Afterwards, Smith publicly expressed his pride in Barassi, enthusing that he had 'really arrived as a coach today'.[84]

ỸỸỸỸỸỸỸỸỸ

Immediately after the fairytale came the nightmare.

Just when the Swans were expecting to progress a step further than they had in 1970, or at the very least maintain their standing, they plummeted like never before. In terms of win/loss ratio and percentage, South Melbourne endured the worst two-year period in its history. After playing off in the 1970 first semi-final, the Swans won just five of their next 44 games – a winning percentage of just 11.36! – to finish last in 1971 (a game and 5.8 percent behind 11th placed Essendon) and second-last (five games behind 10th side Geelong) in 1972. It wasn't a steady slide into oblivion, either – it was a dramatic, immediate decline, which was evident from the opening round of the 1971 season, when they suffered a 105-point drubbing at the hands of – of all teams – Melbourne, at the MCG.

In 1971-72, they lost 39 matches by an average of 42 points – 19 of these defeats were by at least 44 points, and 13 by at least 64 points. Just five of their losses were

---

[83] Geoff Tunbridge. Interview with the author.
[84] *The Sun*, Monday September 28, 1970.

by single-figure margins. And apart from a 72-point win over fellow cellar-dweller North Melbourne in the final round of 1971 (which ended a 10-game losing streak – the worst in Smith's career), their other victories were by just 16, 9, 12 and 15 points respectively.

The reasons for the fall, cited by those who were intimately involved, included complacency, a poor run with injuries, the harsh reality that the playing list was average at best, and renewed off-field tensions, both at committee level, and between the committee and the coach.

Skilton said: 'The worst thing that happened at the end of the 1970 season was we had to stop for the summer. When we came back the next year, we just couldn't get the same momentum going, and we copped a few injuries, and we didn't have the depth of talent to cover those injuries. Before we knew it the season had spiralled out of control and we were struggling just to be competitive, let alone trying to make the four'.[85]

In addition to the retirements of the likes of Paul Harrison (who admittedly had a poor 1970) and former Demons Terry Leahy and Graeme Jacobs (who was a member of Melbourne's 1964 premiership side), the Swans' casualty list included their two key forwards, John Sudholz (who played just two games before returning to the family farm at Rupanyup, near Horsham, 285kms north-west of Melbourne) and Russell Cook (eight games), key defender Tony Haenen (13), rover Haydn McAuliffe (nine), half-forward Keith Baskin (eight) and Shane McKew (one). This represented a mass exodus of experience which proved impossible to replace, especially as the Swans combed the South Melbourne area and their allocated zones – comprising the Riverina and Farrer leagues in New South Wales and the Northern District league on the Victorian side of the border – and found them virtually bereft of talent. Subsequently, their high turnover of players – they tried 46 in 1971, and 45 the next year – was unprecedented in their history. Wayne Walsh explained:

'Norm took a pretty ruthless attitude to what is now known as list management. He always said: "Your first cut is your cruellest cut, but it's your best cut". In other words, players who let you down under pressure will continue to let you down over a period of time, so you're better off getting rid of them. I've always agreed with that. But what happens at a struggling club, if you cut players who are better than the ones coming through, you leave yourself exposed. Norm cleared a couple of players, and then we got some injuries, and we were exposed, and players lost confidence, and we finished last'.

---

[85] Bob Skilton. Interview with the author.

The complacency factor is intriguing. A success-starved club like South Melbourne really had no reason to feel too self-satisfied. Bedford said: 'South had been on the lower rungs of the ladder for so long that I think when we finally made the finals, it was a huge relief and everybody took their eye off the ball and thought: "We're there – it's just going to happen", rather than planning two or three years ahead like the good sides do. I think we just sat back and enjoyed the moment without thinking more towards the future. But even so, the playing group was more to blame for our performances than Smithy. He had a pretty tough job because we really struggled for players, and maybe that's why we only had one good year out of four under Smithy'.[86]

One of the most interesting assessments of the situation came from Bill Stephen. After finishing his second stint as coach of Fitzroy in 1970 and almost dying due to serious illness shortly after, Stephen steadily regained his health and was recruited by Smith to the Swans' cause as a specialist skills coach at the start of 1971. When Clyde Laidlaw left at the end of that season, Smith coaxed Stephen into coaching the reserves. Stephen hadn't wanted the job but, he said, 'there was no-one else'. Stephen observed: 'It was never more evident to me than in those two years at South that no matter how good a coach you are, you won't achieve anything if you haven't got the players. They were disciplined, they were fit, they were trained beautifully, well-coached, motivated, etc., but they couldn't win simply because they didn't have the cattle. You need to have a reasonable amount of good players, but they just didn't have them. Their lack of success really hurt Norm. He'd been trying to extract that extra little bit from each player'.[87]

However, the hurt of defeat didn't compare to the pain Smith suffered at the death of his mother. On July 18, 1971 – the day after the Swans had mustered just three goals in a 49-point loss to Hawthorn at the Lake Oval in round 16 – Ethel Smith passed away peacefully in her sleep. She was 85. Smith signed his mother's death certificate, and she was buried in Melbourne Cemetery three days later.

𝗬𝗬𝗬𝗬𝗬𝗬𝗬𝗬𝗬

Norm Smith faced a selection dilemma over Bob Skilton. He had relieved his 32-year-old skipper of his usual roving duties and experimented with him in a back pocket. It was a move that, in the coach's eyes, had been a failure. Skilton openly admitted he had been exposed on a couple of occasions in the last line of defence, but he denied the experiment had backfired.

---

[86] Peter Bedford. Interview with the author.
[87] Bill Stephen. Interview with the author.

'I was happy to go back there,' he said, 'because I was slowing down a bit, and when you're slow in the first place, it's not a good thing! I had two games in the back pocket. In the second game (in round three), we played at Footscray. Old habits die hard, and twice in two minutes I waited at the front of the pack and it went over the back and my opponent, (18-year-old) Graeme Austin, kicked two easy goals. I copped Smithy's wrath because I should have been with Austin rather than waiting at the front. Aside from that, I thought I'd done pretty well in those two games, but because of those two mistakes in two minutes I was back on the ball the following week.'[88]

Although Skilton couldn't recall feeling his spot was under threat, or that he wasn't worthy of a place in the senior line-up, behind closed doors Smith was seriously considering committing the unthinkable: axing Bobby Skilton from the South Melbourne side.

He confided to Hugh McPherson: 'I'd like to drop Bobby from the side. It would hurt me to do that because Bobby has been such a champion and a great clubman, but it's what I think would be the best for him and the side because he really is struggling. But if I dropped Bobby Skilton, the South Melbourne people would lynch me. I more or less have to play him'.[89]

Skilton decided midway through the 1971 season that it would be his last in the VFL. He was battling constant niggles and was taking longer than normal to recover after matches. He said: 'It was taking me four weeks to get over last week, and I had to play next week!' Perhaps as a mark of respect for his champion, Smith did not push Skilton into retirement.[90]

In many ways, Skilton was actually the least of three significant retirements at the Lake Oval at the end of 1971. The others were those of president Brian Bourke and secretary Noel Brady, whose departures were major blows to the coach, who had received their 'total support' and been given *'carte blanche'* to run the football department.[91] Importantly, Bourke had also provided a necessary buffer between Smith and certain committeemen. Thorogood said: 'Brian allowed Norm the freedom to go about his business without having to deal with certain individuals on the committee. But once Brian was gone, it opened up the doors for these critics to attack Norm'.[92]

---

[88] Bob Skilton. Interview with the author.
[89] Hugh McPherson. Interview with the author.
[90] Bob Skilton. Interview with the author.
[91] Clyde Laidlaw. Interview with the author.
[92] Ian Thorogood. Interview with the author.

Brady, who remained in his position until May 1972 under new president Stan Keane, witnessed the transition of power and didn't like what he saw in the new regime. 'The wind had changed,' Brady recalled. 'There was a move against Norm. Small people – who, compared to Norm, were minions – who hadn't reared their heads while Brian was in charge, all of a sudden started to get a bit of power. There was a lot of jealousy and I reckon they thought they would grow by cutting down a tall poppy. Before I left, I warned Norm: "Just watch them". He later told me: "You were right".'[93]

An example of the new regime's intentions was its attempt to dilute Smith's perceived absolute power over his fellow selectors. This view was at odds with the opinions of several men who sat in on selection committee meetings. Thorogood said that while Smith would 'argue violently at times, thump the table and stand up and roar and argue his point, he appreciated if you stood up with another idea, and while it took some time to get the message through, he'd listen'.[94] It might take five minutes to select the starting 18, but another two hours to pick the 19th and 20th men;[95] and at times debate could rage until 2am on a Friday morning – an arduous undertaking considering all of the selectors (except Smith) had full-time jobs[96] – but in the end, 'everyone was happy'.[97] However, there was at least one occasion when Smith did, in fact, force his opinion on the selection panel. Skilton recalled:

> Johnny Murphy got injured and came back through the seconds and could not get a touch. Every week, Norm would bring up 'Murph's' name. After a few weeks, Norm pulled rank and said: 'I don't care if I'm out-voted 4-1, Murphy is playing. If we wait for him to get best-on-ground in the seconds, he might never play again'. We all just did as we were told and 'Murph' was in. Lo and behold, 'Murph' rose to the occasion and was best-on-ground in his first game in the seniors.[98]

After hearing of instances such as these – which only confirmed the views of some committeemen that the coach always got his way in the picking of the team – the new management decided to reduce his power at the selection table. New skipper John Rantall said:

---

[93] Noel Brady. Interview with the author.
[94] Ian Thorogood. Interview with the author.
[95] Bob Skilton. Interview with the author.
[96] Clyde Laidlaw. Interview with the author.
[97] Bill Stephen. Interview with the author.
[98] Bob Skilton. Interview with the author.

In '72, when we were really struggling, the committee, in their wisdom, decided to put another committeeman on the selection committee. That meant it was now made up of Norm, Thurra, myself, and these two committeemen.

Norm rang me one night and said: 'They're going to take the vote off the captain. What do you think of that?'

I said: 'Oh, all right, I suppose'.

'What do you mean all right? There's a principle here! What would happen if I rang Bobby Skilton and told him that they were going to take the vote off the captain? What do you think Skilton would say?'

I said, 'Oh, he'd be a bit upset'.

Norm said: 'And so should you!'

Before we went into the next selection meeting, Norm said to me: 'You know what they're on about tonight, don't you, John?'

Then he gave me a piece of paper and said: 'This is my team; just stick this in your pocket'.

We sat in the selection committee and argued for two hours, and everyone had their say, and finally we've got the team on the board. Everyone's happy. I'm about to go out the door and Norm says: 'Come here, Mopsy. Give me a look at that team. How far out am I?'

It was identical!

He said: 'So how much power have I got?'

He'd manipulated them and let them think they had some power, when he was actually letting them come around to his way of thinking.[99]

In that 1972 season, another, uglier, man-management issue emerged and resulted in talented defender/midfielder Wayne Walsh leaving South Melbourne after a blow-up with Smith. After being thrown on the scrap-heap after just six appearances for Richmond in 1968, Walsh decided: 'If I'm going to have a career in League football, my best chance is under Norm Smith at South'. It proved a wise decision – he played 63 of the next 75 games, earning state selection in 1970. Smith regarded Walsh as 'a fiery, independent character',[100] and there was the odd squabble between coach and player before their ultimate falling out. Walsh recounted an occasion he made an error and the runner came out with a message he repeated verbatim: 'Thanks, prick'. In another match when Walsh was playing in the centre, Smith told him: 'Do it my way or you'll play in the back pocket'.

---

[99] John Rantall. Interview with the author.
[100] Related by Ian Thorogood. Interview with the author.

Walsh replied: 'That wouldn't bother me. Playing in the back pocket at South is like playing in the centre in another side anyway – the bloody ball's always in defence'.

Their relationship reached its breaking point during the Swans' round 10 loss to Collingwood at the Lake Oval. Walsh admitted that he was 'half-daydreaming' during Smith's halftime address and the coach, who had been 'going ballistic', ordered him out of the room. When the same treatment was meted out at a team meeting the next morning, Walsh walked out and never returned.[101] Walsh publicly declared he would never play under Smith again, but the coach remained silent 'for the sake of the club'. In what Smith described as 'a depressing time',[102] Walsh was cleared back to Richmond – against Smith's express wishes.[103]

The coach claimed the committee agreed to make a public statement in support of the coaching panel. The statement was never made, and Smith felt 'it showed South in a poor light'. He also believed his problems with the committee 'came to a head' over the Walsh saga.[104] It was the umpire Blew row all over again. He and president Stan Keane were constantly at loggerheads. Thorogood explained:

> When Stan Keane became president, I think Norm spent most of his time on Tuesday and Thursday nights arguing with him. They were at opposite ends of the way things should be done. None of Norm's plans came to fruition because he took his eye off the ball to mix it with Keane and other committeemen instead of focusing on the players. He shouldn't have allowed it to happen, but others should have just let him get on with coaching the side instead of interfering.
>
> Occasionally I'd notice that Norm wasn't watching from the sidelines and I'd ask him afterwards: 'Norm, what was going on?'
>
> He'd say; 'Oh, I was talking to this committeeman or the president', or whatever the case might be. Those people, with their constant sniping and criticism, distracted Norm. They were challenging him, but at the end of the day, who were they to challenge Norm Smith?
>
> Norm loved Fitzroy, he loved Melbourne and he loved South Melbourne while he was there. He was loyal wherever he went. He really could have turned his

---

[101] Wayne Walsh. Interview with the author.
[102] *Inside Football*, September 16, 1972.
[103] Under Smith's coaching, Walsh's market value literally increased 6-fold. At the end of 1968, South Melbourne had paid Richmond a transfer fee of just $500 for his services. Three-and-a-half years later the Swans sold Walsh back to the Tigers for $8000. He played in three successive Grand Finals and won premierships in 1973-74. Walsh, who was later an assistant coach at Footscray under Mick Malthouse, remained 'appreciative' of what Smith did for his career.
[104] *Inside Football*, September 16, 1972.

back on those guys and concentrated solely on the football, but he felt that it was so necessary that everyone at the club was thinking along the same line. But, with hindsight, it's obvious that the club was heading for destruction.

If Brian Bourke had remained president and kept the dogs at bay, we would have been much better off and who knows where Norm might have taken us.

It was sad to see the downfall of such a great man. He deserved better than the treatment he received.[105]

Smith, too, yearned for Bourke-style leadership, later declaring: 'I believe our troubles started after the fourth match of the 1971 season when... Brian Bourke said that he was thinking of retiring. Brian, a good friend of mine and an extremely capable administrator, eventually went on with his intention to retire and it was a loss the club couldn't afford. The indecision by some members of the committee that followed would never have happened if he had remained in office'.[106]

Tension continued to mount as the Swans lost the last 16 games of the 1972 season (by an average of 41 points). It was, by six games, the worst losing streak in Norm Smith's coaching career. The final straw was perhaps the loss to bottom side North Melbourne in round 17. The previously winless Kangaroos, coached by former Melbourne star Brian Dixon, overran the Swans at Arden Street to win by nine points. Dixon said: 'We only won one game for the year, and that was it. Both teams were really struggling. I desperately wanted to have a victory against Norman as a coach. It was certainly a relief for me: firstly that North Melbourne finally won a game, and secondly that it happened to be against a side coached by the great Norm Smith. We had a beer together after the game. He was typically gracious in defeat'.[107]

However, Smith and many others felt there was little grace, or class, about the way the Swans' committee handled the coaching position at the end of 1972.

About three rounds before the end of the season, Smith, Thorogood and Stephen met with Stan Keane to discuss arrangements for the 1973 season. Smith said later: 'The three of us were virtually told by... Stan Keane that the coaching jobs would be ours again... Stan Keane gave us the impression... that we would be reappointed *without* the positions being advertised'. Smith even told Keane he was prepared to take a pay-cut 'to help the club out'.[108]

---

[105] Ian Thorogood. Interview with the author.
[106] *Inside Football*, September 16, 1972.
[107] Brian Dixon. Interview with the author.
[108] *Inside Football*, September 16, 1972.

Over the next month, unbeknown to Smith, the situation took a dramatic turn. On the morning of Saturday, September 9 – just a week after the final match – he received a brief letter from the committee stating that it would advertise for applicants for all four coaching positions: senior, assistant, reserves and under-19s (which had been held by Neil Crompton). The letter also contained what Smith described as a 'strange statement': that the club hoped he would re-apply for the senior job. He had, in effect, been sacked. And the dishonourable manner in which it was done – via a letter delivered to his home, rather than in person – had a strange sense of deja vu... and left a similarly bitter taste. He felt affronted, and took it as a personal insult.

Smith had been through this – and worse – before, but it didn't make it any easier... particularly when he learned there had been a three-and-a-half day delay between the time the committee had made its decision and the moment he had received his dismissal notice. The committee had sealed his fate the previous Tuesday night and, from what Smith could gather, he and his two off-siders were supposed to have been told personally by Keane. Although there had been opportunities for a face-to-face breaking of the news – the trio was at the Lake Oval on the Thursday night[109] – this did not eventuate. Dumbfounded, Smith revealed: 'No-one approached me'.[110] But that wasn't all. The most hurtful aspect of the episode was that rumours circulated during the week that Smith would be sacked. In utter disgust, Smith claimed: 'Players knew about it before we were told... Certainly we heard the rumours, but we didn't know the full details officially'.[111]

When he was officially informed, he rang Thorogood.

'You're joking,' was Thorogood's reaction.

'I have joked before,' he replied, 'but I'm not joking about this.'

'Well,' said Thorogood, 'you're going to apply for it, of course.'

Smith said: 'Do you really think I will apply for a job as coach of South Melbourne after what we've gone through in trying to build the place up for four years?... My recommendation to you is that you apply for it'.

Thorogood said: 'Norm, there's a thing called loyalty, and there's no way in the world that if they've done that to you that I will apply for the coaching job – even if they ask me'.

The committee did ask Thorogood, but he rejected their offer.[112] Bill Stephen was also approached, and he too declined. Stephen said: 'If they had've offered

---

[109] *Inside Football*, September 16, 1972.
[110] *The Herald*, Saturday September 9, 1972.
[111] *Inside Football*, September 16, 1972.
[112] Ian Thorogood. Interview with the author.

me $1 million, I still couldn't have taken it on. I would've like to have done it, but my friendship with Norm was so strong that I couldn't. And of course I was very friendly with Thurra, too – I was best man at his wedding. There was no way known I was ever going to take it'.[113]

The day he was sacked, Smith went to the MCG to watch Richmond thrash Collingwood in the qualifying final. While there, Alf Brown got the scoop for *The Herald*. Smith told him the Swans players and staff were 'tremendous', and commended committeemen Bill Richards, Jack Roach and Neville Stibbard for their support, before unloading on their board-room colleagues. 'There is a sickness within the committee,' Smith said. 'Too many committeemen are arguing among themselves about who should be president... The committee is in... (a) state of flux'.[114]

He later told *Inside Football* that while he had 'never known a club with supporters who show such tremendous loyalty, even when the side is losing game after game', he had also never encountered a club burdened by 'so many people so critical of what goes on'. This cancerous reality was brought home to him when a Swans official told him: 'There are people around here who would prefer non-success to success so that they can be critical'. Smith was flabbergasted by this mentality, explaining: 'If you don't have loyalty in a club, then it's hard to have success'.[115]

Keane quickly moved to diffuse the situation, saying the committee had been 'very happy' with the job done by Smith and his coaching panel, and expressing his wish that he would re-apply for the position. 'It is not that we're unhappy with the present coaches,' Keane explained, 'but we believe we should try to find out just who is available.' He said the new 10 years' service rule – a controversial, albeit short-lived rule (it lasted just nine months – from August 1972 to May 1973) that enabled players with 10 years' continuous service with a club to change clubs without a clearance – had 'changed the situation tremendously'. Keane added the committee was also keen to attract applications from potential playing coaches, following the 'successes achieved' by Carlton (who were premiers under John Nicholls) and Essendon (fifth under Des Tuddenham).[116] This must have had Smith and his supporters shaking their heads. After he had introduced a comprehensive, ahead-of-its-time coaching structure, the Swans were considering returning to a set-up that most clubs believed was less than ideal.

---

[113] Bill Stephen. Interview with the author.
[114] *The Herald*, Saturday September 9, 1972.
[115] *Inside Football*, September 16, 1972.
[116] *The Sun*, Monday September 11, 1972.

The whole situation was also sub-standard in the minds of many players. *The Sun* reported that a 'mass walk-out' of up to a dozen senior players was likely unless the Smith panel was retained. An anonymous player said at the time: 'It's a dirty business. The way the thing has been handled has made us sick'.[117]

Although Smith appreciated the players' support, he wrote to them, imploring them to be loyal to the club.

> Dear Player
>
> As you are no doubt aware, I, along with Ian and Bill, will not be coaching South next year. This decision was made by us when the committee decided to call for applications for the coaching positions. This, of course, is their prerogative, but I consider it a vote of no-confidence by the committee in Ian, Bill and myself. However, I prefer this to pass without further comment.
>
> During the past week, many of you have contacted me expressing your feelings and indicating your loyalty to me, and for this I am most grateful. However, I feel it is my duty to tell you that whilst I appreciate your loyalty, I must point out that your loyalty to the club must be stronger.
>
> I have enjoyed my association with South Melbourne and have made many friends. In the case of the players, I will always watch with great interest their progress in the football world.
>
> Of late, the club has not enjoyed the success we would have liked, but no-one can ever doubt your keenness to do well and all would admire you for your efforts. At this stage of your career, you may not have the skill or experience, but I am sure that with the enthusiasm you have shown, true rewards will come.
>
> Many thanks for your efforts and loyalty over these past four years and good luck to you all.
>
> Your sincerely,
> Norm Smith

Peter Bedford said later: 'It was very disappointing. When things like that happen, it's always going to cause heartache and upset, and a number of us felt like that'.[118] The committee summoned the players to meet at the Lake Oval

---

[117] *The Sun*, Saturday September 16, 1972.
[118] Peter Bedford. Interview with the author.

for 'summit talks', during which it would outline its plans for the future.[119] It soon emerged that the Swans were chasing 25-year-old West Australian star Mal Brown to be their playing coach, but Brown quickly ruled himself out of contention. After an Australia-wide search for a successor to Smith, the Swans appointed former star Graeme John, then 30, as non-playing coach. After leaving the Swans in mid-1969, John had played briefly with VFA club Port Melbourne.[120]

In the meantime, the Swans players paid for a farewell function for Smith at The George Hotel. A poster adorning a wall announced: 'The Last Supper of NORM SMITH & His Disciples'. Captain Rantall pointedly told *The Sun*: 'The committee is not here. It was not asked'.

Smith expressed his appreciation and pride in the players, saying: 'They have been very good to me and I will never forget this'.[121]

YYYYYYYYY

When Norm Smith left South Melbourne, he also left a legacy that would remain with those who had been associated with him in his four years at the club.

Skilton reflected: 'He was a great coach and a great person, and I'd like to think that for those of us who had the privilege of being close to him, some of that great person rubbed off on us. Smithy did a lot of great things and he did a few things that were probably wrong, but I don't know anybody who's been right every time. But he was right more often than not'.[122]

Smith is warmly remembered at South Melbourne reunions where, Rantall said, 'you get this whole group of players telling "Smithy stories"; stories of a guy who was tough, hard, ruthless and unforgiving; but all of those stories are told with genuine fondness for the man'.[123]

Even those, like Bill Stephen, who had known Smith for decades gained a greater appreciation of him at South. Stephen said: 'I worked under and with a lot of great coaches. I played interstate football under Checker Hughes, Reg Hickey, and playing-coaches like Charlie Sutton, Fred Flanagan and Ken Hands, and I've worked with Barassi, who was a fine coach. But Norm Smith

---

[119] *The Sun*, Wednesday September 20, 1972.
[120] Graeme John did not fare much better than Norm Smith, losing the first 13 games of 1973, to stretch the Swans' losing streak to 29. It was the worst drought in the club's history, and the fifth-worst in VFL history.
[121] *The Sun*, Wednesday October 25, 1972.
[122] Bob Skilton. Interview with the author.
[123] John Rantall. Interview with the author.

was almost a genius. He could teach football like no other coach I've been associated with'.[124]

⚜⚜⚜⚜⚜⚜⚜⚜

Shortly after leaving South Melbourne, Norm Smith received a phone call from Ron Barassi. Nothing unusual about that – they were virtually family – except this time Barassi, the newly appointed coach at North Melbourne, had a proposition.

'How would you like to be my chairman of selectors at North Melbourne?' asked Barassi.

Smith didn't hesitate: 'I'd love to'.

It was the ideal role for a man of his status and health. The background role certainly made Marj far happier. Smith's rapid acceptance of the offer also pleased Barassi. Although years earlier he had wanted to strike out on his own as a coach without the old fox pulling the strings in the background, Barassi had proven that he was nothing if not his own man. He had also proven himself a great coach in his own right – a dual premiership coach and the hottest property in the market. Barassi logically thought: 'If you've got the opportunity to utilise the experience of a man like Norm Smith, why wouldn't you do it?'

In his mind, there was just one unknown about his new arrangement with his mentor. He believed: 'The only potential negative I could think of was how we would have got on, because the roles had almost been reversed – I was in charge. It would have been interesting from that perspective, and I'm sure we would have had our moments where we butted heads on things because we were both very strong in our views, but I don't think it would have been a problem'.[125] Further to this point, *Herald* writer Alf Brown asked Barassi: 'Aren't you looking for trouble?' Barassi was adamant. 'Of course not,' he replied. 'I can handle him.'[126]

Smith himself had no doubt he could handle his new role, and was excited about starting another phase of his football life at his fourth VFL club. He told *Inside Football*: 'I love football… I'm very keen on teaching football… I'm prepared to go anywhere to help football and talk football'.[127]

He assisted the Kangaroos' campaign immeasurably with his influence on the recruitment of John Rantall. Before the season had even finished, North had approached the Swans' skipper with their plan to secure him under the 10-year rule.

---

[124] Bill Stephen. Interview with the author.
[125] Ron Barassi. Interview with the author.
[126] *The Herald*, 1979.
[127] *Inside Football*, late 1972.

Rantall had initially rejected their advances, but finally agreed to think about it. He had attended the St Kilda-Essendon elimination final at Waverley and learned of his coach's 'sacking' over the loudspeakers. He became angry. He felt an enormous sense of loyalty to Smith for resurrecting his career. Rantall turned to his wife and said: 'That's it; I'm leaving South'.[128] He soon received a phone call from Smith, who told him: 'Get out, "Mopsy". This place is gone'.[129]

In the meantime, Smith joined the Kangaroos, who quickly signed veterans in Doug Wade (from Geelong) and Barry Davis (Essendon), and the battle for Rantall's services intensified. On several occasions, North officials informed Smith: 'Mopsy hasn't signed, and South have raised the ante on us. What do you think?'

Each time, his simple response was: 'Just get him'. It became a bidding war between the Kangaroos and the Swans, and Smith strongly believed the 'Roos should get Rantall for any price, within reason. Barassi quickly learned that Smith was Rantall's 'greatest admirer'. North eventually got their man.

Barassi recalled: 'I'm eternally grateful that Norm was so adamant that we get Mopsy, because Mopsy was one of the great unsung heroes of North Melbourne. You could put him on an opposition player and just about forget about that player being a force that day.'[130] Rantall won his first best-and-fairest award at North in 1974, was one of the club's best in a losing Grand Final and was again among the best players in their 1975 premiership – the club's first.

However, Smith would not live to witness such glory. After watching some pre-season training sessions and attending a couple of match committee meetings, his health deteriorated and he was forced to relinquish his position. Barassi lamented: 'It was a real pity, and very sad, that Norm couldn't continue. We became a top side as it was, but perhaps the presence and input of Norm Smith might have brought success even sooner, and might have brought even greater success over a longer period. That's only speculation, but where Norm was involved any level of success was possible'.[131]

---

[128] John Rantall, in an unpublished interview with Peter Ryan from GSP.
[129] John Rantall. Interview with the author.
[130] Ron Barassi. Interview with the author.
[131] Ron Barassi. Interview with the author.

28

A PREMATURE END

[1973]

Norm Smith had never been one to complain about anything, much less his health. He was of the old school of Australian men who would only ever visit a doctor as a last resort.

'Whingeing and moaning is for bloody sooks,' he was heard to say.[1]

But towards the end of 1972, he started suffering disturbing headaches. He had endured headaches of varying degrees for up to a decade – on at least a couple occasions, they had almost rendered him unable to conduct training and when quizzed about it he would only say: 'I've got this bloody headache'.[2] Usually, though, they would subside and he would be able to again function as normal. But they had recently increased in frequency and intensity, and moved into the ultra-delicate territory of splitting migraines, the likes of which no amount of pain-relieving tablets (or relaxation at Rosebud) could cure. He knew something wasn't right, but it took the urging of Marj and Peter to get him to agree to see a doctor in February 1973.

After an initial check-up, he was sent to St Vincent's Hospital for tests. Marj and Peter were naturally concerned, but thought: 'They'll find out what's causing it and just give him some medication to fix it'.[3] But on the night of Tuesday February 27 (Ron Barassi's 37th birthday), they were 'knocked for six' by the gravity of his condition. A doctor ushered Marj and Peter into an unoccupied room. Even then they didn't begin to fear the worst.

'I've got bad news,' the doctor said. 'The tests show that he has a brain tumour. It's inoperable and terminal.'

Marj and Peter were in 'complete shock'. When they composed themselves, they asked: 'Well, how long does he have to live?'

---

[1] Hugh McPherson. Interview with the author.
[2] Brian Dixon. Interview with the author.
[3] Peter Smith. Interview with the author.

A PREMATURE END [1973]

'I can't put an exact time on it,' the doctor said, 'but I'd say within about three months.'

Peter later reflected: 'It was hard to believe that Dad was actually going to die soon, because you thought he was a superman and he'd somehow survive it. But, unfortunately, he had something they couldn't treat'.

Marj and Peter never told Norm the awful truth of his illness. Peter explained: 'Maybe that's just the way things were done back then. Today, if I had a brain tumour and only a few months to live, I'd want to be told because then I might do a few things before I go. But Dad never knew what was wrong with him. He would have known something was wrong though'.[4]

For a short time after he was released from hospital, Smith continued to drive to his factory in North Coburg. But as Russell Brown recounted, he was a mere shadow of his former self. 'Norm really started struggling to get around,' Brown said. 'Sometimes he'd have to physically put both hands around one of his legs to move it. It was really sad to see a bloke who'd been such a fit, strong footballer in a state like that, and there was nothing he or anyone else could do about it.'[5]

Marj often tried, unsuccessfully, to dissuade her husband from going to the factory. He insisted on helping, but he was actually proving more of a hindrance. When he left, the other workers would rectify his mistakes. Marj would tell Russ: 'Sorry, I tried my best to keep him at home but he wanted to come'.[6]

Smith was also losing his renowned ability to work with his hands. His last effective effort at craftsmanship were gifts for his two grand-daughters, Peter's children Samantha ('Sam' – born October 1970) and Felicity ('Flip' – born January 1972). He made each a pedal-operated metal horse with a sulky. But it wasn't long before he was incapable of such handiwork, along with many simpler tasks.

Melbourne premiership player and committeeman Terry Gleeson recalled visiting the Smiths at Rosebud:

> I knew he hadn't been well, but I was surprised how well he looked. He appeared to be in reasonable shape, although he was a bit thinner than normal.
>
> We were just two old mates catching up for a chat, and we reminisced about days gone by. The *only* thing that was slightly amiss with him was that he repeated himself a couple of times. But, apart from that, he was his normal chirpy self.

---

[4] Peter Smith. Interview with the author.
[5] Russell Brown. Interview with the author.
[6] Thelma Brown. Interview with the author.

Marj told me that he'd been in a pretty bad way and he'd been down, but that day he had lifted himself above everything, and she gave me some credit for that; she said: 'Maybe you brought that on'. It was just one of Norm's good days during his illness.

Marj also asked me: 'Who was the player Norm loved the most?'
I said: 'Oh, Barassi'.
Marj said: 'No, he's family. He loved you the most'.

Norm and I had a strong relationship, but that was rather a surprise to me. It really touched me...

I wasn't Norm's special pet or anything because that's so far from the truth. I think he liked the larrikin side of me, so to speak. Take no bullshit type of thing, being truthful and speaking my mind, rather than dodging around it. He generally liked blokes who were like that.[7]

A fortnight after Smith's diagnosis, he collapsed in the bathroom. He fell heavily, and Marj called an ambulance, which rushed him back to hospital. Marj and Peter thought: 'This might happen a lot quicker than we thought. He might not come home again'.

Smith's eldest grand-daughter Sam was not yet three-years-old, but she vividly recalls being taken to see her 'Pop'. It was perhaps her first conscious memory. Sam said: 'Everyone has told me: "Oh, you couldn't possibly remember that; you were too young". Even Nanna Marj said that. But I wasn't dreaming it. How else I can remember the layout of the hospital and where his room and bed was? Until I was about 10, I was convinced that Dad drove me to Heaven to see Pop'.[8]

For the time being, though – and to the relief of close family and friends, and Smith himself – he was cleared to return home just days later.

Margaret Clay recounted a visit to the Smith house that confirmed in her mind that Smith was in rapid decline. 'Norm was feeding the baby (Felicity) in the high-chair,' she said. 'No-one would realise that he could be so soft and tender as to feed a baby – especially in those days because the women did most, if not all, of those things back then. In his own surrounds, Norm was a normal person. The thing that stood out to me was that he'd always had a great memory, a great brain, and I knew he wasn't well then because he said to me: "Margaret, I can't remember. I just can't remember'. That was strange, and sad'.[9]

---

[7] Terry Gleeson. Interview with the author.
[8] Samantha Smith. Interview with the author.
[9] Margaret Clay. Interview with the author.

Smith could no longer shave himself, either. His son would arrive at his parents' house every weekday at 6.30am (and a little later on weekends) to shave him in bed. It was a ritual that personified a son's heartfelt attempts to comfort his father in his final months. It wasn't easy. Although Smith was 'generally OK to sit and talk to', at times – and increasingly so – 'his mind played tricks on him', and he would become disorientated and confused, and repeat himself. He would also become depressed.

Peter said: 'He'd say how he was struggling, so to pep him up and try to disguise the fact that he was actually deteriorating, I'd encourage him by saying things like: "Hey, but you're a bit better than you were last week. It won't be long before you're down at North Melbourne helping Ronny out". That was probably easier to do as his mental state worsened, because he wouldn't remember what he was like the previous week anyway'.[10]

Smith's physical appearance also began to change dramatically. He'd lost about 25 kilograms, and his once strong physique wasted away to give him the disposition of a frail old man. But as a side-effect of his medication to reduce swelling on the brain, he actually became 'fatter' in the face and his neck thickened. The tumour also caused his head to grow slightly out of shape. Marj and Peter took him to see a specialist in Collins Street and overheard someone say: 'Is that Norm Smith?' Normally there would have been no question of Smith's identity, but now, as Peter described, 'he wasn't instantly recognisable as the Norm Smith everyone knew'.[11]

Smith's illness, and its seriousness, became a closely-guarded secret. Only a select few were told in confidence. Peter said: 'The last thing we wanted was for it to come out in the paper. I think a couple of journos knew about it, but they kept a respectful silence which we appreciated'.[12]

In his final three months, during which he was bed-ridden, Smith only let his closest friends see him. Marj also politely turned many others away. Hugh McPherson said: 'For a man who spent his whole life as the centre of attention in large groups of people, it was a very sad way to spend his last few months'.[13] The fact was Smith didn't want people to see him in such a poor state. He wanted to retain his dignity. Among the few people Smith allowed to visit were the Emselles, the Stephens, the Clays, his old friend Harry Edwards, and George Lenne. They would sit at his bedside and just talk, which Smith seemed to appreciate. It also gave Marj a much needed break from her role as a virtual palliative care nurse.

---

[10] Peter Smith. Interview with the author.
[11] Peter Smith. Interview with the author.
[12] Peter Smith. Interview with the author.
[13] Hugh McPherson. Interview with the author.

Bill Stephen said: 'Some days you could tell Norm was having difficulty focusing, but he pretty well knew who you were until the end. They say that even if a person is struggling like that, deep down they know that you're there, and I think that was the case with Norm'.[14]

Smith had no trouble focusing one day when his two granddaughters were playing noisily in the house. Old habits died hard. The disciplinarian in Smith was still alive and well. His eldest granddaughter Sam was tormenting her little sister Felicity. Smith threw a soft, toy teddy-bear at Sam. The bickering stopped. Lesson learnt.[15]

Peter Smith described the desolation of their vigil: 'We were in a constant state of shock that at some stage in the very near future Dad was going to leave us. It was just a day-by-day thing, and he'd get worse each day. It was a downward spiral. You had to get on with what you had to do, and look after him as well as you could, but there was a real hopelessness and an inevitability about it all. It was just a matter of when and where. We just hoped he wouldn't have to go back to hospital and die there'.[16]

During Smith's final days, Margaret Clay visited to support Marj, as she had done for some months. She went to check on Smith and noticed Bill Stephen was in the bedroom sitting beside him. She decided to give the old mates some privacy, but as she went to walk out Smith said: 'Margaret, come back and sit down'.

She took a seat on the other side of the bed. Smith looked warmly into her eyes and said: 'You're one of the family'.

She reflected: 'Norm had a lovely way about him. He made you feel special. Right to the end. Even when he was very ill and you should have been the one trying to make him feel better'.[17]

The Smiths had been dealt a cruel hand. Aside from the fact Smith was the one who was about to lose his life, Marj and Peter had every right to feel robbed. They had enjoyed many wonderful times with him, but both could have been forgiven for feeling they had somehow missed out on large chunks of rewarding, quality time. As Peter said: 'He was a great father; it's just that I had to share him with everybody'. But this was meant to be a new chapter in their lives together, and their relationships with one another: when Smith had taken a step back from the front-line of football coaching, and all the attendant obsessiveness, stress and tension; when they would make up for lost time and do the kinds of things they

---

[14] Bill Stephen. Interview with the author.
[15] Samantha Smith. Interview with the author.
[16] Peter Smith. Interview with the author.
[17] Margaret Clay. Interview with the author.

had been unable to do while Smith was feeding the monster, feeding his obsession. Marj should have been planning their retirement and looking forward to growing old together; Peter should have been arranging their golf club memberships and booking weekends away. Instead, they were both grieving, and preparing for the inevitable end, and wondering how they would cope without their husband and father.

But for all the misgivings, Marj and Peter still felt they had much to be thankful for in the circumstances. They got their wish – that Smith would die at home – and also cherished the fact that he outlived the doctor's estimate by two months and two days. But despite preparing themselves for the inevitable for the previous five months, they were shocked by how suddenly the end came on July 29, 1973 (the birthday of Barassi's daughter Susan; and six years and six days after Len's death). Just three days earlier, Smith had been on the phone to Ron Barassi. He had been 'most enthusiastic' about putting in an appearance at North Melbourne, but his doctor would not allow it.[18]

Peter Smith described his father's last moments:

> It was about nine o'clock on a beautiful, sunny Sunday morning and Dad was in the front room. He was probably waiting for me to come over and shave him. Mum was in the kitchen. The lounge, dining room and kitchen was a big open area, so Mum could see through to the front door. She heard the door open and she thought it was me arriving. But when she looked up, she saw that Dad had opened the door. Shortly after, he called out: 'Mum!' He often called her Mum. She rushed over to him and somehow got him onto their bed. Mum didn't know whether he died in her arms or when he was in bed, but he went peacefully.
>
> I was at home having breakfast with my family when the phone rang. It was Mum, and she told us Dad was gone. I high-tailed it over there. When I got there, the family doctor was with Mum.
>
> It was a bloody tough time. But at least you knew his pain was over. He was out of his misery. He didn't have to suffer any more.[19]

Norm Smith was viewed as a grandfather of football, a statesman of the game, yet he had died at the age of just 57. This fact was not lost on Marj's 90-year-old mother, Elsie Ellis, who mourned: 'Life is cruel. Norm's gone and I'm still here, yet he had a lot of life ahead of him and would have done a lot more great things

---

[18] Ron Barassi, *The Age*, Monday July 30, 1973.
[19] Peter Smith. Interview with the author.

for young people. I can't do that; I'm too old to do anything. He should have been left, and I should have gone'.[20]

ҮҮҮҮҮҮҮҮҮ

The magnitude of Norm Smith's death was captured by *The Sun's* Barrie Bretland, who announced: 'It is true and not the least trite to say the King is dead'.[21]

Some of Smith's friends remember exactly what they were doing when they heard the news. Two examples were Ken Emselle and Clyde Laidlaw. Emselle had played that Sunday for VFA club Prahran and was driving home when he heard of Smith's death on the radio. 'I was so overcome with emotion that I had to pull over and stop the car,' Emselle said. 'Even though I knew it was coming, it still hit me like a ton of bricks.'[22] Laidlaw, meanwhile, was at a local football match when someone said: 'Did you hear that Norm Smith died this morning?' Laidlaw 'nearly fell over'.[23]

Once Smith's cause of death was confirmed as a brain tumour (or variously as a cerebral tumour or brain cancer), many people who had known him for many years began to suspect that perhaps it had first affected him up to a decade before he was diagnosed. Some believed such an early onset of the tumour might have explained certain erratic behaviour, and even a change in personality in the early to mid-1960s when he became more aggressive with an even shorter fuse. Some desperately wanted to believe this, so that their memories of the man weren't tarnished. Don Cordner said: 'If that was the case, it wasn't his fault because he couldn't help it. I've always hoped that the change in Norm's character wasn't his fault; that it was beyond his control'.[24]

One of the many death notices that appeared in newspapers in the following days was submitted by Ted Whitten, who wrote: 'To a man who stood tall, looked you straight in the eye, and called a spade a spade, (and) was a real Demon in his efforts to make a man a real man'. Other tributes flowed from those who had been even closer to Smith. Percy Beames said Smith was 'without a peer in the history of the Melbourne Football Club'; Jim Cardwell revealed that 'knowing Norm was the most important experience I've had in football or am likely to have'; Checker Hughes hailed him as 'probably the greatest coach ever',[25] later emphasising that

---

[20] Marj Lenne. Interview with the author.
[21] *The Sun*, Monday July 30, 1973.
[22] Ken Emselle. Interview with the author.
[23] Clyde Laidlaw. Interview with the author.
[24] Don Cordner. Interview with the author.
[25] *The Age*, Monday July 30, 1973.

'he was a far better coach than I ever was';[26] while Barassi said: 'I class myself very lucky, both in football and in life, for having been associated with him', adding that 'North Melbourne probably don't realise this now, but Norm's death is its greatest loss for the season'.[27]

The VFL's administrative director, Eric McCutchan, echoed the sentiments of many when he said:

> The wonderful contribution Norm Smith made to our game, both at League and club level, will long be remembered. He enjoyed a very dominant personality, which I believe did a great deal towards shaping the characters of a lot of men who passed through his hands. He never rejected a challenge... Norm Smith will be sadly missed in the football sphere.[28]

Ron Carter from *The Age* observed that 'one of the remarkable things' about Smith was that players from all clubs sought his company. 'They wanted to know him, to sit down with him for a talk,' Carter wrote. 'Now, for those who missed out, it's too late.'[29]

🏆🏆🏆🏆🏆🏆🏆🏆

Norm Smith's funeral service was like a sellout football match: jam-packed with little elbow room inside the venue; hundreds of disappointed folk forced to mill around outside; and traffic chaos for miles.

The funeral – held at St John's Presbyterian Church in Essendon from 2pm on Wednesday August 1, 1973 – was described by Ron Barassi as 'an historic football event and a fitting tribute to a man who lived for the sport... Anyone who doubted his greatness – I certainly didn't – would have had those doubts removed at his funeral. They came from everywhere. Even his so-called enemies – those involved in the football politics at Melbourne and South Melbourne'.[30]

More than 800 paid their respects. In addition to the majority of mourners who had either played with or under Smith at Melbourne, Fitzroy or South Melbourne, also present was a virtual who's who of football, including past greats Syd Coventry, Harry Collier, Reg Hickey, Jack Titus, Jack Dyer, Dick Reynolds,

---

[26] Hugh McPherson. Interview with the author.
[27] *Geelong Advertiser*.
[28] *Geelong Advertiser*.
[29] *The Age*, July 30, 1973.
[30] *The Sun*, August, 1973.

Jack Regan, Phonse Kyne, Harry 'Soapy' Vallence, Arthur Olliver, Lou Richards, Bob Rose, Bob Davis, Jack Clarke, Ted Whitten, Allan Jeans and present-day stars like Des Tuddenham, Len Thompson and Alex Jesaulenko.

Fittingly, at Smith's request, the service was conducted by Ken Melville, the former Melbourne vice-captain turned Presbyterian minister. Smith had expressed this wish six years earlier when he first encountered heart problems. Now the day had arrived, and Melville – the only speaker at the service – had prepared a special eulogy. His words were also heard over loud speakers by those outside, most of whom, *The Age* reported, were 'middle-aged people who had seen the Melbourne team, under Smith, sweep to victory after victory in the 1950s and '60s'.[31] Melville said:

> It has been well said that: 'The value of life lies not in the length of days, but in the use we make of them. Satisfaction in life depends not on the number of your years, but on your will'.
>
> Few, if any of us, gathered here today would doubt the applicability of these words to the one whose death we mourn; one held in such respect and deep affection by so many – Norman Smith.
>
> For Norm, in a life curtailed towards the end by illness, and then most sadly cut short by death, exemplified in so many ways supremely in his person the truth of this saying...
>
> We do not need, on this occasion, to recount his achievements in the sphere of football. As player, as colleague, as coach, advisor or friend. Many fine and just tributes have been paid both to the satisfaction he himself found in the game and also to the satisfaction he gave others. Yet we would be wrong to ignore this area of life... His influence there must know no bounds.
>
> There are those of us present who can recall the pleasure they derived from watching Norm as a player, with feelings of admiration for his fine team play, his unselfishness, his persistency and courage, his sheer football skill. There are others present who will recall the memorable experience of having played beside him or even against him. Others again will have played under him as coach, or will have been associated with him in administrative or a host of other ways.
>
> Consider the influence this one man has had on the game of football.
>
> But consider, and even more importantly, Norm's influence on us – the watchers, the players, the colleagues, the friends. Football then was not just the sphere of great achievement for Norm. Remember too that it was sometimes the scene of

---

[31] *The Age*, August 2, 1973.

great pain and disappointment. Football was the vehicle by which he revealed himself as a person. The means by which people came to love and know and respect Norman Smith the man. It is the many facets of his humanity that we acknowledge and hold high, for they excite in us admiration and even a sense of awe.

To meet Norm was indeed an experience to be valued. He was not the coach of Melbourne or Fitzroy or South Melbourne. He was Norm Smith. And you were not a footballer or a supporter or a club secretary. You were Ken or Bill or Jim. And his interest in you was such that often it seemed he considered himself fortunate to be meeting you rather than vice versa. How much one valued his friendship. How much he seemed to value yours. And it was seldom that one did not feel better for the encounter.

He had a remarkable capacity for being at ease with people. Irrespective of their age or background, their status in club or society, their achievements great or small, none were too great for Norm. Equally, none were ever too small or unimportant.

In this latter regard, many young people have been the recipients of his kindness and concern. Even in situations which placed no demand upon him, and from which he himself stood to gain nothing, such as the occasion when, as a spectator at a district cricket match, amongst a handful of people, he sought to cheer up some defeated and dejected cricketers on the opposing side to the one he was supporting. Or the occasion late one night, after speaking at a junior football club dinner, when he deliberately stayed behind while others were leaving, to seek out and chat with some of the younger players.

One remembers, too, the seemingly little things: the keen sense of humour, the twinkle in the eye, the sudden burst of anger, the touch on the shoulder asking for a last-quarter effort, the graciousness in victory, the disappointment but acceptance in defeat, the yarn over a glass of beer, the interest he took in people's personal lives, his uncanny memory for names, his superb ability as an after-dinner speaker.

Each of us here today, and many others besides, possesses a rich treasury of memories concerning Norm. In the many roles he played in life in the field of work, in business; in the sphere of football, as player and coach, or teacher and friend – above all, in his capacity as a friend – we see ourselves as the recipients in the relationship. We recognise and here acknowledge that our lives are the richer for having known Norm and for having been counted among his friends.

One cannot think for long without thinking also of Marj. What delight he took in savouring moments of triumph with her. What support he received in moments of adversity and suffering. We honour him as a husband and as a father and our deepest sympathy goes out to Marj and Peter in their loss, as it does to the members of their family and the others so closely bound by the ties of deep affection.

So Norm is gone from the scene. But in a very real sense, he lives on in the memories we have and the lives that have been influenced by his graciousness, his friendship, his deep humanity.

In this service we express our respect, and acknowledgement of his worth as we see it. But we do more than that. We here declare a word of approval that this man's life, with its strengths and weaknesses, with its achievements and its failures, with its good and bad, this man's life stands approved, not only by man but by God. To that, also we bear witness in this moment of quietness and mystery, of recollection and respect.[32]

The true testament to the quality of a man is to hear his enemies praise him, so the last word goes to an enemy of sorts, Jack Dyer, who was one of Norm Smith's great adversaries both on and off the field. Smith regarded Dyer as a callous basher on the field, and later argued heatedly with him about this shortcoming. Just days after Smith's funeral, the Richmond great wrote in *Melbourne Truth*:

So Smithy is dead. Well, not really. As long as the game is played, Norm Smith will live. He'll live in the memories of all who saw him and he'll live in the record books. Smithy, as a player and coach, was an outstanding man. He personified courage and team effort. And although he had a fiery nature, he was fair on and off the field.

Players from every club will remember him as a man who always had a word of advice for a young player. He was the first to admit he made his share of mistakes, and that made him more of a man.[33]

---

[32] *Inside Football*, August 11, 1973.
[33] Melbourne *Truth*, August 4, 1973.

POSTSCRIPT

Norm Smith's premature death robbed him of the opportunity to accept several lofty honours.

His first posthumous award was life membership of the Victorian Football League (VFL), which he received in 1978, when the VFL changed its criteria to recognise men who had coached at least 300 games.

In 1979, the VFL introduced the Norm Smith Medal, awarded to the player deemed best-on-ground in the Grand Final. League directors chose Smith's name ahead of one of his childhood heroes, Jock McHale, and Ron Barassi.[1]

Fittingly, the first Norm Smith Medal was won by Wayne Harmes, a grandnephew of Norm Smith and a grandson of Len Smith. Harmes, then a 19-year-old with just 42 games' experience, entered football folklore himself that day when, in the dying stages of a tight Grand Final against Collingwood, he knocked the ball back to teammate Ken Sheldon for the winning goal.

When Marj Smith presented Harmes with the medal named in her husband's honour, it was an emotional moment for both. Marj congratulated Harmes with a kiss on the cheek and said: 'Wayne, I wouldn't have kissed anyone else but you'.[2]

Harmes recalled: 'We both broke into tears. (Host) Peter Landy wanted me to say a few words, but I wouldn't have been able to get a bloody word out. Not only had I played in my first premiership, but the family connection with the medal made it all the more special. I still don't think I deserved the medal though'.[3]

Harmes' mother, Norma – a daughter of Len Smith – was also emotional. Watching from the stands, she shed tears of pride for her son and for the memory of her late Uncle Norm.

---

[1] *The Sun*, November 30, 1978.
[2] Norma Harmes. Interview with the author.
[3] Wayne Harmes. Interview with the author.

🏆🏆🏆🏆🏆🏆🏆🏆🏆

On September 2, 1996 – 23 years after his death – Norm Smith received perhaps his greatest individual honour when a panel of experts selected him as the coach of the AFL Team of the Century.[4] As co-selector Greg Hobbs explained, Smith again edged out Jock McHale:

> Barassi was considered, along with a few others, but it was always going to come down to a choice between Norm Smith and Jock McHale. Even though McHale had coached the most premierships, including the record of four in a row, and had also won six premierships in 10 years, the overriding factor – and this is not to denigrate the performances of McHale with Collingwood – was that the game was more professional and tougher when Smith did it. His Melbourne sides were so good that it got to the stage in the '50s and early '60s where everyone hated their guts and people went along just to barrack against them. But Smith and his players absorbed that high-level pressure probably better than any other side before or since. And aside from Barassi, Smith didn't have any superstars, whereas McHale had the Coventrys, the Colliers and so on.[5]

Marj Smith just lived long enough to learn of her late husband's honour. Although she became progressively frail, she had maintained her independence and drove a car until the final months of her life. A doting grandmother of three, she went to lunch every Saturday with her best friend, Margaret Clay, the widow of Fitzroy great Bert Clay. However, she was struck down by a brain haemorrhage and had been in St Vincent's Hospital for a month when the AFL Team of the Century was announced. The morning after the function, her granddaughter Sam visited her and said: 'Guess what? You're the wife of the coach of the century'. The Smith matriarch smiled broadly.[6] She was 'as proud as punch', and the official plaque soon took prime position on her bedside table.[7]

Marj Smith's condition deteriorated when she contracted a serious infection.

---

[4] The panel comprised former VFL president and North Melbourne great Allen Aylett, former Geelong premiership player and coach Bob Davis, former Melbourne premiership player and *The Age* chief football writer Percy Beames, then Carlton coach David Parkin, 1989 Brownlow Medallist Gerard Healy, former umpire Jack Irving, former 3AW broadcaster Bill Jacobs and long-time football writer Greg Hobbs.
[5] Greg Hobbs. Interview with the author.
[6] Samantha Smith. Interview with the author.
[7] Peter Smith. Interview with the author.

POSTSCRIPT

She died on October 30, 1996 – seven weeks after the announcement of the AFL Team of the Century. She was 77.

🏆🏆🏆🏆🏆🏆🏆🏆🏆

When Melbourne selected its Team of the Century in December 2000, it was a virtual formality that Norm Smith would be named coach and also gain selection as a player. Many expected the full-forward role to go to Fred Fanning, the man who kicked a league record 18 goals against St Kilda in 1947. But Fanning wasn't among the squad of 28. Named at full-forward was Norm Smith, alongside his old mate Jack Mueller. Selection panel member Mike Sheahan – the chief writer at the *Herald Sun* – explained:

> I'm very sympathetic to Fanning because I don't think he got the recognition he deserved. I think he was harshly treated in terms of what he'd done - being the closest to 100 goals in a season and kicking the League record number of goals in a match. But I felt Smith achieved more. He was Melbourne's goals record-holder from 1948 until David Neitz broke it (in 2006) and he was such a versatile forward, the consummate team man, who could fit in with however Checker Hughes wanted them to play. He could play as a decoy or as the front man.

Sheahan said the selection of Smith had been reinforced in his mind following a conversation with Hawthorn patriarch John Kennedy in 2008. 'We were talking about the top 50 players of all time and Kennedy instantly remarked: "Norm Smith would have to be right in contention". Smith was the first player he mentioned. That's not to say he thought he was the only player or the best player, but I took it as a massive mark of respect for Smith'.[8]

Controversy also surrounded the glaring omission of Norm Smith from the 'Parade of Champions' at the MCG. Statues were erected of 10 sportspeople – including four football identities: Ron Barassi, Haydn Bunton, Dick Reynolds and Leigh Matthews. Don Cordner, who chaired the seven-member selection committee in 2002, was particularly disappointed by the snub of his former teammate:

> I desperately wanted to a statue of Norm Smith erected outside the MCG, but I was out-voted, and I bitterly regret that. I went along with the nomination of (Dick)

---

[8] Mike Sheahan. Interview with the author.

Reynolds because he was a great player and he played a lot on the MCG where he had a marvellous record; (Haydn) Bunton didn't play much on the MCG but his record speaks for itself; Barassi earns his place; but I strongly objected to Leigh Matthews becoming the fourth footballer to be honoured. That one should have been of Norm Smith because of his association with the Melbourne club and the Melbourne ground. I can only hope that if they decide to erect a fifth football statue that it's of Norm Smith.[9]

Cordner's wish became reality in 2012 (three years after his death) when a Smith statue became the second unveiled by the Melbourne Cricket Club for the 'Avenue of Legends' (The first had honoured cricket great Shane Warne). Sculptor Lis Johnson's superb bronze likeness included an inscription that reads, in part: 'As a coach, he expected no less from his players than from himself – integrity, purpose, drive and putting the team ahead of individuals.' At the time, an emotional Peter Smith, surrounded by family and many of his father's former charges, said: 'Lis has done a sensational job – it's so life-like. She's captured him perfectly, and turned me into a blubbering mess in the process.'[10]

Norm Smith was a football legend in his own lifetime, so when he was awarded official Legend status in the Australian Football Hall of Fame on July 19, 2007, it merely confirmed what many people already knew.

When the Hall of Fame was established in 1996, Smith was among the 136 original inductees as a coach. He became just the 21st Legend, and only the second coach, after Collingwood patriarch Jock McHale entered the realm of Legend two years earlier (following a change to the Hall of Fame constitution that made coaches eligible for Legend status).

Ron Barassi told guests at the Hall of Fame dinner at the Palladium at Crown Casino: 'I feel very proud to be part of this occasion, in which Norm Smith is proclaimed a Legend of Australian Football – AND SO HE SHOULD!'

Barassi then joined 13 of his teammates from Melbourne's 1964 premiership side, and a Norm Smith impersonator with bright red hair, for a hearty rendition of *A Grand Old Flag*. It was also a particularly moving occasion for Smith's family. Peter Smith said at the time:

---

[9] Don Cordner. Interview with the author.
[10] Peter Smith. Interview with the author.

I'm so proud that it's hard to find the words to describe what I feel. When I received the letter from the AFL, I read the first couple of paragraphs and I broke down in tears. I couldn't read on. I threw it on the bench and Tina, my wife, asked me: 'What's the matter?'

I said: 'Have a look at that'.

She said: 'That's fantastic', and it was. But the fact your own father could be officially acknowledged as one of the Legends of the game took a while to fully sink in. Norm would've been flattered but embarrassed about it all. He would've deflected the praise back to the players. He would've said if it wasn't for the players, he wouldn't have been anything as a coach. The team was always paramount."[11]

---

[11] Peter Smith. Interview with the author.

SELECT BIBLIOGRAPHY

BOOKS
Alves, Stan, with Col Davies, *Sacked Coach*, Crown Content, 2002.
Aylett, Allen, as told to Greg Hobbs. *My Game: A Life in Football*, Sun Books, 1986.
Barassi, Ron and Peter McFarline, *Barassi: The Life Behind The Legend*, Simon & Schuster, 1995.
Bartlett, Rhett, *Richmond F.C. – A Century of League Football*, GSP, 2007.
Batchelder, Alf, *Pavilions In The Park*, Australian Scholarly Publishing, 2005.
Bourbon, Stephen (editor), *Tales from the Inner Sanctum*, RecLink, 2003.
Carroll, Lynda, *The Grand Old Flag*, Hardie Grant, 1999.
Collins, Ben, *The Champions: Conversations with Great Players and Coaches of Australian Football*, GSP, 2006.
Craven, John (editor), *Football The Australian Way*, Lansdowne Press, 1969.
De Lacy, Hec (editor), *The Sporting Globe Football Book 1946*.
Donald, Chris, Fitzroy: For the Love of the Jumper, Pennon Press, 2002.
Dowling, Gerard, *The North Story*, Playwright Publishing, Sydney, 1997.
Dunn, John (editor) and Jim Main, *Australian Rules Football – An Illustrated History*. Lansdowne Press, Melbourne, 1974.
Dunstan, Keith, *The Paddock That Grew – The Story of Melbourne Cricket Club*, Cassell Australia, 1974.
Dyer, Jack and Brian Hansen, *The Wild Men of Football*, Southdown Press, 1968.
Dyer, Jack and Brian Hansen, *Captain Blood*, Stanley Paul, 1965.
Frost, Lionel, *Immortals: Football people and the evolution of Australian Rules*, John Wiley & Sons, 2005.

SELECT BIBLIOGRAPHY

Dyer, Jack, with Brian Hansen, *Jack Dyer's The Greatest: The Most Sensational Players of the Century*, Brian Hansen Nominees, 1996.
Hansen, Brian. *The Jack Dyer Story*, Brian Hansen Nominees, 1996.
Hobbs, Greg, *125 Years of the Melbourne Demons: 1858-1983*, Progress Press Group, 1984.
Holmesby, Russell, and Jim Main. *The Encyclopedia of AFL Footballers*, Crown Content, 1998.
Holt, Stephanie and Garrie Hutchinson (editors), *Footy's Greatest Coaches*, Coulomb Communications, 2002.
Hutchinson, Garrie and John Ross (Editors), *The Clubs : The Complete History of Every Club in the VFL/AFL*, Viking, Ringwood, 1996.
Lovett, Michael (editor), *AFL Record Guide to Season 2007*, GSP, 2007.
Lovett, Michael (editor), *AFL Record Season Guide 2008*, GSP.
Pollard, Jack (editor), *High Mark: The Complete Book on Australian Football*, Murray, 1964.
Richards, Lou, as told to Ian McDonald. *Boots And All!*, Stanley Paul, 1963.
Rodgers, Stephen. *Every Game Ever Played – VFL Results: 1897-1982*, Viking O'Neil, 1983.
Sheedy, Kevin, with Warwick Hadfield, *The 500 Club*, News Custom Publishing, 2004.
Sutherland, Mike, Rod Nicholson and Stewart Murrihy, *The First One Hundred Seasons: Fitzroy Football Club 1883-1983*, Fitzroy Football Club, 1983.
Taylor, E.C.H. *100 Years of Football: The Story of the Melbourne FC 1858-1958*, Melbourne Football Club, 1957.
100 Years of Australian Football: 1897-1996, Penguin, 1996.
Walker, Max, *How to Hypnotise Chooks and Other Great Yarns*, Gary Sparke Publications, 1987.
Whitten, Ted, with Jim Main and friends. *EJ*, Wilkinson Books, 1995.

NEWSPAPERS, MAGAZINES & NEWSLETTERS

Melbourne Truth – particularly a four-part series by Norm Smith, ghost-written by Brian Hansen, in March-April 1962.
The Herald
The Age
The Sun – of great assistance was a six-part series by Barrie Bretland in September-October 1967.

The Argus
The Sporting Globe
The Football Record / The AFL Record
Football Life
Footy Fan
Inside Football
Allsport Weekly
Sports Novels
Trident Monthly (Melbourne FC supporters' club newsletter)
Melbourne Football Club annual reports
Fitzroy Football Club annual reports

INTERNET
www.fullpointsfooty.net
www.afl.com.au
Melbourne Football Club site – *www.melbournefc.com.au*
The AFL Database, compiled by AFL's statisticians, Col Hutchinson and Cameron Sinclair.

VIDEO/DVD
Red and Blue: The History of the Melbourne Football Club. Written and narrated by Stephen Phillips. Australian Football Video, 2005.
The Tony Charlton Football Show, Channel Nine, Sunday July 25, 1965. Kindly supplied to the author by renowned writer/broadcaster Stephen Phillips, who aptly described it as 'the best hour of television you will ever see'.

ONLINE BONUS
The famous coaching notes of Len Smith – regarded by many experts as football's Bible – and coaching material gathered by Norm Smith can be accessed for the first time online by logging on and registering at *theredfox.com.au*.

NORM SMITH

An Official Legend of Australian Football

Born: November 21, 1915, at Clifton Hill, Victoria.
Died: July 29, 1973, at Pascoe Vale, Victoria.

THE PLAYER

Melbourne: 1935-48: 210 games, 546 goals.
Fitzroy: 1949-50: 17 games, 26 goals.
TOTAL: 227 games, 572 goals.

Honours: Melbourne Team of the Century (full-forward);
Victorian representative 1941, 1945 (2 games, 2 goals);
Melbourne best and fairest 1938, 1944;
Melbourne leading goalkicker 1938 (80, 31% of team goals),
1939 (54, 17%), 1940 (85, 25%), 1941 (89, 28%); premierships 1939, 1940, 1941, 1948.

THE COACH

Fitzroy: 1949-51 (55 games, 30 wins, 23 losses, 2 draws, winning rate 55%).
Melbourne: 1952-67: 307 games, 195 wins, 107 losses, 5 draws, winning rate 64%.
Finals: 17 wins, six losses, six premierships (1955, 1956, 1957,
1959, 1960, 1964, runner-up 1954, 1958).
South Melbourne: 1969-72: 87 games, 26 wins, 61 losses, winning rate 30%. Finals: 1 loss.
TOTAL: 449 games, 251 wins, 191 losses, 7 draws, winning rate 56%.

Coach of the AFL Team of the Century (1996)
Coach of Melbourne's Team of the Century (2000)